FRIENDSHIP AND SOCIAL RELATIONS IN CHILDREN

FRIENDSHIP AND SOCIAL RELATIONS IN CHILDREN

Edited by
**Hugh C. Foot, Antony J. Chapman,
and Jean R. Smith**

With a New Introduction by
Philip Erwin

Transaction Publishers
New Brunswick (U.S.A.) and London (U.K.)

Library of Congress Catalog Number: 94-15746
ISBN: 1-56000-766-4
Printed in the United States of America

Library of Congress Cataloging-in-Publication Data

Friendship and social relations in children / edited by Hugh C. Foot, Antony J. Chapman, and Jean R. Smith ; with a new introduction by Philip Erwin.
    p. cm.
  Includes bibliographical references and index.
  ISBN 1-56000-766-4
  1. Friendship in children. I. Foot, Hugh C. II. Chapman, Antony J.
III. Smith, Jean R.
HQ784.F7F74 1994
302.3'4'083—dc20   94-15746
                                                                  CIP

Contents

SECTION IV: FRIENDSHIP CLIQUES

Introduction to the Transaction Edition

PHILIP ERWIN

Although systematic programmes of research on children's peer relationships can be traced back at least as far as the 1920s (Renshaw, 1981), it was only in the 1970s that the sheer volume of published research began to make a review and synthesis imperative. At the time of its publication in 1980, *Friendship and Social Relations in Children* was the first major text of its kind. It constituted an important stocktaking in the field. In its emphasis on interdisciplinary research and perspectives it was considerably ahead of its time and even other books which were to appear the following year. In this volume a number of leading researchers reflected on the substantial achievements in the field and, more importantly, tried to look forward to the long journey that still remained for the emerging discipline. In this chapter I examine the dramatic changes that have occurred in our understanding of children's friendships and peer relationships since the original publication of this book. New areas are opening up and traditional areas are being re-evaluated. There has been an increasing move to emphasise the social as much as the individual and dyadic, and qualitative as well as quantitative data. This is a time of great excitement and real progress for the field as a whole.

Despite the undoubted advances in theory and methodology that have occurred in the last thirteen years, the most obvious change has been in the topics that are investigated. I will examine six major trends in the literature on children's relationships. First, the increasing recognition that the social and environmental context of relationships affects their form and function. Second, sex differences have remained the subject of a substantial amount of interest and research. The emphasis, however, has increasingly moved to highlight the factors that affect patterns of sex segregation and sex-role stereotyping. A third trend has extended research on cognitive aspects of relationships beyond children's expectations of friendship. Information processing approaches are portraying the child as a much more dynamic contributor to the process of understanding and relating to others. A fourth extremely important trend has been the recognition that developmental patterns in children's relationships cannot be explained purely in cognitive terms. Greater concern is now being given to what children actually do in their relationships rather than what they say they do or what they are capable of doing. The fifth discernible trend has been an increasing concern with explaining and alleviating children's relationship problems and difficulties. There are now large numbers of fairly recent deficit and training studies. Unfortunately most of these still treat relationship problems as individual difficulties that may be resolved with appropriate individual therapy. Sixth, research is attempting to integrate diverse literatures. This is best illustrated by the literature on attachment and relationships which is increasingly concerned with the implications of attachment for later peer relationships and love. Each of these themes in the current literature is examined in turn.

THE SOCIAL AND ENVIRONMENTAL
CONTEXT OF PEER RELATIONSHIPS

Children's patterns of relating can only be understood within their specific developmental and social contexts. These provide both limitations and opportunities. These contexts include the simple physical characteristics of the environment, physical resources such as toys and play equipment and the social network within which these interactions occur. Different environments will suit different types of children (Montemayor and Van Komen, 1985), though some environments are generally dysfunctional. Some authors have advocated the need for explicit environmental policies for children (e.g., Van Vliet, 1986).

Family organisation

Parents play an important role in setting the social stage upon which children's friendships are played out. Parents may be especially important for preschoolers because of their responsibility for initiating, structuring, and almost totally controlling the frequency of their child's peer contacts (Parke and Bhavnagri, 1989). Parents initiating a higher proportion of peer contact are likely to have children with a large number of different play partners, more consistent companions outside of kindergarten and, for boys, greater peer acceptance (Ladd and Golter, 1988).

In families with more than one child, sibling relationships may also prove to be an extremely important training ground for children's peer relationships (Shantz and Hobart, 1989). Children's relationships with siblings and parents are fundamentally different in their distribution of power and patterns of relating (Baskett and Johnson, 1982). Siblings are likely to have a more similar level of status and power in a relationship. This is likely to lead to higher levels of conflict than characterise relationships with parents, but it also gives children practice at maintaining equal, negotiated pattern of interaction. This is similar to other peer relationships and hence may prove a useful training ground for the child. Sibling and peer relationships also differ in at least two fundamental ways. First, sibling relationships are inescapable and are imbued with family obligations and norms which may distort patterns of interaction. Second, the participants in sibling relationships often differ in age. This may help children to recognise the limits of their social cognitive abilities, but it may also reduce the direct transferability of learning to extra-familial peer relationships.

An important factor affecting socialisation within the family, and ultimately children's relationship expectations, is social class. The impact of social class on social skills and patterns of relating is well established, though more recently less direct patterns of influence have been highlighted. For example, children of more educated and economically advantaged parents receive more encouragement and support for regular participation in community organisations such as youth clubs, the scouts, or brownies. They are more than twice as likely to show such involvements than children of lower social classes. Community involvement provides approved meeting grounds, places to make friends, and the opportunity to acquire and test new social skills (Bryant, 1985). In contrast, children from working-class backgrounds are more likely to use community facilities on an ad hoc basis or to use only those facilities specifically targeted at low-income groups (O'Donnell and Stueve, 1983). In effect this pattern is demonstrating a self-perpetuating cycle of social deprivation which urgently needs to be addressed.

The neighbourhood

Children's patterns of peer relationships are affected by the availability of appropriate peers and the extent to which their encounters are pre-structured by the geography of their neighbourhood (Rubin, 1980). Children living in neighbourhoods with relatively large numbers of peers have more extensive and satisfying friendship networks and share more activities with their friends (Van Vliet, 1981). With preadolescent boys, neighbourhoods with high social densities promote play in large groups and team sports; there is also an increase in the spontaneity of social interactions (Medrich, Rosen, Rubin and Buckley, 1982).

The physical characteristics of a neighbourhood also have a crucial affect on children's patterns of play and friendship. An isolated location or a difficult, hilly terrain makes it hard for children to visit a friend's house casually, on their own, and is an obstacle to many common children's games. Preadolescents from neighbourhoods where houses were widely separated and with fewer footpaths tend to have fewer and more formal friendships. The availability of facilities such as parks and playgrounds also promotes larger circles of friends and more spontaneous and large group play, though neglected play areas which children discover for themselves and keep private from adults are often preferred.

Safety considerations are a major environmental influence on children's patterns of play and how far afield they range. Children will often treat roads and pavements as play areas that are literally on their doorstep. If there are no pavements or the road is busy then safety reasons render these unavailable and may also prevent access to other neighbourhood resources such as parks. This is a major concern for many preadolescents who may come to see themselves as prisoners in their own neighbourhood (Medrich et al., 1982).

The school

Children's patterns of peer relationships in the school classroom have been the focus of a substantial amount of research (see Miller and Gentry, Chapter 6). The physical characteristics of a classroom or school interact with social density, task, and equipment characteristics to determine the social and academic climate that the child experiences. For example, the social climate of the classroom is substantially affected by whether seating is arranged in small groups or rows and columns (see Hallinan, Chapter 12). In formal classrooms, the social climate is experienced as different according to the child's location within it. The front of row-and-column classrooms is associated with attention to academic matters and dependence on teachers. The back has fewer opportunities for attention to academic matters but greater freedom for peer interaction. Pupils' seating choices reflect their weighting of academic and social opportunities (MacPherson, 1984).

A substantial amount of research has also been devoted to examining patterns of relating in the pre-school classroom (Strayer, see Chapter 9). One of the most comprehensive research studies in this area was conducted by Smith and Connolly (1980). This study shows characteristic patterns of interaction in nursery school classrooms differing in their social density, spatial density, and levels of equipment. In larger spaces there are more large-scale activities, such as running about and the active use of apparatus. In smaller spaces there is more use of equipment such as climbing frames and slides, an outlet for otherwise restricted gross motor activity, and more enforced physical contact between children. With higher spatial densities there is a tendency for less group and rough and tumble play.

The high usage of a classroom or play area need not necessarily result in high levels of social interaction. The quantity and type of material resources available to the children in an area is a crucial consideration. Specific types of play resources have been found to produce differential behavioural effects because of their complexity, variety, and amount to do per child. Some toys and materials are also designed to be played with in specific ways and limit the number of users that can be accommodated simultaneously. For example, blocks are typically extremely popular play materials that are played with co-operatively, but they are also associated with high levels of disagreement and conflict (Phyfe-Perkins, 1980). Reducing number of toys per child can lead to more social interaction and creative play, but also more aggression as competition for available resources increases (Smith and Connolly, 1980). Overall, social density and competition for resources are at least as important as spatial density in determining children's social behaviour.

SEX DIFFERENCES IN RELATIONSHIPS

Sex differences in children's and adolescents' patterns of peer relationships have been a concern of psychologists for some considerable time (see Fine, Chapter 11; Savin-Williams, Chapter 13). Research is consistent in indicating a sex difference in patterns of play and friendship throughout childhood. From one to twelve years of age there is a significant trend for same-sex companionship to increase with age (Feiring and Lewis, 1989). This is accompanied by a corresponding increase in the proportion of sex-typed activities during same-sex interactive play (Smetana and Letourneau, 1984). Girls' friendships tend to be intimate and usually with a small number of select others. Boys apparently value intimacy in relationships less and are commonly found in large, activity-oriented groups (Blyth and Traeger, 1988). These sex differences in social behaviour and patterns of relating are common across many cultures, though their extent and expression vary with the sex-roles that are taught (Whiting and Edwards, 1988).

Recent research has focused on the extent to which sex differences in peer relationships are inevitable and, closely related, the origins of observed sex differences. Sex differences in psychological functioning have, in general, proved a controversial area of research. Research has often ignored individual variation, situational constraints, race, social class, religion and other sub-cultural factors. In reality, the sex segregation in children's peer relationships is dynamic, incomplete, less marked in some social situations than others, and varies between cultures.

There are substantial differences in the socialisation of males and females from an early age. Even before entry to nursery school, many parents seek same-sex playmates for their toddlers and encourage sex-appropriate activities (Snow, Jacklin and Maccoby, 1983). Only a rudimentary understanding of gender is needed before children begin to acquire gender stereotypes and show sex-typed behaviour and preferences for peers and toys (Martin and Little, 1990). Later developments in gender concepts are paralleled by an increasing preference for same-sex peers (Huston, 1983).

In an alternative perspective it has been argued that sex segregation is more a matter of group dynamics than sex-roles (Maccoby and Jacklin, 1987). Sex segregation in children's friendships is seen largely as the result of pressures to belong to peer groups. Differences between the sexes are exaggerated and boys and girls are viewed as opposites. Children become quick to criticise or disrupt a companion's sex inappropriate play and such activity usually ends rapidly (Lamb, Easterbrooks and Holden, 1980). Denigrating out-group members enhances a group's identity and consequently improves the child's status within his or her own group, especially if the two groups perceive themselves to be in conflict or competition (Hogg and Abrams, 1988). Even in pre-schoolers there are important sanctions to encourage conformity to gender norms for behaviour and these are likely to override any styles of play which a child possesses on entry to the playgroup (Fagot, 1981). The socially adept child is the individual who can most successfully accommodate to peer gender expectations.

Group dynamics make cross-sex peer relationships difficult in childhood, though girls are generally given more leeway in their violations of sex-roles and 'tomboys' are relatively common (Feiring and Lewis, 1989). Relaxed cross-sex interactions are most likely to occur when children are involved in an absorbing task or when children are not responsible for the formation of groups, such as when activities are structured by adults, or where there are few alternative playmates or witnesses to the boundary violation. Co-operative interactions, such as in small, mixed-sex instruction groups help to reduce stereotyping and produce an increase in integration (Lockheed, 1986).

Origins of sex segregation

In the first two years, if toddlers interact with peers at all it is in pairs. Groups are seldom formed and there is little evidence of any sex bias in children's peer preferences (Hay, Pedersen and Nash, 1982). As boys do not conform to the obedience and order desired by girls, cross-sex associations become unpleasant for girls and they increasingly reject the approaches of boys. From about the age of two girls begin to make more social approaches to other girls. Boys remain gender neutral a little longer but by the age of three they also contribute to the segregation. By five years of age boys show a stronger same-sex preference than girls (LaFreniere, Strayer and Gauthier, 1984).

Initial patterns of segregation provide the opportunity for the sexes to evolve different patterns of play. With age there is an increase in the proportion of sex-typed activities during play with same-sex peers (Smetana and Letourneau, 1984). These patterns of play make cross-sex interactions increasingly problematic and reinforce the sex segregation in children's peer relationships (Eisenberg, Tryon and Cameron, 1984). In pre-schoolers around 35 per cent of friendships may be cross-sex, but with increasing social interest and activity sex segregation becomes more marked. By seven to eight years of age it is virtually complete (Gottman, 1986). Up to the age of nine or ten it is a prime insult to a child to say that she or he likes the activities typical of the opposite sex. Possibly in recognition of this, children's activity groups also segregate at this age (e.g., brownies and cubs) and a number of ritualised mechanisms exist for dealing with the boundary violations that inevitably occur during sex-segregated play (Gottman, 1986).

Sex differences in peer interaction

Strategies for initiating peer contact differ between the sexes and reinforce the sex segregation of middle-childhood. Girls tend to use polite, mature strategies for initiating contact with peers, boys are more likely to issue a higher proportion of commands, nonverbal overtures, aggressive approaches, or simply attempt to join in with an ongoing activity. These strategies are more successful with peers of the same sex. Cross-sex overtures are most successful when using the style of approach appropriate to the sex of the target (Phinney and Rotheram, 1980). These differences, and the problems of adapting to same- and opposite-sex peers, explain why even young children show more approaches to same-sex rather than cross-sex peers. This is a pattern that becomes increasingly marked with age (Serbin, Sprafkin, Elman and Doyle, 1984).

From about eleven or twelve years of age the sex segregation in children's play and relationships starts a relatively consistent and gradual decline. Young adolescents become aware of each other as potential romantic partners but nonetheless follow a pattern of avoiding major cross-sex contact. Cross-sex contacts are initially tentative, often part of contests and games and may be accompanied by much teasing (Thorne, 1986). Gradually a few individuals begin to affirm rather than avoid charges of cross-sex relationships and they may even gain in status through their association with a member of the opposite sex. The same-sex cliques of early adolescence gradually give way to heterosexual cliques and couples in mid- to late adolescence, generally later for boys than girls (Shrum, Cheek and Hunter, 1988).

SOCIAL COGNITION AND RELATIONSHIPS

Social cognitive factors were the focus of much of the early research on children's peer relationships. As such, they received considerable attention in the first issue of this book (see Bigelow and La Gaipa, Chapter 1; Mannarino, Chapter 2; Barnett and Zucker, Chapter 3). They still remain a major focus of research, though the level of analysis has become considerably more sophisticated.

A fundamental principle emphasised by many psychologists is that social behaviour is mediated by perceptual and cognitive processes. These are the foundation on which the child's interpretation of social cues is built. An ability to decode social cues accurately enables children to regulate their social interactions and is predictive of future social status (Rubin and Daniels-Beirness, 1983). An important task is to understand the bases for children's abilities to use social cues and their consequent decisions regarding appropriate action.

In the study of children's peer relationships three interrelated aspects of social cognitive development stand out as having received special attention: social role-taking, children's friendship concepts, and the role of attribution in social behaviour. In combination these three topics emphasise that to relate to others successfully the child must acknowledge his or her independent perspective and interests, possess schemata which distinguish friendship behaviour from other social behaviour, and be able to understand the causes of behaviour to the extent that this affects its interpretation. It is to these topics and related issues that this section now turns.

Social role-taking

Role-taking is an important basis for children's negotiations of their social reality, self-concept, and social relationships. In school-age children, developments in role-taking are reflected in the effectiveness of interpersonal communication. Good role-takers are able to use subtle and often indirect social cues (Hudson, Forman and Brion-Meisels, 1982). This allows them to infer the needs of others accurately and to respond more flexibly, increasing their popularity and ability to maintain mutual relationships (Spence, 1987). Duck's chapter in this book (Chapter 4) highlights a debate over the age of onset of role-taking abilities in children which was raging in 1980. More recent research suggests that this debate is largely founded on differences of definition and research methods (Erwin, 1993). Social role-taking shows a parallel development with other social and cognitive abilities (see Rubin and Pepler, Chapter 8). With naturalistic testing materials even young children reveal a basic understanding that another's perspective and subjective state differs from their own (Denham, 1986). This is shown, for example, by three-year-olds adapting the complexity of their speech when speaking to handicapped or younger children (Guralnick and Paul-Brown, 1984).

Understanding friendship

Children's understandings of friendship are an important basis for their relationships with peers. Clear evidence exists for a relationship between social knowledge and social competence (Mize and Cox, 1990). Inadequate social knowledge often underlies inappropriate or inadequate goals, expectations, and behaviour in children's peer relationships. This effect may be especially marked in the difficult initial encounters of young and socially inexperienced children (Furman and Walden, 1990).

Despite a huge variety of theoretical and methodological approaches, the extensive literature on children's and adolescents' descriptions of their peers is remarkably consistent. With age there is an increase in the number, complexity, flexibility, and organisation of children's friendship concepts. The distinction between friends and non-friends grows more marked with age.

Early attempts to explain changes in children's friendship concepts were heavily influenced by Piaget's theory of cognitive development. These attempts proposed (and presented evidence) that children's friendship concepts develop in an invariant stage-like sequence (see Bigelow and La Gaipa, Chapter 1; Selman, 1980). Later dimensions build on and elaborate simpler, earlier dimensions of friendship understanding. The finding of an invariant sequence in which levels or dimensions of friendship understanding develop is important in implicating cognitive developmental factors. Though this does not eliminate an alternative explanation in terms of the patterns of socialisation which may characterise a given culture. Additional evidence for the determining role of cognitive developmental factors in children's friendship expectations comes from research comparing different cultural and ethnic groups. Although specific friendship behaviours do vary from one cultural or ethnic group to another, the characteristic patterns of developmental change in children's friendship concepts do appear to be invariant (Rotheram-Borus and Phinney, 1990). Recent research has questioned a strict structural-developmental approach. It has been argued that there is a gradual generalisation of the child's social cognitive abilities, moving from an ability to use the skills in only familiar and concrete situations to being able to apply them even in abstract and unfamiliar situations (Schofield and Kafer, 1985).

A substantial amount of research has examined the role of children's friendship concepts in their actual friendship choices, though few specific correlations between relationship concepts and patterns of interaction have been empirically demonstrated. Indeed, Bigelow (1982) argues that there is often little or no correspondence between why children say they behaved in a certain way and the actual factors that influenced their behaviour. Clarification of the relationship between children's social cognitive abilities and their social behaviour is likely to take many years and necessitate the inclusion of a number of additional social and normative factors.

Social cognition, communication, and social relations

Empirical attempts to establish the relationship between social cognitive abilities, communication, and other social variables have made considerable headway in recent years. Over a series of studies a group of researchers have produced a compelling outline of the possible patterns of relationship between a number of variables and children's peer relationships (Applegate, Burke, Burleson, Delia and Kline, 1985; Burleson, Delia and Applegate, 1990; Clark and Jones, 1990; Delia and Applegate, 1990). The variables examined included social class, maternal and child social cognitive abilities, maternal and child communication quality, and children's peer relationships. If the results of these studies are combined, an interesting picture of the role of social cognition in children's peer relationships emerges. The main impact of social class was on the mother's social cognitive style, her perceptions of social contexts and peoples. Maternal social cognitive skills were positively related to the use of reflection enhancing modes of discipline and nurturance and directly predicted the quality of communication with the child. This was in turn related to the child's social cognitive skills. Children's social cognitive skills were good predictors of their level of person-centred, adaptive communication which was predictive of success in peer relations. This account serves to emphasise that the role of social cognition in children's peer relationships can only be fully understood in its social and historical context. It is an important contribution to our understanding of social cognitive influences on children's peer relationships, but it also highlights how much more research remains to be done. Most of the above pattern of relationships between variables was established in young schoolchildren, it is highly likely that it will change developmentally.

Attribution processes

In the previous section, how children describe their friends was examined. It is also important to understand how these characteristics are attributed to others. The role of attribution processes in relationships has been accorded relatively little attention until recently. Even five- and six-year-olds are able to make dispositional attributions, even though they do not typically use trait information in describing themselves and others (Rholes and Ruble, 1984). They appreciate that attributions need to take individual and situational factors into account, but they weight the importance of these factors differently from older children and adults. Trait-like terms are not used much before the age of eight or nine years because children are uncertain about the stability of these traits and do not perceive such information as salient, not because they are unable to make internal attributions

A number of sources of bias have been noted in peer attribution processes. For example, perceptions of a peer's personality are affected by friendship and the peer's social status. Liking will also affect whether many behaviours are seen as intended and how they are evaluated (Hymel, 1986). Being tripped by a friend may be interpreted as an accident, being tripped by a previously aggressive peer may be seen as an assault (Waas and Honer, 1990). In ambiguous situations aggressive children are particularly prone to interpreting aggressive intent in the behaviour of their peers (Dodge and Frame, 1982). It is easy to see how these attributions of aggression ultimately become the basis of self-sustaining peer reputations and why so many social skills training programmes consequently fail to produce long-term effects.

Children's social experiences and popularity affect and are affected by their perception of social situations. Popular school children are more aware of social cues and causes and are more likely than the other sociometric groups to see themselves as personally responsible for their social successes Although all children tend to externalise the causes for failure, this is accomplished in a more sophisticated manner by popular children. Rather than simply putting failure down to luck they invoke explanations such as the motives of other people. Popular children are more accurate in perceiving the effects of their behaviour and justifiably perceive more personal control in their social lives (Earn and Sobol, 1990). These patterns of attribution shown by popular children are an important ingredient underlying their social confidence and success. Rejected children overestimate their social competence (Patterson, Kupersmidt and Griesler, 1990), and where they do perceive social failure they are less likely to externalise blame. This may become an important factor in the deterioration of unpopular children's strategies for initiating relationships, pushing the unpopular child into a cycle of helpless self-blame (Goetz and Dweck, 1980).

SOCIAL SKILLS

Before the late 1970s there were relatively few studies of the social skills involved in children's relationships. Foot, Chapman and Smith's comment on this state of affairs (see Chapter 10) was to prove remarkably timely. A focus on social skills has been a major feature of research on children's friendship over the subsequent dozen years. Children need to establish complementary roles if successful interaction is to ensue. Differences in social skills are most marked between popular and rejected children—the extremes of social status. Perhaps surprisingly, socially withdrawn or neglected children show little difference in skill from their more popular peers, and have a relatively high likelihood of changing status (Rubin, 1985).

For young children, popularity in nursery school is associated with overall levels of giving and receiving positive, reinforcing behaviour (e.g., giving gifts, attention, or acceptance). Popular children are sociable and responsive to the needs of others and to ongoing interaction (Putallaz, 1983); they are relatively non-aggressive and better able to decode the facial expression and emotions of others (Spence, 1987). Popular children often also have specific skills which are deemed attractive, such as an ability at sports. The picture of the neglected child is only marginally different from that of the popular child. They do tend to perceive themselves as less socially competent than their peers, are often less talkative, and receive fewer nominations as being helpful and nice. There is little difference from popular children in terms of assertiveness, self-rated shyness, unhappiness, or feelings of acceptance (Erwin, 1993).

The behavioural characteristics of unpopular or rejected children are almost the opposite of those of popular children. In nursery school children peer rejection is associated with aggressive, hostile forms of behaviour, lower levels of interaction, and generally less mature forms of play (Rubin, Daniels-Beirness and Hayvren, 1982). Problem behaviour, social disagreements, and friction while playing with peers continue to be major correlates of social rejection in school age children (Nowicki and Oxenford, 1989). Rejected children are less likely to give reasons for their disagreements or to suggest constructive alternatives to resolve their disputes. Rejected pre-school and elementary school children show no shortage of attempts to initiate social contacts, though these are often irrelevant and unresponsiveness to ongoing activities (Black and Hazan, 1990). These strategies are more likely to be ignored or rebuffed than to being accepted. Despite these experiences, rejected children also tend to overestimate their evaluation by peers (Patterson et al., 1990).

A word of caution is in order before leaving the apparently straightforward issue of the relationship of aggression to social popularity. In an observational study of first and second graders Shantz (1986) found that when the effects of aggression and conflict were examined separately, with the other factor held constant statistically, conflict was more closely related to peer rejection than was simple physical aggression. Interestingly, being liked by peers was not related to rates of conflict or aggression. Apparently these characteristics are not in themselves a sufficient reason for rejection; the perceived justification for such behaviours is crucial.

The behaviours that contribute to sociometric status show marked changes developmentally. With age the skills required to establish and maintain social status become increasing complex and subtle. The first positive interest in other children occurs at approximately six months of age. In children from six to twelve months of age, approximately 47 per cent of overtures to peers result in a co-ordinated social encounter, though most of these successes consist of single action—response sequences lasting only a few seconds or a minute (Vandell, Wilson and Buchanan, 1980).

Parental influences on children's social skills

Throughout childhood, children's general levels and patterns of sociability are affected by their earlier interactions with caregivers. Infants spending more time interacting with their mothers at six months of age interact more with peers three months later (Vandell and Wilson, 1987). Similar results have been obtained with children in their second year (Vandell and Mueller, see Chapter 7). Even at the first five years of age, children with a background of a successful maternal relationship are more likely to attain high sociometric status with peers (Putallaz, 1987). Disagreeable and demanding behaviour during maternal interactions are reflected in the disagreeable and demanding behaviour of children toward their peers.

The play of young pre-schoolers with an unfamiliar peer seems to benefit from parental assistance, though the way in which the parent fulfils the role of social skills coach is very important (Bhavnagri and Parke, 1991). A major influence on the way this role is fulfilled is the parents' recollection of their own childhood peer relationships. This influences how active a role the parent takes in the child's social relationships, and ultimately the level of social competence displayed by the child (Putallaz, Costanzo and Smith, 1991). The parents of pre-school and first grade children of high sociometric status appear to interact in a sensitive and positive manner with their children. The parents of less popular children are more controlling, directive and intrusive in their interactions (Austin and Lindauer, 1990). A study by Russell and Finnie (1990) examined the guidance given by mothers to their four- and five-year-old children for joining an existing unknown pair of peers at play. The mothers of popular children were more likely to suggest a group-oriented strategy (such as how to integrate with the ongoing strategy) while the mothers of neglected children were more likely to draw attention to play materials. The mothers of less popular children also show more negative and controlling behaviours toward their children. Rejecting parents using frequent prohibitions, controlling behaviour and high levels of physical punishment are more likely to produce aggressive children. Conversely, relationships with a second parent, a sibling or peer can provide a buffer and even moderate the psychological impact of family violence on children (Moore, Pepler, Weinberg and Hammond, 1990).

Familiarity and social responsiveness

There is more affective and reciprocal communication between friends than non-friends (Brachfeld-Child and Schiavo, 1990). Peer social interactions become more frequent, sustained, and mature as newcomers become acquainted (Roopnarine, 1985). A study by Gottman (1983) examined the conversational behaviour of three- to nine-year-old children. Communication patterns accounted for over 80 per cent of the variability in how well the children related to each other at a first meeting and over 90 per cent of the variation in second and third meetings.

Several studies have examined the social assimilation of the young child to pre-school groups. This approach allows a naturalistic and relatively long-term examination of changes in patterns of sociability with growing familiarity. Naturalistic studies have been remarkably consistent in their results. Aggression declines with opportunities to interact with peers in a nursery school. A host of positive measures of social behaviour all increase with pre-school experience (Shea, 1981). Children attending nursery school often show the most marked changes in their behaviour.

Children of three to four years of age who have had prior experience with peers show higher levels of preference for interacting with peers rather than adults and for engaging in social play rather than spending time alone (Harper and Huie, 1985). Prior experience and familiarity with other children appear to be crucial factors in the levels of sociability and social skill that are observed in pre-schoolers. The benefits of good pre-school experience are also carried forward to later adjustment at kindergarten and beyond (Ironsmith and Poteat, 1990). This suggests the obvious possibility of compensatory education programmes. Unfortunately, less sociable children miss more nursery school due to illness, even though their health records were similar to those of popular children before beginning school (Pennebaker, Hendler, Durrett and Richards, 1981). The shy, withdrawn children who would benefit most from the nursery school experience also find it most difficult to cope with, and hence have a higher rate of absenteeism and benefit less from the experience than their more outgoing peers.

In older children, the friendship networks that evolve in new groups are significantly influenced by and likely to reflect pre-existing school based social status. This confirmation of status occurs rapidly, usually within two or three sessions, whether or not the children are previously acquainted (Coie and Kupersmidt, 1983).

RELATIONSHIP PROBLEMS

A major development since the original publication of this book has been a concern with disordered relationships. This has been fuelled by two main factors: first, a belief that understanding disordered relationships will provide insights into the factors which are necessary for successful relationships; second, other branches of psychology, notably clinical and educational psychology, have been increasingly recognising the importance of relationships for adjustment and that basic research may have implications for clinical practice. It is important to note at this point that research in this area is fragmented, at least in part because there is no agreed taxonomy of children's relationship problems (Gottman, 1991).

Although the volume of evidence for an association between early relationship problems and later adjustment is impressive, the quality of the evidence is extremely variable (see Campbell, Chapter 14; Kupersmidt, Coie and Dodge, 1990). A recent review by Asher and Parker (1989) concluded that the evidence for a causal link between childhood relationships and later problems of adjustment is strongest in the association of early aggression with later juvenile or adult criminality.

Defining withdrawal and isolation

Identification of social withdrawal is usually on the basis of teacher, parent or peer reports. Self-reports may also be used (Bierman and McCauley, 1987). These do correlate with other sources, though further research is required to explore the utility of this criterion and how it is affected by individual differences such as age and verbal ability. Any assessment inevitably involves a subjective component, a judgement concerning what constitutes a deficit and what is to be trained. Relationships are complex phenomena and each mode of assessment has its virtues and advocates, and also its disadvantages. The use of multiple criteria is most likely to provide the broadest, balanced picture and avoid bias.

The cause of isolation and the characteristics of the isolated child are an important consideration in devising appropriate interventions (Coie and Koeppl, 1990). Poor peer acceptance is unlikely to be a primary cause, and is often the product of a complex multiple aetiology; it can be a cause and consequence of other problems. Nevertheless, studies have generally been concerned with teaching the individual specific skills, often concerned with how to initiate relationships, rather than the skills and processes involved in maintaining a relationship. This may be a major reason why there have been so many problems in getting the maintenance and generalisation of training effects.

One of three main criteria has characterised most definitions of social isolation and hence the aims of most social skills training studies. Isolation has been defined in terms of rates of interaction, quality of social interaction, or the social consequences of interaction. The social consequence most usually assessed is sociometric status, though this has more to do with popularity than friendship status (Ladd and Asher, 1985). Many studies have used multiple criteria. Unfortunately each separate criterion has its own problems, measures quite different characteristics of a child's relationships and is not always closely related to other criteria. An unfortunate consequence of these many ways of defining social isolation is that there is little agreement in the literature on the criteria which constitute a genuine deficit, justify interventions, and indicate successful outcomes. A global level of analysis does more justice to the complex, multi-faceted nature of children's social relationships but can appear vague and give little indication about what specific behaviours would be measured. The more analytic approach closely related specifies what should be measured but risks losing sight of the complex interrelationships and multiple external influences that also affect the impact of the behaviour.

It is important to distinguish between children of rejected and neglected status as they have considerably different behavioural profiles (Asher, 1985). Active rejection, in comparison to simple neglect, possesses greater stability across time and social groups (Coie and Kupersmidt, 1983). As it is primarily rejection and associated indices of negative status that predict later adjustment (Ladd, 1990), simple withdrawal is not an appropriate indicator of risk at least in early and middle childhood. More than half of children of low sociometric status nonetheless have at least one best person whom they regard as a best friend and who regards them in the same way (Parker and Asher, 1987). For therapeutic interventions, attention would be better focused on aggressive or rejected children.

Amidst all these definitions of social isolation it is important not to lose sight of the child. As Wanlass and Prinz (1982) noted, isolated children do not form a homogeneous group. Individuals differ in the level and type of social contact that they desire and perceive themselves to possess (Patterson et al., 1990). An adequate explanation of relationship problems must explain both the broad pattern of problems that generally characterise the course of relationship development and the differences between individuals in their patterns of relating.

Relationship collapse

The differences in social skills between successful and unsuccessful relators show both what the socially competent child is doing right and what the less competent child is doing wrong, but research has also been directed to the problems deriving from the dynamics of the relationship itself. Several factors can be pinpointed as important in children's relationship problems. First, relationships have history and so previous relationships and patterns of care will influence current patterns of relating. Second, a major source of problems in relationships derives from the characteristics of the participants (see Carter, Carter, and Benson, Chapter 5). Some of these characteristics of individuals are significant in their own right (e.g., various handicaps) and some have an adverse effect mainly because of the way they relate to the characteristics of the other person (e.g., values and patterns of behaviour). Different types of incompatibility are significant at different points in relationships. The disadvantage of a visible handicap, for example, is likely to be greatest in the early stages of a relationship where it may deter others from making social approaches to child. A third broad group of factors affecting the course of relationships derive from the dynamics of the relationships themselves and are not predictable from the behaviour that the partners give and receive in other social contexts (Ross and Lollis, 1989). These three broad groups of factors, the characteristics of the relators and the history and dynamics of the relationship, are interrelated and reciprocally influencing. Their final impact and significance on a child's happiness and social adjustment is also likely to be influenced by the level of support from other current relationships that the child is able to establish and maintain.

Problems with relationships

No matter how socially skilled and popular a child is, he or she will inevitably experience the collapse of a relationship. It is a normal, perhaps even necessary, part of social development and growth. Learning how to cope with losing and changing friends is complementary to the process of learning how to make and keep friends. Changes in the cognitive abilities and interests of the young child are a natural part of development, and any relationships at any age may end as friends develop in different directions or at different rates. Older children seek and possess more intimacy in their peer relationships, but if they collapse this makes the loss correspondingly more painful (Hartup, Laursen, Stewart and Eastenson, 1988). These relationships are considerably less easy to replace than those of younger children (Buhrmester and Furman, 1987).

Children's accounts of friendship termination become more complex as the child becomes more cognitively sophisticated, though they remain considerably less differentiated than their accounts of friendship formation (Bigelow, 1982). The lesser contact with ex-friends than friends, and the typically shorter process of friendship dissolution than build-up, means that there are fewer opportunities to develop finely-detailed accounts of the deterioration and ending of friendship. The reasons for friendship termination are not only an inability to satisfy the requirements for friendship formation. Research by Bigelow and LaGaipa (see Chapter 1) has highlighted some of the explanations which nine- to fifteen-year-old school children give for the collapse of their relationships. In middle-child-hood explanations emphasise conflict and ego-degrading experiences. By adolescence the major cause of relationship difficulties has moved to disloyalty (befriending others and betraying trust) and lack or loss of admiration; these are evident in almost two-thirds of explanations. If continuing references to ego-degrading experiences are included, 82 per cent of responses are explained. Adolescents share their feelings and secrets more, and are more knowledgeable about their friends' feelings. Consequently trustworthiness and being a reliable confidant are important qualities in adolescent friends and important reasons for relationship disputes.

Some relationships are reported as simply drifting apart; other relationships are disrupted by a single major disagreement. Bigelow (1982) argues that friendships often collapse because of the violation of general rules of good conduct, applicable to all social relationships, rather than specific friendship inadequacies. For seven- to ten-year-olds support and conflict are part of the same dimension of a relationship. Support and conflict become differentiated and constituted separate concerns for young adolescents (Berndt and Perry, 1986). With increasing age disagreements are seen as a natural part of relationships and need not necessarily lead to their collapse (Parker and Gottman, 1989). Friends are more critical of one another but are also more likely to explain the bases of their disagreements (Nelson and Aboud, 1985).

With the approach of adolescence the child often becomes very preoccupied with relationships and with the possibility of peer rejection. Greater attributional and role-taking abilities dramatically increase the brooding attention that the adolescent can devote to analysing why a relationship went wrong (Harvey, Weber, Yarkin and Stewart, 1982). Personal attributions of incompetence as the reason for rejection can fundamentally undermine the child's self-esteem and colour future relationships (Goetz and Dweck, 1980). At this age, relationship collapse, and especially rejection by another, is especially painful because of the feelings of insecurity which characterise this time of important changes in social relationships. The seriousness of breaking-up at this age is exacerbated by the limited availability of alternate relationships; most of an adolescent's peers will already be in established relationships.

Events which precipitate the end of a relationship have been given relatively little empirical attention despite their undoubted significance. Major social dislocations such as moving house or going to a new school affect the number and quality of children's friendships. Children's lack of control over extraneous factors which affect their relationships is an important factor in the experience of their loss. These sorts of disruptions are likely to play a more significant role in the lives of children than adults as they find it more difficult to overcome the obstacle of separation and maintain contact through letters, telephone calls and occasional visits (Levinger and Levinger, 1986). Some relationships are strong enough to survive these barriers, but for most they are merely a transitional stage, cushioning the eventual decay of the relationship and acting as dwindling support while new friendships are formed. Events which disrupt relationships can be traumatic experiences for children because of the difficulties of forming relationships in a new, established peer group. This is a considerably more difficult task than would have been the case in the old peer network. This situation is especially significant for older children where stable cliques are likely to exist.

Fortunately, The trauma of these relationship transitions can be considerably eased with a little forethought and an appropriate induction programme, or by the buffer of other relationships such as peers undergoing the same transition, or parents, and sibs with whom there is a good relationship (East and Rook, 1992). The counterpart to this picture of support is that families can also produce or exacerbate stressful life experiences. Children from families under stress are more likely to experience relationship problems and peer rejection (Patterson, Vaden and Kupersmidt, 1991).

IMPROVING PEER RELATIONSHIPS

As a systematic understanding of children's relationships and relationship problems has progressed over the last twenty years or so, so has the interest in intervention and the sophistication of these attempts. Various types of social skills training have received special attention as approaches to improving children's relationships with peers.

Psychological interventions with children are complicated because several professional groups and agencies are often involved, sometimes with conflicting goals and approaches. There may often be relatively little overlap in the factors affecting the child's perceived adjustment in different circumstances (Takac and Benyamini, 1989). Different figures also elicit different behaviours and evaluate behaviour differently. These differences occur both within groups of judges (e.g., teachers often differ in their evaluation of a child's behaviour) and between groups of judges (e.g., different evaluations are often given by parents, peers and teachers). Disagreements are especially marked for the more subtle aspects of behaviour (Ledingham and Younger, 1985).

Several authors have recently described and emphasised the importance of school based programmes for promoting social competence and peer relationships (e.g., Furman, Giberson, White, Gavin and Wehner, 1989). In particular, school-based preventative programmes have many advantages over remedial programmes, not least that they do not stigmatise children or isolate them from their peers (Rook and Peplau, 1982). However, some authors are pessimistic about this role for the education system amidst the onslaught of the mass media, increased mobility, and the growing emphasis on individuality (Cartledge and Milburn, 1980).

Social skills training

Systematic research on social skills training with children is a relatively recent but promising endeavour. It aims to improve social and interpersonal cognitive abilities through the direct instruction and rehearsal of specific skills. Several related studies have provided substantial empirical evidence about the effectiveness of social skills training as an intervention procedure (Ladd, 1981). A major benefit of social skills training lies in the reduction in negative behaviours that it produces (Gresham and Nagle, 1980), probably the major factor in social rejection. Unfortunately, change is often not maintained. Changes in skills are also not necessarily reflected in changes in sociometric status (Erwin and Ruane, in press) presumably because of the limited time-scale of most studies, a weak relation between the measures and the rigidity of the separate interactional sub-systems which exist for popular and unpopular children over the age of four or five years (Ladd, 1983). Not only must skill be improved but the child (or other agency) must also change the social network to which she or he belongs (see Hallinan, Chapter 12).

Social skills training is concerned with the type and organisation of cognitive and behavioural skills necessary for successful social interaction. Problems can arise because of a lack of knowledge of appropriate social behaviour, lack of actual behavioural skills, or lack of ability to monitor and modify ongoing social behaviour (Mize and Ladd, 1990a). Anxiety and emotional factors, much ignored variables in social skills training, can also inhibit skilled performance (Cox and Gunn, 1980). All these factors can be incorporated in social skills training, though different approaches would be used depending on which skills are emphasised (Cartledge and Milburn, 1980). Rotheram (1980) argues for an integrated approach and that manipulating cognitive, behavioural, and emotional factors on their own has consistently proven fruitless.

Social skills programmes have generally been demonstrated to be fairly efficacious with low accepted children, with actively rejected children the picture is less positive. Although a number of programmes have been reported as producing some improvements in some children, "no treatment has produced long-term improvements in the behavioural adjustment and peer status of rejected children" (Bierman, 1989, p. 73). To balance out this conclusion it must be remembered that few intervention programmes for rejected children have even tried to reduce aggressive behaviour directly. It is likely more focused attention on aggressive and disruptive behaviour will improve the effectiveness of interventions (Coie and Koeppl, 1990).

Social skills training programmes

Many social skills training programmes are eclectic in orientation, incorporating modelling, shaping, and direct instruction. Children are commonly treated individually though many of the techniques have also been successfully used with groups (Wilson and Hersov, 1985). Although many studies have used peers in their treatment programmes, trying to change the attitudes and behaviour of a child's peer group is not common, despite the acknowledged significance of peer perceptions and behaviour for maintaining social status (Hollinger, 1987). Although research provides some evidence for the effectiveness of these approaches, the issue of practicality has received little attention (Kohler and Strain, 1990).

It is important that programmes are tailored for specific client groups. The skills taught in intervention programmes are often selected by comparing what popular and unpopular children of a given age and sex are doing, or what produces positive peer reactions. It is also important that skills training programmes take children's cognitive, social and emotional characteristics into account (Mize and Ladd, 1990b). While most studies do tailor their programme to the specific client group, most studies also ignore or give minimal attention to developmental considerations (Furman, 1980). Indicating the importance of this factor, Schneider's (1989) meta-analysis of social skills interventions concluded that techniques such as modelling, which require less cognitive mediation, are most effective with young pre-schoolers. Approaches using direct reinforcement are amongst the most powerful methods with children that have specific, identifiable behavioural deficits that are causing discomfort or developmental risk. More complex multi-technique programmes are more successful with older children.

Social skills training aims to facilitate maintenance and generalisation by not only teaching skills but by promoting understanding of the skills and an ability to monitor and adapt performance (Ladd and Mize, 1983). It produces improvements in skills use that correlate with improvements in the children's knowledge of friendly social strategies (Mize and Ladd, 1990a).

As the above description implies, social skills training relies heavily on verbal communication. Cognitive processes are explicitly acknowledged and the child is involved as an active participant in the training. The process has been conceptualised as much in terms of education as therapy (Goldstein, Gershaw and Sprafkin, 1985). Because of the emphasis on verbal and cognitive factors, this approach has been mainly used on school-age children (in fact, mainly elementary school age), though similar, positive patterns of results have been reported for pre-schoolers (Mize and Ladd, 1990b).

If a child is isolated because of problems other than skills deficits, such as frustration resulting from academic difficulties, then tackling these is likely to be more productive than simply teaching social skills (Coie and Krehbiel, 1984). For rejected children with negative social behaviour both techniques to control the negative behaviour and techniques to improve social skills are necessary to bring about improvements in sociometric status. Even this is likely to produce only limited generalisation due to the reputation which the rejected child has established with his or her peers and the consequent interpretations placed on his or her behaviour (Bierman, Miller and Stabb, 1987). Nonetheless social skills training programmes could include an element to deal with self-control or be combined with other social learning approaches to reduce negative behaviours. Attention could then also be given to the child's social context to facilitate the generalisation and acceptance of the new behaviour patterns.

Some authors have questioned whether social skills training helps to promote friendship or merely superficial relating. As Button (1979, p. 197) notes, 'It is not too difficult to help someone to greet, meet, and converse at a personal level with other people, but the removal of an impediment alone does not compensate for the long history of not having had practice in that give and take, equal and intimate relationship that friendship implies'. But surely this misrepresents social skills training? No one denies close relations are the product of a history of interaction. What social skills training aims to do is simply help isolated children start to relate.

ATTACHMENT AND LATER PEER RELATIONSHIPS

Recent research on children's peer relationships has increasingly tried to examine broader age groups and to integrate findings across different age ranges. Research on attachment and later peer relationships is an excellent example of this, with many interesting controversies in the process of being resolved. This emphasis on the interconnectedness of relationship phenomena and the social network brings the chapter full circle.

The early attachment of a child to its primary caregiver exerts a major influence on later relationships. 'The young child seeks and explores new relationships within the framework of expectations for self and others that emerges from the primary relationship' (Sroufe and Fleeson, 1986, p. 52). But the nature of the cross-age linkages is something that is only beginning to be explored systematically. These expectations include information such as whether attention and affection are reliably available and affect which social information is perceived as relevant and hence noticed and remembered.

Research has demonstrated a connection between a child's early relations and his or her characteristics later in life. The connection between attachment and the form and functioning of later relationships (smoothness, stability, mutuality) is considerably less clear (Hartup, 1986). The continuity of attachment with subsequent relationships is most clearly demonstrated in those peer relationships which are formed soonest after the primary attachment. These are less coloured by other relationship experiences. Quality of attachment is well documented as predicting the expression and control of affections throughout the pre-school years. Several studies have indicated different relationship patterns associated with differing early attachment histories (Erickson, Sroufe and Egeland, 1985). Parents are more effective models and more effective in coaching their children about social relationships in the context of a warm and secure parent-child relationship. The parents of securely attached children also facilitate their children's peer interactions by responding appropriately while their children are with a playmate. Several studies confirm that infants securely attached to their mothers at twelve to nineteen months of age also show more sociable and peer oriented, confident, friendly, co-operative, outgoing, and independent patterns of social behaviour three or four years later in the nursery school (Erickson, Sroufe and Egeland, 1985). They are more likely to successfully initiate play activities with other children, ignore fewer peer bids and to be involved in peer interaction (Jacobson and Wille, 1986). A long-term study followed children for over a decade and found that these differences in social competence are relatively stable characteristics. Ten-year-olds with a background of secure attachment scored significantly higher on 'ego-resiliency', self-confidence, and an overall measure of competence; they scored significantly lower on dependence, were less often isolated and less likely to be the passive recipients of aggression (Sroufe and Jacobvitz, 1989).

Anxious-avoidant toddlers are active participants in play sessions but tend to be hostile, negative and distant. They often refrain from seeking teachers even if physically hurt (Sroufe, 1983). They also elicit more aggression from their partners. Bullying may even be associated with characteristic attachment histories for the victim and victimiser (Sroufe, 1989). Bullies are often the product of rejecting, emotionally distant patterns of parenting. Conversely, their victims are likely to have a background of parental over-involvement.

Anxious-resistant infants show poor peer relationship skills. They often appear helpless, dependent, visibly distressed by the situation, make few approaches to peers and tend to ignore those made to them. They often score higher than anxious-avoidant or securely attached children on measures of social dominance and social participation, but their impulsive behaviour is less effective in that they are also likely to be rated lowest in peer status (LaFreniere and Sroufe, 1985). Ambivalent children actually receive more disruptive, resistance and conflict responses from peers. They will often remain close to or at least oriented toward their teacher (Sroufe, 1983).

The research examined so far clearly shows the impact of attachment on the acquisition of social skills and social orientation, but it does not reveal the effect of mutual quality of attachment on the quality of later longer-term relationships. Recent research has addressed this issue. A study by Park and Waters (1989) found that the quality of a best friend relationship is influenced by the attachment histories of both partners. In this study pairs of four-year-old friends were observed during free play. Where both members were classified as securely attached the interaction was more harmonious, less controlling, more responsive, and happier than was the case in pairs where one member was insecurely attached.

Even in adolescence, quality of relationships with parents may continue to be more important for well-being than those with peers. Maternal support is a major factor in the adolescent's self-esteem (Greenberg, Siegel and Leitch, 1983). In a study of late adolescents, Kobak and Sceery (1988) found first-year college students classed as having secure attachment were rated as less anxious, more 'ego resilient', and less hostile by their peers, and perceived their relations with family and friends as more supportive.

Romantic love

An exciting recent line of research on post-infant attachment has focused on romantic love. A model of romantic love based on the idea that romantic attachments parallel the secure, ambivalent, and avoidant types of child-parent attachments was initially proposed by Hazan and Shaver (1987). They reported that the relative frequency of these three styles of attachment are approximately the same in adults and infants. Subsequent studies have largely confirmed a relationship between these self-reported attachment styles and the subjective experience of love (Feeney and Noller, 1991). A refinement in the theoretical analysis of love qua attachment has suggested that styles of attachment could be conceptualised in terms of two underlying dimensions, the individual's model of Self and Other (Bartholomew, 1990). For many purposes it may be more useful to think of attachment in terms of a relative placement on these two dimensions rather than simply a small number of types such as secure or insecure (Brennan, Shaver and Tobey, 1991). While such typologies are easier to deal with in diagnostic and social policy terms, they undoubtedly obscure some of the rich variety of forms that attachment takes.

The ways in which adults describe their childhood attachments and their experience of love show impressive parallels, but we must be cautious in how we interpret this evidence. Two closely related problems prevent the simple conclusion that children's early attachments establish a pattern for their later romantic relationships. First, there is little direct evidence for a continuity between patterns of childhood attachment and romantic. It is simply similar patterns that have been noted in these two phenomena. Second, there are problems in relying on people's recollections of childhood relationships. Current experiences may well colour our memories of earlier relationships (Miller, 1989). At the very least it seems likely that our perceptions of current and past relationships are affecting each other.

The above lines of research show the increasing influence of attachment concepts on our general thinking about personal relationships across the whole lifespan. These developments in attachment theory and research are important because they establish an important continuity in our understanding of relationships. They also establish important connections between bodies of literature and hence open up new lines of research in previously discrete area of research.

CONCLUSION

Research on children's relationships has come a long way since this book was originally published in 1980. Although I have examined only a few strands of the vast amounts of research currently being produced, it is evident that major advances have been made. A researcher returning to the area after an absence would scarcely recognise the terrain. The current picture of children's friendships and peer relationships that research presents is considerably more balanced and mature, even though it still has numerous theoretical and methodological shortcomings to address. Considerable optimism may be derived from the fact that current knowledge has advanced sufficiently to be of practical utility. Children can and are being helped by the products of research over the past fourteen years. At the current accelerating rate of research progress, the field holds much promise for progress over the next fourteen years.

REFERENCES

Applegate, J. L., Burke, J. A., Burleson, B. R., Delia, J. G., and Kline, S. L. (1985). Reflection enhancing parental communication. In L. E. Sigel (Ed.), *Parental Belief Systems: the Psychological Consequences for Children*. Hillsdale, N.J.: Erlbaum.

Asher, S. R. (1985). An evolving paradigm in social skill training research with children. In B. H. Schneider, K. H. Rubin, and J. E. Ledingham (Eds.), *Children's Peer Relations: Issues in Assessment and Intervention*. New York: Springer-Verlag.

Asher, S. R., and Parker, J. G. (1989). Significance of peer relationship problems in childhood. In B. H. Schneider, G. Attili, J. Nadel, and R. P. Weissberg (Eds.), *Social Competence in Developmental Perspective*. Dordrecht: Kluwer.

Austin, A. B., and Lindauer, S. K. (1990). Parent-child conversation of more-liked and less-liked children. *Journal of Genetic Psychology*, 151, 5–23.

Bartholomew, K. (1990). Avoidance of intimacy: An attachment perspective. *Journal of Social and Personal Relationships*, 7, 141–178.

Baskett, L. M., and Johnson, S. M. (1982). The young child's interaction with parents versus siblings: A behavioral analysis. *Child Development*, 53, 643–650.

Berndt, T. J., and Perry, T. B. (1986). Children's perceptions of friendship as supportive relationships. *Developmental Psychology*, 22, 640–648.

Bhavnagri, N. P., and Parke, R. D. (1991). Parents as direct facilitators of children's peer relationships: Effects of age of child and sex of parent. *Journal of Social and Personal Relationships*, 8, 423–440.

Bierman, K. L. (1989). Improving the peer relations of rejected children. In B. B. Lahey and E. E. Kazdin (Eds.), *Advances in Clinical Child Psychology*, vol. 12. New York: Plenum.

Bierman, K. L., and McCauley, E. (1987). Children's descriptions of their peer interactions: useful information for clinical child assessment. *Journal of Clinical Child Psychology*, 16, 9–18.

Bierman, K. L., Miller, C. M., and Stabb, S. (1987). Improving the social behavior and peer acceptance of rejected boys: effects of social skills training with instructions and prohibitions. *Journal of Consulting and Clinical Psychology*, 55, 194–200.

Bigelow, B. J. (1982). Disengagement and development of social concepts: toward a theory of friendship. Paper presented to the International conference on Personal Relationships, University of Wisconsin at Madison, July.

Black, B., and Hazen, N. L. (1990). Social status and patterns of communication in acquainted and unacquainted preschool children. *Developmental Psychology*, 26, 379–387.

Blyth, D. A., and Traeger, C. (1988). Adolescent self-esteem and perceived relationships with parents and peers. In S. Salzinger, J. Antrobus, and M. Hammer (Eds.), *Social Networks of Children, Adolescents and College Students*. Hillsdale, N.J.: Erlbaum.

Brachfeld-Child, S., and Schiavo, R. S. (1990). Interactions of preschool and kindergarten friends and acquaintances. *Journal of Genetic Psychology*, 151, 45–58.

Brennan, K. A., Shaver, P. R., and Tobey, A. E. (1991). Attachment styles, gender and parental problem drinking. *Journal of Social and Personal Relationships*, **8**, 451–466.

Bryant, B. (1985). The neighborhood walk: Sources of support in middle childhood. *Monographs of the Society for Research in Child Development*, **50** (3, Serial No. 210).

Buhrmester, D., and Furman, W. (1987). The development of companionship and intimacy. *Child Development*, **58**, 1101–1113.

Burleson, B. R., Delia, J. G., and Applegate, J. L. (1990). Effects of mothers' disciplinary and comforting strategies on children's communication skills and acceptance by the peer group. Paper presented to the Fifth International Conference on Personal Relationships, Oxford University, Oxford, England. July.

Button, L. (1979). Friendship patterns. *Journal of Adolescence*, **2**, 187–199.

Cartledge, G., and Milburn, J. F. (1980). *Teaching Social Skills to Children*. New York: Pergamon.

Clark, R. A., and Jones, J. (1990). Parental reflection enhancing communication, children's person centered communication skills, and children's success in peer relationships. Paper presented to the Fifth International Conference on Personal Relationships, Oxford University, Oxford, England. July.

Coie, J. D., and Koeppl, G. K. (1990). Adapting intervention to the problems of aggressive and disruptive rejected children. In S. R. Asher and J. D. Coie (Eds.), *Peer Rejection in Childhood*. New York: Cambridge University Press.

Coie, J. D., and Krehbiel, G. (1984). Effects of academic tutoring on the social status of low-achieving, socially rejected children. *Child Development*, **55**, 1465–1478.

Coie, J. D., and Kupersmidt, J. (1983). A behavioral analysis of emerging social status in boys' groups. *Child Development*, **54**, 1400–1416.

Cox, R. D., and Gunn, W. B. (1980). Interpersonal skills in the schools: Assessment and curriculum development. In D. P. Rathjen and J. P. Foreyt (Eds.), *Social Competence*. New York: Pergamon.

Delia, J. G., and Applegate, J. L. (1990). From cognition to communication to cognition to communication. Paper presented to the Fifth International Conference on Personal Relationships, Oxford University, Oxford, England. July.

Denham, S. A. (1986). Social cognition, prosocial behavior, and emotion in preschoolers: Contextual validation. *Child Development*, **57**, 194–201.

Dodge, K. A., and Frame, C. L. (1982). Social cognitive biases and deficits in aggressive boys. *Child Development*, **53**, 620–635.

Earn, B. M., and Sobol, M. P. (1990). A categorical analysis of children's attributions for social success and failure. *Psychological Record*, **40**, 173–185.

East, P. L., and Rook, K. S. (1992). Compensatory patterns of support among children's peer relationships: A test using school friends, nonschool friends, and siblings. *Developmental Psychology*, **28**, 1, 163–172.

Eisenberg, N., Tryon, K., and Cameron, E. (1984). The relation of preschoolers peer interaction to their sex-typed toy choice. *Child Development*, **55**, 1044–1050.

Erickson, M. F., Sroufe, L. A., and Egeland, B. (1985). The relationship between quality of attachment and behavior problems in preschool in a high-risk sample. *Monographs of the Society for Research in Child Development*, **50**, 147–166.

Erwin, P. G. (1993). *Friendship and Peer Relations in Children*. Chichester: Wiley.

Erwin, P. G. , and Ruane, G. (in press). The effects of a short-term problem solving programme with children. *Counselling Psychology Quarterly*.

Fagot, B. I. (1981). Continuity and change in play styles as a function of sex of child. *International Journal of Behavioral Development*, **4**, 37–43.

Feeney, J. A., and Noller, P. (1991). Attachment style and verbal descriptions of romantic partners. *Journal of Social and Personal Relationships*, **8**, 187–215.

Feiring, C., and Lewis, M. (1989). The social networks of girls and boys from early through middle childhood. In D. Belle (Ed.), *Children's social networks and social supports*. Chichester: Wiley.

Furman, W. (1980). Promoting social development: Developmental implications for treatment. In B. B. Lahey and E. E. Kazdin (Eds.), *Advances in Clinical Child Psychology*, vol. 3. New York: Plenum.

Furman, W., Giberson, R., White, A. S., Gravin, L. A., and Wehner, E. A. (1989). Enhancing peer relations in school systems. In B. H. Schneider, G. Attili, J. Nadel and R. P. Weissberg (Eds.), *Social Competence in Developmental Perspective*. Dordrecht, Netherlands: Kluwer.

Furman, L. N., and Walden, T. A. (1990). Effect of script knowledge on preschool children's communicative interactions. *Developmental Psychology*, **26**, 227-233.

Goetz, T. E., and Dweck, C. S. (1980). Learned helplessness in social situations. *Journal of Personality and Social Psychology*, **39**, 246-255.

Goldstein, A. P., Gershaw, N. J., and Sprafkin, R. P. (1985). Structured learning. In L. L'Abate and M. A. Milan (Eds.), *Handbook of Social Skills Training and Research*. New York: Wiley.

Gottman, J. M. (1983). How children become friends. *Child Development Monographs*, **48**, (3).

Gottman, J. M. (1986). The world of coordinated play: same- and cross-sex friendship in young children. In J. M. Gottman and J. G. Parker (Eds.), *Conversations of Friends: Speculations on Affective Development*. Cambridge: Cambridge University Press.

Gottman, J. M. (1991). Finding the roots of children's problems with other children. *Journal of Social and Personal Relationships*, **8**, 441-448.

Greenberg, M. T., Siegel, J. M., and Leitch, C. J. (1983). The nature and importance of attachment relationships to parents and peers during adolescence. *Journal of Youth and Adolescence*, **12**, 373-386.

Gresham, F. M., and Nagle, R. J. (1980). Social skills with children: responsiveness to modeling and coaching as a function of peer orientation. *Journal of Consulting and Clinical Psychology*, **18**, 718-729.

Guralnick, M. J., and Paul-Brown, D. (1984). Communicative adjustments during behavior-request episodes among children at different developmental levels. *Child Development*, **55**, 911-919.

Harper, L. V., and Huie, K. S. (1985). The effects of prior group experience, age, and familiarity on the quality and organization of preschoolers' social relationships. *Child Development*, **56**, 704-717.

Hartup, W. W. (1983). Peer relations. In E. M. Hetherington (Ed.), *Handbook of Child Psychology (vol. 4): Socialization, Personality, and Social Development*. New York: Wiley.

Hartup, W. W. (1986). On relationships and development. In W. W. Hartup and Z. Rubin (Eds.), *Relationships and Development*. Hillsdale, N.J.: Erlbaum.

Hartup, W. W., Laursen, B., Stewart, M. I., and Eastenson, A. (1988). Conflict and friendship relations of young children. *Child Development*, **59**, 1590-1600.

Harvey, J. H., Weber, A. L., Yarkin, K. L., and Stewart, B. E. (1982). An attributional approach to relationships breakdown and dissolution. In S. W. Duck (Ed.), *Personal Relationships, vol. 4: Dissolving Personal Relationships*. London: Academic Press.

Hay, D. F., Pedersen, J., and Nash, A. (1982). Dyadic interaction in the first year of life. In K. H. Rubin and H. S. Ross (Eds.), *Peer Relationships and Social Skills in Childhood*. New York: Springer-Verlag.

Hazan, C., and Shaver, P. (1987). Romantic love conceptualized as an attachment process. *Journal of Personality and Social Psychology*, **52**, 511-524.

Hogg, M. A., and Abrams, D. (1988). *Social Identifications*. London: Routledge.

Hollinger, J. D. (1987). Social skills for behaviorally disordered children as preparation for mainstreaming: Theory, practice, and new directions. *Remedial and Special Education*, **8**, 17-27.

Hudson, L. M., Forman, E. R., and Brion-Meisels, S. (1982). Role-taking as a predictor of prosocial behavior in cross-age tutors. *Child Development*, **53**, 1320-1329.

Huston, A. C. (1983). Sex typing. In P. H. Mussen and E. M. Hetherington (Eds.), *Handbook of Child Psychology (vol. 4): Socialization, Personality, and Social Development* (4th edition). New York: Wiley.

Hymel, S. (1986). Interpretations of peer behavior: affective bias in childhood and adolescence. *Child Development*, **57**, 431-445.

Ironsmith, M., and Poteat, G. M. (1990). Behavioral correlates of preschool sociometric status and the prediction of teacher ratings of behavior in kindergarten. *Journal of Clinical Child Psychology*, **19**, 17-25.

Jacobson, J. L., and Wille, D. E. (1986). The influence of attachment patterns on developmental changes from the toddler to the preschool period. *Child Development*, **57**, 338-347.

Keller, M., and Wood, P. (1989). Development of friendship reasoning: A study of interindividual differences in intraindividual change. *Developmental Psychology*, **25**, 820-826.

Kobak, R. R., and Sceery, A. (1988). Attachment in late adolescence: Working models, affect regulation, and representation of self and others. *Child Development*, **59**, 135-146.

Kohler, F. W. and Strain, P. S. (1990). Peer assisted interventions: Early promises, notable achievements, and future aspirations. *Clinical Psychology Review*, **10**, 4, 441-452.

Kupersmidt, J. B., Coie, J. D., and Dodge, K. A. (1990). The role of peer relationships in the development of disorder. In S. R. Asher and J. D. Coie (Ed.), *Peer Rejection in Childhood*. Cambridge University Press.

Ladd, G. W. (1981). Effectiveness of a social learning method for enhancing children's social interaction and peer acceptance. *Child Development*, **52**, 171-178.

Ladd, G. (1983). Social networks of popular, average and rejected children in social settings. *Merrill-Palmer Quarterly*, **29**, 282-307.

Ladd, G. W. (1990). Having friends, keeping friends, making friends, and being liked by peers in the classroom: predictors of children's early school adjustment. *Child Development*, **61**, 1081-1100.

Ladd, G. W., and Asher, S. R. (1985). Social skills training and children's peer relations. In L. L'Abate and M. A. Milan (Eds.), *Handbook of Social Skills Training and Research*. New York: Wiley.

Ladd, G. W., and Golter, B. S. (1988). Parents management of preschoolers peer relations: Is it related to children's social competence? *Developmental Psychology*, **24**, 109-117.

Ladd, G. W., and Mize, J. (1983). A cognitive-social learning model of social skills training. *Psychological Review*, **90**, 127-157.

LaFreniere, P. J., and Sroufe, L. A. (1985). Profiles of peer competence in the preschool: interrelations between measures, influence of social ecology, and relation to attachment theory. *Developmental Psychology*, **21**, 56-69.

LaFreniere, P., Strayer, F. F., and Gauthier, R. (1984). The emergence of same-sex affiliative preferences among preschool peers: A developmental/ethological perspective. *Child Development*, **55**, 1958-1965.

Lamb, M. E., Easterbrooks, M. A., and Holden, G. W. (1980). Reinforcement and punishment among preschoolers: Characteristics, effects, and correlates. *Child Development*, **51**, 1230-1236.

Ledingham, J. E., and Younger, A. J. (1985). The influence of the evaluator on assessments of children's social skills. In B. H. Schneider, K. H. Rubin, and J. E. Ledingham (Eds.), *Children's Peer Relations: Issues in Assessment and Intervention*. New York: Springer-Verlag.

Levinger, G., and Levinger, A. C. (1986). The temporal course of close relationships: some thoughts about the development of children's ties. In W. W. Hartup and Z. Rubin (Eds.), *Relationships and Development*. Hillsdale, N.J.: Erlbaum.

Lockheed, M. E. (1986). Reshaping the social order: the case of gender segregation. *Sex Roles*, **14**, 617–628.

Maccoby, E. E., and Jacklin, C. N. (1987). Gender segregation in childhood. In E. H. Reese (Ed.), *Advances in Child Development and Behavior*, vol. 20. New York: Academic Press.

MacPherson, J. C. (1984). Environments and interaction in rows-and-column classrooms. *Environment and Behavior*, **16**, 481–502.

Martin, C. L. and Little, J. K. (1990). The relation of gender understanding to children's sex-typed preferences and gender stereotypes. *Child Development*, **61**, 1427–1439.

Medrich, E. A., Rosen, J., Rubin, V., and Buckley, S. (1982). *The Seriousness of Growing Up: A Study of Children's Lives Outside School*. Berkeley: University of California Press.

Miller, J. B. (1889). Memories of peer relations and styles of conflict management. *Journal of Social and Personal Relationships*, **6**, 487–504.

Mize, J., and Cox, R. A. (1990). Social knowledge and social competence: Number and quality of strategies as predictors of social behavior. *Journal of Genetic Psychology*, **151**, 117–127.

Mize, J., and Ladd, G. W. (1990a). Toward the development of successful social skills training for preschool children. In S. R. Asher and J. D. Coie (Eds.), *Peer Rejection in Childhood*. New York: Cambridge University Press.

Mize, J., and Ladd, G. W. (1990b). A cognitive social learning approach to social skills training with low-status preschool children. *Developmental Psychology*, **26**, 388–397.

Montemayor, R., and Van Komen, R. (1985). The development of sex differences in friendship patterns and peer group structure during adolescence. *Journal of Early Adolescence*, **5**, 285–294.

Moore, T., Pepler, D., Weinberg, B., and Hammond, L. (1990). Research on children from violent homes. *Canada's Mental Health*, **38**, 19–23.

Nelson, J., and Aboud, F. E. (1985). The resolution of social conflict among friends. *Child Development*, **56**, 1009–1017.

Nowicki, S., and Oxenford, C. (1989). The relation of hostile nonverbal communication styles to popularity in preadolescent children. *Journal of Genetic Psychology*, **150**, 39–44.

O'Donnell, L., and Stueve, A. (1983). Mothers as social agents: structuring the communities activities of school aged children. In H. Z. Lopata and J. H. Pleck (Eds.), *Jobs and Families*. Greenwich, Conn.: JAI.

Park, K. A., and Waters, E. (1989). Security of attachment and preschool friendships. *Child Development*, **60**, 1076–1081.

Parke, R. D., and Bhavnagri, N. P. (1989). Parents as managers of children's peer relationships. In D. Belle (Ed.), *Children's Social Networks and Social Supports*. New York: Wiley.

Parker, J. G., and Asher, S. R. (1987). Peer relations and later personal adjustment: Are low accepted children at risk? *Psychological Bulletin*, **102**, 357–389.

Parker, J. G., and Gottman, J. M. (1989). Social and emotional development in a relational context. In T. J. Berndt and G. W. Ladd (Eds.), *Peer Relationships in Child Development*. New York: Wiley.

Patterson, C. J., Kupersmidt, J. B., and Griesler, P. C. (1990). Children's perceptions of self and of relationships with others as a function of sociometric status. *Child Development*, **61**, 1335–1349.

Patterson, C. J., Vaden, N. A., and Kupersmidt, J. B. (1991). Family background, recent life events and peer rejection during childhood. *Journal of Social and Personal Relationships*, **8**, 347–361.

Pennebaker, J. W., Hendler, C. S., Durrett, M. E., and Richards, P. (1981). Social factors influencing absenteeism due to illness in nursery school children. *Child Development*, **52**, 692–700.

Phinney, J. S., and Rotheram, M. J. (1980). Influence of sex of speaker and respondent on the type and success of young children's social overtures. Paper presented to the British Psychological Society Developmental Section Annual Conference, Edinburgh, September.

Phyfe-Perkins, E. (1980). Children's behavior in preschool settings: A review of research concerning the influence of the physical environment. In L. G. Katz (Ed.), *Current Topics in Early Childhood Education*, vol. 3. Norwood, N. J.: Ablex.

Putallaz, M. (1983). Predicting children's sociometric status from their behavior. *Child Development*, **54**, 1417–1426.

Putallaz, M. (1987). Maternal behavior and children's sociometric status. *Child Development*, **58**, 324–340.

Putallaz, M., Costanzo, P. R., and Smith, R. B. (1991). Maternal recollections of childhood peer relationships: Implications for their children's social competence. *Journal of Social and Personal Relationships*, **8**, 403–422.

Renshaw, P. D. (1981). The roots of peer interaction research: A historical analysis of the 1930s. In S. R. Asher and J. M. Gottman (Eds.), *The Development of Children's Friendships*. Cambridge: Cambridge University Press.

Rholes, W. S., and Ruble, D. N. (1984). Children's understanding of dispositional characteristics of others. *Child Development*, **55**, 550–560.

Rook, K. S., and Peplau, L. A. (1982). Perspectives on helping the lonely. In L. A. Peplau and D. Perlman (Eds.), *Loneliness: A Sourcebook of Current Theory, Research and Therapy*. New York: Wiley.

Roopnarine, J. L. (1985). Changes in peer-directed behavior following preschool experience. *Journal of Personality and Social Psychology*, **48**, 740–745.

Ross, H. S., and Lollis, S. P. (1989). A social relations analysis of toddler peer relationships. *Child Development*, **60**, 1082–1091.

Rotheram, M. J. (1980). Social skills training programs in elementary and high school classrooms. In D. P. Rathjen and J. P. Foreyt (Eds.), *Social Competence*. New York: Pergamon.

Rotheram-Borus, M. J., and Phinney, J. S. (1990). Patterns of social expectations among Black and Mexican-American children. *Child Development*, **61**, 2, 542–556.

Rubin, K. H. (1985). Socially withdrawn children: An "at risk" population? In B. H. Schneider, K. H. Rubin, and J. E. Ledingham (Eds.), *Children's Peer Relations: Issues in Assessment and Intervention*. New York: Springer Verlag.

Rubin, K. H., and Daniels-Beirness, T. (1983). Concurrent and predictive correlates of sociometric status in kindergarten and grade one children. *Merrill-Palmer Quarterly*, **29**, 337–352.

Rubin, K. H., Daniels-Beirness, T., and Hayvren, M. (1982). Correlates of peer acceptance and rejection in early childhood. *Canadian Journal of Behavioral Sciences*, **14**, 338–349.

Rubin, Z. (1980). *Children's Friendships*. London: Fontana.

Russell, A., and Finnie, V. (1990). Preschool children's social status and maternal instructions to assist group entry. *Developmental Psychology*, **26**, 603–611.

Schneider, B. H. (1989). Between developmental wisdom and children's social skills training. In B. H. Schneider, G. Attili, J. Nadel, and R. P. Weissberg (Eds.), *Social Competence in Developmental Perspective*. Dordrecht, Netherlands: Kluwer.

Schofield, M. J., and Kafer, N. F. (1985). Children's understanding of friendship issues: Development by stage or sequence? *Journal of Social and Personal Relationships*, **2**, 151–165.

Selman, R. L. (1980). *The Growth of Interpersonal Understanding*. New York: Academic Press.

Serbin, L. A., Sprafkin, C., Elman, M., and Doyle, A-B. (1984). The early development of sex differentiated patterns of social influence. *Canadian Journal of Social Science*, **14**, 350–363.

Shantz, D. W. (1986). Conflict, aggression and peer status: an observational study. *Child Development*, **57**, 1322–1332.

Shantz, C. U., and Hobart, C. J. (1989). Social conflict and development. In T. J. Berndt and

G. W. Ladd, *Peer Relationships in Child Development*. New York: Wiley.

Shea, J. (1981). Changes in interpersonal distances and categories of play behavior in the early weeks of preschool. *Developmental Psychology*, **17**, 417–425.

Shrum, W., Cheek, N. H., and Hunter, S. M. (1988). Friendship in school: Gender and racial homophily. *Sociology of Education*, **61**, 227–239.

Smetana, J. G., and Letourneau, K. J. (1984). Development of gender constancy and children's sex-typed free play behavior. *Developmental Psychology*, **20**, 691–696.

Smith, P. K., and Connolly, K. J. (1980). *The Ecology of Preschool Behavior*. Cambridge: Cambridge University Press.

Snow, M. E., Jacklin, C. N., and Maccoby, E. E. (1983). Sex of child differences in father-child interaction at one year of age. *Child Development*, **54**, 227–232.

Spence, S. H. (1987). The relationship between social-cognitive skills and peer sociometric status. *British Journal of Developmental Psychology*, **5**, 347–356.

Sroufe, L. A. (1983). Infant-caregiver attachment and patterns of adaptation in preschool: the roots of maladaptation and competence. In M. Perlmutter (Ed.), *Minnesota Symposium on Child Psychology*, vol. 16. Hillsdale, N.J.: Erlbaum.

Sroufe, L. A. (1989). Relationships and relationship disturbances. In A. J. Sameroff and R. N. Emde (Eds.), *Relationship Disturbances in Early Childhood*. New York: Basic Books.

Sroufe, L. A., and Fleeson, J. (1986). Attachment and the construction of relationships. In W. W. Hartup and Z. Rubin, (Eds.), *Relationships and Development*. Hillsdale, N.J.: Erlbaum.

Sroufe, L. A., and Jacobvitz, D. (1989). Diverging pathways, developmental transformations, multiple etiologies and the problem of continuity in development. *Human Development*, **32**, 196–203.

Takac, R., and Benyamini, K. (1989). Criteria for children's adjustment in school, peer group, and youth movement. *School Psychology International*, **10**, 257–263.

Thorne, B. (1986). Girls and boys together...but mostly apart: Gender arrangements in elementary schools. In W. W. Hartup and Z. Rubin (Eds.), *Relationships and Development*. Hillsdale, N.J.: Erlbaum.

Van Vliet, W. (1981). The environmental context of children's friendships: An empirical and conceptual examination of the role of child density. *EDRA Environmental Design Research Association*, no. 12, 216–224.

Van Vliet, W. (1986). The methodological and conceptual basis of environmental policies for children. *Prevention in Human Services*, **4**, 59–78.

Vandell, D. L., and Wilson, K. S. (1987). Infants interactions with mother, sibling, and peer: Contrasts and relationships between interaction systems. *Child Development*, **58**, 176–186.

Vandell, D. L., Wilson, K. S., and Buchanan, N. R. (1980). Peer interaction in the first year of life: An examination of its structure, content and sensitivity. *Child Development*, **51**, 481–488.

Waas, G. A., and Honor, S. A. (1990). Situational attributions and dispositional inferences: The development of peer reputation. *Merrill-Palmer Quarterly*, **36**, 2, 239–260.

Wanlass, R. L., and Prinz, R. J. (1982). Methodological issues in conceptualizing and treating childhood social isolation. *Psychological Bulletin*, **92**, 39–55.

Whiting, B. B., and Edwards, C. P. (1988). *Children of Different Worlds*. Cambridge, Mass.: Harvard University Press.

Wilson, P. and Hersov, L. (1985). Individual and group psychotherapy. In M. Rutter and L. Hersov (Eds.), *Child and Adolescent Psychiatry* (2nd edition). Oxford: Blackwell.

Preface [1994]

Phil Erwin, in his new introductory chapter, has plotted the major trends in research that have taken place since the volume was originally published in 1980. Some of these changes were perhaps predictable. Broadening research interest to take account of social and environmental contexts of relationships was one domain which we might confidently have expected to occur. Also predictable was the continued trend for exploring dysfunctional relationships and the role which peer rejection and neglect were likely to play in later childhood and adult relations.

But the late 1970s and early 1980s saw some exciting new directions for research which the book at that time could scarcely begin to foretell. Interest in children's theories of mind was just surfacing and this led to much more sophisticated conceptualizations of children's cognitive processes. We learned a lot more of the subtleties of children's thinking and we learned to recognize that children are capable of cognitive functioning in ways that had hitherto been untapped. The methodological innovations in exploring children's explanations and justifications for action and thought were setting the scene for new and intriguing models of the development of cognitive processing.

Coupled with this interest in children's theories of mind was the much clearer appreciation of the intimately interwoven relationship between cognitive and social development. We started to see relationships as resources which equip individuals to face new social situations, make new friends and confront new challenges. Relationships therefore serve many different functions: they buffer us from stress;they are 'practice' for the construction of later more mature relationships;and, above all, they provide the context for the development and manifestation of basic competencies.

The idea of children serving as resources for other children is particularly appealing. In informal group settings and in formal educational settings, the 1980s and early 1990s have seen the development of research programs which have been exploring the ways in which children's learning and cognitive development can be facilitated by interactive group processes: cooperative learning, peer tutoring and collaborative problem-solving. Close relationships are characterized by more effective dialogue. Friends are more willing to voice their opinions to each other than are non-friends; they are more inclined to listen to advice from their friends, to criticize and to negotiate. Friends also have to learn to manage their

xxxvii

relationships with each other, at least the relationships that matter to them. Their interactions take more effort, more care and discipline, more planning and control. It is exactly these regulative functions which render these relationships so valuable as the launching ground for children's acquisition of new knowledge.

It would be interesting to speculate what new insights the next fourteen years of research will hold. Our best bet is that we will gain better conceptualizations of the manner in which children acquire understanding of their social worlds through sharing their ideas with others. Time will tell.

HUGH C. FOOT
ANTONY J. CHAPMAN
JEAN R. SMITH

November 1993

Preface [1980]

Most people take their friendships for granted and rarely consider how barren life would be without them. However, having friends is not purely a desirable objective in itself; in developmental terms it is an important social achievement and an index of the proficiency with which we can establish and maintain long-term relationships with others. To the researcher interested in the growth of social competency, therefore, the characteristics of children's friendship relations would seem to provide an ideal starting-point. Yet it is surprising how few studies have focused upon friendships during childhood and adolescence, when the foundation stones of intimate adult relationships are laid.

The investigation of children's social competence through their friendships has distinct advantages by virtue of the status that friendships occupy as 'high-intensity' relationships. Processes and skills that occur during normal peer relations may appear all the more strikingly during friendship relations: such processes as cooperation, modelling and accommodation are more readily identified, more sharply defined and more easily analysed. From a practical point of view the study of friendship also highlights the trainability of social skills in young children. Findings from friendship research are already forming the basis of training programmes specifically designed to cultivate successful social relations in early childhood.

This volume sets out to give an account of different facets of friendships throughout childhood. It is a compilation of review chapters written by some of the leading researchers who have drawn together current findings and ideas in the major research areas of children's friendships and social relations. The volume is designed for all those with academic and applied interests in children's social development. Amongst psychologists it will be of particular interest to those working in the fields of social, developmental, and educational psychology. It will also appeal to sociologists and ethologists whose interests lie in the aetiology, culture, and organization of children's social groups. For those who are professionally concerned with children in teaching, in child care, or in social work there is also much of value in the book. Several chapters deal specifically with children's relationships in the classroom, their conceptions of their peers and the development of friendship cliques.

HUGH FOOT
ANTONY CHAPMAN
JEAN SMITH

Introduction

HUGH C. FOOT,
ANTONY J. CHAPMAN,
and
JEAN R. SMITH

To a large extent psychological interest in children's friendships has been a spin-off from a much broader growth of research in children's social relationships. In common with the contributors to this volume and other researchers of children's interactions, we essentially envisage friendship as a fundamental, albeit special kind of, social relationship, and the emphasis in the title upon friendship *and* social relations is intended to highlight the general social context in which friendships occur. Hartup (1978a, b) stresses the contribution that friendships make to the development of social competency and mature social behaviours in children. La Gaipa (1978) regards friendships as the building blocks for maintaining the social systems of children and adolescents at all levels. Understanding the formation, dynamics and terminations of their friendships is dependent upon a wider structural knowledge of their progress in other social contexts.

It is perhaps for this very reason that explanatory accounts of friendship development have adopted the primary standpoints of social development theory. In one sense this is a desirable state of a affairs inasmuch as theories about friendship should reflect, or be easily translatable into, the terms of more general developmental theories. In another sense, however, it may impose a somewhat constraining perspective upon the ways researchers might wish to proceed both in their thinking and in the nature of their empirical work. In the introduction to their 1975 volume, *Friendship and Peer Relations*, Lewis and Rosenblum have argued that psychoanalytic and Piagetian theories of human development have so dominated research in social development, particularly in terms of child-care practice, that they have 'led to a suppression of active study of children's early social behaviour other than that directed toward the parents' (p. 1).

1

However, the position does appear to be changing in more recent years: researchers are becoming more eclectic in their research approaches and less dogmatically affiliated to particular theoretical frameworks. Of course no one would deny that sound theory is much needed, particularly in this important area of social development. However, adopting a long-term strategy, we believe that a 'loosening up' on the reins of traditional developmental theory is necessary at the present time, giving scope for more divergent and adventurous thinking, more basic data collection of all kinds, and a wider application of research techniques drawn from other branches of psychology and the social sciences.

In some measure this book represents a step in this direction. Within the study of children's friendships, we have deliberately sought sociological and ethological as well as psychological perspectives; and we have aimed at presenting a broad array of theoretical and methodological approaches which in our view serve to open the field up and prompt fresh kinds of attack upon research problems. To this extent the positions represented in this volume are relatively diverse and they draw widely upon thinking in a number of theoretical areas. Nevertheless, we do see this as a healthy sign, even if in the short term there are some definitional and conceptual conflicts which prevent the erection of a single, coherent, theoretical framework.

This is not to suggest that there is not already ample room for improvements in conceptual clarity and methodological standardization. Even on some elementary definitional issues there may be few agreed maxims to follow. For example, we are continually surprised to find in studies comparing 'friends' with 'non-friends' how many researchers fail to provide an adequate description of their 'non-friend' control samples. From a definitional point of view, a 'non-friend' might be the term applied to any companion from a complete stranger to a person with whom one is quite well acquainted but does not actually number amongst one's chosen friends. In psychological terms these types of non-friends are poles apart, particularly amongst young children who are so much more apprehensive and uncertain than adults in the presence of a genuine stranger. Even if the sample is known in these terms, there is, of course, an inevitable problem in dichotomizing friends and non-friends for comparison purposes; this is a problem which is all too rarely acknowledged in the nursery/classroom situation where the majority of studies are undertaken. The children in a given class all know each other to a greater or lesser extent but most sociometric studies, as a prelude to behavioural observation, only require each child to identify his/her three, four or at most five best friends (Austin and Thompson, 1948; Durojaiye, 1969; Kay and McKinney, 1967; Mabe and Williams, 1975; Miller and Maruyama, 1976). Such a cut-off tends to polarize all the remaining children into a homogeneous group of non-friends and no further interest is taken in the differing degrees of acquaintanceship or positive affect that characterize the child's relationship with them. The dichotomy between friends and non-friends, therefore, ignores what is in essence a continuous dimension of friendly affect.

Standardization of the procedures used for determining friendship choices is another much needed development for sample selection. In the sociometric method numerous procedural variations have proliferated and it is not clear how such variations may influence the final samples selected. Many of these variations are probably trivial and are adopted justifiably to suit the demands of the experimental or classroom situation. For example, whether the sociometric test requires oral or written responses, whether it limits the number of choices allowed each child (cf. Lindzey and Byrne, 1968), how it prescribes the number and nature of the criteria upon which the choices are to be made, and whether the choices made are ranked or unranked, weighted or unweighted, are all decisions which to some extent depend upon the research setting, the cognitive level of the subjects and the precise experimental purpose. However, other procedural points, which seem rarely to have troubled researchers, may also be crucial. Little consideration, for example, is given to whether the sociometric test should be administered by the researcher—who is unknown on the first occasion that s/he meets the children—or by the teacher who is, of course, well known. Such a variation might lead to widely disparate choices on the part of a child for all sorts of reasons, in much the same way as an adult will modify his/her criticism or praise for another according to the known relationship between the 'victim' and the companion with whom s/he is conversing at that moment. Even less consideration appears to have been given to whether the sociometric test should be administered to children in a group or individually. Most researchers have chosen to administer the test to a group, hence demanding written responses (Austin and Thompson, 1948; Ausubel, 1954; Bonncy, 1942, 1946, 1971; Davitz, 1955; Durojaiye, 1969; Mabe and Williams, 1975; Schulman, Ford, Bush and Kaspar, 1973; Thorpe, 1955). In many cases this decision was no doubt based upon expediency rather than upon any scientific rationale. From our experience however, working both inside and outside the classroom, we are convinced that children's choices of their best friends are at least partially—if not substantially—affected by momentary factors like besides whom they are standing or sitting when they complete the test, or whose eye they happen to catch as they scan the room in search of those to be chosen. Individual testing, despite the time it takes, does obviate the risk of arbitrarily prompted choices. These and many similar issues are analysed in the chapters that follow.

Before proceeding to review the scope and content of the book, we should like to return briefly to our opening comments concerning the social context in which friendships take place in order to address the more general issue of the functions of children's friendship relations. Friendships tend to be formed between age-peers, even though a higher proportion of children's interactions are with adults (especially parents) or with other children of different ages, such as siblings and their friends (Barker and Wright, 1955). While there is a growing interest in mixed-age interactions, stimulated largely by the work of Hartup and colleagues (Hartup, 1978a, b; Lougee, Grueneich and Hartup, 1977), there are apparently no studies which have examined friendships between companions of widely differing ages. Lewis and Rosenblum (1975) consider the function of peer relationships to be much less clear than the relationship between an infant and his/her caretaker adult. In purely hedonistic terms, and in evolutionary terms, this cannot be disputed, but we are less pessimistic than Lewis and Rosenblum that any statements of the function of peer relations can be no better than 'merely assumptions'. The fact that children do tend to select age-peers as their friends, or at least children whose cognitive abilities and social skills are comparable to their own, is more than purely suggestive that children need to engage in accurate social-reality testing from their interactions. They need to know how unique are their own experiences, under what rules of behaviour others operate in similar circumstances, what are merely parental quirks in control and discipline, and what are the universal social and moral norms. As Hartup (1978a) argues, social adaptation 'requires skills in both seeking help (dependency) and giving it (nurturance); being passive and being sociable; being able to attack others (aggression) and being able to contain one's hostility; being intimate and being self-reliant' (p. 132). Such skills can only be fostered in those peer interactions in which the child is on a roughly equal footing with his companions. These views of the functional value of childhood peer relations are held by many of the authors in this book and in particular by Strayer, by Vandell and Mueller, and by Rubin and Pepler.

STRUCTURE AND CONTENT

The chapters in this volume have been grouped under four main headings which appear to us to reflect the current major foci of empirical research into children's friendships. These groupings were derived on the basis of our adopting a problem-oriented strategy rather than in any sense a chronological, developmental approach. Nevertheless, the book's coverage extends right across childhood from the early social relations of preschool children into late adolescence. Thus most phases of cognitive and social development are considered in terms of their bearing upon changes in children's conceptions of friendship and in their characteristic friendship behaviours. These changes are, of course, substantial. As Hartup (1978a) says of the development of peer relations, it 'proceeds from simple organizations to complex hierarchies, from loosely differentiated interchanges to differentiated interaction, and from primitive awareness of the needs of others to reciprocal relations based on complex attributions' (p. 147).

Section 1 : Friendship values

This section is devoted to children's views and expectations of their friends, with particular emphasis upon changes in developmental stage. The basis for a developmental scale of friendship is outlined in Chapter 1 by Brian Bigelow and John La Gaipa who point out that age is not a sufficiently accurate indicator of social development for plotting the changes in children's friendship values. They are concerned with understanding the relationship between a child's developmental stage and his/her friendship values and behaviours with peers. Extending this scale from childhood into adolescence enables a richer analysis of the cognitions surrounding the decay of friendships as well as their growth.

Just as Bigelow and La Gaipa are concerned about understanding the social and cognitive dimensions of children's development as a framework for studying friendship values, so Anthony Mannarino—in Chapter 2—takes up the issue of defining in what ways friendships may be characterized as unique types of interpersonal relationships, differing from other kinds of associations. In elaborating his contention that the concept of reciprocity is the essential ingredient of friendship he stresses the need for researchers, when selecting 'friends', to ensure that their methodologies are sensitive to the mutuality of friendships and do not, as is all too frequently the case, accept unidirectional choices. Mannarino proceeds with an analysis of the theoretical perspectives of Gesell and Sullivan, arguing both that these authors' works have been sadly neglected by present-day developmental psychologists, and that they merit attention by virtue of the comprehensiveness and integrative power of their theories.

In the final chapter of this section, Chapter 3, David Barnett and Karl Zucker draw upon their study of children's expectancies and perceptions of their peers as a basis for determining the quality of their interpersonal behaviour. They describe the derivation of their Paired Hands Test (PHT), a projective device designed to investigate the 'others-concept' by measuring changes along a qualitative dimension of friendliness and hostility. Their basic interest in the test is to establish a tool whereby children's friendly behaviour, despite its operational complexity, can be adequately predicted. Their results are clearly encouraging in terms of establishing the PHT as a useful index for exploring a child's general expectancies about others; and preliminary findings suggest that the measure relates to other variables such as sex, socioeconomic status and intelligence.

Section 2 : Processes of acquaintance

The recent research on processes of acquaintance stems largely from earlier attempts to isolate specific determinants of friendship choice, and it is probably in this area of friendship that most studies have been conducted over the past 50 years. Variables that have been systematically explored range from propinquity or geographical proximity (cf. Furfey, 1929; King and Easthope, 1973; Seagoe, 1933; Wright, 1969) through similarity of socioeconomic status (cf. Bonney, 1946, 1949; King and Easthope, 1973; Nash, 1973) and race (cf. Asher, 1973; Carter, DeTine, Spero and Benson, 1975; Mabe and Williams, 1975; Singleton, 1974), to personality factors and intelligence (cf. Bigelow, 1977; Bonney, 1946; Duck, 1976, 1977). In addition to identifying relevant factors in friendship formation, current research is also moving towards an analysis of processes such as information synthesizing and inference making, which represent more dynamic and fruitful approaches to understanding acquaintance.

In Chapter 4 Steve Duck, David Miell and Heather Gaebler address themselves to the process of acquainting amongst children. They are concerned with children's developing skill in interpreting others' behaviours and in making inferences about personality. Clearly this process is a prerequisite for abstracting relevant information necessary for successful acquainting and for choosing friends. It is their view that the child's search for information about another person is essentially the same, or at least it involves the same mechanisms, as the adult's search, but that this information-seeking is complicated by maturational changes in social and cognitive skills. Friendship formations have clear implications for learning about the processes of interaction and for construing personality.

The importance of considering the cognitive stages of development in peer friendships is echoed strongly in Chapter 5 by Donald Carter, Susan DeTine-Carter and Forrest Benson, who outline the development of racial awareness, racial preferences and interracial acceptance in the classroom. In reviewing the evidence for interrace friendships they examine black–white acceptance in both academic and social terms. Early contact, socioeconomic status, scholastic and athletic achievement, teacher attitudes, and black–white classroom ratios are amongst the most significant variables that influence interracial acceptance. The authors outline some of the strategies that might be adopted to promote such acceptance.

The issue of peer acceptance in desegregated school settings is further examined in Chapter 6 by Norman Miller and Kevin Gentry who cast doubts on the rationale used to support desegregation policies, namely that the normative achievement values of the predominately white, middle-class children are laterally transmitted to the minority non-white children. Miller and Gentry devote much of their chapter to reviewing recent research usage of the sociometric technique. After considering some methodological issues concerning the collection and analysis of sociometric data, they examine various models of classroom sociometric popularity based upon different sources of influence, for example, demographic, structural features surrounding children's family circumstances, upbringing and parental attitudes, and teachers' attitudes and influence. Research findings on birth-order effects, personality, social skills and normative influences are reviewed insofar as they relate to these models of popularity. Miller and Gentry conclude *inter alia* that the teachers' evaluations are crucial as a source of normative information and influence, a factor which Carter, DeTine-Carter and Benson have also identified as important.

Section 3 : Dynamics of friendship

The emphasis in this section is upon, first, the interactive skills which children need to develop in order to form and maintain satisfactory peer relations and, second, upon the qualitative nature of their friendship relationships. In particular there is a focus upon identifying those social skills, patterns of behaviour and organizational characteristics which differentiate friendly peer interactions from other interactions.

Vandell and Mueller's inquiry of peer relations and friendships (Chapter 7) pursues the theme that very young children under 2 years of age are capable of engaging in fairly extended and sophisticated social interactions. These authors sketch out the foundations of social behaviour in terms of early social skills that find their optimal expression in early friendships. Even at 12 months of age infant friends can be distinguished from infant strangers, and by 2 years mutual preferences are becoming evident. This account of early sociable behaviour embraces many relationship variables (with mother, with older siblings and other older children, and with toys) which facilitate the development of social skills and foster the child's coming to terms with social reality.

A similar global perspective of young children's social relations is taken in Chapter 8 by Kenneth Rubin and Debra Pepler whose primary focus is upon social-cognitive development. They examine the shift away from egocentrism into increasing social awareness of others' feelings and viewpoints, and they argue that many of a young child's utterances, which in Piagetian terms might be regarded as egocentric nonsense utterances, do have communicative value. Play, likewise, is seen from a very early age as serving an 'intellectual adaptive function' which at the very least stimulates the development of social-cognitive abilities. Drawing upon Selman's (1976) structural model of perspective-taking, Rubin and Pepler outline their position that 'different forms of play and peer interaction reflect different levels or stages of social-cognitive development' (p. 20). They also review evidence that perspective-taking skills are enhanced by play, particularly by thematic or fantasy play.

The ethological approach to interactive behaviour adopted by Floyd Strayer in Chapter 9 provides a sharp contrast to the psychological enquiries of Vandell and Mueller and Rubin and Pepler. While the latter have focused upon the implications of friendships and peer relations for the development of adaptive social skills and perspectives in the individual child, Strayer has examined the organization or structure of children's social groups as wholes. Such a perspective, of course, reflects the kind of explanatory system which a biological framework demands and Strayer, quite appropriately, draws attention to the types of inquiry employed by ethologists. In reviewing the results of four separate studies of different groups of preschool children, he sets out to analyse group structure in terms of the coordination among the various dyadic social relationships which may vary in both quality and complexity. His analysis of the dimensions of organization includes a consideration of conflict and dominance relations, affiliative activity, cohesive bonds and prosocial and altruistic relations. The study of the interrelationships between these functions helps substantially in our understanding of the regulatory mechanisms that cultivate and sustain stable group structures.

The final chapter in this section by the editors of this volume, Chapter 10, provides a behavioural analysis of friends' dyadic interactions in terms of the exchanges of non-verbal cues. We are convinced that a detailed and molecular analysis of relatively brief periods of interaction can reveal considerable information about the subtleties and unique characteristics of friendship behaviours which are often overlooked in more molar, descriptive accounts. Taking dyads as our basic social unit, we have explored the interplay and patterning of non-verbal behaviours between friends and developed a measure of the degree of response-matching or reciprocation of responses that occurs between them. Our view of reciprocity as the key to developing friendships (a view shared by Mannarino) rests upon Patterson's (1976) dual model of interpersonal intimacy.

Section 4 : Friendship cliques

Within the structure of this volume the chapters in Section 4, more than in any other section, do reflect a grouping based upon age or developmental stage. Cliquing is a term rarely applied to children younger than 8 or 9 years of age and is most frequently applied to adolescent peer relations. Acceptance into a close and integrated group of friends with a relatively permanent and stable structure is the forerunner to the establishment of mature and lasting adult relationships. Research in this area has focused upon the formation and maintenance of such cliques, upon the subculture which they reflect and upon the norms, roles and structures which they develop.

One marked feature of the existing research is the paucity of studies on girls' friendship cliques. Most of the authors refer to this lacuna, arguing that it reflects the comparative scarcity of female adolescent cliques or gangs in real life. Richard Savin-Williams specifically draws attention to the few studies that are existent; even his own naturalistic observations of female groups are derived from 'staged' settings (summer camp for girls) rather than from spontaneously occurring groupings in a mixed-sex environment. The growing disparity between boys' and girls' patterns of friendship with increasing age is also considered in other chapters of this volume (e.g. Chapter 10).

In the first chapter of Section 4, by Gary Alan Fine, preadolescent male cliques are examined, namely cliques extending from 9 to 12 years. His review of the natural history of these friendships draws mainly upon anthropological sources and upon data derived from participant observation in real-life settings (little league baseball teams). Fine characterizes friendships during this period as occurring through a preoccupation with work-related activities, talk about sex and opportunities for aggressive outlets. He also emphasizes the emergence of an idiosyncratic subculture peculiar to each group which nonetheless is no more than a variant of a larger culture within society as a whole. Fine's ideas concerning the relationships between subcultures is in many ways closely allied to Miller and Gentry's notions of the cultural transmission of norms and values presented in Chapter 6.

In Chapter 12 Maureen Hallinan reviews observational and sociometric studies of adolescent friendship cliques, with a view to identifying both the processes that contribute to the formation and maintenance of cliques and the forms of influence that cliques wield over their members. She then outlines the various ways in which clique structures can be detected from sociometric data and describes a longitudinal study of cliquing amongst schoolchildren in several public and private schools. Evidence of the adoption of a distinctive set of values, or even the emergence of a subculture was a major finding for most of the cliques studied, and certain structural uniformities were identified among different cliques.

As already mentioned, Savin-Williams specifically explores female adolescent cliquing. He draws upon comparative data from cross-cultural studies and from non-human primate groups to build up a remarkably consistent picture of adolescent females dramatically reducing their relations with peers of either sex, and forsaking many of their childhood play groups. Their attention is largely directed either towards developing intense personal friendships with a single other female or towards the family group as a whole. Savin-Williams' own observational study of girls at a 5-week summer camp is concerned with detecting the dominance–submission relations of the girls in four cabin groups. Even in this setting, which is ideal for promoting in-group formation, none of the cabin groups became a cohesive whole, the girls preferring instead to split into pairs and threesomes. Although status differences emerged, further structural analysis of group organization was barely feasible.

In the final chapter of the book, Chapter 14, Anne Campbell directs attention to the role of friendship and peer relations in encouraging anti-social behaviours. In considering the social aetiology of delinquent behaviour she draws a sharp distinction between society's diagnosis of the malaise and frustrations purported to be associated with boys' delinquency and the pressures and conflicts purported to be associated with girls' delinquency, which is still largely treated as though it were a clinical, rather than a social, problem. Changing female roles and opportunities are already being reflected in changes in female crime rates and a reappraisal of female delinquency is long overdue.

As we have already indicated, the contributed chapters as a whole represent the major realms of current research interest in children's friendships. Despite our earlier comment about not necessarily seeking a consistent, easily reconcilable, array of theoretical positions, there are in fact many points of coincidence, many common themes and many shared perspectives between authors. One view which is voiced by many of the contributors is that an understanding of the child's concepts of, and expectations about, his/her friends has to be dependent upon an awareness of the child's general level of social and cognitive development. Many of the theories espoused in this book point directly towards the parallelism between friendship values and behaviours and the stage of social development reached.

REFERENCES

Asher, S. R. (1973). The influence of race and sex on children's sociometric choices across the school year. Unpublished manuscript, University of Illinois.

Austin, M. C., and Thompson, G. G. (1948). Children's friendships: a study of the bases on which children select and reject their best friends. *Journal of Educational Psychology*, **39**, 101–116.

Ausubel, D. P. (1954). *Theory and Problems of Adolescent Development*. New York: Grune and Stratton.

Barker, R. G., and Wright, H. F. (1955). *Midwest and its Children*. New York: Harper and Row.

Bigelow, B. J. (1977). Children's friendship expectations: a cognitive-developmental study. *Child Development*, **48**, 246–253.

Bonney, M. E. (1942). A study of social status on the second grade level. *Journal of Genetic Psychology*, **60**, 271–305.

Bonney, M. E. (1946). A sociometric study of the relationship of some factors to mutual friendships on the elementary, secondary and college levels. *Sociometry*, **9**, 21–47.

Bonney, M. E. (1949). Relationships between social success, family size, socioeconomic home background and intelligence among school children in grades III to IV. *Sociometry*, **12**, 36–48.

Bonney, M. E. (1971). Assessment of efforts to aid socially isolated elementary school pupils. *Journal of Educational Research*, **64**, 359–364.

Carter, D. E., DeTine, S. L., Spero, J., and Benson, F. W. (1975). Peer acceptance and school-related variables in an integrated junior high school. *Journal of Educational Psychology*, **67**, 267–273.

Davitz, J. R. (1955). Social perception and sociometric choice in children. *Journal of Abnormal and Social Psychology*, **50**, 173–176.

Duck, S. W. (1976). Interpersonal communications in developing acquaintance. In G. Miller (Ed.), *Explorations in Interpersonal Communication*. New York: Sage.

Duck, S. W. (1977). Personality similarity and friendship choice: similarity of what, when? In S. W. Duck (Ed.), *Theory and Practice in Interpersonal Attraction*. London: Academic Press.

Durojaiye, M.O.A. (1969). Patterns of friendship and leadership choices in a mixed ethnic junior school: a sociometric analysis. *British Journal of Educational Psychology*, **39**, 88–89.

Furfey, P. H. (1929). Some factors influencing the selection of boys' chums. *Journal of Applied Psychology*, **11**, 47–51.

Hartup, W. W. (1978a). Children and their friends. In H. McGurk (Ed.), *Issues in Childhood Social Development*. London: Methuen.

Hartup, W. W. (1978b). Peer relations and the growth of social competence. In M. W. Kent and J. E. Rolf (Eds.), *The Primary Prevention of Psychopathology. Vol. 3: Promoting Social competence and Coping in Children*. Hanover, Pennsylvania: University Press of New England.

Kay, C. L., and McKinney, J. P. (1967). Friendship fluctuation in normal and retarded children. *Journal of Genetic Psychology*, **110**, 233–241.

King, R., and Easthope, G. (1973). Social class and friendship choice in school. *Research in Education*, **9**, 16–24.

La Gaipa, J. J. (1978). Friendship as a system. Paper presented at the London Conference of the British Psychological Society, December.

Lewis, M., and Rosenblum, L. A. (1975). *Friendship and Peer Relations*. New York: Wiley.

Lindzey, G., and Byrne, D. (1968). Measurement of social choice and interpersonal attractiveness. In G. Lindzey and E. Aronson (Eds.), *The Handbook of Social Psychology*, Vol. 2. Reading: Massachusetts: Addison-Wesley.

Lougee, M. D., Grueneich, R., and Hartup, W. W. (1977). Social interaction in same- and mixed-age dyads of preschool children. *Child Development*, **48**, 1353–1361.

Mabe, P. A., and Williams, J. E. (1975). Relation of racial attitudes to sociometric choices among second grade children. *Psychological Reports*, **37**, 547–554.

Miller, N., and Maruyama, G. (1976). Ordinal position and peer popularity. *Journal of Personality and Social Psychology*, **33**, 123–131.

Nash, R. (1973). Clique formation among primary and secondary school children. *British Journal of Sociology*, **24**, 303–313.

Patterson, M. L. (1976). An arousal model of interpersonal intimacy. *Psychological Review*, **83**, 235–245.

Schulman, J. L., Ford, R. C., Bush, P., and Kaspar, J. C. (1973). Evaluation of a classroom program to alter friendship practices. *Journal of Educational Research*, **67**, 99–102.

Seagoe, M. V. (1933). Factors influencing selecting of associates. *Journal of Educational Research*, **27**, 32–40.

Selman, R. L. (1976). Social-cognitive understanding: a guide to educational and clinical practice. In T. Lickona (Ed.), *Moral Development and Behavior*. New York: Holt, Rinehart and Winston.

Singleton, L. (1974). The effects of sex and race in children's sociometric choices for play and work. Urbana, Illinois: University of Illinois.

Thorpe, J. G. (1955). An investigation into some correlates of popularity among elementary school children. *Journal of Educational Psychology*, **42**, 257–276.

Wright, P. H. (1969). A model and technique for studies of friendship. *Journal of Experimental Social Psychology*, **5**, 295–309.

FRIENDSHIP VALUES

CHAPTER 1

The Development of Friendship Values and Choice

BRIAN J. BIGELOW
and
JOHN J. LA GAIPA

...AND WE WOULD GO EVERYWHERE TOGETHER...

She and all my friends were mad at me for two months for something I didn't do. Do you know what it's like not to have anyone to talk to for two months? I almost went crazy, and I'm not kidding.

(Anonymous)

INTRODUCTION

The conceptual basis of friendship in children and adolescents is explored in the context of cognitive developmental changes. Relatively little is known as yet about what children expect from their friends, how these expectations change over time and the impact of such social cognitions on friendship choice. This chapter is concerned with the way the child organizes his/her thoughts about what to anticipate and value in a peer, and how this organization evolves over time. Such social cognitions are likely to influence how a child interacts with his/her peers. We are also concerned with how these cognitions are translated into the child's 'real-life' experiences: his/her choices, rejections and compromises in friendship.

15

Friendship 'values' and 'expectations' refer to those anticipatory qualities or behaviours that are highly valued in others. These terms are used almost interchangeably. There are times when children feel they cannot expect what they value; and hence our distinction between the two terms. Though expectations involving friendship are not as rigidly institutionalized as in other roles, they are nonetheless socially sanctioned. To be disloyal to a friend without cause may endanger a person's interpersonal credibility. These values and expectations are presumably acquired during socialization in much the same way as moral judgements, and assorted cultural values. An implicit assumption here is that the child's organismic or neurological development serves as a constraining factor in this process.

This chapter is divided into five parts. This first part presents a theoretical discussion of cognitive development. Different approaches are briefly described, and some of the key issues are discussed. The purpose of this part is to provide a theoretical framework for the subsequent treatment of friendship values and expectations. The second part describes the construction of a developmental scale of friendship for locating individuals on the basis of their spontaneous verbal expressions of friendship. The third part deals with the implications of the child's developmental level in influencing friendship and a review of recent original empirical data. These implications are examined in terms of a decision-making task. Preferences are expressed for hypothetical friends who systematically differ in their developmental friendship levels. Comparisons are also made with children's actual dyadic partners, the degree of reciprocity expressed and the differences with age from hypothetical choices. By reporting new data, the fourth part extends this developmental scale to three age groups: middle childhood, early adolescence, and late adolescence. The objective here is to establish the validity of this instrument for differentiating children and adolescents. This part goes beyond friendship expectations to incorporate the growth and decay of friendship, wherein the larger social context of friendship is examined here. The fifth part provides brief descriptions of personal accounts involving the growth and termination of friendship. The purpose here is to investigate the role of social cognitions involving friendship choice with a view toward appreciating more fully the dynamics involved in its growth and decay. Though cognitive development is viewed as important, other agents of social change are also considered.

Approaches to cognitive development

It is risky to generalize about friendship from adults to children. During childhood, the unfolding of cognitive, physical and emotional abilities are under more drastic change than at most any other time. Plotting the developmental course of friendship expectation development is therefore a necessary step towards understanding how children conceive of and choose their friends.

In our review of friendship development, it is not our intention to provide support for one developmental theory or another. Each has its own degree of validity, depending on the behaviours and concepts involved. However, we were concerned that there is a detectable developmental sequence underlying friendship. With such a sequence one can delve logically into plausible reasons for changing thought processes associated with age.

For our purposes, cognitive development can be sorted into three major groupings. (For more exhaustive reviews, see Emmerich, 1968; Zigler and Child, 1969). The first kind of development can be termed 'stage-free' structural. Here the emphasis is on the continuous distinctions that occur over age and the qualitative reorganizations that take place in emerging new concepts.

The second type of research on cognitive development is set apart mainly due to lack of concern with organismic changes. Concepts, such as moral values, are conceived as internalized social information that subscribes to effects of particular reinforcement contingencies. The types of concepts dealt with in this section which support this view are typically ones that are not sensitive to changing thought processes.

The third aspect of conceptual development is an extension of structural theory, with the stage construct invoked as a constraining factor in cognitive development. Here, stages have not only descriptive but predictive value and developmental sequencing is couched in terms of logically discontinuous clusters of emergent concepts.

'Stage-free' structural development is perhaps best exemplified in Werner's orthogenetic principle (1957), which states: 'Whenever development occurs, it proceeds from a stage of relative globality and lack of differentiation to a stage of increasing differentiation, articulation, and hierarchic integration' (p. 126). The most common application of Wernerian theory is in person perception, an inherently vital element in friendship. With children, the results are in the expected direction. Concepts become more differentiated with age through their increase in number, the advanced ones are more complex and subjective, and earlier notions tend to fade with age (e.g. Gollin, 1958; Werner, 1961; Yarrow and Campbell, 1963). A more thorough study in this regard was by Scarlett, Press and Crockett (1971). Along with the increase in frequency of constructs used to describe a hypothetical peer, there was a shift from egocentric to non-egocentric and from concrete to abstract modes of expression with age. More recently, Montemayor and Eisen (1977) extended orthogenetic theory to children's self-concepts between the ages of nine and seventeen. Although these authors used written data, Scarlett, Press and Crockett (1971) and Livesley and Bromley (1973) showed similar changes in self-concept (cf. Shantz, 1975, for an excellent review of the literature on the development of social cognition).

While the above studies certainly show that concepts of peers increase in complexity with age, there is no clear indication as to why some children progress from one conceptual level to another and others do not. There is ample evidence to indicate that for a broad range of content areas, including friendship, the move to abstract thinking is neither necessary nor inevitable (e.g. Bigelow, 1977; Flavell, 1977; Piaget, 1932). This results in an admixture of abilities with age. Even with children's expressions of aggression, age is not a guarantee of change (Hartup, 1975). In fact, Wohlwill (1970) goes so far as to say that chronological age is of questionable value as a developmental variable. The sufficient conditions for further developmental movement are still only speculative. Not all types of concepts need occur in a fixed order and issues of cognitive development may well be less relevant for certain kinds of concepts such as similarity and liking (cf. Byrne and Griffitt, 1966, 1969). Any developmental investigation must first select variables appropriate to ontogenetic change.

Following this line of thought, it is one thing to argue that matters of conceptual structure apply to select kinds of variables that have a logically predetermined sequence. It is another thing to maintain that there are no structural constraints on the learning of abstract feelings. Even in friendship, where affective forces have an inherently strong bearing on further learning, it would seem difficult for a child to internalize a value that is not understood. It therefore makes sense that efforts to simulate the socialization process, such as applying imitative social learning on stages of Piagetian (1932) moral judgements, ultimately found that comprehension of learned values is more likely to be maintained in terms of the natural direction of development (cf. Bandura and MacDonald, 1963; Bandura and Walters, 1963; Cowen, Langer, Heavenrich, and Nathanson, 1969). These finding are consistent with those of Kohlberg (1969), Rest, Turiel and Kohlberg (1969) and Turiel (1966, 1969). Turiel and Rothman (1972) found, however, that at early levels of development this result is not as likely. This foreshadows our own data on friendship choice reported in the third part of this chapter on friendship values and choice.

The main criteria that set cognitive-developmental theory apart are those dealing with equilibration and stages. Both of these constructs have come under criticism lately. In particular, what has served to complicate matters is that there appear to be methodological problems in detecting sequences and stages. It would appear that all that is needed would be to validate the sequencing of social conceptions, such as with friendship, against standard sets of Piagetian tasks (e.g. Rardin and Moan, 1971). However, Brainerd (1973b) has found that the order of acquisition of concrete-operational tasks, such as transitivity, conservation, and class inclusion of length and weight is different from that reported in previous studies (cf. Inhelder and Piaget, 1964; Piaget, 1952; Piaget and Inhelder, 1941; Piaget, Inhelder and Szeminska, 1960). Brainerd (1973a) uses a different method, whereby the child judges the correct solution to a task, avoiding difficulties associated with verbal explanation and erroneous under-assessments of one's logical ability. Since social concepts may be inherently verbal, it is difficult to see how a judgements-only procedure could be employed on tasks used for verifying the sequence with which these concepts evolve. It remains to be seen whether nonverbal techniques can be devised, such as the use of pictures arranged in a sequence to tell a concept-descriptive story. At least one thing stands out: children develop certain cognitive skills earlier than verbally weighted procedures suggest (cf. Miller, 1976).

While the issues of sequencing and equilibration for Piagetian object-sorting tasks have received some validating support (e.g. Kuhn, 1972), the stage construct has clearly lost some of its original meaning. As Flavell (1971, 1977) has aptly pointed out, to conceive of the child as developing logical operations in an abrupt 'metamorphosis-like' manner is theoretically naive. (For critical reviews of stage symmetry, see Brainerd, 1973a, 1976, 1977, 1978.) A more realistic expectation is to observe the component operations ultimately forming a unified whole. Moshman (1977) confirmed this expectation by observing that combinatorial operations begin asynchronously but reach full maturity when the entire stage is well developed. Thus, stages do not have to be 'quantum' leaps of cognition, as long as consolidation eventually occurs. This is a more dynamic use of the term 'stage'. The process of staging earmarks the transitional period of qualitative developmental change. The usefulness of stage theory ultimately depends on its ability to predict further development. As a descriptive device in reporting developmental data, its use is unparalleled. Clearly, the over-use of stage conceptions of development has led to some effort to validate their empirical value. In particular, the review of the moral judgement literature by Kurtines and Greif (1974) produced a reanalysis of Kohlberg's (1969) six stages resulting in three orthogonal stages. Similarly, Bigelow (1977) cluster analysed children's written friendship expectations and reached a parallel conclusion. This three-stage hierarchy is perfectly consistent with the prelogical, concrete-operational and formal-operational distinctions employed in Piagetian theorizing. However, children may express themselves linguistically in terms of stages, but develop the referent level dimensions individually. Brainerd (1973b) proposes an attractive solution to the problem, whereby each emergent concept may be viewed as having its own structure, rather than one which is necessarily shared within a stage. Applying.equilibration in this more molar sense may allow for an empirically reliable developmental sequence consistent with a theoretically sound model. Clearly, social concepts 'clock in' at different times in development (Hartup, 1978). The precision of this temporal sequence depends largely on the reliability of the developmental scale used, coupled with procedures sensitive enough to detect when each dimension initially occurs. It is a matter for future research whether experiments using nonverbal assessments of subjects' social concepts will replicate the evidence that now seems to hold for developmental sequencing. Entanglements between method and theory currently leave the field ripe for further contributions.

TOWARDS A DEVELOPMENTAL SCALE OF FRIENDSHIP

This brief review of the literature on general cognitive development suggests that age-related changes in conceptions of friendship can be understood as a specific instance of more basic changes in the development of social cognitions. Certainly, there is little that is intrinsically unique to friendship expectations from a cognitive-developmental perspective. Age, however, provides only a very crude indicator of social development. As we have noted previously, there are considerable variations among children of the same age, presumably resulting from different rates of neurological growth as well as in their different social experiences. So it seemed necessary to develop a procedure for classifying children according to their dominant developmental level independently of chronological age.

Why would one want to know where a child or adolescent could be located on such a developmental scale of friendship? Prior research on friendship suggests that children who have expectations developmentally behind their peer group are more likely to be socially rejected (La Gaipa and Wood, 1973; Miller and Stone, 1951; Wood, 1976). The present study is more precisely concerned with the interaction between a child's developmental level and those of his/her peers in friendship formation and dissolution. Do children choose friends that are at the same or different developmental levels? From a theoretical point of view, why do children prefer friends at the same or different levels? Consequently, if developmental factors affect interpersonal affection, there is all the more reason to measure them as accurately as possible.

Construction of the developmental scale

Children from grades I to VIII (6–14 years old) were asked to write an essay in class about their expectations of best friends. There were 60 subjects, 30 of each sex, at each grade level, resulting in 480 children in the Canadian sample, and 480 in an age-equivalent Scottish sample. The essays were independently coded by two graduate students by means of 21 friendship dimensions[1] in terms of the importance attached to each one. These analyses resulted in 11 dimensions which increased significantly over grade level in each sample. The grade level where a dimension initially onset was defined so as to make sure that it did not drop down to a non-significance after onset was established. These dimensions were then rank-ordered for onset within each sample and the two rankings obtained from the two samples were then compared. A high correlation was obtained across cultures ($\rho = 0.78$, $p < .01$). In order to enhance the rigour of the sequence without eliminating too much of its content, the two least reliable dimensions in the sequence (friend as giver of help and incremental prior interaction) were removed.

Rank orders were then averaged for the remaining nine dimensions, resulting in the following developmental scale (two dimensions—character admiration and propinquity—had the same average rank order):

Stage 1:
(1) Common activities;
(2) Evaluation;
(3) Propinquity;
Stage 2:
(4) Character admiration;
Stage 3:
(5) Acceptance;
(6) Loyalty and commitment;
(7) Genuineness;
(8) Common interests; and
(9) Intimacy potential.

Using these nine dimensions as variables, cluster analysis verified the proposed stage conception of development. A dimension within a stage correlated positively with its class members and correlated non-significantly or inversely with dimensions in other classes.

As is evidenced by the above developmental sequence, the specific manner in which friendship values develop over time is much more gradual than stage theory would suggest. Standard stage theory (cf. Kohlberg, 1969) implies little stage mixture in a child's response. Quite the contrary was observed. What is noteworthy, however, is that variability in the frequency of using a particular concept is associated with stage-related changes in the use of other concepts. As was anticipated, there was some error in predicting the stage membership of admiration, and loyalty and commitment. They could have gone together but their interface values made this unlikely. Apparently, there may be more to loyalty than simple admiration of character, as it is included in the third stage. As we shall see in the fourth part of this chapter, this distinction becomes more important for friendship growth than decay. The only sex difference in the scale was intimacy potential, initially a typically female attribute in this sample.

As is supported by our results, it is commonly suggested that universal sequencing occurs in cognitive development. Indeed, Flavell (1972) argues that it is difficult to see how it could be otherwise. Brainerd (1978) goes a step farther by suggesting that these sequences do not need to be verified. Psychological research, on the other hand, does not stop with logical positivism. The more dimensions that are included in the sequence, the closer adjacent ones are conceptually and perceptually, and the room for blurring them is potentially greater. The simultaneous onset of propinquity and admiration is a case in point. Obviously, the onus on the investigator to use methods which sharpen the subject's powers of discrimination. The value of this precision is to build a sequence that is also *functionally* useful, containing dimensions which are necessary *and* sufficient to predict the next step in the learning sequence.

Assuming a simple additive model of development (cf. Flavell, 1977), the friendship expectation sequence makes good *post hoc* theoretical sense. For example, proximity necessarily precedes common activities and common activities occurs before evaluation. One cannot like a person one has not met. Evaluation onsets before admiration, the latter being a refinement of the former. Acceptance occurs after admiration because one's appreciation of a person's character is more global than valuing one's personality. Since loyalty incorporates notions of admiration and acceptance, it must occur after them. Since one can be loyal to a person, admire him/her and tolerate his/her weak points without being able to abstract his 'real' self from his/her facade, genuineness must follow loyalty. If one really knows what a person is like, one is in a position to determine whether his/her personality and interests are similar to one's own. At this point the framework is suitable for intimate communication. In retrospect, the problems with propinquity may well have been due to the fact that it is such an obvious aspect of the acquaintance process that it may well have been overlooked by the younger children.

Concerning sequences, the reader should consult Flavell (1977) and Emmerich (1968) to appreciate the alternatives to the one pattern presented here. Even with regard to friendship concepts, there are no doubt further refinements *within* groups. More importantly, each successive concept is not merely an addition to those preceding it, but integrates and subordinates earlier ones. A classic example is intimacy potential which is a separate and distinct notion connoting acceptance, loyalty, commitment, genuineness and common interests. On the issue of hierarchical displacement, Bigelow (1977) found that in *absolute* terms there is no shedding of earlier concepts. For *relative* frequency, there is displacement. This happens because dimensions typically show a rapid initial gain over age, followed by a plateau. It is an open question whether, at some time in life, there is ever complete decay in earlier friendship concepts. Perhaps friendship cannot survive independently of factors such as proximity and common activities. Likewise, a relationship that depends on intimacy potential can hardly thrive without authenticity and unconditional positive regard (Maslow, 1954).

FRIENDSHIP VALUES AND CHOICE

Methodological considerations

In this section we attempt to bridge the gap between what children expect in their best friendships and how they actually go about selecting a best friend. Historically, the division between thought and action has been of profound interest to social science. The value of extracting a concept's reinforcement value in a dyadic interpersonal bond, such as friendship, is rather self-evident. It brings additional data to bear on the validity of the developmental sequence and allows one to investigate in more depth the mechanisms of developmental movement across friendship concepts. At the present time, the interface between existing and emergent concepts is the subject of considerable controversy and speculation.

The literature on children's choice of friends is sparse. It is true that there have been numerous studies on the sociometry of peer interactions (see Hartup, 1975, 1978). Typically, however, these investigations dealt with the frequency of who likes whom and the degree of reciprocated affection. To some extent we are involved with this line of inquiry, but only insofar as it serves as an interpretive vehicle for understanding the mechanics of how a child's ideal friendship translates to real-life relationships. An examination of a child's ideal preferences of a hypothetical peer frees choice from the unwieldy situational demands inherent in a field setting. The differences between actual and ideal friendship choices then provide valuable clues for detecting the reasons for subsequent change in the interactions between peers and the possible dissolutions and reformations of friendship bonds.

Admittedly, a review of the cognitive and developmental parameters of preference is a trifle premature. It cannot be assured that a child who has developed an understanding of a given concept will be able to verbalize it effectively. With this in mind, a child's preference for a given concept may reveal it is beginning to dawn on his/her awareness or alternatively that the concept has remained submerged and unexpressed for some time. We can only assume, for the time being,that comprehension and expressive ability are tightly related.

In order to avoid pitfalls inherent in becoming obsessively embroiled in the stage controversy, experimental parameters of friendship preference were defined in terms of the overall sequence. Also, since stage clustering is statistically dependent on the overall sequence, it was expected that the best predictor of friendship choice is in terms of the child's dominant position in the sequence. Incidentally, we found that it was difficult to control for the child's ability to perceive choice alternatives equally across age. A younger child, due to his relatively limited perspective, is less capable of considering a wealth of different kinds of concepts. Evidence bearing on this point is presented below, but our own data, at least, serve to indicate that older children have more 'conceptual variance' in their ability to express themselves at levels distant from their dominant one. Bearing further on this point, Hartup's (1978) review of the sociometric literature suggests that most children habitually interact with children of different age groups. Clearly, the older child can teach the younger more effectively than a peer or parent, such as shaping appropriate ways to express aggression. With few exceptions, children are physically and mentally better matched than adult–child bonds. By the same token, playing with a younger child provides the older child with an opportunity to demonstrate his/her superiority through effective use of social and emotional strategies not within the immediate grasp of a youngster. Whether these general interaction patterns appear in friendship choices is another matter. To complicate matters further, there is no conclusive evidence which locates the precise time when children begin to differentiate friendship from other types of social roles. Our own data suggest that age and type of choice condition are important in this respect.

The lack of information on the child's distinct meaning of friendship is offset somewhat by data on the development of empathy—a vital element in mutual understanding. The indications are that the child begins to acquire social role-taking perspectives at about 8 years of age. Until s/he can see him/ herself from the other's point of view, it seems improbable that s/he can envisage what it would be like to befriend another based on that other person's expectations of friendship. Several approaches to social role-taking (Feffer, 1959, 1971; Feffer and Gourevich, 1960; Selman and Byrne, 1974) are generally in line with Flavell's (1968) observations. Decentred communication does not initially appear until about the eighth year and undergoes successive developmental changes of an empathic nature.

Investigations of friendship expectations have partially helped to define the age range in which this form of attachment is meaningful to the child. Reisman and Shorr (1978) conducted open-ended interviews with children from grades II to VIII (7–14 years old) and adults from 15 to 65 years of age. At all age levels, subjects mentioned that they liked to talk about problems with their friends. Moreover, most children felt that they had a friend and that the friend was instrumentally useful in some way. Friends were not necessarily same-age peers, which is reflective of Hartup's review (in press) concerning whom the child associates with. Consistent with our own data, concepts such as talking about personal problems and secrets, and expressions of commitment and loyalty, did not occur significantly until early adolescence.

Conceptual frameworks for friendship choice

There are several theoretical avenues by which to approach the problem of friendship expectations and choice. The dearth of research on the cognitive-developmental parameters of preference is more than compensated for in speculation. From the standpoint of a fixed sequence of development, there are basically five points of view. These are: the 'Platonic view' (Kohlberg, 1969; Rest, Turiel and Kohlberg, 1969), personal construct theory (Bannister and Fransella, 1971; Duck, 1977a, 1977b; Kelly, 1955), conceptual development (Harvey, Hunt and Schroder, 1961), the effectance motive (Turiel, 1966; White, 1959), and equilibration (Piaget, 1960, 1970).

The Platonic view has implicit origin in Plato's *Republic*, where the plebeians intuitively looked to their 'philosopher king' for moral and political leadership. The inference is that children inherently appreciate moral and social reasoning more advanced than their own, even though this reasoning may be beyond their grasp in terms of their ability to express what they hear. The Platonic view is applicable to any cognitive-developmental sequence incorporating logically necessary steps to which matters of judgement apply. The prediction here is that children prefer others who are more advanced than themselves without regard to what specific developmental level is preferred. The main problem with this view is that without comprehension of the condition preferred, it is difficult to tell what cues are being used as a basis of preference. Without additional data, it seems premature to embrace the Platonic view as more than an intriguing explanation of preference.

Perhaps the most comprehensive treatment of preference resides in personal construct theory. Kelly (1955) defined a personal construct as a psychological element with which an individual derives anticipated meaning from replicated events. Hence, constructs are experiential rather than ontogenetic, even though a developmental structure could be superimposed on this system. Constructs are the conceptual vehicles with which a person defines his world, his self-concept, and the people with whom he relates. Concerning friendship preference, Duck (e.g. 1973) found that convergent ideologies or similarity prevails in adult friendships. For a cognitive-developmental study, the implications are not entirely clear. However, similar friendship expectations ought to elicit the greatest attraction. As we shall see, this is a complex matter.

Conceptual development theory delineates certain assumptions reminiscent of the stage issue. Concepts stemming from structurally similar systems supposedly elicit approach tendencies, whereas structurally dissimilar systems provoke avoidance reactions. Since the self is defined from this position in terms of one's friendship expectations, the implication here is that friendship choice is for those who share same-stage values. Problems previously discussed on the stage issue cast doubt on the predictive value of this approach.

The effectance motive was first proposed by White (1959) and describes an organism's intrinsic drive to master progressively more difficult material without necessarily requiring external incentives to do so. While this notion is appealing, the concept of equilibration (Piaget, 1970) is more elegant than these other accounts of developmental movement because it integrates conceptual information processing and effectance motive notions. However, a limitation of equilibration is that it does not appear to explain fully the potential difference between the degree of assimilation of particular concepts in the sequence and the preference shown for such concepts. There are numerous examples of people preferring others that they seemingly do not quite understand. The Platonic view compounds this problem. It is not known how far ahead a child can validly appreciate thoughts without having them fully internalized. Presumably, responses to concepts derive from fertile intellectual soil.

Various predictions are possible on the basis of the notion of equilibration. Assuming that exposure to another's concepts of friendship creates disequilibrium with the child's own position in the developmental sequence, resolution of this tension should be in terms of preference for the next level in the sequence. An alternative strategy for children incapable of this move may be that of regression to the next lower position in the sequence.

A further prediction would be that conceptual development as reflected in friendship expectations is not predictive of friendship choice. It could be argued that such a prediction would only be useful simply to exhaust the possible alternative findings. Such a position is not necessarily an empty one in view of the role-taking studies reviewed earlier. These studies would lead us to expect younger children to behave precisely in this way. A child must be capable of taking another person's point of view in order to distinguish the differences and to base his preference on them. The point here is that role-taking ability may be a limiting condition for applying equilibration to preference.

Experimental analysis of friendship choice

The major objective in the first experiment was to determine the relationship between friendship choice and two indices of a person's level of development regarding friendship. The first index was the person's dominant position in the developmental sequence, derived from spontaneous expressions of friendship expectations. The second index was obtained from the percentage of information comprehended in the level of expectation most preferred in best friends. The correspondence between these two indices was also established.

The developmental friendship scale (Bigelow, 1977) was used to select a series of statements on friendship. For each of the eight dimensions making up this scale, four reliable statements were extracted from previous content analyses (Bigelow, 1974) and transcribed onto audio-cassette. Duplicate recordings were then made to provide material suitable for both sexes.

A total of 31 subjects of both sexes between 9 years 11 months and 11 years 11 months were obtained from the sixth and seventh forms (grades V and VI) of a progressive Scottish primary school. The mean age was 10 years 9 months. Subjects were known to be within the average range of intelligence. Individual interviews were recorded on audio-tape and analysed in order to establish the dominant position of the subjects in the developmental sequence. A semi-structured interview technique was used to 'zero-in' on the qualities valued in friendship by the use of successive discriminations, a technique suggested by Kiss' (1972) recursive content analysis. The kind of questions asked included the following: 'What do you want or expect in a best friend?' 'What do you mean by that notion of friendship?' 'How are best friends different from other kinds of friends?' Only responses matching the meanings of the ideal statements embodied in the developmental scale were coded. Where ties occurred between levels, the most advanced one was used to place each child into his dominant level on the scale.

After a 2-week interval, the friendship choice and comprehension phases of this study were conducted. Each child was presented with the four cassette recordings of friendship expectations: one level below, one above, two above, and one at his/her own level, as determined by his/her classification from the interview. The tapes were first played in their entirety and then presented separately for preference responses. At this time the child was asked to choose the person on the tape as his/her first, second, third, or least-preferred best friend. The child was asked to imagine that each tape was a person about his/her own age and sex, and to listen to what she/he expected or wanted in a best friend. At the end of the session, each child was asked to recite what his/her first choice had said about best friends.

Examination of where the 31 subjects has been classified located one at Level 2; two Level 3; 21 at Level 4; and seven at Level 5. Next, we looked at the preference data to find out the friendship choices made by children at each level. A critical aspect of this analysis was to determine the distance between a child's dominant position and the position of the preferred friend. For instance, if a child were at Level 3 and his/her friendship choice were at Level 4, then his/her choice responses were coded as $+1$, indicating that s/he preferred a friend at a higher developmental level than his own. On the other hand, if s/he chose a friend at Level 2, his/her choice responses were coded as -1, indicating s/he preferred a friend at a lower level than his/her own.

A Friedman analysis of variance by ranks indicated that preference was significantly affected ($p < .025$) by the relative level of the bogus peer. Sex differences were non-significant. The $+1$ condition was most preferred. Of the 31 subjects, 14 chose the $+1$ friend, eight chose the -1 friend, and five preferred the $+2$ condition. Rather unexpected was the finding that only four subjects preferred a friend at the same level as their own. The $+1$ and -1 conditions together accounted for 77 per cent of the preferences, whereas only 50 per cent was expected by chance. Most of the subjects remembered best what was said by the bogus peer that they preferred. Of the 31 subjects, 27 remembered information presented by their first choice friend. It should be noted, again, that these 'first choice' friends were generally at a different developmental level. The data suggest, then, that contrary to the Platonic view, preference was directly related to comprehension, but not necessarily its upper limit, and that both related, in turn, to spontaneous expression.

According to personal construct theory, the finding that only four subjects chose their own level in a best friend was unexpected. Yet, by definition, all 31 subjects expressed themselves at their own level, the condition most refused. Because subjects remembered what was said by their first choice friend, there is the likelihood that the $+1$ choice was in reality a direct response to the experimental conditions. It makes no sense to us to assume that they were at the

+ 1 level all along; this runs contrary to their classification responses. More-over, the classification session was more thorough. There is the ever present possibility that recapitulation scores were affected largely by short term recall.

The − 1 findings seem to further weaken the intuitive Platonic view that people should inevitably seek friends at a higher level of development than their own. Moreover, the theoretical notion of consensual validation, implied in the similarity hypothesis, was not supported. Consequently, the equilibration view received the most support because of the preferences found for the + 1, − 1 choice distributions. It should be noted, however, that Piagetian theory is not very explicit regarding the conditions under which developmental regression may occur, that is, the − 1 movement. Further data using socio-metric choices provide a different picture.

The second experiment sought to explain why children perform at one developmental level as measured by their spontaneous expressions and yet perform at a different level in choosing friends. Essentially the same basic design was used with a somewhat younger sample of children, and instead of asking what they expected from a best friend, the instructions were also in terms of an ideal or 'perfect' best friend. Sociometric data were also collected regarding their actual friendship choice.

In this experiment usable data were collected from 51 of a sample of 61 subjects responding to the question on expectations regarding an ideal best friend. The subjects were from the fourth and fifth primary forms (grades III and IV), of a regular Scottish primary school. Of the 61 subjects, the mean age for the fourth form was 8 years 9 months, ranging from 8 years 2 months to 9 years 1 month. For the fifth form, the mean age was 9 years 7 months, ranging from 9 years 1 month to 10 years 2 months. These children were mainly from working-class families. Intelligence scores were not available.

The 51 subjects were classified as follows: 13 at Level 1, 18 at Level 2, eight at Level 3 and 12 at Level 4. As one can see, the distribution was somewhat more evenly spread across the levels and the average level was somewhat lower than in the first experiment.

The actual best friends were identified by means of a sociometric test. The children were asked to name their best friends. A total of 39 children cited a classroom peer as a best friend. Hence, it was possible to compare a person's developmental level with the developmental level of his actual best friend. Forty-four per cent of the children named as best friend another child that was at the same level of development as measured by the friendship scale. This was a significant result ($p < .001$), and one which is consistent with personal construct theory.

Next, we looked at the relationship between developmental level of recipro-city of friendship. A total of 39 children who had named a best friend in the same class were examined to locate reciprocated and non-reciprocated friend-ships. Mutual choice pairs existed for 26 children. The developmental levels of children in the reciprocal and non-reciprocal groups were compared. No significant differences were found, suggesting that *mutual* affection is unrelated to the developmental levels of friendship participants. This is an important fact in the light of hypothetical preference data.

The hypothetical preference for best friends showed a significant distribution ($p < .005$) in favour of the $+1$ and -1 conditions. The $+1$ condition was chosen by 12 subjects and the -1 by 15, this constituting 73 per cent of the sample ($n = 37$). Contrary to sociometric data, only four of these children indicated a same-level choice. In this younger sample, there was a tendency to recall at a level which varied according to the condition most preferred, and also in direct proportion to the subject's dominant position in the scale. Subjects who chose the $+2$ condition recalled equally at the $+1$ and same-level, whereas $+1$ choosers recalled more consistently at the $+1$ level. This was also true of -1 choosers. However, this consistency broke off for a separate group of Level 1 subjects ($n = 12$), an analysis of which showed that equal preference for $+1$ and same-level conditions was followed by recall at the same level. Unlike the older age group in the previous experiment, spontaneous response strength was virtually zero at adjacent levels. Thus, preference increased in intuitiveness with decreases in age and dominant developmental level. Also, since there was no consistent preference distribution for the 9-year-olds, we can only conclude that age and developmental level are not simply two sides of the same psychometric coin.

Overall, the consolidation towards $+1$ preference with age across the two studies was accompanied by more spontaneous response strength and recall ability at the $+1$ level. Since the Platonic view does not account for -1 choices and does not uniformly apply across age groups, at this point the equilibration view seems to best fit these data. The disadvantage of equilibration in this case is that where it applies best is precisely where the linguistic overlap between levels is greatest. Future studies would do well to vary linguistic skill at the $+1$ level to determine the extent of interaction between cognitive and verbal abilities. It would appear, then, that for the less advanced children the psychological and linguistic distance between levels is greater than for the older, more advanced children.

From the standpoint of reciprocity, actual friendships do correspond to ideal choices in the sense that both types of preferences tend to avoid same-level dyads with age. This makes sense because this developmental admixture provides the required social stimulus for developmental change, dissolution and reaffirmation of friendships. The paradox is that as friendship stability increases with age, the discrepancy in the cognitive levels between friends also increases. Judging by the prevalence of $+1$ preferences with age, the tensions leading to dissolution should also grow with age. Two people in a dyad cannot both be the $+1$ choice. Perhaps it is fortunate that the -1 condition was almost as strongly preferred, a result that would surely reduce tensions between agemates. This, together with reciprocity in friendship, may be the saving grace of continued affection.

The findings for change scores are even more striking. The developmental difference between actual and ideal friendship levels is such that ideal preference outstrips differences found for actual friendships. For -1 choosers ($n = 12$), 80 per cent preferred an ideal friend one or more levels below the sociometric, actual friend. For $+1$ choosers ($n = 15$), 100 per cent wanted an ideal friend one or more levels more advanced than their actual friends. These data suggest an inherent dissatisfaction with actual friendship relationships. These preference data, then, show that there are inevitable tensions inherent in friendship development and choice consistent with the very logic of development implied in equilibration.

These preference data correspond quite closely to the role-taking literature reviewed earlier. By the age of 10 years, the child acquires the capacity to take several points of view into account. At the same time, the child begins to consolidate his friendship preferences toward the $+1$ condition. Also, his peer relationships become more developmentally mixed as he now can relate more closely to others who are not the same as himself. Had sociometric data been available for the 11- and 12-year-olds, we may have been able to extend this point. Perhaps the increasing tension between real and ideal friendships eventually leads to Vecerka's (1925) 'negative stage' where children in adolescence change friends rapidly in seeking those with whom they can relate on an intimate level.

It is of interest to note that, unlike that for recall ability, the present data failed to suggest any noticeable effect of dominant level on the condition most preferred. Age level alone accounted for the changes in preference scores. Attributing this to role-taking theory, there may well be a separate experiential factor operating in conjunction with cognitive development in determining friendship preference. Equilibration does not appear to prosper in an experimental vacuum.

GROWTH AND DECAY OF FRIENDSHIP: THE TENSIONS OF COMPROMISE

Critical experiences and the meaning of friendship

In the previous sections, it was suggested that children's conceptions of friendship can be traced to more general changes in cognitive development (Bigelow, 1977; Bigelow and La Gaipa, 1975; La Gaipa and Bigelow, 1972). The specific details regarding the mechanisms involved are still not fully understood. Many writers also make the assumption regarding the extent to which changes in cognitive development are linked to social experiences (Hartup, 1978). Even at a lower level of analysis, there are many unanswered questions regarding the interplay between positive and negative social experiences and the acquisition of conceptions of friendship. In the words of the systems analyst, we do not know the catalysts that affect the entropy of the relationship. The bridge between what children think and what children do has not been crossed. As we have already noted, children often do not choose friends who share the same conceptions of friendship.

In the previous two experiments, subjects were asked to indicate a preference for a best friend from among persons expressing different views or conceptions of friendship, but in real life such rational deliberations are unlikely. Friendship choice involves a redefinition and restructuring of one person's perception of another as a result of specific kinds of experiences. It is not the same kind of decision as choosing among different automobiles. Moreover, the notion of friendship choice may be more relevant to the decay of friendship than to its growth. We suspect that the specifics of breaking, rather than making, a friendship are more sensitive to the various stages in the decision-making process.

Certainly, what children value in friendship and what they have experienced are not necessarily the same, almost by definition. But what children recall as salient and critical social experiences regarding specific friends may provide some insights. Descriptions of critical incidents may then help us to identify important impressions regarding the development and dissolution of friendship.

A further study was designed to establish if the developmental scale was useful for analysing the social experiences of children that are likely to be relevant to the growth and decay of friendship. A second objective was to find out if this scale was effective in discriminating children across a broader age range. The age range was extended from the previous studies to include three age groups: middle childhood, early adolescence, and late adolescence. The mean ages for these groups were 9 years 1 month, 13 years 1 month and 16 years 11 months. In approximate terms, each sample was evenly divided by sex.

The study again took place in the classrooms during regular sessions. To maintain comparability of the data, the first of three tasks was the same. The children were initially asked to write down what they expected from a best friend. The responses to this question were categorized under the label of 'ideal friend' to differentiate them from responses to 'actual friends' involving growth and decay experiences.

The next two sets of instructions were designed to tap critical experiences leading to growth and termination of friendship. To tap growth experiences, the subjects were asked to think about their best friends:

Can you remember something that one of these friends did that made you feel closer to him or her? Write down something really important to you that made you like this person a great deal more.

To tap experiences leading to the decay of friendship, the subjects were asked to think about someone who once but no longer was their friend.

Think about someone who stopped being your best friend because this person did something that really hurt your feelings. What made this friendship break up? Write down something really important to you that made you like this person a great deal less.

Content analysis of critical incidents

In order to conduct a content analysis of the responses, the friendship coding system had to be revised so it could handle the negative as well as the positive side of each friendship construct. Otherwise, it would be difficult to code the reasons given for the termination of friendships. Moreover, a few distinctions were made within some of the categories. The dimensions that were subdivided include loyalty and commitment, admiration, and similarity. In addition, the dimension of conflict was included in order to code statements involving physical, verbal and non-specific references to aggression. A total of 20 dimensions was used in this coding system. In practice, 10 of these dimensions accounted for 95 per cent of the responses, again supporting the use of the briefer, eight-item developmental scale.

Table 1.1 presents the results of the content analysis employing the eight friendship dimensions ordered in terms of the developmental scale cited earlier in this chapter. Two dimensions, ego reinforcement and helping, are also included in the table. They are no part of the developmental scale, but they accounted for a significant amount of the responses. It should be noted that the data for early and late adolescents have been collapsed in this table because of the few differences obtained. The specific differences are mentioned later in this chapter.

Overview of age-related differences

A brief description of the findings in Table 1.1 are given below. Subsequently, some examples and excerpts are provided. Essentially, in middle childhood the major expectations involve evaluation and common activities. The term evaluation refers to such qualities as being 'nice' and 'considerate', that is global descriptive terms. The growth of friendship in this age group is again described in terms of common activities. In addition, ego reinforcement and helping are often mentioned. The termination of friendship appears to be due mainly to conflict and ego-degrading experiences.

In adolescence, loyalty and commitment are viewed as essential qualities in a best friend. But the core growth experiences are quite similar to the findings for middle childhood. The decay of friendship is again described in terms of

Table 1.1. Dimensions used in describing ideal friends (values) and social experiences with actual friends (growth and decay)

Developmental scale Dimensions	Level	Ideal friends Values		Actual friends Growth		Actual friends Decay	
		Child	Adolescent	Child	Adolescent	Child	Adolescent
Common activities	1	32%	36%	39%	25†	02%	01%
Evaluation	2	58	17†	10	02†	06	03
Admiration	3	28	16†	04	02	16	27†
Acceptance	4	01	15†	03	07	02	05
Loyalty and commitment	5	08	59†	06	17†	18	36†
Genuineness	6	03	24†	02	04	06	11
Common interests	7	00	05†	01	06†	00	02
Intimacy potential	8	00	27†	03	12†	01	02
Ego reinforcement		05	11	24	24	31	19*
Helping		20	21	18	24	03	00

*p < .05 } One-tailed test of significance of difference between proportions. The N for children is 142 and the N for adolescents is 308.
†p < .01.

disloyalty, whereas the lack of admiration, that is, low moral character are labels used to explain decay.

Developmental trends are quite apparent in Table 1.1, particularly for changes in values from childhood to adolescence. Evaluation and admiration decrease from childhood to adolescence. On the other hand, dimensions higher on the scale show an increase with age. The same developmental trends are evident for the growth of friendship, though fewer dimensions are involved. Developmental trends are also somewhat evident with regard to the breakup of friendship. Adolescents cite loyalty and commitment, or the lack thereof, much more often as well as noting ego-degrading experiences less often than children.

Sex differences

The various analyses reported in this chapter were initially broken down by sex, but collapsed because of the few sex differences obtained. Any that appeared were mainly found in the adolescent samples. This is typical of the studies we have done on friendship (see La Gaipa, 1977b; La Gaipa and Engelhart, 1978). In middle childhood the only sex difference was that females describe their expectations of a best friend in more global, affective terms than males (68 per cent versus 48 per cent).

The major sex differences was that females are more concerned than males with loyalty and commitment in a best friend. In late adolescence, females place more value on this dimension than males (75 per cent versus 52 per cent), and much of this is with regard to maintaining confidentiality, i.e., intimacy of information (55 per cent versus 35 per cent). Loyalty and commitment also appears to be critical with regard to the termination of friendship. Females cited acts of disloyalty more often than males in both early (47 per cent versus 21 per cent) and late adolescence (47 per cent versus 32 per cent).

Sex differences regarding the disclosure of 'intimate' information were not as dramatic as expected. In early adolescence, females emphasize intimacy more than males (23 per cent versus 9 per cent) and again in late adolescence (60 per cent versus 40 per cent), but no sex differences were found in the contribution of intimacy to growth or decay. It could be that children do not feel that they have to be this specific about the kinds of intimate information involved.

The results of this study provide only limited support for an often cited study by Douvan and Adelson (1966), which reported that boys are less concerned than girls with the affective elements in friendship. We find, instead, little if any difference in the value placed on emotional support and helping, ego reinforcement, acceptance and genuineness, and even the differences cited above are such as to suggest that there is considerable overlap between the males and females.

Sex differences were found, however, in progression along the developmental scale of friendship. We determined the frequency distributions for each age group that were developmentally behind, 'on-target' and advanced. The data on the percentage that are advanced for their age group capture much of the difference. In middle childhood, no sex difference was found in the numbers that were advanced (24 per cent versus 36 per cent). In early adolescence, females were somewhat ahead (44 per cent versus 28 per cent). In late adolescence, many more females were advanced developmentally (65 per cent versus 39 per cent). Much of the superiority found for late adolescent females is due to the greater emphasis placed on intimacy, a Level 8 variable.

Early and late adolescence

Separate analyses of developmental changes during the adolescent years also have not been reported because so few differences were found. The 17-year-olds, as compared to the 13-year-olds, place less value on good moral character in a best friend. It is also less important that a best friend is 'nice' or that s/he provides ego support. In late adolescence intimacy is emphasized much more than in early adolescence (50 per cent versus 16 per cent). Genuineness is also cited more often as the basis for the growth of friendship, and the absence of this quality is cited more often as a reason for breaking up a relationship. We found also that adolescents want friends that are loyal and trustworthy and that provide a reliable source of support in an emotional crisis. In data reported in this chapter, we found no difference in the importance placed on loyalty (57 per cent versus 63 per cent).

Ideal versus actual friendships

The developmental scale of friendship was also used to code each subject's response in terms of its highest position on the eight-point scale. The developmental nature of friendship values was clearly evident by examining the mean developmental level for the children in the three age groups: middle childhood, early adolescence, and late adolescence ($\overline{X}$s = 2.28, 5.25 and 6.47). Developmental changes were also found regarding the descriptions of 'growth' experiences ($\overline{X}$s = 2.61, 3.48 and 4.32). An unexpected finding was the lack of any significant developmental trends regarding 'decay' experiences ($\overline{X}$s = 4.04, 3.96 and 4.15). In middle childhood the same developmental level was evident in responding to questions involving 'ideal' and 'actual'. In adolescence, however, a higher level of development was apparent in 'ideal' than in 'growth' statements. This finding is consistent with Piagetian theory that the concept of 'ideal' is a distinctive feature of formal thought, a characteristic of adolescents (Inhelder and Piaget, 1958). We suspect that part of the difference between 'ideal' and 'actual' is that many adolescents may lack the interpersonal skills needed for implementing their ideals.

There are several implications of the difference between 'ideal' and 'real'. The discrepancy is important in social development in that it may be an impetus to growth. This notion is critical in Piaget's theory of equilibration. A major source of growth is the attempt to reduce disequilibrium resulting from such discrepancies. A second implication is in terms of the notion of self-fulfilling prophecy. Insofar as we have expectations that a friend should be authentic, the likelihood is increased that such a friend will try to be more authentic. This discrepancy may eventually lead to cynicism and a subsequent modification or rejection of such ideals. Alas, La Gaipa (1979) found a general downward trend in friendship values from early to late adolescence for social acquaintances and good friends as opposed to best friends.

What do the growth variables have in common that differentiate them from the decay variables? The growth variables (intimacy, helping and common activities) seem to involve benefits and rewards derived from friendship, and as such lend themselves to a social exchange interpretation (cf. La Gaipa, 1977a). The growth of friendship appears to be facilitated by the exchange of intimate information, emotional support, and doing things together. But the decay of friendship is not simply the breakdown of social exchange. Less than 1 per cent of the respondents made such remarks as 'he stopped helping me' or 'she stopped sharing intimate information'. Instead, the reasons given for decay included statements regarding such characteristics as disloyalty, phoniness and comments that have a moralistic overtone. The termination of friendship appears to involve redefinitions and negative labelling of the other person rather than lack of benefits and rewards. The termination of friendship, then, may be better explained by attribution theory than a social exchange theory. Needless to say, a breakdown in communications is likely to contribute to such negative labelling.

PERSONAL ACCOUNTS

To obtain a comprehensive view of the growth and dissolution of friendship, it is necessary to go beyond cognitive parameters. The meaning of a social experience cannot be explained simply in terms of organismic capacity. The larger social context has to be considered. Two approaches that have helped us to understand children's friendships are ethogeny and structuralism. Ethogeny (Harré, 1977; Harré and Secord, 1972) examines behaviour from the actor's point of view. The explanation of a pattern of social interaction is sought in the 'reasons, rules, meanings and the like taken into account by the participants' (Harré and Secord, 1972, p. 132). Personal reports or accounts is the major technique used. What people say about themselves and others is viewed as relevant to the explanation of behaviour. 'It is essential to take self reports seriously in arriving at adequate explanations of behaviour' (Harré and Secord, 1972, p. 7).

Structuralism seeks to identify 'patterns' rather than cause–effect relationships. The search for patterns is affected by the 'sensitizing' concepts (Blumer, 1969) that the investigator employs. An inductive analysis of the descriptions and accounts provided by people influences the preference given for a theoretical model. An examination of the free descriptions obtained in this research has led us to favour a structural-ethogenic approach. This approach has helped us to make some sense out of such statements, such as one made by a male adolescent in describing the termination of a friendship: 'After we broke up, he would publicly taunt me, and his new friends would taunt me'.

A literal description would be that this is an instance of adolescent cruelty. But the teasing by the former friend would have more complete meaning if looked at from a higher systems level. The teasing might simply reflect his own attempts to demonstrate his new loyalties and his efforts to integrate himself into the new group. The teasing, then, could be interpreted in terms of the interdependency between the clique and the dyad. Such an interpretation is conjectural, but it suggests hypotheses generated from these descriptions that are testable by a more deductive approach if such is preferred by an investigator.

Values and expectations

In middle childhood, the expectations of 9-year-old children are fairly straightforward. They value kindness, politeness, sharing and particularly the lack of aggressive tendencies. Some children in this age group also judge their friends in terms of how they deal with others. 'Someone to play with and have fun with, to care for you, and to share things. No fighting and no horsing around. And to have respect for each other.'

For early adolescence, in the 13-year-old group, a wide range was noted in what is valued and expected, perhaps reflecting the heterogeneity in this age group in the cognitive level of development regarding formal operations. The range extends from the moralistic views of middle childhood to the loyalty and genuineness more characteristic of late adolescence. 'They should like you a lot, be kind to you, tell you their problems, and play games with you. Someone to talk to and care a lot about. Without good friends, life is just a bore. A best friend should not be mouthy and say things to people about you as soon as you turn your back.'

During late adolescence most of the friendship expectations characteristic of early adolescence tend to recur. Loyalty is expected, particularly with regard to the confidentiality of information. There is also an increasing awareness of the role of friendship in personal growth and social development as well as a more realistic outlook toward friendship. 'Best friends are necessary because you need someone to know you better than you know yourself. A friend should not always have to be there to help you when in need because that is not always possible.'

Growth experiences

The kinds of experiences cited in middle childhood involve common activities, helping and ego support. 'I liked her more when she helped me when I fell into a ditch. We started giggling and laughing when we are together. When I was crying, she hugged me, and that's a nice feeling.' The same kinds of themes are reported by 13-year-olds, though expressed with somewhat more articulation. Instances were also noted of inferences as to the nature of the relationship on the basis of the acts of the other. 'She takes the time to hear what I have to say even if it is useless. She won't make fun of what I do. She helps me with things I don't understand. She makes me feel wanted.' 'When other people called me names, she stuck up for me.' The descriptions of friendship among 17-year-olds begins to approximate those which have been written by essayists and philosophers on this subject. But underneath the growing appreciation of friendship, we still can sense such notions as 'A friend in need is a friend indeed'. The dramatic context in which friendships develop is also apparent:

> I know that whatever problem I have, I can discuss it with her. I got into trouble and I mean big trouble. I thought I was pregnant. She was there just to listen to me, to help me, and not to lecture. She wasn't one of those girls who would say: 'Did you love him? What was it like?' Now she is my best friend. I believe a friend like this happens only once in a lifetime, and that it is priceless.

Termination of friendship

In his review of the literature on children and their friendships, Hartup (1978) calls attention to the special qualities that hold for friendship as opposed to popularity, adult-peer or socially governed relationships. The dyadic bond of friendship is particularly susceptible to dissolution because there are few external sanctions holding it together. Duck (1977b) notes that work on lapsed relationships is almost non-existent, and that 'it is not clear, therefore, what general principles apply to the breakdown of relationships' (p. 197).

What is currently referred to as 'termination of friendships' was designated 'instability of friendships' in early research on children. Such research focused on the documentation of the instability of such relationships rather than on isolating their antecedent conditions (Challman, 1932; Hagman, 1933; Jersild and Fite, 1937). Green (1933a, 1933b) observed that friendship was indexed by the number of acquaintances at the ages of two and three. Not until the child is five, does friendship begin to take on any real meaning in terms of continuous experiences with the same person. There is an increase in stability from 6 to 10 years of age, although there is still considerable variation among children (Miell, 1977). It is not until the child is 12 years old that the notion of friendship implies an expectation of some kind of permanence of a relationship. Stability is not very characteristic of children's friendships until about 16 years of age.

The use of such words as 'breakdown' and 'instability' in describing children's friendships implies an unnecessary value judgement. There is the suggestion that it would be somehow 'better' if children did not change friends so often. Such a viewpoint would be contrary to the notion that a variety of different friendships facilitates social development. We also suspect that such concepts as 'breakdown' and 'instability' are inaccurate insofar as we lack benchmarks as to the quality of the relationship that was discontinued. We suspect that what are often defined as children's friendships might be more accurately labelled as acquaintances in adolescence if the same criteria of friendship were applied. Most children's friendships are quite superficial. It might be more accurate to say that children's interaction patterns are highly variable over time.

We suspect that a major reason why children's friendships are so fragile is that they lack the cognitive foundation necessary for appreciating and understanding the meaning of friendship. Moreover, the deeper level of communication essential for intimate friendships is impossible without an adequate conceptual framework of what friendship is all about. It is for this reason that we have focused on cognitive development. But the mechanisms operating in maturational and organismic changes are not yet fully understood. The abstract thought required for thinking about the more intense forms of friendship is not necessarily a cultural universal. Ontogenetic changes are not to be regarded as inevitable (Bigelow, 1974; Flavell, 1977; Kohlberg, 1969). All people do not attain the same level of cognitive or moral development simply by growing older.

The social skills required to establish and maintain a friendship cannot be explained solely in terms of cognitive development. Personality and psychosocial developments also contribute to the acquisition of social cognitions involving friendships. The nature of social experiences during different phases of development are likely to influence not only the friendship values that are acquired but how they are implemented into friendship acts and deeds.

It was noted earlier that 9-year-old seek to explain the decay of friendship in terms of experiences that are ego-degrading—disloyalty and the lack of moral character. What was not pointed out is that 30 per cent of the children cite conflict as the major reason. What is particularly characteristic of 9-year-olds is that the causal explanations often centre on the precipitating event instead of on the antecedent conditions. What appear to be reported are the termination rituals and strategies instead of the causes. 'How' the friendship broke up is more likely to be described than 'why' it broke up. This kind of response is found in all age groups, but is more pronounced among middle childhood. Moreover, the range of termination strategies is greatest in this age group, varying from simple avoidance to physical aggression. 'All of a sudden she got mad and didn't pay any attention to me for no reason. She just ignored me. She just kept on doing gymnastics and talking to her sister. I asked her what was the matter, but she wouldn't talk to me. Now she frowns at me a lot at school.' Nine-year-olds most often report that a verbal declaration was made that the friendship was over. But, it is evident that change is often resisted.

In early adolescence, we find a mixture of direct and indirect confrontations varying from simple avoidance tactics to verbal declarations. Resistance is still alluded to but without the physical aggression found in middle childhood:

> She said she didn't like me anymore so I just think it's not worth having a friend that doesn't like you. I tried to keep her as a friend, but finally realized she didn't want to be my friend, and this made me hate her. She got another one of our friends to tell me she didn't want me around anymore. She said I just didn't fit in because I wasn't real cool like her, and she didn't like my friends.

As we have indicated earlier on, one likely cause of termination is differences in the rate of social development of members of the dyad. This contributes to disparity in social status and dissimilarity in life style. In responding to such episodes, comments were often made on a narrow conception of the moral character of the departed friend. Doubtless for some people, these kinds of negative comments become more sophisticated in adult years. However, it may come as a surprise to note that few dramatic changes occur in the personal accounts of early and late adolescents. The termination strategy of simply ignoring the other continues. What is different is the increasing reference to heterosexual relationships.

> My friend started hanging around with another girl. They went necking with their boyfriends, and I wasn't that kind. I was really hurt when my best friend dumped me for that sex symbol. She thought she was too good for us. She would pretend she didn't know us. It was like saying we weren't good enough for her now that she had better friends. I went out with her boyfriend and she gave me prank phone calls, and called me all kinds of names. She even wrote things about me on the walls of the bathrooms in school. I really hate her now. I never did anything wrong for her to do that.

SUMMARY

In this chapter, we have done some of the much-needed spade work in learning more about the changing processes involved in the development of friendship. As our tentative yardstick of cognitive development, the friendship expectation scale proved invaluable in providing a common linguistic denominator containing the parameters for an experimental inquiry of friendship preference. As one crosses the distance from childhood to adolescence, one is more reliably interested in befriending another who is one developmental level more advanced than ourselves. Paradoxically, 'real-life' choices are most similar during earlier years, becoming more widely scattered with age. Thus, as children consolidate their friendship ideals, they are also evidently better at coping with friendships containing an assortment of expectations.

Fortunately for the adolescent, this increasing disparity between one's 'ideal' and 'real' friendships brings with it a virtual armoury of strategies with which to dissolve the inadequate relationship. Empirical data, together with personal accounts, show that the virtues which foster a best friendship are often not simply the opposites of the reasons given for its demise. Perhaps it is fortunate that friendship is indeed a rather fragile institution, which, in the final analysis, must succumb to the dynamics of individual differences in cognitive development.

NOTES

1. The coding system can be obtained from either author. See Bigelow and La Gaipa (1975) and Bigelow (1977) for complete details.

REFERENCES

Bandura, A., and McDonald, F. (1963). Influence of social reinforcement and the behavior of models in shaping children's moral judgment. *Journal of Abnormal and Social Psychology*, **67**, 274–281.

Bandura, A., and Walters, R. (1963). *Social Learning and Personality Development*. New York: Holt, Rinehart and Winston.

Bannister, D., and Fransella, F. (1971). *Inquiring Man: The Theory of Personal Constructs*. Harmondsworth: Penguin.

Bigelow, B. J. (1974). The development of children's friendship expectations: a cognitive and behavioural perspective. Unpublished Doctoral Dissertation, University of Dundee.

Bigelow, B. J. (1977). Children's friendship expectations: a cognitive-developmental study. *Child Development*, **48**, 246–253.

Bigelow, B. J., and La Gaipa, J. J. (1975). Children's written descriptions of friendship: a multidimensional analysis. *Developmental Psychology*, **11**, 857–858.

Blumer, H. (1969). *Symbolic Interactionism: Perspective and Method*. Englewood Cliffs, New Jersey: Prentice-Hall.

Brainerd, C. J. (1973a). Neo-Piagetian training experiments revisited: is there any support for the cognitive-developmental stage hypothesis? *Cognition*, **2**, 349–370.

Brainerd, C. J. (1973b). Order of acquisition of transitivity, conservation, and class inclusion of length and weight. *Developmental Psychology*, **8**, 105–116.

Brainerd, C. J. (1976). Cognitive development and concept learning: an interpretive review. *Psychological Bulletin*, **84**, 919–939.

Brainerd, C. J. (1977). Response criteria in concept development research. *Child Development*, **48**, 360–366.

Brainerd, C. J. (1978). The stage question in cognitive-developmental theory. *Behavioral and Brain Sciences*, **2**, 173–213.

Byrne, D., and Griffitt, W. (1966). A developmental investigation of the law of attraction. *Journal of Personality and Social Psychology*, **4**, 699–703.

Byrne, D., and Griffitt, W. (1969). Similarity and awareness of similarity of personality as determinants of attraction. *Journal of Experimental Research in Personality*, **3**, 179–186.

Challman, R. C. (1932). Factors influencing friendship among preschool children. *Child Development*, **3**, 146–158.

Cowen, P. A., Langer, J., Heavenrich, J., and Nathanson, M. (1969). Social learning and Piaget's cognitive theory of moral development. *Journal of Personality and Social Psychology*, **11**, 261–274.

Douvan, E., and Adelson, J. (1966). *The Adolescent Experience*. New York: Wiley.

Duck, S. W. (1973). *Personal Relationships and Personal Constructs: A Study of Friendship Formation.* London: Wiley.

Duck, S. W. (1977a). Inquiry, hypothesis and the quest for validation: personal construct systems in the development of acquaintance. In S. W. Duck (Ed.), *Theory and Practice in Interpersonal Attraction.* London: Academic Press.

Duck, S. W. (1977b). *The Study of Acquaintance.* Farnborough: Teakfield.

Emmerich, W. (1968). Personality development and concepts of structure. *Child Development,* **39,** 671–690.

Feffer, M. H. (1959). The cognitive implication of role-taking behavior. *Journal of Personality,* **27,** 152–168.

Feffer, M. H. (1971). Developmental analysis of interpersonal behavior. *Psychological Review,* **77,** 197–214.

Feffer, M. H., and Gourevich, V. (1960). Cognitive aspects of role-taking in children. *Journal of Personality,* **28,** 383–396.

Flavell, J. H. (1968). *The Development of Role-taking and Communication Skills in Children.* New York: Wiley.

Flavell, J. H. (1971). Stage-related properties of cognitive development. *Cognitive Psychology,* **2,** 421–453.

Flavell, J. H. (1972). An analysis of cognitive-developmental sequence. *Genetic Psychology Monographs,* **86,** 279–350.

Flavell, J. H. (1977). *Cognitive Development.* Englewood Cliffs, New Jersey: Prentice-Hall.

Gollin, E. S. (1958). Organizational characteristics of social judgment: A developmental investigation. *Journal of Personality,* **26,** 139–154.

Green, E. H. (1933a). Friendships and quarrels among preschool children. *Child Development,* **4,** 327–353.

Green, E. H. (1933b). Group play and quarrelling among preschool children. *Child Development,* **4,** 302–307.

Hagman, E. P. (1933). The companionship of preschool children. *University of Iowa Studies in Child Welfare,* **7,** No. 4, 1–69.

Harré, R. (1977). Friendship as an accomplishment: an ethogenic approach to social relationships. In S. Duck (Ed.), *Theory and Practice in Interpersonal Attraction.* London: Academic Press.

Harré, R., and Secord, P. F. (1972). *The Explanation of Social Behavior.* Totowa, New Jersey: Roman and Littlefield.

Hartup, W. W. (1975). The origins of friendship. In M. L. Lewis and L. A. Rosenblum (Eds.), *Friendship and Peer Relations.* New York: Wiley.

Hartup, W. W. (1978). Children and their friends. In H. McGurk (Ed.), *Issues in Childhood Social Development.* London: Methuen.

Harvey, O. J., Hunt, D. E., and Schroder, H. M. (1961). *Conceptual Systems and Personality Organization.* New York: Wiley.

Inhelder, B., and Piaget, J. (1958). *The Growth of Logical Thinking from Childhood to Adolescence.* London: Routledge and Kegan Paul.

Inhelder, B., and Piaget, J. (1964). *The Early Growth of Logic in the Child.* London: Routledge and Kegan Paul.

Jersild, A. T., and Fite, H. D. (1937). Children's social adjustment in nursery school. *Journal of Experimental Education,* **6,** 161–179.

Kelly, G. A. (1955). *The Psychology of Personal Constructs.* New York: Norton.

Kiss, G. R. (1972). Recursive concept analysis. Unpublished manuscript, Medical Research Council Speech and Communication Unit, University of Edinburgh.

Kohlberg, L. (1969). Stage and sequence: the cognitive-developmental approach to socialization. In D. A. Goslin (Ed.), *Handbook of Socialization Theory and Research.* Chicago, Illinois: Rand McNally.

Kuhn, D. (1972). Mechanisms of change in the development of cognitive structures. *Child Development,* **43**, 833–844.

Kurtines, W., and Greif, E. B. (1974). The development of moral thought: review and evaluation of Kohlberg's approach. *Psychological Bulletin,* **81**, 453–470.

La Gaipa, J. J. (1977a). Interpersonal attraction and social exchange. In S. W. Duck (Ed.), *Theory and Practice in Interpersonal Attraction.* London: Academic Press.

La Gaipa, J. J. (1977b). Testing a multidimensional approach to friendship. In S. W. Duck (Ed.), *Theory and Practice in Interpersonal Attraction.* London: Academic Press.

La Gaipa, J. J.(1979). A developmental study of the meaning of friendship in adolescence. *Journal of Adolescence,* **2**, 1–13.

La Gaipa, J. J., and Bigelow, B. J. (1972). The development of childhood friendship expectations. Paper read at the Meeting of the Canadian Psychological Association, Montreal.

La Gaipa, J. J., and Engelhart, R. S. (1978). Sex differences in self-disclosure and friendship. Paper read at the meeting of the Southeastern Psychological Association, Atlanta, March.

La Gaipa, J. J., and Wood, H. D. (1973). The perception of friendship by socially accepted and rejected children. Paper read at the meeting of the Eastern Psychological Association, Washington, D.C.

Livesley, W. J., and Bromley, D. B. (1973). *Perception in Childhood and Adolescence.* London: Wiley.

Maslow, A. H. (1954). *Motivation and Personality.* New York: Harper.

Miell, D. (1977). The stability of children's friendships: a developmental study. Unpublished manuscript, University of Lancaster.

Miller, D. P., and Stone, M. E. (1951). The prediction of social acceptance by means of psychoanalytic concepts. *Journal of Personality,* **20**, 162–174.

Miller, S. A. (1976). Nonverbal assessment of conservation of number. *Child Development,* **47**, 722–728.

Montemayor, R., and Eisen, M. (1977). The development of self-conceptions from childhood,to adolescence. *Developmental Psychology,* **13**, 314–319.

Moshman, D. (1977). Consolidation and stage formation in the emergence of formal operations. *Developmental Psychology,* **13**, 95–100.

Piaget, J. (1932). *The Moral Judgment of the Child.* London: Routledge and Kegan Paul.

Piaget, J. (1952). *The Child's Conception of Number.* New York: Humanities Press.

Piaget, J. (1960). The general problems of the psychological development of the child. In J. M. Tanner and B. Inhelder (Eds.), *Discussions on Child Development,* Vol. 4. New York: International Universities Press.

Piaget, J. (1970). Piaget's theory. In P. H. Mussen (Ed.), *Carmichael's Manual of Child Psychology.* Vol. 3. New York: Wiley.

Piaget, J., and Inhelder, B. (1941). *Le developpement des quantities chez l'enfant.* Neuchatel: Delachaux et Niestle.

Piaget, J., Inhelder, B., and Szeminska, A. (1960). *The Child's Conception of Geometry.* London: Routledge and Kegan Paul.

Rardin, D., and Moan, C. (1971). Peer interaction and cognitive development. *Child Development,* **42**, 1685–1699.

Reisman, J. M., and Shorr, S. I. (1978). Friendship claims and expectations among children and adults. *Child Development,* **49**, 913–916.

Rest, J., Turiel, E., and Kolberb, L. (1969). Level of moral development as a determinant of preference and comprehension of moral judgements made by others. *Journal of Personality,* **37**, 225–252.

Scarlett, H. H., Press, A. N., and Crockett, W. H. (1971). Children's descriptions of peers: a Wernerian developmental analysis. *Child Development*, **42**, 439–453.

Selman, B. L., and Byrne, D. F. (1974). Structural-developmental analysis of levels of role taking in middle childhood. *Child Development*, **45**, 803–806.

Shantz, C. U. (1975). The development of social cognition. In E. M. Hetherington (Ed.), *Review of Child Development Research*, Vol. 5. Chicago: University of Chicago Press.

Turiel, E. (1966). An experimental test of the sequentiality of developmental stages in the child's moral judgment. *Journal of Personality and Social Psychology*, **3**, 611–618.

Turiel, E. (1969). Developmental processes in the child's moral thinking. In P. Mussen, J. Langer, and M. Covington (Eds.), *New Directions in Developmental Psychology*. New York: Holt, Rinehart and Winston.

Turiel, E., and Rothman, G. R. (1972). The influence of reasoning on behavioral choices at different stages of moral development. *Child Development*, **43**, 741–756.

Vecerka, L. (1925). Das social Verhalten von Madchen wahrend der Reifenzeit. In Fisher (Ed.), *Quellen und Studien Zur Jugend*. Jena, 41–121.

Werner, H. (1957). The concept of development from a comparative and organismic point of view. In D. B. Harris (Ed.), *The Concept of Development*. Minneapolis: University of Minnesota Press.

Werner, H. (1961). *Comparative Psychology of Mental Development*. New York: Science Editions.

White, R. (1959). Motivation reconsidered: The concept of competence. *Psychological Review*, **66**, 297–333.

Wohlwill, J. F. (1970). The age variable in psychological research. *Psychological Review*, **77**, 49–64.

Wood, H. D. (1976). Predicting behavioral types in preadolescent girls from psychosocial development and friendship values. Unpublished Doctoral Dissertation, University of Windsor.

Yarrow, M. R., and Campbell, J. D. (1963). Person perception in children. *Merrill-Palmer Quarterly*, **9**, 57–72.

Zigler, E., and Child, I. L. (1969). Socialization. In G. Lindsey and E. Aronson (Eds.), *Handbook of Social Psychology*, Vol. 3. Cambridge, Massachusetts: Addison-Wesley.

CHAPTER 2

The Development of Children's Friendships

ANTHONY
P. MANNARINO

Friendship development is currently being investigated within a diverse set of theoretical and research frameworks, many of which are reviewed in this volume. The intention of this chapter is threefold. First, an attempt is made to delineate the major dimensions of friendship and to differentiate it from other childhood social variables. Second, theoretical perspectives of Arnold Gesell and Harry Stack Sullivan, both of whom contributed much to our current understanding of children's friendships, are presented. Third, the empirical research on children's conceptions of friendship is critically reviewed.

DIMENSIONS OF FRIENDSHIP

Webster's *New Collegiate Dictionary* (1973) defines friendship as one person's attachment to another through affection and/or esteem. This definition, although concise, does not sufficiently delimit the boundaries of friendship. Indeed an essential objective in the study of friendship is to isolate its major dimensions and to differentiate it from other interpersonal relationships. Attempting to characterize children's friendships, Hartup (1975) has suggested three basic qualities. First, children exhibit unique behaviours such as talking, laughing, and sharing, in the presence of a friend. Friendships also entail differentiated reactions to separation such as mood changes and a desire to regain proximity through a visit. Finally, Hartup has posited that special conceptual and linguistic categories are applied to friendship. Concepts such as 'chum', 'friend', 'to like', 'to dislike', and 'enemy' represent various aspects of friendship. Unfortunately, little is known about the relationship between these concepts and friendship formation. Research is needed in all these three areas of friendship so that our understanding of children's close interpersonal relations will be multidimensional in nature.

A recent study by Cabral, Volpe, Youniss and Gellert (1977) suggests that children's friendships are markedly different from other childhood social relations. These researchers studied children from 7 to 17 years old who were provided with stories in which a child shares confidential information with a parent, friend, or acquaintance but then learns that this confidence has been breached. Subjects were requested to describe what effect the broken confidence would have on the relationship. Findings indicated that parents were granted the privilege of making information that had been private public because they were perceived as doing it for the child's 'own good', whereas friends were expected to abide by reciprocal agreements as part of the friendship. Acquaintances, on the other hand, could break confidences but such transgressions might prevent the relationship from becoming a friendship. This investigation suggests that friendships are reciprocal in nature and are clearly distinguishable from other interpersonal relationships.

It is the contention of the present author that this concept of reciprocity is *the* essential component of friendship and that it should be included in any definition of the term. To elaborate, two individuals can be said to have a friendship only if the affection and/or esteem that one expresses toward the other is reciprocated. Of course, it is probably difficult to determine if the number and intensity of feelings conveyed by one individual to the other are equally reciprocated. One nonetheless expects some return of positive regard in order for the friendship to be maintained. Most studies of children's friendships, however, have not included a criterion of reciprocity or mutuality. Thus, an investigator who purports to examine the bases of children's friendships by simply asking children to identify reasons why they 'like their best friend' fails to account for the possiblity that a designated best friend may not direct positive feelings toward the subject. In some instances, children may create the illusion that their positive feelings are reciprocated but this perception may have no basis in reality. Indeed in the above illustration it is the bases of liking, not friendship, that are apparently being examined. A major task confronting researchers is to devise innovative experimental methodologies that are sensitive to the mutuality and reciprocity of children's friendships.

The most extensively studied childhood social variable has been peer group acceptance. In order to demarcate clearly the boundaries of friendship, there is a need to distinguish empirically these two concepts. This task is not easy to accomplish as the sociometric techniques designed to measure peer group acceptance or popularity are repeatedly used, albeit in a somewhat modified fashion, to assess friendship formation. Thus, for example, instead of requesting children to name three peers with whom to play after school or with whom to do a group project (as is frequently the case with the measurement of peer group popularity), children are directed to name other children they like best or are their best friends to determine their friendship status. Research by Livesay (1972) and Mouton, Blake and Fruchter (1960) has demonstrated, however, that sociometric techniques are highly correlated, regardless of the criteria used. Accordingly it appears that, by employing essentially the same sociometric techniques to measure both peer group acceptance and friendship, researchers have treated the two variables in an empirically identical manner. To overcome this methodological obstacle but still retain the sociometric strategy in the study of friendship, researchers might ensure that a child's selection of best friends is reciprocated by those friends. A better solution, and one which has been discussed previously and will be reiterated throughout the chapter, is for developmentalists to design alternative strategies of investigating friendship relations in children, particularly ones responsive to the reciprocal 'give and take' nature of this relationship. Such an innovative approach can be found in the recent work of Chapman, Smith, Foot and Pritchard (1979) who have simultaneously utilized sociometric ratings, teacher ratings, and behavioural observations in their study of friendship.

In addition to methodological concerns, there is research evidence which suggests that social acceptance and friendship must be differentiated. In a thorough review of the literature, Hartup (1970) found peer group acceptance to be related to all of the following characteristics: sociability, cooperation, friendliness, self-esteem, socioempathy, low anxiety, intelligence, academic achievement, birth order, children's names, sex and ethnicity. This impressive list implies that a child high in peer status also ranks high on other traits and behaviours that foster academic success and overall personal competence. In no way, however, does a child's level of peer group acceptance suggest anything about his personal intimacy with other children, his age, or his capacity to form and maintain close friendships. In fact, some researchers have reported that peer group status and diverse indices of friendship are empirically unrelated (Horrocks and Buker, 1951; Hunt and Solomon, 1942; Mannarino, 1975). As Hartup (1975) astutely observed, 'the correlates of popularity cannot be used as a data base for formulating assumptions concerning the ontogenetic significance of early friendships' (p. 24).

The preceding discussion illustrates that defining the scope of friendship relations in children is a complex task. Because it is experienced in a highly subjective manner, friendship is difficult to operationalize. Additionally, because of the interactive nature of friendship, research techniques that isolate one variable while controlling all others may not be sensitive to the bidirectionality of this close interpersonal relationship. Despite these obstacles the present author has suggested that the boundaries of friendship can be defined if attempts to operationalize it include a criterion of reciprocity or mutuality and also insure that it is clearly differentiated from other childhood social variables.

The remainder of this chapter is devoted to a presentation of the theoretical foundations of children's friendships and a review of the empirical data on children's conceptualization of friendship. The discussion focuses on children's friendships from the preschool era to preadolescence.

CHILDREN'S FRIENDSHIP: THEORETICAL BASES

The area of social development in children generally suffers from a lack of integrative theorizing. This is particularly true in the study of friendship development, although as this book demonstrates, creative theoretical approaches are beginning to emerge. In this author's view, the two principal theoretical contributions in this area have come from Gesell and Sullivan whose writings are of many years' standing. Their hypotheses and perceptions with respect to the development of children's friendships are extremely enlightening and still influence the thinking of contemporary developmentalists. A discussion of their theories now follows.

Arnold Gesell: The normative-developmental approach

Gesell proposed a comprehensive developmental theory (Gesell and Ilg, 1949; Gesell, Ilg and Ames, 1956). He conceptualized development as a gradual patterning of processes with each succeeding year bringing forth characteristic behaviours and trends. To test his formulations, Gesell conducted a longitudinal study in which observations, interviews, and a variety of other instruments were utilized to gather data on children from birth through to 16 years of age. His approach was normative in that a given child's developmental status was determined by comparing his development on a particular variable to the norms for his age group.

At the core of Gesell's theory were his concepts of 'reciprocal interweaving' and 'spiral reincorporation' (1945). By the former term, he referred to the unevenness of development as counterbalanced systems fluctuate in ascendancy, with each alternatively achieving dominance during the course of ontogenesis, With respect to spiral reincorporation, Gesell posited that early developmental patterns partly reoccur within subsequent developmental periods, although at higher levels of organization.

Gesell's observations on children's friendships fit nicely into his overall conceptual scheme. Thus, he theorized that with each age level characteristic friendship patterns emerge. For example, he observed that 3-year-olds demonstrate a preference for one companion, often of the opposite sex, and begin to use the word 'friend' whereas 4-year-olds frequently select a same-sex friend. Friendships during this era are marked by both fighting and cooperation and dissolve readily during play due to the egocentric nature of preschoolers' interactive styles (Gesell and Ilg, 1949). By 6 years of age, children enjoy having friends and spending time with them; nonetheless, friendships come apart easily as during the preschool period. As Wenar (1971) remarked, however, the alternation of periods of quarrelling and cooperation, far from being detrimental to children's notions of friendship, enables them to learn that differing and resolving differences are basic components of close interpersonal relationships.

Gesell and Ilg (1949) found that 'best' friend relationships appear at approximately 8 or 9 years of age. Unlike the previous developmental period, friendships are more stable and do not dissolve for insignificant or petty reasons. There is a heightened sense of mutuality as friends now respond in a reciprocal manner and maintain their friendships despite occasional conflict. The greater cognitive flexibility of this age level probably contributes to these advances. In discussing Gesell's observations of friendship at 10 and 11 years, Wenar (1971) noted that children have a variety of friends 'who are often adapted to specific occasions, such as a best friend to play ball with, a best friend to work with, a best friend to talk to' (p. 271). Additionally, preadolescent friendships are marked by greater emotional intensity and closer interaction, increased tolerance of conflict, and added stability when compared with earlier friendship relations.

According to Gesell, friendship development follows the same ontogenetic course as other behaviours. Thus, there are periods of equilibrium and disequilibrium as the child vacillates between unstable relationships with many children and more intimate, focused attachments to close friends. Nevertheless, with increasing age, children's friendships progress toward greater maturity as mutuality and reciprocity, the keystones of friendship, become more evident.

This rather brief presentation of Gesell's observations on children's friendships barely scratches the surface of the enormous contribution he made to developmental psychology. What sets his theoretical notions apart from the writings of many contemporary researchers is that he succeeded in integrating his theory and data on the ontogenesis of friendship into a wider developmental framework. Accordingly, his basic axioms of reciprocal interweaving and spiral reincorporation apply not only to children's friendships but to all major behavioural systems that exhibit developmental change. Such a systematic approach to children's friendships is all too infrequent in the current literature where isolated hypotheses and fragmented research data predominate.

Gesell's maturational perspective is not widely esteemed by many present-day developmentalists who prefer a learning or interactionistic viewpoint on development. There are also those who criticize him for emphasizing the 'average' child and thereby overlooking individual differences. Nonetheless, his use of systematic observations, in the long run, might prove to be more sensitive to the bidirectionality of friendship relations than today's supposedly more sophisticated experimental methodologies. As naturalistic observation becomes increasingly refined with the emergence of such techniques, as for example, behavioural categories, coding systems, and time sampling, this approach may provide some methodological advances in the investigation of friendship development.

Harry Stack Sullivan: a clinician's view of friendship

Sullivan's social development theory and in particular his observations on children's friendships (Sullivan, 1952, 1965) are rarely mentioned in either contemporary child development journals or textbooks. Perhaps some see his major contributions as coming in the clinical arena, specifically his extensive work on schizophrenia and psychiatric interviewing, and have therefore overlooked his developmental theorizing. Or, maybe his theory has been too closely linked with Freud's ideas and has not been evaluated on its own merits. In either case, Sullivan's formulations about children's friendships remain a largely untapped reservoir of developmental knowledge.

Sullivan was one of a number of theorists who gradually divorced themselves from the orthodox psychoanalytic tradition because of Freud's lack of emphasis upon social relationships. In fact, in some ways his ideas bear a closer resemblance to those of Adler (1927) who was the first theorist to propose the notion of an innate social interest. In his theoretical discussions, Sullivan (1952) postulated that throughout the developmental sequence, children have a need for interpersonal relationships which vary from one period to the next. During childhood (which he somewhat idiosyncratically defined as occurring between 2 and 4 years old) the child is not sufficiently ready to engage in peer relationships outside the family. This early focus on family members to fulfil social needs is a function of the child's insecure personality. According to Sullivan, due to feelings of helplessness and general anxiety, the young child is heavily preoccupied with building his 'self dynamism' which largely evolves from experiences of approbation and/or disapproval from the parents. The self therefore grows to resemble evaluations made of the child by 'significant others' in his life. Sullivan proposed the term 'reflected appraisal' to describe this self-developing process.

Sullivan (1965) theorized that the juvenile era occurs between 4 and 9 years old and is uniquely characterized by a need for playmates. As Mullahy (1970) noted, the child's social interest during this period is quite general and self-oriented. As a result of the child's egocentric nature, peer relations are initiated and maintained not out of a sincere concern for others but due to the need to enhance his/her own status and popularity. (Of course, peer relationships can evolve for similar reasons during later developmental periods but Sullivan suggested that self-oriented social relationships are characteristic of the juvenile era.) The juvenile period is therefore marked by high levels of competition. The cooperation and conformity that do emerge are self-motivated as the child attempts to achieve greater personal prestige in the eyes of his peers.

Despite the self-orientation of the juvenile era, Sullivan proposed that the development of 'social accommodation' is a positive outcome of this period. By this term, he referred to the child's ability to learn and grasp how many slight differences in interpersonal style and cognitive perspective there are. This developmental advance is the product of reduced ego-centrism which results from increased peer interaction. In this regard, Sullivan's notions resemble the previously discussed observations of Gesell who noted that children's gradual understanding and resolving of differences in interpersonal style are critical elements in early friendships. Nonetheless, Sullivan strongly believed that during the juvenile era the child remains predominantly insensitive to the personal worth of others and is not truly interested in their welfare or happiness.

With preadolescence, intimate interpersonal adjustment becomes the crucial challenge of life. Sullivan (1953) hypothesized that a need for interpersonal intimacy develops through maturation and experience. Specifically, a new type of interest evolves in which a member of the same sex becomes a 'chum' or close friend. Within this relationship, the preadolescent develops a genuine sensitivity to the individual concerns of his chum—not a self-centred sensitivity, but a sincere interest in the welfare of the other human being.

Two significant developments are associated with a 'chum relationship'. First, Sullivan proposed that the intimacy of this close interpersonal experience provides a validation of the preadolescent's self-worth. In Sullivan's own words, 'through mutual interaction, the necessity for thinking of the other fellow as right and for being thought of as right by the other leads to a resolution of the uncertainty as to the real worth of the personality' (1953 p. 52). Thus, honest communication with his/her best friend enables the preadolescent to realize that his/her thoughts and feelings are similar to those of someone else. Sullivan labelled this process 'consensual validation of the self'. Conversely, failure to establish a chum relationship contributes to a lowering of self-perceptions. The preadolescent without a close friend is deprived of the opportunity to communicate openly with a peer and his ideational symbols are therefore not validated. Doubts as to the real worth of the personality result with a diminished self-esteem being the final outcome.

The other significant consequence of a chumship is that the preadolescent develops a 'sense of humanity' as the interests of another become as important as his/her own. Although Sullivan was not entirely clear with respect to this matter, he seemed to suggest that the specific sensitivity and 'other' orientation displayed toward the chum eventually transcend this relationship and become a general altruistic perspective. For Sullivan, a chum represented one instance of humanity for the preadolescent. As both youngsters communicate openly, the preadolescent begins to appreciate the common humanity of people since s/he shares many qualities with his/her chum. A compassion for fellow men is therefore extended not only to friends but also to those who are not known. Thus, becoming sensitive to the needs of one individual results in greater interpersonal insight and also a greater probability that the preadolescent will demonstrate continued sensitivity in subsequent social encounters.

The predictive nature of a chum relationship was in fact supported by a study of adults of both sexes as part of the larger Berkeley Guidance Study (Maas, 1968). In this investigation, adults were classified as 'warm' or 'aloof' based on their capacity for intimate relationships as measured by test protocols and a Q-sort after an interview. It was reported that the warm group had more enduring and mutually satisfying chumships during preadolescence than the aloof group. These data had been collected earlier as part of a longitudinal research strategy. Although the follow-back research tactic employed in this study is not as adequate for predictive purposes as a follow-up design (Ricks, 1970), it was clearly demonstrated that preadolescent peer relations can have specific implications for adult intimacy.

Apart from the Maas (1968) study, the present author was unable to locate any empirical investigations conceptualized and designed from a Sullivanian theoretical perspective. Of indirect relevance, however, is a developmental study of children aged from 8 to 21 years old in grades IV–XVI by Byrne and Griffitt (1966). These researchers found that beginning at 9 or 10 years of age, children choose as friends other children whose attitudes are similar to theirs. Such results imply that preadolescent friendships evolve largely out of a need to select peers who can reinforce one's attitudes and ideas. In Sullivanian terms, one seeks to validate consensually one's ideational symbols.

Recently the present author completed a broad investigation of friendship patterns in preadolescent boys (Mannarino, 1976; 1978a). Utilizing a Sullivanian framework, he hypothesized that children with a chum relationship would exhibit higher self-concepts and greater levels of altruism than those without this close friendship. The subject population comprised boys selected from grade VI of an elementary school from one of the white, upper middle-class suburbs of a metropolitan area. Three criteria of a 'chumship' were used. First, a measure of friendship stability was included in which subjects were requested to name their three best friends in order of preference (cf. Horrocks and Buker, 1951; Thompson and Horrocks, 1947). Two weeks later the identical procedure was followed. Only those children whose best friend from the initial measure remained as their best or second best friend were considered to have a

Table 2.1.   Chumship checklist

---

1 Play games in which you both take turns being the leader.
2 Walk to school together.
3 Help out when one of you gets behind in his work.
4 Talk about girls.
5 Share each other's games, bat and ball, etc.
6 Tell each other things you wouldn't tell anyone else.
7 'Stick up' for each other if an older boy is picking on one of you.
8 Sit together on school bus.
9 Try to be on same side when choosing teams for football or baseball, even if he is not the best player.
10 Do 'fun' things together, such as going to the movies or ball games.
11 Tell each other if one of you has done something wrong.
12 Phone each other about school assignments.
13 Talk about what you want to be when you grow up.
14 Sleep over at each other's house.
15 Talk about your parents.
16 Find it hard to disagree with him on important things.
17 Go on a vacation or short trip with him and his family.

From Mannarino (1976). Copyright 1976 by the American Psychological Association. Reprinted by permission.

stable friendship. The second criterion involved the Chumship Checklist (see Table 2.1) designed by the author, in keeping with Sullivan's notions of a chumship, to evaluate whether or not the preadolescent male communicates honestly with his friend and is sensitive to his needs and interests. A pilot study (Mannarino, 1975) indicated that the checklist's internal consistency is of the order of $p = .85$. This correlation was considered sufficient to warrant further use of the checklist in the main part of the investigation. In this regard, only those subjects who checked at least 10 of the 17 items were considered to exhibit a chum relationship. Finally, each subject was asked to specify whether he would rather spend his spare time with his best friend or group of friends. Subjects who indicated a preference for their best friend satisfactorily met this criterion.

Thirty of the original 92 subjects qualified for the chumship group by meeting all three criteria. A second group of 30 subjects was then selected who did not maintain this close friendship, as evidenced by failing to meet at least two of the three criteria, but who were equal to those in the chumship group with respect to level of peer group acceptance and intelligence. Peer popularity was assessed by means of a sociometric questionaire while intellectual status was determined by taking the most recent IQ score that the subject had on his permanent academic records.

There were two measures of altruism. The first was the altruism sub-scale of the *Scale of Social Responsibility* (Harris, 1957). This instrument measures children's attitudes toward 'concern for others'. The second method was a behavioural measure, a modified version of the new standard prisoner's dilemma game. This modification permitted children to play selfishly or altruistically with an unfamiliar peer in order to accumulate points to be exchanged for prizes at a local fast-food restaurant. The *Piers–Harris Children's Self-concept Scale* (Piers and Harris, 1969) was used to assess the level of self-concept. Results indicated that on both the self-report and behavioural measures, preadolescent males involved in a chum relationship displayed significantly greater levels of altruism than those without this friendship. Additionally, the former group exhibited significantly higher self-concepts than the latter group. These data were interpreted as supporting Sullivan's notions that a chum relationship provides consensual validation of the preadolescent's self-worth and contributes to his developing sense of human sensitivity and interpersonal empathy.

Despite the statistical significance and implications of its findings, the above project suffered from a number of methodological shortcomings. That it was a correlational design precludes any definitive statements about the direction of causality. Thus, altruism and positive self-perception may contribute as much to the development of chum relationships and are just as plausible an argument as the reverse line of reasoning. Furthermore, the examination of friendship patterns was not intensive, as at no time was the interaction of a preadolescent and his best friend specifically observed. A related problem was the fact that a criterion of mutuality, previously emphasized as a crucial element in defining friendship, was not included. Nevertheless, the results of this investigation suggest that best friendships potentially play a critical role in the socialization process during the preadolescent era. Most importantly, though, it was demonstrated that Sullivan's theoretical notions about friendships can be tested. Given the lack of systematic theory in the area of friendship development, his work certainly merits reexamination and further empirical analysis.

CHILDREN'S CONCEPTIONS OF FRIENDSHIP

The discussion to this point has primarily been devoted to defining friendship and to providing theoretical bases for the study of friendship development. Unfortunately, as indicated earlier, the empirical studies of children's friendships have often not stemmed from any systematic theoretical framework. This has resulted in fragmentation of existing data. Investigators have been at least partly successful, though, in integrating research and theory in the study of children's conceptualization of friendship. In particular, in recent years, there has been increased theoretical and research interest in how children think about friendship, the language of friendship, and the relationship between these factors and the formation and maintenance of close interpersonal relationships. The following section is a review of studies in this area.

Almost without exception, the empirical research on children's conceptions of friendship has only included as subjects children over the age of 6 years old. Nonetheless, there are a few things that we do know about how children think and talk about friendship during the preschool era. It is generally agreed that by 3 or 4 years old, children begin to use the word 'friend' (Gesell and Ilg, 1949; Wenar, 1971). It is unlikely, however, that they possess a sophisticated internalized understanding of the concept of friend given the cognitive limitations of this period. Yet, at a behavioural level, it is evident that preschoolers are learning to appreciate some of the special qualities of friendship. As described in the previous section, both quarrelling and cooperation characterize the friendships of this era (Gesell and Ilg, 1949). Thus, preschoolers demonstrate some understanding that differing and resolving differences are integral components of close interpersonal relationships. One might also conjecture, as Piaget (1965) has done with respect to middle childhood, that frequent interaction with a friend during the preschool period reduces the child's egocentrism as s/he is confronted by the friend's behavioural dissimilarities.

There exists a significantly greater wealth of data on children's conceptions of friendship during middle childhood and preadolescence. This line of research has not evolved in a vacuum, however, as it is closely connected to both previous and ongoing research in the field of person perception. In fact, cognitive-developmental theory (Piaget, 1960; Werner, 1957) has been utilized as a conceptual framework by investigators in both areas. One of the major postulates of this theoretical approach is that during the course of development, behaviour becomes increasingly more differentiated and complex but also more integrated into a hierarchically organized structure. Werner labelled this process the 'orthogenetic principle'. This developmental tenet was first supported in the person perception field by the work of Gollin (1958) who found in children from 10 to 16 years of age that the use of more differentiated and inferential concepts in interpersonal description increased monotonically with age.

Other studies in the general area of person perception have been consistent with Gollin's findings. Signell (1966) reported in a study of children aged from 9 to 16 years of age that older children employed functionally more complex concepts than younger children when describing familiar peers while Maddock and Kenny (1973), in a study of impression formation, found that 12-year-olds exhibited more differentiated and integrated impressions than either 10-or 8-year-olds. Scarlett, Press and Crockett (1977) conducted an investigation, using grade I, III and V boys of 6 to 11 years old, specifically conceptualized from a Wernerian developmental perspective. They hypothesized that, with increasing age, children would use a greater number of constructs to describe their peers. Additionally, it was suggested that abstract concepts would show a monotonic increase while egocentric constructs would demonstrate a monotonic decrease with age. All three hypotheses were supported by the data.

   The above studies have a direct bearing on the research on children's conceptions of friendship. Taken together, they suggest that as children grow older,
they develop a more complex and hierarchically-organized conceptual system
with which to think about their peers. Older children are more precise and
abstract in their social judgements and more logically systematic in their evaluations of interpersonal relationships. Based on these findings, we would expect
that older children would have a larger reservoir of concepts to describe a
friendship relation than younger children and that the former group would
utilize more abstract and complex dimensions than the latter group in thinking
about friendship. The work of Rosenbach, Crockett and Wapner (1973),
however, demonstrates that such a hypothesis may not always be easy to
support. In a study of impression formation comparing groups of 6- and
7-year-olds, 12- and 13-year-olds, and 18- and 19-year-olds, all male, they
discovered that the degree of differentiation and level of integration of impressions increased monotonically with age but that strong emotional involvement
with the individual described reduced the developmental level of the impressions
formed of him. Since emotional involvement is an essential component of
children's friendships, at least from preadolescence upward, these findings
imply that a child's conceptual system functions less adequately in relation
to a friend than a non-friend.
   Despite the intriguing nature of both the methodology and results of the
Rosenbach et al. study, researchers directly studying children's conceptions
of friendship have accumulated data highly discordant with its results. In all
three studies reviewed below, the criterion of friendship was whether the subject
liked or disliked a designated peer. Additionally, although not always acknowledged, the cognitive-developmental viewpoint served as a theoretical base.
Thus, in the previously cited study, Scarlett et al. (1971) noted that male subjects
in grades I, III and V used significantly more constructs to describe liked than
disliked boys. Also, in a large-scale study of children ranging in grade from
kindergarten through the college level, Peevers and Secord (1973) reported
that older children produced more differentiated statements about both
friends and non-friends than younger children but, regardless of age, disliked
peers were described with fewer, more egocentric terms than liked peers.
Livesley and Bromley (1973) have detected a similar trend in a study of 320
children aged from 7 to 15 years old. They reported that, irrespective of age, a
greater number of phrases were used to characterize liked than disliked peers.
   The consistency of these findings across diverse subject populations and
experimental settings is impressive. Contrary to Rosenbach et al., they support
the notion that a more organized and developmentally more advanced conceptual system is in operation when children are requested to describe a friend
than a non-friend. Such findings are not unexpected, though, given that it is
likely that children have more prolonged and varied experiences with friends
than non-friends. These experiences can provide the child with a broader base

of information with which to represent verbally a friend than may be the case with a non-friend with whom interaction is probably more limited and restricted. Moreover, the discrepancy between the results of these studies and the Rosenbach *et al.* project can be accounted for, at least in part, by the fact that the former studies employed liking as an index of friendship while Rosenbach *et al.* examined the degree of emotional involvement as one interpersonal criterion. Intuitively, these two indices do not seem equivalent.

One must be cautious, nonetheless, in unequivocally accepting the research findings on children's conceptualization of friendship in the light of the friendship criterion, namely, like or dislike for a peer, utilized in all three studies. In the first place, this measure includes no assessment as to whether the liked peer reciprocates the positive feelings exhibited by the subject. Therefore, the mutuality of the relationship remains indeterminate. Additionally, the extent of one's like or dislike of a peer provides no data about the nature of the child's involvement or interaction with him. It is certainly conceivable that a youngster is liked merely because s/he displays those qualities esteemed by the peer group while a disliked peer is low on these characteristics. Accordingly, it appears that these studies, although purporting to examine the conceptual dimensions of friendship, have actually investigated peer group popularity and its correlates in children's conceptual systems. Until more precise, sensitive measures of friendship are designed, research in this area will continue to have methodological drawbacks.

Bigelow and La Gaipa have developed an interesting and innovative approach to the study of children's conceptualization of friendship (Bigelow, 1977; Bigelow and La Gaipa, 1975, and this volume). Adopting the cognitive-developmental model discussed earlier, Bigelow originally proposed in his thesis work that the expectations children have of their best friends follow a stage-like, invariant sequential process during ontogenesis. To test this hypothesis, he studied 480 children from 6 to 14 years old in both Canada and Scotland and asked them to write an essay about what they expect from a best friend. Content analyses revealed that 11 of the 21 friendship expectation dimensions formulated *a priori* increased with age. Moreover, those that did increase emerged in a relatively fixed sequence, the developmental trend indicating a shift from concrete, egocentric dimensions in the youngest children to an intermediate scociocentric stage and finally to abstract empathic dimensions in the oldest children. It is important to note, however, that almost half of the friendship expectation dimensions did not change with age. Two in particular, ego reinforcement and reciprocity of liking, were significant expectations of a best friend at all ages. This latter finding is consistent with the present writer's emphasis upon including a criterion of mutuality in all investigations of friendship. Bigelow himself concluded that 'the more cognitive aspects of friendship may change over time but the affective value may remain basically unchanged' (1977, p. 251). Although La Gaipa and Bigelow's (1972) written essay technique may not be equally appropriate to all ages and their intermediate sociocentric stage was based upon only one friendship expectation dimension, this work is noteworthy for its sound theoretical foundation and the expansiveness of the cross-cultural comparison.

Selman and his associates (Selman, 1976; Selman and Jacquette, 1977), have similarly hypothesized that friendship awareness develops in a hierarchical, invariant sequence. Momentary awareness of a friend as playmate was suggested as the first stage followed in order by stages described respectively, as 'unilateral help-giving', 'inconsistent cooperation', 'mutual sharing', and 'autonomous interdependence'. Analyses of standardized interviews conducted with 225 subjects of both sexes, aged from 4.5 to 32 years, revealed a monotonic increase in friendship awareness scores between the ages of 6 and 15 years. For this latter group, average increases amounted to nearly two stages, from average scores near stage two to averages near stage four. Thus, the research of both Selman and Bigelow has supported a cognitive-developmental model for children's conceptions of friendship which parallels the invariant sequential, stage approach posited by Piaget and Werner for intellectual development and Kohlberg (1963) for moral development.

A recent study by the present author has shed some additional light upon children's conceptions of friendship (Mannarino, 1978b). This investigation was designed to explore whether children with a stable best friendship differ in their conceptualization of this interactive process from children with an unstable best friendship. A measure of friendship stability and the child's preference with regard to spare time, both of which were described earlier in this chapter, served as two indices of friendship. The final criterion was a test of mutuality to assess whether the child who is selected as best friend reciprocates by also naming the subject as best friend. A total of 27 of the original 81 subjects, all males in grader VI, satisfied all three criteria and were designated as the best friendship group. This group was matched on IQ and peer group acceptance with a second group of 27 subjects who failed to meet at least two of the three criteria. All subjects then responded to the seventeen item Chumship Checklist to determine the nature of their interactive patterns with their best friends. Results indicated that the stable best friendship group checked a significantly greater number of checklist items than the unstable best friendship group. Despite overall group differences, though, only five items significantly discriminated between the two groups. Two of the discriminating items, 'Walk to school together' and 'Sleep over at each other's house', seem to focus on the amount of time the best friends spend together. This finding suggests that frequency of interaction may promote close, stable friendships.

Two checklist items, 'Talk about what you want to be when you grow up' and 'Talk about your parents' appear to involve the sharing of personal thoughts and feelings and also significantly differentiated the groups. This finding is in accordance with Bigelow's (1977) research in which he noted that self-disclosure (intimacy) emerges as an important expectation of best friends during preadolescence. The last item which discriminated between groups was 'Phone each other about school assignments'. It is worth pointing out that less than 20 per cent of the youngsters in the unstable best friendship group checked this item (the lowest percentage obtained for any item) while 56 per cent of those in the stable best friendship group did so. Nonetheless, it is difficult to surmise what it is about the nature of school assignments that contributes to this finding. Perhaps only in the context of a stable friendship do children feel sufficiently comfortable to ask for help with academic subjects.

We thus see a remarkable degree of consistency in the research on children's conceptions of friendship. With increasing chronological age, children develop a progressively more differentiated and hierarchically organized conceptual system with which to think and talk about their interpersonal relationships. Children apparently utilize this system in a more effective manner with friends than non-friends as the former group is more elaborately and less egocentrically described than the latter group. Lastly, there appears to be a developmental progression in children's conceptions of friendship with joint activities and propinquity serving as common denominators of preschool friendships, conformity and cooperation marking the friendships of middle childhood, and loyalty, mutuality, and self-disclosure characterizing preadolescent friendships.

CONCLUSIONS

This chapter has focused primarily upon three major aspects of friendship development in children: the definition and scope of friendship, its theoretical foundations in developmental psychology, and the research on children's conceptions of friendship. Probably the major conclusion to be drawn is that the study of children's friendships is still in its earliest days. Whereas other childhood social variables such as group formation and peer popularity have been fairly extensively researched, friendship development has received only sporadic attention. In the author's opinion, there exists a critical need for normative-developmental data tracing friendship formation from the preschool era through preadolescence. Currently, we have bits and pieces of knowledge but a comprehensive approach spanning the major developmental periods is lacking.

The present writer suspects that the study of children's friendships has not achieved greater prominence in the social development literature because of the tremendous difficulty in operationalizing empirically this relationship. Whereas aggression, attention-seeking, or prosocial behaviours are observable acts that are readily quantifiable, friendship can only be defined in a dyadic sense and successfully measured behaviourally by techniques sensitive to the two-person interactive process. Because the latter procedure is a complicated task, researchers have often used indirect measures of friendship such as socio-metric techniques. As discussed in depth previously, these—when used alone—have proven to be seriously inadequate. To overcome this methodological handicap, the author has designed the Chumship Checklist which provides data with respect to the interactive styles of children and their best friends. An alternative solution is to utilize the sophisticated behavioural observation methods which are extensively employed in the study of other children's behaviours. This technique can be responsive to the reciprocity of friendship if researchers develop behavioural codes that specifically address this quality of the relationship (cf. Foot, Chapman and Smith, 1977; Foot, Smith and Chapman, 1979). Observational data, combined with information from child interviews (including joint interviews with the child and his friend present), teacher and parent ratings of friendship, and measures of friendship stability, would contribute to a broad-based data bank on friendship development in children.

To foster the study of children's friendships, it is also essential that develop-mentalists begin to examine the role of friendship in the socialization process of childhood. Although the family is still considered the major translater of society's norms to children, the peer group is now recognized as an important socializing agent. Unfortunately, 'peer group' has all too frequently referred to peer group popularity with no special emphasis placed on friendships. Certainly the results of some research (Mannarino, 1976; 1978a) reviewed in this chapter suggest that friends may play a more significant role in the socialization process than was once thought.

With respect to children's conceptions of friendships, although this area is currently receiving more attention, we still know very little about how young children think about friendship. In fact, not one study reviewed included as subjects children under 6 years of age. This would appear to be for a number of reasons. First, school-age children are more accessible as research subjects than preschoolers because of their school participation. Moreover, the grade divisions in most schools lend themselves to convenient research groupings. Perhaps the most critical reason, though, is that it is difficult to design research instruments appropriate to the cognitive and emotional developmental status of preschoolers. Written essays, paper-and-pencil self-reports, or complex behavioural manipulations are typically beyond their comprehension. Inter-views, even by skilled individuals, are also not particularly suitable given that preschoolers are not characteristically facile in expressing themselves verbally. In view of the fact that a number of developmental theorists (Erickson, 1950; Piaget, 1962) have proposed that preschoolers most effectively communicate their thoughts and feelings through play, one alternative might be to examine more systematically children's play to assess how the concept of 'friend' fits into this symbolic network.

There has been, additionally, little investigation of sex differences in children's conceptions of friendship. Since some developmentalists have suggested that at least during adolescence, girls' friendships are marked by greater emotional intimacy and less affected by where they 'fit' into the 'group' than boys' friendships (Douvan and Gold, 1966; Wenar, 1971), it would be interesting to discover the precursors of these differences and whether younger boys and girls think differently about friendship. Also, the influence of parents and siblings on children's conceptions of friendship remains an unexplored area.

This chapter could not properly conclude without reiterating two points: namely, that integrative theorizing is essential to the study of friendship development and that the empirical investigation of children's friendships must stem from theory. Research in this area remains fragmented and often not tied to any systematic conceptual framework. This deficiency has been partly overcome in the study of children's conceptions of friendship where the cognitive-developmental model has been adopted by a number of investigators. Hopefully, researchers examining other dimensions of friendship will provide a theoretical foundation for their work as well. In particular, theory and research sensitive to the bi-directionality of friendship relations are critical. Only when this reciprocity and mutuality, which are the cornerstones of friendship, are carefully examined will we be able to draw more definitive conclusions about the essential components of children's close interpersonal relationships.

REFERENCES

Adler, A. (1927). *Practice and Theory of Individual Psychology*. New York: Harcourt, Brace and Jovanovich.

Bigelow, B. J. (1977). Children's friendship expectations: a cognitive-developmental study. *Child Development*, **48**, 246–253.

Bigelow, B. J., and La Gaipa, J. L. (1975). Children's written descriptions of friendship. *Developmental Psychology*, **11**, 857–858.

Byrne, D., and Griffitt, W. (1966). A developmental investigation of the law of attraction. *Journal of Personality and Social Psychology*, **4**, 699–703.

Cabral, G., Volpe, J., Youniss, J., and Gellert, B. (1977). Resolving a problem in friendship and other relationships. Unpublished manuscript, Catholic University.

Chapman, A. J., Smith, J. R., Foot, H. C., and Pritchard, E. (1979). Behavioural and sociometric indices of friendship in children. In M. Cook and G. D. Wilson (Eds.), *Love and Attraction*. Oxford: Pergamon Press.

Douvan, D., and Gold, M. (1966). Modal patterns in American adolescence. In L. W. Hoffman and M. L. Hoffman (Eds.), *Review of Child Development Research*. Vol. 2. New York: Russell Sage.

Erikson, E. H. (1950). *Childhood and Society*. New York: Norton.

Foot, H. C., Chapman, A. J., and Smith, J. R. (1977). Friendship and social responsiveness in boys and girls. *Journal of Personality and Social Psychology*, **35**, 401–411.

Foot, H. C., Smith, J. R., and Chapman, A. J. (1979). Non-verbal expressions of intimacy in children. In M. Cook and G. D. Wilson (Eds.), *Love and Attraction*. Oxford: Pergamon Press.

Gesell, A. (1945). *The Embryology of Behavior*. New York: Harper.

Gesell, A., and Ilg, F. L. (1949). *Child Development*. New York: Harper.

Gesell, A., Ilg, F. L., and Ames, L. B. (1956). *Youth: The Years from Ten to Sixteen*. New York: Harper.

Gollin, E. S. (1958). Organization characteristics of social judgment: a developmental investigation. *Journal of Personality*, **26**, 139–154.

Harris, D. B. (1957). A scale for measuring attitudes of social responsibility in children. *Journal of Abnormal and Social Psychology*, **55**, 322–326.

Hartup, W. W. (1970). Peer interaction and social organization. In P. Mussen (Ed.), *Carmichael's Manual of Child Psychology*. New York: Wiley.

Hartup, W. W. (1975). The origins of friendship. In M. Lewis and L. A. Rosenblum (Eds.), *Friendship and Peer Relations*. New York: Wiley.

Horrocks, J. E., and Buker, M. E. (1951). A study of the friendship fluctuations of pre-adolescents. *Journal of Genetic Psychology*, **78**, 131–144.

Hunt, J., and Solomon, R. L. (1942). The stability and some correlates of group status in a summer camp group of young boys. *American Journal of Psychology*, **55**, 33–45.

Kohlberg, L. (1963). Moral development and identification. In H. W. Stevenson (Ed.), *Child Psychology*. Chicago: University of Chicago Press.

La Gaipa, J. J., and Bigelow, B. J. (1972). The development of childhood friendship expectations. Paper read at the Meeting of the Canadian Psychological Association, Montreal.

Livesay, K. K. (1972). Sociometric criteria of choice and personal-social adjustment. Unpublished manuscript, Indiana State University.

Livesley, W. J., and Bromley, D. B. (1973). *Person Perception in Childhood and Adolescence*. London: Wiley.

Maas, H. S. (1968). Preadolescent peer relations and adult intimacy. *Psychiatry*, **31**, 161–172.

Maddock, R. C., and Kenny, C. T. (1973). Impression formation as a function of age, sex and race. *Journal of Social Psychology*, **89**, 233–243.

Mannarino, A. P. (1975). Friendship patterns and altruistic behavior in preadolescent males. Unpublished manuscript, Ohio State University.

Mannarino, A. P. (1976). Friendship patterns and altruistic behavior in preadolescent males. *Developmental Psychology*, **12**, 555–556.

Mannarino, A. P. (1978a). Friendship patterns and self-concept development in pre-adolescent males. *Journal of Genetic Psychology*, **133**, 105–110.

Mannarino, A. P. (1978b). The interactional process in preadolescent friendships. *Psychiatry*, **41**, 308–312.

Mouton, J., Blake, C., and Fruchter, B. (1960). The reliability of sociometric measures. In J. L. Moreno (Ed.), *Sociometric Reader*. Illinois: Free Press of Glancor.

Mullahy P. (1970). *Psychoanalysis and Interpersonal Psychiatry*. New York: Science House.

Peevers, H. B., and Secord, P. F. (1973). Developmental changes in attribution of descriptive concepts to persons. *Journal of Personality and Social Psychology*, **27**, 120–128.

Piaget, J. (1960). *Psychology of Intelligence*. Totowa, New Jersey: Littlefield, Adams and Co.

Piaget, J. (1962). *Play, Dreams and Imitation in Childhood*. New York: Norton.

Piaget, J. (1965). *The Moral Judgment of the Child*. New York: Free Press.

Piers, E. V., and Harris, D. B. (1969). *The Piers–Harris Children's Self-concept Scale*. Nashville: Counselor Recordings and Tests.

Ricks, D. F. (1970). Life-history research in psychopathology: retrospect and prospect. In M. Roff and D. Ricks (Eds.), *Life-history Research in Psychopathology*. New York: McGraw-Hill.

Rosenbach, D., Crockett, W. H., and Wapner, S. (1973). Developmental level, emotional involvement, and the resolution of inconsistency in impression formation. *Developmental Psychology*, **8**, 120–130.

Scarlett, H., Press, A., and Crockett, W. (1971). Children's descriptions of peers: a Wernerian developmental analysis. *Child Development*, **44**, 439–453.

Selman, R. L. (1976). Toward a structural analysis of developing interpersonal relations concepts: research with normal and disturbed preadolescent boys. In A.D. Pick (Ed.), *Minnesota Symposia of Child Psychology*. Vol. 10. Minneapolis: University of Minnesota Press.

Selman, R. L., and Jacquette, D. (1977). Stability and oscillation in interpersonal awareness: a clinical-development analysis. In C. B. Keasey (Ed.), *The Nebraska Symposium on Motivation*. Vol. 25. Lincoln: University of Nebraska Press.

Signell, K. (1966). Cognitive complexity in person perception and nation perception: a developmental approach. *Journal of Personality*, **34**, 517–537.

Sullivan, H. S. (1952). *Conceptions of Modern Psychiatry*. New York: Norton.

Sullivan, H. S. (1953). *The Interpersonal Theory of Psychiatry*. New York: Norton.

Sullivan, H. S. (1965). *Personal Psychopathology*. New York: Norton.

Thompson, G. G., and Horrocks, J. E. (1947). A study of the friendship fluctuations of urban boys and girls. *Journal of Genetic Psychology*, **70**, 53–63.

Webster's New Collegiate Dictionary (1973). Springfield, Massachusetts: G. and C. Merriam.

Wenar, C. (1971). *Personality Development: From Infancy to Adulthood*. Boston: Houghton Mifflin Company.

Werner, H. (1957). *Comparative Psychology of Mental Development* (revised edition). New York: International Universities Press.

CHAPTER 3

The Others-Concept: Explorations into the Quality of Children's Interpersonal Relationships

DAVID W. BARNETT
and
KARL B. ZUCKER

Writing from the perspective of an emerging 'experimental ecology of human development', Bronfenbrenner has stated that 'much of contemporary developmental psychology is the science of the strange behavior of children in strange situations with strange adults for the briefest possible periods of time' (1977, p. 513). The study of friendship has good potential for withstanding such criticism, for children's friendships can be studied as they naturally occur and within the parameters of acceptable psychological research. Moreover, the prosocial aspect of friendship is in keeping with the growing interest in the study of prosocial behaviour in children (Gottman, Gonso and Rasmussen, 1975; Mussen and Eisenberg-Berg, 1977; Yarrow, Waxler, Barrett, Darby, King, Pickett and Smith, 1976), as an alternative to a focus on violence and aggression. The research reviewed in this chapter incorporates several dimensions which relate to friendship on a global level. The central focus is the significance for interpersonal behaviour of a child's perceptions of other persons along a qualitative dimension of friendliness and hostility. The studies centre around behavioural observations of children's cooperative play in an approximation of a natural setting. The results from these studies have been related to an emerging, interactive construct, which has been referred to as the 'others-concept'.

THE OTHERS-CONCEPT: DEFINITION AND
REVIEW OF RELATED CONCEPTS

The others-concept

The others-concept is defined as a person's general expectancies about other people along a positive–negative continuum (Barnett and Zucker, 1975). The construct refers to how a person perceives people in general, not necessarily any one particular person. Similar constructs have been suggested in the literature, but they have a somewhat different emphasis. The others-concept is similar to George Mead's 'generalized other', but for Mead this meant an organization of the role of others (Mead, 1934). He thought of the generalized other as a conception which a person derives from his experiences of other participants' related roles in a given situation (cf. Lindesmith and Strauss, 1968). Another similar construct is Jourard's 'other-concept' which he defined as the 'beliefs one holds concerning someone else's personality' (Jourard, 1958). His concept, however, refers to one other person rather than to people in general. The 'life position' of 'You're OK' described in the literature dealing with transactional analysis most closely approximates the meaning implied in the others-concept construct (cf. Berne, 1961; Harris, 1969).

The others-concept is considered by the present authors to be parallel to the self-concept, with a similar importance in personality research and education. Rather than an inward look, the others-concept refers to an individual's capacity to make judgements and predictions about the behaviour or potential behaviour of other persons. These assumptions regarding other people are perhaps best thought of as developmental in nature and are based on generalizations from specific learning incidents with significant persons in one's environment.

The question that the others-concept helps to answer is how predictions and assumptions about other people are made when available information is minimal and ambiguous. Within the context of research reported in this chapter, children have been given the opportunity to assign meaning to photographs or slides depicting possible social interactions. Questions arise as to the origins of those meanings and the value of the information in predicting the behaviour of the person making the judgements.

The self-concept

In order to clarify further what is meant by the others-concept, a few statements about the self-concept may be helpful. There has been a needed shift in the conceptual frameworks surrounding the self-concept away from persons' 'traits' or 'attributes' towards 'an analysis of interaction in an explicitly described context of relations' (Cottrell, 1970, p. 66). One might consider the 'self–other organization' (Cottrell, 1970) as well as a self-situational organization.

In a review article, Shavelson and his co-workers explore their concerns about the construct validity of the self-concept (Shavelson, Hubner and Stanton, 1976). They point out the increasing research interest in children's self-concepts, and interest in the enhancement of the self-concept through educational programmes, especially for disadvantaged children (p. 408). In addition to stressing positive self-concepts as an important outcome of programmes, many researchers view the self-concept as a potentially important 'moderator variable'; that is, a variable that helps to account for differences in achievement outcomes and perhaps, along with other variables such as motivation, for children's responses to various treatments (p. 408).

Shavelson et al. (1976) outline what they consider to be seven critical features necessary in defining the self-concept construct.

(1) It is organized: the infinite number of experiences yielding perceptions of oneself are encoded or categorized.
(2) The self-concept is multifaceted: it may reflect idiosyncratic categories concerning domains such as school ability, physical characteristics, and various social milieus.
(3) The hierarchical nature of self-concept is stressed, ranging from a broad base of individual experiences in particular situations to a general self-concept.
(4) The general self-concept is stable, but at the same time much variability may exist for an individual in different situations.
(5) The self-concept is developmental and relates to learned experiences.
(6) The self-concept is evaluative: a person describes and evaluates his/her own performance in a particular situation or in a class of situations against ideal standards or in comparison with the performance of peers or perceived evaluations of significant others.
(7) The self-concept is differentiable from other constructs with which it is theoretically related.

These features of the self-concept would also appear to apply to the others-concept.

It is important also to note the interrelationship of the self-concept and others-concept. Galluzzi and Zucker (1977) reviewed the literatures they judged to be pertinent to this topic. They found that Wylie (1961) had cited 21 studies that, in general, found a positive relationship between self-acceptance and acceptance of others. Additional studies showing this relationship have been reported (McCandless, 1967; Richmond, Mason and Padgett, 1972; Robinson, 1967; Stock, 1949; Suinn and Hill, 1964; Williams, 1962). Also, many prominent theorists have stressed the importance of both self-acceptance and acceptance of others in effective psychosocial functioning (Adler, 1927; Berne, 1961; Fromm, 1964; Harris, 1969; Horney, 1950; Rogers, 1951; Sullivan, 1953).

Evaluating the others-concept

The Paired Hands Test (PHT) (Barnett and Zucker, 1973, 1975, 1977; Zucker and Barnett, 1977) has been used exclusively for evaluating the others-concept to date, although the authors consider the concept to be of sufficient importance to warrant attention apart from any specific assessment technique. The PHT makes use of 20 slides (or photographs), each showing one black hand and one white hand in a relationship which implies an interaction between the hands. The pictures are shown one at a time and the subject is asked to indicate what s/he thinks the hands are doing by selecting one statement out of five presented for each slide. The statements describe possible interactions between people chosen from the verbatim responses received from children in response to the question, 'What do you think the hands are doing?' and scaled by a Thurstone-type technique along a continuum ranging from extremely positive to extremely negative interactions between the hands. The test has gone through several revisions (Barnett and Zucker, 1973, 1975, 1977; Zucker, 1976; Zucker and Barnett, 1977; Zucker and Jordan, 1968).

Both the others-concept and the PHT originated from a need to find a way to evaluate possible increases in friendliness among children already presumed to be fairly friendly. Zucker and Jordan (1968) designed the original version of the PHT; and it was used in 1966 to study possible changes in friendliness among children attending a Children's International Summer Village, sponsored by an organization whose major purpose is to provide opportunities for developing friendships across national boundaries. More recent studies have led to the development of the others-concept as a theoretical construct and to the viewing of the PHT as a measure of the extent to which children interact with others in a warm, non-threatening, non-abrasive, cooperative, helpful manner (Barnett and Zucker, 1973, 1975, 1977).

The PHT-E (for elementary school-aged children in approximately grades III to VI, from 8 to 11 years old) has gone through several revisions. Zucker and Jordan (1968) used 15 colour photographs of hands. In nine photographs there were two hands in varying juxtapositions to each other, one hand belonging to a black person and the other to a white person. The other six photographs were of single hands, three black and three white. Barnett and Zucker (1973) used a PHT form showing nine slides of two white hands in meaningful but ambiguous interactions between the hands. A group administration procedure using slides that were very similar in format to the 1968 bi-racial photographs was developed. This represented a significant change from the open-ended response approach used in 1968. Verbatim responses were collected from

Table 3.1. Qualitative dimension of friendliness–hostility used to scale the Paired Hands Test and results of the scaling study

Scale Value	7	6	5	4	3	2	1
Descriptions provided for judges to anchor scaling	Very warm; very kind; very close feeling	Very enjoyable; helping; playing together; very cooperative	Pleasant interaction without necessarily close feeling; working together; cooperation; friendly competition	Perfunctory; indifferent; business like	Annoying competition with some hostility; practical joke	Very rude; competition with strong hostility; very unpleasant	Cruel; physical hurt; severe hostility
Mean value for all statements included under scale position	6.83	5.85	4.90	4.18	2.92	2.19	1.15
Standard deviations for statements included under scale position	0.08	0.19	0.28	0.15	0.25	0.23	0.14
Number of statements in scale position	11	16	17	9	17	16	14

children, and appropriate statements were selected and rank ordered by judges along a friendliness–hostility dimension. The procedure has been reported in more detail elsewhere (Barnett and Zucker, 1973).

To improve reliability and validity, the PHT-E was lengthened to include 11 new poses (suggested by Burzynski, 1972) in addition to those in the 1973 study. The present form of the PHT-E includes 20 photographs or slides of black and white hands interacting. Five choices for each of the new photographs were adapted from a collection of verbatim responses.

A Thurstone scaling technique was used to place each statement along the friendliness–hostility dimension. After four separate scaling attempts, equal-appearing intervals were obtained between statements included under each of the seven scaling categories. Table 3.1 shows the results of the final scaling study in which each statement was rated along a seven-point scale of a friendlines–hostility dimension. The close correspondence between the actual mean values for all statements included under the scale positions, and the relatively small standard deviations for the seven categories of statements, supported the feasibility of an equal-appearing interval scale. The results obtained from the scaling study allowed assignment of a numerical value to each statement for the purpose of scoring. A high score, in studies completed after 1973, reflects the frequency of positive statements chosen and also the magnitude of the choices. Research has been done to support the efficacy of the others-concept on the continuum of developmental levels from school-aged children through to adults.

Black–white hand combinations were chosen for the current test form because, in exploratory studies in which results from photographs showing two white hands were compared to the black–white combinations, it has been found that most children obtained similar scores, although there were some note-worthy exceptions. It was for this reason that the authors thought that their first priority should be a study of how people feel about other people regardless of colour. The racial factor, however, presents a challenging area for future research.

Research hypothesis

Although the others-concept may eventually be studied in other ways, the PHT has been used to assess children's others-concepts in research up to the present. The PHT, as a projective test, presents the subject with ambiguous stimuli and requires him/her to order or assign meaning to the stimulus (Zubin, Eron and Schumer, 1965). Zubin *et al.* offer the following assumptions relating to an experimental approach to projective techniques: ' ... [the] response to stimulation is determined and predictable and not accidental; ... test behavior is ... a small sample of lawful behavior ... [and] directly reflects inner personality and behavior in other situations ... [and the] indirect approach characteristic of these tests insures a spontaneous and representative response ... ' (p. 12–13). The major premise is that an individual's basic personality structure adds purpose and unity to an individual's behaviour. The PHT samples a child's perceptions of how two people involved in a social interaction are feeling about one another along a positive–negative continuum and, by inference, reveals whether his/her perceptions of others tend to be positive, negative, neutral or inconsistent.

Although the studies have produced other useful data, the basic premise of the research has been that children who perceive social interactions differently— for example, in more friendly or more hostile manners—will exhibit different social behaviours. The relationship between PHT scores and social interactions has been explored through a systematic method of behavioural observations with extreme scoring children. The general hypothesis tested in a series of experiments is that children with more positive others-concepts (those with high PHT scores) will interact in small group situations in more positive and task-related ways than children with lower others-concepts.

Methodological concerns

Many methodological concerns persist in this complex area of research en-compassing, as it does, the areas of personality assessment, development of the others-concept as a personality construct, and prediction of children's social behaviours. The danger of over-simplification is great; one must usually tolerate violations of strict or exemplary research designs in order to accomplish even basic objectives. Several writers have presented their concerns and dis-cussed the possibilities for new directions in personality research.

In a series of critical and thought-provoking writings, Mischel (1968, 1973, 1977) has outlined theoretical and practical problems in the area of personality assessment. A basic question, relative to this chapter, is whether there is a unity of traits in personality organization which can, in fact, predict complex social behaviours. An extensive review of all the issues involved would be outside the scope of the present discussion. The major concerns are presented within the context of incremental validity and utility. Mischel questions the value of test-derived personality descriptions. They ' ... are valuable to the extent that they provide significant increments in valid information over other less readily available or less economical sources' (1968, p. 104). Utility of the information depends on 'the value of the predictions and treatment decisions to which they lead in the individual case' (p. 104). Another global concern is the assumption, popular especially with self-report inventories of the type which were developed in the 1920s, ' ... that what a person says he does reflects his typical overt behavior and that self-reports about traits therefore provide an accurate shortcut to the measurement of life behavior outside the test' (1968, p. 75). Projective techniques, as well as objective tests, have not fared well in Mischel's analysis in terms of their incremental validity and utility for individual cases, nor in terms of providing indirect evidence of internal predispositions (p. 145).

More recently, Mischel (1977) elaborated on the multiple determinism of behaviour, contextualism, and interactionism. He asserted that ' . . . if human behavior is determined by many interacting variables—both in the person and in the environment—then a focus on any one of them is likely to lead to limited predictions and generalizations' (p. 246). Another important point which he made, pertinent to the research under discussion, is that ' . . . even a relatively simple "stimulus" or "situation" may produce a variety of often unpredictable specific (and weak) effects depending on a large number of moderating variables and the many different ways in which the particular "subjects" may view them and transform them' (p. 247).

In considering the environment's impact on the subject and how variables considered to be personal attributes mediate and define one's environment, Mischel (1973, p. 279) has spoken of the 'phenomenological impact' of the environment. He has questioned how environmental operations produce their effects on an individual (Mischel, 1977, p. 247). Among other variables that Mischel noted are competencies, constructs, expectancies, and subjective values (p. 247).

One may wonder what to include as the cognitive aspect of the person—environment interaction. Obvious inclusions, relatively devoid of controversy, follow the consensus approach of the social learning theories (Bandura, 1977, p. 23) and relate to attentional processes (perceptual set) and retentional processes (symbolic coding, cognitive organization). Mischel (1977) made the following pertinent comment on 'person variables': ' . . . people differ in how they encode, group, and label events and in how they construe themselves and others' (p. 251). He continued, in considering the interface of personality and cognition, with the following point: ' . . . an adequate approach to how people understand their world—including events, sentences, and people—will have to take account of how they organize information in meaningful, hierarchical, rule-guided ways' (p. 252).

The controversy and concern regarding the personality traits which Mischel addressed has been explored by Bem and Allen (1974). In addition to the ceiling correlation of $+0.30$ typically found in behavioural research with personality measures, they have noted that in some important studies, such as those by Hartshorne and May on the nature of character (cf. Hartshorne and May, 1928, 1929; Hartshorne, May, and Shuttleworth, 1930), that very little consistency was found in various measures of 'moral character' (Bem and Allen, 1974). A major concern is the relevance of a particular scale or trait for a given individual. They made the point that some traits may be relevant for some persons and, therefore, will yield consistent descriptions of behaviours: ' . . . only the behavior of consistent individuals can be meaningfully characterized by the investigator's construct ... ' (p. 512). The experimenter must determine how many individuals share the experimenter's 'partitioning of the world ... ' into a particular trait dimension (p. 512). Bem and Allen demonstrated significant improvements in predictions of behaviours (including friendliness) by a self-report technique dividing 'those who are cross-situationally consistent on a particular trait and those who are not' (p. 512).

Similarly, in an important review of personality research devoting special attention to the question of traits and psychometric procedures, Hogan, DeSoto and Solano (1977) noted many criticisms of traditional approaches to personality measurement, but they defended the use of tests. The major points of their article bear reiterating here. The first is that the concept of trait is misleading; it may be better defined as 'stylistic consistencies in interpersonal behavior' (p. 256). In questioning whether tests measure traits, three properties of useful scales are listed: '(a) persons tend to receive the same scores on different occasions; (b) on any given occasion there will be variations in the scores within a group; (c) these variations will be associated in a theoretically predictable way with variations in other scores for the same group derived in other ways' (p. 256). Hogan *et al.* stress that 'using tests entails no particular theoretical commitment'. They offer a balanced position between persons interested in trait-like or personal variables and researchers who focus on situationally specific behaviour.

By briefly reviewing the above points, one can readily grasp the complexity of relevant personality research within a social milieu. In the others-concept research to be described in the following pages, an attempt has been made to take these concerns into consideration.

BEHAVIOURAL STUDIES OF CHILDREN'S SOCIAL INTERACTIONS

The basic premise of the research to be described in this section is that children who perceive social interactions differently—for example, in a more friendly or in a more hostile manner—will exhibit social behaviours consistent with their perceptions. A relationship between PHT scores and social interaction has been explored through a systematic method of behavioural observations of extreme-scoring children. The general hypothesis that the present authors have been testing in a series of experiments is that children with more positive others-concepts (those with high PHT scores) interact in small group situations in more positive and task-related ways than children with more negative others-concepts.

The children under study

Essentially, three separate groups of children have been included in a series of investigations which will now be reviewed together. In the 1973 study,

there were 26 girls and 17 boys, all in grade IV (generally 9-year-olds) at the Indiana State University Laboratory School, Terre Haute, Indiana. The 1975 study also made use of Laboratory School children; there were 12 boys and 12 girls included in the study. They were distributed across grades IV, V, and VI, approximately 9–11 years old). The procedures in the 1977 study were more complicated than in the two earlier studies and have been reported in more detail elsewhere (Barnett and Zucker, 1977). A total of 1,235 children in grades IV, V, and VI in Terre Haute and Indianapolis were administered the PHT. Of these children, those from the three schools in Terre Haute were included in the behavioural part of the study. Children at these schools were identified as high or low scorers if they were at least 1.25 standard deviations above or below the mean. The 1.25 standard deviation cut-offs brought behavioural differences into sharp focus while still providing a sufficient number of children for the statistical analysis. Two hundred and eleven children were originally studied in the groups but, because of the initial selection procedures and concerns with time delays between testing and behavioural observations, only 120 of those children originally studiedfell in the classification 1.25 standard deviations from the overall mean. The procedure was modified because the experimenters used an overall mean for all three schools in the final analysis, whereas the originally planned experimental procedure required that means for each school be used for assignment of children to groups.

Recording of social behaviours

Children's comments while they worked together on various assigned tasks in groups of three or, in several studies, four, comprised the social behaviours which were analysed in most of this research. The time allowed for each task was usually 15 minutes. In one study the groups were videotaped so that non-verbal behaviour could also be codified (Barnett and Zucker, 1973), but in the other studies a system using audiotapes of individual children's comments recorded through a unidirectional microphone worked satisfactorily. The range of the children's verbal comments was remarkable when one considers that they were simply asked to perform a brief, structured task (intended by the experimenters to be enjoyable). Examples of actual statements made by children working on the tasks are as follows:

'It's kind of hard.'
'They can see your white underwear.'
'Why don't you put the puzzle into the Coke bottle?'
'I'm scared.'
'We ain't going to have nothing done [shout]!'
'That piece is too little.'
'I've got three pieces, you big tub.'
'Come on now and get this done or I'll blast your heads off.'

The following are examples of various tasks which were used in three separate studies: assembling a steamboat with Tinkertoys (from a model which was to be copied), working a jigsaw puzzle matching domino faces, and making a poster with magic markers after deciding together what its content should be. The instructions given to the Tinkertoy Boat Model task give an idea of how these tasks were introduced to the children:

> I want you to pretend that you are settlers on the Mississippi River about 100 years ago. The neighbouring town has made a boat to take their crops to market. Here is a model of it. You now realize that you have to build one too, or you won't be able to get supplies for the winter. You have 15 minutes to build one just like this one. (Included in the 1975, 1977 studies.)

The tasks themselves seemed to become important variables. Originally, they were not considered to be of direct interest. The individual effects of the tasks were not systematically studied to any great extent except in the 1975 study because of the confounding effects of having differing procedures and tasks at different schools and also different demographic features that characterized the children. Some of the tasks were repeated, with only a very slight variation, for the different experiments. In the 1975 study the experimenters wanted to avoid repeating the same task with the same children on five different occasions. However, it became apparent that the tasks differed as to the interest and enthusiasm generated, the challenge presented, the group processes elicited, and the frustrations involved. Matching domino faces seemed to be relatively uninteresting to the children while other tasks, such as making posters with magic markers or assembling a large, very complicated model of a steamboat with Tinkertoys, seemed to be inherently more interesting. Even when the tasks did not elicit differences between high- and low-scoring children, the range of behaviours persisted to a large degree.

Analysis of social behaviours

A system of categorizing the children's comments was developed to provide behavioural observations that could be statistically and reliably analysed. Each response was judged on two dimensions. The first dimension was that of being task-related (identified by T) or non-task-related (identified by N). Task-related items were defined as responses which relate directly to the tasks. They could be either instructions, questions, suggestions, or comments. Non-task-related responses were those considered to be irrelevant to the tasks, such as conversations, comments, or noises which were not concerned with solving the problem or completing the tasks.

The second dimension required judging whether a statement was positive ($+$) or negative ($-$). A plus response was one that might be a helpful suggestion or one that merited compliance, agreement, or support. A negative statement was one which would typically evoke anger, seeming abrasive or hostile in an actual or implied way. In the examples of children's comments given earlier, 'It's kind of hard' was coded $T+$; 'They can see your white underwear' was coded $N-$; 'Why don't you put the puzzle piece into the Coke bottle?' was coded $T-$; and 'You love that guy?' was coded $N+$.

In a pilot study, a transcription was typed of all comments for each child, and judges did their coding from this transcription. In the larger study judges coded verbal comments as they listened to the tapes. When two judges listened independently to the tapes, the correlations between the codes they assigned were 0.99 for the $T+$ (sample size = 5,570), 0.98 for $N-$ (sample size = 2,813), 0.96 for $N+$ (sample size = 2,462), and 0.93 for $T-$ (sample size = 1,607). The $T+$ and $N-$ categories are less ambiguous and are perhaps most important because they demonstrate opposite types of responses, while the $T-$ and $N+$ categories combine dimensions. The $N-$ category may be most influenced by social inhibitions and pressures to conform. It is interesting to note the general, prosocial findings of this research in that the largest percentage of all responses was in the $T+$ category.

Some findings

The studies consistently demonstrated that children who have high others-concepts (as measured by the PHT) tend to interact more positively in small groups than people who have low others-concepts. The subjects who had positive others-concepts showed a tendency to be more cooperative, goal-directed, and pleasant. The subjects who had negative others-concepts were found to be less cooperative and goal-directed, and they also showed a tendency to be more abrasive, and sometimes rude, with other members of their groups.

It should be emphasized that the differences between subjects with high others-concepts and low others-concepts were not always readily apparent. Frequently they were not obvious, and there were occasions when individuals with high others-concepts acted negatively, and vice versa. The overall results were substantiated only by coding blindly more than 12,000 separate behaviours of nearly 300 subjects and then comparing the totals. When this was done, the experimental data clearly demonstrated that in general a person who has a high others-concept is more likely to interact positively with others than a person with a low others-concept. In the largest study (sample size = 211) there was a significant difference on the $T+$ dimension at the 0.001 level ($F = 28.94$; $df = 1,416$; $p < .001$). A result of this magnitude was not noted in a school-by-school analysis; however, some statistically significant and predicted results were found in individual schools.

The data also revealed (as might be expected) that some situations more than others brought out differences between individuals with high or low others-concepts. In the situations which did not bring out differences, group trends

Table 3.2. Means and standard deviations of frequency of $T +$ statements by high others-concept and low others-concept children during five different tasks

	Task I Boat model	Task II Dominoes	Task III Farm tractor	Task IV Puzzle	Task V Poster
High others-concept					
($n = 12$)	32.9	50.5	26.6	44.3	41.0
Standard deviation	10.2	16.7	11.3	32.0	27.7
Low others-concept					
($n = 12$)	17.5	48.4	19.3	27.7	19.9
Standard deviation	11.7	21.6	11.8	27.2	11.0
t-Values	2.06*	0.78	1.27	1.43	2.53*

*Significant at the .01 level.

revealed that the high- and low-scoring children had behaved similarly on the coded dimensions, rather than that a reversal had taken place. When statistically significant behavioural differences were found, however, they were always in the direction of high-scoring subjects' behaving more positively than low-scoring subjects. Table 3.2 illustrates this point.

In the 1975 study (Barnett and Zucker, 1975) the groups of children met over a 5-week period with only the tasks varying. The findings indicated that there were significant differences on two tasks. When proportions of comments, rather than frequencies, were analysed, Task III (Farm tractor) also yielded statistically significant findings. The results could most logically be attributed to differences in the tasks, although other variables may be involved.

Critique of the behavioural studies

For statistical analyses the frequencies and proportions of coded categories of behaviour were used. Qualitative differences were not included as a part of the formal analyses. As discussed earlier, situational influences that would tend to hide consistencies within individuals with regard to their perceptions of other people, and that would be predictable from psychometric information, were not systematically studied. However, contemporary thinking regarding the complex interactions among personal variables (in this instance the children's perceptions as indicated by their PHT scores) and situational influences suggests the necessity of integrating both points of view. For example, the large complicated puzzle seemed to elicit behavioural differences between high- and low-scoring children in one situation (a specific school and group of children), but when included in another study, did not elicit significant differences. In other words, situations may change even when tasks are held constant. Complex interactions among child variables, group variables, and tasks could not be explored adequately at that time. Nevertheless, despite the powerful moderating effect of situations on an individual's expression of behaviour, significant differences were still maintained in the predicted direction for overall group effects in each experiment.

One interesting line of inquiry, admittedly a post hoc insight, was prompted following a review of Bem and Allen's (1974) discussion of concerns relating to the consistency of overt behaviours from situation to situation and the prediction of consistent behaviours from psychometric data. Some children who scored consistently in the high or low range on the PHT were identified from test-retest results which were available for a small number of the children who had participated both in the behavioural study and in a test-retest reliability study. The small sample size and the *post hoc* procedure do not warrant statistical treatment of these scores; however, the consistency found in coded behaviours seems promising. There were four children who had scored low on the PHT both times they were tested and for whom the behavioural data were available. Their proportions of $T+$ behaviours were 0.39, 0.35, 0.37, and 0.23. In contrast, five children were found who had scored high on the PHT both times they were tested and for whom the behavioural data were available. Their proportions of $T+$ behaviours were 0.27, 0.79, 0.60, 0.94, and 0.89. Thus, all of the children who had scored low consistently on the PHT had engaged in $T+$ behaviours a relatively small percentage of the time that they had participated in the group activities. In contrast, four out of the five children who had scored high consistently on the PHT had engaged in $T+$ behaviours a relatively high percentage of the time. A possible implication is that some psychological scales may not be relevant for some children. It seems plausible that if children who were inconsistent in their responses on the PHT were removed from the study (or studied in a different manner), the behaviours expressed in the small group situations would gain consistency.

In summary, there is need for further exploration into interactions among personal and situational variables. More research relating to the prediction of social behaviours from psychometric information is also needed. Finally, available data suggest that interaction between individuals and particular scales or instruments would be a fruitful topic to explore.

RESULTS OF NORMATIVE, DEMOGRAPHIC, AND CORRELATIONAL STUDIES

The preceding section included a discussion of how the quality of children's social interactions can be partly understood in terms of a combination of interacting factors, one of which is the others-concept. Although many factors, both situational and personal, must be better understood in order to comprehend more fully the quality of children's interactions and friendships, the focus of the present chapter is on the others-concept and its role in helping to illuminate this highly complex topic.

It would be anticipated that the others-concept of any given individual has been influenced by both environmental and personal determinants, and this is supported by empirical findings. Group research has found variations in PHT scores to be associated consistently with variables such as sex and socioeconomic status. While many considerations preclude inferring that the PHT score of any given individual is an exact reflection of his/her others-concept, or that correlations between others-concept and other variables apply in all cases, consistent findings in normative, demographic, and correlational research indicate that the variables discussed below tend to be related to a person's others-concept.

The sex of the subject is one such variable. Most others-concept research which has been carried out to date has been undertaken in the USA (usually in the Midwest). In these studies a consistent finding has been that females have more positive others-concepts than males (Barnett and Zucker, 1973, 1975, 1977; Zucker and Barnett, 1977; Zucker and Jordan, 1968). Although the question of *why* this is so remains to be answered, this recurrent sex difference is, in itself, significant for what it may imply concerning the quality of children's interactions and friendships, at least in midwestern USA. It suggests the probability of warmer and more positive interactions occurring among girls than among boys. This is consistent with Bakan's thesis that femininity is 'more closely bound with larger interpersonal relationships' or what he calls 'communion' (Bakan, 1966, p. 23), and with Maccoby and Jacklin's (1975) conclusion that boys are more aggressive than girls.

There is a difficulty, however, with such a conclusion. In the one cross-national study of the others-concept, Burzynski (1980) found that such a sex difference does not occur in Ireland. In a study of more than 3,400 children, mostly in the 10–12-year-olds age range, he found no sex differences in others-concepts among the approximately 1,000 children he tested in Northern Ireland and only a slight, but not statistically significant, sex difference among his other subjects who lived in the Republic of Ireland. In order to account for this, it is necessary to learn more about the environmental factors which influence people's others-concepts and how these factors vary in different locations.

Socioeconomic status is another variable which has been found to be related to others-concept in a consistent manner. In general, studies, including Burzynski's in Ireland, have repeatedly shown that children whom teachers judge as coming from higher socioeconomic backgrounds have more positive others-concepts as a group than children who are judged to come from lower socioeconomic backgrounds (Barnett and Zucker, 1977; Burzynski, 1980; Zucker and Barnett, 1977). It appears from data presently available that this difference is stronger at the elementary school age and gradually decreases as people approach adulthood (Zucker and Barnett, 1977). These findings prompt the inference that some environmental factors which bring about differences in children's others-concepts lose their impact after those children have other exposures among which school is, perhaps, of utmost importance.

In addition to the experiences associated with being male or female, and the influences which result from having different socioeconomic backgrounds, data have accumulated which begin to show how other factors are related to the others-concepts people acquire. Black children living in a moderate size city in midwestern USA have been found as a group to have others-concepts quite similar to those of white children from a low socioeconomic background who live in the same community, while black children living in a larger city where schools were being integrated at the time of testing were found to have lower others-concepts. The difference in others-concept between black and white secondary-level students was found to be small and not statistically significant, and among freshmen entering college mean scores for black and white subjects were almost identical (Zucker and Barnett, 1977). It appears that the experience of being black in the USA has an impact on a child's others-concept, but that this experience can only be understood in terms of many other factors.

Likewise, Burzynski's data show that the experience of growing up in Northern Ireland, as compared with growing up in the Republic of Ireland, is likely to be associated with lower others-concepts in children. The 1,059 children in his Northern Ireland (Belfast area) sample had a mean PHT score lower than the mean score for the 2,312 children in the Republic of Ireland (Dublin area), and this difference was statistically significant. A possible explanation is that the tensions and strife experienced by children in the Belfast area affect their others-concepts.

A discussion of variables which have been found to be related to the others-concept cannot be limited to the factors thus far reported. Other more personality-related variables must also be included. One of these is the degree to which an individual has adjustment problems. Hart (1975) found that children who were described by their teachers as having the kinds of symptoms typically associated with learning disabilities and emotional disturbances had lower others-concepts as a group than their classmates. Galluzzi and Zucker (1977) found that children who had positive others-concepts and positive self-concepts, as measured by the Piers–Harris Self-concept Scale (Piers and Harris, 1969), were better adjusted personally and socially, according to results obtained on the California Test of Personality (Thorpe, 1953), than children who had low self-concepts and low others-concepts, high self-concepts and low others-concepts, or low self-concepts and high others-concepts. 'Adjustment' is, of course, a nebulous term having many different definitions and aspects, but the results of these two studies suggest strongly that at least some of the aspects of adjustment, however it is defined, are likely to have a significant relationship to a person's others-concept.

Since perceptual processes are considered by many psychologists to be interrelated with personality variables (Blake and Ramsey, 1951), one might conjecture that children who have positive others-concepts as a group possess some different personality attributes from children who possess negative others-concepts. In an unpublished study Kirchhoff (1977) demonstrated just that. She gave the Children's Personality Questionnaire (Porter and Cattell, 1975) to high- and low-scoring children in grades V and VI (mostly aged 9–11 years) and found statistically significant differences as follows: those with positive others-concepts (the high scorers on the PHT) were more forthright, self-disciplined, sensitive, conforming, conscientious, and spontaneous than those with negative others-concepts. In another unpublished study, Houser (1977) found a low positive, but significant, correlation (0.40) between internal locus of control using the Nowicki–Strickland Locus of Control Scale (Nowicki and Strickland, 1973) and positive others-concept among the same group of children.

Another personal quality of people which has been found to be related to others-concept is their stage of moral development, as conceptualized by Kohlberg (1971). Whiteman, using Rest's Defining Issues Test (Rest, 1974), found the others-concepts of students in grades VII–XII (mostly aged 12–18 years) who scored at the higher stages of moral development to be significantly higher as a group than those of children who scored at the lower stages (Whiteman, 1976; Whiteman, Zucker and Grimley, 1978). Thus, as Whiteman had hypothesized, it appears that there is a relationship between how people perceive other people and the concerns they appear to have about others as reflected in their moral judgements.

A discussion of people's personal attributes which have been found to be related to their others-concepts would not be complete without a reference to intelligence level. This variable was saved until the end because of the unclear data which have been obtained up to now. In large-scale studies of children's others-concepts, teachers' judgements of children's intelligence levels have been found consistently to be as significantly related to others-concept as are their judgements of socioeconomic status. As a group the children they judge as highly intelligent consistently have had more positive others-concepts than the children judged as less intelligent. The problem with this finding, however, is that socioeconomic status is a confounding factor. The teachers' judgements of socioeconomic status correlated highly with their judgements of intelligence level. No carefully controlled study in which these two variables are separated has yet been carried out. However, several studies involving children who were either enrolled in special classes for the educable mentally retarded or screened as possible candidates for such classes suggest that, as a group, these children often do not have more negative others-concepts than 'normal' children of their age bracket (Hart, 1975; Zucker and Barnett, 1977). The relationship between the variable of measured intelligence and others-concept clearly needs to be investigated more systematically and thoroughly.

A number of environmental variables and more personal qualities which have been demonstrated through research to have some meaningful relationship to a child's others-concept have been discussed in this section. A more comprehensive understanding of these relationships will develop when their interrelationships are explored. For example, Galluzzi is currently studying the relationship of self-concept and others-concept of regular class children to student and teacher perceptions of classroom environment.

Although much still needs to be learned about the complexities of the interactions among the many variables which are related to children's group behaviour, the trends which were discussed in this section represent some significant beginnings. Some of the variables which are likely to have a bearing on a child's others-concept are surfacing. In the previous section of this chapter, the relationship between others-concept and actual behaviour was discussed. As factors which help to account for variations in others-concept among different children become better understood, another link in the chain to better comprehension of the quality of children's social interactions and friendships is added.

AREAS FOR FURTHER RESEARCH

The others-concept is a relatively new construct. Although the present authors believe that it can be very useful for conceptualizing group processes and behaviour, and therefore can provide a helpful approach to understanding some aspects of children's friendships, much research with this construct still needs to be carried out. There are so many avenues which will need to be explored that only a scattering of the kinds of considerations which seem important to the authors are covered in the following pages.

Further conceptual development and theoretically-oriented research is very much needed. Research must be conducted which will more clearly and accurately delineate convergent and discriminant criteria in order to improve construct validity. Much still needs to be learned about the meaning of an individual PHT score. Research up to now has focused upon extreme-scoring individuals, but the meaning of a more average score needs to be investigated. It is possible to obtain an average score on the PHT, the only instrument which has been used in others-concept research up to now, by responding relatively neutrally to all the photographs or by fluctuating between positive and negative responses. Which of these approaches is used by any given individual may have other ramifications. Moreover, some individuals fluctuate in their responses on retest more than others, as already noted. Considerations such as these need to be explored in order to sharpen the utility of the others-concept as a construct and widen its possible application.

Specific facets of the others-concept will need to be studied separately. For example, drawing from experience with the self-concept, it can be conjectured that it would be profitable to evaluate separately how children perceive adults, specific categories of adults such as teachers, other children, males, females, superiors, subordinates, and so on. The possibilities are overwhelming, but that does not justify avoiding the issue.

More behavioural studies would also presumably have good potential for enhancing understanding of the others-concept construct. The behavioural studies summarized earlier in this chapter have helped to fill a gap which is often found in personality assessment research, namely, the relationship between test scores and behaviour. Much more knowledge about the behaviour of people who have a specific kind of others-concept is needed, however. This knowledge can only be acquired through carefully planned, systematic, painstaking behavioural research.

There is also a need for more demographic, correlational, and normative studies. Each of the studies of this type which has been conducted in the past has contributed in some fashion to the accumulation of knowledge presently available on the others-concept. There were many questions identified in the last section which still need to be clarified regarding the variables which have been studied, such as sex, socio-economic status, and intelligence, and their relationship to the others-concept. Additionally, there are many other variables which need to be explored, such as whether a person grows up in an urban or a rural setting, regional differences in others-concept, subcultural differences, and other national differences. The relationship of any of these variables to the others-concept will be complex, of course, and will probably have to be approached in a variety of new and creative ways. For example, sex differences in others-concept have so far been studied in terms of the traditional male–female dichotomy, but have never been explored in terms of psychological masculinity and femininity or androgyny.

Children's friendships and social interactions will become more understandable and predictable as the complex interrelationships between personal variables, such as the others-concept, and situational factors are explored. This is another area in which the surface has only been scratched. People act differently depending upon the characteristics of the other people who are with them, the activities in which they are engaged, the pervading psychological climate, and the settings in which those activities take place (e.g. school, playground, neighbourhood, home, prison, retail store). Again, the research challenge might appear to be overwhelming, but little by little, more understanding can be gained through systematic and thoughtful research.

Another area which needs to be explored further is how to improve the quality of children's interpersonal relationships. This is, of course, a highly practical goal which has far-reaching ramifications for the mental health of individuals and society. A general hypothesis which can be offered on the basis of the material discussed in this chapter is that improvement in children's others-concepts will lead to improvement in the quality of their interpersonal relationships. Obviously, other factors must be taken into consideration, many of which have been suggested in this chapter. Practical research related to intervention strategies would very likely contribute to theoretical knowledge as well.

Reference to intervention strategies and research having direct applications would not be complete without mentioning the topic of ethnic and racial attitudes. People would not have positive others-concepts as defined in this chapter if they perceived only people of their race in a positive light. In order to have a positive others-concept as measured by the PHT one must perceive people in general, regardless of colour, in a positive way. This is assured by the composition of the PHT photographs which are comprised of black and white hands interacting. As mentioned earlier, several studies which made use of all white hands or all black hands have been carried out in the past. Soon a larger study of this type is to be initiated to explore the variable of racial and ethnic attitudes and its relation to other findings which have been reported in this chapter. This, too, is an area which has many theoretical and practical ramifications.

The quality of children's interpersonal relationships and friendships is a complex topic with many facets, as is evidenced by the variety of material presented in the present volume. A child's concept of self and others should be considered in a broad context. The present chapter has focused on a child's others-concept, stressing this construct's significance for the topic of concern. Data have been surveyed showing how the others-concept construct can help contribute to the overall understanding of children's interpersonal behaviour and friendships within the framework of an interactionistic and contextualistic model; the importance of reciprocal influences among many interacting personal and situational variables has been especially emphasized.

REFERENCES

Adler, A. (1927). *The Practice and Theory of Individual Psychology*. New York: Harcourt, Brace and World.

Bakan, D. (1966). *The Duality of Human Existence*. Chicago: Rand McNally.

Bandura, A. (1977). *Social Learning Theory*. Englewood Cliffs, New Jersey: Prentice-Hall.

Barnett, D. W., and Zucker, K. B. (1973). An exploration into children's interpersonal behavior as related to their perception of social interactions. *Psychology in the Schools*, **10**, 61–66.

Barnett, D. W., and Zucker, K. B. (1975). The others-concept and friendly and cooperative behavior in children. *Psychology in the Schools*, **12**, 495–501.

Barnett, D. W., and Zucker, K. B. (1977). Validating a measure of children's others-concept through population and behavior variables. *Journal of Personality Assessment*, **41**, 131–143.

Bem, D. J., and Allen, A. (1974). On predicting some of the people some of the time: the search for cross-situational consistencies in behavior. *Psychological Review*, **81**, 506–520.

Berne, E. (1961). *Transactional Analysis in Psychotherapy*. New York: Grove Press.

Blake, R., and Ramsey, G. (1951). *Perception: An Approach to Personality*. New York: Ronald Press.

Bronfenbrenner, U. (1977). Toward an experimental ecology of human development. *American Psychologist*, **32**, 513–531.

Burzynski, P. (1972). Perception of social interaction and social behavior among adults: an adult form of the Paired Hands Test. Educational Specialist Thesis, Indiana State University.

Burzynski, P. (1980). A cross-national investigation of the others-concept using the Paired Hands Test. Doctoral Dissertation, Indiana State University.

Cottrell, L. S., Jr. (1970). Some neglected problems in social psychology. In Stone, G. P., and Farberman, H. P. (Eds.), *Social Psychology through Symbolic Interaction*. Waltham, Massachusetts: Xerox College Publishing.

Fromm, E. (1964). *The Heart of Man*. New York: Harper and Row.

Galluzzi, E., and Zucker, K. B. (1977). Level of adjustment and the self-and-others-concept. *Psychology in the Schools*, **14**, 104–108.

Gottman, J., Gonso, J., and Rasmussen, B. (1975). Social interaction, social competence, and friendship in children. *Child Development*, **46**, 709–718.

Harris, T. (1969). *I'm OK, You're OK*. New York: Harper and Row.

Hart, S. (1975). The others-concept and children with special needs. Paper presented at the meeting of the American Psychological Association, Chicago.

Hartshorne, H., and May, M. A. (1928). *Studies in the Nature of Character*. Vol. 1. New York: Macmillan.

Hartshorne, H., and May, M. A. (1929). *Studies in the Nature of Character*. Vol. 2. New York: Macmillan.

Hartshorne, H., May, M. A., and Shuttleworth, F. K. (1930). *Studies in the Nature of Character*. Vol. 3. New York: Macmillan.

Hogan, R., DeSoto, C. B., and Solano, C. (1977). Traits, tests and personality research. *American Psychologist*, **32**, 255–264.

Horney, K. (1950). *Neurosis and Human Growth*. New York: Norton.

Houser, D. (1977). Relationship of locus of control and others-concept in children. Paper presented at the annual meeting of the American Psychological Association, San Francisco.

Jourard, S. (1958). *Personal Adjustment*. New York: Macmillan.

Kirchhoff, L. (1977). Personality trait comparisons between high and low others-concept children. Paper presented at the annual meeting of the American Psychological Association, San Francisco.

Kohlberg, L. (1971). Stages of moral development as a basis for moral education. In C. M. Beck *et al.* (Eds.), *Moral Education*. Toronto: University of Toronto Press.

Lindesmith, A., and Strauss, A. (1968). *Social Psychology*, third edition. New York: Holt, Rinehart and Winston.

Maccoby, E., and Jacklin, C. (1975). *The Psychology of Sex Differences*. Stanford, California: Stanford University Press.

McCandless, B. R. (1967). *Children: Behavior and Development*. New York: Holt, Rinehart and Winston.

Mead, G. (1934). *Mind, Self and Society*. Chicago, Illinois: University of Chicago Press.

Mischel, W. (1968). *Personality and Assessment*. New York: Wiley.

Mischel, W. (1973). Toward a cognitive social learning reconceptualization of personality. *Psychological Review*, **80**, 252–283.

Mischel, W. (1977). On the future of personality measurement. *American Psychologist*, **32**, 246–254.

Mussen, P., and Eisenberg-Berg, N. (1977). *Roots of Caring, Sharing, and Helping*. San Francisco, California: W. H. Freeman.

Nowicki, S., and Strickland, B. R. (1973). A locus of control scale for children. *Journal of Consulting and Clinical Psychology*, **40**, 148–154.

Piers, E. V., and Harris, D. B. (1969). *Piers–Harris Children's Self-concept Scale*. Nashville, Tennessee: Counselor Recordings and Tests.

Porter, R., and Cattell, R. (1975). *Children's Personality Questionnaire*. Champaign, Illinois: Institute for Personality and Ability Testing.

Rest, J. R. (1974). *Manual for the Defining Issues Test*. University of Minnesota, unpublished manuscript.

Richmond, B., Mason, R., Jr., and Padgett, H. (1972). Self-concept and perception of others. *Journal of Humanistic Psychology*, 12, 103–111.

Robinson, S. A. (1967). A comparison of expressed acceptance of self and of others and responses on the Blacky pictures of two adolescent groups (Doctoral Dissertation, University of California, Los Angeles).*Dissertation Abstracts*, 28, 1311A. (University Microfilms No. 57–11, 713).

Rogers, C. R. (1951). *Client-centered Therapy*. Boston: Houghton Mifflin.

Shavelson, R., Hubner, J., and Stanton, G. (1976). Self-concept: validation of construct interpretations. *Review of Educational Research*, 46, 407–441.

Stock, D. (1949). An investigation into the interrelations between the self-concept and feelings directed toward other persons and groups. *Journal of Consulting Psychology*, 13, 176–180.

Suinn, R., and Hill, H. (1964). Influence of anxiety on the relationship between self-acceptance and acceptance of others. *Journal of Consulting Psychology*, 28, 116–119.

Sullivan, H. S. (1953). *The Interpersonal Theory of Psychiatry*. New York: Norton.

Thorpe, L. P. (1953). *California Test of Personality, Elementary, Form AA*. Monterey, California: California Test Bureau/McGraw-Hill.

Whiteman, J. (1976). An examination of the relationship between moral development and the perception of others (Doctoral Dissertation, Indiana State University).*Dissertation Abstracts*, 37, 4124B.(University Microfilms No. 77–1609).

Whiteman, J. L., Zucker, K. B., and Grimley, L. K. (1978). Moral judgment and the others-concept. *Psychological Reports*, 42, 283–289.

Williams, J. (1962). Acceptance by others and its relationship to acceptance of self and others: a repeat of Fey's study. *Journal of Abnormal and Social Psychology*, 65, 438–442.

Wylie, R. (1961). *The Self-Concept*. Lincoln, Nebraska: University of Nebraska Press.

Yarrow, M. R., Waxler, C. Z., Barrett, D., Darby, J., King, R., Pickett, M., and Smith, J. (1976). Dimensions and correlates of prosocial behavior in young children. *Child Development*, 47, 118–125.

Zubin, J., Eron, L. D., and Schumer, F. (1965). *An Experimental Approach to Projective Techniques*. New York: Wiley.

Zucker, K. B. (1976). The others-concept: its place in the schools. *The School Psychology Digest*, 5, 4–12.

Zucker, K. B., and Barnett, D. W. (1977). *The Paired Hands Test Manual*. Dallas, Texas: McCarron-Dial Systems.

Zucker, K. B., and Jordan, D. (1968). The Paired Hands Test: a technique for measuring friendliness. *Journal of Projective Techniques and Personality Assessment*, 32, 522–529.

PROCESSES OF ACQUAINTANCE

CHAPTER 4

Attraction and Communication in Children's Interactions

STEVE DUCK,
DAVID K. MIELL
and
HEATHER C. GAEBLER

It is a curious fact about social psychological research into interpersonal attraction that it has tended to follow the pattern that individuals themselves employ when they become acquainted: in other words, the researcher has become acquainted with the cues that influence and promote interpersonal attraction in the same order as individuals become acquainted with the cues that influence and promote liking for one another. Thus, many early studies were concerned with 'public factors' like the physical or sociological characteristics that influence choice (Perrin, 1921; Seagoe, 1933) whilst the emphasis of more recent work falls on behavioural style (Argyle and Dean, 1965) and on private factors like effects of cognitive characteristics of acquainting partners (Byrne, 1971; Kelvin, 1977). Indeed it is possible to structure most research findings in a way that reflects this development (Duck, 1977).

In the case of children's friendships the research is similar in pattern but different in detail: some early work concentrated on the role of 'objective' factors in children's choice behaviour (e.g. social status of parents—Potashin, 1946; place of the home—Seagoe, 1933; IQ score—Bonney, 1946). Subsequent work has looked at the influence of behavioural style (Campbell and Yarrow,

89

1961); considered the ways in which behaviour (and the meaning behind it) alters with age (Rubin, 1972); considered the qualitative changes in cognition that accompany individual growth (Rardin and Moan, 1971); and has lately related all this to theories of cognitive development, particularly those concerned with the development of moral or empathic concepts (Bigelow, 1977; La Gaipa and Bigelow, 1972; Smither, 1977).

What is lacking is a statement of the conceptual similarities and differences in the qualitative nature of *adults'* and *children's* personal relationships. We believe there are many similarities which are not confined to those that are manifested by the parallel ways in which researchers have dealt with the two topics. For example, if one attends to the factors which have been shown to influence adult relationship growth then there is a marked parallelism between the way in which adult acquaintances develop with time and the basis on which children form their relationships at different ages: both start with the influence of the objective characteristics of the partner (like physical attractiveness, status); are subsequently influenced by behavioural style (e.g. non-verbal activity, level of aggressiveness); become centred on the understanding of motives behind the observed behaviour (e.g. by means of attribution or role taking); and ultimately focus on the character that lies behind the motives (e.g. by trait description or comprehension of another's personality characteristics).

Adult acquainting may be conceived to be a communicative process with the ultimate aims of obtaining the maximum amount of information about the detail of the partner's personality (notably about his personal constructs, cf. Duck, 1973). Adult acquainting, in this view, is motivated by a search for support for one's own 'personality' provided in the form of similarity in most cases (see Duck, 1976, 1977; and below). The progress of adult relationships is restricted by the limits imposed upon what one *can* know about another person after given lengths of time spent acquainting, by a need for context in order to make useful inferences about the partner's personality and so on. Clearly in the case of children the limits are going to derive from the child's imperfect skills in social interaction: before the child can employ the crucial kind of search for personality detail that is essential to successful adult acquainting, s/he must be able to appreciate what s/he discovers and must therefore have developed the ability to interpret another person's behaviour in relevant terms. In the case of children's friendships then, our analysis must concentrate on how these skills develop if we are to elucidate the parallelism between children's and adults' acquainting. In children the acquaintance sequence is complicated (and limited) by the fact that children are learning in many different areas of 'cognitive' and 'social' competence at the same time as they are learning to interpret, and themselves produce, the behaviours that are implied by a given stage of relationship development.

COMMUNICATION AND SELF-VALIDATION IN ACQUAINTANCE

To complete the above analysis it is necessary to consider briefly the motive for adult acquainting and the sense in which acquaintance can be conceived as a communicative process in the service of this motive. We then consider how it may apply to children's friendships and we review some literature on children's friendship choice in an attempt to test the utility of the model.

Need for effectance

In our analysis, following Byrne and Clore (1967) and Duck (1976, 1977), the motivational force for acquaintance is a 'need for effectance' (White, 1959), that is, a need to evaluate one's competence at dealing with the world, to establish that one has adequate perceptual and behavioural apparatus for conducting one's daily life satisfactorily. To the extent that one's attitudes or beliefs or opinions or styles of behaviour or personality constructs are shared by other people, they can be validated by the consensus of those other people (consensual validation), particularly in cases where the attitudes or constructs cannot be validated by other than social means (Festinger, 1954). In the present context, the notion of consensual validation can be used to predict that similarity is, in certain circumstances, highly reinforcing (Byrne, 1971). A search for similarity of attitudes and personality constructs thus characterizes much interpersonal interaction as an attempt to satisfy one's need for effectance and to validate one's view of the world. Essentially, then, for adults, the relationship between personality, similarity and friendship is a very important *functional* one: friendship is an essential process in the validation of one's personality constructs and so contributes to personal growth and psychological integrity. But since one cannot know the extent of such support or similarity provided by a perfect stranger (because one has not yet found out about *his* personality), acquaintance—the process of getting to know someone— can usefully be regarded as a communication process which has as its central goal the discovery of information about the partner's personality, in the service of the need for effectance (Duck, 1976, 1977).

Acquaintance as communication

An approach based on the view we have taken above will clearly be concerned with the way in which developing acquaintance serves to provide information about the partner's personality. However, most research on interpersonal attraction in adults has been concerned with the factors that make a person initially attractive to another person. We might also note that this has also been true of studies of children's choice and that this has led to a serious deficiency in theoretical conceptions of the nature of acquaintance development in children. In particular it has done little to encourage the establishment of a tradition of longitudinal studies into relationship development.

The research on adults' attraction to strangers has concerned a variety of stimuli such as physical attractiveness (Perrin, 1921), non-verbal behaviour (Allgeier and Byrne, 1973), sociological information (Byrne, Clore and Worchel, 1966), attitudinal stimuli (Byrne, 1971), and personality characteristics (Duck, 1973). As stimuli that provoke attraction and liking, these attributes of persons can generally be conceptualized within a reinforcement–affect model (Clore, 1977). However, if one makes the insubstantial assumption that attraction to strangers is a starting point for a developing acquaintance, then the effectiveness of such cues or attributes in promoting liking must also be explained in the context of developing acquaintance. Do they 'work' because they are simply and inherently attractive or do they somehow help individuals to serve the need for effectance? Taking this latter view, Duck (1976, 1977) has argued that attributes or cues (like physical attractiveness, or non-verbal behavioural style, or sociological status, or beliefs) are attractive insofar as—and for the reason that—they inform the observer about a partner's probable personality at an appropriate point in a developing acquaintance. Acquaintance is thus communication in the sense that, in an ordered and sequential way, the observer attends to various features of his/her partner in order to extract information from them about his partner's personality (Duck, 1976, 1977). Essentially, the sequence begins with contextual information (such as socioeconomic status, dress, physical appearance) that casts little direct light upon a partner's personality but is useful background. The sequence ends—much later—with the precise and sophisticated detailed knowledge about the partner's personality that is available after the more personal exchanges of an extended series of interactions. Communicative, information gathering affects liking and intimacy growth by means of the predictive inferences that are formed by each person into a general model of his partner's personality. The model can then be compared with the person's own personality, in order to deduce the likely level of similarity existing between the two.

In the present context it is important to note that such a process is probably mediated by several complex skills: some (implicit) theory of 'personality'; an ability to take another's viewpoint in order to judge his reasons for doing things (and hence his likability); shrewdness, accuracy of perception, ability to distinguish the relevant from the irrelevant; an appreciation of the significance of 'extraneous' cues (like physical attractiveness, non-verbal style, etc.); and various other skills both social and cognitive. These take on importance in this context precisely because they are things that children lack and have to acquire as part of a developing social sensitivity. Furthermore, Duck (1973) has argued that the assessment of personality support from another person is the usual basis for decisions about suitability as a friend. Where such support is inadequate the partner will, if possible, be 'filtered out' (i.e. discarded) from the pool of potential friends and other partners will be sought. Extending this idea to children's friendships, we argue that, if children are developing the skills outlined above and are testing their competence in various new ways, their relationships will be liable to be unstable. This, as we shall show below, is because these new skills take time to master and use in socially functional ways. This view assumes that, like adult acquainting, children's friendship is best seen as a communicative process where information is gathered systematically in the service of a need for effectance. In the latter case, however, it is complicated and restricted by the fact of the simultaneous acquisition and growth of social and cognitive skills.

Children's communication and self-validation

In our view it violates both commonsense and the Occam's razor principle to assume, without proof, that children's friendships are based on essentially different mechanisms from those upon which adult friendships are based. Indeed, Byrne and Griffitt (1966) showed that the reinforcing effects of consensual validation were operative by at least 9 years of age. However, we wish to go further and argue that children's friendship processes are originally imperfect (but gradually improving and developing) approximations to the set of principles governing adult acquainting. Clearly, if children's acquainting is based on the same underlying motivation then such acquainting will be severely limited in the early years (0–5 years old) since children have underdeveloped concepts of enduring personality (Livesley and Bromley, 1973). The prediction follows that as such concepts of personality develop in sophistication, so will the basis of children's friendship also become more like that of adults.

Equally, the nature of the information gathered in acquaintance will be constrained by the children's abilities at different ages to understand the relevance of given cues (like non-verbal behaviour, smiling and eye-contact) to personality interpretation. Each type of information will be relevant and significant for children in terms only of their present abilities to discriminate, present knowledge of social rules, normative behaviour or verbal skills, and their present concepts of personality. Since children are developing their skills at role taking, at describing other people, at perceiving what types of behaviour are appropriate in different circumstances, and at assessing moral problems (to specify only a few developments), our argument suggests that they will wish to assess and evaluate the efficacy of these developing discriminations, in the service of the need for effectance. Further, it is plausible that a child's ability to detect certain kinds of information is something that develops progressively. Each development is then a new part of their view of the world; each needs its value assessed and will be tested *primarily*, we argue, through social interaction and friendship. Friendship is thus strictly functional to personal development.

One study supporting the principles of such a view, but conducted on adolescent subjects, was completed by Duck (1975) using Kelly's (1955) *Reptest* measure of personality. Testing of adolescents of different ages (12, 14, 16 years old) revealed that the personality similarities associated with friendship partners not only were significantly higher than those associated with other, random, pairings within the population, but also were different in type at the three ages. Those aspects of personality which were developing and increasing proportionately with age (e.g. psychological constructs—descriptions of others' motives and character) also began to assume proportionately greater significance among those similarities that correlated with friendship choice.

Some (pseudomethodological) theoretical issues

Since the work on childhood relationships has not so far been conducted within the above framework nor derived specifically from the principles outlined, this chapter will seek out such a structure in previous research in a way that is consistent with the above suggestions. To achieve this goal, comparisons must be made between studies with different theoretical and methodological characteristics. However, one point that we wish to stress in doing this is that many of the apparently methodological differences between studies are actually disguised theoretical and substantive differences (Duck, 1977; Levy, 1977). This is especially true within the framework above where many differences in experimental methods act to convey subtly different information to subjects in ways that have concealed the (lack of) comparability between studies. In this context, when one study measures 'popularity' by means of unreciprocated choices (e.g. Rubin, 1972) whilst another measures 'popularity' by means of the number of mutual choices (e.g. Dymond, Hughe and Raabe, 1952) and yet a third concerns not popularity but 'friendship' as its dependent variable (e.g. Austin and Thompson, 1948), the studies are not necessarily informing about the same things even if they claim to be. They are realizing different aspects of the acquaintance process, where different causal factors may be influential: the causes of popularity (how *many* people like someone) are not necessarily the same as causes of friendship (how *much* someone likes someone else); neither are the underlying psychological mechanisms necessarily identical (La Gaipa and Wood, 1973). Equally, popularity is an expression of liking by general consensus, whilst friendship is a *relationship* that has, of itself, to be managed and maintained as a continuing entity (Duck, 1977). The skills that are required in order to recognize that someone is attractive (popular) will centre on the ability to detect and evaluate certain key cues (e.g. physical attractiveness, friendliness, generosity) whilst the ability to maintain and continue a particular relationship will depend on the performance of certain role-based behaviours (e.g. the ability to 'be a friend' to someone), on having the concept of the role of 'friend', and on the ability of partners to reciprocate adequately in communicative interaction. It is therefore necessary to be alert to the distinctions between the studies which measure and seek to explain popularity, those that measure and seek to explain friendship and, within this latter set, those that operationalize friendship as mutual choice only and those that operationalize it as choice—whether mutual or unreciprocated. It is extremely likely that measures of 'children's friendship' which base themselves on these different criteria are drawing different and essentially non-comparable conclusions about not only the nature and causes of friendship in childhood but also what it means to children and how the concept develops and matures.

As an example of the subtleties that some workers have overlooked it may be observed that Waldrop and Halverson (1975) in the course of a study on sex differences in friendship, noted a distinction between *extensive* and *intensive* peer relations: extensive relations involve playing with groups of others whilst intensive ones centre around one selected individual. Clearly children who habitually adopt one mode rather than another are different in psychological terms in ways that a simple experimental instruction to 'name your three best friends' may obscure. We extend this point, however, to the assertion that the choice of measure by which to identify the subject of study is not *simply* a methodological issue. The choice of measure expresses the researcher's implicit theory about the nature of the phenomenon that he is investigating and his implicit view of the major factors involved (Duck, 1977).

A further pseudomethodological issue concerns the stability of children's friendship choices over time. Previous findings have been highly inconsistent (see Mouton, Blake and Fruchter, 1955, for a review) although this is partly accounted for by the age factor. Stability increases with age, approaching asymptote about 12 years of age (Busk, Ford and Schulman, 1973). Yet researchers have so far failed to ground this empirical finding within developmental theory. From a developmental approach it may be predicted that observed changes in sociometric choice over usual test-retest intervals of 2 months or more (e.g. Northway, 1968) may be confounding: (i) changes in the child's basis for selection as social concepts develop (cf. Bigelow, 1977; Livesley and Bromley, 1973); with (ii) a certain basis for selection which characteristically leads to instability of choice. Regarding this latter, the findings of Bigelow and La Gaipa (1975) suggest that, prior to about 11 years of age, children do *not* possess 'normative expectations' (which function to maintain relationships). Instead, young children's friendship choices will be largely contingent upon factors which are themselves liable to fluctuate with the child's subjective experience of each particular interaction (e.g. 's/he played with me today', 's/he gave me a sweet'). Whereas previous studies have failed to consider test-retest intervals of less than 1 week, it follows from the developmental approach that sociometric choices of young children should change over very short intervals. To test this hypothesis children aged between 5 and 11 years of age were asked whom they liked best in their class on six separate occasions over a fortnight (Miell and Duck, 1978). Results significantly supported the main hypothesis and showed marked developmental trends of increasing stability toward the empirically established asymptote (Busk, Ford and Schulman, 1973) presumably reflecting a gradual acquisition of normative expectations. Here again, then, the theoretical implications of a seemingly 'methodological' point (choice of test-retest interval) are important for the conceptualization of a well-known aspect of friendship in children. Alas, until workers adopt a paradigmatic approach to children's friendship, with agreed frameworks and definitions, the essentially theoretical nature of such 'methodological' disputes will often be obscured.

ATTRACTION AND LIKING IN CHILDREN

Just as adult liking is multidetermined, so too is the liking of children for one another. Just as some factors act to predispose adults to like one another whilst entirely different factors precipitate a relationship, so it is with children. Just as some factors promote initial attraction in adults whilst others prolong and continue the development of intimacy over time in adult relationships, so we claim in this chapter that the nature of the cues which are salient in children's friendship differ as a function of the age of the children being studied. The sections that follow thus describe not mutually exclusive influences on liking in children but complementary ones; not things that invariably precipitate relationships but ingredients of a complex mixture of causality.

Sociological and casual correlates of liking

One clear influence on the likelihood of relationship formation is simple opportunity. The more certain one is of encountering another person again, the more worthwhile it may seem to invest the time necessary to establish a relationship. Hence it is plausible to expect that such things as closeness of parental domicile, frequency of interaction, equivalence of age or intelligence (and hence an increased likelihood of being placed in the same school classroom) and spatial distance in the classroom itself will be constraints upon or facilitators of children's friendship choice. Indeed, these factors are, in a general sense, found to have intuitively predictable effects (Bonney, 1946; Potashin, 1946), although they seem to be clearly the kind of factors that predispose one child to relate to another rather than being precipitators of given acquaintances. Thus Seagoe (1933) found that propinquity was a strong factor in the selection of associates among children and that, in general terms, such things as mental age and intelligence exerted less than the expected effects. Byrne (1961), however, reports that *functional* proximity in the classroom has more effect on peer relationships and interaction than other forms of propinquity. It is clear, however, that there is no simple effect of such factors and that they interact with other factors. Thus Austin and Thompson (1948) showed that, when children were asked to give reasons for selecting and rejecting peers, propinquity and similarity of interests were given as the next most important factors after personality characteristics. It is unclear how one should interpret these latter findings, however, since they predate systematic attempts both to assess the validity of measures used in this context and to investigate the nature of 'personality' from a child's point of view. Since children's notions of personality (and the constructs that are appropriate to describe it) develop with age (see below) the simple adoption of a measure that appears adequate to adult observers or experimenters may be rather rash.

On the whole, then, and with the above reservations, the findings from children are consistent with those from adults that were being conducted about that time (e.g. Festinger, Schachter and Back, 1950, on residents of a housing estate; Willerman and Swanson, 1952, on college sororities). These combine to show that whilst propinquity acts to facilitate relationship the full functional explanation of them derives from other factors. The choice to interact again and to continue to interact more intensively is based on other cues.

One such cue in the case of adults is physical attractiveness (Berscheid and Walster, 1974). In the case of children, if it can be shown that they also respond to such cues, then certain assumptions have to be made. Favourable responses to physical cues presume that children are able to identify such cues, that they attach significance to them, whether or not they are the same cues conveying the same meaning as for adults (Duck and Gaebler, 1976), or else that children have developed at least some form of physical attractiveness stereotype, whether it is the same as the adult one or not. Work by Dion (1973, 1974; Dion and Berscheid, 1974) suggests that children do possess such a stereotype by quite an early age (3–6 years of age) and that it probably is acquired, in part, from adult responses to attractive and unattractive children. It has also been shown (Dion and Berscheid, 1974) that physical attractiveness influences the popularity of all but the youngest children (4 years of age and below) and that physically unattractive children are often attributed with unpleasant or antisocial behaviour tendencies.

It also seems plausible in the context of children's interactions that ratings of popularity may be based upon—and physical attractiveness cues are influential through the mediation of—the development of sex stereotypes. Williams, Bennett and Best (1975), for example, showed that awareness of adult sex stereotypes was present even in kindergarten children but that knowledge of them increased to asymptote in a similar manner in boys and girls as they proceeded to grade II (6 years of age). It is noteworthy that both the sex stereotype and the physical attractiveness stereotypes operate to produce in perceivers expectations about the personality or behaviour of others (Dion, Berscheid and Walster, 1972; Williams *et al.*, 1975) and that this fact is consistent with our hypothesis here that such casual and 'sociological' factors exert their influence on friendship and attraction through the meaning that they have for personality/behavioural model formation. In adults such cues are important influences on friendship precisely for this reason (Duck, 1977; Duck and Craig, 1975, 1977), but in children it is unclear so far whence these expectations could be derived. It seems plausible that (especially at an early age) children, in learning to associate outward appearance and observable behaviour (that is, learning that the two may be related), come not only to develop a more sophisticated and stable view of personality but also subsequently to use induction as the basis for making inferences from one to the other (e.g. deducing that physically attractive people have friendly personalities).

Behaviour in interactions

Given the assumption that much learning *about* social relationships is taking place in childhood (Hartup, 1978) it is likely that much of it occurs *in* social relationships. Green (1933) conducted a study of play and quarrelling in preschool children in an attempt to assess the influences of such behaviour on the development of friendly relationships or the acquisition of 'socialized' patterns of action. Amongst several findings were the observations that friendship indices increased regularly with age whilst the ratio of quarrelling to friendship decreased regularly with age. However, mutual quarrellers were more friendly than average and mutual friends more quarrelsome, such that Green (1933) regarded quarrelling as a part of friendly social intercourse at the ages studied. It was concluded that 'play that includes quarrelling and making up is excellent training and probably teaches children to minimize their grievances and to be good sports' (p. 251). Thus the experience of play and interaction with others appears to provide the context for the formation and use of normative expectations about the appropriateness of different kinds of behaviour in specific circumstances.

Equally important in the child's development of concepts of attractiveness and an appreciation of the likability of certain behaviours is a developing awareness of the consequences of one's own behaviour for others. Whilst this is dealt with at greater depth later in this chapter, it may be briefly noted that Long and Lerner (1974) have examined the ways in which children come to establish a concept of 'deserving' by means of delayed gratification for kindly acts, whilst Barrett and Yarrow (1977) have shown that development of pro-social behaviour depends in large measure on the ability of the child to make accurate inferences about others' behaviour. The attractiveness of behaviour is thus related not solely to the stimulus properties of the behaviour itself (e.g. 'dirty' behaviour is disliked) nor to the consequences that it has for the observer (e.g. assertiveness may be liked or respected even when it occasions aggression against the observer) but to the observer's beliefs about the intentions behind it and the type of personality or character that it reveals (Duck, 1977).

Lastly, we suggest that a developed concept of the attractiveness of *one's own* behaviour is acquired by reference to the reactions of other people to oneself. Many theories about need for affiliation (Byrne, McDonald and Mikawa, 1963; Mehrabian and Ksionzky, 1974) are based on the assumption that individuals acquire a notion of the rewardingness of association with other people from their past experiences of reinforcement received from other people. Indeed, Campbell and Yarrow (1961) suggest that initial responses of peers to a child often influence or even determine his subsequent behaviour and consequent popularity. It is tempting to conclude from this that an individual's self-esteem is largely determined by early experiences. However, as with much work on interpersonal attraction that seeks the origins of attractiveness, it is often asserted but seldom demonstrated that such factors originate in childhood. One could as easily postulate that such things as others' behaviour are attractive in their own right for children and that self-esteem is developed more by adolescent experiences than childhood ones. It is clear, however, that the possibility exists that not only one's own attractiveness to others but also one's own response to others' reactions to oneself is established in childhood. Childhood play is an obvious source for developing comprehension of both the relative attractiveness of different sorts of action and the 'meaning' of others' behaviour (Shaver, 1975).

Describing others' behaviour: social perception

Abilities to interpret others' behaviour, to construe its causes and to make causal attributions are essential ingredients of adult social interaction as much as they are a basis for assessing the attractiveness of others' personalities— and hence are an influence on adult personal relationships. Clearly children need to, and do, develop such abilities during maturation although there are several components to this complex skill that have to be acquired. First, the child has to appreciate that certain attributes of others can, if used wisely, give information about their personality characteristics. It should be noted, however, that the significances of such attributes or cues are not absolutes but vary from person to person, even between adults. Thus the child needs must construct his/her own characteristic style of detecting personality information from others' physique, behaviour, attitudes and so on. S/he must also deduce the meaning of those cues to which s/he attends, a meaning that may be personal and peculiar to him/herself. This phenomenological perspective is consistent with the arguments above and emphasizes the multidimensional nature of the communicative and perceptual skills that the child needs to acquire. Second, in order to appreciate any personal meaning of the cues that s/he decides are significant, the child needs to develop a concept of what 'a personality' or a stability in other people (and himself) amounts to, as well as developing the discriminative perceptual abilities. Third, the child has to learn—and to learn to use correctly—the kinds of terms that are appropriate for describing the discriminated cues. Fourth, the child has to acquire some conceptualization of the logical relationship and inferential nexus of the terms used to describe others' behaviour—that is to discover the ways in which such terms are thought to correlate. Fifth, the child has to acquire the realization that such terms can be used to *explain* behaviour as well as to describe it, through the process of inference to dispositions. Sixth, since communication is a reciprocal process, the child must learn not only to deduce things from others' behaviour but also to transmit information to them about his/her own personality. This will facilitate *their* perception of *his/her* personality characteristics. Clearly this reciprocity will facilitate the communication of information relevant to their *mutual* decision to become (and stay) friends. Also the later of these communicative and interpretative skills amount to a growing ability to make attributions (Shaver, 1975). They will thus depend on and relate to the development of a child's ability to understand the perspective of other people than him/herself, since a differentiated interpretation of someone's behaviour depends on a recognition of the situational pressures, environmental influences and personal requirements that may have influenced him/her to act as s/he did. Hence it presumes the ability to take the other person's perspective in order to assess what these situational and personal influences may have been. These aspects of the attribution process are now discussed in turn.

Decoding of non-verbal cues

There is little evidence about the ways in which children learn to attend to and interpret cues such as non-verbal signals (or their relationship to speech) which are fundamental firstly to the conduct of adult social interaction (Wiener, Devoe, Rubinow and Geller, 1972) and secondly to interpretation of adult behaviour in terms of underlying states, motives and personality characteristics. However, Bugenthal, Kaswan and Love (1970) indicate the differences that exist between adults' and children's abilities to interpret non-verbal/verbal inconsistency (which, to an adult, usually suggests 'sarcasm'—for example, a negative message said with a smile). Whilst adults have little difficulty divining the true message, children usually either misunderstand or read all inconsistent messages as negative in effect.

Cognitive abilities developed in interaction

On the other hand, Campbell and Yarrow (1961) have shown that children who had acquired greater social effectiveness and were more popular, did have a correspondingly greater ability to interpret other people's behaviour. The content of their views about others did not differ systematically from the views of less effective and less popular children but the interpretative quality of their perceptual reports did differ. This suggests the intriguing hypothesis that children who have developed greater levels of descriptive sophistication will be more able to interact satisfactorily with others and should be more effective and popular. One wonders how far such skills can be actively taught, in view of their obvious social significance: at the moment they seem to be allowed to develop haphazardly from play alone.

In an attempt to examine the relationship between play preference, ego-centrism, popularity and classification skills, Rubin and Maioni (1975) observed and classified children's play and role taking abilities. Support was found for the view that type of play was related to age and cognitive ability. Hence the ability to interact successfully with others at a given age is consequent upon the achievement of a level of cognitive functioning that corresponds to that of those with whom one interacts. The better able one is to comprehend the behaviour of others in the terms that they themselves employ, the greater the communication and the greater the functional support that partners provide for each other—by validating the newly-acquired ways of describing other people. Changes in description should thus relate *functionally* to friendship (Duck, 1977).

Development of personal description

How do such descriptions of other people change with age? Peevers and Secord (1973) have indicated some ways in which the description of others' behaviour or characteristics develops with age, particularly showing a remarkable increase of differentiation in description. Peevers and Secord (1973) noted three levels of differentiation: *undifferentiated*, where the target person was described in terms of his relation with the environment (e.g. 'He lives in a big house'); *simple differentiated*, where the target person was described in terms of global labels (e.g. 'He's nice'); and *differentiated*, where the personal properties of the target were described (e.g. 'He's a good athlete'). The depth of description also increased in the sense that, with age, describers become increasingly aware of the specific situational, temporal or internal states of others. They also develop a more causal/explanatory approach to comments about other people rather than being purely descriptive. Other evidence suggests that children are not only learning how to describe others but are also gaining some insights into the appropriateness of certain behaviours in certain circumstances (i.e. an understanding of normative behaviours)—a background which is essential for the interpretation of the actions of a given individual in a particular situation. For example, Long and Lerner (1974) and Lerner and Reavy (1975) have examined ways in which prosocial behaviour is influenced by one's understanding of what happens to others in similar circumstances.

The progressive development of these descriptive skills (and the awareness of the social significance of the relationship between a given actor's performance and the general norm) is perhaps second in importance to an understanding of *how* they are learned and *why* they change and develop. We know of no work that has examined these important causal questions so as to illuminate the ways in which popularity and unpopularity are *caused* by growth (or failure of growth) in the cognitive skills implied in and necessary for social interaction. However, this may be because—as the next section shows—researchers are undecided about the nature and significance of changes or development in such social/cognitive skills in any case, and cannot therefore take decisions about how such developmental differences function in relation to friendship and attraction.

Social and cognitive development: understanding others' personalities

Following largely on suggestions by Piaget (1959, 1962), many workers have set out to show that social capacities are related to the cognitive developments that take place with age. Specifically it is predicted that social abilities and popularity should relate to the ability to take the role of the other (variously, interchangeably and confusingly called also 'empathy', decentering, perspective taking, social insight). Dymond *et al.* (1952), using a projective test and a social insight test, both of which required the subject to take the role of another actor, showed an increase with age (from 7- to 11-year-olds) in the ability to take another's viewpoint. They showed also a relationship between social insight and popularity. However, this result is difficult to interpret in view of the fact that the correlation between the sociometric measure and the projective test was near zero. The authors suggested that, while children become progressively more aware of (and better able to assess) the feeling of others accurately, they also become aware of the fact that some feelings are 'safe' to admit and others need defences. In other words, the task that children must learn to perform adequately is not solely the task of *recognizing* in others (whether as a result of cognitive development or not) increasingly subtle social characteristics, but also the task of learning the social significance of the occurrence of such traits in the interpretation of others' personality structure. Hence the task illuminates the problems that children face in assessing the attractiveness of another person which, we would predict, will depend at first on the learned attractiveness of certain cues and subsequently on the ability to assess from the cues the structure and attractiveness of the underlying personality.

Further evidence on the relationship between cognitive and social abilities comes from Feffer and Gourevitch (1960) who gave children of various chronological ages a projective role-taking task along with a series of impersonal cognitive tasks developed by Piaget and his co-workers. These performances were analysed in terms of the concept of balanced decentring, that is, the ability to shift from one aspect of a situation to another in a balanced yet flexible manner. The findings suggested a correspondence between the ability to decentre on physical tasks and on social ones. However, as we have previously noted, the interpretation of these results is dependent on the resolution of certain 'methodological' issues that actually have important theoretical force. This is perhaps best evidenced by a detailed consideration of the Borke/Chandler and Greenspan debate and its subsequent development.

The Borke/Chandler and Greenspan debate

The debate began with a study by Borke (1971). She reported that young children—as early as 3 years of age—have the capacity for recognizing that others have feelings which vary according to the situation in which the individual finds him/herself. This depended somewhat on the particular emotion being identified—happiness, it appears, is easier to distinguish than anger or sadness, whilst fear is the most difficult. Borke concluded that previous findings (supporting Piaget's position that children remain primarily egocentric until about 7 years of age) were due to a too heavy reliance on verbal skills, such that verbal incompetence rather than egocentrism was being detected in the very youngest children and was mistaken for a psychological orientation. Borke's own method avoided this source of confusion and involved a multiple-choice technique which required the child merely to point to a representation of a facial expression, supposedly provoked by the events in a story told to the child.

Chandler and Greenspan (1972) objected to Borke's conclusions on the grounds that her procedure failed to satisfy an important condition necessary for a behaviour to qualify as truly empathic, since for this to occur an individual must be able to anticipate what someone feels or thinks, not merely in a particular situation (whose antecedents are not fully understood by the subject) but also when the thoughts and feelings are different from the subject's own. Thus Chandler and Greenspan (1972) argue that what appear to be correct attributions of another's feelings in Borke's experiment are likely to be reached through a process of stereotyping and projection, and hence are in a sense not truly empathic.

Conceding to Borke the point that previous research has relied overmuch on verbal meanings, Chandler and Greenspan conducted an experiment using cartoons depicting affectively-charged sequences. After identifying the affective state of a central character the subjects were shown a sequel where the central character was joined by a second child who had not been present when the affective state was evoked. The central character was then shown to behave in a manner consistent with his evoked affective state. Subjects were then asked to tell the story from their point of view as well as that of the bystander and a measure of egocentrism was derived from the degree to which the description manifested interference from the additional knowledge of the antecedents that was available to the subject. In this way, Chandler and Greenspan argued, the subject was required to take a viewpoint measurably different from his own. Whilst few subjects had difficulty in identifying the affective state of the central character (consistent with Borke), there were age-related differences in perspective taking ability, with younger subjects tending to confuse their own perspective with those of the uninformed bystander. This seems to show that young children can anticipate the affective reactions of others without being able to take another's perspective.

In a rejoinder, Borke (1972) accepted that differences in operational definitions were responsible for the differing conclusions, but argued that both sets of results were consistent with the view that development of empathy is a continuous rather than a discontinuous process and that sensitivity to the affective responses of others (whether achieved through projection, identification or stereotype) represents the beginning of such a process—a 'prereflective empathic ability'. Borke thus conceded that 'relativistic' empathy does not appear until later, although she maintains that an awareness of the feelings and variation of the feelings of others with the situation is present very early, with its roots in the emergence of the concept of 'self'.

What emerges from this debate is a picture of a theoretical argument arising from the use of different methodologies. More recently, Smither (1977) has noted that the concept of empathy itself is one fraught with both methodological and theoretical ambiguities. The major point of interest here is in her linguistic analysis of the term 'empathy' itself, which she has demonstrated to be a non-unitary concept, involving many related skills all of which develop with age.Thus the positions taken by Chandler and Greenspan (1972) and Borke (1972) are not necessarily incompatible, within Smither's comprehensive analysis. Empathy, she argues, involves more than labelling of affect but presupposes some conceptual schema or context within which the emotions of others are interpreted. Such a context, as we have argued, must come to include an ability in the empathizer to comprehend the beliefs, evaluations and comments that the other makes about the world. Indeed many emotions such as envy, shame and pride require rather this type of contextual information than the direct behavioural cues available. Thus Smither distinguishes between 'contagious' or 'natural' expression of emotion and 'intentional role-taking'— a more socially based form of expression, involving finer discriminations between self and other and understanding of normative behaviour. Within such a framework, Borke's findings would appear to correspond to the former ability (i.e. interpretation of contagious expression) whilst Chandler and Greenspan's clearly involve other levels of discrimination. Borke's comments about experience are thus pertinent here: as such 'relativistic' abilities develop, there will be an increasing reliance on such socially-based expression of emotion, including use of language, and we would expect an accompanying increase in the range of predictability by the child of others' emotional responses. In conclusion, both Borke, and Chandler and Greenspan, used limited concepts and different methodologies to delineate what are probably aspects of a more generally developing set of skills and this is reflected in their apparent disagreement. However, the position is complicated by the work of Turnure (1975) who used a different set of measures and found that decentring increased with age regardless of whether a physical or social task was involved. However, there was a *simple* correspondence between performance on social role taking and on Piagetian tasks—a finding that Turnure put down to methodological differences in previous studies. We are inclined to agree that the methodological differences are important but disagree that their only importance is at the methodological level. We conclude, with Borke, that the issue is not 'egocentrism versus empathy', nor even how empathy may be fostered, but the way in which a *variety* of skills are interrelated, and how individual differences in the ability come to develop.

Cognitive and psychological factors in interaction

There are other aspects of cognition that, according to our analysis, should relate to friendship (i.e. to actual social performance, rather than simply to social concepts), and indeed the relationship between friendship and cognition should be a two-way affair in that children can learn *from* social interaction as well as having concepts *about* it. One can see in the work of Rardin and Moan (1971) an important link in this context between this view and some of the previous points. These workers proposed that peer relations (as opposed to social concepts) developed in a manner parallel to the development of physical concepts and they found support for this idea. More exciting, however, was the reverse of this proposal, namely that a child's cognitive development could be directly affected by the quality of his peer interactions, as judged by popularity rankings. This proposal was supported in the case of development of social concepts but not in the case of physical ones. Rubin (1972) however, found that, whilst the ability to take another person's point of view may play a causal role in the attainment of popularity during early school years, factors other than egocentrism or decentring ability became relevant determinants of popularity later on (grades IV–VI: that is, 8–10 years old).

Whilst it does seem plausible that popularity and ability to take the role of the other should be related somehow, it is more interesting in our view to examine the *causal* links that exist between the two. It is plausible that the factors which people learn to notice are affected by the personal relationships that they establish at given points in childhood and that their ability to detect (and respond favourably to) personality similarity may be likewise determined. Since the derivation of such friendship expectations is comprehensively treated in Chapter 1 of this volume, we will simply observe the parallels between the kinds of expectations that children have of friends at given ages and the character of the interaction between them at that time. Indeed La Gaipa and Wood (1974) showed that a person's friendship behaviour was often deduced by subjects from knowledge about that person's personality traits. Equally, Duck (1977) has observed the ways in which personality characteristics (such as style of thought, cognitive complexity, chronic anxiety states) influence the choices of friends made by adults. Clearly an individual's expectations about friendship and about other people influence his/her friendship behaviour— the interesting question is whether they were *derived from* it during childhood.

Self-validation

Children appear to learn most about interaction from their peers (Hartup, 1978; and above). Play is a central area for the learning of the dynamics of interaction, in terms of role acquisition, and interpretation of social cues that affect ultimately the child's ability to conceptualize his/her social world (Rubin and Maioni, 1975). There are a number of reasons why this should be so that have been mentioned above (e.g. it necessitates the taking of others' perspectives and the integration of them into the individual's conceptual system). Questions remain, however, about what is truly being learned, what mediates the influence of such factors, and precisely how the conceptual changes that are taking place affect the child's relationships. Our argument has been that such conceptual changes have to be learned as *functional* in social relationships and the mere acquisition of the ability to use new conceptual structures cannot account for their retention, which can be explained only if the child discovers their value for him/her in social relationships. Thus, we have argued, an essential part of the causal impact that these changes have upon an individual is the fact that they need to be *tested* once acquired. They can be evaluated in two ways: either by finding others who use or share them and thus validate them consensually; or by discovering the extent to which they lead to more sophisticated ways of dealing with other people (a version, in fact, of the first point, since finding that others' behaviour can be explained by one's new concepts is a way of validating the concepts through the mediation of others).

Kohn (1966) has argued that young children do, to a considerable extent, create particular types of social environment by the type of behaviour that they manifest and that this is one way in which continuity of personality development may be maintained. This may be interpreted to mean that the child's personality and the nature of his/her relationships will be a result of both the choices of associates *available* to him/her (Gaebler, 1978) and the choices actually made. Clearly here is a complicated reciprocal relationship not well documented as yet (Kirchner and Vondracek, 1975).

One aspect of this development and validation of self-concept is self-esteem, since this will determine the child's relationship expectancies (whether s/he expects to be liked or disliked). Certainly this is true of adult relationships

(Walster and Walster, 1965) although whether this is true of children—and, if so, at what ages—remains to be demonstrated. An important finding by Kirchner and Vondracek (1975), supporting the hypothesis that early interaction with peers considerably affects the kind of interaction that occurs later, was that amongst very young children (3–6 years of age) the *major* source of self-esteem was from peers.

From the above discussion it appears that popularity can mediate self-esteem and vice versa. It certainly seems plausible on the basis of present evidence that many adult social characteristics may be the result of childhood experiences in interactions with peers.

LEARNING AND FRIENDSHIP

Amidst all the other forms of conceptual, perceptual, cognitive, behavioural and social development that are taking place in childhood, the child has to learn to apply these developments to social interaction and has to learn to see different forms of social relationship as distinct. This presumably involves notions about what 'friendship' means ('conceptual learning'), how it is performed or indicated to other people (both to those who are its object and to others who are not), and the nature of the relationship once it is established and maintained ('behavioural learning'). It has also become clear that much learning takes place as a *result* of friendship ('learning consequent on friendship'). It is not, indeed, as obvious as it may seem at first sight that the development of all these things should be temporally coincident. It is an empirical question whether the onset of a particular way of looking at other people is necessarily or immediately translated into a behavioural pattern that reflects the new cognition—or indeed whether children should immediately appreciate (or predicate behavioural change on) new conceptual abilities. Thus the discussion that follows does *not* presume that these three forms of learning (conceptual, behavioural and consequent learning) are closely or clearly related in any obvious way. Much research will need to be done before the precise interrelationships between the three become clarified.

Learning about 'friendship' as a concept

A large amount of work by La Gaipa and his associates (see Chapter 1) has been concerned both directly and indirectly with the way in which children's concepts about friendship develop. Particularly, La Gaipa and Bigelow (1972), Bigelow and La Gaipa (1975) and Bigelow (1977) have examined the ways in which friendship expectations develop with age. The findings suggest three stages of friendship expectancy development: the *situational* stage (where expectations concern 'common activities', 'propinquity' and 'evaluation'); the *contractual* stage (where expectations relate to normative 'character admiration'—for example, 'He doesn't get into trouble'); and the *internal-psychological* stage (involving acceptance, loyalty, commitment, genuineness, intimacy potential and common interest expectations). These findings, although they concern friendship expectancies rather than the factors that predispose individuals to find another person attractive, bear an obvious similarity of style to the proposals we have made here concerning the communicative nature and stages of acquaintance. Also worth noting is the fact that other versions of this sequence (Selman and Jaquette, 1977) deal with friendship awareness in a way that almost exactly parallels Levinger and Snoek's (1972) and Levinger's (1974) model of growth of attraction in adult relationships. Thus Selman and Jaquette note five stages of friendship awareness (0—momentary physical playmate; 1—one-way assistance; 2—fairweather co-operation; 3—intimate, mutual sharing; 4—autonomous interdependence). Levinger (1974) talks of four stages of relationship growth (0—Zero contact; 1—unilateral awareness; 2—bilateral surface contact; 3—mutuality: this stage is actually a continuum). This once again emphasizes our point about parallels between children's relationship growth (with age) and adults' relationship growth (over a shorter period of time).

Also worth noting is the possibility that those who fail to learn such friendship expectancies and also those who fail to learn the (possibly independent) skills of performing behaviour relevant to them, could be rejected by others and may then suffer deleterious effects on their self-esteem and subsequent adult relationships. In consideration of children who may be said to lack an appreciation of the value of stability in social relationships (Miell, 1978), it is unlikely that they would be chosen as friends by others who possess a stability concept. If one child is alone 'unstable' among his/her classmates, each of whom has a large number of others who meet the stability criterion for friendship s/he is likely to be unpopular (under-chosen). While s/he remains unpopular, his/her chances for the development of a stability concept may be greatly minimized as, indeed, may his/her opportunities for other aspects of development.

Learning to be friends

Whilst the evidence suggests that the learning of friendship expectancies is sequentially invariant on the whole, and something that occurs in many different populations, the evidence on the learning of the 'mechanics' of relationship maintenance is something that is less well documented. This is rather surprising in view of the fact that the adequate maintenance of relationships (rather than initial attraction to someone else) is the primary determinant of satisfaction with them. In adults, many relationships that seem promising actually collapse for various reasons evidently associated with lack of personality support (Duck and Allison, 1978) and these collapses and failures lead to feelings of loneliness, despair and social worthlessness (Peplau and

Perlman, 1977). In the absence of evidence one way or the other, it seems plausible to propose that some of the collapses of relationships that occur are due to complex incompatibilities of the partners (as suggested by Duck and Allison, 1978) but that the largest percentage of those that recurrently involve the same individual may be directly attributable to that person's failures to learn, as a child, how to be friends.

From the evidence given above, it seems that children who lack the social/ cognitive developmental level of their age peers, or who fail to acquire the age-appropriate concepts of friendship and social relationships will be socially disadvantaged, since their cognitive deficiences will lead to less adequate social opportunities for interaction with other children. La Gaipa and Wood (1973) presented evidence to show that unpopular children who were socially withdrawn differed from the normal children in the concepts that they had about friendship and they appeared to be behind in social development as a result of decreased contacts consequent on the lack of usual friendship expectancies. La Gaipa and Irwin (1976) showed similar results with disturbed adolescent girls and suggest that this perception of self by these individuals tended to create differences in the reciprocal role relationships that develop in normal intense female adolescent friendships. It was suggested by these authors that disturbed adolescents tended to be rejected as friends by others because they were more prone to violate confidences or over-expose the friendship—that is, they had not developed an awareness of the normative frameworks within which friendships operate successfully.

Learning from friendship

If cognitive/social development leads to increased opportunities for social encounter and to popularity, then those who enjoy advanced development should also enjoy more opportunities to learn about others, about friendship, about social relationships and about others' personality structure. They should thus not only gain more frequent opportunities to engender deep relationships but should also learn more about the nature of personal relationships as a result of their experiences and opportunity. Waldrop and Halverson (1975), indeed, noted that there are age-related differences and comparabilities in the preferred pattern of play in children from 2 years 6 months old to 7 years 6 months old. Children who were socially capable at 2 years 6 months were more likely to be sociable at 7 years 6 months. However, highly social boys tended to have *extensive* peer relations (i.e. they played with groups of others) whilst highly social girls tended to have *intensive* peer relations (i.e. they usually played with one or two other specific girls).

Furthermore, Hartup (1978) reports several other studies indicating the various social competencies which are acquired through friendship and peer interactions (e.g. sociability, as opposed to social withdrawal; mastering of aggressive impulses; sexual socialization) and also indicates a relationship between poor social interaction and subsequent social conduct (e.g. low peer acceptance correlates with delinquency and with likelihood of receiving 'bad conduct' discharges from the Services).

It is not entirely inconceivable, but not yet empirically supportable, that many inadequacies that are reflected in other ways (e.g. alcoholism, neurosis) are derived from an inadequate 'friendship style' (Duck, 1977). Whilst the causal links are not clearly established, nor the direction of causality plainly clarified, some evidence is provided by La Gaipa (1977) to show that such 'abnormal' populations do have characteristically odd views of the nature of friendship, such as may be derived in childhood.

IMPLICATIONS AND CONCLUSIONS

The above analysis provides a framework for reviewing the motivational forces at work in children's acquainting in terms of the need to obtain validational support for personality at progressively more 'adult' levels. Such a framework helps explain *how* children develop social concepts and *why* the initial uncertainty of them, when newly acquired, provokes the individual to use them and test them out in social relationships. It is also clear that considerable future analytic effort should be brought to bear on the constraints imposed by the process of *cognitive* (as opposed to social) development: that is, the extent to which children's acquainting is limited at given ages by the type of communication of which they are capable when it comes to describing other people (particularly children's learned capabilities in using personality descriptions or assessing other people's personalities from their behaviour).

Two things are notable, given this background: first, that the different skills that children need to acquire in order to become fully functioning members of society are very much left for them to pick up as best they may; second, that, given the complexity of the factors that have been identified in our analysis, the present state of knowledge makes it imprudent to draw conclusions that are not predicated on a call for an increase of research effort into the issues. In our view it would be both foolish and dangerous to extrapolate too freely from the present analysis without considerable cross examination and investigation of it. For example, it appears to cast up the simple suggestion that more educational effort should be directed towards the inculcation of certain sociable skills. This, however, is a suggestion that must be based first on a firmer empirical rock than we have been able to expose; and, second, has far-reaching implications for the nature of education and the role of the psychological researcher in society. Is it indeed the purpose of psychological research in this area to make recommendations for the restructuring of the educational system? What importance is the development of sociable abilities to be given in education? These are large primary questions that must be answered before it becomes plausible to begin the practical work of defining goals, establishing criteria and beginning to train the necessary abilities. Given, then, that we recognize clearly the risks of oversimplification of the issues, we offer the following speculative proposals on the basis of our above analysis.

As is clear from the above, whilst communication about friendship and the nature of social relationships would seem to be ultimately more important in children's development than are the factors relating to popularity, it is actually the latter that give children the best opportunities of interacting with others in a way that permits the greatest learning about social relationships. Whilst research workers have often considered the ways in which cognitive development and growth leads a child to develop social awareness, less work—and less unambiguous work—has been done on the implications that this has for social interaction. Yet it is possible that cognitive development may affect social interaction in ways that set a pattern for adult social relationships and this is a possibility with important educational implications. Particularly, it suggests that educators should, perhaps, devote more attention to the social patterns in the classroom and the ways in which these relate to educational achievement. Smither (1977) has also pointed out that the child's development of an ability to express emotion in ways that facilitate understanding by others will affect his opportunities for educationally helpful interaction with them. We hope also to have shown some of the implications of friendship for learning about (and development of) personality constructs—such that popular children or those with a network of friendships are presented with greater opportunities for learning in various spheres of social life.

We would therefore speculate that educators should attend closely to the social patterns that exist within the classroom and that researchers should examine the predicted relationships between social interactions and educational achievement. We suggest that Seagoe (1933), Austin and Thompson (1948), and others, may have made the wrong interpretation of the direction of causality in the observed correlation between friendship and similarity of educational achievement: we argue that childhood friendship may cause similarity of achievement and not vice versa.

However, whilst these educational speculations may be of some interest, we, as social psychologists, are naturally interested more in the implications of our analysis for personal growth and the acquisition of sociability. Unfortunately, it is here that the risk of oversimplified deduction from our analysis is greatest. For example, it would be easy to suggest that the skills of relating need to be more openly discussed and deliberately transmitted during childhood and adolescence to ensure that faulty relational skills are identified and modified in their formative years. However, we have traced out above not only the immense intricacy of some of these 'skills' themselves but also the complex relationship of sociability and cognitive growth, the intertwining of sociable concepts and sociable activity, the influence of peers and of adults, the nature of conceptual development about other people, and the problems of making relationships *work*. We would therefore be loath at this stage to do more than point to such avenues of further enquiry. In this context we feel it may be productive to note the parallels between childhood ontogenesis and the route that is followed in forming relationships between adults. We have therefore stressed this parallelism throughout the chapter.

We have also discussed the ways in which personality growth and self-esteem level may be influenced by childhood social experiences. In this respect we would predict interactive effects of teachers and peers on the reputations and labels that children acquire. Self-attribution and other theorists may wish to argue that once a child is labelled in a given way by a teacher in class (e.g. 'That was stupid'), his/her peers may begin to respond to him/her as if the label were the reification of a trait (e.g. 'He is a stupid person') and, in time, s/he may come to perceive him/herself as being preemptively that kind of person (e.g. 'I am nothing but a stupid person'). The point is not that the teacher gives out the label but that the peers pick it up, possibly because they already have some affective response to the other child which the label serves to reinforce. It is plausible that opinions of peers about a given individual may shape and influence their responses to him/her and hence may affect the individual's direction of personality growth.

These speculations are derived from the view that peer interaction and friendship is based on, and in turn comes to serve the function of, self-validation. It is, in our view, of major importance for both theoretical work and social policy that all aspects of childhood friendship be seen as *functionally* related to personality development and individual growth—and it is for future research to give this important possibility the exploration it deserves.

REFERENCES

Allgeier, A. R., and Byrne, D. (1973). Attraction towards the opposite sex as a determinant of physical proximity. *Journal of Social Psychology*, **90**, 213–220.

Argyle, M., and Dean, J. (1965). Eye-contact, distance and affiliation. *Sociometry*, **28**, 289–304.

Austin, M. C., and Thompson, G. G. (1948). Children's friendships: a study of the bases on which children select and reject their best friends. *Journal of Educational Psychology*, **39**, 101–116.

Barrett, D. E., and Yarrow, M. R. (1977). Prosocial behavior, social inferential ability and assertiveness in children. *Child Development*, **48**, 475–481.

Berscheid, E., and Walster, E. H. (1974). Physical attractiveness. In L. Berkowitz (Ed.), *Advances in Experimental Social Psychology*. Vol. 7. New York: Academic Press.

Bigelow, B. J. (1977). Children's friendship expectations: a cognitive-developmental study. *Child Development*, **48**, 246–253.

Bigelow, B. J., and La Gaipa, J. J. (1975). Children's written descriptions of friendship: A multidimensional analysis. *Developmental Psychology*, **11**, 857–858.

Bonney, M. E. (1946). A sociometric study of the relationship of some factors to mutual friendships on the elementary, secondary and college levels. *Sociometry*, **9**, 21–47.

Borke, H. (1971). Interpersonal perception of young children: egocentrism or empathy? *Developmental Psychology*, **5**, 263–269.

Borke, H. (1972). Chandler and Greenspan's 'ersatz egocentrism': a rejoinder. *Developmental Psychology*, **7**, 107–109.

Bugenthal, D. E., Kaswan, J. W., and Love, L. R. (1970). Perception of contradictory meanings conveyed by verbal and nonverbal channels. *Journal of Personality and Social Psychology*, **16**, 647–655.

Busk, P. L., Ford, R. C., and Schulman, J. L. (1973). Stability of sociometric responses in classrooms. *Journal of Genetic Psychology*, **123**, 69–84.

Byrne, D. (1961). The influence of propinquity and opportunity for interaction on classroom relationships. *Human Relations*, **14**, 63–69.

Byrne, D. (1971). *The Attraction Paradigm*. New York: Academic Press.

Byrne, D., and Clore, G. L. (1967). Effectance arousal and attraction. *Journal of Personality and Social Psychology*, **6**, 1–18.

Byrne, D., Clore, G. L., and Worchel, P. (1966). Effect of economic similarity-dissimilarity on interpersonal attraction. *Journal of Personality and Social Psychology*, **4**, 220–224.

Byrne, D., and Griffitt, W. (1966). A developmental investigation of the law of attraction. *Journal of Personality and Social Psychology*, **4**, 699–702.

Byrne, D., McDonald, R. D., and Mikawa, J. (1963). Approach and avoidance affiliation motives. *Journal of Personality*, **31**, 21–37.

Campbell, J. D., and Yarrow, M. R. (1961). Perceptual and behavioural correlates of social effectiveness. *Sociometry*, **24**, 1–20.

Chandler, M. J., and Greenspan, S. (1972). Ersatz egocentrism: a reply to H. Borke. *Developmental Psychology*, **7**, 104–106.

Clore, G. L. (1977). Reinforcement and affect in attraction. In S. W. Duck (Ed.), *Theory and Practice in Interpersonal Attraction*. London: Academic Press.

Dion, K. K. (1973). Young children's stereotyping of facial attractiveness. *Developmental Psychology*, **9**, 183–188.

Dion, K. K. (1974). Children's physical attractiveness and sex as determinants of adult punitiveness. *Developmental Psychology*, **10**, 772–778.

Dion, K. K., and Berscheid, E. (1974). Physical attractiveness and peer perception among children. *Sociometry*, **37**, 1–12.

Dion, K. K., Berscheid, E., and Walster, E. H. (1972). What is beautiful is good. *Journal of Personality and Social Psychology*, **24**, 285–290.

Duck, S. W. (1973). *Personal Relationships and Personal Constructs: A Study of Friendship Formation*. London: Wiley.

Duck, S. W. (1975). Personality similarity and friendship choices by adolescents. *European Journal of Social Psychology*, **5**, 70–83.

Duck, S. W. (1976). Interpersonal communication in developing acquaintance. In G. Miller (Ed.), *Explorations in Interpersonal Communication*. New York: Sage.

Duck, S. W. (1977). *The Study of Acquaintance*. London: Teakfield, Saxon House.

Duck, S. W., and Allison, D. (1978). I liked you but I cannot live with you. *Social Behavior and Personality*, **6**, 43–47.

Duck, S. W., and Craig, R. G. (1975). Effects of type of information upon interpersonal attraction. *Social Behavior and Personality*, **3**, 157–164.

Duck, S. W., and Craig, R. G. (1977). The relative attractiveness of different types of information about another person. *British Journal of Social and Clinical Psychology*, **16**, 229–233.

Duck, S. W., and Gaebler, H. C. (1976). Physical attractiveness and ratings of popularity by children and teachers. *IRCS: Research on Psychology and Psychiatry*, **4**, 143.

Dymond, R. F., Hughe, A. S., and Raabe, V. L. (1952). Measurable changes in empathy with age. *Journal of Consulting Psychology*, **16**, 202–206.

Feffer, M. H., and Gourevitch, V. (1960). Cognitive aspects of role-taking in children. *Journal of Personality*, **28**, 383–396.

Festinger, L. (1954). A theory of social comparison processes. *Human Relations*, **7**, 117–140.

Festinger, L., Schachter, S., and Back, K. (1950). *Social Pressure in Informal Groups*. New York: Harper.

Gaebler, H. C. (1978). Liking and disliking in young children of different ages. Unpublished manuscript, University of Lancaster.

Green, E. H. (1933). Friendship and quarrels among pre-school children. *Child Development*, **4**, 237–252.

Hartup, W. W. (1978). Children and their friends. In H. McGurk, (Ed.), *Issues in Childhood Social Development*. London: Methuen.

Kelly, G. A. (1955). *The Psychology of Personal Constructs*. New York: Norton.

Kelvin, R. P. (1977). Predictability, power and vulnerability in interpersonal attraction. In S. W. Duck (Ed.), *Theory and Practice in Interpersonal Attraction*. London: Academic Press.

Kirchner, E. P., and Vondracek, S. I. (1975). Perceived sources of esteem in early childhood. *Journal of Genetic Psychology*, **126**, 169–176.

Kohn, M. (1966). The child as a determinant of his peers' approach to him. *Journal of Genetic Psychology*, **109**, 91–100.

La Gaipa, J. J. (1977). Testing a multidimensional approach to friendship. In S. W. Duck (Ed.), *Theory and Practice in Interpersonal Attraction*. London: Academic Press.

La Gaipa, J. J., and Bigelow, B. (1972). The development of friendship expectations. Paper presented at the meeting of the Canadian Psychological Association, Montreal, July.

La Gaipa, J. J., and Irwin, K. (1976). The administration of the children's friendship expectancy inventory to emotionally disturbed adolescent females. Unpublished manuscript, Windsor, Ontario, Canada.

La Gaipa, J. J., and Wood, H. D. (1973). The perception of friendship by socially accepted and rejected children. Paper delivered to the Eastern Psychological Association, Washington, DC.

La Gaipa, J. J., and Wood, H. D. (1974). An approach to the study of friendship in terms of implicit personality theory. Paper read to Canadian Psychological Association, Windsor, Ontario.

Lerner, M. J., and Reavy, P. (1975). Locus of control, perceived responsibility for prior fate and helping behavior. *Journal of Research in Personality*, **9**, 1–21.

Levinger, G. (1974). A three-level approach to attraction: toward an understanding of pair-relatedness. In T. L. Huston (Ed.), *Foundations of Interpersonal Attraction*. New York: Academic Press.

Levinger, G., and Snoek, D. (1972). *Attraction in Relationship: A New Look at Interpersonal Attraction*. Morristown, New Jersey: General Learning Press.

Levy, P. (1977). Methodological versus substantive issues in psychology: a meaningless distinction? Unpublished Manuscript, University of Lancaster.

Livesley, W., and Bromley, D. (1973). *Person Perception in Childhood and Adolescence*. London: Wiley.

Long, G. T., and Lerner, M. J. (1974). Deserving, the 'personal contract' and altruistic behavior in children. *Journal of Personality and Social Psychology*, **29**, 551–556.

Mehrabian, A., and Ksionzky, S. (1974). *A Theory of Affiliation*. Lexington, Massachusetts: Lexington Books.

Miell, D. K. (1978). Stability in children's friendship choice: a developmental study. Unpublished manuscript, University of Lancaster.

Miell, D. K., and Duck, S. W. (in preparation). Stability of choice in young children's friendship preferences: the case of short test-retest intervals.

Mouton, J. S., Blake, R. R., and Fruchter, B. (1955). The reliability of sociometric measures. *Sociometry*, **18**, 7–48.

Northway, M. L. (1968). Stability of young children's social relations. *Educational Research*, **11**, 54–58.

Peevers, B. H., and Secord, P. F. (1973). Developmental change in attribution of descriptive concepts to persons. *Journal of Personality and Social Psychology*, **27**, 120–128.

Peplau, L. A., and Perlman, D. (1977). Blueprint for a social psychological theory of loneliness. Paper presented at the British Psychological Society, Welsh Branch, International Conference on Love and Attraction, Swansea.

Perrin, F. A. C. (1921). Physical attractiveness and repulsiveness. *Journal of Experimental Psychology*, **4**, 203–217.

Piaget, J. (1959). *The Language and Thought of the Child*. London: Routledge and Kegan Paul.

Piaget, J. (1962). *Play, Dreams and Imitation in Childhood*. London: Routledge and Kegan Paul.

Potashin, R. (1946). Sociometric study of children's friendship. *Sociometry*, **9**, 48–70.

Rardin, D. R., and Moan, C. E. (1971). Peer interaction and cognitive development. *Child Development*, **42**, 1685–1699.

Rubin, K. H. (1972). Relationship between egocentric communication and popularity among peers. *Developmental Psychology*, **7**, 364.

Rubin, K. H., and Maioni, T. L. (1975). Play preference and its relationship to egocentrism, popularity and classification skills in preschoolers. *Merrill–Palmer Quarterly*, **21**, 171–179.

Seagoe, M. V. (1933). Factors influencing selection of associates. *Journal of Educational Research*, **27**, 32–40.

Selman, R. L., and Jaquette, D. (1977). Stability and oscillation in interpersonal awareness: a clinical-developmental analysis. In C. B. Keasey, (Ed.), *The Nebraska Symposium on Motivation*. Vol. 25. Lincoln: University of Nebraska Press.

Shaver, K. G. (1975). *An Introduction to Attribution Processes*. Cambridge, Massachusetts: Winthrop.

Smither, S. (1977). A reconsideration of the developmental study of empathy. *Human Development*, **20**, 253–276.

Turnure, C. (1975). Cognitive development and role-taking ability in boys and girls. *Developmental Psychology*, **11**, 207–209.

Waldrop, M. F., and Halverson, C. F. (1975). Intensive and extensive peer behavior: longitudinal and cross-sectional analyses. *Child Development*, **46**, 19–26.

Walster, E., and Walster, G. W. (1965). The effect of expecting to be liked on choice of associates. *Journal of Abnormal and Social Psychology*, **67**, 402–404.

White, R. W. (1959). Motivation reconsidered: the concept of competence. *Psychological Review*, **66**, 297–333.

Wiener, M., Devoe, S., Rubinow, S., and Geller, J. (1972). Nonverbal behavior and nonverbal communication. *Psychological Review*, **79**, 185–214.

Willerman, B., and Swanson, L. (1952). An ecological determinant of differential amounts of sociometric choices within college sororities. *Sociometry*, **15**, 326–329.

Williams, J. E., Bennett, S. M., and Best, D. L. (1975). Awareness and expression of sex stereotypes in young children. *Developmental Psychology*, **11**, 635–642.

CHAPTER 5

Interracial Acceptance in the Classroom

DONALD E. CARTER,
SUSAN
L. DETINE-CARTER
and
FORREST W. BENSON

Concern regarding interracial understanding and acceptance has become prominent over the past two decades in the United States as the state-financed schools attempt to provide truly integrated education. Similarly, with the influx of immigrants, British schools are beginning to encounter the problems of multi-racial education.

This chapter treats interracial friendship as an extension of same-race interaction. Discussion about the development of racial awareness and preferences of the young child to the more sophisticated racial attitudes of the adolescent is based on attraction theory superimposed on cognitive stages of social development. First, a brief overview of attraction theory is presented, then a description of the variables associated with attraction and acceptance is presented, which shows the influence of level of cognitive development on the child during the preschool and early school years (between 3 and 8 years old) and the middle school years (between 8 and 14 years old). Finally, research findings are integrated with practical methods of promoting interracial peer acceptance in the classroom.

COGNITIVE ASPECTS OF SOCIAL DEVELOPMENT

This section applies Levinger's (1974) levels of pair relatedness to interracial contact in the classroom and the general development of racial attitudes. Levinger's theory of social relationships contains three levels of interaction.

Level 1. Unilateral awareness

There is no interaction between persons; however, there is momentary impression formation by the observer, as observing a passerby. The majority of person perception, ethnic stereotypes and attraction research has been devoted to this level of interpersonal behaviour (Brigham, 1971; Griffitt, 1974). Unilateral awareness provides the child with the foundation for race awareness and, thereafter, it is influenced by the salience of race to the child.

Level 2. Surface contact

Interaction between persons is transitory, as at a first meeting, and with persons frequently encountered but only casually addressed (e.g. greeting a neighbour on the way to work). Some surface relations go beyond this point but stay within social roles and transmit little unique information about the individuals involved. 'Surface encounter is useful for learning whether the other is a person whom one would like to get to know better, to share more with, or to build a mutual relationship with' (Levinger, 1974, p. 104). This would appear to be the level of most contact between peers and teacher–child in a structured classroom. The child takes on the externally structured role of student. Responsiveness at this level of contact would be the lowest level or origin of interracial acceptance. Working on a class project together would indicate interracial acceptance, but could be interaction at only this surface level.

Level 3. Mutuality

This level is perceived as a continuum from minor intersection (friendly interaction) between the pair to major intersection (love relationship). Self-disclosure, trust, and empathy are aspects of these relationships. Behaviour coordination and emotional investment are involved here, as each learns to accept and accommodate the other's attitudes and behaviours. At the upper limits of this level, 'I' and 'you' become 'we'. Shared awareness is also important. 'At level 3, two persons not only know much about one another, but each one further knows what he knows about him. Still further, each knows that the other knows that he knows it; and so on' (Levinger, 1974, p. 106). Thus, each partner 'assumes responsibility for the other's feelings and outcomes in the relationship' (Lickona, 1974, p. 47). It is at this level of interracial peer acceptance that friendships are formed and personal ideas are interchanged regarding the various academic and social aspects of the environment. To some extent these friendship pairs will vary depending on the task involved (e.g. academic, social, physical). For a child to be able to succeed academically, a mutual bond is often beneficial. However, even these situations could remain at the surface level.

In addition to the three levels of interpersonal interaction, Levinger (1974) postulates a zero point, where no contact exists. Some aspects of ethnic stereotypes are based at this point, since the person has no contact with the ethnic group but is aware of its existence through others' descriptions. This zero point is also significant in the development of racial awareness, as the colour concepts of black and white take an affective meaning prior to their cognitive application to racial groups (Stabler, Johnson, Berke and Baker, 1969).

According to Piaget (1950) there is parallel development of social and cognitive structure. Support for this contention is provided by Goldschmid (1968) for popularity, Rardin and Moan (1971) for social skills and peer relations, and Davidson (1976) for prejudice and tolerant ethnic attitudes (related to Kohlberg's moral development stages, which is an extension of Piaget's theory). Blatt's study (unpublished, cited in Kohlberg, 1969) also establishes the relationships between conceptual development of friendship and moral stages of development, which also parallel cognitive stages of development, while Bigelow (1977) relates friendship expectations to Kohlberg's cognitive developmental stages. This relationship between cognitive and social development is assumed to influence the interracial behaviour of children.

RACIAL AWARENESS AND IDENTIFICATION OF 3- TO 8-YEAR-OLDS

Since Lasker's (1929) study, researchers have been concerned with the development of racial attitudes or prejudices in children. Numerous studies have dealt with the topics of: racial awareness, racial identification, racial preferences, and interracial acceptance or rejection among young children. The findings in these areas will be summarized with the major focus on the more recent research, since reviews of the literature are available (Brand, Ruiz and Padilla, 1974; Goodman, 1964; Jones, 1972; Porter, 1971).

Numerous definitions are found for the terms associated with this area. We have chosen the following as most appropriate. 'Racial awareness' is defined as 'knowledge of both the visible differences between racial categories and the perceptual cues by which one classifies people into these divisions' (Porter, 1971, p. 22). 'Racial identification' is defined as the ability and willingness to classify one's self as a member of a particular racial group. 'Racial preference' refers to the predilection of one racial group over another with no indication of rejection of the latter. The term 'interracial acceptance' will be reserved for the situation in which an individual perceives an other-race group member as equally able to fulfil his needs in a given situation. The opposite pole is rejection, while tolerance is at the lowest limit of acceptance. Although few researchers have operationally defined these terms, preferring to use such terms as 'racial attitudes' and 'prejudice', the significance of these distinctions is apparent. The young child between the ages of 3 and 6 years, approximately speaking, is cognitively incapable of the concrete operations necessary to formalize such attitudes or prejudices. Therefore such terminologies are unnecessary and even absurd.

The majority of studies of racial awareness prior to 1970 have used the doll techniques originated by Clark and Clark (1939, 1947). The Clarks presented each black subject with two brown baby dolls with dark hair and two white dolls with yellow hair, all sexless and identical except for skin and hair colour. The 3- to 7-year-old subjects were asked to respond to each of seven questions by choosing one doll.

Other methods employed to measure racial awareness are: photographs (Fox and Jordan, 1973; Morland, 1958, 1966; Ohsako, 1973), family groups (Goodman, 1952; Porter, 1971; Simon, 1974) and various modifications of the doll technique controlling for skin colour (Greenwald and Oppenheim, 1968; Simon, 1974), hair colour (Hraba and Grant, 1970) and doll's sex (Porter, 1971).

The majority of studies dealing with racial awareness have two major flaws. No validity or reliability data are offered and most researchers interpret their data in terms of racial awareness rather than simply knowledge of 'colour'. With the exception of two studies using a third doll (i.e. Greenwald and Oppenheim, 1968; Simon, 1974), the forced choice situation consists of two possible responses, white or brown. The white question usually appears first; therefore, if the child has any conceptualization of the colour 'white' he will choose correctly. It is, then, only a process of elimination to choose the 'coloured' doll as the 'not-white' choice. It is apparent that the questions proposed to detect racial knowledge or awareness only distinguish children at various levels of colour knowledge. The amount of inaccuracy among whites and blacks in choosing the 'negro' doll verifies this fact.

When the number of questions used to evaluate racial awareness is increased, the degree of awareness decreases sharply, even among 5-year-olds (Morland, 1958; Porter, 1971). In a comparison study of six measures of racial awareness with a sample of 85 black and white 3- to 7-year-olds, Ballard and Keller (1976) conclude that the picture technique is the most reliable and valid, and tests involving the most stimuli are more reliable. New techniques and situations including various skin colour stimuli and racial classification tasks are therefore needed.

Conclusions concerning the racial awareness of the young child between 3 and 6 years of age from the available research are limited. However, the following trends appear:

(1) The three-year-old black or white child is aware of colour differences but not necessarily racial differences (Porter, 1971). This colour differentiation becomes more accurate with age (Johnson, 1977; and most doll studies indicate this), and the achromatic colours (black and white) are distinguished before secondary hues (Johnson, 1977).

(2) The young child tends to relate white with positive objects or adjectives and black with negative attributes or items (Stabler *et al.*, 1969).

(3) By the fourth year, colour becomes affectively laden even though the child lacks a highly developed understanding of race; this is acquired earlier for black children (Crooks, 1970; Goodman, 1952; Porter, 1971). Pure colour recognition takes a rapid spurt at 4 years of age (Morland, 1958, 1966).

(4) At 5 years of age the child becomes more conceptually sophisticated; s/he realizes that biological features are connected to social categories. Social evaluations of race and racial awareness appear to occur almost simultaneously.

(5) Contact in desegregated settings seems to increase racial awareness of children (Porter, 1971).

(6) Preschool children who appear to have negative other-race attitudes can become less 'prejudiced' through experimental treatment and/or reinforcement procedures (Best, Smith, Graves and Williams, 1975; Horton, 1973; Katz, 1973a, b; Parish, Fleetwood and Lentz, 1975; Serbin, Tonick and Sternglanz, 1977).

The research to date concerning racial identification has been extremely limited methodologically and frequently over-interpreted. The Clarks (1974) first observed that young blacks misidentified themselves using a forced choice doll technique with the question: 'Which doll looks like you?'. Sixty-six per cent of their 254 3- to 7-year-olds identified with the white doll. Other studies have replicated this technique or used a similar one, some including white samples, concluding that about 10–15 per cent of blacks misidentify (Datcher, Savage and Checkosky, 1973; Hraba and Grant, 1970) and to a greater extent than whites (Morland, 1958, 1966; Porter, 1971). However, these conclusions must be questioned in view of more recent studies, more sophisticated designs and the following general criticisms:

(1) The racial identity question is always presented last, after the preference questions, to prevent potential distortion of the data due to ego involvement (Clark and Clark, 1947). However, previous responses made to preference items may influence the results in the opposite direction; that is, black

children acquiring typical black–white connotations of bad–good highly instilled by society may then refuse to identify with a black doll which they have previously described negatively. Identification has almost unanimously been based on a single response.

(2) Only two studies controlled for racial awareness (Morland, 1958; Porter, 1971). Obviously, this factor must be included since low awareness subjects may be producing higher percentages of misidentification. Porter (1971) found that: (i) although colour knowledge is positively related to identi-fication, (ii) blacks with higher colour salience identify less accurately, indicating awareness alone does not account for misidentification; (iii) black and white children with high own-race choice on attitude questions identify most correctly; and (iv) all the black children with high own-race preference and high term knowledge classify themselves correctly. She concludes that correct self-identification measures not only knowledge of race or personal appearance, but positive attraction to racial membership for all children and group identity (feelings about own racial status) for many black children.

(3) The amount of misidentification among blacks is related to skin colour; that is, light-skinned blacks' misidentification is extensive (80 per cent in the Clark and Clark study). When a third doll (mullato) is introduced, black misidentification decreases to 25 per cent, and white misidentification increases, making them about equivalent (Greenwald and Oppenheim, 1968).

(4) Most samples have been drawn from preschool settings; in the older studies, the children were segregated. The current studies have indicated more blacks identifying with black stimuli, especially in an integrated setting, and even more importantly in settings where staff or contact-adults have stressed cooperation, cultural differences, and cultural pride (Crooks, 1970; Fox and Jordan, 1973; Horton, 1973; Kirn, 1973; Simon, 1974).

Considering the more current trend, the major conclusions to be drawn concerning racial identification among young children are:

(1) Identification increased with age for blacks and whites.
(2) Racial identification develops similarly to sexual identification, but girls tend to use sex for identification more than race (Adair and Savage, 1974).
(3) Preschool programmes emphasizing positive integrated contact are critical in the development of positive self-concept and racial identity especially among blacks (Crooks, 1970; Horton, 1973; Kirn, 1973).

Whether the 'Black Movement' or changes in research methodology is accounting for changes in racial identification is still undetermined, and further research is needed.

From the point of view of developmental theory, the preschool child can only function at Levinger's first two levels: awareness and surface contact. He is simply not cognitively ready for mutual relationships. Thus, interracial peer acceptance at this age is determined by the child's awareness of race differences and the salience of race in the determination of surface contact attraction. Given the high valence of sex identification, the process of centring could reduce the effect of race in preschool situations. Since the child has usually had little influence from outside the family, the expression of race awareness and stereotyping is primarily a function of imitation, modelling, and identification. However, the stereotyping could be considered unintentional, as the child reasons from the particular to the particular and is not logical.

RACIAL PREFERENCE AND ACCEPTANCE OF 3- TO 8-YEAR-OLDS

Studies of racial attitudes of children can be categorized into four basic designs: (1) verbalized attitudes; (2) preferences for photographs/line drawings; (3) doll choices; and (4) disguised or projective measures. A summary of conclusions for each category is presented.

Verbalized attitudes

Very few studies have analysed children's attitudes or verbal comments. The following conclusions emphasize that attitudes expressed are highly determined by the stimuli and technique employed.

(1) Many children will verbalize colour differences of stimuli presented (79 per cent of white children: Radke and Trager, 1950; Radke, Trager and Davis, 1949).
(2) Most comments made by black and white children are unrelated to colour or race (63–77 per cent: Porter, 1971).
(3) Use of race in interpreting stimuli is low; 12–13 per cent for whites and 0–2 per cent for blacks. When the child is made to acknowledge racial composition of the stimuli, other-race rejection increases considerably due to the leading technique used (for whites, 68 per cent; for blacks, 22 per cent: Radke and Trager, 1950; Radke et al., 1949).
(4) Unfavourable opposite-race comments are fairly low: 2 per cent for black children and 18 per cent for white children (Porter, 1971); or about 25 per cent for all children (Goodman, 1952). However, the high percentage for whites is highly contaminated by clean/dirty references to colour— 32 per cent (Porter, 1971); and review of comments of all children indicates that mimicry of adult models is taking place.
(5) Favourable opposite-race comments are few: 6 per cent for blacks and 9 per cent of whites (Porter, 1971); although own race preferences are

exhibited on positive items, no differences have been reported on negative items indicating that neither racial group exhibits greater anti-other-race feelings than anti-own-race feelings (Katz, Sohn and Zalk, 1975).

(6) Interpretations of research are difficult since the more vocal children are over-represented, many comments fall into two or more categories, percentages are confounded by other variables, and race of the experimenter influences results (Katz *et al.*, 1975).

Preference of photographs/line drawings

Two picture techniques have been used: group pictures and single stimulus persons or pairs. Results for the first technique show that all children prefer a white majority classroom or white stimuli (Koslin, Koslin, Cardwell and Pargament, 1969; Morland, 1958, 1966). However, older blacks decrease in this preference by 8 years of age (Morland, 1962) to a point of significant own-race preference (Koslin, Koslin *et al.*, 1969) or show no consistent pattern of preference (Koslin, Amarel and Ames, 1970). Preferences of white group stimuli may simply be due to familiarization; however, studies reporting type of contact experienced are inconsistent. Two studies interpret segregated whites as less accepting of blacks (Morland, 1962, 1966), while two others find no difference (Koslin, Koslin *et al.*, 1969; Koslin *et al.*, 1970). As previously mentioned, other factors may be influencing preferences (i.e. racial composition, sex).

Results using the second technique are:

(1) Colour cues are most distinctive, shade cues are secondary and facial cues the least distinctive for all children. However, significant differences occur for age, race and level of prejudice. Younger children (7– to 9-year-olds) attend to shade cues; they do not attend to facial features as do older children (12-year-olds). Blacks and high-prejudice children judge colour as more differentiating among pairs of stimuli, whereas low-prejudice children judge colour differences as less distinguishing among pairs (Katz *et al.*, 1975).

(2) Desegregation reduces white preference of blacks and whites (Koslin, Amarel and Ames, 1969) especially for older white children (7-year-olds), but change for blacks is less noticeable or little change is exhibited with age (Williams, Best and Boswell, 1975).

(3) Desegregation *per se* may not be as important as quality of contact since desegregated schools show opposite results (Williams *et al.*, 1975) and preferences vary in relation to anticipated interaction situations (Kiesler, 1971).

(4) Young children use other variables to determine preferences (Adair and Savage, 1974; Kircher and Furby, 1971). Girls use sex significantly more than boys as a determining factor (Adair and Savage, 1974).

(5) The stimulus-pair situation is a conflict situation for young white children asked to use labels such as good and bad (Cantor and Paternite, 1973) and more familiar pairs are more difficult to label (Cantor, 1972).

Doll choices

The number of studies dealing with racial preferences determined by doll choices (usually forced) is great and the resultant inconsistencies are confusing. Therefore, the older studies will be summarized and emphasis will be placed on more recent research with the fewest methodological problems.

By utilizing the three preference questions originated by Clark and Clark (1939) and by interpreting the findings of various authors, the following statements can be made regarding racial preferences of young black and white, segregated and desegregated, children between the ages of about 3 years old to 8 years old.

(1) White children prefer the white doll. The percentages vary from 48 per cent (Hraba and Grant, 1970) to 100 per cent (Crooks, 1970, control group only). However, a few recent studies indicate no real preference exists, white or black, especially for 3- and 4-year-olds (Katz and Zalk, 1974), when open-ended questions are used (Lerner and Buehrig, 1975), or for children raised with adopted other-race children (Simon, 1974).

(2) Many studies indicate that blacks prefer the white doll but less than whites; the percentages range from 30 per cent (Hraba and Grant, 1970) to 76 per cent (Asher and Allen, 1969). However, a few studies indicate that this preference decreases with age (Asher and Allen, 1969; Clark and Clark, 1947) and is stronger among boys (Asher and Allen, 1969).

(3) Whites' preference for the black doll (and mulatto doll in Greenwald and Oppenheim, 1968) is substantially less than their preference for the white doll: 16–49 per cent (Hraba and Grant, 1970). However, it appears to be greater for integrated whites (Datcher et al., 1973), or at least for males (Porter, 1971).

(4) Blacks' preference for the brown doll (or mulatto) varies from 12 per cent (Crooks, 1970, control group) to what many authors refer to as the 'majority' preferring black to as high as 82 per cent reported (Ward and Braun, 1972). Banks (1976) cites five studies indicating blacks' preference for black stimuli. It is related to high self-concept (Ward and Braun, 1972), increases in a positive integrated setting when positive attitudes prevail (Crooks, 1970) and increases when a black experimenter does the testing (Kirn, 1973). It is somewhat related to skin colour and socioeconomic status (Porter, 1971).

(5) The use of dolls is highly questionable for determining racial preferences of children, and therefore many factors should be controlled: racial awareness, hair colour, skin colour, sex of dolls and subjects, equal

attractiveness and familiarization of dolls, type of contact (desegregated, integrated, segregated) experienced by the children and situational open-ended questions used to determine preferences.

Disguised or projective measures

Disguised or projective techniques have been infrequently used in surveying racial bias or attitudes. These are presented from least disguised to most disguised.

A few studies have proposed that black and white children's use of perceptual cues are distinct. Katz (1973b) reported that 3– to 5-year-olds have more difficulty learning to differentiate faces of another race than their own. Black children learned more quickly to discriminate pairs of racial stimuli varying in shade; performance of younger children increased when reinforcement was given by an other-race adult; and all children learned more easily when the lighter shade face of the pair was reinforced, supporting previous research that a light preference exists among children. Two other studies revealed that white children (7 and 11 years of age) use facial cues more than colour cues of nonsense faces, and labelling of stimuli changes their judgement of similarity of cues; but black children use colour to distinguish faces, and labelling does not influence their judgements (Katz and Seavey, 1973). Training of children either to label or to differentiate perceptual cues results in a significant reduction of prejudice scores on a multiple choice projective test, especially on negative items and among older children (11-year-olds). It may be that training to individuate members of another race makes it difficult to retain negative attitudes (Katz, 1973b).

Banks and Rompf (1973) asked 6– to 8-year-olds to reward black and white players in a ball toss game for individual trials and then to name the overall winner, even though the two players performed equally well. Black and white subjects preferred the white player quantitatively (rewards), but were biased toward their own race qualitatively (winner) regardless of the race of the experimenter. Blacks may learn to over-reward the white player, but show racial pride by proclaiming the black player the winner. However, the positive stereotype of American society regarding the black athlete may be influencing the results.

As early as 2 years 6 months or 3 years of age the child acquires the knowledge of colours with achromatics recognized before most chromatics (Johnson, 1977). Investigators have found that even young children associate white with the positive and good, and black with the negative or bad, whether they are categorizing objects (Stabler et al., 1969) or adjectives (Williams and Roberson, 1967). Williams et al. (1975) report that pro-white bias increases until 7 years of age and then decreases for white children, but moderate pro-white bias remains fairly constant for black children to 9 years of age. Boswell and Williams

(1975) report a correlation of 0.40 between racial attitudes and colour meaning, which they interpret as a fear of the dark experience. However, Palmer (1973) found the opposite of colour prejudice for integrated 3- and 4-year-olds but not for 8- to 10-year-olds. Simon (1974) found that 3- to 8-year-old white children living in multi-ethnic families were less biased with regard to the connotative meanings of the colours black and white, than previously found by Williams and Roberson (1967). Only the adjectives 'clean' and 'dirty' retained high positive and negative valence, respectively.

Although there are some inconsistencies, it appears that the critical factors influencing racial preferences or bias are age of the children and amount of positive contact with other-race members. In dealing with the young child we must remember that 'an important component of what is identified as racial bias in preschool children may be learned, not in the context of race, but in the context of colour' (Boswell and Williams, 1975, p. 153).

Reviewers of racial preference have concluded that prevalence of blacks' preference for white stimuli has decreased since 1966 with a corresponding increase in preference for black stimuli (Butler, 1976). However, in a review of 25 studies of black children, Banks (1976) reinterprets the results as compared to deviations from chance selections. He concludes that 69 per cent of the studies show no preference; 25 per cent show black preference; 6 per cent show white preference and, therefore, the phenomenon of black preference for white stimuli has never been shown to exist.

Acceptance

Patterns of interracial acceptance at the preschool level have been conducted primarily through observation. Although some researchers have tried socio-metric choice on an individual basis (Orost, 1971), Gottman (1977) has found the relationship between sociometric choice and observed acceptance among 3- to 5-year-olds is zero, but the correlation between sociometric rejection and negative interaction is moderate ($r = 0.30$). Porter's (1971) results substantiate this, as she found no relationship between observed playmate choice and expressed attitudes on a doll choice measure among 5-year-olds, except for one group of white children who had rejected blacks on the attitude measure; they selected blacks most frequently as playmates. In general, observed black–white play patterns have shown no racial preferences, as interactions are observed at the chance level (Goodman, 1964; Porter, 1971).

Developmentally, the typical preschool child has not reached sufficient cognitive maturity to engage in mutual relationships. However, some kinder-garten children, and most children by 7 years of age, will have begun to engage in elementary mutual relationships. In terms of interracial implications, the primary school child (5–7 years old) should be aware of racial differences and be able to perceive individuals as members of a racial group and as having other characteristics at the same time. Thus, with differentiation, selection of friends becomes increasingly based on similarity of interests and activities.

ACCEPTANCE AND PREFERENCE OF 8- to 14-YEAR-OLDS

Research in interracial acceptance during the middle school years has produced varied and conflicting results (Carithers, 1970; St. John, 1975). Armor (1972) reviewed five busing for desegregation studies, primarily involving middle school children. He concluded 'The data suggest that, under the circumstances obtaining in these studies, integration heightens racial identity and consciousness, enhances ideologies that promote racial segregation, and reduces opportunities for actual contact between the races' (p. 102). Pettigrew, Useem, Normand and Smith (1973) criticized Armor's selection of studies and generalizations.

Other research indicates that acceptance is behaviour-related rather than race-related. Behaviour resulting from the frustration of non-achievement in the classroom reduces acceptance. Katz (1964) summarized studies comparing black and white achievement and ability for desegregated schools and found a definite discrepancy in scores favouring whites. Singer (1967) studied black and white children in grade V (10-year-olds) in segregated and desegregated schools. She found that desegregated whites see black peers as more aggressive and non-achieving. However, they were more willing to associate with blacks than segregated whites. As Glidewell, Kantor, Smith and Stringer (1966) point out, this aggressive classroom behaviour is probably the result of a child being less healthy, less intelligent, lacking in interpersonal skills, and from a lower class. This results in rejection by peers, further lowering of self-esteem, and frustration that leads to either hostile aggressive behaviour or withdrawal, leading to further rejection by others.

Additional evidence for this circular process theory is reported. Anderson's (1966) study showed that desegregated IV, V and VI 8- to 12-year-old blacks scored higher on an 'antisocial attitudes' scale than segregated blacks. Katz (1968) found that individuals try to obtain the achievement standards of their peers and this particularly relates to lower-class blacks who are usually low achievers. Ausabel and Ausabel (1963) concluded that lower class alienation results from frustration due to the inability to meet school standards. Pettigrew (1969) found ' ... the inability, typically black, to meet academic and social standards of the middle class white majority may directly initiate rejection by teachers and peers alike, leading to defensive responses' (p. 4). It appears that blacks want to be accepted and are frustrated by their inability to keep up with white peers, and this may stimulate antisocial behaviour.

Armor's (1972) discussion of the Ann Arbor study indicates that, although blacks lose their peer status when moved to an integrated school, their ratings are more positive toward their white peers, which agrees with Katz's (1968) assertion that white teachers and students have high prestige value for the blacks. In a comparison study between bused black students and non-bused white students over a 6-month period, Benson (1969) found no *significant* change in academic and social acceptance of black students. However, there was a tendency toward increased academic acceptance and blacks showed stronger other-race acceptance than same-race acceptance. Another investigation (Benson and Carter, 1971) of newly-integrated 9- to 13-year-old students, in two schools, showed that after 6 months blacks and whites preferred their own racial group for satisfaction of social needs and academic recognition. Although differences between means were significant, they were small. However, the younger children perceived both races as equivalent satisfiers of academic and social needs after 6 months and no change was evidenced in a 2-year follow-up. This result is quite different from the findings of Gerard, Jackson and Conolley (1975). They found limited change in the acceptance of Mexican Americans and blacks over a 6-year period of desegregation. Although there was some increase in peer acceptance for the minorities, the ratings were received from within the minority group itself. However, there are at least three important differences between these studies: (1) In the Benson and Carter (1971) study, the busing was voluntary; (2) Benson and Carter allowed the students to rate all their classmates, while Gerard *et al.* (1975) obtained only three choices; (3) the classroom composition was between one-quarter and one-third black in the Benson and Carter (1971) study, whereas Gerard *et al.* (1975) reported only about 20 per cent minority per classroom. In their conclusion, Gerard *et al.* (1975) suggest that one condition that must be satisfied if a child is to get along well in a setting of ethnic cleavage is: 'his subgroup must be large enough for him to find congenial associates' (p. 238).

In a 2-year study of sociometric acceptance of 5,000 elementary school students, Wrightstone, McClelland and Forlano (1966) found that, after the first year, blacks tended to select fewer blacks and more whites as first choice, indicating that acceptance generally improves with continued contact. Carter, DeTine, Spero and Benson (1975) studied acceptance of black and white children in grades VII and VIII (12- and 13-year-olds) in an integrated school after 1 or 2 years of integration. Blacks perceived whites as equally capable of satisfying their academic needs but preferred their own race for their social needs. Whites preferred their own race for satisfaction of both academic and social needs. However, the academic preference for whites by whites seems realistic since black students had consistently lower grade point averages than white students. The most important finding was that grade point average, rather than race, was the major determinant of social and academic acceptance by all groups except social acceptance by black males. This is consistent with the Glidewell *et al.* (1966) review of the relationship between intelligence and social acceptance and academic achievement and social acceptance; and Buswell's (1951) causality hypothesis, namely, that achievement determines classroom status.

Sex was also found to be a more prominent determinant than race in acceptance by white and black females (Carter *et al.*, 1975). These findings are substantiated by St. John and Lewis (1975) who found sex is 'a much more important source of cleavage than is race' (p. 351), and grade point average is a 'consistently important factor in peer-group popularity' (p. 352) among grade VI students. DeTine (1975) also found that the academic and social acceptance of 9- and 10-year-old students was best predicted by grade point average and achievement scores, as they appeared as major predictor variables in five of six regression equations. However, their acceptance was much less predictable than the older students' acceptance. Carter *et al.* (1975) were able to explain 20–50 per cent of the academic acceptance variance, while DeTine (1975) found that the same variables accounted for only 14–34 per cent of the academic acceptance variance for 9- and 10-year-olds. Social acceptance was less predictable in both studies.

One experimental study indicates that contact does not necessarily lead to acceptance; it is interaction with common goals that promotes interracial acceptance. DeVries and Edwards (1972) compared a traditional grade VII (12-year-olds) mathematics class without teams or games to three experimental groups: one with games but no teams, one with teams but no games, and one with teams and games. A sociometric measure was used after 20 treatment days. Their results indicate that teams do reduce race and sex barriers to student interaction, consistent with previous studies (Mann, 1959; Witte, 1972). Individual success produced team success, therefore, it was to the advantage of all to help and be helped by others.

Developmentally, thinking about social situations becomes more complex during the middle school years. It would seem that stereotyping occurs because the child is unable to differentiate other persons from the environment (centring). With decentration, the child can differentiate between persons and stereotyping and prejudice should be reduced (8-year-olds). This is somewhat supported by Davidson (1976), as she found smaller frequencies of negative ethnic comments in 10- to 13-year-old children than in 7-year-olds. However, with increased cognitive capacity, positive racial contact during this period is critical to prevent the cognitive process of over-generalization toward racial groups or stereotyping. 'With co-consciousness and mutual role-taking, typically well developed by the age of 10–11, attraction-in-relationship should be significantly more dependent upon shared attitudes than it would be before the development of reciprocal consciousness' (Lickona, 1974, p. 43). Thus, interracial friendship, like any other, will be based on areas of common interest and concern.

TRENDS IN INTERRACIAL ACCEPTANCE

In spite of conflicting results, studies of interracial peer acceptance and pre-ferences yield some general trends.

(1) Almost all studies support the conclusion that whites prefer whites, and most early studies found that blacks also prefer whites. Although there is some current support for blacks' preference for whites (Gerard, 1969; Wolf and Simon, 1975), Carithers' (1970) review suggests that this may be changing. Two supportive studies report equal ratings given to both groups by blacks (Benson and Carter, 1971; Carter et al., 1975). St. John and Lewis (1975) found that black boys and white boys and girls receive the same friendship ratings from each racial group, while black grade VI 11-year-old girls receive higher own-race acceptance.

(2) There is little agreement about the effects of interracial contacts on attitude change, for, as Carithers (1970) states, 'Most attitudinal research...has erred in being too simplistic and atheoretical' (p. 40). However, most researchers agree that the earlier the contact the better, and that frequency of contact is not as important as type of contact to stimulate interracial acceptance.

(3) Academic acceptance is greater than social acceptance in schools (Benson and Carter, 1971) and not necessarily race-related but achievement-related at least for white acceptance of blacks (Carter et al., 1975; DeTine, 1975). Gerard et al. (1975) would disagree, however.

(4) Social acceptance is also achievement-related (St. John and Lewis, 1975) but to a lesser extent than academic acceptance (Carter et al., 1975; DeTine, 1975).

(5) The child's acceptance of others is more sex-linked than race-related: that is, sex is a more potent determinant of friendship choice than race (Carter et al., 1975; Criswell, 1937, 1939; Damico, 1975; Raths and Schweickart, 1946; St. John and Lewis, 1975; Singleton, 1974).

(6) Socioeconomic status has been found to be an influential variable in most acceptance studies (Campbell, 1964; St. John, 1970: Weinberg, 1968). Hyman (1969) summarized 12 studies and concluded that whites' increased acceptance and positive attitudes toward blacks were related to social status. This was supported by St. John and Lewis (1975), as they found that the social acceptance of blacks and whites by white children in grade VI was related to socioeconomic status. Further support is given by Glock et al. (1975) who found prejudice to be related to economic deprivation. However, St. John and Lewis (1975) found that socioeconomic status was unrelated to social acceptance by black grade VI students (12-year-olds), and Gerard et al. (1975) did not find socioeconomic status to be related to white acceptance of minority students (5- to 12-year-olds) following integration.

(7) Although a positive self-concept is frequently associated with peer acceptance (DeTine, 1975; Long and Henderson, 1966; Trent, 1957), Hartup (1970) points out, 'we would predict that popular children have more

positive self-concepts than less popular. However, research evidence does not consistently confirm this prediction' (p. 390).

(8) Athletic ability has been found to be a relevant variable in interracial peer acceptance, particularly among boys (Brown and Bond, 1955; DeTine, 1975; Gerard et al., 1975; McGraw and Tolbert, 1953).

(9) Black–white ratios in the classroom, the grade, and the school are considered as important variables influencing interracial peer acceptance. When the proportion of blacks is less than 50 per cent, black students' achievement increases and social acceptance is enhanced (Coleman, 1966; St. John, 1975; United States Commission on Civil Rights, 1967; Weinberg, 1968). Carter et al. (1975) found low correlations between racial composition below 53 per cent black and peer acceptance. However, the black–white ratio contributed to the prediction of social and academic acceptance by black and white females, to academic acceptance by black males and to social acceptance by white males. Weinberg (1968) concluded that the nature of white friendships with black children varied with racial composition of the classroom. In a predominantly white classroom, white children have a larger element of choice as to whether or not they develop a friendship with a black classmate. Thus, they can choose more spontaneously and the result is a more intimate relationship. In predominantly black classrooms, however, the choice is a narrower one, and resulting relationships are less spontaneous and intimate. McPartland's (1968) study of high school students (14- to 18-year-olds) supports this: 'as the proportion of students from other races increases in a student's classes, the proportion of those who have close friends outside of their own race increases' (p. 236). However, he also found that 'the highest percentage of teachers reporting racial tension was 13.9 per cent, occurring among those who had between 50 and 74 per cent whites in their class' (p. 138). St. John and Lewis (1975) found that the ratio was unrelated to social acceptance among 12-year-old whites, that black boys were more popular in majority black classes, and that black girls were more accepted by whites in majority white classes. Although studies are not in total agreement concerning the ideal racial composition, it seems clear that racial compositions of the classroom, of the grade, and of the school (Koslin, Koslin, Pargament and Waxman, 1972) are related to peer acceptance.

(10) The number of years in an integrated school has yielded inconsistent results with regard to interracial acceptance (Gerard et al., 1975; McPartland, 1968; St. John and Lewis, 1975). However, as St. John (1972) points out, 'whether previous interracial experience facilitates subsequent experiences depends of course on the nature of the prior contact' (p. 12), which is related to the contact hypothesis literature (Amir, 1969).

(11) Teacher attitude has been found to be related to interracial acceptance in the classroom. Gerard et al. (1975) found that teacher bias was related to

whites' acceptance of minority students as friends and St. John and Lewis (1975) found a significant relationship between whites' interracial acceptance and teachers' fairness. Weinberg (1968) reviewed desegregation studies and concluded that the tone of leadership provided by teachers influenced the students' acceptance of integration.

(12) Age has frequently been associated with interracial acceptance, as Criswell (1937) found little racial valuation prior to grade V, with some evidence for continuing cleavage throughout the 14- to 18-year-old high school years. (Dwyer 1958; St. John, 1964). The research, however, has yielded conflicting results. Selection of peers by race occurs early in the educational process, but the degree of acceptance has not been thoroughly studied. When given an opportunity to rate all their peers, students' racial cleavage is less evident than when friendship choices are listed or abstract racial attitude measures are used.

Numerous variables have been found to be associated with interracial peer acceptance in an integrated school and some have been discussed previously. Additional variables are: school environment, administrative style, staff racial balance, equal status contact, fear and threat, belief systems and attitude similarity, classroom grouping procedures, personality, prejudice and other ethnic attitudes, personal space, and styles of interaction and communication. The major problems with the research literature in this area are that a limited number of variables have been included in each study, and various techniques and methods have been used. Since interracial acceptance is a multi-faceted behaviour, researchers need to examine and/or control as many of these variables as possible before more definite conclusions can be made.

PROMOTING INTERRACIAL PEER ACCEPTANCE

Strategies to improve interracial peer acceptance are based on extensive research and observations of what 'works'. These include: inservice education; multi-ethnic curriculum; classroom and school activities; supportive services; and administrative role.

Inservice preparation of teachers is a critical step in the implementation of integration. Inservices should encourage: honesty between staff and teachers; an understanding of minority group culture, behaviour, language and mannerisms; an understanding of the right of minority students to a sense of school 'ownership'; and the need to have curriculum and school activities that meet minority needs (Love, 1977).

The effectiveness of staff preparation has been shown to reduce racial prejudice of white teachers (Robinson and Preston, 1976) and promote positive attitudes in high school students (Lachat, 1972). Swick (1973) found teacher racial attitude change was enhanced by contact with parents and community organizations. Reviews of inservice education (Swick, 1974) and prejudice reduction research (Cook, 1950) suggest that teachers should be given human relations training focused on their ethnic-racial perceptions of minorities.

A multi-ethnic curriculum should portray the contributions of minority groups, give examples of positive multi-ethnic interaction, act as a catalyst for the discussion of racial issues, and provide achievement models for minority students. In a review of multi-ethnic curricula, Banks (1972) concludes: (1) programmes with general or global objectives are not likely to be successful; (2) courses which consist primarily or exclusively of lecture presentations have little impact; (3) diverse experiences, such as seminars, visitations, committee work, guest speakers, movies, multimedia materials, and workshops, combined with factual lectures, are more effective than any single approach; (4) community involvement and contact are the most productive techniques; (5) psychotherapy and *T*-grouping are also promising strategies.

Six-week sessions utilizing multi-ethnic curricula have been found to produce positive racial attitudes in 5- and 6-year-old students (Westphal, 1974), increased patterns of biracial interaction of junior high (Gajendra, McDonald and McDonald, 1971) and high school students (Breckheimer and Nelson, 1976).

What goes on in the classroom is the real issue in integration. The mere physical placing of students in the classrooms is not enough. Under the teacher's direction, successful participation of all students is essential. This involves complex social and psychological factors including self-image, achievement motivation, ethnic understanding, and social skills. Intervention techniques that promote peer acceptance should include opportunities for students to participate and feel successful in a variety of socially rewarding activities (Asher, Oden and Gottman, 1977). Children can be given special classroom roles (e.g. chairperson of a classroom party) to encourage them to participate and 'be a star'. The importance of taking part in visible valued classroom roles is demonstrated by Chennault (1967) who paired isolates with popular children to produce skits for their classroom twice a week for 5 weeks. The isolates significantly improved their sociometric ratings; however, Rucker and Vincenzo (1970) found that this positive change is only maintained with continued participation.

Reinforcement techniques have been utilized to enhance interracial interaction. Hauserman, Walen and Behling (1973) reinforced black and white children in grade I with candy for sitting with each other in the lunch-room and interracial interaction increased and generalized to the classroom. However, behaviour regressed when reinforcement was terminated. Therefore, for reinforcement to 'work' it must be faded out gradually so that true friendships become the reinforcers or reinforcement must be used that can be easily maintained; that is, verbal comments by the teacher, which have been shown to increase cross-sex play among preschool whites (Serbin *et al.*, 1977).

Classrooms that promote successful experiences and help children feel a sense of accomplishment are likely to promote peer acceptance. Learning activities that would provide a variety of interactions could include learning centres, small group lessons, learning games, varied written assignments, opportunities for choice of school work, experiments, building or making things (e.g. models), intercultural murals, peer tutoring, and small group team projects. Reduced bias in children under 6 years of age has resulted from using neutral conditioning in story groups (Parish *et al.*, 1975), and separately using stories with racial connotations and biracial activity groups (Best *et al.*, 1975). Charlesworth and Hartup (1967) found that positive social responses among preschool children occurred more frequently during play in contrast to table activities (puzzles, art work). Although there seems to be less conflict, aggression, or confusion when materials are abundant and children move individually from activity to activity, interaction is greater when preschool children work with no activity options and move en masse (Doke and Risley, 1972).

Many children who lack the social skills to make friends can be taught necessary social behaviours. Asher *et al.* (1977) stated that some of the behaviours needed to be liked and have friends include responding positively, communicating accurately, being expert, and initiating a relationship. Numerous studies indicate that acceptable behaviour varies with the situation. For example, positive non-verbal behaviour in a lower-class school helps develop friendship while it tends to contribute to being disliked in a middle-class school (Gottman, Gonso and Rasmussen, 1975).

Helping a child learn a skill valued by his peer group should enhance acceptance. Studies of the effect of low status black children teaching higher status white children (Cohen and Roper, 1972) and interaction in creative work groups (Cohen, Lockheed and Lohman, 1976) found black children earned equal status through the treatment activities. The inability to initiate new friendships can be corrected by simple role-playing to offer a greeting, attempt to include (want to play?), or give information (Gottman *et al.*, 1975). Shaping, modelling, and coaching have been shown to help children make friends. Zimmerman and Brody (1975) found that there are distinct differences in interaction patterns of black and white grade V and VI boys (10- to 12-year-olds) but these patterns are altered through use of television modelling. In interracial dyads contact increased through learning each other's play style. Oden and Asher (1977) found coaching grade III and IV children to make friends increased friendships. Obviously student age, teaching style, and school environment are crucial variables in the successful utilization of these techniques.

Extra-curricular activities should be established to offer opportunities for students of different social and cultural backgrounds to associate in pursuit of common goals and to develop common interests (United States Commission on Civil Rights, 1976). McPartland (1968) found that adolescent black 'students in racially similar classes who were active in extra-curricular activities less frequently chose all Negro friendship groups' (p. 317), were more likely to value future interracial associations, and had more positive racial attitudes.

A situation to be avoided is the formation of a small group of students who dominate the social system of the school and set the climate for values and behaviour codes. Minority students must not be left out of the mainstream of school life, develop feelings of alienation, develop a completely separate social system, or cluster together only at specific locations.

A sound instructional programme for an integrated school includes a variety of supportive services: counselling; psychological and remedial testing; and specialized resource rooms.

Many guidance counsellors and social workers possess the training to deal with the pupil dynamics of integration. They often are the only personnel in a building who logistically can deal with problem prevention, early problem resolution, and crisis situations. They do not have the handicap of a punitive authoritarian image with children; are usually perceived as helping, open, and receptive to the needs of students; and function as community liaisons. Beker (1967) found these functions to facilitate observed acceptance and interracial interaction of 6- to 14-year-old students, when performed by an integration specialist assigned to each school. Strub (1974) found that small group counselling of racially mixed high school students improved their interracial interaction. Sussman (1973) stated that students found satisfaction in receiving peer counselling in a multi-ethnic junior high school.

In the USA, the school principal is ultimately responsible for the educational outcomes. Turnage (1972) surveyed all the junior and senior high school principals of desegregated schools in the state of Virginia. They responded as feeling they: 'faced an almost overwhelming problem of human relations, relevancy of education to the needs of subgroups, conflicts, and pressures from within and without' (p. 42); encouraged positive interracial cooperation and acceptance but were uncertain about the best way to accomplish it; acquired additional responsibility without an increase in power-status and without a clear role definition in desegregation; knew that community support of desegregation was tenuous; and perceived little evidence of official support.

The school integration process should encourage interracial acceptance as well as improve achievement by minimizing sources of fear and threat (Katz, 1964, 1968; Weinberg, 1975). Fear of the unknown and preconceptions of the threats of integration seem to be the basis of a variety of problems. These problems include lower achievement, anti-social behaviour, withdrawal, verbal or overt aggression, and racial cliques. Katz (1964, 1968) points out the need for a variety of tension-reducing strategies. These strategies will be successful only if teachers are properly prepared, experienced supportive staff is available, and fair and consistent policies and rules are established by the administrator.

Probably the most important aspect of interracial peer acceptance in the classroom is the flexibility of each person involved in the process. Everyone, the parents, the school staff, and the students, must be willing to accept change and endeavour to promote understanding.

REFERENCES

Adair, A. V., and Savage, J. (1974). Sex and race as determinants of preferences, attitudes and self identity among black preschool children: a developmental study. *Journal of Social and Behavioral Sciences*, **22**, 94–101.

Amir, Y. (1969). Contact hypothesis in ethnic relations. *Psychological Bulletin*, **71**, 319–342.

Anderson, L. V. (1966). The effects of desegregation on the achievement and personality patterns of Negro children. Unpublished Doctoral Dissertation, George Peabody College for Teachers.

Armor, D. (1972). The effects of busing. *The Public Interest*, No. 28, 90–126.

Asher, S. R., and Allen, V. L. (1969). Racial preference and social comparison processes. *Journal of Social Issues*, **25**, 157–166.

Asher, S. R., Oden, S. L., and Gottman, J. M. (1977). Children's friendships in school settings. In L. G. Katz (Ed.), *Current Topics in Early Childhood Education*. Vol. 1. Norwood, New Jersey: Ablex.

Ausabel, D., and Ausabel, P. (1963). Ego development among segregated Negro children. In H. A. Passow (Ed.), *Education in Depressed Areas*. New York: Teachers College, Columbia University.

Ballard, B., and Keller, H. R. (1976). Development of racial awareness: task consistency, reliability, and validity. *Journal of Genetic Psychology*, **129**, 3–11.

Banks, J. A. (1972). Imperatives in ethnic minority education. *Phi Delta Kappan*, **53**, 266–269.

Banks, W. C. (1976). White preference in blacks: a paradigm in search of a phenomenon. *Psychological Bulletin*, **83**, 1179–1186.

Banks, W. C., and Rompf, W. J. (1973). Evaluative bias and preference behavior in black and white children. *Child Development*, **44**, 776–783.

Beker, J. (1967). A study of integration in racially imbalanced urban public schools— a demonstration and evaluation. Final report. Educational Resources Information Center, Document Number ED 013857.

Benson, F. W. (1969). A comparison of social and academic acceptance among core city students and non-core city students in October and May of a school year. *Child Study Center Bulletin*, **5**, 84–87.

Benson, F. W., and Carter, D. E. (1971). The effects of a bussing program for racial balance on peer acceptance. Paper presented at the meeting of the American Educational Research Association, New York City, February.

Best, D. L., Smith, S. C., Graves, D. L., and Williams, J. E. (1975). The modification of racial bias in preschool children. *Journal of Experimental Child Psychology*, **20**, 193–205.

Bigelow, B. J. (1977). Children's friendship expectations: a cognitive developmental study. *Child Development*, **48**, 246–253.

Boswell, D. A., and Williams, J. E. (1975). Correlates of race and color bias among preschool children. *Psychological Reports*, **36**, 147–154.

Brand, E. S., Ruiz, R. A., and Padilla, A. M. (1974). Ethnic identification and preferences: a review. *Psychological Bulletin*, **81**, 860–890.

Breckheimer, S. E., and Nelson, R. O. (1976). Group methods for reducing prejudice and discrimination. *Psychological Reports*, **39**, 1259–1268.

Brigham, J. C. (1971). Ethnic stereotypes. *Psychological Bulletin*, **76**, 15–38.

Brown, W. H., and Bond, L. B. (1955). Social stratification in a sixth grade class. *Journal of Educational Research*, **48**, 530–543.

Buswell, M. (1951). The relationship between the social structure of the classroom and the academic success of the pupil. Unpublished Doctoral Dissertation, University of Minnesota.

Butler, R. O. (1976). Black children's racial preference: a selected review of the literature. *Journal of Afro-American Issues*, **4**, 168–171.

Campbell, J. D. (1964). Peer relations in childhood. In L. Hoffman and M. Hoffman (Eds.), *Review of Child Development Research*. Vol. 1. New York: Russell Sage Foundation.

Cantor, G. N. (1972). Use of a conflict paradigm to study race awareness in children. *Child Development*, **43**, 1437–1442.

Cantor, G. N., and Paternite, C. E. (1973). A follow-up study of race awareness using a conflict paradigm. *Child Development*, **44**, 859–861.

Carithers, M. W. (1970). School desegregation and racial cleavage, 1954–1970: a review of the literature. *Journal of Social Issues*, **26**, 25–47.

Carter, D. E., DeTine, S. L., Spero, J., and Benson, F. W. (1975). Peer acceptance and school-related variables in an integrated junior high school. *Journal of Educational Psychology*, **67**, 267–273.

Charlesworth, R., and Hartup, W. W. (1967). Positive social reinforcement in the nursery school peer group. *Child Development*, **38**, 993–1003.

Chennault, M. (1967). Improving the social acceptance of unpopular educable mentally retarded pupils in special classes. *American Journal of Mental Deficiency*, **72**, 455–458.

Clark, K., and Clark, M. (1939). The development of consciousness of self and the emergence of racial identification in Negro preschool children. *Journal of Social Psychology*, **10**, 591–599.

Clark, K., and Clark, M. (1947). Racial identification and preference in Negro children. In T. M. Newcomb and E. C. Hartley (Eds.), *Readings in Social Psychology*. New York: Holt.

Cohen, E. G., Lockheed, M. E., and Lohman, M. R. (1976). Center for interracial cooperation: a field experiment. *Sociology of Education*, **49**, 47–58.

Cohen, E. G., and Roper, S. S. (1972). Modification of interracial interaction disability: an application of status characteristic theory. *American Sociological Review*, **37**, 643–646.

Coleman, J. S. (1966). *Equality of Educational Opportunity*. Washington, DC: United States Government Printing Office.

Cook, L. A. (Ed.) (1950). *College Programs in Intergroup Relations*. Chicago: American Council on Education.

Criswell, J. H. (1937). Racial cleavage in Negro-white groups. *Sociometry*, **1**, 81–89.

Criswell, J. H. (1939). A sociometric study of race cleavage in the classroom. *Archives of Psychology*, No. 235.

Crooks, R. C. (1970). The effects of an interracial preschool program upon racial preference, knowledge of racial differences and racial identification. *Journal of Social Issues*, **26**, 137–143.

Damico, S. (1975). Sexual differences in the responses of elementary pupils to their classroom. *Psychology in the Schools*, **12**, 462–467.

Datcher, E., Savage, J. E., Jr., and Checkosky, S. F. (1973). School type, grade, sex, and race of experimenter as determinants of racial preference and awareness in black and white children. In *Proceedings, 81st Annual Convention American Psychological Association*. Washington, DC: American Psychological Association.

Davidson, F. H. (1976). Ability to respect persons compared to ethnic prejudice in childhood. *Journal of Personality and Social Psychology*, 34, 1256–1267.

DeTine, S. L. (1975). Correlates of peer acceptance in grades four and five in two integrated schools. Unpublished Master's Thesis, State University of New York, College at Buffalo.

DeVries, D. L., and Edwards, K. J. (1972). *Student Teams and Instructional Games: Their Effects on Cross-race and Cross-sex Interaction*. Baltimore: Center for Social Organization of Schools, John Hopkins University.

Doke, L. A., and Risley, T. R. (1972). The organization of day-care environments: required vs. optional activities. *Journal of Applied Behavior Analysis*, 5, 405–420.

Dwyer, R. J. (1958). A report on patterns of interaction in desegregated schools. *Journal of Educational Sociology*, 31, 253–256.

Fox, D. J., and Jordan, V. B. (1973). Racial preference and identification of black, American Chinese, and white children. *Genetic Psychology Monographs*, 88, 229–286.

Gajendra, K., McDonald, V., and McDonald, B. (1971). Teaching race in schools: some effects on the attitudinal and sociometric patterns of adolescents. *Race*, 13, 187–202.

Gerard, H. B. (1969). Factors contributing to adjustment and achievement. Progress Report, May 1969. Educational Resources Information Center, Document Number ED 035 501.

Gerard, H. B., Jackson, T. D., and Conolley, E. S. (1975). Social contact in the desegregated classroom. In H. B. Gerard and N. Miller (Eds.), *School Desegregation*. New York: Plenum Press.

Glidewell, J. C., Kantor, M. B., Smith, L. M., and Stringer, L. A. (1966). Socialization of social structure in the classroom. In L. Hoffman and M. Hoffman (Eds.), *Review of Child Development Research*. Vol. 2. New York: Russell Sage Foundation.

Glock, C., Wuthnow, R., Piliavin, J., and Spencer, M. (1975). *Adolescent Prejudice*. New York: Harper and Row.

Goldschmid, M. L. (1968). The relation of conservation to emotional and environmental aspects of development. *Child Development*, 39, 579–589.

Goodman, M. E. (1952). *Race Awareness in Young Children*. Reading, Massachusetts: Addison-Wesley.

Goodman, M. (1964). *Race Awareness in Young Children*. Second edition. New York: Collier Books.

Gottman, J. M. (1977). Toward a definition of social isolation in children. *Child Development*, 48, 513–517.

Gottman, J., Gonso, J., and Rasmussen, B. (1975). Social interaction, social competence, and friendship in children. *Child Development*, 46, 709–718.

Greenwald, H. J., and Oppenheim, D. B. (1968). Reported magnitude of self-misidentification among Negro children—artifact? *Journal of Personality and Social Psychology*, 8, 49–52.

Griffitt, W. (1974). Attitude similarity and attraction. In T. L. Huston (Ed.), *Foundations of Interpersonal Attraction*. New York: Academic Press.

Hartup, W. W. (1970). Peer interaction and social organization. In P. H. Mussen (Ed.), *Carmichael's Manual of Child Psychology*. New York: John Wiley.

Hauserman, N., Walen, S. R., and Behling, M. (1973). Reinforced racial integration in the first grade: a study in generalization. *Journal of Applied Behavioral Analysis*, 6, 193–200.

Horton, R., Jr. (1973). Black parent-child participation in preventive-intervention programs: implications for self-concept values and racial identification. Unpublished Doctoral Dissertation, University of Michigan.

Hraba, J., and Grant, J. (1970). Black is beautiful: a re-examination of racial preference and identification. *Journal of Personality and Social Psychology*, **16**, 398–402.

Hyman, H. H. (1969). Social psychology and race relations. In I. Katz and P. Gurin (Eds.), *Race and the Social Sciences*. New York: Basic Books.

Johnson, E. G. (1977). The development of color knowledge in preschool children. *Child Development*, **48**, 308–311.

Jones, J. M. (1972). *Prejudice and Racism*. Reading, Massachusetts: Addison-Wesley.

Katz, I. (1964). Review of evidence relating to effects of desegregation on the intellectual performance of Negroes. *American Psychologist*, **19**, 381–399.

Katz, I. (1968). Factors influencing Negro performance in the desegregated school. In M. Deutsch, I. Katz and A. R. Jensen (Eds.), *Social Class, Race and Psychological Development*. New York: Holt, Rinehart and Winston.

Katz, P. A. (1973a). Stimulus predifferentiation and modification of children's racial attitudes. *Child Development*, **44**, 232–237.

Katz, P. A. (1973b). Perception of racial cues in preschool children: a new look. *Developmental Psychology*, **8**, 295–299.

Katz, P. A., and Seavey, C. (1973). Labels and children's perception of faces. *Child Development*, **44**, 770–775.

Katz, P. A., Sohn, M., and Zalk, S. R. (1975). Perceptual concomitants of racial attitudes in urban grade-school children. *Developmental Psychology*, **11**, 135–144.

Katz, P. A., and Zalk, S. R. (1974). Doll preferences: an index of racial attitudes. *Journal of Educational Psychology*, **66**, 663–668.

Kiesler, S. B. (1971). Racial choice among children in realistic situations. Unpublished Manuscript, University of Kansas. As cited in J. M. Jones (1972), *Prejudice and Racism*. Reading, Massachusetts: Addison-Wesley.

Kircher, M., and Furby, L. (1971). Racial preferences in young children. *Child Development*, **42**, 2076–2078.

Kirn, K. G. (1973). Racial identification and preference in young children as a function of race and sex of the experimenter and child. Unpublished Doctoral Dissertation, University of Florida.

Kohlberg, L. (1969). Stage and sequence: the cognitive-developmental approach to socialization. In D. A. Goslin (Ed.), *Handbook of Socialization Theory and Research*. New York: Rand-McNally.

Koslin, S. C., Amarel, M., and Ames, N. (1969). A distance measure of racial attitudes in primary grade children: an exploratory study. *Psychology in the Schools*, **6**, 382–385.

Koslin, S. C., Amarel, M., and Ames, N. (1970). The effect of race on peer evaluation and preference in primary grade children: an exploratory study. *Journal of Negro Education*, **39**, 346–350.

Koslin, S. C., Koslin, B. L., Cardwell, J., and Pargament, R. (1969). Quasi-disguised and structured measure of schoolchildren's racial preferences. In *Proceedings, 77th Annual Convention American Psychological Association*. Washington, DC: American Psychological Association.

Koslin, S., Koslin, B., Pargament, R., and Waxman, H. (1972). Classroom racial balance and students' interracial attitudes. *Sociology of Education*, **45**, 386–407.

Lachat, M. A. (1972). A description and comparison of attitudes of white high school seniors toward black Americans in three suburban high schools: an all white, desegregated and an integrated school. Unpublished Doctoral Dissertation, Teachers College, Columbia University.

Lasker, B. (1929). *Race Attitudes in Children*. New York: Holt.

Lerner, R. M., and Buehrig, C. J. (1975). The development of racial attitudes in young black and white children. *Journal of Genetic Psychology*, **127**, 45–54.

Levinger, G. (1974). A three-level approach to attraction: toward an understanding of pair relatedness. In T. L. Huston (Ed.), *Foundations of Interpersonal Attraction*. New York: Academic Press.

Lickona, T. (1974). A cognitive-developmental approach to interpersonal attraction. In T. L. Huston (Ed.), *Foundations of Interpersonal Attraction*. New York: Academic Press.

Long, B. H., and Henderson, E. H. (1966). Self-social-concept of disadvantaged school beginners. Paper presented at the meeting of the American Psychological Association, New York City, September.

Love, B. J. (1977). Desegregation in your school: behavior patterns that get in the way. *Phi Delta Kappan*, **59**, 168–170.

Mann, J. H. (1959). The effect of interracial contact on sociometric choices and perceptions. *Journal of Social Psychology*, **50**, 143–152.

McGraw, L. W., and Tolbert, J. W. (1953). Sociometric status and athletic ability of junior high school boys. *Research Quarterly*, **24**, 72–80.

McPartland, J. (1968). The segregated student in desegregated schools. Final report to the Center for the Study of Social Organization of Schools. Educational Resources Information Center, Document Number ED 021944.

Morland, J. K. (1958). Racial recognition in nursery school children in Lynchburg, Virginia. *Social Forces*, **37**, 132–137.

Morland, J. K. (1962). Racial acceptance and preference of nursery school children in a southern city. *Merrill–Palmer Quarterly*, **8**, 271–280.

Morland, J. K. (1966). A comparison of race awareness in northern and southern children. *American Journal of Orthopsychiatry*, **36**, 22–31.

Oden, S., and Asher, S. R. (1977). Coaching children in social skills for friendship making. *Child Development*, **48**, 495–506.

Ohsako, T. (1973). Race awareness in eight, ten, and twelve year old boys. Unpublished Doctoral Dissertation, Michigan State University.

Orost, J. (1971). Racial attitudes among white kindergarten children from three different environments. Paper presented at the meeting of the American Educational Research Association, New York City, February.

Palmer, E. L. (1973). Colour prejudice in children as a function of race, age, and residence neighbourhood. Paper presented at the meeting of the American Psychological Association, Montreal, August.

Parish, T. S., Fleetwood, R. S., and Lentz, K. J. (1975). Effect of neutral conditioning on racial attitudes of children. *Perceptual and Motor Skills*, **40**, 695–701.

Pettigrew, T. F. (1969). The Negro and education: problems and proposals. In I. Katz and P. Gurin (Eds.), *Race and the Social Sciences*. New York: Basic Books.

Pettigrew, T. F., Useem, E. L., Normand, C., and Smith, M. S. (1973). Busing: review of the evidence. *Public Interest*, No. 30, 88–118.

Piaget, J. (1950). *The Psychology of Intelligence*. New York: Harcourt-Brace.

Porter, J. D. R. (1971). *Black Child, White Child: The Development of Racial Attitudes*. Cambridge, Massachusetts: Harvard University Press.

Radke, M. J., and Trager, H. G., (1950). Children's perceptions of the social roles of Negroes and whites. *Journal of Psychology*, **29**, 3–33.

Radke, M. J., Trager, H. G., and Davis, H. (1949). Social perceptions and attitudes of children. *Genetic Psychology Monographs*, **40**, 327–447.

Rardin, D., and Moan, C. (1971). Peer interaction and cognitive development. *Child Development*, **42**, 1685–1699.

Raths, L., and Schweickart, E. F. (1946). Social acceptance within interracial school groups. *Educational Research Bulletin*, **25**, 85–90.

Robinson, T. W., and Preston, J. D. (1976). Equal-status contract and modification of racial prejudice: a reexamination of the contact hypothesis. *Social Forces*, **54**, 911–924.

Rucker, C. N., and Vincenzo, F. M. (1970). Maintaining social acceptance gains made by mentally retarded children. *Exceptional Children*, **36**, 679–680.

Serbin, L. A., Tonick, I. J., and Sternglanz, S. H. (1977). Shaping cooperative cross-sex play. *Child Development*, **48**, 924–929.

Simon, R. J. (1974). An assessment of racial awareness, preference, and self-identity among white and adopted non-white children. *Social Problems*, **22**, 43–57.

Singer, D. (1967). Interracial attitudes of Negro and white fifth grade children in segregated and unsegregated schools. Unpublished Doctoral Dissertation, Columbia University.

Singleton, L. (1974). The effects of sex and race on children's sociometric choices for play and work. Educational Resources Information Center, Document Number ED 100520.

Stabler, J. R., Johnson, E. E., Berke, M. A., and Baker, R. B. (1969). The relationship between race and perception of racially related stimuli in preschool children. *Child Development*, **40**, 1233–1239.

St. John, N. H. (1964). De facto segregation and interracial association in high school. *Sociology of Education*, **37**, 326–344.

St. John, N. H. (1970). Desegregation and minority group performance. *Review of Educational Research*, **40**, 111–133.

St. John, N. H. (1972). Desegregation: voluntary or mandatory? *Integrated Education*, **10**, 7–17.

St. John, N. H. (1975). *School Desegregation: Outcomes for Children*. New York: Wiley.

St. John, N. H., and Lewis, R. G. (1975). Race and the social structure of the elementary classroom. *Sociology of Education*, **48**, 346–368.

Strub, R. F. (1974). The perceptions of selected groups regarding the effect of cross-cultural group counseling on reducing tension in a racially mixed school. Unpublished Doctoral Dissertation, University of South Dakota.

Sussman, M. B. (1973). The development and effects of a model for training peer-group counselors in a multi-ethnic junior high school. Unpublished Doctoral Dissertation, University of Miami.

Swick, K. J. (1974). Challenging pre-service and inservice teacher's perception of minority group children: a review of research. *Journal of Negro Education*, **43**, 194–201.

Swick, K. J. (1973). An investigation of an experimental urban teacher preparation program: implications for teacher preparation. Unpublished Doctoral Dissertation: University of Connecticut.

Trent, R. D. (1957). The relation between expressed self-acceptance and expressed attitudes toward Negroes and whites among Negro children. *The Journal of Genetic Psychology*, **91**, 25–31.

Turnage, M. (1972). The principal: change agent in desegregation. *Integrated Education*, **10**, 41–45.

United States Commission on Civil Rights (1967). *Racial Isolation in the Public Schools*. Washington, DC: United States Government Printing Office.

United States Commission on Civil Rights (1976). *Fulfilling the Letter and Spirit of the Law: Desegregation in the Nation's Public Schools*. Washington, DC: United States Government Printing Office.

Ward, S. H., and Braun, J. (1972). Self-esteem and racial preference in black children. *American Journal of Orthopsychiatry*, **42**, 644–647.

Weinberg, M. (1968). *Desegregation Research: An Appraisal*. Bloomington, Indiana: Phi Delta Kappa.

Weinberg, M. (1975). The relationship between school desegregation and academic achievement: a review of research. *Law and Contemporary Problems*, **39**, 240–269.

Westphal, R. (1974). The effects of primary grade level inter-ethnic curriculum on racial prejudice. Unpublished Doctoral Dissertation, University of Southern California.

Williams, J. E., Best, D. L., and Boswell, D. A. (1975). The measurement of children's racial attitudes in the early school years. *Child Development*, **46**, 494–500.

Williams, J. E., and Roberson, J. K. (1967). A method for assessing racial attitudes in preschool children. *Educational and Psychological Measurement*, **27**, 671–689.

Witte, P. H. (1972). The effects of group reward structure on interracial acceptance, peer tutoring, and academic performance. Unpublished Doctoral Dissertation, Washington University.

Wolf, R. L., and Simon, R. J., (1975). Does busing improve the racial interaction of children? *Educational Researcher*, **4**, 5–10.

Wrightstone, J. W., McClelland, S. D., and Forlano, G. (1966). *Evaluation of the Community Zoning Program.* New York City: Bureau of Educational Research, Board of Education of the City of New York.

Zimmerman, B. J., and Brody, G. H. (1975). Race and modeling influences on the interpersonal play patterns of boys. *Journal of Educational Psychology*, **67**, 591–598.

CHAPTER 6

Sociometric Indices of Children's Peer Interaction in the School Setting [1]

NORMAN MILLER
and
KEVIN
W. GENTRY

The sociometric technique was pioneered by Moreno (1934), who first used it to measure peer acceptance in a school setting. As a measurement technique it provides a rich source of data from which to make inferences about a wide variety of social psychological processes including friendship, social exchange, interpersonal power, and interpersonal attraction. Consequently, it is not surprising to note that it has been employed extensively in sociological and psychological research beginning more than 50 years ago (Almack, 1922). In his thorough review, Hartup (1970) points out that no aspect of children's social behaviour has received more attention than peer acceptance or popularity. The fact that most sociometric research focuses upon children rather than adults may reflect the importance that psychologists ascribe to the socializing influences of peers during the course of psychological development; the average child spends a larger portion of time with peers than with his or her parents. Perhaps, too, school children are the most frequent object of sociometric study because the classroom maintains them in captive, 'stable' groups, thereby facilitating research. This chapter reviews current research that uses the sociometric technique to examine correlates of peer popularity. It considers

145

evidence on the relation between popularity and personality attributes, social skills, physical attractiveness, birth position, and school desegregation.

For comprehensive reviews of earlier studies of children in the classroom setting, the reader is referred to Glidewell, Kantor, Smith and Stringer (1966), and to Hartup's (1970) comprehensive review. Additionally, Asher, Oden, and Gottman (1979) provide a brief review of sociometric and non-sociometric studies of children's friendships both in and out of school settings. Although generically termed *sociometric instruments*, many different techniques are employed in assessing interpersonal attraction within given social groups. A discussion of methodological issues in the conduct of sociometric investigations can be found in Lindzey and Byrne (1968).

METHODOLOGICAL CONSIDERATIONS

It should also be noted that an extensive literature primarily attends to the mathematical and psychometric properties of sociometric data. Social choice data were originally examined in the form of *sociograms*, graphic depictions of who chooses whom within a group. Mathematical representations were soon applied that were less cumbersome than the drawing of sociograms. Prior to the widespread availability of high speed computers, however, they nevertheless entailed appreciable hand-analysis. Katz' (1950) punched card technique, or the scalogram board technique, originally developed for Guttman's (1950) scalogram analysis (see Glanzer and Glaser, 1959) are examples of early innovations. With the advent of the high speed computer, however, the application of complex mathematics to sociometric data has resulted in a rapid sophistication of techniques for their analysis. Indeed, more effort has been devoted to the development of procedures for analysis than to the refinement of alternative techniques for collecting sociometric data.

Sociometric data are most easily and perhaps most often arrayed as chooser (rows) by chosen (columns) matrices. This arrangement, first suggested by Forsyth and Katz (1946), enables the application of matrix algebra to identify various complex structural properties of groups, and additionally simplifies the counting of choices received by any one individual. Subsequent to the computer age, the methodological literature soon began to swell with articles detailing and comparing the application of increasingly more complex matrix operations to sociometric analysis. Among the techniques available are directed graph theory (e.g. Flament, 1963; Harary, 1969; Harary, Norman and Cartwright, 1965), factor analysis of choice matrices (e.g. Macrae, 1960), multidimensional scaling (e.g. Reynolds, 1976), economic or input–output models (Hubbell, 1965; Roistacher, 1974), and other combinations of matrix manipulation schema. At the time of writing, at least five computer packages for the analysis of sociometric data exist (Alba and Guttman, 1971; Alt and Schofield, 1975; Johnson-Lenz, 1977; Naugher, 1976; Rosen and Abrams, 1970).

A number of researchers have compared different procedures for analysing sociometric data (Bonacich, 1972; Lankford, 1974; Nosanchuk, 1963). Among methodological sophisticates, however, little general agreement emerges regarding the relative superiority of the alternative techniques. Consequently, the researcher's choice among sociometric analytic techniques is more or less arbitrary, and can be made to suit the data at hand. Additionally, the more sophisticated or complicated analytical techniques are most often concerned with identifying cliques, choice patterns, cohesion indices, and so on, whereas more substantive research has relied on less esoteric or sophisticated measures, attempting instead merely to describe popularity and social conditions in classrooms. Thus, the majority of studies in the existing literature simply count the number of choices received by an individual, compare these to the number of choices received by other individuals in the group, and relate these scores to other variables theoretically predicted to be related to popularity. For example, Roff, Sells and Golden (1972), in their report of a large study of social adjustment in children—in which they employed sociometric measures—concluded, for various reasons, that the use of these complex matrix methods was unnecessary. It seems likely, however, that more refined indices such as clique measures do identify something about the structure of social groups that is distinct from a simple popularity index based upon sociometric nominations. This is illustrated well by correlations between clique membership scores and popularity nominations.

Table 6.1 presents for illustrative purposes data from a study of school desegregation (Gerard and Miller, 1975). In this research, a multiethnic sample of about 1,750 children, their parents, and their teachers were extensively premeasured prior to the implementation of a desegregation program and then remeasured successively over the next 5 years. The study sample included almost all the minority children in the Riverside, California Unified School District within grades kindergarten to VI (5- to 11-year-olds) and a set of white children from the receiving schools who were matched with the minority children on grade and sex. Although the initial study sample contained over 1,750 children, sociometric data were collected from all children in classes that contained sample children. Thus, there were full sociometric data from over 10,000 children in approximately 300 classrooms.

Our analyses of these data use the strong components procedure to identify cliques[2] (Harary et al., 1965). This method defines cliques as those groups in which all members share at least some mutual friends. It requires all possible pairs of clique members to be reciprocally 'reachable' from one another. This definition does not specify any upper or lower limit on the number of steps (intermediary persons) that are necessary to reach any one clique member from any other, and thus might be too loose (unrestrictive) if applied to data where children made unrestricted choices. In our own data however, children made a total of nine choices, three for a friend, three for a play partner, and three for someone with whom they would like to work. Our preliminary work with these clique isolation techniques suggested that a lenient definition rather than a more restrictive definition of a clique was called for, in that overly restrictive limitations on the number of steps necessary to reach one clique member from another, or other restrictions, in many instances resulted in the identification of no cliques whatsoever in the array of approximately 700 classrooms. We expect that further work will help us to clarify some of these methodological issues—issues that are influenced by considerations of both data and method.

Table 6.1 presents the correlation of clique membership scores with the raw popularity data from which the former were derived. Inspection reveals several points. First, as shown in the lower portion of Table 6.1, popularity nominations do show stability from one year to the next. As seen in the upper portion of Table 6.1, however, the strength of the relation between clique membership and popularity is at best rather moderate. Furthermore, the year-to-year reliability of clique membership is low. That clique membership from year-to-year is less stable than raw popularity seems understandable. Whereas popularity reflects status, clique membership—being an aspect of the classroom social structure—seems more vulnerable to changing interpersonal processes that occur from one year to the next. It seems likely that the lower reliability of the clique membership scores is also exacerbated by the fact that it is a dichotomous variable and that in the vast majority of classrooms the strong components clique isolation procedure isolates only a single clique.

The notion that clique identification reveals something distinct from popularity lies, of course, at the heart of sociological studies of complex organizations, such as the historically important work of Roethlisberger and Dickson (1939) on a Western Electric production section and Homans' (1950) reanalysis of the sociometric data from the 14 men who worked in the Bank Wiring Room. Similarly, studies of community structure and influence systems, which also initially tended toward qualitative analysis depend upon clique identification (Dahl, 1961; Hunter, 1953). More recent technical developments, however, now make quantitative analysis distinctly possible, even in community studies where the sheer numbers of persons and remoteness of links between them formerly seemed an insurmountable problem (Rossi, 1960). Network analysis, the identification and analysis of social networks, also rests upon procedures for isolating cliques. Although earlier work in network analysis paralleled sociometric analysis in linking specific persons by means of direct social interaction (Mitchell, 1969), more recent work relaxes the definition of social interaction to include, for instance, money flow and transmission of organizational information (Turk, 1973). Similarly, it relinquishes its focus on individuals to view organizations or other social groupings as the unit of analysis, studying, for example, overlapping leadership in corporate entities (Levine, 1972).

Table 6.1. Correlations among popularity and clique membership scores, and test-retest reliability of popularity scores

Clique membership and popularity*: sociometric choices received

	Predesegregation			Post-1-year			Post-3-years		
	Seating	Play	Work	Seating	Play	Work	Seating	Play	Work
Clique index									
predesegregation	0.21	0.18	0.19	0.09	0.08	0.08	0.07	0.07	0.04
Post-1-year	0.10	0.07	0.07	0.24	0.20	0.23	0.13	0.08	0.06
Post-3-years	0.03	0.00	0.03	0.01	0.00	0.00	0.08	0.04	0.04

Test-retest correlations for three measures of popularity†

Seating choices received

Year	1966	1967	1968	1969	1971
1966		0.39	0.30	0.26	0.16
1967			0.38	0.31	0.21
1968				0.39	0.26
1969					0.35

Playing choices received

Year	1966	1967	1968	1969	1971
1966		0.42	0.35	0.32	0.16
1967			0.53	0.43	0.32
1968				0.53	0.34
1969					0.34

Work choices received

Year	1966	1967	1968	1969	1971
1966		0.35	0.30	0.31	0.22
1967			0.39	0.38	0.20
1968				0.46	0.37
1969					0.37

* r values greater than 0.06 are significant at $p < .05$, two-tailed. Ns for a given correlation vary from 738 to 1,534, and represent only Riverside School Study children.

† All tabled correlations are significant at $p < .01$. Data from the years 1968 and 1971, although not discussed in the text, are included for the additional information they provide.

Although some form of directed graph theory underlies most computer procedures for clique indentification, another recent innovation is block modelling, as developed by White and his associates (Boorman and White, 1976; Lorrain and White, 1971; White, Boorman and Breiger, 1976). Whereas graph theory focuses on the units that are connected with one another, block-modelling is as equally concerned with units lacking any relationship. It attempts to group clusters of units that are structurally equivalent in terms of the pattern of interrelation (or lack of it) among its members. Thus, it ultimately attempts to delineate positions within a structure or to define social roles, thereby emphasizing the interchangeability of those occupying a given position.

Whatever the particular approach to clique identification or structural analysis of social groups, data reduction becomes a necessity in the study of many large network or influence systems within communities. In studies of the social relations within large American high schools where children typically move from one class to the next and classes do not have substantially over-lapping memberships, the need for data reduction also arises. As indicated earlier, factor analysis (Freeman, 1968; Macrae, 1960) and cluster analysis (Bailey, 1975) provide one type of alternative; multidimensional scaling (Guttman, 1968; Lingoes, 1972; McFarland and Brown, 1973; Reynolds, 1976) offers another. For an interesting application of multidimensional scaling procedures to the analysis of coalitional structures within a community see the work of Laumann and his associates (e.g. Laumann and House, 1970; Laumann and Pappi, 1976). More recently, network sampling procedures have been recommended and used (Capobianco, 1970; Granovetter, 1976; Niemeijer, 1973; Tapiero, Capobianco and Lewin, 1975). The fact that a sociometric study of a middle size American college with 5,000 students will contain over 12,000,000 potential lines of association emphasizes the impetus to adopt sampling approaches.

A review of the literature concerned with techniques for analysing socio-metric data and/or the actual analysis of such data suggest an important caveat for the investigator who is about to initiate sociometric measurement or is faced with a body of sociometric data that requires analysis. Specifically, whether or not sophisticated matrix or other more powerful techniques are used, or are usable, often depends on the nature of the data to be studied, and thus in part upon the subjects from which data are gathered. For example, while Hallinan (1976), Cohen (1977), and others were able to use and gain interesting information with more complicated techniques, these same pro-cedures may yield little additional information in other data sets. Although future work may reveal relations among sample size, sample characteristics, measurement error, and the appropriateness or usefulness of matrix methods, it is important to emphasize this specificity of method to data and subjects. Conclusions regarding the general usefulness or appropriateness of various statistical or aggregation techniques should not be drawn on the basis of the outcomes of a single study, no matter how large it may be in terms of sample size or number of measures. In larger samples, the care taken in administering measures may not be as great as that employed in smaller studies; differences among those who administer the measures may add to the variance. Increasing measurement error, which necessarily reduces the intercorrelations among sociometric measures and other variables, might seriously erode the usefulness of more sophisticated analytical techniques as in Roff *et al.* (1972). (See Holland and Leinhardt, 1973, for a discussion of the structural implications of measurement and error in sociometric data.)

A final procedural refinement is important to the investigator planning to gather and analyse sociometric data. Recent evidence suggests that a roster-and-rating procedure (Roistacher, 1974) is superior to peer nomination methods wherein children nominate one or more classmates for various interaction situations such as playmates, work partners, best friend, and so on. In the roster-and-rating procedure the child gives a rating on numerical scales to all the members of a class who are listed on a class roster. The roster-and-rating method is thought to minimize measurement error by: decreasing the likelihood of a student not being chosen because s/he was momentarily forgotten; providing an index of a child's acceptance by *all* group members, since each child is rated by all of his/her classmates; and by removing constraints on the child making choices that might result in measurement error (Hallinan, 1974, 1976; Holland and Leinhardt, 1973; Singleton and Asher, 1977).

MODELS OF SOCIOMETRIC POPULARITY

Hartup (1970) provides a review of pre-1970 investigations concerning correlates of children's sociometric acceptance by peers, from which the following brief summary is derived. This review reveals a consistent picture of those social attributes that covary with peer acceptance. Friendliness, sociability social visibility, and outgoingness are all positively related to acceptance, and this relation is unaffected by age level. Interestingly, however, a lack of sociability does not necessarily predict the child will be actively rejected. Other indicators of social flexibility, such as compliance, cooperation, and acceptance of others are positively correlated with peer popularity, suggesting that a child's popularity may be due to a willingness to tailor his behaviour to the demands of peaceful and efficient group functioning (Moore, 1967).

Numerous studies reveal positive relations among various global measures of psychological adjustment and acceptance. For example, evidence seems to support the conclusion that anxious children are less popular than non-anxious children. However, another indicator of adjustment, high self-esteem, has not been consistently found to be related to popularity. Similarly, two behavioural manifestations of a lack of adjustment, aggressiveness and dependency, have been shown to be inconsistently (in the case of the former) or complexly (in the case of the latter) related to the child's popularity. Family adjustment and a psychologically positive family environment, when reflected in child rearing styles, also leads to the child's acceptance by peers. Research dealing with a child's scholastic aptitude, as reflected by IQ and achievement measures, presents a clear picture of a positive relation between these attributes and the child's popularity.

Finally, popularity also appears to be associated with other less malleable characteristics of the child, such as athletic skill, early onset of pubescence, physical attractiveness, 'normalcy' of given name, lateness of birth position, and of course, the child's sex, ethnicity, and social class. And, although Hartup (1970) laments the dearth of research on group dynamics among children, he notes findings relevant to our later section on the effects of group cooperative experiences on popularity. Specifically, it was known as long as two decades ago that group success experiences produce more positive peer evaluations (Heber and Heber, 1957).

Given these past findings, one can envisage numerous models to explain the sociometric popularity of schoolchildren. One might focus on familial antecedents. Various alternatives within this class are possible. For instance, one type of model might primarily include demographic factors such as race or social class; similarly, it might include structural variables, such as the type of family unit; whether or not one parent is absent from the home; whether an extended family or unrelated adults live in the home; what birth position the child occupies among siblings; the age of parents relative to that of the child; etc. Of course, many of such structural variables may in turn be related to demographic variables.

Another possibility is a model that attends more directly to psychological factors themselves, rather than to the structural or demographic factors from which they might emerge. For instance, the amount of overall parental reinforcement that a child receives might be critical. The child who is a product of a warm, reassuring, positive home may be more appealing to others than one from a cold, punitive, hostile environment who feels unwanted, rebuked and worthless. A model based on this reasoning predicts positive correlations between the positivity of the trait ratings that a child receives from his parents and his ability to attract friends in school. Parenthetically this model also predicts positive correlations between parental and teacher perceptions on a general evaluative factor. A version of this model might also see certain personality traits as emerging from such parental treatment and consequently these traits might in turn be related to their popularity.

A model which takes an entirely different emphasis assigns to the teacher a more prominent causal role regarding a child's friendships within the school setting. In this view, regardless of whatever precipitates it, the teacher's attitude toward the child sets the tone for the response of other classmates. In other words, a child's classmates model their teacher's attitude toward him/her. Thus, if liked by his/her teacher, s/he is also likely to be popular among his/her peers. In contrast to the preceding model, an alternate view puts both the teacher's attitude and peer attitudes as independent responses to a child's characteristics, whatever their origin. The important feature differentiating this model from the preceding one is that it does not place the teacher's reaction to the child in the position of being causally antecedent to peer evaluation and behaviour. Note however, that it does not preclude the possibility of similar evaluative responses by both peers and teacher.

Throughout our examination of data in the sections that follow we attempt to comment on their bearing upon the plausibility of these alternative models.

BIRTH ORDER, PERSONALITY AND SOCIAL SKILLS

Reviewing the effects of birth position on peer popularity, Hartup (1970) concluded that birth order appeared to account for a significant portion of the variance in children's peer relations. He further implied that personality factors might mediate this relation. Recent work suggests that differential acquisition of social skills by children of differing birth position accounts for the relation between birth order and popularity rather than other dimensions of personality (cf. Oden and Asher, 1977). In confirmation of earlier findings (Schachter, 1964; Sells and Roff, 1964), Miller and Maruyama (1976) found later-born children to be more popular than early-born children. In considering the explanation of such effects they argued that the interaction among siblings within the home requires that younger children, being less powerful than their older brothers and sisters, must develop more effective interpersonal skills in order to obtain a modicum of favourable outcomes; they must develop powers of negotiation, accommodation, tolerance, and the capacity to accept less favourable outcomes. Alternatively, it is of course logically possible that first-borns having the greater power that accompanies age, may develop an interpersonal preference for interacting with less powerful others; similarly, they may develop an autocratic, authoritarian style with accompanying negative personality traits. The emergence of such negative characteristics in older children might also make them less popular than their younger siblings.

To ascertain which of these processes result in the greater popularity of later-borns relative to first-borns—the positive traits of later-born children or the negative characteristics of first-borns—Miller and Maruyama compared the popularity of first-born children to that of children with no siblings. If first-borns' dominance over their younger siblings results in an autocractic interpersonal style, which subsequently detracts from their popularity, children without siblings should be as popular as last-borns, in that both lack younger siblings to exploit. Alternatively—if later-borns must acquire positive interpersonal skills—only children (as well as other first-borns) should both be less popular than later-borns, since both first-born and only children lack the opportunity that younger siblings can provide for acquiring positive inter-personal skills.

Analyses revealed only children to be most similar in popularity to first-born children. Thus, it seems that only and first-born children are perhaps less popular because of a *failure* to acquire positive interpersonal skills, rather than because first-born children develop and use coercive power techniques. Additionally, Miller and Maruyama's (1976) data tend to refute Hartup's (1970) implicit contention that personality factors other than those related most directly to social skills mediate the birth-position/popularity relation. Not only were no ordinal position differences found on personality measures of self-esteem, anxiety, field dependence, achievement motivation, and delay of gratification, but neither were there differences in intelligence or school achievement among popular and unpopular children, or among children of different birth position.

Smith, Tedeschi, Brown and Lindskold (1973) also investigated the relation-ship between peer popularity and personality. Although they found no sex dif-ferences on separate measures of trust, self-esteem, and internal–external con-trol administered to children in grades IV, V and VI (9- to 11-year-olds), the pattern of intercorrelations among the measures was different for males and females. For males, popularity was accompanied by self-trust, self-esteem, and an orientation toward internal control. For females, popularity was not significantly related to any of these personality dimensions. The authors interpret this sex difference in terms of socialized sex-role demands, arguing that for males, normative pressures call for self-confidence and self-reliance. Thus, for example, boys who demonstrate trust or reliance in others may give the impression of incompetence or naivety, resulting in low acceptance by their similarly-socialized peers. For females, however, the normative pressures in regard to these particular personality dimensions may be less strong, and the traits consequently remain unrelated to popularity. These results suggest that normative pressures and learned skills of impression management in-fluence popularity.

Other research also attempts to document such differences in interpersonal skills. In a series of reports based on a sample of 20 children who were longi-tudinally tracked through grades kindergarten II, IV and VI (5- to 11-year-olds) Rubin (1971, 1972, 1973) found that in kindergarten and grade II (5- to 7-year-olds) the most popular children were least egocentric. Egocentrism was defined as an embeddedness of one's own view, or an inability to shift mental perspective between one's own and another's viewpoint. Thus, although it is thought that egocentrism diminishes with increasing levels of development, the ability to take another's viewpoint is clearly an interpersonal skill, and children may differ in the degree to which they develop it. For example, Waldrop and Halver-son (1975) found consistency in sociability, as measured by various observational indices, at the age of 2 years 6 months and again at the age of 7 years 6 months. An egocentric child, appearing to be selfish, or lacking empathy and sympathy, might consequently experience little peer acceptance. Interestingly, however, when he included his entire set of longitudinal measures, Rubin (1973) found that 11 measures of egocentrism were unrelated to sociometric popularity. Thus, the evidence provided by Rubin on the relation between egocentrism and popularity remains mixed and unclear. Deutsch (1975) provides additional related evidence; female preschoolers who were least egocentric were more popular on an observational measure of popularity but not on a sociometric measure similar to that used by Rubin (1973). Taken together, these findings suggest either that egocentrism and sociometric popularity are related only at certain developmental stages, or alternatively, that sociometric and observational measures of popularity are related only at certain ages—that is, at ages other than the preschool level.

Although the evidence provided by Rubin and Deutsch lacks definitiveness, other work does support the idea that children with greater social skills tend to be more popular. In a study by Gottman, Gonso and Rasmussen (1975), in which children provided a popularity score by listing an unspecified number of their peers as best friends, a number of different dimensions of social skills were measured. These included tasks in which the child was required to: label emotions in facial expressions, send cue words to a listener, take the visual perspective of another and demonstrate successfully how to make friends. The nature and frequency of interactions with peers and teachers was assessed with classroom observations. The results indicated that popular children, in contrast to their unpopular agemates, were socially more skilled and interacted differently with their peers. Specifically, relative to unpopular children, they had greater knowledge of how to make friends, they distributed and obtained more positive reinforcement, such as giving or receiving verbal approval or a token, and they spent less time daydreaming.

Mannarino's (1976) results also suggest that preadolescent males who have relatively stable friendships are more likely to be skilled at initiating or maintaining friendship relations. Controlling for popularity, and comparing grade VI boys who had a stable, fairly strong friendship with at least one peer to those who did not, Mannarino found that boys who did have 'chums' were more likely to have an altruistic orientation, as measured by a questionnaire and by scores on a modified prisoner's dilemma game. Drawing upon Sullivan's (1953) theorizing, Mannarino suggests that the specific interpersonal sensitivity generated within a chum relationship may generalize to become a more general concern for the welfare of others. Within the context of the present discussion, the presence of an altruistic orientation among boys with stable friendships can be interpreted as evidence of their greater knowledge, ability, or skill at making and keeping friends. Indeed, Mannarino's second friendship selection criterion, the Chumship Checklist, selects subjects who report engaging in behaviours that foster intimacy and reciprocity, such as 'tell each other things you wouldn't tell anyone else', and 'stick up for each other if an older boy is picking on one of you'. Additional work might profitably investigate the relation between Mannarino's Chumship Checklist and some of the other indicators of social facility or skill reviewed here.

Roistacher (1974) administered a sociometric instrument to 1 204 junior high school males, together with seven-point scales on which they could indicate how well they liked each of their peers, and how similar to themselves they perceived their peers to be. Well-liked boys received the same number of sociometric choices as others, but had a higher proportion of their choices reciprocated. Although Roistacher's detailed analyses cannot be thoroughly discussed here, his theoretical interpretation of the results provides an interesting addition to the question of the relation between social skill and popularity. He suggests that social success results from lower costs of obtaining information about potential friends and better allocation of effort, rather than merely having contact with more people. In other words, as found by Gottman *et al.* (1975) and Miller and Maruyama (1976) in their younger samples, popularity results from a knowledge of how to make friends and comfortably interact with them. The greater knowledge among Roistacher's subjects included that of how to allocate friendship-making effort, as well as an ability to discern which peers would be likely to reciprocate one's friendship choices.

To some extent, skill at athletics can be viewed as a component of social skill, insofar as most school related athletic activities include social interaction in combination with some motor skill. Coleman (1961) reported that the values of high-status cliques focused more on athletic and social skills than on academic excellence. Roistacher (1972) found that among junior high school males, members of larger-than-average cliques reported significantly more participation in athletics than did boys in smaller cliques. Thomas and Chissom (1973) found that gross motor skill differentiated males of high and low sociometric status. Indeed, Asher, Oden and Gottman (1979) have suggested that the general variable operating here is that of *expertness*: being good at something that is valued by other children leads to popularity. It is interesting to speculate about the extent to which these findings are specific to educational systems that are structured to emphasize individual competitiveness rather than cooperation.

Taken together these studies provide support for the view that certain kinds of skills, abilities, and attitudes toward others, act to make one more desirable as a friend. Irrespective of differences among children in their racial-ethnic background, the development of these traits is related to such structural variables as birth position. Their development apparently does not seem to depend on specific behaviours of parents; nor do the characteristics that make one desirable as a friend seem to be related to other personality traits that seem less likely to contribute directly to the quality of one's social interactions.

NORMATIVE INFLUENCES

Social psychologists have long been interested in processes whereby group norms are formed, maintained, and changed. As indicated earlier in our discussion of models of popularity, the teacher occupies a most important role in the classroom setting and consequently becomes a likely candidate as a source of influence. Children who rank high in terms of the similarity of their values to those of the teacher frequently emerge as most popular in the classroom (Glidewell *et al.*, 1966). As children develop their own values and attitudes, however, those of the teacher should diminish in impact. Thus, such effects should appear most strongly in the elementary grades and tend to disappear in the junior and senior high school years.

Gerard, Jackson and Conolley (1975) provide data that illustrate the impact of the teacher's values in multiethnic classrooms in which white children were numerically predominant. To generate teacher bias scores, they used an index based on the teacher's evaluation of a child's academic motivation. Those teachers whose academic expectations for a minority child were under-estimated relative to that child's actual academic performance in the preceding year, and whose expectations for white children were overestimated in terms of their actual previous performance, were defined as biased. Teachers who exhibited this bias were compared to those who tended not to underestimate the ability of minority children relative to that of white children. Examining the friendship nominations received by children in these two types of classes, they found that the more biased a teacher was toward minority children, the fewer friendship choices those children received from whites. Interestingly, this effect appeared only for friendship choices. On choices for schoolwork playground partner there was no relationship between a teacher's bias and the popularity of minority children among their white peers.

Gerard *et al.* favour a modelling explanation of these results, wherein the teacher sets the example by his/her treatment of the minority children in a class and the white children follow that example. Their failure to find a relation between either playground or schoolwork popularity and teachers' bias suggests, as does Hallinan's (1976) work, that the teachers' value system cannot or does not predominate in other settings, such as the playground. The different outcomes for playground or mutual schoolwork situations makes sense, in that choices for these latter dimensions are less pure as measures of friendship; for instance, playground choices undoubtedly also reflect athletic ability, and schoolwork choices must depend in part on scholastic talent.

More recent analyses of these same data further reveal that in both 1966 (prior to desegregation) and in 1967 and 1969 (after desegregation) clique members were rated more favourably by their teachers than were isolates (Gentry and Miller, 1978). These ratings were made on an array of adjective trait dimensions; when subjected to factor analysis, they yielded two factor

Table 6.2.   Teachers ratings of isolates and clique members

	Evaluation factor			Activity factor		
	Predesegregation	Post 1	Post 3	Predesegregation	Post 1	Post 3
Isolates	31.71*	30.79	32.34	26.36	26.67	28.98
Members	33.28	33.52	33.55	29.49	28.99	29.31

*Higher scores indicate more favourable ratings.

scores, one representing evaluation, and the other an activity-related content domain. The first factor primarily reflects the ratings the child received on such traits as: prone to anger; difficult to discipline; prone to tantrums; disobedient; demanding; not helping; and impatient. The second primarily reflects the ratings the child received from the teacher on the items: not energetic; submissive; fearful; slow; weak-willed; dependent; and cautious. The means for these measures at three points in time are presented in Table 6.2. (Higher scores reflected relatively more favourable ratings.) It should be noted that although the means are arrayed similarly in all years, the 1969 differences between isolates and clique members are not significant, 3 years after the implementation of the desegregation programme.

Our own data further suggest that the child's parents may not have such strong effects as does the teacher. Specifically, the child's parents rated the child on the same dimensions as did the teacher. When subjected to varimax rotation, the parent ratings show virtually the same factor structure as those found for teachers. Analysis, however, reveals no differences between the ratings that isolates and clique members receive from their parents. Other analyses that examine the relation between these same parental ratings and popularity as reflected by peer nominations do not substantially change this picture. Although some of the correlations attain significance, the picture they present is not a consistent one and the overall strength of the relations, as can be seen from inspection of Table 6.3, is rather weak. If anything, the correlations of parent ratings with friendship popularity, as opposed to popularity for school work or playground partner, are weakest. This is especially true in the case of the first factor, which is a general evaluative factor. In accord with this, among three racial-ethnic groups, black children receive more favourable evaluations from their parents than do white or Mexican-American children, yet they are least popular among their classmates.

Taken together, these results argue against any model which sees popularity as arising directly from the overall reinforcement level, approval, or positive regard that a child receives in the home setting. Instead, they emphasize the role of the teacher and they tend to support a model in which his/her evaluation of a child has normative impact. Before stopping with this conclusion, however,

Table 6.3.   Correlation of parent ratings on evaluation and activity factors with popularity

Predesegregation

Sociometric criterion	Father's ratings		Mother's ratings	
	Evaluation	Activity	Evaluation	Activity
Seating	0.05†	0.04	0.12†	0.04
Play	0.00	0.01	0.00	0.09†
Work	0.08†	0.08†	0.14†	0.05†

*Post-1-year parent ratings**

	Evaluation	Activity
Seating	0.08†	0.06†
Play	0.00	0.07†
Work	0.05	0.14†

Post-3-years

	Father's ratings		Mother's ratings	
	Evaluation	Activity	Evaluation	Activity
Seating	0.04	0.16†	0.03	0.07
Play	0.05	0.16†	0.01	0.09†
Work	0.00	0.10†	0.02	0.13†

*Only one parent was interviewed in this year, usually the mother.
† $< .05$.

it is important to note that Hallinan (1976) questions the validity of generalizing the findings of classroom sociometric studies. In considering the comparison of sociometric outcomes in traditional classrooms to those obtained in alternative classrooms, she raises three criticisms (see Chapter 12): (1) that structural characteristics of the classroom such as physical arrangement, grouping practices, and pedagogical techniques are not considered; (2) that most sociometric studies examine only cross-sectional data (but see Gerard et al., 1975, for an exception); and (3) that often only data description techniques are employed, and that more powerful statistical techniques are thus required.

With these criticisms in mind, she compared the sociometric choice patterns of open, semi-open, and traditionally structured classrooms. Results indicated that, as predicted, open classrooms were less characterized by skewed hierarchal distributions of choices which contain relatively large numbers of isolates and stars; instead, they were more likely to foster mutual friendships of longer duration, and were more likely to break down 'psychologically uncomfortable' asymetric and intransitive relationships among children. Hallinan thus demonstrates that these methods of alternative education do seem to improve the social climate in the elementary school. Free interaction seemingly reduces the importance and unequal distribution of popularity, increases contact, and fosters the formation of mutual, lasting friendships. In addition, her contentions call attention to the possibility that the teacher's potency as a source of normative impact may be diminished in classrooms that depart from the typical social and physical configurations found in American education.

Turning instead to other sources of normative influence on children, how might other aspects of parental behaviour influence a child's friendships? Employing a subset of data from the same data set as Gerard *et al.* (1975), Orive and Gerard (1975) suggested that a minority child's success in establishing friendly interpersonal relationships with white agemates depends on the degree to which his/her parents have developed contacts in the white community. Minority parents who rarely associate with whites may not have acquired behaviours that are appropriate in terms of the norms of the white community. Not having acquired them, their children cannot model such behaviours, and consequently they are not as attractive to their white agemates. Combining the number of choices the child received on all three sociometric criteria, Orive and Gerard found that the more extensive his father's contact with mixed-ethnic organizations which contained white adults, the more acceptance a minority boy received from his white classmates; his mother's contact with whites was unrelated to his popularity. Curiously, however, neither father nor mother contact was related to girls' popularity. Yet, when the minority father reported *less* contact with relatives, minority girls were more popular with their white peers. These data indirectly suggest, at least for boys, that those whose parents cannot or do not model or directly teach the norms of the majority will be less popular. Knowledge of prevailing norms is thus an antecedent of a skill enabling the child to be popular or unpopular, at least with the members of the group enforcing those norms.

A study of older children (Cohen, 1977) points indirectly to the importance of parental values and attitudes. Cohen provides a detailed investigation of the sources of homogeneity in the attitudes and habits of adolescent clique members. Employing data from Coleman's (1961) Newlawn High, he found impressive homogeneity, as indexed by similarity among the scores of clique members' responses to a set of 18 questionnaire items. The questionnaire measured 'a range of attitude and habits in areas of concern to adolescents' such as intention to go to college, frequency of dates, etc. Detailed analyses compared the strength of three possible sources of clique homogeneity: conformity to social or normative pressures within cliques; the rejection or departure of those who deviate most from other clique members; and the tendency to select persons similar to existing clique members as group replacements or additions. Both conformity pressures and the tendency to add new or replace leaving members with similar peers worked to produce greater homogeneity among those within as opposed to those outside of cliques. The strongest source of attitude homogeneity, however, was *initial homophilic selection*—the tendency of those initially forming a clique to choose one another on the basis of similarity.

Cohen's careful work suggests that cliques are homogeneous in traits and attitudes primarily because individuals tend to *form* relationships and cliques on the basis of attitude and value similarity. A particularly interesting implication of this overriding importance of initial selection is that newly-formed relationships (and groups) within a stable population tend to be more uniform than older ones. This is due to the fact that as members of a school population become better acquainted with one another through the passage of time, they also become better able accurately to identify and pick similar cliquemates (Cohen, 1977; Newcomb, 1961).

Since Cohen (1977) only examined peers as a source of homogeneity among clique members, his results do not directly isolate the source of peer group norms and uniformity. For example, no data on the effects of teachers or parents were included. Morever, as he notes, if peers are similar at the time of their friendship choice, their similarity cannot have been produced by any mutual pressure. To take an example, students might select one another on the basis of mutual college plans. Because there is a positive relation between socioeconomic status and college attendance, college-bound peers would unintentionally tend to choose friends whose parents possessed high social status. In this case, then, the similarity between friends, rather than being the result of mutual influence processes, is more probably a reflection of the similarity between their respective parents. Parental influence thus seems very powerful, and may outweigh the importance of other factors such as classroom organization or pedagogical technique (Hallinan, 1976). Further, Cohen's results indicate that the effects of parental influence persist even among older children in the more open high school environment.

It is important to note that in studying children in stable or 'captive' school or classroom groups, non-school influences tend to be ignored. Although some of the studies reviewed have gathered data from parents, to our knowledge no study has systematically investigated children's friendships and peer relations outside the school setting and examined their relation to peer relations within the school setting. The prevalence of the neighbourhood school concept as a guiding policy in school districts throughout the country automatically results in a child's neighbourhood peers also being his schoolmates. The advent of mandatory busing programmes to combat segregation and the increased enrolment in private schools portends an increasing number of children whose neighbourhood playmates are not their schoolmates. Consequently, it is possible that a child might be relatively unpopular in the school setting, not assimilating any of the values of his school peers and instead drawing his values, norms, and social skills from neighbourhood peers and from siblings.

PHYSICAL ATTRACTIVENESS

The burgeoning research on the effects of physical attractiveness has shown that it not only affects first impressions and attitudes (Clifford and Walster, 1974; Mills and Aronson, 1965), but long-term relations as well (Murstein, 1972). Others act differently toward attractive as opposed to unattractive persons, in general behaving more favourably toward them (Athanasiou and Greene, 1973; Barocus and Karoly, 1972; Mims, Hartnett and, Nay, 1975; West and Brown, 1975). Other research shows that even exactly identical behaviour by attractive and unattractive persons elicits different responses from others (Snyder, Tanke and Berscheid, 1977). At the same time, other studies do reveal differences in the behaviours of attractive and unattractive persons. For example, attractive persons are more frequently referred for counselling services, yet receive more favourable clinical prognoses (Barocus and Black, 1974; Barocus and Vance, 1974). Additionally, they are less likely to be juvenile delinquents (Cavior and Howard, 1973).

Because there are strong tendencies to view others as integrated and consistent units (Asch, 1952) this array of evidence suggests that it should not be too surprising to find that physical attractiveness affects sociometric nominations. Although attractive persons judge themselves to be more popular (Berscheid, Dion, Walster and Walster, 1971; Walster, Aronson, Abrahams and Rottmann, 1966) little direct evidence exists other than Dion and Berscheid's (1974) findings with preschool children.

Maruyama and Miller (1975, 1978) present additional data that largely confirm the expected results. Among white and Mexican-American children, those rated more attractive by independent judges were sociometrically more popular among their school-mates. More recent analyses of these data tend to confirm this same outcome for measures of clique membership (Gentry and Miller, 1978). Interestingly, and somewhat anomalously, no relation was found for black children. In part, this can be traced to the fact that most of the positive relations found between physical attractiveness and other variables (e.g. first impressions, teacher and parent ratings, and favourable personality traits) were reversed for black children. For them, physical beauty was a detriment. Given these unexpected reversals, the absence of a positive relation between the popularity and the physical attractiveness of black children may be more understandable, although the generally negative outcomes found for attractive black children on other variables remains a puzzle.

Lerner and Lerner (1977) report similar findings for rural white grade IV and VI children (9- and 11-year-olds). Instead of using sociometric nominations to assess popularity, they used peer nominations of the boy or girl for whom each of nine positive and negative attributes most aptly applied. As shown by Gentry and Miller (1978) such scores, especially with regard to positive attributes, are related to sociometric popularity. In the Lerners' data, nominations for positive traits (other boys and girls like him/her, most want as friend, happy, etc.) were positively related to physical attractiveness whereas a negative relation was found for negative nominations.

SCHOOL DESEGREGATION[3]

As stated in the legal decisions that guide public policy in the United States, the purpose of school desegregation is often phrased in ambiguous if not platitudinous terminology: for example, to 'reduce the harms of segregation', 'provide equal educational opportunity', or 'improve education for all children'. Sometimes these aims have been interpreted by the courts as requiring the redistribution of the students within a district so that each school is a racial-ethnic microcosm of the district, containing the same proportions of students from each racial-ethnic background as found in the district as a whole. Indeed, in the court cases that immediately followed the historic Brown decision, in which the United States Supreme Court ruled that separate schools for black children were inherently unequal, the courts often seemed to interpret proportional redistribution as the goal of desegregation. In recent years, however, court decisions have tended to emphasize more concrete goals other than numerical redistribution, such as reducing the educational achievement gap that characterizes the academic performance of white and minority students. Stephan (1978), Gerard and Miller (1975), Miller (1979) and others have interpreted the 1954 Brown decision as not only attempting to redress this particular problem, but also as concerned with other tangible goals: aiming to improve inter-ethnic relations and to raise the self-concepts of minority children.

In the social science theorizing that has been concerned with achieving these three goals, the hypothesis of 'the lateral transmission of values' has occupied a major explanatory position. As will be shown, peer acceptance, and consequently sociometric data, play a pivotal role in this theorizing.

The lateral transmission of values hypothesis is really a theoretical model concerned with how beneficial desegregation effects are achieved. It contains a number of distinct components. It suggests that: (a) there is a specific set of values that facilitate achievement; (b) these values are in fact possessed by many, if not most of the white, middle-class children, but by lesser proportions of lower-class and minority children; (c) inter-racial mixing of minority children into classrooms that have a numerical majority of middle-class white children, and consequently, also have a white, middle-class norm structure, will result in minority children internalizing these achievement-related values; and (d) in conjunction with the higher achievement level that is normative in the middle-class school, possession of these values will lead to improved academic achievement.

The logic behind the process just described is deeply rooted in experimental social psychology. The notions of: (a) specific values facilitating achievement (e.g. McClelland, 1961); (b) social influence processes resulting in the norms of the majority being passed onto the minority (e.g. Asch, 1952; Jones and Gerard, 1967); and (c) within limits, performance levels being responsive to standards (e.g. Atkinson, 1964); have all been well documented, at least within the laboratory. Further evidence has suggested that achievement-related values have in fact been more prevalent in white children than in minority children (e.g., Mussen, 1953). Given the laboratory evidence supporting the notions comprising the lateral transmission of values hypothesis, social scientists concerned with minority academic performance interpreted their findings in terms of value transmission although other interpretive alternatives were in fact available (Coleman, Campbell, Hobson, McPartland, Mood, Wernfeld and York, 1966; Crain and Weisman, 1972).

The 'value' dimensions in the lateral transmission of values hypothesis presumably can bring about academic achievement change in two different ways. First, they can have a direct normative influence on achievement; that is, simply behaving in ways consistent with the values that are predominant could affect achievement. An alternative view would argue that the values which are internalized induce changes in personality, which in turn produce changes in achievement. This latter sequence, which can be drawn more clearly from the social psychology literature cited earlier, appears to be the one implied by Coleman *et al.* (1966), and by Crain and Weisman (1972). Taking as an example a specific aspect of achievement motivation—locus of control—they emphasize that as compared to segregated minority children, minority children in desegregated classrooms exhibit a greater tendency to perceive themselves as in control of their environment.

Regardless of the choice between the two models suggested above, there seem to be two additional variables that mediate the value transmission hypothesis. First, unless minority children are accepted by their white peers, value transmission seems unlikely to occur. Support for this proposition has been provided by the United States Commission on Civil Rights (1967), which found achievement of black children to be related to: (a) a lack of racial tension; (b) having a close friend who is white; and (c) the percentage of white students in the classroom. Therefore, peer acceptance occupies a pivotal position in the transmission of values hypothesis.

Second, teachers may produce effects paralleling those of peers. That is, teachers provide an additional set of salient values. However, insofar as: (a) there is little reason to believe that teachers in white schools hold basic educational values that differ much from those held by teachers in minority schools; and (b) any results of differing expectations for children tend to affect ongoing processes rather than outcomes (e.g. Brophy and Good, 1974), this latter source of influence might be seen as somewhat less important.

To summarize, we have suggested that the lateral transmission of values hypothesis follows logically from previous research and provides a plausible model for examining the effects of school desegregation. It proposes that values mediate the relation between background influences and achievement. Given that middle-class white children are numerically preponderant in the classroom, the values of minority children can presumably be changed by: (a) favourable inter-racial contact resulting in (b) minority children acquiring the values of the white children, which *may* (c) lead to change in personality structure of the minority children, and will (d) result in higher achievement by minority children. Thus, in this model acceptance by their white classmates is critical for improvement in the academic performance of minority children.

If peer acceptance plays such an important role in the theorizing about beneficial desegregation effects, it becomes important to examine factors that affect a white child's prejudice against minority children. Likewise, since reciprocity of 'liking' plays such an important role in attraction and friendship, it becomes equally important to examine minority prejudice toward white children.

Westman and Miller (1978) selected children who exhibited an extreme increase or decrease in prejudice following desegregation. Prejudice was measured by children's responses to an ethnic pictures test, in which degrees of in- and out-group acceptance and rejection are reflected in the preference ranks assigned by the white, Mexican-American and black children to same— and other—sex facial colour pictures of children from these three racial groups.

Using this index, children who tend distinctly and exclusively to prefer the pictures of those who belong to their own racial ethnic group can be compared to those whose preferences are not influenced by race. A detailed analysis of the correlates of this outgroup prejudice shows that prejudice among children is related to their intelligence. Children whose postdesegregation prejudice decreased had higher IQ scores than did children whose prejudice increased, although this difference was not manifested on scholastic achievement tests or on classroom grades. Similarly, differentiation between children whose prejudice increased and those whose prejudice decreased were pronounced in teacher's ratings; the less prejudiced children were rated more favourably. Finally, those whose prejudice decreased as desegregation continued received more sociometric nominations as schoolwork partners.

This result for schoolwork popularity can be seen as consistent with those for intelligence and for teacher ratings: the child with greater intellectual ability is less prejudiced, receives more favourable ratings from the teacher, and is sociometrically more popular on the schoolwork criterion, which is perhaps most directly relevant to the arena of intelligence and achievement. One explanation for these results, as previously implied, is that rejection *by* others leads to a rejection *of* others, in this case members of the outgroup. Of course, the causal direction could be reversed, such that *being* prejudiced makes one less desirable in the eyes of others and thus leads to rejection (non-acceptance) by them. As Westman and Miller (1978) note, however, the failure to find differences between prejudiced and unprejudiced children on the play-partner and seating partner sociometric popularity indicators appears to weaken this latter interpretation to the extent that the difference in popularity was specific to the 'schoolwork situation'.

Since no meaningful or consistent differences between children whose prejudice increased and those whose prejudice decreased were found on an array of personality measures (including self-attitudes, self-esteem, and anxiety), these results give no support to a view that sees prejudice as a form of displaced hostility stemming from the self-hatred that underlies low self-esteem, high anxiety and a sense of rejection by others. Instead, they support the cognitive sophistication interpretation suggested by Glock et al. (1975). This latter view, emphasizing the role of cognitive complexity, sophistication, and cynicism in curtailing the development of prejudice, builds upon an earlier discussion of stereotypes which emphasizes their substantial basis in truth (Campbell, 1956, 1962). Prejudice, as well as representing an explanation of group differences via completion of self-fulfilling prophecies, more fundamentally rests on the perception that true group differences do exist. Cognitive sophistication promotes immunity to prejudice by enabling one to deal more effectively with the truth component of stereotypes. It enables one to discriminate between relative versus absolute differences, to curtail their over-generalization, and by increasing one's understanding of how such differences arise, to resist prejudicial responses to them.

Let us turn next, however, to studies that more directly examine the lateral transmission of values hypothesis. The findings of Gerard and Miller (1975) must be considered disappointing to anyone advocating a lateral transmission of values approach to desegregation. Riverside voluntarily implemented a desegregation programme backed by community support; further, the percentage of minority children in Riverside was 20 per cent, a proportion presumably beneficial for school desegregation (e.g. United States Commission on Civil Rights, 1967). Given these and other factors (see Hendrick, 1975), Riverside should have provided a good environment both for producing successful desegregation and for examining the lateral transmission of values hypothesis.

Despite the promotive environment that seemingly existed, there was no positive effect of desegregation on achievement test scores for minority children, although the achievement scores of white children were not adversely affected. The predesegregation scholastic achievement deficits that characterized minority children were not made up, but continued to increase as grade-in-school increased. Desegregation produced a decrease in the class grades of the minority children and improvement in the grades of white children. This stemmed from two facts. Since white children on the average perform at a higher scholastic level than do minority children, the desegregated classrooms contained a wider range in children's performance levels. At the same time, teachers typically employ a single set of norms when they grade their students, assigning approximately the same number of As, Bs, etc. from one year to the next. This grade normalization consequently resulted in poorer grades for the minority students and better grades for the white students.

The achievement results, however, do not in and of themselves constitute disconfirmation of the lateral transmission of values hypothesis. Despite the general lack of academic benefit following desegregation, it was still possible that those few minority students who did in fact improve academically were those who had been accepted and did adopt the values of the white children.

Turning first to analyses of the personality measures they show simply no support whatsoever for the lateral transmission of values hypothesis. Though some personality changes among minority children may be interpreted as consistent with it, these effects were so minimal and so inconsistent that they preclude the possibility that personality measures importantly predict achievement and mediate academic benefit. Any impact of white children on minority children, 'is most assuredly not mediated by changes in basic personality structures' (Miller, 1975, p. 302). Reanalyses of the Riverside data using 'causal model' approaches (McGarvey, 1977; Maruyama, 1977), clearly reaffirm this conclusion.

Consistent with the version of the lateral transmission of values hypothesis that postulates direct normative influence, however, minority children accepted by whites did in fact perform better than their peers who were not accepted (see Gerard et al., 1975). Nevertheless, several considerations temper this result. First, as suggested earlier, inter-racial acceptance was in fact low. Therefore, any benefits of promotive cross-racial interaction would be restricted to a small number of minority students. Second, consistent with the preceding reasoning, the positive relation between acceptance and achievement was primarily due to differences between minority children who had been high achievers in the segregated classrooms. Third, inter-racial acceptance resulted at best in maintaining past achievement levels, not improving them. The most important point, however, is that although the results are consistent with direct normative influence they are not conclusive. Gerard et al. 's (1975) analyses do not speak on the causal direction of the relation between a minority child's popularity and his academic performance.

Subsequently, two dissertations using a maximum likelihood structural equation approach to these data (cf. Joreskog, 1973) sought to test path analytic causal models (Maruyama, 1977; McGarvey, 1977). Maruyama, examining cross-sectional data from the data set, found that in the predesegregation year the peer acceptance of white children was positively related to the evaluations they received from teachers and parents and to their achievement. His evaluation of the causal processes seemed to indicate that peer acceptance did mediate the favourable effect of adult evaluations on achievement. Additionally, the black child's acceptance by white peers was directly related to achievement, as in the predesegregation all-minority classroom. McGarvey (1977) on the other hand, addressed the issue more directly. Rather than comparing static cross-sectional models of pre- and postdesegregation data, he tested a longitudinal model. When whites were considered apart from minorities, academic ability caused popularity in the postdesegregation year. This effect was not primarily mediated by increases in the child's popularity prior to desegregation (as was the case among minorities); predesegregation academic ability made a causally independent contribution to postdesegregation popularity. This was not the case for minority children, whose academic ability alone was not enough to gain them popularity in the desegregated setting. In a similar vein, Blanchard, Weigel and Cook (1975) found that the competence of blacks interacted with situational factors in affecting liking ratings received by them, while competence alone affected the ratings of liking received by whites.

These findings provide little support for a view that puts peer acceptance as an antecedent of the minority child's academic achievement in the predominantly white classroom. Additionally, they force us to reconsider the results obtained by Maruyama (1977). With the advantage of retrospective wisdom, it can now be seen that Maruyama's findings—based as they were on static cross-sectional analyses—only found support for the normative influence model because, prior to testing the model, he specified the direction of the relation between acceptance and academic achievement to be in accord with it. Given McGarvey's results, in which the causal relation between variables is specified by the temporal design rather than intuition or prior theorizing, Maruyama's positive path should be reversed to show (in accord with McGarvey) that it is academic ability which leads to acceptance.

To our knowledge, Lewis and St. John (1974) provide the only other test of the normative influence model. They too focus on the relation between popularity and academic achievement of black students in the desegregated classroom. Drawing from the findings of the United States Commission on Civil Rights (1967) cited earlier, they too argued that the academic success of black students would be contingent upon peer acceptance. They proposed a path model with socioeconomic status (SES) and percentage of white students as background variables external to the model; either: (a) past grade point average (GPA) or IQ (Otis Group administered test); or (b) popularity with whites as intervening variables; and present GPA or reading achievement as the criterion.

Though their data could perhaps be fitted as readily to other models, Lewis and St. John did seem to find support for the normative influence model. Popularity was related to GPA, though not to reading achievement. In the light of these findings, Lewis and St. John (1974) suggested that, 'the social process that best explains the beneficial effect of acceptance by white peers on black achievement is probably .the lateral transmission of achievement-oriented norms and/or skills' (p. 89). More recently, however, Maruyama and Miller

(1978) have reanalysed these same data, again using a structural equation approach to the data analysis (Joreskog, 1973). These latter procedures are superior to path analysis procedures in that they treat specific measures as indicators of the latent theoretical variables, thereby taking a more sensible approach with regard to measurement error and reliability. They also contain procedures for testing the goodness of fit of the specific model to the data. Reanalysis failed to confirm Lewis' and St. John's view that the popularity or acceptance of minority children by their classmates results in subsequent scholastic achievement gains. Instead reanalysis supported the opposite causal sequence: peer acceptance was the result of, not the cause of, good academic performance.

In conclusion existing research now appears to offer little, if any, support for either version of the lateral transmission of values hypothesis. In part the failure to find unambiguous support for a causal relation between peer acceptance and academic achievement in the desegregated setting may reflect the fact that sociometric choices and inter-racial contact are so strongly curtailed to within-race choices for both the minority and white child alike (Gerard et al., 1975; Stephan and Rosenfield, 1978) and further, that the influence of race on these preferences seems to increase if not remain constant after desegregation (Stephan, 1978). In Rosenberg and Simmons' examination of integrated schools, sociometric measures showed as much as 96 per cent of third choices for friend by black students to be within-race choices (Rosenberg and Simmons, 1971). Even in a school setting that probably came as close as is possible to meeting Allport's (1954) or Cook's (1969) criteria for beneficial inter-racial contact, Schofield and Sagar (1977) found little decrease in the extent to which race determined social interaction patterns among children in a middle school. If the desegregated school setting is indeed so strongly characterized by an absence of inter-racial contact and interaction, there is little opportunity for normative influence to operate. To put it somewhat differently, if the friendship choices and social interactions of black children were entirely restricted to other black children, it would be logically impossible to find a relation between acceptance by their white classmates and scholastic performance.

The preceding presentation and discussion of data suggest the need for some re-examination of the circumstances under which normative influence occurs. Indeed, one might well question why theorists had such expectations in the first place. What are the circumstances under which persons accept group norms and behave in accordance with them? More specifically, what circumstances would lead minority children to adopt norms that support scholastic achievement?

Although the answers to such questions have received considerable if tangential attention in discussions of the circumstances necessary for beneficial inter-racial contact (Allport, 1954; Amir, 1976; Cook, 1969; Schofield, 1978), important considerations have not been addressed. Norms will not be accepted without contact with the dominant group. Yet resegregation within the classroom commonly occurs after the implementation of desegregation programmes (Gerard and Miller, 1975; Rosenberg and Simmons, 1971; Schofield, 1978; Silverman and Shaw, 1973). Even with substantial contact, two important ingredients for increasing normative influence may be missing from most desegregated classrooms: first, white students must make their own acceptance of minority children and their friendship towards them contingent upon the minority child's adoption of White scholastic achievement norms; second, minority children must perceive that their acceptance by white classmates is indeed contingent upon adopting such norms. In the normal classroom it is not at all certain that the overt behaviour which supposedly reflects the internalization of scholastic achievement norms, namely good scholastic performance, does in fact exert strong influence on children's friendship choices either within racial ethnic groups or between them. Nor is it clear that children would or could verbalize such norms as being important in their friendship selection. Nor is it clear that those minority children who are accepted by their classmates more frequently exhibit behaviours that reflect acceptance of scholastic achievement norms. Instead, it seems more likely that socioeconomic similarity, common interests, teacher behaviour, and a variety of other factors operate to influence friendship patterns. Consequently, there is little reason to expect to find confirmation of the normative influence model.

Perhaps implicitly recognizing some of these doubts about the lateral transmission of values model, a number of researchers have worked to develop specific classroom procedures to improve academic performance. At the same time, others devised procedures aimed primarily at improving intergroup relations within the learning context. At least five distinct groups of researchers are currently engaged in implementing and evaluating outcomes of various cooperative learning techniques: Aronson and his colleagues (see Aronson, Bridgeman and Geffner, 1978); Cook and his associates (see Weigel, Wiser and Cook, 1975); the Johnsons (Johnson and Johnson, 1974); the Sharans (Sharan and Sharan, 1976); and Slavin and his predecessors (see Slavin and DeVries, 1979).

Each has developed cooperative procedures that contain features which distinguish them from others, yet all implicitly impose principles that work to enhance inter-racial attraction and friendship. First, they restructure the classroom setting so as to increase substantially the amount of inter-racial interaction in the classroom. Secondly, although the reward structures that they employ differ along several dimensions, they all tend to reinforce explicit positive behaviours on the part of children towards their classmates: helping; attending and listening to; rooting for; commiserating with; depending upon; etc. More importantly, these behaviours are reinforced across as well as within racial-ethnic boundaries. Thirdly, by their very nature, they tend to make explicit a norm structure that endorses inter-racial cooperation.

Although some combination or integration of these separate research efforts is required, a fairly consistent positive picture is revealed by all. In general, cooperative learning experiences have salutory effects on a wide range of children's outcomes, including achievement, individual psychological health, and interpersonal and inter-ethnic acceptance, trust and liking (cf. Johnson and Johnson, 1974).

Whereas the lateral transmission of values hypothesis places peer acceptance as causally antecedent to minority scholastic improvement, it seems likely that cooperative learning procedures exert independent and direct influence upon each of these variables. Thus, while they contain features that should work to enhance intergroup acceptance as argued above, it seems likely that their effects upon learning are not mediated by changes in social relationships and attitudes. Instead, it seems likely that when scholastic improvement occurs, it stems from enhanced motivation, greater participation and interest, and more time actively spent in learning activity.

While it is too soon to view cooperative learning as a panacea for educational ineffectiveness as well as inter-racial intolerance, it does seem to offer more promise than does a reliance upon the passive and indirect influence process that lies at the heart of the lateral transmission of values hypothesis—an influence process which, in its dependence upon a level of intergroup interaction and acceptance that does not often seem to empirically emerge, seems doomed to failure.

CONCLUSION

This chapter has presented recent information on methodological developments and issues with respect to sociometric data. Additionally, it has summarized recent empirical research concerned with the relation of popularity, as measured sociometrically, to other variables. Finally, it has examined in some detail the role of sociometric peer acceptance in desegregated school settings, concluding that current data provide relatively little confirmation of its supposed critical theoretical role (as specified by the lateral transmission of values hypothesis) in producing scholastic benefit to minority children.

NOTES

1. We wish to particularly acknowledge support from National Institute of Mental Health Grant R 03–MH 26094. The new data presented in this article were collected as part of a larger study on school desegregation in Riverside, California, in cooperation with the Riverside Unified School District. The project was supported by National Institute of Health Grants HD–02863 and HD–6255, the Rockefeller Foundation, the Regents of the University of California, the United States of Education Grant OEG–1–7–070375–5246, and the California State Department of Compensatory Education

(McAteer Act). We also acknowledge a NIMH Special Research Fellowship, a Haynes Foundation Summer Research Award and a James McKeen Cattell Fellowship all of which facilitated the preparation of this manuscript.

2. The Riverside sociometric data are arrayed as chooser-by-chosen matrices, allowing complex matrix methods to be applied. For this purpose we employed the 'SOCIO program', tailored by Johnson-Lenz (1974, 1977) to an IBM 1800 computer and written specifically for our data. Within this program, many algorithms for clique identification are available, all based on directed graph theory (Harary, Norman and Cartwright, 1964). We have chosen to report the results of only one such method, the strong components matrix. The SOCIO program allows the number of cliques in a classroom to be counted and also allows a score to be assigned to each subject reflecting whether or not the subject belongs to a clique. It is this latter score that was computed for all subjects in our sample and which we employed in our research to be reported here.

3. We thank Geoffrey Maruyama for assistance with this section.

REFERENCES

Alba, R., and Gutman, M. (1971). *SOCK—A Sociometric Analysis System*. New York: Bureau of Applied Social Research.

Allport, G. (1954). *The Nature of Prejudice*. Reading, Massachusetts: Addison-Wesley.

Almack, J. C. (1922). The influence of intelligence on the selection of associates. *School Society*, **16**, 529–530.

Alt, J. E., and Schofield, N. (1975). Clique: a suite of programs for extracting cliques from a symmetric graph. *Behavioral Science*, **20**, 134–135.

Amir, Y. (1976). The role of intergroup contact in change of prejudice and ethnic relations. In P. A. Katz (Ed.), *Towards the Elimination of Racism*. New York: Pergamon Press.

Aronson, E., Bridgeman, D. L., and Geffner, R. (1978). The effects of a cooperative classroom structure on students' behavior and attitudes. In D. Bar-Tal and L. Saxe (Eds.), *Social Psychology of Education: Theory and Research*. Washington, DC: Hemisphere.

Asch, S. E. (1952). *Social Psychology*. Englewood Cliffs, New Jersey: Prentice-Hall.

Asher, S. R., Oden, S. L., and Gottman, J. M. (1979). Children's friendships in school settings. In L. G. Katz (Ed.), *Current Topics in Early Childhood Education*. Vol. 1. Hillsdale, New Jersey: Erlbaum.

Athanasiou, R., and Greene, P. (1973). Physical attractiveness and helping behavior. *Proceedings of the 81st Annual Convention of the American Psychological Association*, **8**, 289–290.

Atkinson, J. W. (1964). *An Introduction to Motivation*. Princeton, New Jersey: Van Nostrand.

Bailey, K. D. (1975). Cluster analysis. In D. R. Heise (Ed.), *Sociological Methodology*. San Francisco: Jossey-Bass.

Barocus, R., and Black, H. K. (1974). Referral rate and physical attractiveness in third grade children. *Perceptual and Motor Skills*, **39**, 731–734.

Barocus, R., and Karoly, P. (1972). Effects of physical appearance on social responsiveness. *Psychological Reports*, **31**, 495–500.

Barocus, R., and Vance, F. L. (1974). Physical appearance and personal adjustment counseling. *Journal of Counseling Psychology*, **4**, 96–100.

Berscheid, E., Dion, K., Walster, E., and Walster, G. W. (1971). Physical attractiveness and dating choice: a test of the matching hypothesis. *Journal of Experimental Social Psychology*, **7**, 173–189.

Blanchard, F. A., Weigel, R. H., and Cook, S. W. (1975). The effect of relative competence of group members upon interpersonal attraction in cooperating inter-racial groups. *Journal of Personality and Social Psychology*, 32, 519–530.

Bonacich, P. (1972). Factoring and weighting approaches to status scores and clique identification. *Journal of Mathematical Sociology*, 2, 113–120.

Boorman, S. A., and White, H. C. (1976). Social structure from multiple networks. II. Role structures. *American Journal of Sociology*, 81, 1384–1446.

Brophy, J. E., and Good, T. L. (1974). *Teacher-student Relationships: Causes and Consequences*. New York: Holt, Rinehart and Winston.

Campbell, D. T. (1956). Enhancement of contrast as a composite habit. *Journal of Abnormal and Social Psychology*, 53, 350–353.

Campbell, D. T. (1962). Stereotypes and the perception of group differences. *American Psychologist*, 22, 817–829.

Capobianco, M. F. (1970). Statistical inference in finite populations having structure. *Transactions of the New York Academy of Science*, 32, 401–413.

Cavior, N., and Howard, L. R. (1973). Facial attractiveness and juvenile delinquency among black and white offenders. *Journal of Abnormal Child Psychology*, 1, 202–213.

Clifford, M. M., and Walster, E. (1973). The effects of physical attractiveness on teacher expectations. *Sociology of Education*, 46, 248–258.

Cohen, J. M. (1977). Sources of peer group homogeneity. *Sociology of Education*, 50, 227–241.

Coleman, J. (1961). *The Adolescent Society*. Glencoe, Illinois: Free Press.

Coleman, J. S., Campbell, E. Q., Hobson, C. J., McPartland, J., Mood, A. M., Wernfeld, F.D., and York, R. L. (1966). *Equality of Educational Opportunity*. Washington, DC: Office of Education, HEW.

Cook, S. W. (1969). Motives in a conceptual analysis of attitude-related behavior. In D. Levine (Ed.), *Nebraska Symposium on Motivation, 1969*. Lincoln, Nebraska: University of Nebraska Press.

Crain, R. L., and Weisman, C. S. (1972). *Discrimination, Personality, and Achievement: A Survey of Northern Blacks*. New York: Seminar Press.

Dahl, R. A. (1961). *Who Governs: Democracy and Power in an American City*. New Haven, Connecticut: Yale University Press.

Deutsch, F. (1975). Observational and sociometric measures of peer popularity and their relationship to egocentric communication in female preschoolers. *Developmental Psychology*, 10, 745–747.

Dion, K., and Berscheid, E. (1974). Physical attractiveness and peer perception among children. *Sociometry*, 37, 1–12.

Flament, C. (1963). *Applications of Graph Theory to Group Structure*. Englewood Cliffs, New Jersey: Prentice-Hall.

Forsyth, E., and Katz, L. (1946). A matrix approach to the analysis of sociometric data: preliminary report. *Sociometry*, 9, 340–347.

Freeman, L. C. (1968). *Patterns of Local Community Leadership*. Indianapolis: Bobbs Merril.

Gentry, K. W., and Miller, N. (1978). *Peer Relations and School Desegregation*. Unpublished manuscript, University of Southern California.

Gerard, H. B., Jackson, T. D., and Conolley, E. S. (1975). Social contact in the desegregated classroom. In H. B. Gerard and N. Miller (Eds.), *School Desegregation*. New York: Plenum Press.

Gerard, H. B., and Miller, N. (1975). *School Desegregation*. New York: Plenum Press.

Glanzer, M., and Glaser, R. (1959). Techniques for the study of group structure and behavior. I. Analysis of structure. *Psychological Bulletin*, 65, 317–332.

Glidewell, J. C., Kantor, M. B., Smith, L. M., and Stringer, L. A. (1966). Socialization and social structure in the classroom. In M. L. Hoffman and L. N. Hoffman (Eds.), *Review of Research in Child Development*, No. 2. New York: Russel Sage Foundation.

Glock, C. Y., Wuthnow, R., Piliavin, J. A., and Spence, M. (1975). *Adolescent Prejudice*. New York: Harper and Row.

Gottman, J., Gonso, J., and Rasmussen, B. (1975). Social interaction, social competence, and friendship in children. *Child Development*, **46**, 709–718.

Granovetter, M. (1976). Network sampling: some first steps. *American Journal of Sociology*, **81**, 1287–1303.

Guttman, L. (1950). The basis for scalogram analysis. In S. A. Stouffer, L. Guttman, E. A. Suchman, B. S. Lazarsfeldt, S. A. Star, and J. A. Clausen (Eds.), *Measurement and Prediction*. Princeton, New Jersey: Princeton University Press.

Guttman, L. (1968). A general nonmetric technique for finding the smallest coordinate space for a configuration of points. *Psychometrika*, **33**, 469–506.

Hallinan, M. T. (1974). *The Structure of Positive Sentiment*. New York: American Elsevier.

Hallinan, M. T. (1976). Friendship patterns in open and traditional classrooms. *Sociology of Education*, **49**, 254–265.

Harary, F. (1969). *Graph Theory*. Reading, Massachusetts: Addison-Wesley.

Harary, F., Norman, R. Z., and Cartwright, D. (1965). *Structural Models: An Introduction to the Theory of Directed Graphs*. New York: Wiley.

Hartup, W. W. (1970). Peer interaction and social organization. In P. H. Mussen (Ed.), *Carmichael's Manual of Child Psychology*, Vol. II (third edition). New York: Wiley.

Heber, R. F., and Heber, M. E. (1957). The effect of group failure and success on social status. *Journal of Educational Psychology*, **48**, 129–134.

Hendrick, I. E. (1975). The historical setting. In H. B. Gerard and N. Miller (Eds.), *School Desegregation*, New York: Plenum Press.

Holland, P., and Leinhardt, S. (1973). The structural implications of measurement error in sociometry. *Journal of Mathematical Sociology*, **3**, 85–112.

Homans, G. C. (1950). *The Human Group*. New York: Harcourt Brace Jovanovich.

Hubbell, C. H. (1965). An input–output approach to clique identification. *Sociometry*, **28**, 377–399.

Hunter, F. (1953). *Community Power Structure*. Durham, North Carolina: University of North Carolina Press.

Johnson, D. W., and Johnson, R. T. (1974). Instructional goal structure: cooperative, competitive, or individualistic. *Review of Educational Research*, **44**, 213–240.

Johnson-Lenz, P. (1977). The SOCIO data analysis system. Unpublished manuscript, 695 Fifth Street, Lake Oswego, Oregon 97034.

Jones, E. E., and Gerard, H. B. (1967). *Foundations of Social Psychology*. New York: Wiley.

Joreskog, K. G. (1973). A general method for estimating a linear structural equation system. In A. S. Goldberger and O. D. Duncan (Eds.), *Structural Equation Models in the Social Sciences*. New York: Seminar Press.

Katz, L. (1950). Punched card technique for the analysis of multiple level sociometric data. *Sociometry*, **13**, 108–122.

Kleck, R. D., Richardson, S. A., and Ronald, L. (1974). Physical appearance cues and interpersonal attraction in children. *Child Development*, **45**, 305–310.

Lankford, P. M. (1974). Comparative analysis of clique identification methods. *Sociometry*, **37**, 287–305.

Laumann, E. O., and House, J. S. (1970). Living room styles and social attributes: the patterning of material artifacts in a modern urban community. In E. O. Laumann, P. Siegel and R. W. Hodge (Eds.), *The Logic of Social Hierarchies*. Chicago: Markham.

Laumann, E. O., and Pappi, F. U. (1976). *Networks of Collective Action*. New York: Academic Press.

Lerner, R. M., and Lerner, J. V. (1977). Effects of age, sex, and physical attractiveness on child–peer relations, academic performance, and elementary school adjustment. *Developmental Psychology*, **13**, 585–590.

Levine, J. H. (1972). The sphere of influence. *American Sociological Review*, **37**, 14–27.

Lewis, R., and St. John, N. (1974). Contribution of cross-racial friendship to minority group achievement in desegregated classrooms. *Sociometry*, **37**, 79–91.

Lindzey, G., and Byrne, D. (1968). Measurement of social choice and interpersonal attractiveness. In G. Linzey and E. Aronson (Eds.), *The Handbook of Social Psychology*, Vol. II. Reading, Massachusetts: Addison-Wesley.

Lingoes, J. C. (1972). A survey of the Guttman–Lingoes nonmetric series. In R. Shepard, A. K. Romney and S. B. Nerlove (Eds.), *Multidimensional Scaling: Theory and Applications in the Behavioral Sciences*. New York: Seminar Press.

Lorrain, F. P., and White, H. C. (1971). Structural equivalence of individuals in social networks. *Journal of Mathematical Sociology*, **1**, 49–80.

McClelland, D. C. (1961). *The Achieving Society*. Princeton, New Jersey: Van Nostrand.

McFarland, D., and Brown, D. (1973). Social distance as a metric: a systematic introduction to smallest space analysis. In E. O. Laumann (Ed.), *Bonds of Pluralism: The Form and Substance of Urban Social Networks*. New York: Wiley.

McGarvey, W. E. (1977). Longitudinal factors in school desegregation. Unpublished doctoral dissertation, University of Southern California.

Macrae, D., Jr. (1960). Direct factor analysis of sociometric data. *Sociometry*, **23**, 360–371.

Mannarino, A. P. (1976). Friendship patterns and altruistic behavior in preadolescent males. *Developmental Psychology*, **12**, 555–556.

Maruyama, G. M. (1977). A causal model analysis of school desegregation. Unpublished doctoral dissertation, University of Southern California.

Maruyama, G., and Miller, N. (1975). *Physical Attractiveness and Classroom Acceptance*. SSRI Research Report 75-2, Social Science Research Institute, University of Southern California.

Maruyama, G., and Miller, N. (1977). The effects of physical attractiveness and race on essay evaluation. Paper presented at the meeting of the Psychonomic Society.

Maruyama, G., and Miller, N. (1978). Re-examination of normative influence processes in desegregated classrooms. Unpublished manuscript, University of Southern California.

Miller, N. (1975). Summary and conclusions. In H. B. Gerard and N. Miller (Eds.), *School Desegregation*. New York: Plenum Press.

Miller, N. (1979). Principles and social policy relevant to successful school desegregation. In W. Stephan (Ed.), *Desegregation: Past, Present, and Future*. New York: Plenum Press.

Miller, N., and Maruyama, G. (1976). Ordinal position and peer popularity. *Journal of Personality and Social Psychology*, **33**, 123–131.

Mills, J., and Aronson, E. (1965). Opinion change as a function of the communicator's attractiveness and desire to influence. *Journal of Personality and Social Psychology*, **1**, 173–177.

Mims, P. R., Harnett, J. J., and Nay, W. R. (1975). Interpersonal attraction and help volunteering as a function of physical attractiveness. *Journal of Psychology*, **89**, 125–131.

Mitchell, J. C. (1969). *Social Networks in Urban Situations*. Manchester: Manchester University Press.

Moore, S. G. (1967). Correlates of peer acceptance in nursery school children. In W. W. Hartup and N. L. Smothergill (Eds.), *The Young Child*. Washington, DC: National Association for the Education of Young Children.

Moreno, J. L. (1934). *Who Shall Survive?* Washington, DC: Nervous and Mental Disease Publishing Company.

Murstein, B. I. (1972). Physical attractiveness and marital choice. *Journal of Personality and Social Psychology*, **22**, 8–12.

Naugher, J. R. (1976). A system for the collection and computer analysis of sociometric data for research and classroom purposes. *Dissertation Abstracts International*, **36**, 12–A7957–7958.

Mussen, P. H. (1953). Differences between the TAT responses of negro and white boys. *Journal of Consulting Psychology*, **17**, 373–376.

Newcomb, T. M. (1961). *The Acquaintance Process*. New York: Holt, Rinehart and Winston.

Niemeijer, R. (1973). Some applications of the notion of density. In J. Boissevain and J. C. Mitchell (Eds.), *Network Analysis: Studies in Human Interaction*. The Hague: Mouton.

Nosanchuk, T. A. (1963). A comparison of several sociometric partitioning techniques. *Sociometry*, **26**, 112–124.

Oden, S., and Asher, S. R. (1977). Coaching children in social skills for friendship making. *Child Development*, **48**, 495–506.

Orive, R., and Gerard, H. B. (1975). Social contact of minority parents and their children's acceptance by classmates. *Sociometry*, **38**, 518–524.

Reynolds, T. J. (1976). The analysis of dominance matrices: extraction of unidimensional orders within a multidimensional context. Unpublished doctoral dissertation, University of Southern California.

Roethlisberger, F. J., and Dickson, W. J. (1939). *Management and the Worker*. Cambridge, Massachusetts: Harvard University Press.

Roff, M., Sells, B., and Golden, M. M. (1972). *Social Adjustment and Personality Development in Children*. Minneapolis: University of Minnesota Press.

Roistacher, R. C. (1972). Peer nominations, clique structures, and exploratory behavior in boys at four junior high schools. Unpublished doctoral dissertation, University of Michigan.

Roistacher, R. C. (1974). A microeconomic model of sociometric choice. *Sociometry*, **37**, 219–238.

Rosen, R., and Abrams, P. (1970). *CHAIN: A Sociometric Linkage Program*. New York: Bureau of Applied Social Research, Columbia University.

Rosenberg, M., and Simmons, R. G. (1971). *Black and White Self-esteem: The Urban School Child*. Washington, DC: American Sociological Association.

Rossi, P. H. (1960). Power and community structure. *Midwest Journal of Political Science*, **4**, 390–401.

Rubin, K. H. (1971). Egocentrism in early and middle childhood: a factor analytic investigation. Unpublished doctoral dissertation, Pennsylvania State University.

Rubin, K. H. (1972). Relationship between egocentric communication and popularity among peers. *Developmental Psychology*, **7**, 364.

Rubin, K. H. (1973). Egocentrism in childhood: a unitary construct? *Child Development*, **44**, 102–110.

Schachter, S. (1964). Birth order and sociometric choice. *Journal of Abnormal and Social Psychology*, **68**, 453–456.

Schofield, J. W. (1978). School desegregation and intergroup relations. In D. Bar-Tal and L. Saxe (Eds.), *Social Psychology of Education: Theory and Research*. Washington, DC: Hemisphere Publishing Company.

Schofield, J. W., and Sagar, H. A. (1977). Peer interaction patterns in an integrated middle school. *Sociometry*, **40**, 130–138.

Sells, S. B., and Roff, M. (1964). Peer acceptance–rejection and birth order. *Psychology in the Schools*, **1**, 156–162.

Sharan, S., and Sharan, Y. (1976). *Small Group Teaching*. Englewood Cliffs, New Jersey: Educational Technology Publications.

Silverman, I., and Shaw, M. E. (1973). Effects of sudden mass desegregation on interracial interaction and attitudes in one southern city. *Journal of Social Issues*, **29**, 133–142.

Singleton, L. C., and Asher, S. R. (1977). Peer preferences and social interaction among third-grade children in an integrated school district. *Journal of Educational Psychology*, **69**, 330–336.

Slavin, R. E., and DeVries, D. L. (1979). Learning in teams. In H. Walberg (Ed.), *Educational Environments and Effects: Evaluation and Policy*. In press.

Smith, R. B., III, Tedeschi, J. T., Brown, R. C., Jr., and Lindskold, S. (1973). Correlations between trust, self-esteem, sociometric choice, and internal–external control. *Psychological Reports*, **32**, 739–743.

Snyder, M., Tanke, E. D., and Berscheid, E. (1977). Social perception and interpersonal behavior: on the self-fulfilling nature of social stereotypes. *Journal of Personality and Social Psychology*, **35**, 656–666.

Stephan, W. G. (1978). School desegregation: an evaluation of predictions made in Brown vs. The Board of Education. *Psychological Bulletin*, **85**, 217–238.

Stephan, W. G., and Rosenfield, D. (1978). *The effects of desegregation on race relations and self-esteem*. Unpublished manuscript, University of Texas at Austin.

Sullivan, H. S. (1953). *The Interpersonal Theory of Psychology*. New York: Norton.

Thomas, J. R., and Chissom, B. S. (1973). Differentiation between high and low sociometric status for sixth-grade boys using selected measures of motor skill. *Child Study Journal*, **3**, 125–130.

Tapiero, C., Capobianco, M., and Lewin, A. (1975). Structural inferences in organizations. *Journal of Mathematical Sociology*, **4**, 121–130.

Turk, H. (1973). *Interorganizational Activation in Urban Communities: Deducations from the Concept of System*. ASA Rose Monograph Series. Washington, DC: American Sociological Association.

United States Commission on Civil Rights. (1967). *Racial Isolation in the Public Schools*. Washington, DC: United States Government Printing Office.

Walser, E., Aronson, V., Abrahams, D., and Rottman, L. (1966). Importance of physical attractiveness in dating behavior. *Journal of Personality and Social Psychology*, **4**, 508–516.

Waldrop, M. F., and Halverson, C. F., Jr. (1975). Intensive and extensive peer behavior: longitudinal and cross-sectional analyses. *Child Development*, **46**, 19–26.

Weigel, R. H., Wiser, P. L., and Cook, S. W. (1972). The impact of cooperative learning experiences on cross-ethnic relations and attitudes. *Journal of Social Issues*, **28**, 1–19.

West, S. G., and Brown, T. J. (1975). Physical attractiveness, the severity of the emergency, and helping: a field experiment and interpersonal simulation. *Journal of Experimental Social Psychology*, **11**, 531–538.

Westman, G., and Miller, N. (1978). *Concomitants of Outgroup Prejudice in Desegregated Elementary School Children*. SSRI Research Report, Social Science Research Institute, University of Southern California.

White, H. C., Boorman, S. A., and Breiger, R. L. (1976). Social structure from multiple networks. I. Blockmodels of roles and positions. *American Journal of Sociology*, **81**, 730–780.

SECTION III

DYNAMICS OF FRIENDSHIP

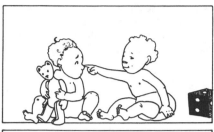

CHAPTER 7

Peer Play and Friendships during the First Two Years

DEBORAH L. VANDELL
and
EDWARD C. MUELLER

At 20 months, Percy and Steven are sitting at opposite ends of a rocking boat. Percy screeches. Steven laughs. Percy screeches. Steven laughs. The cycle is repeated several times. Then Steven begins to crawl from the rocking boat. Percy vocalizes, 'ah,' smiles, and then reaches to Steven and touches his head and shoulders lightly with several pats. Steven walks away (Marvin, 1977, p. 4).

Zeke and Samual are both six months old. This visit is their second one with each other. Zeke and Samual are sitting about 10 inches from each other. Samual waves both arms as he looks at Zeke. Samual then looks down at his own foot and moves his foot back and forth across the carpet. He then leans forward and touches Zeke's foot as he looks at Zeke's face. Zeke then reaches over and touches Samual's face. Samual leans away from Zeke. Zeke looks at Samual and vocalizes. Samual leans forward again and touches Zeke's foot. Zeke smiles and vocalizes as he looks at Samual. Touching, smiling, and vocalizing with periodic looks at the face of the other baby continue for the next few minutes until Zeke loses his balance and falls over (Vandell, in preparation, boydyad # 6-session 1 observation).

A dog approaches the children (former inmates in a German concentration camp) who are terrified. Ruth (about $3\frac{1}{2}$ years) though badly frightened

181

herself, walks bravely to Peter who is screaming and gives him her toy rabbit
to comfort him. She comforts John next by lending him her necklace ...
Paul (about $3\frac{1}{2}$ years) loves eating corn flakes. He has just started eating when
Miriam, who is not sitting next to him, drops her spoon. Paul at once stops
eating and picks up the spoon for her before continuing (Freud and Dann,
1951, p. 136–137).

The observations of Marvin, Vandell, and Freud and Dann were chosen to
begin this discussion of early peer play and friendship because they illustrate
two points that are pursued in this chapter. The first point is that very young
children (infants and toddlers, in fact) are capable of engaging in fairly extended
and sophisticated social interactions. While this point is not as surprising today
as it once was, it must still serve as a starting point for this discussion. The second
point then follows from the establishment of peer interaction. If infants and
toddlers are capable of complex interactions, do they also exhibit specific
peer preferences? That is, do they have friendships?

In 1975, Lewis and Rosenblum edited a volume entitled *The Origins of
Behaviour : Friendship and Peer Relations* which in its title promised to examine
just these issues. Unfortunately, however, the examination of peer infant
relations was still in its infancy when that book was being prepared; and the
bulk of the volume was devoted to descriptions of early peer interaction (the
necessary first step, but still not an analysis of friendship). Only one of the
empirical papers in the collection (Lewis, Young, Brooks and Michalson,
1975) explicitly considered the issue of friendship. Still, the anecdotal comments
of other contributors (Hartup, 1975; Yarrow, 1975) suggested that infant–
toddler friendships might not be unreasonable.

In the present chapter, the quest for understanding peer interaction and
friendship during the first 2 years is resumed. Since the study of early peer
relations is now in its 'toddlerhood', it is possible to address the issue of friendship in more detail.

As a part of this process, the present chapter is divided into five sections.
First, there is a description of early social interaction and play. This section
provides an index of social skills which an infant might bring to bear on early
friendships. The second section then examines early friendships explicitly.
It examines what might be meant by the term 'friend' during infancy as well as
how common the 'friendship' phenomenon might be. The third section
then investigates a related phenomenon, namely popularity. Popularity is
differentiated from friendship and the studies of infant popularity are examined
for their revelations concerning friendship. In the fourth section the possible
origins of early peer relations are examined. Questions about the effects of
parents, siblings, and objects on peer interactions are addressed. Finally, in
the fifth section, the implications of peer play and peer friendships for child
care are explored. In this final section, the relevance of the play and friendship
research for the development of environments for children is discussed.

SOCIAL BEHAVIOUR, SOCIAL INTERACTION AND PEER PLAY

During the 1920s and 1930s, a group of studies (Bridges, 1933; Buhler, 1927; Klein and Wander, 1933; Maudry and Nekula, 1939; Mengert, 1931) illustrated the range of peer social encounters possible during the first 2 years. For example, Buhler (1927) described the reactions of infants when the babies' mothers came to a milk depot in New York City. During the visits the unfamiliar infants were placed together in a crib facing each other and their reactions were recorded. In a second classic of the period, Bridges (1933) recorded the social behaviours of a group of Canadian orphanage babies as they engaged in their regular morning activities. From 9 months onward, the babies were regularly placed together in groups; and Bridges outlined what occurred during these regular visits. Like Bridges (1933), Maudry and Nekula (1939) also observed institutionalized children (in this case, low-income Viennese children who were in the temporary custody of an orphanage). Rather than observing the regular morning activities, however, Maudry and Nekula placed dyads of infants together in an experimental manipulation. A series of objects were introduced and removed in a systematic order. The babies' reactions to the objects and to each other were then recorded.

Recently there has been a continuation of these research traditions. Eckerman, Whatley and Kutz (1975) and Ross and Goldman (1976) adopted situations analogous in some ways to Buhler's observations. Unfamiliar infants were brought into an unfamiliar situation and observed together. In observations that paralleled Bridges', Vincze (1971) observed institutionalized (and familiar) infants as they interacted as part of their regular day. Lee (1973), Mueller and Rich (1976), and Vandell and Mueller (1977) adopted situations similar to Bridges' in terms of naturalistic observation of regularly occurring morning activities. Familiar infants (who were members of playgroups) were observed as they played together without outside interference. Finally, DeStefano (1976) and Vandell (in preparation) have systematically varied the objects available to infant peers in a situation somewhat analogous to Maudry and Nekula's.

In these various studies separated by time and place, three types of peer activities have been described: social behaviour, social interaction, and peer play. Before proceeding with a discussion of peer friendship each of these activities should be discussed. One can argue that each represents a necessary ingredient out of which early peer friendship are formed.

Peer social behaviour

Studying social behaviour in infancy presents special difficulties. A major problem is how to determine whether a 6-month-old or a 10-month-old infant is, in fact, directing a social behaviour to a peer. For example, when an infant touches another child, is the infant simply exploring the other child as he might an inanimate object or is there some awareness of the personal identity of the other child? When an infant smiles, can one assume that the facial expression has any social intent? Obviously, the preverbal child cannot be asked his intention; so how might intention be inferred?

Several researchers (Becker, 1977; Bridges, 1933; Bronson, 1975; Mueller and Brenner, 1977) have resolved this dilemma in a similar way. They have adopted visual regard as the criterion. If one child looks at another child (especially at the other child's face) while exhibiting another behaviour, then a social behaviour is said to have occurred. Thus, if a child smiles while looking at another child's face, a social smile is registered. Similarly, if a child takes a toy while looking at the second child's face, a *social take* is typically recorded.

Using this criterion, a remarkable consistency has been recorded in the appearance of peer social behaviour (Mueller and Vandell, 1979). Even in institutionalized children (Bridges, 1933; Maudry and Nekula, 1939; Vincze, 1971), in children reared in fairly extreme poverty (Buhler, 1927), and in children deprived of extensive peer experience (Eckerman *et al.*, 1975; Ross and Goldman, 1976; Shirley, 1933), the range of peer social behaviours and the order of those behaviours' appearance have been similar.

As one would expect, simple looking at the peer appears first, by about 2 months of age (Bridges, 1933; Lichtenberger, 1965; Vincze, 1971). It is on this base that other social behaviours build. Social touching has been reported by three to four months (Lichtenberger, 1965; Shirley, 1933; Vincze, 1971). Peer-directed smiles and vocalizations have been observed in 6-month-old infants (Bridges, 1933; Buhler, 1927; Maudry and Nekula, 1939; Vincze, 1971). When they are able to creep or crawl, infants have been found to approach, follow, and reach for each other (Bridges, 1933; Durfee and Lee, 1973). By 12 months of age, a whole repertoire of peer social behaviours has appeared. In fact, it can be argued that many of the crucial behavioural elements of subsequent friendship are present by 12 months. The toddlers will offer and receive toys. They will laugh and smile at the peer. They will imitate the peer's activity.

It would be a mistake, however, to over-estimate the skills one sees in these 12-month-olds. During the first year, many of the social behaviours appear as isolated social behaviours (Becker, 1977; Lee, 1973; Vandell, in preparation). In these one-way contacts, the infant directs a social behaviour to another infant and elicits no response from the second child. Lee, in looking at 6- to 10-months-olds, found 60 per cent of her infants' social behaviours to be of this one-way variety.

In essence, these early social behaviours can be seen as the building blocks for early interaction (Mueller and Lucas, 1975). As a first step in interaction, the isolated social behaviours do not elicit a response. When the social behaviour of one child does succeed in eliciting a social behaviour from the second child, however, a social interaction can be said to occur (Becker, 1977; Bronson, 1975; Mueller and Brenner, 1977; Mueller and Vandell, 1979).

Social interaction

While one-way contacts were common encounters in the first year, peer social interactions have also been recorded (Becker, 1977; Durfee and Lee, 1973). These elicited responses are a notably more difficult accomplishment than are one-way contacts. Not only must child A direct a behaviour to child B, but child A must make the behaviour interesting enough to elicit a response from B. For B's part, he must not only direct a social behaviour to A, but that behaviour must come fairly rapidly (Becker, 1977; Goldman and Ross, 1977; Vandell, 1977). Vandell (1977), for example, found that if a social response were to occur, it usually happened within 1.8 sec of A's social behaviour. The break between A's behaviour and B's behaviour when not in interaction was more in the order of 30 sec. In somewhat older children (3 years 6 months of age), Lieberman and Garvey (1977) have noted a similar rapidity of interaction. The most common pause in their children's behaviours during interaction was 1.5 sec. After 1.5 sec, the probability of responses dropped off markedly.

It will be noted from this description of social interaction that no reference has been made to the content of the interactions. In fact, content can vary widely during social interactions. A sequence like 'John hits Sam. Sam grabs John and John then cries' represents an interaction of three units as does a more pleasant sequence like 'John smiles at Sam. Sam laughs and touches John. John kisses Sam.' In the analysis of the social interaction sequences, the requirement of turn alternation can be seen as more critical than content; and many of the studies of early interaction have focused on this alternation (Becker, 1977; Mueller and Brenner, 1977; Vandell, 1977; Vandell and Mueller, 1977).

Becker (1977), for example, outlined the development of interaction sequences in 9-month-olds observed with the same social partner over a 3-week period. She found sequences of at least three units in length in 18 per cent of her subjects' peer behaviours. During the second year, Vandell (1977) recorded even longer sequences, with sequences up to 24 exchanges in 22-month-olds.

While content is not the major determinant of interaction, an observation should still be made concerning the content of the exchanges. Most of the social interactions observed in the infants and toddlers have had a distinctly serious tone. Mueller and Brenner (1977) reported that 70 per cent of the interactions they observed in playgroup toddlers were affectively neutral. Similarly, Rubenstein and Howes (1976) have noted the predominance of affectively neutral encounters in their sample of home-reared toddlers. In both studies, positive affect was relatively infrequent when compared to neutral affect.

It may be only with the mastery of social interaction that positive affect is expressed during interaction. The results of Ross and Goldman's study (1976) of 12- to 24-month-olds support such a hypothesis. Ross and Goldman found positive affect to be most common in interactions involving 2-year-olds and least common with 1-year-olds. The 18-month-olds showed a variable pattern of positive affect. With an older partner, positive affect was more prevalent than with a younger partner.

Ross and Goldman argued that this positive affect served a special function in the interactions. The smiles and laughter were seen as acting as metacommunication between the children. According to Ross and Goldman, they marked the special case, 'This is a game'. If they are correct, then just as social interaction may grow out of social behaviours, infant games may grow out of social interaction. Play may represent those special cases of social interaction which have been freed of the serious business of learning to interact.

Peer social play

The problems discussed earlier in defining social behaviour are compounded by the difficulties inherent in the attempt to define play. The range of activities that have been included within the concept of play is extremely broad (Bruner, Jolly and Sylva, 1977; Garvey, 1977; Millar, 1968). Consider several situations that might be included under the rubric of play. Two infants pat each other for 30 sec. They smile and vocalize repeatedly. A 4-month-old lies in her crib. She bounces her crib by arching her back and then slamming down onto the bed. A mobile jiggles and the baby stares intently. She repeats the activity 10 times. A father and son engage in a game of checkers. The son's brow is creased and he looked very serious. The father suggests stopping the game; and the son violently protests.

One conclusion that could be drawn after examining this range of possible play activities is that play is a meaningless topic for scientific study. Schlosberg (1947), for example, has drawn just such a conclusion. Schlosberg argued that there are simply too many divergent strands of activities involved to be meaningfully integrated into a single coherent concept. More recently Garvey (1977) also has noted the special difficulties in studying play. As Garvey pointed out, play, like Proteus, keeps changing shape, with the characteristics and functions of play varying developmentally and situationally. Despite Schlosberg's argument and the difficulties inherent in defining play, however, the study of social play has proceeded.

Millar (1968) has begun by arguing what play is not. According to Millar, play is not simply an explosion of surplus energy. Nor did Millar see play as simply a practice of instinctual or necessary skills. What play is, according to Millar, is an attitude of pleasure and enjoyment. It was seen as *any activity* that is approached in a less serious way and with a lack of constraint.

In identifying play as an attitude, Millar (1968) is reminiscent of Piaget's (1962) definition of play. In observing the sensory-motor child, Piaget also argued that play is marked by a lack of constraint and less seriousness. When Piaget observed Laurent and Jacqueline, he noted that play appeared only after the children had mastered a given activity or task. Until then, the children were very intent on the task at hand. With mastery, however, the activity appeared to be engaged in for its own sake and with pleasure. The hallmarks of play, according to Piaget, were then repetition and positive affect.

Garvey (1977) has adopted similar criteria of enjoyment and repetition. According to Garvey, even when the play is not actually accompanied by positive affect, it is still positively valued. To these features, Garvey then added four additional characteristics. According to Garvey, play has no extrinsic goals. Rather, the underlying motivation for play is intrinsic with the means being more important than the ends. Second, Garvey argued that play must be spontaneous and voluntary, not obligatory. One cannot make someone play. Third, Garvey contended that play must include active engagement on the part of the player. According to Garvey, play cannot be passive. And finally, Garvey saw play as more than a harmless aberration. Garvey argued that play has an important role in cognitive and social development.

Each of the definitions of play given thus far has included all types of play as well as play at various ages. Goldman and Ross (1977), however, have completed an analysis of social play and games that is especially relevant for this chapter. Goldman and Ross videotaped the social interactions of 48 toddlers in a laboratory playroom. The videotapes were then analysed for the presence of *infant games* using four criteria. Like Garvey (1977), Goldman and Ross first looked for active involvement; and in keeping with the topic of *social* play, this involvement needed to be mutual and with each other. As a second requirement, Goldman and Ross then expected *turn alternations* to occur. Each child had to act and then wait for a response from the partner. One should note that these first two criteria correspond to the definition of social interaction given in the previous section. It was only in the two final criteria that the special case of infant games emerged.

These two criteria, repetition and non-literality, often occurred together. Non-literality referred to the different meaning behaviours had during games and during ordinary circumstances. This non-literality could be marked in several ways. Smiles and laughter, for example, acted as the non-literal markers which distinguished rough and tumble play from agonistic encounters. A push or shove accompanied by laughter and smiles was seen as qualitatively different from that same activity accompanied by a frown. Similarly,.smiles and laughter help distinguish a playful 'offer and receive' sequence from a more serious exchange of material.

The non-literality of infant games was also apparent in turn repetition, the fourth characteristic of infant games. When an action was repeated over and over, it became apparent that the activity itself was the ultimate goal. For example, when a toddler offered a toy repeatedly, it became apparent that the child was more concerned with the act of distribution and less concerned with the end product of the distribution.

Using these four rather stringent criteria, Goldman and Ross found 28 examples of infant games in the 24 dyads they observed. These games ranged from 8 to 280 sec in duration with the number of turn alternations ranging from four to 31. These games were found to be of three types. The first and simplest games were imitative. Within this category, Goldman and Ross described mutual patting, laughing, and in some cases, imitative vocalizations. Other researchers (Buhler, 1927; Vincze, 1974) have also described games of this type in babies as young as 6 months old. The second type of game was more complex and included complementary roles. For example, one child vocalized and another child laughed through at least two exchanges, or one child banged a toy and another child vocalized through at least two rounds. Peak-a-boo games which Vincze (1974) described in infants as young as 10 months old would be of this complementary sort. It was only in the third and final type of game that the two toddlers took reciprocal roles. In reciprocal games, one child might offer an object which the other child received; or, one child might chase the second child who was the chasee.

In examining Goldman and Ross' protocols as well as the descriptions of Buhler, Vincze, and Mueller, one is struck by the complexity of the social play which was observed. Still, these studies may be an under-estimation of early social skills and games. Some of the studies (Bridges, 1933; Vincze, 1974) observed institutionalized children and it is possible that some of these infants were retarded. At the same time, those studies (Buhler, 1927; Goldman and Ross, 1977) of non-institutionalized children, while not having the problems of institutionalization, may have had other limiting factors. These latter studies tended to observe unfamiliar, peer inexperienced children on a short-term basis. Mueller and Vandell (1979) have compared data indicating that situational constraints such as unfamiliar setting, unfamiliar children, and lack of peer experience can signficantly lessen the amount and complexity of the interactions observed.

In view of these limiting factors, it may be that early peer friendships can provide the optimal expression of the early peer social skills. The infants would not only be familiar with each other but they would have a better opportunity to develop a repertoire of interactions and games with an infant friend. Thus, one might argue that just as parent–child interaction can act as a best approximation of the adult–child system, friend–peer interaction can be a particularly good index of early peer interaction competence.

Early peer friendship may act as a best approximation of early social competence for a second reason. Friendships can be seen as a culmination of infant social skills, a culmination that emerges only after social behaviour, interaction, and play have appeared. In this approach, social behaviours are the simplest social skill. However, over time—and with an opportunity to be with other children—social interactions (the sequencing of social behaviours) would develop. Then, with the mastery of social interaction, there is evidence that the special case of peer social play can develop. In play, the special features of positive affect and repetition are added to ordinary social interaction. Friendship may then be conceptualized as a fourth level of social competence.

EARLY PEER FRIENDSHIPS

Since it is apparent that infants and toddlers can play together, the next issue to address is whether 1- and 2-year-olds are also capable of developing friendships. The description from Freud and Dann (1951) which introduces this chapter suggests that such friendships are possible. Unfortunately, however, Freud and Dann were describing somewhat older children who had experienced a very atypical infancy. Reared in a concentration camp with little adult attention, the children turned to each other for emotional support. When brought to England after the Second World War, the children showed a deep and persistent bond to each other. They protected each other when threatened. They would interrupt their own favourite activities in order to help each other. When they were apart, they continually asked for each other.

Still other anecdotes suggest that friendships during the first 2 years may be possible under less traumatic conditions as well (Marvin, 1977; Yarrow, 1975). Yarrow, for example, has briefly described two 16-month-old friends. She outlined how when one came into a room and saw his friend sobbing, he frowned, then walked over to his friend, patted him, and gave him a toy.

One of the authors of this chapter has his own friendship anecdote. Loren, his son, began playing with Robert when the two boys were 8- and 10-months-old. After 5 months, Robert and Loren then joined the same playgroup. During the playgroup, the boys actively chose one another as the preferred playmate; and in their play, the two boys showed the most sophisticated play of the playgroup. Years later when Robert moved away, he continually asked for Loren and Loren repeatedly for Robert.

Even with these anecdotes, however, one may wonder about more empirical support concerning early peer friendships. It may be asked whether these anecdotes highlight the unusual case. As a first step in addressing this question, two preliminary questions must be addressed. First of all, one must ask what is meant by friendship in children, especially infants and toddlers. The second question then follows from the first. How might one measure these friendships?

Definition of early friendships

Several definitions have been proposed for friendship in older children. For example, Selman (1975) has described friendship in terms of trust and intimacy.

According to Selman, this level of trust and intimacy is based on an individual's level of interpersonal awareness. Bigelow (1977) has argued that friendship can be conceptualized in both concrete and abstract terms. Bigelow's investigations indicated that friendships in younger children were characterized by giving help and sharing activities while friendship in older children incorporated more abstract qualities such as genuineness and intimacy. Gamer (1977) has argued that friendship implies mutual support. According to Gamer, a friend is an individual upon whom one can rely.

It is quite clear that facets of each of these definitions are inappropriate for 1- and 2-year-olds. Obviously, infants will not demonstrate Selman's higher levels of interpersonal awareness. In addition, genuineness and intimacy are probably not important factors for toddlers. Still, there are other aspects of friendship which are not beyond 1- and 2-year-olds.

In Gamer's and Bigelow's definitions, friendship was at least partially defined in terms of particular and specific behaviours. Friends did certain things like help one another and share in activities. Friends did not hurt one another. Implicit also was the idea that one can place greater expectations on friends.

As outlined in the first section, infants and toddlers are capable of social behaviours which include some of these potential friendship indicators: they can offer and receive objects (i.e. share); they can engage in mutual activities; they are capable of agonistic and non-agonistic encounters; and they can show positive and negative affect during interactions. Thus, it appears that toddlers have at least the bricks for building early friendships.

Toddlers may also be capable of a second characteristic implicit in the definitions of friendship in older children. In the studies of older children it is assumed that friends will choose to play with one another in preference to other children. This mutual preference is expected in the global sense of total number of behaviours directed to the friend as well as in the differential use of specific behaviours. Thus, friends are expected to show more evidence of play, sharing, positive affect, and proximity seeking with each other than with others. One may wonder if any less of an expectation can be placed on friendships during the first 2 years.

In combining these criteria, it is then possible to arrive at least at a working definition of peer friendship during the first 2 years. Early peer friends may be characterized by: (a) a greater frequency of certain behaviours such as proximity seeking, sharing, positive affect, and play; and (b) a mutual preference with the two friends specifically preferring each other as interaction partners.

Measures of friendship

Following directly from the definition of early friendship, one may be able to develop several techniques for studying friendships. As was the case with the definition of friendship, the studies on older children suggest several directions for potential research. Many of the studies of older children have used socio-metric techniques (Eder and Hallinan, 1977; Foot, Chapman and Smith, 1977; Gottman, Gonso and Rasmussen, 1975). In these studies children were asked with whom they liked to play, who their friends were, and with whom they liked to spend time. In a second approach, children were still interviewed, but they were questioned concerning the attributes they associated with friends (Bigelow, 1977; Bigelow and La Gaipa, 1975; Peevers and Secord, 1973; Selman and Jacquette, 1977). Using such an approach, children have been found to describe friends in terms of prosocial criteria such as support, loyalty, trust, and reciprocity. In contrast to the first two approaches, a third approach has not adopted interview techniques for studying friendship. On the contrary, these studies (Marshall and McCandless, 1957) observed children during their play to see with whom they played. Specific behaviours and preferences were recorded through direct observation; and the friendship analyses were then based on these direct observations.

Obviously, studying friendship during the first 2 years presents some special difficulties. First, one must determine the potential opportunity for making friends. Certainly two children who live in separate houses across town and who only see each other for 10 minutes in a laboratory situation can hardly be classified as friends. Thus, before trying to study friendship, it must be asked how much contact do infants have with each other during the first 2 years.

These figures vary considerably. In a review of sibling caretaking in a variety of non-Western cultures, Weisner and Gallimore (1977) reported that sibling caretaking (which occurred in many cultures) enhanced the probability of infant–peer contact; and they implied that such peer contacts were not un-common events. As for Western infants, Goldman and Ross (1977) noted that 28 per cent of the first-born toddlers they observed interacted at least two or three times a week with another same-aged child. Thirteen per cent interacted daily with another child. Lewis et al. (1975) reported that 22 per cent of their 1-year-olds participated in regular playgroups, while 28 per cent of their 18-month-olds did. Vandell (in preparation) has found that even many 6-month-olds have regular peer experience. Only 30 per cent of her first-born, home-reared infants had never had contact with another infant, while 60 per cent were with another baby at least once a week. Forty per cent were with other babies three or four times a week. Mother's Day Out and shared baby sitting were common experiences for these middle-class/upper-middle-class babies. Thus, one can conclude that for at least a number of babies there is an opportunity for friendships to develop in infancy; but do they, in fact, do so?

Toddlers cannot be asked who their friends are as they would be in a socio-metric study nor can they be asked to describe friendship characteristics as they might in an interview. Instead, modifications must be introduced. In a modification of the sociometric approach (Lewis et al., 1975; Rubenstein and Howes, 1976), *mothers* were asked to identify their infants' friends. The infants with their mother-identified friends were then observed. Other studies (Vandell, 1978), however, have taken a second approach. Direct observation of the infants was used as the method of determining the friendships, that is, what the infants did with particular children was used as the friendship determinant.

Consider these two types of studies in detail. Using maternal reports of the infant friendships, Lewis *et al.* (1975) compared the interaction characteristics of peer friends and peer strangers. A 'friend' was defined as a child with whom the focal infant had played at least twice a week over the previous 2 weeks and once a week over the preceding 2 months. The 'stranger' was a same-aged infant with whom the focal baby had not had previous contact. The 1-year-old focal infants were brought into the laboratory on two occasions, once with the reported friend and once with a peer stranger. Significant differences were found in the child–friend and child–stranger dyads. More proximal contacts and positive affect were found between infant 'friends'. The infant 'friends' also imitated one another more often. Three times more negative affect was found with the 'strangers'. At the same time, there were no differences in the child–friend and child–stranger dyads in the frequency of distal contacts like vocalizing and looking. When one compares these behaviours with the definitions of friendship developed earlier (friends are more likely to express positive affect and to maintain proximity, they are less likely to make one another unhappy), one might conclude with Lewis *et al.* that friendship are possible in the second year.

In a second study, Lewis *et al.* (1975) experimentally manipulated friendship to see if a similar pattern might result. Eight dyads of 1-year-old strangers were observed in a laboratory playroom. Mothers were then instructed to have the two babies visit each other two or three times in their homes during the next week. The following week the infants were videotaped once again in the laboratory, followed by three more home visits. Two of the dyads were then videotaped a third time with each other. The remaining six infants were videotaped with a peer stranger.

A pattern of results similar to those of the first study was found. There was an increase in the frequency of proximal contacts between peers with increased exposure to each other. This pattern was then reversed for the six infants who were viewed with the peer stranger in the third visit and further strengthened for the two infants observed with the 'friend'.

An additional study of early peer relations has adopted maternal reports of peer experience as a potential friendship index. Like Lewis *et al.*, Rubenstein and Howes (1976) asked mothers if their infants had a consistent peer playmate or friend. 'Consistent' was defined as meaning playing together for two or three times a week for at least 4 months. The focal infants were then observed twice in the child's home, once with only the mother present and once with the friend, the friend's mother, as well as the child's own mother present.

Rubenstein and Howes found that the peer's presence had a significant impact on the child. The child interacted significantly less with the mother when the peer was present. In over 60 per cent of the 10-sec periods when the friend was present, focal child and friend were interacting. They characteristically vocalized to each other, exchanged toys, and imitated each other. Negative interactions were uncommon. In 19.8 per cent of the periods, the infant friends played together (defined as mutual awareness of reciprocal responding). Specifically, six of the pairs engaged in run–chase. Pushing–pulling the peer on a toy was seen in three toddler pairs. Two pairs engaged in fantasy play (like talking to one another on play telephones). If the hallmark of friendship is mutually shared interest in one another, Rubenstein and Howes' children do indeed qualify as friends.

Interestingly enough, the focal child's play with objects was also affected by peer friend's presence. Higher levels of object play were associated with the peer's presence. Thus, Rubenstein and Howes not only support the possibility of friendship occurring, but also the hypothesis that early friendship might facilitate infant development.

Unfortunately, however, in each of these studies a problem in interpretation exists because of the use of maternal reports. The variable being manipulated may not be friendship but simply the familiarity of the children. Just because two infants spend time together regularly does not make them friends.

Now it is time to consider direct assessment of early friendship. In line with the criteria for friendship outlincd earlier, several such assessments are possible. For example, one could observe toddlers with equally familiar peers in a group setting and see which peers choose whom. Friendship would then be defined as the dyadic preferences of two children. Another possibility is that a friendship pair might direct more specific behaviours like proximity seeking, touching, and smiling to each other than they do to other children.

Vandell (1978) has addressed both of these possibilities in a study of six toddler boys. The boys were the only members of a university playgroup which met for 3 hours daily over a 6-month period. The boys were all very familiar with each other, so the issue of differential familiarity was not the issue.

The boys were videotaped as they engaged as a group in free play. Because of the difficulty in focusing on all of the children simultaneously, each child was videotaped for 5 minutes, using a random order. Six of these 5-minute observations were made of each child during three separate periods (at 16, 19, and 22 months old). Each 5-minute observation was then analysed in terms of: (1) who interacted with whom; (2) who initiated the interactions; (3) what types of social behaviours were used during the interactions (positive affect, negative affect, sharing, agonistic actions); and (4) the presence of infant games.

Conclusions about the possibility of peer friendships in these six boys were determined by the measures of friendship that were adopted. The first measure examined was differential rate of interaction initiations. It was hypo-thesized that friends would be more likely to initiate interactions with each other than they would be to initiate interactions with other children in the playgroup. Using this criterion, two children, Tony and Steven, showed evidence of friendship but this mutual preference was seen only at 22 months old. Before that time, peer preferences were apparent with each of the six children choosing another child more frequently than others, but the second child never reciprocated this preference by primarily initiating interactions with the first child. Using this criterion of mutual initiation preference, then, friendships only emerged at 22 months old and only for two children.

Tony and Steven showed stronger evidence of friendship using other measures. For example, when friendship was defined in terms of a predominance of positive interaction (determined by the inclusion of positive affect and/or sharing in the social interactions), Tony and Steven were once again friends. With this measure, in all three periods, Tony and Steven were the most likely of any of the possible dyads to have positive interactions.

A third possible friendship index was also considered. Each social interaction sequence was analysed in terms of Goldman and Ross's four criteria of infant games: mutual engagement, turn alternation, non-literality, and repetition. Using these criteria, games were reported only at 22 months old. Once again, Tony and Steven represented the most likely friendship dyad.

In addition to looking at the six children in the group situation, Vandell (1978) also examined the possibility of early peer friendships in a dyadic setting. At 16, 19, and 22 months, the same six toddler boys were videotaped in every possible dyadic combination (15 dyads). For these dyads, each pair was separated from the group and then videotaped together for 15 minutes.

Evidence of reciprocal preferences in the interaction initiations was apparent in the dyadic setting, just as it was in the group situation. In the dyadic setting, however, friendship pairings occurred in all three periods; and the pairings were somewhat different from the group setting. The most initiations at 16 months old occurred for the Tony–Roy dyad. Tony and Peter had the most interactions at 19 months old. Tony and Steven was the most common dyad at 22 months old. In each case, both children most frequently chose to initiate interaction with each other more than with any other child.

Two points may be apparent in this outline of friendship pairs. First, during dyads, the preferences were not stable over time. Tony, the child chosen most often as a 'friend' by other children, differentially selected different partners over the 6 month period. Still, a second point should be noted. The pairing of Tony and Steven appeared late in the year in both the dyad and group settings.

The specific content of the social behaviours of each of the dyads was also analysed. First, positive interactions were studied. As was the case in the group study, positive interactions were those that included either positive affect, or sharing, or both. The results using the positive interactions as a friendship index closely paralleled the mutual preference measure. Tony and Roy had the most positive interactions of any dyad in the first period. Tony and Peter were tied with Tony and Steven for most positive interactions in the second period. Tony and Steven had the most positive interactions in the last period.

Finally the prevalence of infant games was compared. Once again, if an interaction was coded as an infant game, it was not coded as a positive interaction. Even so, the frequency of infant games closely paralleled the mutual initiation and positive interaction results. Roy and Tony played the most games at 16 months old and Peter and Tony played the most games at 19 months old.

Summary of friendship analyses

In each of the friendship analyses presented in this section, it appears that the concept of friendship is a viable one during the first 2 years of life. Lewis *et al.* illustrated that infant 'friends' could be differentiated from infant strangers even at 12 months old. Rubenstein and Howes reported friendship dyads across the second year. By 22 months old, according to Vandell's data, friendships defined as mutual preferences in interaction initiation were apparent. Finally, as indicated in this section there appears to be some stability in friendship choices over time. In the Vandell study, the dyad of Tony and Steven occurred repeatedly. Furthermore, Tony's presence in all friendship pairs suggests that friendship formation may depend on *personal* characteristics as well as *reciprocal* factors.

PEER POPULARITY

In this discussion of friendship, there are several reasons for also considering the related issue of popularity. The characteristics of popular children may help to clarify why some children are better liked than other children. At the same time, the characteristics of unpopular or avoided children may help specify why some children do not have friends. In a sense, popularity may represent a simpler case than friendship. Friendships are, after all, by definition, dyadic and reciprocal; two children must be mutually involved for a friendship to result. Popularity, on the other hand, implies only a one-way preference. This one-way preference of several children is then focused on a single child or a limited number of children. The popular child need not reciprocate these differential preferences. Still, one might assume that the popular child's behaviour has some distinguishing characteristics that make that child's behaviour more desirable than other children's behaviour. Some researchers (Gottman *et al.*, 1975) working with older children have found just such a relationship.

Focusing on infants and toddlers, Lee (1973) also has examined the issue of peer popularity. Lee examined a group of five infants who were the only participants in a university day-care centre. Written commentaries of the social encounters during the children's regular morning activities were made. From these commentaries, Lee abstracted a record of interaction partners as well as a record of the frequency and kind of social behaviours used by the children.

Lee noted two children in particular. These infants were the most preferred infant (i.e. the most popular) and the least preferred infant (i.e. the child nobody wanted to spend time with). Within these designations, Lee found that most of the infants made similar selections with Jenny being consistently the most popular infant and Patrick being consistently the least popular child.

Of special interest to this discussion, Lee found revealing differences in the interaction characteristics of the two babies. Jenny was *less* likely to initiate interactions than was Patrick; Patrick was a very frequent initiator in the child care centre. Jenny's mode of initiating was also very different from Patrick's. Patrick was more likely to 'grab' the other children, while Jenny was more likely to use an unobtrusive 'look' as her way of initiating interactions. In terms of interaction responsiveness, Patrick engaged in mutual interactions *only when* he initiated the interactions. Jenny's behaviours were as likely to be reciprocal in those cases when she responded to others as in those cases when she initiated the interactions.

Lee's (1973) data also pointed to a relationship between infant popularity and friendship. The one child (Amy) in the playgroup who did not avoid Patrick had very different interactions with Patrick than did the other children. With Amy, Patrick's behaviours more closely resembled Jenny's behaviour with the other children. Patrick was unlikely to grab Amy, and he was responsive to Amy's initiations. He allowed Amy to take a more active role in interactions.

In her friendship analyses, Vandell (1978) also examined the possibility of early popularity. When her toddlers were examined in terms of their most and least preferred social partners, clear peer preferences and avoidances were apparent. For example, at 16 months old, the most preferred child had 24 interactions initiated to him while the least preferred child had only two attempts to interact with him. At 22 months old, the other infants initiated 15 interactions with the preferred infant and only four interactions with the least preferred infant.

In contrast to Lee's analysis, however, Vandell did not find a relationship between the behaviour of the least and most preferred infants and their relative ranking. For example, the most frequent initiator (who was also the infant most likely to use intrusive behaviours like 'grab') was *not* the most avoided child in the playgroup. Instead, the least preferred child was a very quiet, inactive child. Also, contrary to expectation, the responsiveness of the infant to the partner's initiation did not affect popularity. Those infants who were more likely to respond positively to another child's initiation were no more frequently selected as interaction partners than were those other infants with more negative responses. Finally, the identification of the most and least preferred partners varied across time. Three different children were the most preferred infant at each of the three different time periods; and the three other infants had the dubious honour of being the least preferred child during one of the three periods.

What do these results mean for a friendship analysis? First of all, they suggest that the concept of *popularity* may be reasonable for this age of infant, at least in terms of being chosen more often as an interaction partner. Still, when compared with the earlier friendship analysis, popularity appears to be more fleeting. Further, the behaviours that characterized friends were not yet those that characterized 'popular' infants. With these differences, one may then conclude that even during infancy it is very important to distinguish between the two terms.

ORIGINS OF EARLY PEER RELATIONS

A basic assumption underlying the concept of friendship developed in the previous sections is that repeated experience with the same child is a necessary condition for friendship. Becker (1977), Mueller and Brenner (1977), and Lewis *et al.* (1975) among others have pointed to the value of such repeated exposure for the development of social interaction and play. At the same time, however, peer exposure alone is probably not the only factor contributing to the development of early interaction and friendship. In this section, other possible contributors to early peer relations and friendships are explored.

Mother–child relations

In discussing the origins of friendship, the most obvious possibility is the mother–child interaction system. On the one hand there is Freud's admonition that the mother–child relationship is the prototype for all subsequent relationships. At the same time, social learning theory argues that, since most infants spend most of their time with their mothers, they probably generalize peer relations from this earlier predominant experience. Similarly, the thrust of attachment theory has been to emphasize the critical nature of the infant's bond with the mother on subsequent development. The question, then, is whether the empirical work supports the hypothesis that peer relations grow out of parent–child relations.

At one level, the reply seems to be inevitably 'yes'. The studies of non-human primates (Harlow and Harlow, 1969; Ruppenthal, Arling, Harlow, Sackett, and Suomi, 1976; Suomi, 1977) as well as studies of human infants (Ainsworth and Bell, 1970; Lewis, 1976; Provence and Lipton, 1963) show that babies do not develop very well in the absence of contact and affection. Since parents are typically the source of this affection and contact, the centrality of parental contact is reinforced.

In addition to the role of the mother as a provider of physical contact and affection, researchers have outlined the central role of parents in creating a sense of efficacy in their infants (Lewis, 1976; Watson, 1977). During the first months, infants are notably inept with objects; but with adults, infants are able to create fairly clear-cut contingencies. Lewis (1976) has argued that from these contingencies the child begins to develop self-competence: 'If I do this, something happens'. In their absence, the infant develops 'learned helplessness' instead. Still, self-competence and the need for physical contact are fairly global prerequisites for subsequent peer relations. Are there other more direct connections between the adult–infant and infant–peer systems? Other lines of evidence support this possibility.

Bridges (1933) in her description of the development of early social behaviour outlined the appearance of infant social behaviours with adult caregivers and with peers. Bridges noted that social behaviours like smiling and vocalizing appeared first with adults. It was only after a lag of about 3 months that the behaviours then appeared in peer-directed activities. Bridges interpreted this lag as meaning that an infant generalizes his social behaviour from adult to child. Unfortunately, however, Bridges' study has some methodological characteristics that may have contributed to this lag. Before 9 months old, the infants did not have regular contact with peers, while they did have regular contact with adults. It may be that peer interaction would have developed in parallel to the adult–child behaviours if given the opportunity. Or, it is even possible that if the peer contacts were initially greater than the adult–child contacts, perhaps adult–child relations would have grown out of the peer relations.

More recently, Eckerman et al. (1975) have also examined the relationship between adult–child interaction and child–child interaction. Eckerman et al. compared the peer interactions of home-reared toddlers with those same toddlers' mother–child interactions. They found that the behaviour to peers resembled more closely what the infants did with their mothers than what the infants did with inanimate objects. At the same time, however, the initial frequency of behaviours was greater with the mother. Like Bridges, Eckerman et al. interpreted this lag as suggesting that the peer system generalized out of the mother–child system. In Eckerman et al.'s study as in Bridges', however, the evidence of mother–child interaction being the source of peer interaction is still circumstantial. While there may be a direct effect on the peer system, one must turn to other studies for such test.

Lieberman (1976) has provided one such test. Lieberman examined the relationship between the mother–child and child–child interaction systems over time. Specifically she analysed the relationship between security of child attachment to the mother at 3 years old and responsiveness to peers 4 months later. Her results indicated that children's low home anxiety with their mothers was significantly correlated with the children's peer social competence (competence included measures of responsiveness to peer, number of chains in interaction, and reciprocal behaviour). At the same time, Lieberman's results argued that the mother–child system was only one of the determinants of peer interaction. Previous peer experiences also contributed to peer social competence. Those children with more nursery school experience were more socially skilled than other children.

Of course, Lieberman's subjects were somewhat older than the 1- and 2-year-olds who are the focus of this chapter. Vandell (1977), however, has examined these same issues in younger children. In this study, toddlers were observed with both mothers and peers at 16, 19, and 22 months old; and significant cross-lag relations were found between the two systems. The mothers' behaviour to their sons at 16 and 19 months old appeared to influence significantly their sons' behaviour with peers at 22 months old. In each case, it appeared that the specific content of the mothers' behaviour influenced the type of behaviour the sons then used with peers. Specifically, mothers who frequently offered toys to their sons had sons who subsequently were frequent toy offerers to their peers. Mothers who frequently used negatives with their sons and who frequently seized toys from their sons had sons who were subsequently more aggressive with their peers.

While these data seem to offer a clear indication of the important role of the parent–child system to subsequent peer interaction, such a conclusion is an over-simplification of a more complex relationship. First, the direction of influence was not always from parent to child. On the contrary, the child's interaction with peers also significantly influenced subsequent parent–child interactions. This influence was particularly apparent in the length and complexity of interaction sequences. Specifically, those infants who had characteristically longer interaction sequences with peers at 16 and 19 months old then had significantly longer interactions with parents at 22 months old. It appeared that skill at social interaction with peers significantly affected the parent–child system and not vice versa.

This direction of influence is reasonable in the light of the demands made by the two systems. The early peer relationship can foster the development of interaction in ways that parent–child interaction cannot. First, infants seem to have to work much harder for a social response from a peer than from a parent (Bronson, 1974; Eckerman et al., 1975). While a parent is likely to respond to an unclear, ambiguous social signal, peers are less likely to respond to a sloppy signal. Furthermore, peer interactions are, by necessity, more child-directed than are parent–child interactions. In peer interaction, the infants must assume the sole responsibility for initiating and maintaining the interactions. The net result, then, is that infants are forced to develop more advanced social skills if they hope to succeed. From this pressure, one might hypothesize that the parent–child system would also benefit. This enhancement over time is precisely what was found by Vandell (1977).

The issue of parental influence on peer interaction is further complicated by discrepancies in parent and peer behaviour. Even though specific maternal behaviours appear to shape subsequent peer–toddler behaviours, there are still significant differences in the behaviours found in the two systems. In Vandell's (1977) comparison, the toddlers used significantly more aggression and positive affect with peers than with their mothers. With their mothers, the toddlers were much more likely to use vocalizations and gestures. Furthermore, the pattern of vocalizations and motor behaviours varied across time in the two systems. The toddlers became increasingly vocal between 16 and 22 months old with their mothers, while the proportion of motor behaviours increased with peers. Eckerman *et al.* have suggested still other basic differences in the two systems. They have argued that peers are able to present more novel and interesting social behaviours. They also feel that the peer's activities may be more easily duplicated than those of adults.

The picture, then, is much more complex than the one painted at the beginning of this section. While the mother–child relationship is certainly important to the development of peer relations, its role is not merely a simple transfer from the mother to peer. On the contrary, both systems appear to influence the other. Furthermore, both systems with their unique qualities appear to be important in development.

Older siblings and other older children

Another possible contributing factor to early peer relations may be interactions with older siblings and other older children. In their intermediate position between adults and infant peers, older children may be well suited to maximize the advantages associated with the two other types of interaction. For example, older child–infant interactions may lessen the inequities associated with adult–child interaction. Older children may be less dominant than parents in terms of the active initiation and maintenance of interactions. One may also expect the older child to be a less persistent initiator than the parent, thus forcing the infant to take a more active role. Furthermore, the older child may be less accepting and responsive than a parent of an infant's ambiguous attempts at interaction. If the infant hopes to interact with the older child he may have to develop much clearer social behaviours.

At the same time, the older child has more social skills than an infant peer; and these greater skills should allow the child to be more responsive than an infant. Early peer interactions are sometimes hampered because one of the infants fails to respond regardless of the other infant's best effort (Bronson, 1975). These failures are probably less likely to occur with a somewhat older child.

Ross and Goldman (1976) have data that support this view of older children facilitating interaction. Ross and Goldman examined 18-month-olds with 1-year-olds and with 2-year-olds. While these children are not widely spaced in age, they still support the hypothesis that somewhat older children may facilitate interaction. The 18-month-olds had more frequent and more complex interactions with a 2-year-old partner than they had with a 1-year-old partner.

In addition to the levels of social skills reflected in older children affecting the amount and complexity of interaction, older children may facilitate peer interactions in another way. They may facilitate the recognition of the peer as a potential social partner. They may especially help the infant who has not been exposed to other infants recognize another infant as a peer. An infant who has been around only adults may have more difficulty generalizing to peers than a child who has not been exposed to older children. The overall size, the facial configuration, and skills of older children could help mark the transition.

Thus far, we have presented hypotheses about why older child–infant interaction should facilitate interaction. There is, of course, another possibility. The interactions with older children could be of such a negative nature that they would result in an infant's avoidance of peers and an overall depression of peer interaction.

In what may be a surprise to those people who remember having their heads held down in a toilet by an older sibling, the limited data suggest that experience with older children (including siblings) can facilitate peer interaction. Shirley (1933) presents some of the oldest data in this regard. Looking at infants in a semi-structured situation in which the two infants were placed facing each other, Shirley found that those infants with older siblings were more likely to initiate interactions with peers than were infants without siblings. Shirley also found that the infants with older siblings were more socially responsive with a peer. The mothers also reported that the infants more frequently laughed, kicked, and played with their older siblings than they did with adults.

Kelly's observations (1976) of 40 3-year-olds in a nursery school yielded similar results. Half of the children had older siblings; half did not. Kelly found that the non-sibling children initiated significantly fewer peer interactions than did those children with older brothers and sisters. At the same time, the non-sibling children showed significantly more teacher-directed behaviour and solitary play.

DiBona's examination (1974) of six 12-month-olds in a playgroup also suggested a sibling effect. The three infants with older siblings were the three children who were most likely to use agonistic behaviours such as pushing, hitting, and taking toys. The three infants with no older siblings engaged in fewer behaviours overall, and, in particular, fewer agonistic behaviours.

In looking at 32 first-born 6-month-olds, Vandell (in preparation) has further indications that experience with older children can have a facilitative effect on peer interactions. While this research is still in progress, some trends

are clear. Those infants who were around older children on a regular basis (at least once a week) were significantly more likely to direct social behaviours to their peers than were infants without this experience.

It would be a mistake, however, to assume that the evidence concerning peers and older siblings is without controversy. Bronson (1975), Goldman and Ross (1977), and Lieberman (1976) did not find significant sibling effects in their observations of early peer interaction. With the wide range of observation conditions, subject populations, and type of measures adopted, the reasons for these discrepancies have not been untangled. A direction for future research is to begin this process.

Objects

Both of the potential sources of peer relations (siblings and parents) outlined above focus on experiences outside of the peer system as sources of subsequent peer interaction. In both cases, the implicit assumption is that peer relations grow out of other social experiences. Another possibility, however, is based on a different assumption. The focus on objects, in particular toys, as a source of peer interaction reflects the autonomous nature of the peer system. The lines of evidence regarding the role of objects are clear.

First, the majority of early peer encounters occur around objects. Maudry and Nekula (1939) found that all of the play encounters they observed in 6- to 8-month-olds incorporated objects. In 16- to 18-month-olds, 96 per cent of the play activities were around the objects. Mueller and Brenner (1977) reported that at least 83 per cent of the contacts they observed in toddlers were around objects. Goldman and Ross (1977) have also noted the importance of objects in many of the infant games they observed in toddlers. Games using balls, for example, were the most common games they observed.

Mueller and DeStefano (1973) have described how object-centred contacts might foster subsequent interaction. According to Mueller and DeStefano, the objects can both 'invite' and 'demand' social interaction. Consider the demand side first. A child is playing with a desired toy. A second child sees the toy, wants it, and tries to take it. The first child then has two choices. S/he can relinquish the toy or s/he can act. If s/he wants to keep the toy, s/he is forced to recognize the presence of the other child. At the same time, objects can encourage social interaction in a more subtle way by inviting social interaction. In this circumstance, contacts around the same or similar objects invite the mutual discovery of inter-person contingencies. Through the objects, infants can discover their control over the peer. Mueller and DeStefano (1973) have provided an example which illustrates how this mutual discovery of inter-personal contingencies might work.

The observation begins with two toddlers, Loren and Robert, being attracted to the same toy train. Loren is pushing the train's smoke stack and the train makes an interesting noise. Robert comes over to the toy. In the meantime, Loren begins to pull the train with Robert in pursuit. Loren then notices Robert following and changes direction several times, running back and forth across the room. Robert watches and then imitates Loren's running. Loren then imitates Robert. By this time, both children are looking at each other and making excited sounds. The purely object-centred contact allowed the toddlers to discover their mutual control over each other.

In view of the proposed importance of objects to early peer contacts, an additional question to pose is what happens to early peer interaction in the absence of objects. In this regard, the research (DeStefano, 1976; Maudry and Nekula, 1939; Vandell, in preparation) has suggested various reactions depending on the age of the child and the social skills of the child.

Vandell (in preparation) has looked at peer encounters in 6, 9, and 12-month-olds. The infants were observed for 15 minutes on three separate occasions at each age (for a total of nine visits per child). For each visit, an infant was observed with another child of the same sex and same age. For 10 minutes of the observation, several toys were present; and for 5 minutes no toys were present. These two situations were then counterbalanced across the dyads.

The presence and absence of toys appeared to have a significant effect on the amount and kind of interactions observed. Interesting enough, this effect was related to the level of the infants' social skills. Those infants who showed more social skills in the object present condition had a different response to the no-toys condition than did those infants with fewer skills. (The higher level of social skill was marked by more social behaviours, by more social responses, and by more interaction sequences.) The more socially skilled infants turned to each other or to each other's clothing, when all the toys were removed. Thus, in the no-toys condition, two infants began playing with one of the infant's shoes. Another child began exploring and manipulating the partner's face. With no toys, however, the less skilled infants responded differently. Unlike their more skilled counterparts, they did not turn to one another as objects. They simply cried.

DeStefano (1976) has examined the effect of different kinds of objects as well as no-objects on older infants. He observed 18-month-old infants in four situations: (1) no-toys present; (2) only small manipulatable toys like small balls and pull toys present; (3) only large toys like slides and rocking boats present; and (4) both large and small toys present. DeStefano found that the amount and tone of the interactions were affected by the four object conditions.

Interactions were least common in the small toys condition and most common in the large toy and no-toy conditions. The type of encounters that occurred in the large toy and no-toy conditions was different, however. Positive affect was more likely in the large toy condition, while negative affect was significantly more common in the no-toy condition. In the no-toy condition, the toddlers were likely to do what the most skilled 6- and 9-month-olds did; that is, turn the other child into an object.

IMPLICATIONS OF EARLY PEER PLAY AND FRIENDSHIP FOR CHILD CARE

Several themes have emerged in this discussion of early peer friendships that may be relevant for child care planning. First of all, it appears that peer interaction must be seen as part of a larger social system. The infant's interactions with parents, older children, and peers are all part of a social network and as such each may influence the other. Nothing in this discussion, then, supports the argument that infants do not need mothers or that infants do not need cross-aged interaction. At the same time, however, there appears to be an autonomy between the systems. Significant differences in each of these systems have been noted; and these differences can be seen as playing their own role in development. Specifically, one can argue that children may benefit from the special experiences which peer interaction can offer.

This value of peer experience has been well documented in older children. Hartup (1977), for example, has outlined the special role of peers in the development of a child's control of aggression, in a child's sexual knowledge, and in a child's moral judgements. Hartup has argued that the unequal nature of adult–child interaction does not facilitate these aspects of development.

Other researchers (Freud and Dann, 1951; Furman, Rahe and Hartup, in press; Novak and Harlow, 1975) have outlined the special role of peer interaction in additional areas. Freud and Dann, for example, provided an early example of the potential of peers as social rehabilitators. The children they studied were reared in a German concentration camp and their caretakers were, not surprisingly, preoccupied with their own survival. What was surprising to Freud and Dann was that the infants were relatively (although not totally) normal. The infants used each other as love substitutes.

More recently, Novak and Harlow (1975) have further examined the possibility of peers acting as social rehabilitators. Novak and Harlow described isolation-reared Rhesus monkeys who had a range of bizarre characteristics. Previous attempts to rehabilitate similar monkeys through exposure to skilled juvenile monkeys, objects, and adult females had failed. When 'he isolated monkeys were placed with slightly younger normal peers, however, successful rehabilitation occurred. The infants were better able to modulate their aggression; they were better able to respond appropriately to other monkeys.

Furman, Rahe and Hartup (in press) have recently concluded a similar manipulation with human children. Three groups of children were selected from a series of nursery schools. One group was composed of children who were designated by their teachers as social isolates, as children who had great difficulty interacting appropriately with other children. The second group of children was the same age as the first group, but was described as very socially skilled. The third group was composed of very socially skilled children, but these children were 16 months younger than the children in groups one and two. Skilled and unskilled children were then paired for 10 play sessions. Furman *et al.*'s results corresponded directly to Harlow's work. The greatest success at rehabilitation was associated with the younger skilled peer and the older unskilled child playing together.

The thrust of the work with older peers, then, is to illustrate the value of peer experience. There are similar suggestions that infants and toddlers may benefit from such an experience. In a study of playgroup toddlers, Mueller and Brenner (1977) described the complexity of social behaviours and social interactions of toddlers with 1 month versus 4 months of peer experience. They found those toddlers with more experience had significantly more complex social behaviours and interactions than did those toddlers with less experience. In a study of 9-month-olds, Becker (1977) also found that the frequency of interactions and the complexity of social behaviours were influenced by peer familiarity. Her 9-month-olds became increasingly socially skilled with peer exposure.

As a special case of interaction, early friendships seem to maximize some of the benefits associated with early peer interaction. Across various studies, the early friendships were characterized by infant games, highly pleasant and sophisticated exchanges. The friendships were also characterized by evidence of mutuality and reciprocity. Negative and aggressive contacts seemed to be minimized in friendship.

If one accepts the premise that these early peer relationships are desirable, the next issue is how such relationships might be facilitated. The existing literature makes some suggestion in this regard. First of all, repeated experiences with the same child seem to act as a necessary prerequisite to peer relations (Becker, 1977; Mueller and Brenner, 1977; Vandell, 1977). The evidence of little social interaction in peers seems to come in examination of peer strangers (Bronson, 1975). Even with regular exposure, however, not all situations may be equally beneficial. DeStefano (1976) has illustrated the crucial role that objects can play in the amount and tone of interactions. Large non-portable toys seemed to maximize positive interactions, while small, manipulatable toys seemed to discourage interactions. Negative affect was maximized in a no-toys condition. In designing the playroom to facilitate interactions, one would not want only small toys.

The size of the child-care group also appears to affect early interaction. Vandell and Mueller (1977) have compared the early peer interactions in a group setting of four to six children with peer interactions which occurred in a dyadic setting. They found fewer interactions to be registered in the group situation. They also found growth over time in terms of number and kind of interactions to occur only in the dyadic setting. While further work is necessary, it may be that infants' and toddlers' peer relations would most benefit from a smaller group.

The situation in which children meet and interact is yet another potentially important factor. Becker (1977) and Rubenstein and Howes (1976) have supported the idea of greater frequencies of interaction in familiar settings. Infants observed in their own homes attempted to interact more than did those infants who were observed in someone else's home. It seems reasonable that unfamiliar laboratory situations would further depress the amount of interaction observed.

When taken as a whole, then, generalizations about child-care planning can be drawn. If early peer interactions and friendships are valued, their development may be fostered through: (a) allowing the infants to spend time together regularly; (b) varying the kind and number of toys; and (c) adopting a familiar playroom. The number of children present at any point in time may also be important.

REFERENCES

Ainsworth, M., and Bell, S. M. (1970). Attachment, exploration, and separation: illustrated by the behavior of one-year-olds in a strange situation. *Child Development*, **41**, 49–67.

Becker, J. (1977). A learning analysis of the development of peer-oriented behavior in nine-month-old infants. *Developmental Psychology*, **13**, 481–491.

Bigelow, B. J. (1977). Children's friendship expectations: a cognitive developmental study. *Child Development*, **48**, 246–253.

Bigelow, C. J., and La Gaipa, J. J. (1975). Children's written descriptions of friendship: a multidimensional analysis. *Developmental Psychology*, **11**, 857–858.

Bridges, K. M. B. (1933). A study of social development in early infancy. *Child Development*, **4**, 36–49.

Bronson, W. (1974). Mother–toddler interaction. *Merrill–Palmer Quarterly*, **20**, 275–301.

Bronson, W. (1975). Peer–peer interactions in the second year of life. In M. Lewis and L. A. Rosenblum (Eds.), *The Origins of Behavior: Friendship and Peer Relations*. New York: Wiley.

Bruner, J., Jolly, A., and Sylva, K. (1977). *Play*. New York: Basic Books.

Buhler, C. (1927). Die ersten sozialen Verhaltensweisen des Kindes. In C. Bühler, H. Hetzer and B. Tudor-Hart (Eds.), *Soziologische und Psychologische Studien uber das Erste Lebensjahr*. Jena: Gustav Fischer.

DeStefano, C. (1976). Environmental determinants of peer social behavior and interaction in a toddler playgroup. Unpublished doctoral dissertation, Boston University.

DiBona, L. (1974). A correlation of birth order and peer directed high power tactics. Unpublished paper, Boston University.

Durfee, J. T., and Lee, L. C. (1973). Infant–infant interaction in a daycare setting. Presented at the Annual Meeting of the American Psychological Association, Montreal, August.

Eckerman, C. O., Whatley, J., and Kutz, S. (1975). Growth of social play with peers during the second year of life. *Developmental Psychology*, **11**, 42–49.

Eder, D., and Hallinan, M. (1977). Sex differences in children's friendships. Unpublished manuscript, Stanford University.

Foot, H. C., Chapman, A. J., and Smith, J. R. (1977). Friendship and social responsiveness in boys and girls. *Journal of Personality and Social Psychology*. **35**, 401–411.

Freud, A., and Dann, S. (1951). An experiment in group upbringing. *The Psychoanalytic Study of the Child*, **6**, 127–168.

Furman, W., Rahe, D. F., and Hartup, W. W. (in press). Social rehabilitation of low-interactive preschool children by peer intervention. *Child Development*.

Gamer, E. (1977). Children's reports of friendship criteria. Paper presented at the annual meeting of the Eastern Psychological Association, Boston, April.

Garvey, C. (1977). *Play*. Cambridge, Massachusetts: Harvard University Press.

Goldman, B., and Ross, H. (1977). Social skills in action: an analysis of early peer games. Unpublished paper, University of Waterloo.

Gottman, J., Gonso, J., and Rasmussen, B. (1975). Social interaction, social competence, and friendship in children. *Child Development*, 46, 708–718.

Harlow, H., and Harlow, M. (1969). Effects of various mother–infant relationships on rhesus monkey behavior. In B. M. Foss (Ed.), *Determinants of Infant Behaviour*. Vol. 4. London: Methuen.

Hartup, W. (1975). The origins of friendships. In M. Lewis and L. Rosenblum (Eds.), *The Origins of Behavior: Friendship and Peer Relations*. New York: Wiley.

Hartup, W. (1978). Children and their friends. In H. McGurk (Ed.), *Issues in Childhood Social Development*. London: Methuen.

Kelly, K. R. (1976). The effects of peer and sibling exposure on social development in young children. Unpublished paper, Boston University.

Klein, R., and Wander, E. (1933). Gruppenbildung in zweiten Lebensjahr. *Zeitschrift fur Psychologie*, 128, 257–280.

Lee, L. C. (1973). Social encounters of infants: the beginnings of popularity. Paper presented at the International Society for Behavioral Development, Ann Arbor, August.

Lewis, M. (1976). The origins of self-competence. Paper presented at the National Institute of Mental Health Conference on Mood Development, Washington, DC.

Lewis, M., and Rosenblum, L. A. (1975). *The Origins of Behavior: Friendship and Peer Relations*. New York: Wiley.

Lewis, M., Young, G., Brooks, J., and Michalson, L. (1975). The beginning of friendship. In M. Lewis and L. A. Rosenblum (Eds.), *The Origins of Behavior: Friendship and Peer Relations*. New York: Wiley.

Lichtenberger, W. (1965). Mitmenschliches Verhalten eines Zwillingspaares in seinen ersten Lebensjahren. *Ernst Reinhardt Verlag*, Monograph.

Lieberman, A. (1976). The social competence of preschool children: its relations to quality of attachment and to amount of exposure to peers in different preschool settings. Unpublished doctoral dissertation, Johns Hopkins University.

Lieberman, A., and Garvey, C. (1977). Interpersonal pauses in preschoolers' verbal exchanges. Paper presented at the Bienniel Meeting of the Society for Research in Child Development, New Orleans, March.

Marshall, H., and McCandless, B. (1957). A study of prediction of social behavior of preschool children. *Child Development*, 28, 149–159.

Marvin, C. (1977). Sympathy and affection in the peer interaction of one year olds. Unpublished doctoral dissertation. Ohio State University.

Maudry, M., and Nekula, M. (1939). Social relations between children of the same age during the first two years of life. *Journal of Genetic Psychology*, 54, 193–215.

Mengert, I. G. (1931). A preliminary study of the reactions of 2-year-old children to each other when paired in a semi-controlled situation. *Journal of Genetic Psychology*, 39, 393–398.

Millar, S. (1968). *The Psychology of Play*. Harmondsworth, Middlesex: Penguin Books.

Mueller, E., and Brenner, J. (1977). The origins of social skills and interaction among playgroup toddlers. *Child Development*, 48, 854–861.

Mueller, E., and DeStefano, C. (1973). Sources of toddlers' peer interaction in a playgroup setting. Unpublished paper, Boston University.

Mueller, E., and Lucas, T. (1975). A developmental analysis of peer interaction among toddlers. In M. Lewis and L. A. Rosenblum (Eds.), *The Origins of Behavior: Friendship and Peer Relations*. New York: Wiley.

Mueller, E., and Rich, A. (1976). Clustering and socially-directed behaviours in a playgroup of 1-year-old boys. *Journal of Child Psychology and Psychiatry*, **17**, 315–322.

Mueller, E., and Vandell, D. (1979). Infant–infant interaction. In J. Osofosky (Ed.), *Handbook of Infant Development*. New York: Wiley Interscience.

Novak, M., and Harlow, H. (1975). Social recovery of monkeys isolated for the first year of life. *Developmental Psychology*, **11**, 453–465.

Peevers, B., and Secord, P. (1973). Developmental changes in attribution of descriptive concepts to persons. *Journal of Personality and Social Psychology*, **27**, 120–128.

Piaget, J. (1962). *Play, Dreams and Imitation*. New York: Norton.

Provence, S., and Lipton, R. (1963). *Infants in Institutions*. New York: International Universities Press.

Ross, H. S., and Goldman, B. M. (1976). Establishing new social relations in infancy. In T. Alloway, L. Krames, and P. Pliner (Eds.), *Advances in Communication and Affect*. Vol. 4. New York: Plenum Press.

Rubenstein, J., and Howes, C. (1976). The effects of peers on toddler interaction with mother and toys. *Child Development*, **47**, 597–605.

Ruppenthal, G. C., Arling, G. A., Harlow, H. F., Sackett, G. P., and Suomi, S. (1976). A ten-year perspective on motherless mother monkey behavior. *Journal of Abnormal Psychology*, **85**, 341–348.

Schlosberg, H. (1947). The concept of play. *Psychological Review*, **54**, 229–231.

Selman, R. (1975). Interpersonal thought in childhood, preadolescence, and adolescence: a structural analysis of developing conceptions of peer relationships. Paper presented at the Annual Meeting of the American Psychological Association, Chicago, August.

Selman, R., and Jacquette, D. (1977). Stability and oscillation in interpersonal awareness: a clinical-developmental analysis. In C. B. Keasey (Ed.), *The Nebraska Symposium on Motivation*. Vol. 25. Lincoln: University of Nebraska Press.

Shirley, M. (1933). *The First Two Years: A Study of Twenty-five Babies*. Minneapolis: University of Minnesota Press.

Suomi, S. (1977). Peers, play, and primary prevention in primates. In M. Kent and J. Rolf (Eds.), *The Primary Prevention of Psychopathology: Promoting Social Competence and Coping in Children*. Hanover, New Hampshire: University Press of New England.

Vandell, D. L. (1977). Boy toddlers' social interaction with mothers, fathers, and peers. Unpublished doctoral dissertation, Boston University.

Vandell, D. L. (1978). Friendship and popularity during the second year of life. Paper submitted for publication, University of Texas at Dallas.

Vandell, D. (in preparation). Social behavior and interaction in six- to twelve-month-olds. University of Texas at Dallas.

Vandell, D., and Mueller, E. (1977). The effects of group size on toddler social interaction with peers. Paper presented at the Bienniel Meeting of the Society for Research in Child Development, New Orleans, March.

Vincze, M. (1971). The social contacts of infants and young children reared together. *Early Child Development and Care*, **1**, 99–109.

Vincze, M. (1974). Az egyuttes tevekenyseg alakulasa egy cgyutt nevelkedo csoportban 3 honapos kortol 2-½ eves korig. *Pszichologiai Tanulmanyok*, **10**, 289–295.

Watson, J. (1977). Smiling, cooing and 'the game'. In J. Bruner, A. Jolly, and K. Sylva (Eds.), *Play: Its Role in Development and Evolution*. New York City: Basic Books.

Weisner, T., and Gallimore, R. (1977). My brother's keeper: child and sibling caretaking. *Current Anthropology*, **18**, 169–190.

Yarrow, M. R. (1975). Some perspectives on research on peer relations. In M. Lewis and L. A. Rosenblum (Eds.), *The Origins of Behavior: Friendship and Peer Relations*. New York: Wiley.

CHAPTER 8

The Relationship of Child's Play to Social-Cognitive Growth and Development

KENNETH H. RUBIN
and
DEBRA J. PEPLER

It has long been thought that the young child is incapable of, or ·at least has some major difficulties in, understanding that other people can have view-points, opinions, intentions, and feelings different from his/her own. This line of theoretical speculation follows mainly from the early work of Piaget (1926, 1932, 1951) concerning the development of children's abilities to think about their social worlds (or to social-cognize). Thus, when children fail to take the points of view of social others into account, Piaget describes their thoughts as egocentric in nature. Moreover, he believes this mode of thought to predominate during the preoperational years, declining by 7 or 8 years of age when children are able to decentre socially and to consider reciprocal relations.

How then does such egocentric thought manifest itself in the behaviours of young children? What are the mechanisms through which such immature social-cognizing is overcome? In this chapter, we describe briefly the course of social-cognitive development in childhood, focusing mainly on the early stages of development. Moreover, we attempt to describe how the development of peer interaction and peer play serves both to reflect and possibly to cause social-cognitive growth.

209

EGOCENTRISM IN CHILDHOOD: THE PIAGETIAN POSITION

The first Piagetian treatment of the development of egocentrism in childhood is to be found in *The Language and Thought of the Child* (Piaget, 1926). In this classic work, Piaget noted that the speech of the young, preoperational stage child is often neither addressed to, nor adapted to, a listener. Indeed, often a listener is not even necessary for speech to occur: Empirical support for this position emanated from an original series of studies in which the naturalistic speech of children was dichotomized as being non-social (i.e. egocentric) or social. In one study, 38 per cent of 1 500 remarks made by two 6 years 6 months old children was found to be of a repetitious, playful, or collective monologue character. Higher percentages of egocentric speech were subsequently found for 3- to 5-year-old children, while lower percentages were found for 7- to 8-year-old children. Thus, in accordance with his theory, Piaget found the proportion of non-social speech to decrease, and the proportion of social speech to increase, with increasing age. Similar findings have subsequently been reported by Fisher (1934) and by Kohlberg, Yaeger, and Hjertholm (1968).

The most prevalent explanation for the large proportion of non-social utterances during naturalistic conversations has stemmed from Piaget's suggestion that young children lack both the skill and the will to communicate. The former argument concerning the skill dimension has been accepted by many as being an appropriate evaluation of the early communicative data. However, the suggestion that young children lack the will to communicate has been a contentious one—so much so, that in a reply to Vygotsky (1962) vis à vis the forms and functions of non-social speech, Piaget reversed his original position (Piaget, 1962). To this end, Piaget concluded that preschool children do have a desire to communicate with others and that such a social will has a biological basis, being present in the infant from birth (Piaget, 1977). We elaborate on this view in a later section of this chapter.

The Piagetian position concerning egocentrism during communication has also received major support in the recent literature concerning referential communication. Typically, referential communication studies are carried out in laboratory settings. A child is asked to describe a novel figure to an auditor who must choose this figure from a number of other such novel forms. The listener is separated from the speaker by a partition thereby disallowing visual (gestural) communication. Such paradigmatic investigations of communicative skill have generally reported competence to increase with age (see Glucksberg, Krauss, and Higgins, 1975, for an extensive review of this literature). One of the explanations for the linear development of referential communicative abilities with age has typically been the decline of egocentric modes of thought.

The inability to take the role of the other has been thought to underlie social dysfunctions in areas other than communication. For example, Piaget and Inhelder (1956) and Flavell (1968), among others, have reported that young children are less able to take the literal, spatial viewpoints of others than are older children. Thus, when a child is asked to choose from a number of pictures how another person seated opposite her/him might see a three-object spatial display, s/he often responds 'egocentrically'; that is, s/he chooses the picture that portrays how the display looks to him/her.

In studies of empathic awareness or the ability to share another's emotional response, preoperational stage children have been found to display egocentric behaviours. For example, when asked to consider simultaneously how two adults in an unfamiliar situation feel about each other and about the situation itself, young children have been found to be less able to empathize with these 'others' than are older, concrete operational children (Feffer, 1959; Rothenberg, 1970). Moreover, when asked to predict what others are thinking (e.g. Miller, Kessel, and Flavell, 1970) similar findings are reported. That is, role-taking skills increase with age as a supposed function of the decline of egocentric thought (Rubin, 1973).

In summary, the Piagetian position vis à vis social-cognitive development is that children come to take the figurative and literal perspectives of others; they come to cognize correctly about social, non-observable traits of others, by the concrete and formal operational years. Such abilities are enhanced by the demise of egocentric thought and the onset of decentration skills (i.e. the ability to think simultaneously about more than one aspect of a social situation).

EGOCENTRISM IN CHILDHOOD: SOME RECENT VIEWS

In recent years, investigators concerned with the development of social-cognition have become increasingly critical of the original Piagetian theory and research. Citing definitional and methodological difficulties, these researchers have begun to conduct in-depth, more complex analyses of children's social thoughts and behaviours. For example, recent studies of the naturalistic dyadic interactions of preschoolers have revealed such young children to be most effective social communicators (Garvey and Hogan, 1973; Mueller, 1972). These writers stress that while Piaget concentrated on the 35 per cent of speech which was non-social, he neglected the 65 per cent which was social in nature. Thus, in both the Garvey and Hogan (1973) and Mueller (1972) studies, as in the original Piaget report, preschoolers were found to be communicatively successful approximately 65 per cent of the time.

Further communication studies have indicated that the Piagetian egocentric category of word play and repetition may take on distinct social overtones much of the time. For example, an egocentric nonsense utterance on the part of one child may elicit a like response from his/her play partner. A word play game between the social partners thus evolves, enabling the children to come into contact and subsequently to interact cooperatively. One point to consider in such early repetitious, word-play games is that children who use such verbal schemes may be demonstrating the will to communicate or to initiate social encounters, but that they may be lacking the mature, verbal skill to do so.

   The early skill to communicate has also been demonstrated in recent studies of referential communication. In these reports (Evans and Rubin, in press; Maratsos, 1973), preoperational aged youngsters who were given the opportunity to supplement their verbalizations with gestures were found to be as effective communicators as their older, concrete operational counterparts.

   Concerning the ability to take the literal viewpoint of others, Flavell (1977) has reported data which clearly indicate that the rudiments of non-egocentric spatial perspectivism are present as early as 2 and 3 years of age. For example, Flavell describes a paradigm in which both sides of a card are shown to a young child. On one side of the card is drawn a cat, while on the other side there is a dog. The child is typically asked, 'What do you see?', and 'What do I see?'. According to Flavell, even 2-year-olds are able to master this elementary, social-cognitive problem.

   As for the identification of how others feel, Borke (1971) has presented data supporting the existence of empathic, non-egocentric responses in children as young as three years. Moreover, Hoffman (1976) has suggested that the basis of empathy is present not long after birth.

   Finally, cognitive or conceptual perspective-taking skill has been shown to exist in a rudimentary fashion in 3- and 4-year-olds. Marvin, Greenberg, and Mossler (1976) played a series of videotapes, one of which included a child actor entering his grandmother's house (the tapes were augmented by oral descriptions concerning where the actor was going) to youngsters between 2 and 6 years old. Their mothers were then invited into the laboratory and both mother and child viewed the videotape minus the auditory augmentation. Each child was subsequently asked whether or not his/her mother knew where the actor was going. Correct responses to such questions which demanded elementary inferential skills were evident as early as 3 and 4 years of age.

   In summary, recent research has amply demonstrated that preschool-aged children are quite capable of making socio-centred responses in simple laboratory or naturalistic settings. That is, when the task demands are not too strenuous, rudimentary forms of role-taking skill appear evident prior to the concrete operational period of development. These data, however, may be countered once again by observations of children's naturalistic behaviours in child–adult and child–child social groups. Allow us, now, to provide you, the reader, with the following anecdotal observations of the senior author's daughter, when she had just turned 3 years old.

   I
      Dad: 'Amy, what are you doing upstairs?'
      Amy: 'This' [loud voice]
      Dad: 'Amy, you know that I can't see what you are doing! What is it you are up to?'
      Amy: 'I'm doin' this!' [in a louder voice]

II

After playing 'hide-n-seek' with Dad and having successfully sought and caught Dad, it becomes Amy's turn to hide.

   Amy: 'OK, now it's my turn. You count to 10 and I'll hide.'
   Dad: [Shuts eyes and counts to 10] 'Ready or not, here I come!' Dad turns around only to find Amy standing in the corner of the same room, face to wall, 'hiding' from Dad.

III

Amy and Leslie (a 4-year-old female companion) are playing with playdough at the same table. Both children are concentrating intently on their own products. After about 5 minutes Amy toddles to the couch, snuggles up to her blanket and falls asleep. Leslie continues to make playdough cookies never bothering to note the whereabouts of her companion. After about 10 minutes Leslie turns around and says 'Hey Amy, look at this!' Amy, not being where Leslie is addressing her, and in fact, being blissfully asleep, fails to respond.

In the meanwhile, Leslie does not bother to wait for a verbal or attentional response and continues to make cookies. A full 3 minutes later she says 'I'm through', gets off her chair and to her surprise finds her little friend lying on the couch. She then runs up to Amy's mother who has viewed the entire episode and remarks, 'Hey I think Amy's asleep!'

These three anecdotes, which are probably familiar to those readers who are parents, demonstrate quite nicely the Piagetian notion of childhood egocentrism. While preschoolers may, for the most part, carry on clear social conversations with their peers and parents, and while they may, for the most part, be quite well-meaning in their social encounters, they do slip-up at times. In short, preschoolers often display an over-abundance of the assimilative adaptation process (Piaget, 1970). Thus, you are thought to be able to see what your child sees, even though she is a full staircase above you. Or, you are not thought to see your child when her eyes are closed. Or, two best friends may engage in varying activities within an 8-ft perimeter and not know what the other is doing.

All of these examples clearly demonstrate that under certain conditions young children do think and behave quite differently from adults. This should not be interpreted as meaning that preschoolers are totally bereft of social-cognitive skills. We are merely suggesting that these abilities are not as well formed or developed as those of their older, concrete or formal operational counterparts.

Given the above data concerning the existence of both egocentric and social thought processes in young children, and given very recent reports that the available set of laboratory role-taking measures do not generally correlate to any great degree (Kurdek, 1977; Rubin, 1978), the following argument may ultimately prove highly reasonable. It may well be that the lack of significant correlations between role-taking measures is the result of their tapping different levels of social-cognitive skill. This argument is best supported by Rubin's (1978) study in which a measure of 'sequential role-taking' (i.e. the ability to consider multiple, alternative thoughts, emotions, etc., in a sequential but not simultaneous fashion: cf. Selman, 1976a) was not significantly correlated with measures of simultaneous role-taking skill. The latter measures, however, were found to be significantly interrelated. Given that the measures of interest had previously been shown to have an acceptable degree of inter-observer and test-retest reliability (Kurdek, 1977), it is likely that the Rubin results stemmed from the fact that different levels of role-taking skill were being assessed. Consequently, the approach to be taken in subsequent sections of this chapter is to consider social-cognition as evolving in a stage-like manner from rudimentary forms in early childhood to complex forms in later childhood and early adolescence.

WHY CHILDREN THINK AND ACT EGOCENTRICALLY: THE PIAGETIAN VIEW

While the following statement may be somewhat surprising to many, it is nevertheless true that Piaget (1977) assumes the infant to be psychologically *social* from almost the day of its birth. The infant smiles, coos, and tries to make contact with others as early as the second month of life. According to Piaget, the early predispositions toward establishing social relationships 'come from within', that is they are inherited. Unfortunately, to Piaget these early tendencies are manifested egocentrically, so that the only viewpoint to be considered in early social interactions is that of the infant or the young child him/herself. Since there is little knowledge of, or experience with, either the rules or signs which are exemplified by the language and moral values of society, thought remains egocentric.

The process by which children move into active, cooperative, societal membership may be described in a grossly oversimplified fashion as follows. First, when a child is faced with a social-cognitive discrepancy, the mental structures (schemes) which the child had previously formed, are thrown into a state of imbalance. To return the mind to a state of cognitive homeostasis or equilibrium, the child either assimilates the external elements into the evolving or existing structures of the organism, or s/he modifies the existing schemes to meet the demands of the external world (i.e. s/he accommodates). Thus, in dyadic social situation, if two children are engaged in parallel play and suddenly one of the partners decides that s/he desires the toy which is being held by the other, a number of solutions to the social problem is possible. The assimilator will: (a) not take into account the fact that the other will be sad/angry if s/he grabs the toy away; and (b) may believe that it will actually cause no emotional response in the other. On the other hand, the accommodator will: (a) be aware that grabbing the toy away may cause grief or anger; and (b) will adjust his/her behaviour to the situation at hand (e.g. say 'please'; offer to trade the toy; ask to share; or whatever).

The assimilative manner of thinking obviously has implications for the development of early social behaviours and social relations. For example, researchers have often cited egocentric thought as a major causative factor for observations that preschoolers are less likely than older children to engage in altruistic behaviours (Mussen and Eisenberg-Berg, 1977), and cooperative and sociodramatic play (Rubin, Watson, and Jambor, 1978). Likewise, the greater incidences of peer conflict (Dawes, 1934), and both practice and parallel play (Rubin et al., 1978) in the early years have been attributed to egocentrism.

How does Piaget account for the decline of egocentric thought? As mentioned before, the source of motivation to become a truly social being comes from within. Moreover, this motivation is often elicited by the child's experience of an optimal level of discrepancy between external events and internal structures. Given too great a discrepancy between external events and one's own mental schemes, one becomes either too bored or too aroused, and as a result assimilatory processes take precedence. Take, again as an example, the typical parallel play situation. All participants in such play situations: (a) probably do not care what is going through the minds of their proximity-mates; and (b) if they bothered to think about their mates' thoughts and emotions, would probably perceive them as being similar to their own. This play situation may thus be considered conceptually and socially redundant. In short, the social situation poses no special accommodative problem.

There are other social situations, however, where one child actively insists on a construction of events different from that of his/her play partner. While involved in mural painting one child may say to another: 'If you put blue and yellow together it will make green'. If the other child had, to that period of time, believed the only consequence of mixing colours to be messy paintbrushes (and if the discrepant notion offered is interesting to the child), then the situation becomes accommodatively and socially relevant.

It should be noted that discrepant viewpoints do not always lead to peaceful solutions. When children beg to differ concerning issues of importance to them, conflicts often ensue, not only in their minds but also in their actions. The numerous peer conflicts observed by researchers concerned with early child interaction certainly attest to the validity of this position (e.g. Dawes, 1934; Hartup, 1974; Maudry and Nekula, 1939). In turn, these conflicts, if they occur with regularity, have the power of forcing the child to compromise, to accommodate, to take the point of view of the other. Given sufficient experience in such peer group encounters, the child comes to realize that: (a) survival in the social world; as well as (b) popularity among one's peers, are marked by compromise and socialized thoughts.

The development of socialized thinking is believed to have reached a fine point by the onset of concrete operations; that is, between 7 and 11 years of age. Thus, role-taking, moral development, and other social-cognitive abilities are seen as *faits accomplis* by this period. This somewhat simplistic view of the development of social-cognition reveals the 'all-or-none' position of Piaget's theory concerning the nature of egocentric thought. Children are either able to perspective-take or they are not able to do so.

Therein lies our first criticism of the Piagetian description of the rise and fall of egocentric thought. Recent research has made it abundantly clear that egocentrism is not a unitary construct (Rubin, 1978). Moreover, there appear to be distinct stages of perspective-taking skill which encompass the ages between infancy and adolescence (Selman, 1976a, b). Thus the all-or-none position of Piagetians appears tenuous at best.

Our second criticism of the Piagetian position stems from an apparent inconsistency vis à vis the causes of the decline of egocentric thought and conversely the onset of social thought in childhood. As outlined above, Piaget (1932) feels strongly that peer interaction and peer conflict serve to decrease egocentric thinking and to increase accommodation (and thus compromise) in young children. On the other hand, play, during which much peer interaction takes place, is seen as pure assimilation or as the most characteristic reflection of egocentric thought. As a result, one may come away with the opinion, following a reading of Piaget's position concerning play, that such activity is not particularly conducive to the onset of socialized thought. We, of course, beg to differ from Piaget. It is our belief that the Piagetian definition of play as pure assimilation is unreasonably restrictive. We view the phenomenon of play as being inextricably tied to peer interaction in early childhood, both serving to reflect and, at the very least, stimulate the development of social-cognitive abilities.

The position that play serves an intellectual adaptative function is made clear in the following section. However, at this point we should like to whet the reader's appetite with some initial support for our viewpoint. Consider the concept of sociodramatic play. Such activity is a highly complex form of social interaction which involves making a distinction between literal and non-literal contexts (Garvey, 1977), understanding the roles and perspectives of play partners (Smilansky, 1968), and accommodating rather than assimilating when there are role conflicts (Matthews, 1977). The existence of sociodramatic play episodes in preoperationally aged children indicates that: (a) play is not merely a reflection of pure assimilation and egocentrism; and (b) that elementary perspective-taking skills do exist in early childhood.

SOCIAL-COGNITIVE DEVELOPMENT AND PLAY

We now reach a critical point in the chapter. In this section we examine one of the more detailed and creative models of social-cognitive development; that is, the six-staged hierarchical model of Selman (1976a, b). To Selman, perspective-taking first emerges when children are approximately 3 years of age and continues to develop until cognitive maturity is reached. The theoretical model gains initial empirical support from a series of studies (Selman, 1976b; Selman and Byrne, 1974) in which children were asked to respond to dilemmas posed in short stories. Thus, the original data base was largely verbal in nature—a phenomenon which exists in much of the social-cognitive literature (e.g. Chandler, 1973; Kohlberg, 1976; Rest, 1976; Rothenberg, 1970).

While we concur with the stage approach to the study of social cognition as well as with the description of the characteristics inherent in each of Selman's (1976a, b) stages, we also feel strongly that reliance on verbal report data may provide an inadequate and inaccurate picture of the development of social-cognitive abilities (Rubin and Trotter, 1977). Thus, it is our position that one can just as easily, and much earlier in the life-span, infer such competencies from the nature of peer interaction and play. In short, in paraphrasing Hoffman (1976), we believe that the rudiments of role-taking skills are present as early as 2 years. Moreover, we are of the opinion that the ages cited by Selman as being normative for his stage model are actually overestimates, at least as concerns his first three stages. Those overestimates appear to result from Selman's reliance on complex verbal assessment rather than on observations of naturalistic indices of perspective-taking skill.

In this section we hope to provide support for our position that different forms of play and peer interaction reflect different levels or stages of social-cognitive development. Since the focus of this chapter is on early and middle childhood we will only concern ourselves with the first three stages of Selman's model.

Stage zero

It is noteworthy that Selman's first stage, 'egocentric role-taking' is not thought to appear until the child is approximately 3 years old. This first stage of role-taking is characterized by the child's ability to differentiate between the physical self and physical others. Thus, in infancy and toddlerhood, the child comes to define the self as a separate entity from others in his/her environment (Mead, 1934). The first stage is also characterized by the child's ability to understand that others can have feelings and thoughts, and that these traits can be different from his/her own. According to Selman, 3- to 6-year-olds can accurately label the feelings of others only when their own feelings match those of the others in a given social situation (Selman, 1976b), or when the situation or other person is familiar to the child. In short, the ability to 'read' or to predict the emotions of others is based on familiar and observable characteristics.

We agree with the general psychological viewpoint that one of the major problems facing the sensorimotor child is that of mastering the concepts of person permanence and self definition. However, we also believe that the positive characteristics of the Stage 0 perspective-taking child are, for the most part, evinced by the time the child is 3, or at the most, 4 years of age.

In our conceptualization of the development of social-cognitive skills, the groundwork is laid during the first year or so of life. Recent observations of parent–infant interaction demonstrate that between 7 and 17 months, infants come to develop a set of social anticipations and a sensitivity to the rules of such 'baby games' as peek-a-boo (Bruner and Sherwood, 1976). Since infants do not show separation or any other anxiety behaviours during the typical peek-a-boo game, it may be that such youngsters are able to differentiate between the literal event of 'mother-departing' and the playful game of momentary disappearance. Both the ability to understand the rules of peek-a-boo and the ability to anticipate certain behaviours on the part of a playmate (in this case mother or father) may involve the very basic skill of taking notice of, or having one's own perspective concerning the physical actions of others. Moreover, these elementary skills build the base upon which later game—playing behaviours which involve complex perspective-taking skills are built.

Further evidence for the early appreciation of rule structure in infant and toddler games stems from the recent work of Goldman and Ross (1978). These researchers found turn-taking to occur in the play of 12- to 24-month-old dyad participants. The skills cited by the authors as those demonstrated in turn-taking included: (a) the ability to distinguish between the actions of self and those of others; (b) the ability to wait for the partner to take his/her turn; (c) the ability to deal with the problem of simultaneous behaviours; and (d) the ability to employ violations of the turn-taking pattern in an effort to reestablish mutual engagement. From these behaviours one may infer that infants and toddlers are not only aware that others exist as separate entities from themselves, but also that these others can and do behave in certain predictable ways.

The recent studies of Mueller and his colleagues (Mueller and Lucas, 1975; Vandell and Mueller, this volume) provide a conceptual framework for the development of social skills and social-cognition during the infant and toddler years. In a first stage of social interaction, contacts appear to centre around objects. Thus in the earliest of social contacts between infants, one play partner is likely to duplicate the physical effects produced by the other partner with toys or other objects. These imitative behaviours demonstrate the infant's awareness of the actions of others.

During the second stage of toddler social interaction, the participants appear to behave in particular ways in order to elicit contingent behaviours from each other. For example, the initiator of a social interaction may bang a stick and wait for a subsequent response from his/her playmate. Such anticipatory behaviours, seen both in the work of Mueller and Lucas (1975) and Goldman and Ross (1978) reflect the infant's or toddler's ability to think about, or to make predictions about the behaviours of others who share his/her play environment. That is, 'If I bang with this stick, you will also bang with a stick'. While not indicating a reflection on the thoughts of others, these anticipatory behaviours based on contingent relationships, appear to mirror Selman's Stage 0 abilities which require that a child be able to predict that another feels (overt expression) the same way as s/he does in a given situation.

Finally, during the third stage of toddler social interaction, exchanges become reciprocal and early games take on the form of intercoordinated actions. For example, in ball games one child acts as the thrower while the play partner acts as receiver. For a game to take place, the partners must reverse roles, the thrower becoming receiver and vice versa. Such a role-exchange demonstrates an even more sophisticated awareness of the other, an awareness which may include thinking about the effects of one's own behaviours on those of the play partner.

In summary, recent studies of infant and toddler play demonstrate that children younger than 3 years of age are capable of thinking about others as well as about the behaviours of others. As in Selman's Stage 0, cognitions about others during the first 3 years appear to concern physical, overt properties. Taking the conservative line, it may well be that the intent of such early social interactions is egocentric. For example, one may engage in a seemingly social behaviour merely 'to make an interesting sight last', that sight being a particular response from a play partner. It may then be argued that the skills evident in early social games are rudimentary and do not constitute true social competencies. Infant and toddler 'games' may thus mirror Piagetian circular reactions of a social nature (Mueller and Lucas, 1975). Nevertheless, such behaviours are elementary forms of social-cognitive development—forms which may, in fact, be of a Stage 0 genre.

Although the perspective-taking skills of the Stage 0 child are highly limited, it is our belief that they are present prior to, rather than after, 3 years as Selman (1976a) suggests. Initial support for our position has come from the above description of early toddler social interactions. Further supportive data stem from both anecdotal and experimental reports. For example, Hoffman (1976) has described a number of incidents in which toddlers were able to 'read' accurately the emotions of others in familiar situations. Hoffman recounted an anecdote in which one 15-month-old grabbed a toy from an agemate. The agemate's reaction, which was to cry, elicited a consoling response from the source of distress. This consoling response first consisted of the donation of the aggressor's teddybear to the playmate. Realizing that the teddybear did not make the playmate happy, the aggressor ran from the room and retrieved the playmate's security blanket—the result, a cessation of crying. This anecdote, and many others like it provide further non-laboratory evidence that Stage 0 perspective—taking is in the repertoire of toddlers.

Finally, Borke (1971) has provided laboratory data to bolster our argument. Children as young as 3 years old were shown to differentiate correctly between the happy and sad responses of story characters. Again, these data appear to support the claim that correct identification of emotions in familiar situations is evident earlier than proposed.

Stage 1

The second stage in Selman's model perspective-taking has been labelled 'social informational role-taking'. Children in this stage are generally from 6 to 8 years old. At Stage 1, the kindergarten and early elementary school child comes to understand that the self and the other have potentially different interpretations of the same social situation. People can feel and think in different ways because they are in different situations. The child at Stage 1 cannot judge her/his own actions from the perspective of others. S/he is unable to understand that others can make inferences about her/his thoughts and/or feelings, while s/he is simultaneously engaged in the same inferential process vis à vis these others. Thus, the Stage 1 child engages in unidirectional perspective-taking. Selman (1976b) also notes that at this stage children come to distinguish between intentional and unintentional behaviours and correspondingly, that people, particularly the self, have evaluative abilities.

Evidence for the possibility that Stage 1 occurs earlier than the model suggests stems from the work of Garvey concerning the social play of children from 3 to 5 years old. To Garvey (1977), social play cannot occur until children become able to distinguish play from reality, that is children must interpret their playmates' gestures as non-literal and thus playful. While elementary forms of such a distinction were cited above (Bruner and Sherwood, 1976), the play/non-play differentiation becomes all the more clear when phrases like 'it's just pretend' or 'you aren't really a wicked witch' appear in the play of preschoolers. It is quite likely that the ability to distinguish play from reality requires the child to focus, not only on the actions, but also on the intentions of a playmate whose thoughts may be different from his/her own at the time. Thus, from observations of preschool play one may infer Stage 1 perspective-taking skills.

A second ability cited by Garvey as being essential for social play is that of rule abstraction. To play in a social context, children must be able to infer the rules governing the particular social situation as well as be able to understand collectively the rules. According to Garvey, there are two types of rules which govern social play. First there are general procedural rules such as turn alternation—rules which appear evident as early as 1 year old (Goldman and Ross, 1978). Second, there are situation specific rules which apply to particular play episodes. An example of the latter form of social rule may be extracted from a 'pretend you are sick' game (Garvey, 1976). Garvey noted that the 'sick' child in this anecdote, momentarily forgot his role and when his play partner telephoned for a doctor, he answered the call himself. The partner, however, was quick to point out the role violation of the previously accepted rules of the 'game': 'No, you're not the doctor, you're sick'. This play episode nicely demonstrates that children of preschool age are able, not only to take on a role different from their own, but also to conceptualize role expectations for play partners different from the role expectations for the self. These seemingly mature behaviours are tempered, however, by the difficulty of children to stick to the preassigned and previously agreed upon roles.

In summary, if one were to accept the age ranges cited by Selman as normative for Stage 1 of his model, one would not expect preschool children to be able to conceive of role expectations and rules governing play. However, such traits do exist, thereby supporting our claim that one may infer perspective-taking skills from the play behaviours of children at earlier ages than one might expect from verbal indices of such skills.

It is noteworthy that the play behaviours of preschool and kindergarten children have typically been categorized as being parallel and associative in nature (Parten, 1932; Rubin, 1977). The latter category, associative, finds children engaged in games or dramatic exercises involving others where each partner is unilaterally intent on his/her own behaviour (Millar, 1968). Thus, the play of 4-year-old children often reveals a focus on one perspective at a time, either their own or the other's, without a coordination of viewpoint—clearly a behavioural analogue to Selman's Stage 1. It follows that the play of children at this stage should show little evidence of an understanding of reciprocity, agreed upon social roles, and hierarchies within sociodramatic, cooperative exercises. Moreover, the understanding and display of competitive, zero-sum games should be alien to Stage 1 perspective-takers. Such games also involve the appreciation of sophisticated notions of reciprocal rather than unidirectional relationships. Evidence that such sophisticated play patterns rarely occur during naturalistic peer interactions of 4- and 5-year-olds stems from the recent observational work of the senior author (Rubin, 1977; Rubin, Maioni, and Hornung, 1976; Rubin et al., 1978).

To recapitulate, the work of Garvey demonstrates that dramatic play occurs with regularity among preschool children. However, the modal pattern of spontaneous dramatic play in preschoolers is one in which the child fails to assume a non-changing role within a previously agreed upon status hierarchy. This form of associative-dramatic play and the conceptual requirements for its display appear to demand the role-taking skills characteristic of Selman's Stage 1.

Laboratory support for the belief that Stage 1 perspective-taking occurs at earlier than 6 years of age stems from the work of Marvin and his colleagues. As mentioned earlier, Marvin et al. (1976) employed a simplified perspective-taking task in which children were individually shown a videotaped story and were then asked whether or not their mothers (who had not viewed the story) knew how the episode ended. These researchers found that children as young as 4 years of age could differentiate their own perspective from those of others.

More recently, Ruble, Higgins, Akst, and Loebl(1977) studied preschoolers' abilities to use social comparison processes in evaluating the achievement behaviours of other children. These workers found that with the increased salience and importance of the social comparison information (e.g. showing an event to be judged on film rather than reading a story) 4- and 5-year-olds could evaluate the achievements of others based on the relationship between an individual's performance and a set of norms. One finding of note was that such young children could best engage in the social comparison process when the achievement to be judged consisted of an overt, motor behaviour rather than a more covert, cognitive behaviour. Thus, as in Selman's Stage 1, the preschoolers were able to evaluate the behaviours of others when those behaviours were highly visible and probably meaningful to the child him/herself.

Finally, Darley, Klosson and Zanna (1978) have found that preschool-aged children can consider the concept of extenuating circumstances when asked to suggest just and fair punishment allocations for antisocial behaviours. For example, preschool children consistently judged a story character more kindly if s/he aggressed in an effort to rescue a younger sibling than if the character aggressed for no justified reason. In short, these recent data concerning the ability to judge intent and to employ elementary social comparison strategies provide support for our notion that Stage 1 perspective-taking skills are available to children by 4 or 5 years of age, and that such skills are detectable through observations of children's play.

Stage 2

The last Selman social-cognitive level we shall deal with in this chapter has been given the label the 'self-reflective role-taking' stage. Children in this perspective-taking stage are usually between the ages of 8 and 10 years. The characteristics of Stage 2 perspective-takers include an awareness that others think or feel differently from the self, and an ability to take the 'second person' perspective, that is to think that 'he is thinking of me in such a way' or that 'he knows that I am feeling happy'. The child cannot, however, make inferences about the self and the other simultaneously or mutually, but only sequentially. Thus, s/he cannot step 'outside' the dyadic situation and 'view' it from the perspective of a third person.

It is noteworthy that the play behaviours of children during the middle-childhood years (6 to 10 years of age) seem to reflect sequential perspective-taking skills. For example, sociodramatic play involves the simple coordination of perspectives (Rubin, 1977; Smilansky, 1968): 'you be the doctor and I will be sick'. Moreover, such play involves the ability to stick to the previously agreed upon roles for extended periods of time. However, the child does not appear to be able to step outside the play situation to consider the mutuality of the relationship between the two play characters, one of whom is him/herself. To be a 'writer' or 'director' of a self-planned play episode one would have to consider who would make the best 'doctor' or 'patient' or 'villain'. Such conceptualization, which has not heretofore been investigated, would appear to be one behavioural analogue to Stage 2 perspectivism. Our best guess is that between 6 and 8 years of age, such skills come to the fore.

Another form of child's play which is evinced in middle-childhood is the simple, competitive game with rules. One of the major distinctions between this game form and the games of infants, toddlers, and preschoolers earlier described (Garvey, 1977; Goldman and Ross, 1978) is its competitive nature. The competitive games of this age group generally do not have ultimate or fixed winners. As Sutton-Smith (1971) notes, the 'sides' or roles chosen for these games are transitory and winning is episodic. For example, the games of hide-and-seek, frozen tag, and dodge-ball all necessitate an understanding of reciprocal relationships and role-reversibility, both of which are Stage 2 perspective-taking skills. However, one need not simultaneously consider points of view from the 'third person' perspective (Stage 3) to engage in such early competitive games. One is only required to keep in mind that 'when you are it, I have to flee or to hide' and 'when I am it, you have to flee or hide'. There is little need to speculate about strategies based on recursive thought processes ('if I do this, s/he will do that, so I will ... '). Such skills appear necessary for games like chess or draughts or organized sports which are probably reflective of simultaneous, Stage 3 perspective-taking skills, and which effectively develop in behavioural form to some degree at around 9 or 10 years of age (Sutton-Smith, 1971).

It should be further noted that children between the ages of 6 and 10 years have difficulty planning attack and defence game strategies simultaneously (Sutton-Smith, 1971). Instead the focus appears to be an attack or defence while considering the prospective actions of the self and the other ('I will attack and you will flee'). This form of game playing skill most certainly mirrors the sequential perspective-taking skills of Selman's (1976a) Stage 2 children.

In summary, we have attempted to demonstrate that the varying levels of perspective-taking skill in early and middle childhood are paralleled (and during the infancy and preschool periods, preceded) by particular forms of play and peer interaction. The question which remains is whether or not peer play is anything more than a simple reflection of social-cognitive growth and development. More precisely phrased, can peer play cause social-cognitive growth?

PLAY AND PEER INTERACTION AS CAUSAL VARIABLES

We should note hastily that a number of psychologists of high repute have considered play to be essential to the development of cognitive skills. Bruner

(1972), for example has noted the importance of play for the development of tool use and construction activities. Piaget (1951) regarded symbolic play as a necessary precursor to the development of games with rules and to a mature moralistic outlook. Smilansky (1968) claimed sociodramatic activities helped develop cognitive, creative and social skills. Two points are worth mentioning from the outset. First, the forms of play thought to be most important in the development of social competence and social-cognition are symbolic or dramatic play with peers (Rosen, 1974; Rubin and Maioni, 1975; Saltz and Johnson, 1974; Smilansky, 1968). Second, the evidence supportive of this notion is promising and growing, but still fairly inconclusive.

Why is it that dramatic (or thematic or pretense) play with peers should cause the development of social-cognitive skills? To Mead (1934) dramatic play was seen as fundamental to the development of the self-concept. Thus, to establish a separate self-identity, Mead believed that the child must figuratively get 'outside him/herself and view him/herself from some other perspective. Dramatic play was seen as the prime vehicle for this. By taking the role of another in play, the child was thought to gain a reflection of him/herself as different from, but related to others.

Similarly, Vygotsky (1966) and Singer (1973) noted that representational play, characterized by dramatic play themes, was an important precursor to the development of cognitive and social-cognitive skills. Both of these influential psychologists have indicated the significance of representational play in liberating the child from the 'here and now'. In short, such behaviour was thought to promote abstract thought, the development of imagery, and verbal coding skills. Singer (1973), as well as Smilansky (1968) and Lieberman (1977), also reflected on the importance of make-believe play for the development of creativity, divergent thinking, and an understanding of social roles and the institutions within which they operate.

As for the field of pedagogy, preschool programmers such as Weikart, Rogers, Adcock, and McClelland (1970), Kamii and DeVries (1977), and Spivack and Shure (1974), advocate the use of sociodramatic training to promote cognitive, social and social-cognitive functioning.

Ironically, Piaget, the one person whose theoretical viewpoints have inspired the development of the study of social-cognition saw little causal role for play in the development of role-taking skills. Play, particularly symbolic play, to Piaget (1951) exemplified the subordination of reality to the whims of the child's ego. Thus, play was viewed as 'pure assimilation', a clearcut example of the child's egocentric viewpoint of the world. As such play, to Piaget, reflected the inadequacy of early thought. The role of imaginative play was seen merely as a manner of exercising newly developed cognitive skills.

While it is not often easy to disagree with Piaget, we feel strongly that he has underestimated the power of play in determining the development of social-cognitive skills. First, as Sutton-Smith (1966) has pointed out, Piaget's definition of play as 'pure assimilation' may be unreasonably restrictive. If one considers the phenomenon of dramatic or symbolic play, one may readily infer that such activities have accommodative properties as well. For example, children who engage in imaginative play tend to 'conserve' the imaginative identities of play objects despite contra-indicative stimuli. A child may call a block his/her pet dog, and persist in calling it by that label and in acting toward it as if it were a dog, despite the fact that it never barks, sniffs around, bites postmen, or urinates on neighbours' lawns. (Perhaps we should all have pet blocks!) This conservation of identity in the preschool years certainly pre-dates the quantitative forms of conservation found a few years later.

Moreover, the child demonstrates the operation of reversibility during pretence play. While enacting a role the child never forgets his/her true identity. The child who is playing 'Wonder Woman' certainly runs to Mommy when she is told: 'I am leaving now, Amy. If you don't come you will have to stay at Daddy's office all day!' Likewise, a lump of clay undeliciously scattered with beans and toothpicks may be treated as a cake, but never really eaten. Certainly both of these examples reveal early decentration and reversibility skills. That is, the child, in her/his early symbolic play is: (a) able to realize simultaneously that s/he can play a role and be him/herself or that a lump of clay can be just that, as well as a birthday cake (decentration); and (b) the child realizes that s/he can revert to being him/herself after the play episode is over. Thus, regarding our earlier discussion of Garvey's (1976) work, it may well be that elementary cognitive forms of decentration and reversibility underlie the child's ability to distinguish fantasy from reality.

These views imply that dramatic play may be a useful mechanism which compels the child to conserve the identity of peers and the self through the world of make-believe. Moreover, the decentration skills evoked by socio-dramatic play may cause the child to regard his/her behaviours from his/her own role perspective and from the perspectives of his/her peers simultaneously.

While such a position is conceptually plausible, the true test of whether or not peer play serves as a causal variable in the development of social-cognitive skills rests with empirical research. In this regard, we should be among the first to point out that the data supportive of this position, to this date, are promising, but not sufficiently strong to make some final conclusive statement. Unfortunately many of the problems rest not with the findings themselves, but with the methodologies employed in the studies.

STUDIES RELATING PLAY AND SOCIAL-COGNITIVE DEVELOPMENT

First, much of the research linking play and social-cognition is correlational in nature. For example, Rubin and Maioni (1975) observed the free play behaviours of children and found a significant positive correlation between the frequency of dramatic play and scores on classification and role-taking tasks, both of which purportedly require the development of decentration skills. Notably they found a negative relationship between the frequency of functional, practice play and these same cognitive tests.

In another study, Rubin (1976a) found a significant positive correlation between observed incidence of associative play in preschoolers and scores on a role-taking task (Borke, 1971) as well as a negative correlation between unoccupied and parallel play and role-taking skill. Thus, active peer interaction was positively correlated with social-cognitive development, while passive peer-interaction was negatively correlated with such development. Still more recently, Cragg (1977) found a significant positive relationship between kindergarten group play and both role-taking and sharing behaviours.

In subsequent studies, Rubin (1976b) has found that children who initiate and with whom other children initiate active interchanges are less verbally egocentric in naturalistic settings than their less social preschool agemates.

Johnson (1976) recently made the point that lower socioeconomic status preschoolers have been found consistently to display less sociodramatic and symbolic play than their middle-class agemates (e.g. Sigel and McBane, 1967; Smilansky, 1968). He linked these findings to the fact that lower-class preschoolers also tend to be less able to come up with alternative uses for objects (divergent thinking), to classify (Sigel and McBane, 1967) and to role-take (e.g. Bearison and Cassel, 1975) than their middle-class counterparts. Since all of these latter skills require the ability to decentre, Johnson's conceptual leap made some sense. In order to bolster his case, Johnson found that the frequency of sociodramatic play units in preschoolers was significantly related to their performance on a test of decentration skills, that is, divergent thinking.

While these studies do indicate some link between decentration and social-cognitive abilities and play, their correlational nature does not allow us to capture the elusive causal variable. The results reported above may just as easily indicate that role-taking or decentration skills are prerequisite to dramatic or social play. Recently, however, a number of researchers have carried out training studies in attempts to consider the directionality of the play/social-cognition relationship.

One of the first attempts to train cognitive and social skills through play was that of Smilansky (1968). Working with disadvantaged Israeli children, Smilansky found sociodramatic play training to lead to greater verbal communication skills, more positive affective behaviour and less aggression. These latter abilities have been thought by some (e.g. Mussen and Eisenberg-Berg, 1977) to be somewhat dependent on the development of social-cognition; that is the better able a preschooler is to role-take, the less likely s/he will be to engage in egocentric speech and aggressive behaviours and the more likely s/he will be to display altruistic acts (e.g. Rubin and Schneider, 1973). Unfortunately, much of the Smilansky data are non-quantitative in nature, and one cannot be entirely certain of the significance of her findings.

More recently Saltz and Johnson (1974) examined the effects of thematic play tuition on disadvantaged preschool children's intellectual and social-cognitive skills. In a nutshell, their results indicated significant differences on the role-taking measure between those who received training where they listened to a story (*Little Red Riding Hood*), and then enacted it and those who did not have such a tuition experience. Unfortunately, their choice of a post-test only social-cognitive assessment was flawed in two ways. First, the authors had no way of knowing whether role-taking skills were equivalent at the outset of the training programme. More important, however, was the fact that the particular test of role-taking used in the study (Borke, 1971) only tapped the very first of Selman's (1976a) levels of social-cognitive development. If the authors were attempting to claim that thematic play tuition caused the development of a social-cognitive understanding of reciprocity, the choice of a Selman Stage 2 or Stage 3 measure would have been far more appropriate (e.g. Chandler, 1973).

Rosen (1974) also investigated the effects of sociodramatic play training on social skills and role-taking. Two different groups of disadvantaged pre-schoolers received teacher initiated tuition in sociodramatic play for 10 1-hour sessions. The results indicated that the training group increased their cooperative and role-taking skills significantly more than did two comparison groups, one of which engaged in musical activities and the other of which engaged in non-fantasy activities. While improvement in role-taking was noted, it is important to point out, once again, that the tests examined the lowest of Selman's levels and failed to tap either the concepts of reciprocity or decentration.

In a fourth study, Fink (1976) examined the effects of tuition in thematic play on the development of perspective-taking skills. Thirty-six kindergarteners were assigned to one of three groups: (a) thematic play tuition (children were instructed to engage in four play exercises over a 4-week period: for example, 'playing zoo'); (b) a group which received extra free-play activity in the non-directive presence of the experimenter; and (c) a non-treatment control group. Only the first group showed significant pre-test to post-test increases in the understanding of both kinship relations and social-role conservation (e.g. a doctor can also be a wife, mother, and so on), both ostensibly measures of social-cognitive decentration skills.

A fifth source of data concerning the causal relationship between imaginary role-play and role-taking skills stems from the applied work of Spivack and Shure (1974). In a series of studies (Spivack and Shure, 1974), these writers have found that when small groups of preschoolers are tutored in role-play and thematic play exercises they are more likely to improve social problem-solving skills than are their agemates who have received no such training.

The ability to solve such social problems as getting a desired toy from a peer in a socially acceptable manner has been thought by some to necessitate role-taking skills. While the Spivack and Shure data are highly promising, it must be added hastily that their curriculum is not solely built around role-play and imaginary-play techniques. For example, small group tuition is also given to teach children relational terms ('same'/'different'). Thus, the role of tutored play in the development of social-problem solving is not yet known.

The five sources cited above provide us with promising but inconclusive support for the notion that sociodramatic play causes social-cognitive growth. One problem with the training studies is that the outcome measures of role-taking skill are either inappropriate or ill-conceived. In the cases of the Saltz and Johnson (1974), Rosen (1974), and Fink (1976) studies, the perspective-taking tasks did not tap the more mature Selman levels. In the Spivack and Shure (1974) studies the outcome measures are primarily verbal assessments of social problem-solving skills. Krasnor and Rubin (1978) have recently pointed out that verbal assessments of social-problem solving abilities are very poor predictors of children's behavioural solutions to the same problems in natural settings.

A second problem with the above reports rests with the dilemma of ascertaining whether or not it is the sociodramatic play experience or the tuition experience which leads to social-cognitive gains. As Smith (1977) correctly points out in his comments concerning the Rosen (1974) study, 'it remains a distinct possibility that there were differences between the kind of tuition given in fantasy/sociodramatic play and that given in music or non-fantasy activities (Rosen's other two groups). It would be relevant to have detailed observations of the actual tuition experiences of the different groups' (p. 135). This same commentary is appropriate vis à vis the Saltz and Johnson (1974) and Fink (1976) studies as well.

Taken together, there appears to be limited empirical support for the premise that sociodramatic play causes social-cognitive growth and development. There is even less empirical support for the premise that sociodramatic free play serves an accommodative role in cognitive development. As Smith (1977) points out the crucial variable may be adult tuition rather than sociodramatic play. At this point in time the theoretical basis for arguing that play serves a causal role in growth and development is stronger than the empirical support for such a proposition. However, recent naturalistic observational research may provide the theorists with some welcome supportive data. Take, for example, the work of Matthews (1977). This researcher noted that in some same-sex fantasy play dyads, children assumed specific sex-role positions (e.g. mother and father) and had smoothly functioning relationships. Thus, in some cases fantasy play was assimilative in that the children's similar perceptions of the roles of mothers and fathers determined their role-play behaviours. However, in other cases, disagreements ensued concerning the sex-role appropriateness of each other's play behaviours. These play conflicts were observed to lead to different perceptions of sex-appropriate behaviours given relevant changes or compromises in subsequent fantasy play. In short, Matthews revealed the accommodative function of fantasy play in the development of person-perception or role-taking skill.

We had earlier noted the causal importance of peer conflicts in the decline of egocentric thought. The recent Matthews work, as well as that of Garvey and Berndt (1975) shine light on the possibility that conflict in fantasy play serves an accommodative function. Further support for our contention will hopefully be produced in future research endeavours. Perhaps with more carefully designed training studies, or better still, with some sequential analyses (e.g. Gottman and Notarius, 1977) of naturalistic observations of fantasy play, peer interaction, and peer conflict, the causal relationship between play and social-cognitive competence will be ascertained.

CONCLUSION

We have, in this chapter, described the phenomenon of social-cognitive development, or more particularly the development of perspective-taking skills in childhood. In plotting the course of social-cognitive development we have taken the position that a number of levels of perspective-taking ability exist (Selman, 1976a, b) and that these levels are mirrored by various forms of children's play behaviours and social interactions. Finally, we have reviewed some promising data which suggest that play, specifically thematic or fantasy play, encourages growth in perspective-taking skills. Such play, which forces its participants to adopt novel social roles, and which often elicits peer conflict concerning social expectations and conformity, appears to serve as a valuable medium for promoting social-cognitive growth.

While the empirical research concerning the causal role of children's play and peer interaction in the onset of perspective-taking skills is still fairly inconclusive, it is hoped that future research will be pleasantly informative. Until such time occurs, we may sensibly conclude that: (a) children enjoy playing with peers; (b) sociodramatic or fantasy play appears to be logically and functionally related to social decentration and perspective-taking; and (c) tuition in such play among small groups appears to be a productive exercise. Given these conclusions, it is probably worthwhile for teachers and parents to encourage and participate in the sociodramatic play of their pupils and children.

REFERENCES

Bearison, D. J., and Cassel, T. Z. (1975). Cognitive decentration and social codes: communicative effectiveness in young children from differing family contexts. *Developmental Psychology*, **11**, 29–36.

Borke, H. (1971). Interpersonal perception of young children: egocentrism or empathy? *Developmental Psychology*, **5**, 263–269.

Bruner, J. S. (1972). Nature and uses of immaturity. *American Psychologist*, **27**, 1–28.

Bruner, J. S., and Sherwood, V. (1976). Peekaboo and the learning of rule structures. In J. S. Bruner, A. Jolly and K. Sylva, (Eds.), *Play—Its Role in Development and Evolution*. Harmondsworth, Middlesex: Penguin Books.

Chandler, M. (1973). Egocentrism and antisocial behavior: the assessment and training of social perspective-taking skills. *Developmental Psychology*, **9**, 326–332.

Cragg, S. (1977). The effects of empathy, role-taking and play on altruism. Unpublished manuscript, University of Waterloo.

Darley, J. M., Klosson, E. C., and Zanna, M. P. (1978). Intentions and their contexts in the moral judgments of children and adults. *Child Development*, **49**, 66–74.

Dawes, H. (1934). An analysis of 200 quarrels of preschool children. *Child Development*, **5**, 139–157.

Evans, M. A., and Rubin, K. H. (in press). Hand gestures as a communicative mode in school-aged children. *Journal of Genetic Psychology*.

Feffer, M. H. (1959). The cognitive implications of role-taking behavior. *Journal of Personality*, **27**, 152–168.

Fink, R. S. (1976). Role of imaginative play in cognitive development. *Psychological Reports*, **39**, 895–906.

Fisher, J. L. (1934). Language patterns of preschool children. *Child Development Monographs*, **15** (Monograph).

Flavell, J. (1968). *The Development of Role-taking and Communication Skills in Children*. New York: Wiley.

Flavell, J. H. (1977). *Cognitive Development*. Englewood Cliffs, New Jersey: Prentice Hall.

Garvey, C. (1976). Some properties of social play. In J. S. Bruner, A. Jolly and K. Sylva (Eds.), *Play—Its Role in Development and Evolution*. Harmondsworth, Middlesex: Penguin Books.

Garvey, C. (1977). Play with language. In B. Tizard and D. Harvey (Eds.), *Biology of Play*. Philadelphia: Lippincott.

Garvey, C., and Berndt, R. (1975). The organization of pretend play. Paper presented at the Symposium, Structure in Play and Fantasy, American Psychological Association, Chicago.

Garvey, C., and Hogan, R. (1973). Social speech and social interaction: egocentrism revisited. *Child Development*, **44**, 562–568.

Glucksberg, S., Krauss, R. H., and Higgins, E. T. (1975). The development of communication skills in children. In F. Horowitz (Ed.), *Review of Child Development Research* Vol. 4. Chicago: University of Chicago Press.

Goldman, B. D., and Ross, H. S. (1978). Social skills in action: an analysis of early peer games. In J. A. Glick, and K. A. Clarke-Stewart (Eds.), *Studies in Social and Cognitive Development*. Vol. 1. New York: Gardner Press.

Gottman, J., and Notarius, C. (1977). Sequential analysis of observational data using markov chains. In T. Kratochwill (Ed.), *Strategies to Evaluate Change in Single Subject Research*. New York: Academic Press.

Hartup, W. W. (1974). Aggression in childhood: developmental perspectives. *American Psychologist*, **29**, 336–341.

Hoffman, M. (1976). Empathy, role-taking, guilt, and development of altruistic motives. In T. Lickona (Ed.), *Moral Development and Behavior: Theory, Research and Social Issues*. New York: Holt, Rinehart and Winston.

Johnson, J. E. (1976). Relations of divergent thinking and intelligence test scores with social and non-social make believe play of preschool children. *Child Development*, **47**, 1200–1203.

Kamii, C., and DeVries, R. (1977). Piaget for early education. In M. C. Day and R. K. Parker (Eds.), *The Preschool in Action*. Boston: Allyn and Bacon.

Kohlberg, L. (1976). Moral stages and moralization: the cognitive-developmental approach. In T. Lickona (Ed.), *Moral Development and Behavior*. New York: Holt, Rinehart and Winston.

Kohlberg, L., Yaeger, J., and Hjertholm, E. (1968). Private speech: four studies and a review of theories. *Child Development*, **39**, 692–736.

Krasnor, L. R., and Rubin, K. H. (1978). Preschoolers' verbal and behavioral solutions to social problems. Paper presented at the Annual Meeting of the Canadian Psychological Association, Ottawa, June.

Kurdek, L. (1977). Components and correlates of cognitive perspective-taking. *Child Development*, **48**, 1503–1511.

Lieberman, J. N. (1977). *Playfulness: Its Relationships to Imagination and Creativity*. New York: Academic Press.

Maratsos, M. P. (1973). Nonegocentric communication abilities in preschool children. *Child Development*, **44**, 697–700.

Marvin, R. S., Greenberg, M. T., and Mossler, D. G. (1976). The early development of conceptual perspective-taking: distinguishing among multiple perspectives. *Child Development*, **47**, 511–514.

Matthews, W. S. (1977). Sex role perception, portrayal, and preference in the fantasy play of young children. Paper presented at the Biennial Conference of the Society for Research in Child Development, New Orleans, March.

Maudry, M., and Nekula, M. (1939). Social relations between children of the same age during the first two years of life. *Journal of Genetic Psychology*, **54**, 193–215.

Mead, G. H. (1934). *Mind, Self and Society*. Chicago: University of Chicago Press.

Millar, S. (1968). *The Psychology of Play*. New York: Penguin Books.

Miller, P. H., Kessel, F. S., and Flavell, J. H. (1970). Thinking about people thinking about . . . : a study of social cognitive development. *Child Development*, **41**, 613–623.

Mueller, E. (1972). The maintenance of verbal exchanges between young children. *Child Development*, **43**, 930–938.

Mueller, E., and Lucas, T. (1975). A developmental analysis of peer interaction among toddlers. In M. Lewis, and L. A. Rosenblum (Eds.), *Friendship and Peer Relations*. New York: Wiley.

Mussen, P., and Eisenberg-Berg, N. (1977). *Roots of Caring, Sharing and Helping*. San Francisco: Freeman.

Parten, M. (1932). Social participation among preschool children. *Journal of Abnormal Psychology*, **27**, 243–269.

Piaget, J. (1926). *The Language and Thought of the Child*. London: Routledge and Kegan Paul.

Piaget, J. (1932). *The Moral Judgement of the Child*. Glencoe, Illinois: Free Press.

Piaget, J. (1951). *Play, Dreams and Imitation in Childhood*. New York: Norton.

Piaget, J. (1962). Comments on Vygotsky's critical remarks. In L. S. Vygotsky (Ed.), *Thought and Language*. Cambridge, Massachusetts: MIT Press.

Piaget, J. (1970). Piaget's Theory. In P. H. Mussen (Ed.), *Carmichael's Manual of Child Psychology*, Vol. 1. New York: Wiley.

Piaget, J. (1977). *Science of Education and the Psychology of the Child*. New York: Penguin Books.

Piaget, J., and Inhelder, B. (1956). *The Child's Conception of Space*. London: Routledge.

Rest, J. (1976). New approaches in the assessment of moral judgment. In T. Lickona

(Ed.), *Moral Development and Behavior*. New York: Holt, Rinehart and Winston.

Rosen, C. (1974). The effects of sociodramatic play on problem-solving behavior among culturally disadvantaged preschool children. *Child Development*, **45**, 920–927.

Rothenberg, B. (1970). Children's social sensitivity and the relationship to interpersonal competence, intrapersonal comfort, and intellectual level. *Developmental Psychology*, **2**, 335–350.

Rubin, K. H. (1973). Egocentrism in childhood: a unitary construct? *Child Development*, **44**, 102–110.

Rubin, K. H. (1976a). The relationships of social play preference to role taking skills in preschool children. *Psychological Reports*, **39**, 823–826.

Rubin, K. H. (1976b). Social interaction and communicative egocentrism in preschoolers. *Journal of Genetic Psychology*, **129**, 121–124.

Rubin, K. H. (1977). The play behaviors of young children. *Young Children*, **32**, 16–24.

Rubin, K. H. (1978). Role-taking in childhood: some methodological considerations. *Child Development*, **49**, 428–433.

Rubin, K. H., and Maoini, T. L. (1975). Play preferences and its relationship to egocentrism, popularity, and classification skills in preschoolers. *Merrill–Palmer Quarterly*, **21**, 171–178.

Rubin, K. H., Maioni, T. L., and Hornung, M. (1976). Free play behaviors in middle- and lower-class preschoolers: Parten and Piaget revisited. *Child Development*, **47**, 414–419.

Rubin, K. H., and Schneider, F. W. (1973). The relationship between moral judgment, egocentrism, and altruistic behavior. *Child Development*, **44**, 661–665.

Rubin, K. H., and Trotter, K. T. (1977). Kohlberg's moral judgment scale: some methodological considerations. *Developmental Psychology*, **13**, 535–536.

Rubin, K. H., Watson, K. S., and Jambor, T. W. (1978). Free play behaviors in preschool and kindergarten children. *Child Development*, **49**, 534–536.

Ruble, D. N., Higgins, E. T., Akst, L., and Loebl, H. H. (1977). Integration of social comparison information in young children's achievement evaluations. Unpublished manuscript, Princeton University.

Saltz, E., and Johnson, J. (1974). Training for thematic-fantasy play in culturally disadvantaged children: preliminary results. *Journal of Educational Psychology*, **66**, 623–630.

Selman, R. L. (1976a). Social-cognitive understanding: a guide to educational and clinical practice. In T. Lickona (Ed.), *Moral Development and Behavior*. New York: Holt, Rinehart and Winston.

Selman, R. L. (1976b). Toward a structural analysis of developing interpersonal relations concepts: research with normal and disturbed preadolescent boys. In A. D. Pick (Ed.), *Minnesota Symposium on Child Psychology*. Minneapolis, Minnesota: University of Minnesota Press.

Selman, R. L., and Byrne, D. (1974). A structural-developmental analysis of levels of role-taking in middle childhood. *Child Development*, **45**, 803–806.

Sigel, I. E., and McBane, B. (1967). Cognitive competence and level of symbolization among five-year-old children. In J. Hellmuth (Ed.), *Disadvantaged Child*, Vol. I. New York: Brunner-Mazel.

Singer, J. L. (Ed.) (1973). *The Child's World of Make Believe*. New York: Academic Press.

Smilansky, S. (1968). *The Effects of Sociodramatic Play on Disadvantaged Children: Preschool Children*. New York: Wiley.

Smith, P. K. (1977). Social and fantasy play in young children. In B. Tizard and D. Harvey (Eds.), *Biology of Play*. Philadelphia: Lippincott.

Spivack, G., and Shure, M. B. (1974). *Social Adjustment of Young Children*. San Francisco: Jossey-Bass.

Sutton-Smith, B. (1966). Piaget on play: a critique. *Psychological Review*, **73**, 111–112.

Sutton-Smith, B. (1971). A syntax for play and games. In R. R. Herron and B. Sutton-Smith (Eds.), *Child's Play*. New York: Wiley.

Vygotsky, L. S. (1962). *Thought and Language*, Cambridge, Massachusetts: MIT Press.

Weikart, D. P., Rogers, L., Adcock, C., and McClelland, D. (1970). *The Cognitively Oriented Curriculum*. Urbana, Ill.: ERIC/NAEYC Publications.

CHAPTER 9

Child Ethology and the Study of Preschool Social Relations

FLOYD F. STRAYER

ETHOLOGICAL APPROACHES TO SOCIAL BEHAVIOUR

Ethology usually is described as a specialized discipline within biology concerned with the direct observation of naturally occurring units of behaviour. Such concerns certainly distinguish ethologists from any other behavioural scientists. However, efforts to define ethology soley in terms of its methodological orientation fail to capture essential differences between biological and more traditional psychological approaches to the study of social behaviour. The inadequacy of such a methodological distinction between ethology and psychology is most apparent in the field of child development, where a strong emphasis upon the description and analysis of naturally occurring maturational changes has had a long and important history (cf. Barker, 1930, 1965; Chittenden, 1942; Dawe, 1943; Emmerlich, 1964; Gellert, 1961, 1962; Piaget, 1926, 1948, 1951, 1952, 1954; Shirley, 1933; Washburn, 1932). Nevertheless, the form of naturalistic description most often employed in developmental psychology differs from that found in ethological research. This difference in the use of observational methods reflects a more basic divergence in the conceptual frameworks which underlie psychological and ethological approaches to behaviour.

Fundamental distinctions between the conceptual orientations in ethology and those in other behavioural disciplines have been repeatedly emphasized by researchers actively engaged in the comparative biological study of behaviour (e.g. Bateson and Hinde, 1976; Blurton Jones, 1972; Kummer, 1971; Tinbergen, 1963). Kummer (1971) provides perhaps the most concise summary of the network of explanatory systems which constitute the biological framework for analysing behaviour. Each type of explanation described by Kummer is associated with a limited set of specific questions about the nature of behaviour.

The first and most basic type of question concerns the organization, or structure of the behavioural phenomena which are of interest. The commitment to providing an adequately detailed descriptive account of behavioural elements characteristic among members of a species provides a common focus in the preliminary stage of all ethological research. Many of the most important advances in child ethology during the past decade have dealt directly with this problem of specifying the diversity of behavioural units which can be observed among young children (e.g. Blurton Jones, 1972; Blurton Jones and Leach, 1972; Brannigan and Humphries, 1972; Grant, 1969; Leach, 1972; McGrew, 1970, 1972; Smith and Connolly, 1972). Although these descriptive studies seldom contribute directly to our understanding of children's social relationships, they reflect a basic assumption in ethology that qualitative differences in complex phenomena, such as social relationships or interaction episodes, cannot be understood without a detailed consideration of qualitative differences in individual action patterns which constitute social exchange between individuals.

Following the development of an adequate behavioural inventory, ethological researchers usually begin systematically to consider questions concerning the immediate causation or the immediate function of selected behavioural elements. Although these same two problems have dominated psychological theory and research, they play a somewhat different role in ethological investigations. Perhaps most importantly, analysis of the immediate antecedents—and consequences of different behavioural elements—permits a regrouping of units included in the behavioural repertoire into larger categories defined in terms of common causal factors (Tinbergen, 1950) or common outcomes (Hinde, 1970). Thus for the ethologists, research on causation and function has two quite different benefits. First, such research provides information concerning the factors which influence, or control the occurrence of behaviour. This information contributes directly to an increase in the accuracy of prediction and control of behavioural phenomena, which is apparently a universal objective within the behavioural sciences. Second, the same information facilitates the reorganization of the behavioural inventory, and thus contributes to a deeper appreciation of basic similarities among morphologically distinct behavioural units. This latter insight is essential for the inductive derivation of important classes or categories of behaviour (i.e. aggressive behaviour, affiliative activity, etc.).

Finally, in addition to questions about immediate causation and function, a complete ethological analysis includes consideration of the historical context for behaviour. This latter interest raises questions concerning behavioural ontogeny and phylogeny. Such questions also involve an interest in antecedents and consequences of behaviour, but within the larger time-frame necessary for evolution and development. It is perhaps this historical, comparative emphasis which distinguishes ethology most clearly from traditional psychology, and permits it to offer a vast number of descriptive models which can be used to generate testable hypotheses about human social behaviour.

SOCIAL ETHOLOGY AND SOCIAL ORGANIZATION

Although the preceding discussion suggests a fairly comprehensive and unified conceptual orientation in ethological research, the relative attention given to each of these explanatory systems has produced considerable diversity within the field. Crook (1970) argued that there are two quite distinct approaches evident in modern ethology. The first focuses more directly upon the organization of individual action patterns, their causation and development. Without its emphasis upon the comparative analysis of naturally occurring behaviour, this branch of ethology would be indistinguishable from modern psychology. The second approach, called 'social ethology' (Crook, 1970) or 'sociobiology' (Wilson, 1975), deals more directly with questions about organization of social behaviour, the coordination of activity between individuals, and the evolutionary history of social structures. According to Crook (1970), the development of social ethology as a distinct branch of biological research occurred as a result of the increasing quantity of information about social behaviour among non-human primates. Given both the complexity and diversity of primate societies, an analysis of individual differences in behavioural activities necessitated a detailed consideration of the organization of stable relationships within the social group.

One of the most important advances in the development of social ethology entailed the formulation of an empirical approach to the evaluation of social organization. Although it was evident to even the earliest primatologists (e.g. Yerkes, 1928; Zuckerman, 1932) that the integration of individuals within a stable social group places important limitations upon each of their activities, it was not clear how to summarize the patterns of social coordination which provided these contextual constraints on individual social behaviour. In fact, early studies of primate social organization were hampered by both theoretical and methodological problems. Most of the theoretical difficulty involved determining the relative utility of general social concepts, such as dominance, leadership, control roles, affiliative bonds, kinship patterns and playmates, as necessary and/or sufficient dimensions for the description of primate relationships (Chance and Jolly, 1970; DeVore, 1965; Jay, 1968; Jolly, 1972). The corresponding methodological problems entailed the derivation of appropriate operations for the evaluation of these general concepts. With the awareness that standardized operational measures of such concepts failed to predict social behaviour in a group setting (Bernstein, 1970), researchers began to emphasize the descriptive analysis of ongoing social behaviour as a means of identifying basic dimensions of social organization. This trend culminated in the formulation of a more systematic inductive approach to specifying the nature of social relationships and group structures (Hinde, 1976; Hinde and Stevenson-Hinde, 1976).

Hinde's (1976) approach to social organization requires clear distinctions between four different levels of social description. The identification of individual *action patterns* (elementary units of social behaviour) represents the lowest level of behavioural description. Subsequently, the identification of recurrent combinations of such social actions occurring between individuals permits the isolation of qualitatively different *interaction sequences* which summarize dyadic social exchange within the group. Inspection of how the various types of interaction sequences covary across dyadic contexts may suggest specific groupings of social exchange which can be used as converging indices of different dimensions of dyadic *social relationships*. An analysis of the regularity and variability in such sequences permits a discussion of how social relationships differ in both quality and complexity. Finally, having described the nature of social relationships, it becomes possible to explore more general organizing principles which summarize the coordination that exists among relationships. It is exactly such coordination among various social relationships that constitutes *group structures*.

PRESCHOOL SOCIAL ETHOLOGY

Given the relatively recent formulation of specific analytic procedures for the investigation of social organization, it should not be surprising that most ethological studies of preschool social behaviour have failed to provide a detailed consideration of social relationships and group structure. In contrast, the majority of published studies deal primarily with the analysis of single behavioural units and the integration of these units into more extended individual action sequences (Blurton Jones, 1972; McGrew, 1972). The few studies dealing directly with social relationships and group structure have focused almost exclusively upon the descriptive analysis of social dominance (McGrew, 1972; Misshakian, 1976; Strayer and Strayer, 1976). Other researchers have attempted to relate differences in dominance status within the preschool peer group to a variety of other measures of individual differences, that is frequency of received social attention (Abramovitch, 1976), general patterns of social spacing (Abramovitch and Strayer, 1977), differences in social competence (Sluckin and Smith, 1977); and differences in the accuracy of social perception (Strayer, Chapeskie and Strayer, 1978). Ethological researchers are currently developing techniques for the evaluation of friendships among preschool children (Abramovitch, personal communication; Marvin, personal communication), but in the past much less attention was given to more cohesive forms of social bonding. Work in our own laboratory has been directed toward the concurrent analysis of preschool social conflict (agonism), affiliative interaction (peer attachment), and prosocial exchanges (altruistic sequences). The final section of this chapter provides a summary of our preliminary findings concerning the nature of these three social relations. Since this approach to the analysis of social relations draws heavily from methods and concepts developed by animal ethologists, our discussion of preschool social organization will stress comparative information from social ethology whenever possible.

DIMENSIONS OF PRESCHOOL SOCIAL ORGANIZATION

Samples, settings and observational techniques

The following research findings are derived from four separate studies of different social groups during the past 4 years. Three of the studies were conducted in university preschool centres during the second half of the academic year. Thus, these children had at least 4 months of group experience prior to observational sampling. The remaining group of children was observed from the start of their group experience.

The Langara preschool group

Observations at the Langara Preschool Center in Vancouver, British Columbia, were conducted during the summer months of 1973. At the beginning of observations, the group contained 18 children (10 boys and 8 girls). Since one girl left the group early in the observational session, data are presented for only 17 children ranging in age from 3 to 5 years (mean age: 52 months). Observations were conducted both indoors and outdoors using portable video equipment. Primary emphasis in the video samples was given to recording agonistic interaction through the use of matrix completion sampling techniques. In addition, regular instantaneous scan samples were obtained through direct observation of proximity patterns and play activity of each child.

The Simon Fraser preschool group

Observations at the Simon Fraser University Preschool in Vancouver, British Columbia, were conducted during the late spring of 1974. Although this group contained 16 children (8 boys and 8 girls), one boy and one girl were absent for over 25 per cent of the observation days, and thus were eliminated from the sample. The remaining 14 children ranged from 3 to 5 years (mean age: 48 months). Observations were conducted indoors throughout a 4-week period. Daily records of social behaviour were obtained using 5-min focal individual samples. Observations were tape-recorded and transcribed immediately after the observation period.

The Waterloo preschool group

Observations at the Waterloo Center in Waterloo, Ontario, were conducted during a 6-week period beginning in late January and ending in March of 1975. The Waterloo group contained 26 children; but seven children were absent for more than 25 per cent of the observational days, and thus were not included in the final sample. Data are presented for 19 children (10 boys and 9 girls) who ranged in age from 3 to 5 years (mean age: 52 months). The Waterloo Preschool Center contained three rooms which were available during free-play periods. The largest central room was already equipped with video cameras and microphones. This equipment provided a permanent record of social activity during the observation period. Direct observation of focal subgroups provided records of interactions in the two other rooms of the preschool centre.

The Clarke preschool group

Observations at the Clarke Institute of Psychiatry in Toronto, Ontario occurred during the summer months of 1976. The 11 children (10 boys and one girl) who ranged in age from 5 to 7 years (mean age: 74 months) were referred to the Clarke Institute to participate in a summer training programme for the enhancement of social skills. Because of their inability to adjust to social demands from the school setting, none of these children had been able to attend regular school classes. Observations at the Clarke Institute were conducted on 4 days of 6 consecutive weeks using direct observation techniques. Focal individual samples of social interaction were tape-recorded and transcribed immediately following daily observation.

Records of social interaction in all groups were coded using a four item descriptive syntax. For each observed social exchange, the initiator, his action, the target, and the target's response were always noted. If one of the items in the description was unclear, the entire exchange was not coded. Reliabilities for use of the complete coding inventories were assessed using a percentage agreement formula. Comparisons were made between trained observers who coded social interactions from the same video-taped record of preschool free-play. Weekly agreement scores were always above 80 per cent.

Social conflict and dominance relations

Power relations in children, as in other primates, are not chaotic, but are typically organized in terms of a group dominance hierarchy. The concept of 'dominance' provides a good bridge linking ethological and psychological considerations. Dominance is a structural model for a group that describes agonistic relationships observed for all dyads in the group. Its meaning is only in relation to the group, and it is best viewed as an 'emergent property' of groups at the structural level of analysis discussed in the introduction. It is not a property of individuals. While psychologists have tended to focus on 'aggression', and have used the term as an individual descriptor or as a trait concept, ethologists have more characteristically bypassed this focus and have been more concerned with the function and organization of conflict interactions within and for the group.

Dominance essentially involves asymmetrical social relationships. Dyadic dominance describes the relative balance of social power between any two members of a social group, while a dominance hierarchy summarizes the organization of such power relations among all possible dyads within the stable group. In dyadic dominance, one individual typically submits to the other. In group dominance, the hierarchy is governed by a linear rule, such that if **A** dominates **B**, and **B** dominates **C**, then **A** is dominant to both **B** and **C**.

Social dominance has been viewed as a basic dimension of social organization among primates, and has been related to a number of social processes such as group defence (Jolly, 1972), social learning (Strayer, 1976), social innovation (Tsumori, 1967), and social play (Dolhinow and Bishop, 1972). Theoretically, the formation and maintenance of a stable dominance hierarchy functions to minimize intragroup aggression by establishing a relatively stable set of serial perogatives for each group member. Having learned the appropriate power sequence, each individual is able to anticipate and to avoid the adverse consequences of severe and continued aggression.

Figure 9.1 shows a primate dominance hierarchy for a group of macaque monkeys. This matrix represents systematic comparisons of wins and losses among all dyads in the group.

A dyadic matrix provides a useful quantitative representation of differential social participation by all group members in every possible dyadic social context. By listing individuals simultaneously as initiators (in the rows of the matrix) and as targets (in the columns) of social activity, it becomes possible to inspect visually the nature of dyadic social relationships within a stable group. For example, in Figure 9.1 the social relationship between **A** and **B** is summarized in the two cells on either side of the diagonal in the upper left corner of the matrix. **A** initiated five aggressive acts toward **B** where **B** responded with a submissive gesture. In contrast, **B** initiated only one such aggressive–submissive exchange with **A**. Thus, the nature of their social relationship was

INITIATOR	TARGET A	B	C	D	E	F	G	H	I	J	K	L	M	N	O	P	total
♂ A		5	17	6	7	7	7	3	2	7	5	4	3	4	3	6	86
♀ B	1		13	3	4	2	4	1	1	1		6	1		1	2	40
♂ C	1			24	19	18	20	22	4	8	6	13	5	8	4	7	159
♀ D		1			4	5	9	2	2	1		2	3	6		1	36
♂ E						6	7	4	5	3	2	3	4	2	5	3	44
♀ F		2	1	1			3	3	2	8	7	11	2	2	1	7	50
♀ G			2					5	5	5	4	8	2	1	4	4	40
♂ H						1			1	4	3	2	4	2	1	1	19
♀ I										3		1				5	9
♂ J							1				2		1	2	3		9
♂ K												=	=	5	4	2	11
♀ L							1						=	1	3	4	9
♂ M											=	=		=	1	3	4
♂ N												=			2	3	5
♀ O																=	0
♀ P															=		0
total	2	6	32	36	35	38	51	42	22	40	29	49	24	33	31	51	521

Figure 9.1. Dyadic dominance matrix showing aggressive–submissive relations within a group of macaque monkeys

asymmetrical with **A** more often assuming the dominant role. By comparing all such dyadic relationships within a stable group, it is usually possible to discover a single rank-ordering of individuals (as initiators and targets) so that virtually all observed dominance exchanges are located in the upper portion of the dyadic matrix. In Figure 9.1 the letters assigned to each group member reflect their relative status within the group dominance hierarchy. This seriation of individuals was derived by a systematic comparison of dyadic relationships, and represents the best ordering of individuals since it maximizes the number of observed conflict episodes above the diagonal in the dyadic matrix.

The important aspect to focus on is the distribution of interactions within the matrix. This distribution demonstrates very well the linearity of the dominance structure. There are no violations of status ranking since individuals ranked lower in the group never win a majority of conflict encounters with an animal higher in the matrix. This matrix also illustrates an important conceptual point about dominance. It is a general descriptive concept that summarizes stable social relationships evident in the resolution of various forms of naturally occurring conflict. As you can see, the emphasis is on the resolution of sets of interactions rather than on the frequency of individual aggressive acts.

Table 9.1.   Categories and patterns of preschool agonistic behaviour

Behaviour	Description
I Physical attack	
Chase	Rapid pursuit of a fleeing child (McGrew, 1972, p. 107).
Push-Pull	Forceful contact with hands or shoulders which results in the physical displacement (McGrew, p. 82–84).
Hit	Forceful contact with hand or fist (Blurton Jones, 1972, item 15, p. 105).
Kick	Forceful contact with foot or leg (McGrew, 1972, p. 90).
Bite	Contact with teeth to other's limbs or body (McGrew, 1972, p. 52).
Wrestle	Gross grappling movements with another (McGrew, 1972, p. 105).
II Threat gestures	
Face and body posture	Forward flexion of the body accompanied by head raise and chin jut (McGrew, 1972, p. 54).
Intention hit	Movements similar to 'hit' but not resulting in physical contact (McGrew, 1972, 'incomplete beat', p. 70).
Intention kick	Movements similar to kick but not resulting in physical contact (McGrew, 1972, 'incomplete kick', p. 90).
Intention bite	Lunging movement with head and upper trunk accompanied by an open mouth and display of teeth, but not resulting in physical contact (Brannigan and Humphries, 1972, item 16, p. 57).
III Competitive conflict	
Object struggle	Competition over the possession of an object which frequently, but not necessarily is accompanied by 'wrestle' (McGrew, 1972, 'property fights', p. 122).
Supplant	Competition over the use of space or the priority of physical position, if accompanied by physical contact, supplant usually involves gentle touching, rather than physical attack patterns.
IV Submissive gestures	
Help-seeking	Efforts to solicit the intervention of another person during a dyadic agonistic encounter, often entails seeking physical proximity with adults.
Cry-scream	Vocal or verbal protest accompanied by backward movement (Smith and Connolly, 1972, p. 78).
Rapid-flight	Fast locomotor withdrawal, usually in response to 'chase', but also a reaction to other attack and threat patterns.
Cringe	Dramatic reduction in stature with flexion of body and slumping of shoulders, usually accompanied by a movement backwards (McGrew, 1972, 'crouch', p. 88).

Table 9.1. (*Contd.*)

Behaviour	Description
Hand-cover	Covering of face or upper body with arm and hand, usually with fingers spread and palm turned outwards (McGrew, 1972, p. 76).
Flinch	Quick movement, less dramatic than 'cringe', but also reducing stature and increasing social distance (McGrew, 1972, p. 97).
Withdrawal	Locomotor activity which results in a break of inter-personal distance.
V *No response*	
Ignore	Any non-agonistic response to an initiated act from categories I, II and III.

TARGET

INITIATOR	Ro	Ss	Br	If	Td	Sd	Pe	Ir	Cs	Ka	Ch	Ty	Gl	Sa	Me	Ju	Sh	total
♀ Ro		1	3	4	1			1	1		1		7		1			20
♂ Ss	1		7	8	2	1	1	12	3		1	1	4	1			2	44
♂ Br	1	4		7	3	2	2	1		8	1	5	5				1	40
♂ If	3	3	2		3	1	13	3	5	1		8	3			2	1	48
♂ Td	1			3		4	6		8	5	1		1	3		2	1	35
♂ Sd							2	8	11		4		4	3		1		35
♂ Pe	1		1	9	3	4		2		1		7	9	1	1			39
♂ Ir				1	1	1	2		7	5	1	1	1					20
♂ Cs	1	1	1	2	5	11		3			1							25
♀ Ka							1				11		1			1	4	18
♀ Ch	4		4	3	3	2	1					3	11	5		2	2	40
♀ Ty									2				2		8			12
♂ Gl		1	9	3		3	6			11	2			1		7	5	48
♂ Sa		1	4		1	2	1			1			1					11
♀ Me											3							3
♀ Ju				1							1	1						3
♀ Sh								1	1									2
total	12	11	31	40	22	32	36	30	37	14	29	23	53	32	9	16	16	443

Figure 9.2. Dyadic distribution of initiated aggression at Langara

The difference between aggression and dominance can be illustrated by noting that monkey **C** initiates the most aggression but is third in dominance, whereas moneky **B**, who is higher, initiates less aggression than five others who are below her in status.

The determination of social dominance rests on the identification of specific behaviours describing the initiation and termination of conflict episodes. In a recent paper (Strayer and Strayer, 1976), we identified the general categories of naturally occurring social conflict among children, and the specific action patterns which describe them are shown in Table 9.1. The response categories and specific action patterns comprising them are also shown. In particular, submissive response to attacks and threats have been shown to provide the best fit for dominance relations among both primates and children. There are other classes of social conflict as well. Struggles over objects and space have also been used to index dominance relationships. While the use of object/position struggles with young children does provide an index of social dominance, it differs somewhat from the order based on attacks and threats, principally because the loss or perhaps abandonment of an object is not the same as a *submissive* response.

The importance of the submissive response in defining group dominance structure was pointed out by Rowell (1966, 1974) in primate work, and it is evident in our work with children as well (Strayer and Strayer, 1976). Figure 9.2

TARGET

INITIATOR	Ro	Ss	Br	If	Td	Sd	Pe	Ir	Cs	Ka	Ch	Ty	Gl	Sa	Me	Ju	Sh	total
♀ Ro	▨	1	1		1=								1	1				5
♂ Ss		▨	1=	3	1				4	1			1	3		1		5
♂ Br	1=		▨	1	1				1		6		3	2		1		6
♂ If				▨	2	1	8	2	2	1	↕↕		4	2	2	1		5
♂ Td	1=				▨	=	3		7	2			1					4
♂ Sd					=	▨	1	1	4	2	1		↕↕	1				0
♂ Pe					1		▨		1				1=	3				6
♂ Ir								▨	3	2	1							6
♂ Cs					2			1	▨	=	=		1					4
♀ Ka									=	▨	=	9	1			1	3	4
♀ Ch			1↕↕						=	=	▨	=	5	3		1	1	1
♀ Ty											=	▨	1=	=	2			3
♂ Gl				1=					1		1=		▨	=	=	3	5	1
♂ Sa				1↕↕					1			=	=	▨	=			2
♀ Me													=	=	▨	=	=	0
♀ Ju															=	▨	=	0
♀ Sh															=	=	▨	0
total	1	2	2	5	6	4	13	9	18	7	10	11	19	12	2	9	12	142

Figure 9.3. Dominance matrix showing aggressive–submissive relations at Langara

shows all agonistic interactions that were initiated by each child in the Langara group, *regardless* of the target's response. The many entries below the diagonal in this matrix indicate that this class of social activity cannot be used to derive a simple hierarchical structure for the group.

However, when we look specifically at classes of aggression leading to submission, the type of group structure shown in Figure 9.3 has typically been evident. The entries below the diagonal in this latter figure indicate episodes in which the linear dominance prediction was violated and they are a measure of the stability of the dominance structure in terms of its linearity and rigidity. Linearity refers to the extent to which observed dyadic relationships conform to a transitivity rule. In this case, two dyadic relationships were not predicted by the linear dominance model, and are marked with a special symbol. Rigidity refers to the number of episodes in which a less dominant child won in a *minority* of interactions. Five cells in the matrix (a total of only six episodes) show cases where dominance relationships were not completely rigid.

This sort of dominance structure has now been observed and replicated in three samples of young children. Figure 9.4 shows the dominance hierarchy

		Ma	Ch	Ja	Bl	Tl	Jo	Cm	Je	El	Ef	Bk	Em	Eh	Pa	Rs	Rm	Sh	Bp	Ca	total
INITIATOR	♂ Ma	▨	=	2			1		2	1			1		1		1				9
	♂ Ch	=	▨	10	2	1=	1	1	8		1			1			1	↕			26
	♂ Ja		1	▨	4	2	2	1	3		2			10							25
	♂ Bl			1	▨	1=	1	1=								1					5
	♀ Tl	1=	1	1=		▨	1		5	2	8	2		3	1		3		1	2	31
	♂ Jo		1				▨	1						2	1						5
	♂ Cm				1=			▨	=	=	1			1		1					4
	♂ Je			1				=	▨	=	2	2		2							7
	♀ El							=	=	▨	=	1									1
	♂ Ef				1	1			=		▨	1	1=				1				5
	♀ Bk											▨	=	3	1				1		5
	♀ Em											1=	▨	=							1
	♀ Eh						1						=	▨	1						2
	♀ Pa													=	▨	1		2			3
	♂ Rs															▨	1	↕			1
	♀ Rm																▨		1		1
	♀ Sh	1↕											1↕					▨	=	1	3
	♀ Bp																	=	▨	=	0
	♀ Ca																		=	▨	0
total		0	3	16	8	6	7	4	18	3	17	5	5	20	2	5	5	2	5	3	134

Figure 9.4. Dominance matrix showing aggressive–submissive relations at Waterloo

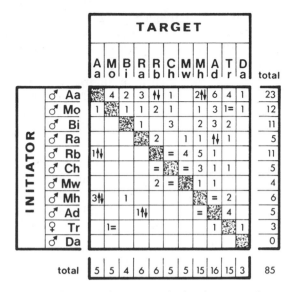

Figure 9.5. Dominance matrix showing aggressive–submissive relations at the Clarke

Table 9.2. Comparison of dominance hierarchies

Group	Linearity	Rigidity
Macaque monkeys	100%	98%
Langara Preschool Group	98%	92%
Simon Fraser Preschool Group	94%	94%
Waterloo Preschool Group	96%	94%
Clarke Preschool Group	92%	88%

obtained at the Waterloo Preschool Center. It is an excellent replication of the Langara structure described above. Figure 9.5 shows the dominance hierarchy obtained at the Clarke clinic. Here too, we see that a stable dominance hierarchy characterizes the dyadic power relationships. These children also have worked out a stable structure for agonistic interactions. The extent of comparability of the three dominance structures is shown in Table 9.2. The Clarke hierarchy is about as stable in terms of both linearity and rigidity as the other two groups. The implication we can draw is that the Clarke children are not deviant in terms of structuring group power relationships. But remember that this hierarchy is based on specific action patterns; and the Clarke children, labelled as 'aggressive' may engage in different *forms* of agonism than other groups.

A comparison of the relative frequency for different categories of social conflict indicated that to some extent this proposition was true. The Clarke group initiated a relatively higher proportion of physical attacks as against threat gestures, while their responses to agonism were similar to the other groups. This finding may indicate that these children were less able, or willing, to ritualize their aggression in more mild forms of threat, and may have been less sensitive to the use of threats as social cues for establishing dominance relations. Other explanations may centre on the fact that this group, with one exception, was composed of boys, and males in all groups have a higher rate of agonism and a higher proportion of physical attacks as against threats than do females. One can also speculate that group functioning is influenced by group composition, and that a unisex group will work out dominance differently than a heterosexual group. It should also be noted that the Clarke group was in the process of group stabilization, a process which initially may result in the higher incidence of physical attacks.

Having considered dominance at the level of group structure, it seems important to examine how it is that total agonism may be constrained by the group dominance structure. In Table 9.3, we see the distribution of total agonism as a function of dominance status. Using a median split to divide the group, among macaques it is clearly the high-dominant animals who initiate agonistic interactions; and they do so among themselves about half the time. For children, the picture is more variable, but we can see that low status children in all groups are the targets of only half the agonistic interaction, and there is some balance in the distribution of conflict. In the Langara, Simon Fraser, and especially the Waterloo group, high status children actually confined the major portion of their agonistic interactions among themselves. In the Clarke group this was not the case. Low status children were targets of aggression by high status children more often than in the other groups. It seems important to note that these same low dominant children frequently violated dominance relations by directing over half of their own aggressive acts toward higher status group members. For the other three samples, only 15 per cent of

Table 9.3. Distribution of agonism as a function of status position of participants in dyadic exchanges

Group	Direction of aggressive acts			
	High to high	High to low	Low to high	Low to low
Macaque monkeys	46%	45%	0%	9%
Langara Preschool Group	35%	28%	13%	23%
Simon Fraser Group	42%	28%	15%	15%
Waterloo Preschool Group	55%	19%	13%	14%
Clarke Preschool Group	23%	46%	20%	12%

aggression by low status children was directed toward high status group members. Perhaps at the Clarke, low status children were less able to inhibit aggression, and consequently were more likely to provoke aggression by higher status children. Thus, although a stable dominance hierarchy was apparent in each of our four groups, total social conflict was differentially contained by the observed status structure.

The comparative construct of group dominance hierarchy has opened up a rich field of study concerning individual differences between children, as well as peer group dynamics. However, the nature of preschool dominance has been more thoroughly investigated by child ethologists than other dimensions of group organization. A more adequate understanding of preschool social relationships and adjustment to the peer group requires more information about the more positive aspects of interaction among young children. The following sections present some preliminary findings concerning two other important aspects of preschool social organization—affiliative bonds and altruistic relations.

Affiliative activity and cohesive bonds

The comparative techniques for analysing social conflict and group dominance hierarchies have proved useful in the description of children's power relationships. However, correspondingly sophisticated methods are not available for the description of cohesive bonds between agemates in a stable group. Theoretically, the relative neglect of positive social relationships is somewhat paradoxical, since the analysis of social dominance makes sense only when one assumes that there are more important cohesive factors which make group membership an attractive option for all individuals. It is exactly such cohesive factors which would lead to the social aggregation of individuals and ultimately necessitate the ritualization of aggressive, anti-social tendencies in the behavioural system we call dominance.

Although the ethological analysis of social bonding has not focused at the level of peer-group organization, considerable progress has been made in the description of primary attachment between parents and offspring. The theoretical works of Bowlby (1969, 1973) and Harlow and Harlow (1965) provide a reasonable conceptual starting point for the analysis of secondary affectional ties which link individual children to agemates in the preschool group.

In our first efforts to detect social bonds and affiliative structures within preschool groups, we relied on techniques which have been employed to assess social proximity patterns within feral groups of Old World monkeys. The procedure simply entailed mapping the location of all group members at regular intervals over an extended observational period. From the resulting behavioural maps, we were able to determine the 'nearest neighbour' of each child in each sample. By comparing the relative frequency that each child was spatially close to other

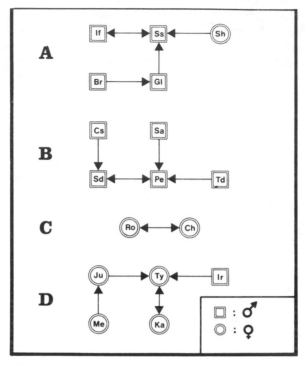

Figure 9.6. Sociometric representation of 'nearest neighbour' relations at Langara

group members throughout the sampling period, we determined the most
frequent nearest neighbour for each child of the group. Figure 9.6 shows the
results of this mapping procedure for the Langara Preschool Center. Four
distinct subgroupings of children were evident. In each subgroup, there was a
focal dyad with two individuals who were most often in close proximity with
each other. The remaining children were most frequently observed in proximity
with one of the children in the focal dyad, except for two children who assumed
a more peripheral role by being in proximity most often with a central but not
focal group member. Identical affiliative networks have recently been identified
in the analysis of nearest neighbour data collected independently on four preschool groups by Abramovitch at the University of Toronto (Abramovitch
and Strayer, 1977). In general, membership and status within the affiliative
networks appear more directly related to a child's gender than to his position
within the social dominance hierarchy. Thus, it seems that these affiliative
networks may reflect a second form of social organization within preschool
groups that may be independent of, or be only indirectly related to, social
dominance.

However, these preliminary sociometric representations of average spacing tendencies do not provide an adequate description of social bonds between children since they fail to distinguish the individual's role in maintaining proximity with other children in the group. A child may be persistently followed by, and thus in proximity to, another group member even though the two seldom engage in positive forms of social interaction. Given this limitation in the behavioural mapping and nearest neighbour procedure, our subsequent analyses of cohesive bonds and affiliative structures have employed observational techniques which parallel the interactional analysis of social dominance and correspond more closely to the conceptual model for the analysis of social organization described in the introduction.

Table 9.4 shows the organization of an affiliative behaviour inventory which

Table 9.4.   Categories and patterns of preschool affiliative behaviour

Behaviour	Description
I Proximity	
Approach	Locomotor activity directed toward another child which ends with attainment of interpersonal space (children are within touching distance if both stretch out their arms).
II Social orientation	
Glance	Brief orientation of the head and face toward another who is within interpersonal distance (McGrew, 1972, p. 56).
Gaze	More extended orientation toward another who is within interpersonal distance (Blurton Jones, 1972, item 27, p. 106).
Look	Extended orientation toward another who is outside interpersonal distance.
III Physical contact	
Hand-to-body	Any gentle hand movement touching the body of another child (Brannigan and Humphries, 1972, item 124, p. 62).
Body-to-body	Gentle body movements touching another child, often includes lateral contact (McGrew, 1972, p. 98, 101 and 103).
Hold-hands	Mutual contact with hands (McGrew, 1972, p. 77).
IV Postural gestures	
Beckon	Hand gesture with repeated motion toward the body (McGrew, 1972, p. 72).
Forward-lean	Flexion of upper trunk toward another who is within interpersonal distance (McGrew, 1972, p. 100).
Head-nod	Rapid up and down movement of the head (McGrew, 1972, p. 57).
Posture-adjust	Small movements of the body which produce a change in physical position in relation to another child who is within interpersonal distance.

Table 9.5.   Transition probabilities between elements in dyadic affiliative exchanges

Initiated action pattern	Response category				
	Proximity	Social orientation	Physical contact	Postural signals	No response
Approach (2302)*	0.00	0.34†	0.00	0.06†	0.59†
Gaze (141)	0.01	0.65†	0.00	0.06	0.28†
Glance (364)	0.00	0.59†	0.00	0.01	0.41†
Look (661)	0.02	0.41†	0.00	0.00	0.57†
Body-body (175)	0.00	0.16†	0.03	0.06	0.75†
Hand-body (166)	0.00	0.30†	0.01	0.04	0.46†
Posture-adjust (228)	0.00	0.35†	0.00	0.04	0.61†

*Number in parentheses indicates the total frequency for each pattern.
†Exchanges selected as regularly occurring forms of interaction.

was used in three more recent studies of preschool social organization. Although the list of action patterns and behavioural categories does not completely describe all possible forms of prosocial behaviour, these activities occur at a relatively high rate in preschool groups and, perhaps more importantly, provide a potential behavioural link for the analysis of primary and peer social attachments.

Having selected these individual action patterns as possible indices of peer attachment, our first task was to determine empirically how these behaviours were organized in typical social exchanges. Table 9.5 shows the transition probabilities between the different forms of behaviour in dyadic exchanges observed at the University of Waterloo Daycare Center. The number in parentheses following each form of initiated action indicates the frequency of dyadic exchanges which began with that particular pattern. The most striking result in this table is the generally high probability that any form of initiated affiliative action will lead to 'no response' from the social target. Over half of all affiliative overtures were apparently ignored by the person to whom they were directed. When the target responded, the most likely form of reaction was a 'social orientation response'. This was especially true for dyadic exchanges that began with a 'social orientation' pattern. Finally, it is important to note that nearly 60 per cent of observed dyadic exchanges began with the 'proximity' pattern—Approach. This finding has been repeated in all three groups observed using the present affiliative inventory, and suggests that the maintenance of interpersonal proximity is a very important part of our assessments of affiliative social behaviour.

Having identified regularly occurring patterns of dyadic affiliative exchange, our second task entailed examining the extent to which these forms of social exchange provided a convergent measure of affiliative activity for particular dyads in the group. Given the high probability of no response to many affiliative initiations, we were initially interested in assessing whether children generally received social responses from some group members, but less often from others. With the exception of visual exchanges initiated from outside personal space (look/look, and look/no response), the dyadic correlations between exchanges beginning with the same affiliative action pattern were reasonably high. These correlations ranged from 0.38 to 0.67 and had a median value of 0.56. Thus there was a strong positive relation between the frequency of acknowledged and ignored affiliative overtures directed toward the same social target. It was not the case that initiators received responses from some children and were usually ignored by others. Instead, it seems that affiliative behaviours were directed toward selected group members who sometimes responded and sometimes ignored the initiated action.

Dyadic correlations between the frequency of initiated exchanges from each of the four general categories of affiliative behaviour were uniformly high. In the Waterloo group, these category correlations range from 0.67 to 0.82 and had a median value of 0.74. Thus there was a high degree of association in the frequency of initiated affiliative activity to specific social targets. This

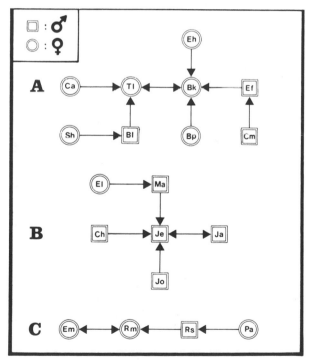

Figure 9.7. Sociometric representation of directed
affiliative activity at Waterloo

finding suggests the general categories of social behaviours which have been used in the analysis of parent–child interaction provide convergent measures of affiliative preferences, or peer attachments within the preschool group.

Given the high degree of association in the dyadic initiation of the present forms of affiliative behaviour, a total interaction score was computed for each directional dyad in the Waterloo group by summing the frequency of all initiated activity. Comparisons of the relative proportion of each child's behaviour that was directed to all possible group members permitted identification of a behaviourally based first preference for each child. These preferences are shown pictorially in Figure 9.7.

The affiliative organization of the Waterloo group consisted of three social networks. The structure of these subgroups was quite similar to those already reported for the Langara sample. Each subgroup contained a focal dyad where members had a reciprocal affiliative preference. In each network, one member of the focal dyad was selected more often as a most preferred target by other group members, and consequently appears as the central individual in the subgrouping. Finally, there were a number of children who appeared more peripheral to the network because their most preferred affiliative target was a central, but not a focal subgroup member.

Very similar results were obtained in the analysis of dyadic affiliative inter-

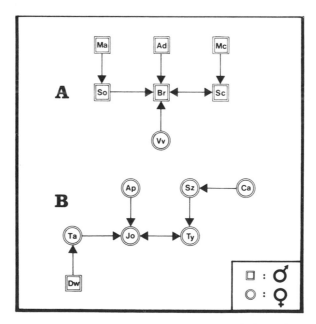

Figure 9.8. Sociometric representation of directed
affiliative activity at Simon Fraser

action in the Simon Fraser project. With this sample, correlations between the major categories of activity ranged from 0.47 to 0.83 and had a median value of 0.61. Once again, examination of behaviourally defined preference revealed distinct affiliative networks; these are shown in Figure 9.8. Each network was again characterized by a focal dyad with a reciprocated affiliative preference, and the majority of children in each subgroup were of the same sex.

The last study in this series produced a somewhat unexpected result. The affiliative structure of the clinical group at the Clarke Institute failed to divide into distinct subgroupings. Furthermore, as shown in Figure 9.9, there were no reciprocal preferences evident in the affiliative network. The particular reasons why this set of children differ from the previous groups are unclear. However, it seems important to emphasize that estimates of weekly stability in affiliative preferences among members of the Clarke group were on the average substantially lower than those of the other preschool groups. The greater variability in the social specificity of peer attachment behaviours among the Clarke children corresponds well with prior clinical reports concerning the difficulty these children had in adjusting to a peer-group. But such interpretations should be examined cautiously, since the variability in social preference may equally well be attributed to social pressures which the children necessarily encountered during the process of group formation.

The identification of two social structures based upon different forms of social activity raises an important question. To what extent does knowledge of group dominance relations facilitate our understanding of affiliative exchanges among preschool children? Figure 9.10 shows the dyadic frequency of social approaches as a function of children's dominance rank. This presentation of affiliative initiations provides a chaotic picture of affiliative activity

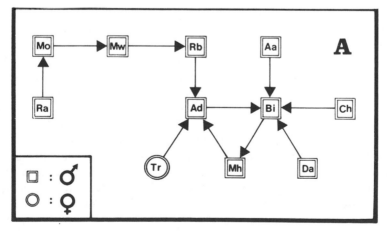

Figure 9.9. Sociometric representation of directed affiliative activity
at the Clarke

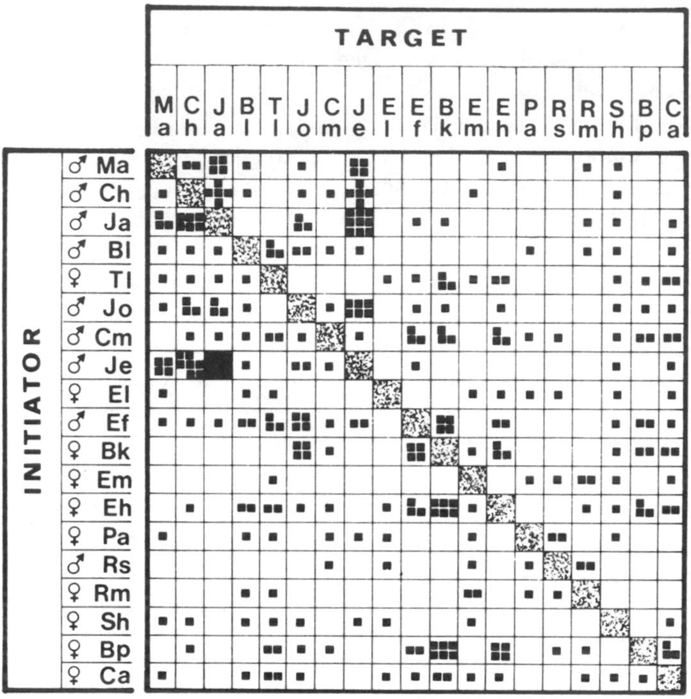

Figure 9.10. Dyadic distribution of affiliative approaches with children ordered according to status within the group dominance hierarchy

within the preschool group. However, when the list of children in the matrix is rearranged according to their status within the affiliative networks, rather than within the dominance hierarchy, as in Figure 9.11, some order begins to appear in the dyadic matrix. The organizing principle for this final matrix is radically different from the one used in assessing asymmetrical power relations. Observations tend to cluster around the diagonal of the matrix in regions quite close to the focal figures in each affiliative network. Some indication of the importance of each network is also evident in this figure. Nearly three-quarters of initiated affiliative activity is directed toward children from the same affiliative subgroup. Thus although the social networks were defined in terms of each child's most preferred affiliative target, the resulting affiliative structure provides the social context for the majority of all children's affiliative behaviour.

Throughout this discussion, we have referred to peer attachment as a possibly unidirectional, that is, not reciprocal, social preference. Future research should attempt to expand this conception of a social bond by exploring reciprocity in attachment behaviours among peers. Certainly, we have discovered a number of reciprocal attachments that would meet our intuitive definitions of friend-

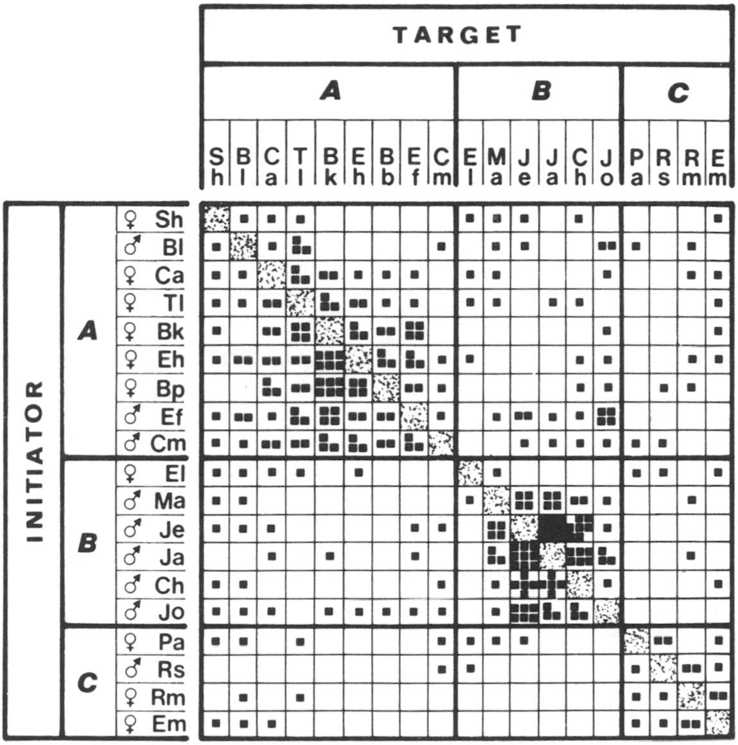

Figure 9.11. Dyadic distribution of affiliative approaches with children ordered according to positions within affiliative networks

ship. It seems quite likely that the number of friendships within each group may have been greater than was evident in our pictorial representation of affiliative networks. Frequency of activity alone seems to provide only one measure of personal attachment. Much more attention must be given to both the quality and sequencing of cohesive social interaction if we hope to provide a more valid measure of early childhood friendships.

Prosocial activity and altruistic relations

The concept of 'altruism' has recently gained prominence as a fundamental construct in the biological analysis of social organization. The work of Hamilton (1964) and Trivers (1971) has clearly demonstrated the evolutionary impact of this class of behaviour. However, little research has been conducted which attempts to identify how social relations may control or regulate naturally occurring altruism, or how altruistic gestures may influence established social relationships. It seems likely that the forms of relationships discussed in the

Table 9.6.   Categories and patterns of preschool altruistic activities

Behaviour	
I Object related activity	
Give	The donation of an object to another (Blurton Jones, 1972, item 25, p. 106).
Offer	Holding out an object toward another but waiting for it to be taken.
Take	Grasping an object from another and bringing it closer (Blurton Jones, 1972, item 6, p. 104). This behaviour was never scored if the children were competing for possession of the object.
Share	Reciprocal exchange of objects, involving three instances of the above patterns.
II Cooperative activity	
Task-cooperation	Any mutual activity directed toward the achievement of a common goal, such as the organization of materials for a play session, or returning materials at the end of the play bout.
Play-cooperation	Mutual activities directed toward a common goal which occur in the context of a play bout as part of the ongoing play activity.
III Helping activities	
Task-help	Assistance given to another child where the activity of the helper was different from that of the person being helped (Smith and Connolly, 1972, p. 79).
Play-help	Helping activity which occurs in the context of a play bout as part of the ongoing play activity.

preceding two sections may have some direct influence on the emergence of 'normative altruism' (Rosenhan, 1970). Unfortunately, the role played by altruistic behaviour in the social organization of preschool groups has been less conspicuous than that of dominance or affiliation. The relative neglect of such prosocial activity may reflect the fact that altruistic behaviour seems to occur relatively infrequently when compared to these other two classes of social activity.

A major goal in our research on preschool altruism involved elucidating how such prosocial activity may serve to strengthen affiliative bonds, and perhaps regulate the amount of agonistic interaction which occurs between young children. In addition to these general questions about group organization, we were also interested in knowing the degree to which prosocial interactions could be described as reciprocal in nature, and the extent to which children direct altruistic actions indiscriminately to all other peer group members, or only to selected individuals.

To examine these questions, spontaneously occurring altruism was recorded during periods of free play at each of the four preschool centres. A descriptive inventory including object-related, cooperative and helpful actions was used to determine the range and nature of altruistic activity among the children. Table 9.6 shows the units of behaviour which were included in this inventory. However, since many of the patterns described in the inventory occurred infrequently, for purposes of analysis, forms of initiation within each category were combined to yield three general measures of initiated and received activity for each child.

When the relative distribution of actions in each of the behavioural categories was examined, it was clear that all groups were similar in that object-related activities occurred most frequently. These activities accounted for nearly one-half of the observed prosocial activity. In addition, for all groups the give/take interaction was observed as the most frequent type of object activity. Cooperative exchanges were the next most frequently occurring category of prosocial activity; these activities comprised nearly one-third of the total actions observed. Play-cooperation accounted for the major proportion of cooperative behaviours recorded. The least frequent prosocial interactions, which included only about one-sixth of the observations, were those which involved helping. Again, the behaviours within this category were similarly distributed for each group with play help/accept being the most frequently recorded type of helping exchanges.

A further similarity in the nature of altruism in each of the groups was the high degree of social specificity evident in the observed behaviour. That is, children directed prosocial actions toward a limited number of peer group members. Close to one-third of all prosocial actions for each child were directed toward the most preferred peer target, while about one-fifth were directed toward the second most preferred. In general, the data for each sample indicated that nearly three-quarters of all prosocial actions by each child were distributed among at most four other children in the group.

In order to assess the extent to which behaviours within the groups were reciprocated, the degree of association between individual rates of initiation and receipt for prosocial actions was examined. The overall correlation showed a significant positive relationship between giving and receiving altruistic behaviour $(r = +0.55, p < .01)$. Separate analyses were also conducted for each group. These latter analyses showed that reciprocity in altruistic behaviour was greatest in the Langara group, where the correlation between initiation and receipt of prosocial behaviour was $+.83$ $(p < .01)$. At Waterloo and Simon Fraser, the index of reciprocity was somewhat lower but still statistically significant $(r = +0.46$ and $+0.55, p$'s $< .05)$. However, reciprocity was not evident in the initiation and receipt of prosocial behaviour for the Clarke children. In this group, there was virtually no relation between rate of initiation and receipt of behaviour $(r = -0.06, p < .10)$. Thus, although reciprocity appeared to characterize the interaction of the normal groups, it did not characterize the altruistic interaction which occurred in the atypical group.

The fact that the great majority of prosocial actions were directed toward a limited number of social targets and that altruistic social interactions were marked by reciprocity (at least in the three typical groups) suggested that the most preferred targets for children's altruism may be closely affiliated with the young 'altruist'. To examine this possibility, both altruistic and affiliative choices were directly compared. Since these comparisons required identification of the most preferred target for both initiated affiliative and altruistic activity, only children with clear preferences in both domains were included in the analysis. Data from the Langara group were not used in this comparison because it was unclear whether preferences based on nearest neighbour data were comparable to those obtained through the use of initiated affiliative activity.

Figure 9.12 shows sociograms depicting the most preferred social targets for altruistic behaviour in the Waterloo, Simon Fraser and Clarke groups. The solid arrows indicate that the target for altruistic behaviour was also the most preferred target for affiliative behaviour, while the open arrows indicate that the preferred target for altruism did not correspond to the affiliative preference. Two-thirds of the altruistic and affiliative preferences were similar in the Waterloo group. Data available from the Simon Fraser group showed a similar degree of correspondence (64 per cent). On the other hand, for the Clarke group, there was only a single example of correspondence between the targets chosen for affiliative and altruistic actions (only 9 per cent of the observed choices were similar). The correspondence between target preferences for these two classes of activity in the normal groups suggests that altruistic behaviour was directed toward those with whom the child maintained a close affiliative bond.

Our second question about the relation between altruism and group organization concerned the possible relationship between dominance status and altruistic behaviour. In order to answer this question rank-order correlation coefficients were computed between position in the dominance hierarchy and the amount of altruistic behaviour initiated and received. In all groups there was no association between dominance status and individual rate of initiated altruism. However, there was a significant relationship between position in the dominance hierarchy and rate of receiving altruistic actions. This correlation was strongest within the Clarke group ($\rho = +0.60$, $p < .05$) and also significant in the order samples (Langara, $\rho = +0.41$, $p < .05$; Waterloo, $\rho = +0.42$, $p < .05$); and Simon Fraser, $\rho = +0.52$, $p < .05$). Thus, altruistic behaviour seemed to be not only directed toward those with whom the normal child was affiliated, but tended also to be directed toward those in the group who were more dominant than the young 'altruist'. The latter finding suggests that altruistic behaviour may be used to appease dominant individuals in the

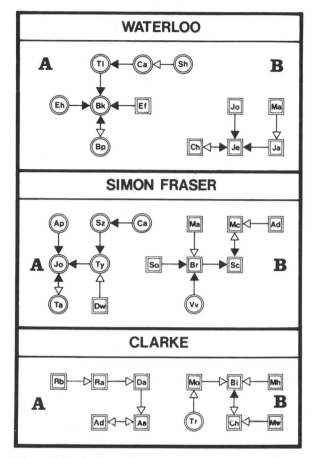

Figure 9.12. Sociometric representation of altruistic and
affiliative preferences at three preschool centres

group, or perhaps to attempt to elicit behaviour incompatible with aggression.

In summary, then, the prosocial behaviour of the groups observed in this study was consistent with respect to the social specificity of normative altruism and with respect to the distribution of acts across the classes of object-related, cooperative and helping activities.In contrast, the prosocial behaviour observed in the atypical group differed from that observed in the normal groups in several ways. There was no evidence for social reciprocity or mutuality in altruistic activities in the Clarke group. Also, there was evidence that prosocial behaviour was not directed toward those with whom the Clarke children most often affiliated. These differences between the clinical and normal groups in conjunction with the earlier differences reported on cohesive bonds suggests that a problem for the atypical group may have been the development and stabilization of positive social bonds.

With regard to the potential functions of altruism in preschool social organization, our results indicate that prosocial activities are directed toward those with whom the child is most closely affiliated as well as those who are ranked higher in the dominance hierarchy. Thus, the social function of altruism for group organization may lie in its signalling and regulating role in relation to both dominance and affiliative interactions. Future systematic exploration of these preliminary findings should perhaps focus on the possibility that altruism may be used to regulate or control these other types of social interaction. Only by identifying how altruism functions in stable social groups will we begin to understand the way in which specific social structures such as affiliative networks and dominance hierarchies contain or influence naturally occurring prosocial behaviour. Such understanding seems critical for a better appreciation of both the psychology and biology of reciprocal altruism.

ACKNOWLEDGEMENT

Research reported in this chapter has benefited greatly from the investment of time and energy by a number of people who participated directly in one, or more, or the observational projects. These people who deserve a strong note of thanks include: Tom Chapeskie, Ingrid Fisher, Harry Fraser, Susan Gamble, Pat Harris, Shielah McConnell, Martin Smith, Janet Strayer, and Susan Wareing. I also want to express my appreciation to the children and staff from each of the facilities where we have worked; their patience and collaboration made our work possible and pleasurable. Finally, I would like to thank the agencies which during the past 4 years have directly or indirectly helped finance portions of this research. These include: Le Conseil des Arts du Canada, the Spencer Foundation, and Le Conseil National de Recherches du Canada.

NOTE

1. The direct observation and analysis of behaviour is a complex and time-consuming business. The present report summarizes the research activities of a group of people who have worked together on various aspects of a single problem. The use of 'we' in the text is meant to reflect this collective effort.

REFERENCES

Abramovitch, R. (1976). The relation of attention and proximity to rank in preschool children. In M. Chance and R. Larsen (Eds.), *The Social Structure of Attention*. Chichester: Wiley.

Abramovitch, R., and Strayer, F. F. (1977). Preschool social organization: agonistic, spacing, and attentional behaviors. In P. Pliner, T. Kramer and T. Alloway (Eds.), *Recent Advances in the Study of Communication and Affect*. Vol. 6. New York: Academic Press.

Barker, M. (1930). A technique for studying the social material activities of young children. *Child Development Monographs*. No. 3. New York: Columbia University Press.

Barker, R. G. (1965). Explorations in ecological psychology. *American Psychologist*, **20**, 1–14.

Bateson, P. P. G., and Hinde, R. A. (1976). *Growing Points in Ethology*. Cambridge: Cambridge University Press.

Bernstein, I. S. (1970). Primate status hierarchies. In L. Rosenblum (Ed.), *Primate Behavior: Developments in Field and Laboratory Research*. New York: Academic Press.

Blurton Jones, N. (1972). Characteristics of ethological studies of human behaviour. In N. Blurton Jones (Ed.) *Ethological Studies of Child Behaviour*. Cambridge: Cambridge University Press.

Blurton Jones, N., and Leach, G. M. (1972). Behaviour of children and their mothers at separation and greeting. In N. Blurton Jones (Ed.), *Ethological Studies of Child Behaviour*. Cambridge: Cambridge University Press.

Bowlby, J. (1969). *Attachment and Loss:* Vol. I. New York: Basic Books.

Bowlby, J. (1973). *Attachment and Loss:* Vol. II. New York: Basic Books.

Brannigan, C. R., and Humphries, D. A. (1972). Human non-verbal behaviour, a means of communication. In N. Blurton Jones (Ed.), *Ethological Studies of Child Behaviour*. Cambridge: Cambridge University Press.

Chance, M. R., and Jolly, C. J. (1970). *Social Groups of Monkeys and Men*. London: Jonathan Cape.

Chittenden, G. E. (1942). An experimental study in measuring and modifying assertive behavior in young children. *Monographs of the Society for Research in Child Development*. Vol. 7, 1–87.

Crook, J. H. (1970). Social organization and the environment: aspects of contemporary social ethology. *Animal Behaviour*, **18**, 197–209.

Dawe, H. C. (1943). Analysis of two hundred quarrels of preschool children. *Child Development*, **5**, 139–157.

DeVore, I. (1965). *Primate Behavior: Field Studies of Monkeys and Apes*. New York: Holt, Rinehart and Winston.

Dolhinow, P., and Bishop, H. (1972). The development of motor skills and social relationships among primates. In P. Dolhinow (Ed.), *Primate Patterns*. New York: Holt, Rinehart and Winston.

Emmerlich, W. (1964). Continuity and stability in early social development. *Child Development*, **35**, 311–332.

Gellert, E. (1961). Stability and fluctuation in the power relationships of young children. *Journal of Abnormal and Social Psychology*, **62**, 8–15.

Gellert, E. (1962). The effects of change in group composition on the dominant behaviour of young children. *British Journal of Social and Clinical Psychology*, **1**, 168–181.

Grant, E. C. (1969). Human facial expression. *Man*, **4**, 525–536.

Hamilton, W. D. (1964). The genetical evolution of social behavior. *Journal of Theoretical Biology*, **7**, 17–52.

Harlow, H. F., and Harlow, M. K. (1965). The affectional systems. In A. Schrier, H. Harlow and F. Stollnitz (Eds.), *Behavior of Non-human Primates*. Vol. 2. New York: Academic Press.

Hinde, R. A. (1970). *Animal Behaviour: A Synthesis of Ethology and Comparative Psychology*, second edition. New York: McGraw-Hill.

Hinde, R. A. (1976). Interactions, relationships and social structure. *Man*, **11**, 1–17.

Hinde, R. A., and Stevenson-Hinde, J. (1976). Towards understanding relationships: dynamic stability. In P. Bateson and R. Hinde (Eds.), *Growing Points in Ethology.* Cambridge: Cambridge University Press.

Jay, P. C. (1968). *Primates: Studies in Adaptation and Variability.* New York: Holt, Rinehart and Winston.

Jolly, A. (1972). *The Evolution of Primate Behavior*, New York: Macmillan.

Kummer, H. (1971). *Primate Societies: Group Techniques in Ecological Adaptation.* Chicago: University of Chicago Press.

Leach, G. M. (1972). A comparison of the social behaviour of some normal and problem children. In N. Blurton Jones (Ed.), *Ethological Studies of Child Behaviour.* Cambridge: Cambridge University Press.

McGrew, W. C. (1970). Glossary of motor patterns of four-year-old nursery school children. In S. Hutt and C. Hutt (Eds.), *Direct Observation and Measurement of Behavior.* Springfield, Illinois: Charles C. Thomas.

McGrew, W. C. (1972). *An Ethological Study of Children's Behavior.* New York: Academic Press.

Misshakian, E. A. (1976). Aggression and dominance relations in peer groups of children six to forty-five months of age. Paper presented at the Annual Conference of the Animal Behavior Society, Boulder, Colorado, June.

Piaget, J. (1926). *The Language and Thought of the Child.* London: Routledge and Kegan Paul.

Piaget, J. (1948). *The Moral Judgement of the Child.* New York: Free Press.

Piaget, J. (1951). *Play, Dreams and Imitation in Childhood.* New York: Norton.

Piaget, J. (1952). *The Origins of Intelligence in Children.* New York: International Universities Press.

Piaget, J. (1954). *The Construction of Reality in the Child.* New York: Basic Books.

Rosenhan, D. (1970). The natural socialization of altruistic autonomy. In J. Macauley and L. Berkowitz (Eds.), *Altruism and Helping Behavior.* New York: Academic Press.

Rowell, T. E. (1966). Hierarchy in the organization of a captive baboon troop. *Animal Behaviour*, **14**, 430–443.

Rowell, T. E. (1974). The concept of social dominance. *Behavioral Biology*, **11**, 131–154.

Shirley, M. M. (1933). *The First Two Years: A Study of Twenty-five Babies.* Institute of Child Welfare Monograph Series No. 7. Mineapolis, Minnesota: University of Minnesota Press.

Sluckin, A., and Smith, P. (1977). Two approaches to the concept of dominance in preschool children. *Child Development*, **48**, 917–923.

Smith, P., and Connolly, K. (1972). Patterns of play and social interaction in preschool children. In N. Blurton Jones (Ed.), *Ethological Studies of Child Behaviour.* Cambridge: Cambridge University Press.

Strayer, F. F., (1976). Learning and imitation as a function of social status in macaque monkeys (*Macaca nemestrina*). *Animal Behaviour*, **24**, 835–848.

Strayer, F. F., Chapeskie, T. R., and Strayer, J. (1978). The perception of preschool social dominance relations. *Aggressive Behavior*, **4**, 183–192.

Strayer, F. F., and Strayer, J. (1976). An ethological analysis of social agonism and dominance relations among preschool children. *Child Development*, **47**, 980–989.

Tinbergen, N. (1950). The hierarchical organization of nervous mechanisms underlying instinctive behaviour. *Symposium of the Society for Experimental Biology*, **4**, 305–312.

Tinebergen, N. (1963). On the aims and methods of ethology. *Zeitschrift Für Tierpsychologie*, **20**, 410–433.

Trivers, R. L. (1971). The evolution of reciprocal altruism. *Quarterly Review of Biology*, **46**, 35–57.

Tsumori, A. (1967). Newly acquired behavior and social interactions of Japanese monkeys. In S. Altmann (Ed.), *Social Communication among Primates*. Chicago: University of Chicago Press.

Washburn, P. (1932). A scheme for grading the reaction of children in a new social situation. *Journal of Genetic Psychology*, **40**, 84–99.

Wilson, E. O. (1975). *Sociobiology: The New Synthesis*. Cambridge, Massachusetts: Belknap/Harvard University Press.

Yerkes, R. M. (1928). *The Great Apes*. New Haven, Connecticut: Yale University Press.

Zuckerman, S. (1932). *The Social Life of Monkeys and Apes*. London: Routledge.

CHAPTER 10

Patterns of Interaction in Children's Friendships

HUGH C. FOOT,
ANTONY J. CHAPMAN
and
JEAN R. SMITH

Recent years have marked a steady and healthy growth in studies of children's friendships. However, the concentration of research effort, as other chapters in this volume attest, has been directed at the genesis and development of friendships rather than at the dynamics of friendship in children's social encounters. Potashin (1946) recognized this lacuna over three decades ago, yet the position is still much the same now as it was then.

Most of the studies of friendship behaviours that do exist are observational in nature, and are aimed at exploring general and comparatively gross patterns of behaviour. Few detailed analyses of specific social behaviours between friends have been undertaken, least of all in terms of their reciprocal implications for the development of interpersonal intimacy. In the first section of this chapter we review the limited empirical research on children's friendship behaviours with particular emphasis upon identifying characteristics or patterns of behaviour that differentiate interactions between friends from those between non-friends. We also pay special attention to friends' social sensitivities and to their responsiveness to each others' more subtle social cues which are of equal, if not more, research interest.

In the second section we consider friendship interactions in the context of social intimacy theory and discuss the appropriateness of Patterson's (1976) model of reciprocation to the behaviours of friends. Finally, in the third section, we sketch out the ways in which we have developed Patterson's notion of reciprocation in our own studies of children's friendships which have examined the temporal patterning of friends' non-verbal behaviours in dyadic interactions.[1]

BEHAVIOURAL CHARACTERISTICS OF CHILDREN'S FRIENDSHIPS

Almost any research paradigm for investigating behavioural components of friends' interactions depends upon an initial selection of children who are friends. This raises the immediate problem that children who identify each other orally as friends may not necessarily interact with each other any more frequently than with other unselected children, although some researchers (e.g. Challman, 1932; McCandless, Bilous, and Bennett, 1961) have taken the frequency of interaction between children as an objective measure of the strength of their friendship. However, the evidence concerning whether sociometric choices of children generally do correspond with preferences manifested in actual play associations is sufficiently confusing to give serious cause for concern about what measure is most valid. Biehler (1954) found high agreement between behavioural and sociometric first choices amongst a group of preschool children, but beyond the first choice a child will select any of several less liked companions to play with, regardless of the sociometric order in which s/he placed them. On the other hand, Chapman, Smith, Foot, and Pritchard (1979) found that only 27 per cent of 4-year-olds interacted most with their stated 'best' friend in the classroom, while in 9-year-olds there was no correspondence at all between sociometric choices and play associations in the playground. Classroom interactions are, of course, often constrained by the children's seating positions and by the teacher, and do not, therefore, provide a valid measure of natural association. Playground interactions are, however, far less constrained beyond the deliberate staggering of playtime for children of different ages/classes in many schools. In the study cited above correlations between sociometric popularity and playground popularity were as low as -0.20.

The essential interest here, however, concerns the behavioural responses of friends when they *are* interacting, irrespective of the relative frequency or infrequency with which they seek each other out in order to interact. In this context one may have renewed faith in the sociometric method. Since Frankel and Potashin (1944), researchers have found sociometry generally adequate for identifying friends as a precursor to exploring behavioural differences between friends and nonfriends, and it is a tribute to the validity and robustness of the method that such relatively stable findings have emerged. Admittedly, much depends upon the age of the children: the method is substantially less reliable when applied to children under the age of 5 or 6 years than when applied to children older than this age.

Prosocial and antisocial behaviours

Most studies are consistent with the view that friendship enhances the emission of all kinds of desirable interactive behaviours. Across a fairly wide age-range, the joint activities of friends are characterized by more generosity, cooperation, integration and sharing (cf. Anderson, 1937; Galejs, 1974), by more democratic and consultative verbal exchange (Lippitt, 1941; Potashin, 1946), by more humour and teasing (Foot, Chapman, and Smith, 1977; Potashin, 1946), by more sociability, affection, cheerfulness and toleration (Charlesworth and Hartup, 1967; Potashin, 1946) and generally by noisier and more exciting behaviour (Philp, 1940).

In terms of task performance, friends and non-friends do not appear to differ in any systematic way. Brady-Smith, Newcomb, and Hartup (1978), for example, had grade I and III children (i.e. 6- and 8-year-olds) performing block-building tasks under competitive and cooperative sets and found no difference between friends and non-friends in the task outcomes. Friends, however, made more reference to questions of equity, issued more commands of mutual intent and engaged in more frequent affective expressions than did non-friends. The investigators concluded that interpersonal attraction facilitates the expressive and reciprocal components of social interaction 'regardless of the superordinate goal structure'. Other evidence also suggests that measures of social responsiveness are particularly sensitive to friendship effects: in comparison with non-friends, friends exchange more mutual glances, smile and laugh at each other more (Foot, Chapman, and Smith, 1977; Potashin, 1946; Schwartz, 1972), are more likely to engage in proximal activities by standing or sitting closer to each other (Aiello and Jones, 1971; Jones, 1971; Jones and Aiello, 1973; Smith, Foot, and Chapman, 1977) or by touching each other (Langlois, Gottfried, and Seay, 1973; Lewis, Young, Brooks, and Michalson, 1975). Also friends are more likely to imitate each other and indulge in gesturing (Lewis et al., 1975).

By contrast non-friends appear to have either of two effects upon each other during interaction. On the one hand they act indifferently towards each other, perform tasks as if they were on their own and are generally much quieter, more bored, and restrained (Philp, 1940; Potashin, 1946). On the other hand non-friends are more likely to strive to impress each other by talking a lot, showing off, poking fun at and embarrassing each other and generally acting more competitively (Philp, 1940). Non-verbal behaviours include more curious and 'watchful' looking behaviours with a marked reduction of mutual gaze. What set of circumstances leads to which kind of reaction is not altogether clear, but the general social context appears to be crucial. A pair of non-friends is more likely to adopt the second, more competitive role when in the company of other children, some of whom may be their friends; whereas it is more likely to adopt the former, quieter role when it is in the absence of other company.

Friendship interactions should not, however, be seen purely as promoting prosocial behaviour. There is ample evidence that friendship also enhances less desirable interactive behaviours. One only has to look at the development of friendship cliques and gangs to appreciate the pressures on individual children to perform anti-social aggressive acts (see Chapter 14). Green (1933), in a study of quarrels and friendship, has emphasized quarrelling as an 'essential part of friendly social intercourse', particularly amongst boys. As Maccoby and Jacklin (1975) argue, it is difficult always to accept that rough and tumble play is positive social interaction; it may start out as exuberantly happy behaviour but may quickly turn into fighting. Such aggression in peer relations is seen by many as a very necessary ingredient for adequate social development.

Hartup (1977, 1978a, 1978b) adopts the view that the child can best achieve an optimal social development through opportunities to interact with individuals whose social and cognitive capacities are similar to his/her own, because it is only through these peer relationships that s/he can acquire a full repertoire of social experiences. Aggression, for example, is largely inhibited by parents, as a consequence of which most of the child's aggression has its outlet in play. Lambert (1974) reported that nearly three times as much aggression occurs during play with peers as during interaction within the family. Peer interaction thus provides the child with an opportunity to experiment aggressively with his/her peers in a way that would not be permitted in adult–child relations. Learning encompasses '(a) effective aggression skills—how to hit in order to defend oneself and how to make another person angry; (b) aggression controls—how to "turn-off" one's own anger and resist the temptation to attack someone else' (Hartup, 1977, p. 5).

The influence of peer relationships upon the control of aggressive behaviour is of particular significance. Patterson, Littman, and Bricker (1967) have demonstrated that feedback from other children clearly serves to escalate and de-escalate rates of aggression among nursery school children. Control from peers also operates powerfully in other directions: Wahler (1967) examined the extent to which prosocial learning in nursery school children can be facilitated by peer rewards: selective attention by peers to instances of cooperation promoted further cooperative acts; positive social overtures and speech by the subjects increased the rate of emission of these desired responses. Such contacts provide the child with experiences of success and failure, both of which are crucial ingredients for a balanced social adjustment. Experiences of this kind are also fostered by friendship with younger and older children. Hartup (1978a) emphasizes the importance for social adaptation of mixed-age interactions, in addition to same-age interactions. 'Social adaptation requires skills in both seeking help (dependency) and giving it (nurturance); being passive and being sociable; . . . being intimate and being self-reliant' (Hartup, 1978a, p. 4–5). Many of these skills are clearly facilitated by having younger or older friends whose lesser or greater degree of social maturity promotes respectively dominant, nurturant behaviour on the one hand and submissive, dependent behaviour on the other.

Sex differences in friendship behaviours

The extent to which there are distinctive patterns and styles of behaviour that differentiate interactions between friends from those between non-friends has also emerged from various studies that have examined sex differences. Preference for same-sex friendships throughout childhood and into adolescence has long been noted with preference percentages in the region of 62–81 per cent (cf. Challman, 1932; Green, 1933; Koch, 1933; Parten, 1933). From a behavioural viewpoint various differences in the qualities of boys' and girls' same-sex friendship interactions have been reported, and comparisons of same- with opposite-sex friendships have been observed. Galejs (1974), for example, studying nursery school children, found same-sex friends to engage in generally more excited behaviours than opposite-sex friends; they were more giggly, happy, attention-seeking and 'grabby' (pulling and shoving). Opposite-sex pairs engaged in more leading, dominating, demonstrating and assisting behaviours. Girls displayed generally more pronounced behaviour in the company of opposite-sex friends, particularly sharing and toleration. Antisocial behaviours such as unfriendliness and unconstructiveness appeared to feature about equally in the interactions of both sexes.

Green (1933) paints a slightly different picture with respect to quarrelling in nursery school children: he found it to be most prevalent in boy–boy friendships, followed by boy–girl friendships and least in girl–girl friendships. It may well be that these behavioural differences between the sexes are in part explained by changing trends in socialization and sex-role expectations in the 40 years that separate Green's and Galejs' studies, but the differences may also be attributable to variations in the size and composition of the play group in which boys and girls habitually tend to play. The greater altruistic/sharing behaviour and the less quarrelsomeness of nursery school girls may reflect their tendency to distribute their interactions across a larger number of playmates than do boys (Clark, Wyon, and Richards, 1969). Direction of causality is, of course, difficult to determine in this relationship. It may be that girls have a natural affinity towards larger groups which fosters the development of prosocial behaviours, but it is equally—if not more—plausible that girls' prosocial behaviours develop for other reasons (e.g. modelling, socialization, sex-role learning), thus equipping them to cope with a larger circle of playmates.

Nevertheless, the evidence of differences between boys' and girls' preferred sizes of playgroups is relatively consistent. Reviews of this evidence (cf. Maccoby and Jacklin, 1975; Waldrop and Halverson, 1975) suggest that there is a dramatic reversal in patterns of playmate choices. Until the age of about 7 years (cf. Waldrop and Halverson, 1975) boys have relatively 'intensive' friendships with a few other same-sex peers, while girls are more 'extensive', better able to cope with a whole group of other children (who are more likely to be of both sexes). But after that age a reverse trend develops, boys more readily merging into larger groups and gangs, and girls fostering single or relatively few 'best friend' relationships. The extent of this cleavage is well illustrated and documented by Savin-Williams in his descriptions of adolescent groups (see Chapter 13) and appears to be a cross-cultural phenomenon (Omark, Omark and Edelman, 1973).

The social sensitivities of boys and girls

Waldrop and Halverson's distinction between intensive and extensive peer relations refers basically to the exclusivity of boys' and girls' friendship patterns. The terms, however, may be somewhat misleading in as much as they seem to imply something about the *depth* of children's friendships. Maccoby and Jacklin (1975), who have considered depth of friendship in relation to sex differences, state categorically (in relation to older children and adolescents) that: 'By definition, girls' friendship patterns are more intimate, by simple virtue of the fact that they are smaller' (p.210). While in practice it is very probable that the fewer friends a child has the more intimate s/he is likely to be with those friends, this is by no means a necessary consequence. Many children, like adults, are able to maintain close intimacy with a substantial number of friends. Indeed, if friendship dissolution may be taken as a measure of the strength of a friendship then at least one study (Shapiro, 1967) shows that the friendships of teenage girls with intensive peer relations, are more prone to dissolution than those of teenage boys with comparatively extensive peer relations.

Despite the qualitative differences in boys' and girls' friendships in terms of size of groupings during childhood and adolescence, the evidence concerning depth and intimacy of friendship is somewhat equivocal, as is the evidence on the relative social sensitivities of boys and girls. Maccoby and Jacklin (1975) have reviewed both issues and have challenged the traditional view that males are more interested in objects and their manipulation, while females show a greater interest in people and a greater capacity for establishing and maintaining inter-personal relations, a view expressed by Garai and Scheinfeld (1968). In arguing that there are essentially no consistent differences between the sexes in their social sensitivities, Maccoby and Jacklin have drawn upon evidence concerning children's reactions to strangers and non-familial adults, their positive social interaction with age-mates and their empathy for interpersonal relationships, as measured, for example, by the explanations they give of the feelings and motives of subjects in storied incidents. What differences emerge from the studies on empathy appear to endorse a sex-typed perspective (cf. Feshbach and Roe, 1968) namely that boys and girls are more sensitive to feelings and relationships surrounding same-sex subjects in predicaments with which they are themselves familiar or might expect to gain familiarity in the future.

Many of the studies which form the basis of Maccoby and Jacklin's conclusions, however, have concentrated either upon children's sensitivities to social cues in a *non-interactive* situation, or upon children's reactions to cues *outside* the immediate interaction. Studies of the former type typically examine the recognition of accuracy of judgement of facial expressions (e.g. Cantor, 1971; Gitter, Mostofsky and Quincy, 1971; Hamilton, 1973; Savitsky and Izard, 1970); studies of the latter type involve, for example, the intervention of the experimenter in terms of his attentiveness or verbal support (e.g. Burton, Allinsmith and Maccoby, 1966; Meddock, Parsons and Hill, 1971; Pawlicki, 1972). Little evidence, however, is available about the social sensitivity of boys and girls to each other during interaction as a function of their interpersonal relationship, and it may well be that Maccoby and Jacklin's conclusions do not generalize this far. In one study of 9- to 12-year-olds that has examined the interaction between friendship and sex on the allocation of toys (Benton, 1971), it was found that female pairs appeared to prefer parity (whether with a friend or not) more than did boys, but they discriminated more against non-friends in terms of making poorer evaluations of them and perceiving them as less friendly. Other findings, not specifically from studies on friendship, also point to girls of all ages being more concerned than boys with equalizing relative outcomes in reward-sharing situations (cf. Vinacke and Gullickson, 1964). This behavioural measure of consideration by girls may at least constitute some confirmation of their enhanced sensitivity to their companion's needs or feelings in interactive situations.

Most of the evidence of sex differences in social sensitivity as a function of friendship stems from the exchanges of non-verbal cues during interaction. In a series of studies by the present authors, overwhelming effects of friendship were obtained on measures of social sensitivity, such as durations and frequencies of laughter, smiling, looking at companion, touching and talking (Chapman, Smith and Foot, 1980; Foot, Chapman and Smith, 1977; Smith *et al.*, 1977). Children were substantially more responsive on all these measures when paired with friends to watch comedy cartoon films than when paired with strangers. Other researchers, mentioned earlier in this chapter, have found effects of friendship for proximity and orientation. Whilst these friendship effects are relatively large and fairly consistent on the whole, there are more subtle sex differences in the relative impact that friendship makes upon some, at least, of these measures. Proximity activities are relatively straightforward inasmuch as most studies that have produced a sex difference have arbitrated in favour of girls and women standing/sitting closer together, facing each other more directly and touching each other more frequently in various social settings (cf. Aiello and Jones, 1971; Guardo, 1969; Jones, 1971; Jones and Aiello, 1973; Langlois *et al.*, 1973). Other measures of social sensitivity amongst boys and girls, however, seem to be influenced by the particular social situation, as well as by the friendship/non-friendship association. Foot, Chapman and Smith (1977), for example, found that the laughter and smiling of 7- and 8-year-old boys and girls with friend companions varied according to the intimacy of the situation: boys laughed significantly more when intimacy was high than when it was low, whereas girls laughed significantly more when intimacy was low than when it was high. The opposite relationship held for smiling: girls smiled more when intimacy was high, boys smiled more when it was low. These results firstly raise an important issue about the preferred level of social intimacy for boys and girls, and secondly throw some light on the differential roles of laughter and smiling in the social interactions of friends.

In relation to the first issue we have argued that boys and girls differ both in their preference for a 'comfortable' level of intimacy and in their sensitivity to changes in the prevailing level of intimacy. Girls' preference for shared cooperative tasks (cf. Leventhal and Anderson, 1970) and their tendency to self-disclose more than boys (cf. Rivenbark, 1971; Walker and Wright, 1976) provide some evidence that the normative level of tolerated intimacy is relatively higher for girls than it is for boys. Fisher and Byrne (1975) concluded from their examination of sex differences in spatial behaviour that females 'can tolerate closer interpersonal contacts than males' (p. 15). This line of reasoning led us to the prediction that girls would be disposed to find a high intimacy situation relatively more tolerable and congenial than a low intimacy situation, and would consequently be more likely to engage in social behaviours that reflect their higher comfort. For boys it was reasoned conversely that they would find a low intimacy situation relatively more congenial than a high intimacy one, and this former situation would evoke more comfortable social behaviours.

In relation to the second issue, the contrasting findings for boys' and girls' smiling and laughter in the context of high and low intimacy conditions provides persuasive evidence for suggesting that these measures of social responsiveness play different roles in children's interactions. It was argued that smiling more directly reflects the congeniality or degree of felt comfort of the situation: hence the greater smiling for girls in their preferred high intimacy situation and for boys in their preferred low intimacy situation. Laughter, by contrast, occurs more frequently and for longer durations in the non-preferred intimacy conditions (low for girls and high for boys). This accords exactly with what would be expected on the basis of Berlyne's (1969), Chapman's (1975a, 1975b) and Rothbart's (1976) views that laughter is a tension-release mechanism, occurring in situations where there is a build-up of tension. The non-preferred intimacy situations clearly qualify as better candidates for evoking arousal than the preferred intimacy situations. Further functional differences in boys' and girls' uses of laughter with friends were suggested by the data: boys, it was speculated, laugh in order to break attention from their companion in a situation that they find *over*-arousing; girls laugh in order to gain attention in a situation that they find *under*-arousing.

Sensitivity to social cues during the course of interaction can also be examined through children's perceptiveness of each others' behaviours. We know of no studies with friends in which children's perceptiveness has been directly measured. Looking at one's companion has often been analysed, of course, but looking and mutual gaze can only be treated as an index of attentiveness or affiliation, not as an evaluative awareness of what the companion is doing. We have collected some subjective data along these lines with boys and girls, sufficient to indicate that it might prove a fruitful line of future inquiry (cf. Foot, Chapman and Smith, 1977). After brief periods of dyadic interaction 7- and 8-year-old boys and girls were asked to gauge their own reactions towards their companions and their companion's reactions towards them. The children's verbal ratings (using three-point scales) of amounts of smiling and looking were compared with overt levels of responsiveness.

A 'perceptive' child was defined as one who rated his or her companion as having smiled or looked 'a lot', 'a little', or 'never', when the companion had in fact been a high, low or rare responder, respectively. Identification of the perceptive children revealed that they were more likely to be with friends than with strangers. . . . (p. 408).

SOCIAL INTIMACY THEORY

As already mentioned in the Introduction to this book, theoretical approaches to the study of children's friendships are relatively diffuse, drawing, perhaps rather haphazardly, upon constructions and models that have been developed to encompass other social psychological phenomena and other dimensions of social interaction. In the remaining sections of this chapter we attempt to outline and adapt a model of social intimacy which is particularly suitable for exploring children's friendship behaviours. The model is basically a behavioural one, but it has the potential for development in terms of cognitive dimensions that take account of a child's values, expectations, attitudes and social perspectives.

One of the basic shortcomings of many of the behavioural studies of friendship until the 1970s has been their concern with exploring the episodic behaviours of individual children *as a function of* their social situation or of their relationship with their peers. In other words, the tendency has been to describe what changes in the child's behaviour have taken place as a result of external social influences impinging upon him/her. These influences are brought about either through direct manipulation of the social environment or through selecting and comparing children who have had, usually on the basis of evidence collected *post hoc*, differential social experiences of one kind or another. This point has been put forward cogently by Schaffer (1974, 1977) in relation to the whole area of socialization processes. Definitions of the process 'were couched entirely in terms of what parents, or society generally, did to the young child, referring to the way in which he was "moulded" into an effective participant or to the manner in which his behaviour was "shaped" by his social environment' (Schaffer, 1974, p. 209). Sears' studies of the relationships between parental practices and child behaviour are typical examples of this one-way perspective of the processes of socialization (cf. Sears, Maccoby and Levin, 1957).

What is needed for an adequate account of children's relationships and interactions with friends, therefore, is a model which recognizes the two-way nature of the interaction, and the fact that the child under observation is just as much impinging upon his/her companion as the companion is upon him/her. In describing mother–child relationships, Schaffer (1974) likens their interaction to a 'kind of ping-pong game when the move of each partner is to an extent dictated by the previous move of the other partner' (p. 212). It is not sufficient, therefore, to focus upon one child's behaviour in a relationship while ignoring the companion's behaviour.

Compensation in interpersonal intimacy

This concern with friendship interaction as a reciprocal process led us to an examination of social intimacy theories which are primarily concerned with the interplay of behaviours between subject and companion during the course of interaction. By far the most widely acknowledged of these theories is the equilibrium model of social intimacy proposed by Argyle and Dean (1965). This theory is built on the basic premise that there is a kind of pressure between interactants for maintaining a comfortable level of interpersonal intimacy. It assumes that individuals are sensitive to varying states of intimacy and guage what is an appropriate or tolerable level for any given encounter, be it with a friend or stranger. The point of balance is a function of the approach tendencies in the situation, which include the satisfaction of affiliative needs and the desire for feedback, and the avoidance tendencies, which include fear of rejection and failure or fear of revealing oneself. The dynamic aspect of the theory concerns the restoration of the equilibrium level if and when that level is disturbed either by one or other of the interactants, or possibly by external stimuli or pressures that impinge upon their interaction. Since intimacy is a composite of a variety of individual behaviours, verbal and non-verbal, a change in any one of these behaviours may disturb the total balance, and pressures to compensate for or counteract the disturbance come into play.

The notion of compensation is crucial and the power of the theory lies in its ability to predict compensatory adjustments in intimacy behaviour by one interactant consequential upon changes in intimacy initiated by the other. For example, if intimacy is raised by closer physical proximity because one or both interactants move in too close, then intimacy along another dimension, such as eye contact or smiling, will inversely decrease.

Corroborative evidence for the Argyle and Dean model is substantial. Patterson (1973a) has provided a thorough review of the empirical studies that tested the theory in the 7 years or so following its formulation. Briefly, the bulk of the supportive evidence concerns the much researched measure of eye contact which has been shown to decrease systematically with increases in physical proximity between interactants (e.g. Argyle and Ingham, 1972; Goldberg, Kiesler and Collins, 1969; Patterson, 1973b; Schulz and Barefoot, 1974; Stephenson, Rutter and Dore, 1972). Findings also suggest that eye-contact is inversely related to intimacy of conversational topic, for example, an interviewer asking increasingly intimate questions (Carr and Dabbs, 1974; Schulz and Barefoot, 1974). A similar inverse relationship has been shown between directness of body orientation and proximity (Aiello and Jones, 1971; Felipe and Sommer, 1966; Mehrabian and Diamond, 1971; Pellegrini and Empey, 1970).

Clearly there are other combinations of intimacy behaviours that remain to be explored, unless the apparent lack of evidence suggests that such studies have been undertaken without producing significant, 'publishable' results. The scope of the original formulation has been modified (cf. Argyle and Cook, 1976) to encompass other non-verbal signals such as form of address, openness of posture and expression of emotion which have more recently been recognized as contributing to overall intimacy. In addition the theory has been refined to include more subtle changes in intimacy behaviours and to take account of the social norms and rules which inevitably contribute such powerful influences in determining the appropriate equilibrium point for intimacy.

Despite this bulk of confirmatory evidence for the equilibrium model, there are a number of studies which do not accord with the notion that *compensation* is the inevitable consequence of intimacy changes. In a more recent and exhaustive review, Patterson (1976) has drawn attention to published research which not only is unsupportive of the compensation notion but is in direct contradiction to it. Perhaps the most impressive examples come from studies involving intimacy of conversational topic, as where interactants are engaged in verbal self-disclosure. Jourard and Friedman (1970) found that their subjects self-disclosed more as a consequence of being touched by the experimenter; and Altman (1973) in his review of self-disclosure studies, reported that most of this work indicates a positive correlation in degree of disclosure by interactants. With respect to purely non-verbal behaviour, too, there is evidence for reciprocation of responses rather than compensation. Breed (1972) found that a confederate who increases intimacy by raising his levels of looking and forward lean produces similar levels of increased responsiveness from the subject. Likewise, Chapman (1975a) found that children listening to a humorous recording engaged in more eye-contact as they sat closer together. Indeed in all our studies quoted to date in this chapter, we have only ever obtained results which suggest that increases in intimacy along one dimension go hand in hand with increases along other dimensions.

Important also, in view of the model shortly to be described, are the findings that upward changes in intimacy are accompanied by positive changes in affect. For example, Carr and Dabbs (1974) found that closer proximity, for the purposes of conducting an interview, led to increased liking of the interviewer by the interviewee; and in Breed's study it was found that increased intimacy (brought about by forward lean, seating orientation and eye-contact) prompted subjects to judge the companions as more interested in them. Admittedly, it is not always the case that increases in immediacy behaviours imply more positive affect. Patterson, Mullens and Romano (1971), in a study of intrusion in a library setting, reported that frequencies of glances at an intruder increased with decreases in interpersonal distances. As the investigators acknowledged, it is plausible that looking was a defence mechanism aimed at warning off the intruder rather than serving its more usual affiliative function.

Before proceeding with our discussion of the reconciliation of these conflicting findings, and their relevance to studies of friendship, brief reference should be made to the almost exclusive use of adult samples in these studies of interpersonal intimacy. In particular, as Russo (1975) points out with reference to eye-contact, 'the interaction between spatial behaviour and other non-verbal behaviours, such as EC, has not been studied with children as subjects' (p. 497). Russo's own study with kindergarten, grade I, and grade VI children in a conversational setting, tended not to support the compensatory model inasmuch as mean length of eye-contact did not increase with increasing distance (although percentage of eye-contact did). The only other study which directly tested the compensation model with respect to children was by Chapman (1975a), in which the intimacy behaviours of 7- to 8-year-old children were explored in a non-conversational setting. Contrary to the notion of compensation, the results showed that the closer together children were seated the more they laughed, smiled and engaged in eye-contact. Evidence favouring the operation of compensatory reactions in children is tangential and comes almost exclusively from studies of children with behaviour disorders, particularly autism. Briefly, it has been argued that the reason why autistic children endeavour to avoid eye-contact (Hutt and Ounsted, 1970; Kanner, 1943) and shun social interaction (Currie and Brannigan, 1970; Richer and Nicoll, 1971) is in order to reduce incoming information to a tolerable level from what is perceived by them as being potentially too arousing or too overwhelming.

In essence it is our view that the processes of interpersonal intimacy work much in the same way for children, albeit at a more embryonic level, as they do for adults. If the evidence just cited for normal children appears to favour a non-compensatory process, then this is not, we would argue, a function of any *process* differences between children and adults but rather a function of the situation they are in. This is clarified shortly as we turn our attention to the reconciliation of the conflicting evidence on compensatory processes in interpersonal intimacy.

Reciprocation in interpersonal intimacy

It was in the light of the contradictory evidence concerning compensatory effects that Patterson (1976) formulated his arousal theory of interpersonal intimacy. Central to Patterson's model is the notion that arousal change is a critical factor in determining variations in expressed intimacy. The assumption is that if one member of an interactive pair changes his level of intimacy to any noticeable degree (above or below the tolerated range) this change will create a state of increased arousal in the other member of the pair. Patterson reviews in some detail the evidence pertaining to this question of the concomitance of arousal changes with variations in intimacy behaviours, which is almost exclusively tied to two dimensions of intimacy: interpersonal distance and eye-contact. Such evidence as exists (which we shall not review here) is encouraging in that it supports the link between intimacy and arousal changes at various levels: there is physiological (e.g. galvanic skin response, heart rate, EEG), behavioural (e.g. facial expressions, fidgetting) and subjective (e.g. ratings of mood, perceived irritability) evidence. There is no reason, other than sheer lack of data why such reactions should not also be expected as a consequence of changes in other intimacy behaviours: touching, smiling and laughter. In fact, as mentioned earlier, laughter has been specifically identified as having primary arousal-reducing properties (cf. Berlyne, 1969; Chapman, 1975b; Rothbart, 1976).

Up to this point Patterson's model appears to be identical to that of Argyle and Dean: it is similarly founded upon the notion that arousal is evoked by changes in intimacy behaviours by one interactant and is the precipitator of appropriate reactions by the other. What is crucial to Patterson is the *affective* state associated with the arousal that has been so evoked: 'it is assumed that the mediating emotional states are a joint product of arousal change and cognition' (p. 239), the cognitions referring to the subject's knowledge and perceptions of the situation and relationship s/he is in. Thus, a state of arousal is necessarily accompanied either by a negative or by a positive affective state, and it is this emotional component which determines the behavioural reaction of the subject to changes in arousal.

> Specifically, it is proposed that negative emotional reactions precipitate compensatory behaviours, returning the interaction to a more comfortable or appropriate level of interpersonal intimacy. Conversely, positive emotional reactions precipitate a reciprocation of the original intimacy behaviours, leading to a new and different level of intimacy. In general both types of reactive changes in the intimacy behaviours probably serve to maximize one's comfort or satisfaction in an interaction. (p. 241).

Thus, Argyle and Dean's compensatory model applies in situations where arousal changes have negative, unwelcomed emotional associations, and reciprocating reactions occur in situations where arousal changes have positive, welcomed emotional associations. This emphasis upon the affective values attached to arousal changes inevitably draws one's attention back to the inter-active situations employed, and it is here that a *post hoc* reconciliation of the evidence has to be attempted. Patterson has argued that the vast majority of studies in which compensation typically occurs have been characterized by subject or design features which are likely to produce negative emotional states. The settings used, for example, are often relatively 'sterile' laboratories, or places where normal interaction is restricted (e.g. libraries). Often subjects know or suspect that they are under observation. Companion variables may also bring an artificial and possibly unwelcome element into the situation: at best subjects may be naive strangers under instructions to conduct a conversation on some specified topic; at worst confederate companions may be used who are programmed to maintain a particular level of intimacy or to follow a particular sequence of intimacy changes. Such manipulations conspire to make the naive subject potentially anxious or apprehensive, and compensatory reactions are hardly a surprising outcome. By contrast those situations in which reciproca-tion has been found are typically more naturalistic and pleasurable. The self-disclosure studies are usually highly naturalistic (as in clinical settings) even if self-disclosure is manipulated for experimental purposes. Chapman's (1975a) study and our joint studies with children (cf. Chapman *et al.*, 1980; Foot, Chapman and Smith, 1977) were conducted in a congenial unconstrained setting with which the children had previously been well familiarized, and in which no demands were placed upon them other than to listen to humorous stories or watch comedy films. Above all, in our studies, the children were friends with each other. Thus, the combination of congenial, familiar surroundings, a pleasurable task and being with a friend companion must, as indeed we are confident it did, optimize the positive emotional state of the child and maximize the chances of eliciting reciprocation of intimacy behaviours.

The value of Patterson's dual model of interpersonal intimacy for studies of children's friendship is that it provides a vehicle for exploring specific predictions about the patterning and sequencing of intimacy behaviours between friends. The fact that children are relatively unsophisticated and can more readily be observed than adults without their being suspicious that they are under observation also makes children ideal subjects for investigation.

FRIENDSHIP AND THE PATTERNING OF INTIMACY BEHAVIOURS

In this section we outline the preliminary ways in which we have tested out and developed Patterson's notion of reciprocation in our recent studies of children's friendships. In addition we draw out some implications from this work which might be pursued in further research.

Matching of overall levels of responsiveness

In general terms, as already indicated, our studies of the non-verbal behaviours of friends appear to support the reciprocation process (Foot, Chapman and Smith, 1977; Foot, Smith and Chapman, 1977, 1979). Children showed greater overall emissions of laughter, smiling and looking in the company of a friend than in the company of a non-friend. This was attributed to the greater positive affect which is associated with arousal changes initiated during interactions with friends, as well as to the generally higher level of intimacy tolerated by friends. Higher levels of responsiveness, of course, are exactly what a social reinforcement or social facilitation model would also predict on the assumption that a friend's responses have more reinforcement value or facilitating strength than a non-friend's responses, and are therefore more mutually enhancing. We argue, however, that the process of reciprocation is not the same as the process of reinforcement.

Given that our basic data consisted of cumulative durations of the non-verbal measures, it might be argued that the reason for the higher levels of responsiveness among friends lay purely in the fact that friends typically share and certainly tolerate more intimate interactions than do non-friends: their equilibrium level is consistently higher from the beginning of an interaction. If reciprocating processes, rather than purely reinforcement processes, formed the basis for determining levels of responsiveness, then it would need to be shown that subjects and companions in their interactive dyads were responding at very similar levels, irrespective of whether their overall rates of responsiveness were high or low.

In exploring reciprocatory processes, therefore, our first interest lay in examining the similarity of overall levels of responsiveness (what we have termed 'response-matching') between subjects and companions in each of our friend and non-friend dyads (cf. Foot, Smith and Chapman, 1977). Our prediction was that friends would response-match more closely than non-friends and this would be true even where overall levels of responsiveness for friend and non-friend dyads were similar, that is, in the overlap between the two distributions of responses. An analysis was undertaken of the data obtained in two studies involving pairs of children watching cartoon films. This analysis consisted of taking the overall duration of each intimacy behaviour (laughing, smiling, looking and talking) from the subject and companion in each dyad, and expressing whichever value was the smaller as a proportion of the larger. Thus, if the subject smiled for a total of 15 sec and the companion for a total of 20 sec, or vice versa, then the proportion was 0.75. For each dyad a set of response-match values was thus generated indicating the proportion of time that one interactant spent laughing, smiling, looking or talking, relative to the other. Values can vary from zero, representing total dissimilarity between subject and companion responses, to unity, representing perfect similarity.

The average response-match values are cited elsewhere (Foot, Smith and Chapman, 1977). Suffice it to say here that significantly higher values (approximately twice as high) were obtained for friend dyads on all measures (except laughing, where a statistical test was not applied in view of the almost complete absence of laughter amongst non-friends). Attention to the low-responding friend dyads in relation to the high-responding non-friend dyads, whose overall levels of responsiveness virtually overlapped, showed that the disparity between their response-match values was just as great as the disparity in the overall values for friend and non-friend dyads. One interesting sex difference was that girl friends appeared to match their amounts of talking very much more closely than did boy friends; this difference, we speculated, might be related to girls' preference for equitable, harmonious relationships in contrast to boys' more competitive, exploitative relationships with their friends.

This analysis of reciprocation, in terms of the overall similarity of levels of responsiveness between subject and companion is, however, very crude and of limited explanatory value. It does not offer a solution to the key questions about reciprocating processes. For example, it tells us nothing about the patterns of influence between subject and companion, that is whether one member of the pair is more initiative of intimacy behaviours and the other more reactive, or whether they initiate and react equally. Above all it provides no indication of how dependent each child's behaviour is upon the behaviour of the other, because it ignores the interplay and temporal sequencing of their responses. Thus, perfect response-matching could as readily be achieved by one child's smiles all occurring during the first minute of interaction, and the other's during the last minute of interaction (totally independent) as by one child's smiles being locked in sequentially to the others' (totally dependent).

Temporal patterning of non-verbal behaviours

An attractive feature of Patterson's model is that it does not assume that for any given encounter there is one stable level or range of tolerated intimacy which the interactants are motivated to maintain, as Argyle and Dean would hold. Interaction is fluid and Patterson's modification allows the interactants, through reciprocation, to shift their level of intimacy upwards or downwards during the course of interaction. One might tap, at successive points in time, an interaction between a boy and girl growing acquainted at a party, for example, and find intimacy level steadily changing. In many ways, therefore, intimacy refers more to specific states of feeling and to the momentary interplay of behaviours, as when two people at a particular point in time share a joke, embrace, or make love, than it does to the long-term, 'average' condition of the relationship between these two people.

It is the dynamic and relatively volatile nature of intimacy which, in our view, necessitates a much more molecular approach to its study. In terms of reciprocation it is essential to plot, on a momentary basis, the sequence and timing of behaviours between subject and companion. Are their interactions characterized by simultaneous bursts of activity (as in Schaffer's ping-pong analogy), interspersed with gaps, or are they responding with little regard to each other's behaviours? If reciprocation is taking place, then it should be evidenced by close and harmonious temporal patterning of subject and companion behaviours.

Our next step, therefore, in developing Patterson's model was to postulate that not only should overall response levels between interacting friends be more similar than those between interacting non-friends, but that, on a momentary basis, specific responses by one should be more closely matched by the specific responses of the other (cf. Foot *et al.*, 1979). In order to test this hypothesis a record was made, from video-tape-recordings, of individual behaviours by subject and companion during test sessions, when, as before, they watched cartoon films. This record provided a basis for analysing the sequence and duration of each laugh, smile and look emitted by each child. The precise form of the analysis and the results obtained are cited elsewhere (Foot *et al.*, 1979). Briefly the response-match index derived in this study referred to the degree of intermeshing (or close temporal occurrence) expressed as a ratio, between the subject's and companion's non-verbal behaviours. These indices showed clearly that behaviours of friends were more closely intermeshed than behaviours of non-friends, and in particular, that there was a strong sex effect: both boys and girls matched their responses more closely to a same-sex than to an opposite-sex companion; and this was true for non-friends as well as for friends. These results are particularly interesting in the context of what was described earlier in the chapter concerning children's preferences for interactions with same-sex companions. Indeed, they lend some weight to the notion that degrees of response-matching may to some extent reflect the strength and intimacy of the relationship.

It is interesting to speculate just what the relationship between a behavioural index of response-matching and interpersonal intimacy might be. Everyday experience provides many instances to support the idea that some kind of relationship might exist between them: two lovers engaging in a rapid, subtle exchange of glances, smiles and touches; close friends savouring the quick cut and thrust of witty word play. Yet it cannot be the simple monotonic relationship that these examples might imply. It is not difficult to find other examples of situations where close response-matching reflects the very opposite of intimacy: two people hurling abuse at each other, or capping each other's sarcasm with yet more cutting remarks.

Obviously the cognitions, purposes and interests of the interactants are crucial variables inasmuch as they determine the affective 'labelling' associated with arousal changes. Yet it is in this area that the theory is at its weakest: just how cognitions combine to determine the affective labelling has not in any sense been worked out. Few interactive situations can be defined entirely in positive or negative emotional terms. Most contain a variety of affective components so that, for example, the total degree of positive affect is the outcome of the extent to which positive components outweigh negative ones. It may well prove to be that reciprocation is not so much a function of the total *amount* of positive affect as it is a function of the qualitative *composition* of the positive and negative affective components which have to be balanced against each other. On the behavioural side, too, it may be that the specific affective components within the interactive situation shape the mode through which reciprocation occurs. For example, pleasurable anticipation of a long-awaited event (where arousal changes have positive affect) might evoke reciprocation during interaction in terms of increased smiling, while actually experiencing the event with the same interactant might provide the occasion for arousal changes that evoke reciprocation along some other completely different dimension. It is not clear, therefore, whether a particular set of reciprocated responses could be predicted from a knowledge of the affective circumstances prevailing at the time of the interaction, or whether other alternative reciprocated responses might equally well have been evoked.

Without specifically addressing ourselves to this question we have made some attempt to look at the association between specific types of subject and companion behaviours. In our most recent study of response-matching (cf. Foot, *et al.*, 1979), we were interested in analysing the emissions of *any* intimacy behaviour (from amongst those that were included in the analysis) by one subject which occurred in closer temporal proximity to *any* intimacy behaviour by the other. The index obtained ignored whether the subject specifically laughed, smiled or looked.

From the records taken from the same video-tape-recordings, a more detailed analysis was subsequently conducted on 'specific' response-matches, that is, occasions when a behaviour was reciprocated in kind: a laugh for a laugh, a smile for a smile, and so on. These data have not been published: they defy statistical analysis because of the small sample size and the large intersubject variability. In general terms, though, the results confirmed the view that friends are more likely to reciprocate in kind than are nonfriends, although this effect is to some extent confounded by the higher overall level of reciprocation amongst friends along any intimacy dimension. Whatever else these results suggest, they appear to favour the operation of reciprocation over pure reinforcement, on the basis that reinforcement does not imply that the same type of response initiated by one interactant will be elicited from the other. However, the effect is relatively weak, and we do not dispute that reinforcement is at least partially responsible for response-matching.

CONCLUSION

Patterson's model undoubtedly suffers some limitations. Most of the so-called intimacy dimensions also serve functions other than expressing intimacy in interaction. Eye-contact, for example, is important in gaining feedback and in synchronizing transitions in conversation (Argyle, Lalljee and Cook, 1968); smiling is sometimes used to mask anxiety (Mehrabian, 1971; Schulz and Barefoot, 1974). However, this consideration is equally characteristic of other theories of interpersonal intimacy. More particularly, the types of affective labels attached to arousal changes need to be defined much more precisely and, for predictive power, it would be useful if the range of reciprocated behaviours could be specified for given situations. Patterson (1977) has acknowledged the need to investigate individual differences with respect to variations in adjustments to arousal (preferences for one mode of reaction rather than another) and to differences in sensitivity to intimacy changes by the partner. Perhaps these differences are linked to basic dimensions of personality, or to habitual styles of interaction. In our studies of response-matching we have found that some children consistently under- or over-matched: in different encounters with friends and non-friends they repeatedly responded more or less to their companion than their companion did to them, irrespective of the overall level of responsiveness in each of these interactions. Such observations as these may help in identifying those children who set the pace of interaction and establish the general level of intimacy in their social encounters with others, and those children who invariably take their cue from the other. More research in this direction is clearly needed.

Despite its weaknesses the model provides a constructive framework for making predictions about children's behaviours during their interactions with friends. As mentioned earlier in the chapter, it is imperative to consider the two-way flow of interaction and the model rightly concerns itself with both subject and companion behaviours and their mutual effect upon each other. There is, encouragingly, renewed interest in the development of methodologies and data management techniques for analysing behaviour streams and the sequencing of social behaviours (cf. Bakeman and Dabbs, 1976; Gottman and Bakeman, 1978).

Our development of the theory shows that refinement is possible in ways that enable more precise predictions to be made. The generality of the model, however, needs to be proven in a wider range of interactive settings, and, since most of the assumptions are based upon research evidence derived from dyads, the implications for triads and for larger groups need to be explored.

NOTE

1. The empirical research reported in this chapter was part of a series of studies on children's social responsiveness in humorous situations, sponsored in the United Kingdom by the Social Science Research Council (Grant HR 3043).

REFERENCES

Aiello, J. R., and Jones, S. E. (1971). Field study of the proxemic behavior of young school children in three subcultural groups. *Journal of Personality and Social Psychology*, **19**, 351–356.

Altman, I. (1973). Reciprocity of interpersonal exchange. *Journal for the Theory of Social Behaviour*, **3**, 249–261.

Anderson, H. H. (1937). Domination and integration in the social behavior of young children in an experimental play situation. *Genetic Psychology Monographs*, **19**, 341–408.

Argyle, M., and Cook, M. (1976). *Gaze and Mutual Gaze*. Cambridge: University Press.

Argyle, M., and Dean, J. (1965). Eye-contact, distance, and affiliation. *Sociometry*, **28**, 289–304.

Argyle, M., and Ingham, R. (1972). Gaze, mutual gaze, and proximity. *Semiotica*, **6**, 32–49.

Argyle, M., Lalljee, M., and Cook, M. (1968). The effects of visibility on interaction in a dyad. *Human Relations*, **21**, 3–17.

Bakeman, R., and Dabbs, J. M., Jr. (1976). Social interaction observed: some approaches to the analysis of behavior streams. *Personality and Social Psychology Bulletin,.* **2**, 335–345.

Benton, A. A. (1971). Productivity, distributive justice and bargaining among children. *Journal of Personality and Social Psychology*, **18**, 68–78.

Berlyne, D. E. (1969). Laughter, humor and play. In G. Lindzey and E. Aronson (Eds.), *Handbook of Social Psychology*. Vol. 3. Reading, Massachusetts: Addison-Wesley.

Biehler, R. F. (1954). Companion choice behavior in the kindergarten. *Child Development*, **25**, 45–50.

Brady-Smith, J. E., Newcomb, A. F., and Hartup, W. W. (1978). Friendship and incentive condition as determinants of children's social problem-solving. Paper presented at APA Convention.

Breed, G. (1972). The effect of intimacy: reciprocity or retreat. *British Journal of Social and Clinical Psychology*, **11**, 135–142.

Burton, R. V., Allinsmith, W., and Maccoby, E. E. (1966). Resistance to temptation in relation to sex of child, sex of experimenter, and withdrawal of attention. *Journal of Personality and Social Psychology*, **3**, 253–258.

Cantor, G. N. (1971). Effects of context on preschool children's judgments. *Journal of Experimental Child Psychology*, **11**, 505–512.

Carr, S. J., and Dabbs, J. M., Jr. (1974). The effects of lighting, distance and intimacy of topic on verbal and visual behavior. *Sociometry*, **37**, 592–600.

Challman, R. C. (1932). Factors influencing friendship among preschool children. *Child Development*, **3**, 146–158.

Chapman, A. J. (1975a). Eye contact, physical proximity and laughter, a re-examination of the equilibrium model of social intimacy. *Social Behavior and Personality*, **3**, 143–155.

Chapman, A. J. (1975b). Humorous laughter in children. *Journal of Personality and Social Psychology*, **31**, 42–49.

Chapman, A. J., Smith, J. R., and Foot, H. C. (1980). Humour, laughter and social interaction. In P. E. McGhee and A. J. Chapman (Eds.), *Children's Humour*. London: Wiley.

Chapman, A. J., Smith, J. R., Foot, H. C., and Pritchard, E. (1979). Behavioural and sociometric indices of friendship in children. In M. Cook and G. D. Wilson (Eds.), *Love and Attraction*, Oxford: Pergamon Press.

Charlesworth, R., and Hartup, W. W. (1967). Positive social reinforcement in a nursery school peer group. *Child Development*, **38**, 993–1002.

Clark, A. H., Wyon, S. M., and Richards, M. P. M. (1969). Free play in nursery school children. *Journal of Child Psychology and Psychiatry*, **10**, 205–216.

Currie, K. H., and Brannigan, C. R. (1970). Behavioural analysis and modification with an autistic child. In S. J. Hutt and C. Hutt (Eds.), *Behaviour Studies in Psychiatry*. Oxford: Pergamon Press.

Felipe, N. J., and Sommer, R. (1966). Invasion of personal space. *Social Problems*, **14**, 206–214.

Feshbach, N. D., and Roe, K. (1968). Empathy in six- and seven-year-olds. *Child Development*, **39**, 133–145.

Fisher, J. D., and Byrne, D. (1975). Too close for comfort: sex differences in response to invasions of personal space. *Journal of Personality and Social Psychology*, **32**, 15–21.

Foot, H. C., Chapman, A. J., and Smith, J. R. (1977). Friendship and social responsiveness in boys and girls. *Journal of Personality and Social Psychology*, **35**, 401–411.

Foot, H. C., Smith, J. R., and Chapman, A. J. (1977). Individual differences in children's social responsiveness in humour situations. In A. J. Chapman and H. C. Foot (Eds.), *It's a Funny Thing, Humour*. Oxford: Pergamon Press.

Foot, H. C., Smith, J. R., and Chapman, A. J. (1979). Non-verbal expressions of intimacy in children. In M. Cook and G. D. Wilson (Eds.), *Love and Attraction*. Oxford: Pergamon Press.

Frankel, E. B., and Potashin, R. (1944). A survey of sociometric and presociometric literature on friendships and social acceptance among children. *Sociometry*, **7**, 422–431.

Galejs, I. (1974). Social interaction of preschool children. *Home Economics Research Journal*, **2**, 153–159.

Garai, J. E., and Scheinfeld, A. (1968). Sex differences in mental and behavioral traits. *Genetic Psychology Monographs*, **77**, 169–299.

Gitter, A. G., Mostofsky, D. I., and Quincy, A. J. (1971). Race and sex differences in the child's perception of emotion. *Child Development*, **42**, 2071–2075.

Goldberg, G. N., Kiesler, C. A., and Collins, B. E. (1969). Visual behavior and face-to-face distance during interaction. *Sociometry*, **32**, 43–53.

Gottman, J., and Bakeman, R. (1978). The sequential analysis of observational data. In M. Lamb, S. Soumi, and G. Stephenson (Eds.), *Methodological Problems in the Study of Social Interactions*. Madison: University of Wisconsin Press.

Green, E. H. (1933). Friendship and quarrels among preschool children. *Child Development*, **4**, 237–252.

Guardo, C. J. (1969). Personal space in children. *Child Development*, **40**, 143–151.

Hamilton, M. L. (1973). Imitative behavior and expressive ability in facial expression of emotion. *Developmental Psychology*, **8**, 138.

Hartup, W. W. (1977). Peer relations: developmental implications and interaction in same- and mixed-age situations. *Young Children*, **32**, 4–13.

Hartup, W. W. (1978a). Children and their friends. In H. McGurk (Ed.), *Issues in Childhood Social Development*. London: Methuen.

Hartup, W. W. (1978b). Peer relations and the growth of social competence. In M. W. Kent, and J. E. Rolf (Eds.), *The Primary Prevention of Psychopathology*. Vol. 3. Hanover: University Press of New England.

Hutt, C., and Ounsted, C. (1970). Gaze aversion and its significance in childhood autism. In S. J. Hutt and C. Hutt (Eds.), *Behaviour Studies in Psychiatry*. Oxford: Pergamon Press.

Jones, S. E. (1971). A comparative proxemics analysis of dyadic interaction in selected subcultures of New York City. *Journal of Social Psychology*, **84**, 35–44.

Jones, S. E., and Aiello, J. R. (1973). Proxemic behavior of black and white first-, third-, and fifth- grade children. *Journal of Personality and Social Psychology*, **25**, 21–27.

Jourard, S. M., and Friedman, R. (1970). Experimenter–subject 'distance' and self-disclosure. *Journal of Personality and Social Psychology*, **15**, 278–282.

Kanner, L. (1943). Autistic disturbances of affective contact. *Nervous Child*, **2**, 217–250.

Koch, H. L. (1933). Popularity in preschool children: some related factors and a technique for its measurement. *Child Development*, **4**, 164–175.

Lambert, W. W. (1974). Promise and problems of cross-cultural exploration of children's aggressive strategies. In J. de Wit and W. Hartup (Eds.), *Determinants and Origins of Aggressive Behavior*. The Hague: Mouton.

Langlois, J. H., Gottfried, N. W., and Seay, B. (1973). The influence of sex of peer on the social behavior of preschool children. *Developmental Psychology*, **8**, 93–98.

Leventhal, G., and Anderson, D. (1970). Self-interest and maintenance of equity. *Journal of Personality and Social Psychology*, **15**, 57–62.

Lewis, M., Young, G., Brooks, J., and Michalson, L. (1975). The beginning of friendship. In M. Lewis and L. A. Rosenblum (Eds.), *Friendship and Peer Relations*. New York: Wiley.

Lippitt, R. (1941). Popularity among preschool children. *Child Development*, **12**, 305–332.

McCandless, B. R., Bilous, C. B., and Bennett, H. L. (1961), Peer popularity and dependence on adults in preschool-age socialization. *Child Development*, **32**, 511–518.

Maccoby, E. E., and Jacklin, C. N. (1975). *The Psychology of Sex Differences*. Stanford: Stanford University Press.

Meddock, T. D., Parsons, J. A., and Hill, K. T. (1971). Effects of an adult's presence and praise on young children's performance. *Journal of Experimental Child Psychology*, **12**, 197–211.

Mehrabian, A. (1971). Nonverbal betrayal of feeling. *Journal of Experimental Research in Personality*, **5**, 64–73.

Mehrabian, A., and Diamond, S. G. (1971). Seating arrangement and conversation. *Sociometry*, **34**, 281–289.

Omark, D. R., Omark, M., and Edelman, M. (1973). Dominance hierarchies in young children. Paper presented at the International Congress of Anthropological and Ethnological Sciences, Chicago.

Parten, M. B. (1933). Social play among preschool children. *Journal of Abnormal and Social Psychology*, **28**, 136–147.

Patterson, M. L. (1973a). Compensation in nonverbal immediacy behaviors: a review. *Sociometry*, **36**, 237–252.

Patterson, M. L. (1973b). Stability of nonverbal immediacy behaviors. *Journal of Experimental Social Psychology*, **9**, 97–109.

Patterson, M. L. (1976). An arousal model of interpersonal intimacy. *Psychological Review*, **83**, 235–245.

Patterson, M. L. (1977). Issues surrounding the arousal model of interpersonal intimacy. Paper presented at the APA Convention, San Francisco, August.

Patterson, G. R., Littman, R. A., and Bricker, W. (1967). Assertive behavior in children: a step towards a theory of aggression. *Monographs of the Society for Research in Child Development*, **32**, (Whole No. 113).

Patterson, M. L., Mullens, S., and Romano, J. (1971). Compensatory reactions to spatial intrusion. *Sociometry*, **34**, 114–126.

Pawlicki, R. E. (1972). The influence of contingent and noncontingent social reinforcement upon children in a simple operant task. *Child Development*, **43**, 1432–1438.

Pellegrini, R. J., and Emprey, J. (1970). Interpersonal spatial orientation in dyads. *Journal of Psychology*, **76**, 67–70.

Philp, A. J. (1940). Strangers and friends as competitors and co-operators. *Journal of Genetic Psychology*, **57**, 249–258.

Potashin, R. (1946). A sociometric study of children's friendships. *Sociometry*, **9**, 48–70.

Richer, J. M., and Nicoll, S. (1971). A playroom for autistic children, and its companion therapy project. *British Journal of Mental Subnormality*, **17**, 132–143.

Rivenbark, W. H. (1971). Self-disclosure among adolescents. *Psychological Reports*, **28**, 35–42.

Rothbart, M. K. (1976). Incongruity, problem-solving and laughter. In A. J. Chapman and H. C. Foot (Eds.), *Humour and Laughter: Theory, Research and Applications*. London: Wiley.

Russo, N. F. (1975). Eye contact, interpersonal distance and the equilibrium theory. *Journal of Personality and Social Psychology*, **31**, 497–502.

Savitsky, J. C., and Izard, C. E. (1970). Developmental changes in the use of emotion cues in a concept formation task. *Developmental Psychology*, **3**, 350–357.

Schaffer, H. R. (1974). Early social behaviour and the study of reciprocity. *Bulletin of the British Psychological Society*, **27**, 209–216.

Schaffer, H. R. (Ed.) (1977). *Studies in Mother–Infant Interaction*. London: Academic Press.

Schulz, R., and Barefoot, J. (1974). Non-verbal responses and affiliative conflict theory. *British Journal of Social and Clinical Psychology*, **13**, 237–243.

Schwartz, J. C. (1972). Effects of peer familiarity on the behavior of preschoolers in a novel situation. *Journal of Personality and Social Psychology*, **24**, 276–284.

Sears, R. R., Maccoby, E. E., and Levin, H. (1957). *Patterns of Child Rearing*. Evanston, Illinois: Row, Peterson.

Shapiro, B. Z. (1967). Dissolution of friendship ties in groups of children. *Dissertation Abstracts*, **27**, (10-A), 3517–3518.

Smith, J. R., Foot, H. C., and Chapman, A. J. (1977). Nonverbal communication among friends and strangers sharing humour. In A. J. Chapman and H. C. Foot (Eds.), *It's a Funny Thing, Humour*. Oxford: Pergamon Press.

Stephenson, G. M., Rutter, D. R., and Dore, S. R. (1972). Visual interaction and distance. *British Journal of Psychology*, **64**, 251–257.

Vinacke, W. E., and Gullickson, G. R. (1964). Age and sex differences in the formation of coalitions. *Child Development*, **35**, 1217–1231.

Wahler, R. G. (1967). Child–child interactions in free field settings: some experimental analyses. *Journal of Experimental Child Psychology*, **5**, 278–293.

Waldrop, M. F., and Halverson, C. F. (1975). Intensive and extensive peer behavior: longitudinal and cross-sectional analyses. *Child Development*, **46**, 19–26.

Walker, L. S., and Wright, P. H. (1976). Self-disclosure in friendship. *Perceptual and Motor Skills*, **42**, 735–742.

FRIENDSHIP CLIQUES

CHAPTER 11

The Natural History of Preadolescent Male Friendship Groups

GARY ALAN FINE

> The boy's reaction to his gang is neither more nor less reasonable than the reaction of a mother to her babe, the tribesman to his chief, or the lover to his sweetheart. (Puffer, 1912, p. 7).

Psychologists have recognized that preadolescence is something more than a way-station to puberty. The period is more significant than as a transition between two stages of sexual development; much of this emphasis focuses on the social components of the period, particularly socialization through peer influences (Hartup, 1978). Friendships characterize this period and may take priority over relations of kith and kin. Parent–peer cross-pressures frequently studied in adolescents (Brittain, 1963; Rosen, 1955) have their origins in this period, where preadolescents are beginning to realize that central issues will be received with a different concern and response by adults than by peers. Some, such as this 12-year-old girl, choose the latter to confide in:

> If I was in trouble, I think I would go to my friends first and see what they think. I don't know if I would go to my mom and dad first. (Konopka, 1976, p. 84).

While Hartup is probably correct that the outcome of peer interaction is general-ly concordant with adult–child interaction, the role of peer influence in this period should not be underestimated.

Examinations of these peer relationships have traditionally had one of two emphases: the importance of the single chum or the importance of the multi-member social group or gang. Is the child's cathexis directed to one individual or to a group? While there is little confrontation between the proponents of these two perspectives, they presuppose different research emphases, and predict different patterns of interaction. Will the preadolescent stay with one chum or will a group meet together maintaining a set of stable relationships. Waldrop and Halverson (1975) suggest that sex differences exist among child-ren's friendships. Girls' friendships tend to be intensive (oriented to chums), while boys tend to have extensive ties (such as gangs). Gruenberg and Krech (1959) suggest that this pattern will differ according to the friendship needs of the individual child, but this answer, though possibly correct, makes social behaviour idiosyncratic and less dependent on developmental regularities than some would admit.

Preadolescence as the chumship period

Perhaps the most influential exponent of the belief that the preadolescent child needs to find a close friend, a 'chum', of approximately the same age is Sullivan (1953). The establishment of this one-to-one relationship with a member of the same sex (in his case, male) characterizes the developmental task of this period. Sullivan rhapsodizes about the potential beneficial effects of this interaction:

> ... in the company of one's chum, one finds oneself more and more able to talk about things which one had learned, during the juvenile era, not to talk about. This relatively brief phase of preadolescence, if it is experienced, is probably rather fantastically valuable in salvaging one from the effects of unfortunate accidents up to then. (p. 227).

Sullivan suggests that this relationship is similar to the psychiatric definition of love. From this perspective it is the single relationship that is central, and the group has a rather peripheral position.

There is considerable evidence to support the importance of the chumship relation at this period. Cottle (1971) documents the tender relationship be-tween two 'disadvantaged' youths as they plan to rocket to the moon. Other cultures also provide evidence of the importance of close ties at this age. Cohen (1967) notes that among the Nigerian Kanuri tribe:

> During childhood the young person usually chose a young age-mate from amongst his siblings or cousins as his ... 'secrets man', the person who knows his most intimate thoughts, hopes and fears. (p. 48).

These chumship relationships are frequently long-lasting, even extending into adulthood, and they appear in some descriptions to exist outside of the context of the peer group (e.g. Hilger, 1952, describing the Arapahoe of central North America). Chumship bonds have been reported among the following North American Indian tribes: the Crow (Lowie, 1935), the Southern Ojibwa (Hilger, 1951), the Micmac (Wallis and Wallis, 1955), the Tübatulabal (Wheeler-Vogelin, 1938), and the Mam (Wagley, 1949). Jamaicans (Cohen, 1966) and Araucanians (Hilger, 1957) are supposed to manifest this behaviour as well. African tribes with this tight friendship pattern include the Hausa (Smith, 1965), the Wolof (Gamble, 1957), and the Tallensi (Fortes, 1949). Tribes in Oceana with chumship relationships include the Trukese (Gladwin and Sarason, 1953), the Trobriand Islanders (Malinowski, 1929), and the people of Manus (Mead, 1930). Clearly friendship bonds are found throughout the globe; that they are not reported for every society or culture region may be related to the lack of a sufficient sample of ethnographies and a lack of specificity among the writers as to the nature of the friendship bonds. It is, of course, reasonable that different regions or tribes maintain different patterns of children's social organization, as is true among adult groups, and more controlled cross-cultural analysis seems highly desirable. The evidence clearly indicates that the chumship pattern is not merely an artifact of European or American socialization, but seems to serve a generally felt human need for interpersonal closeness in the preadolescent period, a need which may be met through group interaction.

Preadolescence as the 'gang age'

Furfey (1926) termed the period of preadolescence the 'Gang Age' and the moniker is not without suitability. Preadolescents do spend time in relatively stable groups. Furfey suggests that preadolescents feel that: 'The really interesting thing is not what one does oneself but what the gang as a whole does. The gang's the thing!' (p. 131). Puffer (1912) states dramatically: 'Without doubt, there is a gang-forming instinct set deep within the soul of boyhood' (p. 25). Empirical evidence for the prevalence of children's groups is found in a retrospective study by Crane (1942). Crane asked Australian college students to recall whether they had been members of gangs during their primary school days. Eighty per cent of the male respondents and two-thirds of the female subjects responded affirmatively. A study by Wolman (1951) of Israeli school children found lower rates of current membership in groups or gangs. In his sample, 29 per cent belonged to a gang or informal neighbourhood group. Whether this difference is due to methodology of data collection, sampling, questions asked, national difference, or definition of gang or group is unclear. However, a substantial percentage of preadolescents do admit to belonging to a group of their peers, and, in admitting this, identify with the group at least to the extent of admitting membership. The largest 'census' of gangs is still Thrasher's (1963) magnum opus. He found that only 1.5 per cent (18 gangs) of the gangs studied were composed of 6- to 12-year-olds; however, 37.5 per cent (455 gangs) had members between 11 and 17 years of age. Unfortunately Thrasher's figures do not allow for an exact determination of the individual ages or the percentage of the preadolescent population involved in those gangs. Preadolescents may even be members of criminal gangs (e.g. Brown, 1965; Shaw, McKay and McDonald, 1938) and engage in illicit activities. The difference between a preadolescent group and a preadolescent gang is a fine one, complicated by related terms such as clique or club; despite different value overlays, they are essentially the same structural form: a group of children in frequent and intense interaction, generally outside direct adult supervision. Because these naturally occurring groups are outside adult control and sponsorship, they have not been observed much, particularly when compared with adolescent gangs in which adults can blend in more easily.

There is evidence that preadolescent groups occur cross-culturally, cutting as wide a global swath as chumship patterns. Han (1949) suggests that in Korea a boy of about 7 or 8 years old will find a group of friends his own age with whom he will go through life. In many societies these groups, as well as providing a social locus for leisure activities, also serve as nuclei for a work group. Preadolescent and early adolescence male groups are used for herding cattle and for taking horses out to pasture (e.g. Skrefsrud, 1942, among the Santal of Eastern India; Weltfish, 1965, describing the Pawnee of the American plains; Wilson, 1951, for the Ngonde of East Africa). As with chumship relationships these cliques are frequently said to last into adult life (Barnett, 1970, describing the Hokkien on Taiwan; Hunt, 1962, among the Tzeltal of Southern Mexico; Schapera, 1930, among the Hottentots of Southern Africa; Spiro, 1949, among the Woleasians of Micronesia). Elwin (1947) in discussing the Gond of India suggests that the communal and organized character of their society makes individual friendships rare. It is by no means definitively proven that social structure or cultural patterning generally have the determinative effect that Elwin suggests, but his suggestion is worth further examination. Research on the relationship between social organization and interpersonal orientation would have considerable value in elucidating this issue.

In Western cultures both the chumship model and the gang model of preadolescence have validity. Both relate to important aspects of preadolescent social development. The child must learn trust and sensitivity to another person (the chum) and must also learn appropriate behaviour and social poise within a collectivity (the gang). Both provide supportive settings in which these important aspects of socialization can be mastered, and in which fear of failure is significantly reduced, though not eliminated entirely.

Issues of analysis

One point deserves early and emphatic mention to avoid charges of overgeneralization. For several reasons we restrict our discussion to male friends in this chapter. This is not because we feel that male friendships (be they chums or groups) are necessarily more frequent (though there is some evidence for this proposition) or more interesting, but from a relative paucity of observational data on females. Most studies in this area, like so many others in the social sciences, focus on males; my own research is no exception to this, and of course, retrospectively, I have only my own preadolescent relationships to generalize from. One should be mindful that males and females may differ in their leisure patterns (Lever, 1976) and relationships (Waldrop and Halverson, 1975), but this issue deserves special treatment, not feasible in this chapter. Rather than treating one group in depth and with confidence, and the other in an inadequate and superficial fashion, it seems preferable to refrain from generalizing to girls. Boys, it is said, will be boys; what girls are is an issue for others.

A second issue is the age limits placed upon preadolescence. The debate on which years adequately describe this period has had a long history, yet it has not been resolved to general satisfaction. For those who see preadolescence as a transition period, its limits are circumscribed by the more exciting periods that surround it—the resolution of the Oedipal Crisis and the onset of puberty. This psychiatric-biological approach generally sets the age limits of this period younger than those who examine the period in its own right or who use a structural end-point, such as the beginning of high school. Psychiatrists and biologists further complicate the issue by suggesting that one should define the period on an individual basis, a view which would seem to de-emphasize the peculiarly social elements of this stage. The most generally accepted definition of the period termed preadolescence seems to focus on 9- to 12-year-olds (Kohen-Raz, 1971), and this is the period that we focus on in this article. It seems advisable to follow a conservative approach rather than include all that might feasibly be termed youthful behaviour.

Two major data sources comprise the basis of this chapter in addition to standard psychological and sociological investigations. First, we have drawn heavily from anthropological investigations, using source material available in the Human Relations Area Files and other anthropological writings. To understand the natural history of friendship requires that we use sources that emphasize field observation, and that means that we must accept descriptive snippets included in general ethnologies. While some anthropologists have focused upon childhood (Hilger, 1952; Mead, 1930; Whiting and Whiting, 1975), even these studies do not focus upon the friendship relation, a fact which makes the investigative process time-consuming. However, the evidence gathered may be sufficient to allow for statements which have some measure of cross-cultural validity.

The second source from which natural data about friendships are gathered is a 3-year participant observation study of preadolescent males (described in Fine and Glassner, 1979). Over the course of the 3 years, Little League baseball leagues in four American communities have been examined: (1) Beanville, an upper-middle class professional suburb of Boston, Massachusetts; (2) Hopewell, an ex-urban township outside of the Providence, Rhode Island metropolitan area—consisting of a string of small towns, beach front land, farms and a campus of the state university; (3) Bolton Park, an upper-middle class professional suburb of St Paul, Minnesota, similar to Beanville except for geographical area, and (4) Sanford Heights, a middle- to lower-middle class suburb of Minneapolis, Minnesota, comprised of a large number of modern mass-produced homes. A research colleague, Harold Pontiff, conducted a parallel investigation of a Little League baseball programme in an urban, upper-middle class area of St Paul, Maple Bluff. The Little League baseball organization was founded in the United States in 1939 for the purpose of allowing boys (aged 9–12 years old) to play organized baseball under adult supervision. The organization has grown enormously to become international, and now comprises over 600 000 players in about 5 000 leagues. Although the programme was designed for males, and for a long time excluded girls from registering, the programme now admits both boys and girls as a result of court-suits, although only 10 girls played in the five leagues in the period under examination. In order to focus our observation, two teams were chosen in each league to be studied intensively, so we have detailed records of the behaviour of players on 10 teams (12–15 players per team), less detailed records of 32 other teams, and information on scores of preadolescents who were not involved in the baseball programme at all. While we can not claim that our sample is wholly representative of American children, it does cover a substantial range of environments. Like the Little League organization itself, the middle-class sample has fewer rural children, urban children, and poor children than would be expected by chance. Thus, attempts to generalize to those groups must be handled with some caution.

In this chapter we first examine some of the content of children's friendship activities, and next discuss a general conceptualization of friendship, and particularly preadolescent friendship, as serving as a micro-culture for its members. We then present a general model for the development and maintenance of friendship ties emphasizing the particular features of the preadolescent period, and conclude with a discussion of the necessary flexibility of the concept of friendship to place it in the interactional context in which it naturally occurs.

CONTENT OF PREADOLESCENT FRIENDSHIPS

Redl (1966) spoke a profound truth about preadolescence in suggesting that it is 'the phase when the nicest children begin to behave in the most awful way' (p. 395). He suggested that two explanations apply to the change in preadolescent behaviour patterns: first, a loosening and restructuring of childhood behaviour patterns; and, second, an orientation to and need for group attachment and stimulation (see also Kohen-Raz, 1971, p. 17). Along with these developmental changes (both individual and social) occurs new conversational and behavioural content. Those who examine friendship from the standpoint of sociometry tend to conceptualize the tie as a social bond without content. While this has reaped a rich research harvest, it has also missed much of what is distinctive about natural occurring friendships.

While we cannot describe all of the behaviours that occur within the context of preadolescent friendships, several basic themes deserve comment in that they represent a marked change from the earlier childhood periods. For this discussion we use a loose definition of friendship, out of necessity more than deliberate strategy, since most observations of children's play have been of groupings of preadolescents more than of distinct chumship pairs or identifiable groups or gangs. However, in certain of these observational studies the groupings examined were defined as groups by the participants (Cikler, 1967; Helanko, 1969) or by adults (Sherif, Harvey, White, Hood and Sherif, 1961; Sherif and Sherif, 1953). Children's friends extend beyond the chumship pair and often beyond the gang, and one would be remiss in omitting these weaker friendship ties from the analysis.

Three types of friendship content seem particularly salient during this period: (1) work-related activity, or activity designed to socialize the child into an adult or adolescent role; (2) the emergence of interest in talk about sex and sexuality; and (3) a wide range of aggressive behaviour—towards peers, adults and objects. This discussion inevitably ignores much childhood behaviour—for example, the more 'childish' play that has been well categorized by folklorists (e.g. Newell, 1963—originally published 1883; Opie and Opie, 1959; Sutton-Smith and Rosenberg, 1961), which seems less distinctively preadolescent.

Work and socialization

It is at the preadolescent period that adults begin to feel that their offspring can and should be trusted with work-related tasks. Perhaps as a function of school in Western social structure, the work related tasks of preadolescents are relatively less time-consuming than in other cultures; there is also the sentiment that the work of childhood is play. Preadolescents, however, are often asked to help with the chores of the community where they live: helping to farm (e.g. Han, 1949) or herd animals (e.g. Skrefsrud, 1942; Wilson, 1936). Younger children are not to be trusted with such responsibilities, or, to the extent that they are, they work only under the direct supervision of adults, and not in self-directed and self-selected groups.

In cultures where work is not a direct part of the activity of friendship groups, friends may play at adult work. It is reported that Mongolian children pretend to go on long caravans, steal sheep and cattle, build shelters, and catch wild horses (Maiskii, 1921). Among the Iroquois of eastern North America boys between 8 and 11 years old play together at hunting and war. They form large groups and wander in the forest for days at a time, often without adults. They sleep in the open, and eat wild roots and berries and whatever small animals they can catch (Quain, 1937). Western society generally cuts preadolescents off from direct adult activities because of the specialized tools necessary for proper role performance. However, boys do enact some adult behaviour in the 'professionalization' of preadolescent sports. So, for example, Little Leaguers in Maple Bluff put charcoal around their eyes to imitate professional ballplayers, and are meticulous in the details of their uniforms. The interest that preadolescents in America have in automobiles (and motor-cycles) is probably a reflection of their desire for adult mastery. Erikson (1963) terms preadolescence as the stage in which the child must learn the 'technological ethos' of his culture, and an interest in gadgets and scientific technology is characteristic of the period. It is appropriate that Cottle (1971) should choose a proposed lunar venture by two preadolescents as symptomatic of the stresses and needs of this period. Imagining oneself as an adult, and performing this role authentically, has appeal for this age group, whether the adult role is technological or athletic.

Sexual topics

The preadolescent period is characterized by an extensive discussion of sex, and some action, though by no means as much as the talk would imply. This is not merely a function of the sexualization of American society (Petras, 1973) but seems to describe other cultures as well (e.g. Gorer, 1938, about the Lepcha of the Himalayas; Steward, Manners, Wolf, Seda, Mintz and Scheele, 1956, about the Puerto Ricans). However, our most extensive data on this phenomenon are Anglo-American.

Gagnon (1972) suggests that the transition between childhood and adolescence is linked to an awakening of sexual impulses. By 12 years old, according to the Kinsey data, 21 per cent of males have masturbated; by 14 years old 72 per cent have done so (Kinsey, Pomeroy and Martin, 1948, p. 500); however, even more significant than actual sexual behaviour (often first occurring in mutual masturbation groups composed of tightly bonded peers (Gagnon, 1972; cf. Pepitone, 1975)) is sexual talk which sometimes seems to dominate the private world of preadolescent males. Gesell, Ilg and Ames (1956) note that: 'Twelve-year-old boys often have bull sessions to discuss matters rather freely, at least as far as the pooled knowledge of the group will permit' (p. 115). On the basis of the observations and tape recordings collected by preadolescent 'assistants' it is clear that these sessions are filled with loud (almost hysterical) giggly laughter, insults, and bravado. These behaviours testify to the anxiety-producing significance of these topics (see also Oxreider, 1976, and Ransohoff, 1975 for analyses of girls' groups). In these situations, the boy opens himself to others, and makes himself vulnerable to attacks. Thus, for direct sexual admissions it is essential that the participants have close friendship relationships with each other.

There is another layer of sexual talk that characterizes preadolescents, which is less directly tied to the presence of close friends. This refers to the 'naughty talk' that often characterizes preadolescent discussions (Knapp and Knapp, 1976). Stone and Church (1968) note: 'boys ... learn to leer before they have learned to giggle' (p. 369). Preadolescents' 'slanguage' is characterized by these sexual references in private; in public, preadolescents have sufficient need for impression management to refrain from their use. In my research in Sanford Heights, for example, a wide range of terms had homosexual or heterosexual connotations to these 'children': 'bitehead', 'blow job', 'eat me out', 'fuckhead', 'finger bang', 'header', 'lick me', 'pusslick', 'prostie', 'scum', 'suck my willy', 'snatchbite', or 'woman bleeder' to name a few of the sexual-based terms used in a community of preadolescents over a 4-month period in the presence of a (trusted) adult. Another set of more esoteric terms (e.g. 'prang', 'Jolly Wally') have the same basic sexual-aggressive meanings, which, because they were unknown to adults, could be used in public. The construct of a latency period does not do justice to the interests of preadolescent boys; Erikson's (1963) view of preadolescence as the calm before the storm of puberty neglects the intensity of interaction among acquaintances. Whether this behaviour serves the function of coping with the child's world (Knapp and Knapp, 1976) or provides a release for sexual tension produced by social pressures and biological developments is not entirely clear. What is apparent is that one will be unable to explain preadolescent male friendship without realizing that sexual material is of great significance to friends' interaction.

Aggression

It is difficult to separate the sexual talk of preadolescents from their aggressive talk and behaviour, because the sexual imagery is frequently aggressive, with a patina of homosexual symbolism. This aggression characterizes much of preadolescent interaction, and requires acclimatization by adults, who must realize that it does not necessarily indicate dislike. Whiting and Whiting (1975) indicate that aggressive behaviour by children in their observational study of six cultures is quite prevalent, comprising 24 per cent of all behaviour to peers. The sexual words given above are used not in erotic situations, but in aggressive or mock-aggressive ones. Boys feel perfectly capable of wishing each other dead ('drop dead', 'I hope you die') when they wish to express disapproval; charges of 'homosexuality' are made to close friends ('Stew's a part-time faggot' or 'Baskins, you fem, you better run good'). Because of the flexibility in friendships these aggressive remarks can be accepted by the target with equanimity—and often with a counter-insult. Preadolescents are proficient at determining the intent of an insult from tone of voice, paralinguistic cues, and situational definition. In a friendship relation insults do not imply hatred; the social implications of being a 'faggot' are thus situationally defined. Serious frustrations in a significant area (such as sports) may lead to interpersonal aggression and thus active hostility and group disintegration (Cikler, 1967). However, more frequently these aggressive behaviours are taken as the temporary interactional perturbations that they are, and may be functional in teaching the child the appropriate use of aggression (Hartup, 1978).

Preadolescent aggression is not always directed within the group; the group may act jointly or in unison against outsiders. The two main objects of this aggression for preadolescent boys are girls of their acquaintance (or boys considered to be 'girls') and anonymous adults, although known adults are rarely attacked directly (Whiting and Whiting, 1975, p. 157). Sometimes preadolescent aggression can be quite striking. I was surprised during my observation in Beanville to hear a group of friends discussing whether rape was really wrong. While the session was filled with wild laughter, the aggressive content (and the sexual content) indicated that on an emotional level the session was not humorous.

Children's pranks also provide evidence of interpersonal aggression. Boys in both Hopewell and Sanford Heights throw eggs at houses, an activity appropriately termed 'egging'. This is similar to a prank of Brahman children, who use a holiday for the same basic end. Brahmans consider it unlucky to catch sight of the moon on the fourth day of one particular month. If the moon is seen one must throw stones at one's neighbour's home to avoid bad luck. 'Children, to be on the safe side, go and throw stones at their neighbour's house whether they have seen the moon or not, for it is too good a chance of stone-throwing to be wasted!' (Stevenson, 1920, p. 332). From my observation and discussions with dozens of children, pranks seem always to be performed with friends—never alone. The playing of a prank requires the social support provided by friends. As part of the research in Sanford Heights 48 of the 50 12-year-olds in the baseball league responded to a series of questions about cultural items, all of which were known to at least some members of the Sanford Heights preadolescent community. Four of these items dealt with aggressive pranks: (1) egging a house; (2) making a funny phone-call (Dressler, 1973; Knapp and Knapp, 1976); (3) playing the Polish Rope Trick, a prank which consists of two boys holding an imaginary rope across a roadway at dusk, hoping to stop cars; and (4) playing Ding Dong Ditch—ringing a doorbell and running away (see Opie and Opie, 1959). The percentages of boys who had performed these pranks were 40 per cent, 52 per cent, 19 per cent and 56 per cent respectively. As part of this interview, players were asked *with whom* they performed these pranks. Combining all pranks for this analysis, 70 partners who played Little League baseball were named (counting a boy only once for each namer even if they performed several pranks together). Each player was also asked whether every other 12-year-old Little Leaguer was one of the boy's five best friends in the League, a close friend, a friend, disliked, or not disliked and not a friend. Of the sample of 70 prank partners, 60 per cent were among the namer's five best friends in the League, an additional 29 per cent were close friends of the namer, but not among the five closest friends, and 9 per cent more were friends. Only one boy was not a friend and another partner was disliked. These last two cases came from the same namer who changed friends during the middle of the season and these were *former* friends. These figures compare with 10 per cent of all boys in the sample who can be named as best friends in the league (assuming boys limit their choices to other 12-year-olds; if they are not limited in this way the expected percentage falls to 5 per cent). In the entire sample, 18 per cent are named as close friends, another 31 per cent are considered friends, 2 per cent are disliked, and 49 per cent are neither friends nor disliked. Friendship is clearly the setting in which aggressive behaviour to outsiders can and does occur. The friendship tie provides the support necessary for breaking the normative rules of adult society, a cross-cultural phenomenon characteristic of preadolescents.

FRIENDSHIP AS A CULTURAL INSTITUTION

Having discussed content that seems to be particularly characteristic of pre-adolescent friendships, it is appropriate to consider the nature of friendship, and to present an approach to friendship that allows for the incorporation of content as an integral part of the friendship relationship, and allows for the description of how this relates to the network of friendship relations in a preadolescent population.

Suttles (1970) speaks of friendship as being a social institution. It is a tie which provides certain needs for its members over a period of time, and is relatively (though not completely) stable. Suttles notes that friendship seems to have three main characteristics: (1) it is a generalized relationship; (2) it is voluntaristic—extending beyond prescribed institutional or organizational affiliations; and (3) it is subject to interpersonal negotiation by its parties to an extent which is unusual in other social relations. Suttles points out that friendships have a private culture with its own internal order and local content.

While the prototype of this private culture is the friendship dyad, one can speak of the friendship group as having a private culture. The case could be argued that each of the dyadic relations in the group has a variant culture, and these variants combine to form the group culture. Culture can be effectively analysed as being located and created within small groups of members in effective interaction. This form of localized culture is termed the 'idioculture' of a group, defined as 'a system of knowledge, beliefs, behaviors and customs, particular to an interacting group, to which members can refer and employ as the basis of further interaction' (Fine, 1979, p. 6). This group culture can be seen as describing the content of relations among a large variety of groups: families, clubs, gangs, and work groups. However, group culture is particularly noticeable when relationships are intense (in friendships rather than friendly relations (Kurth, 1970)) and when relationships are multivalent. A social relationship does not and cannot exist in an interactional vacuum. Members are continually engaged in constructing a meaningful reality and a history (McBride, 1975) that becomes indicative of the unity of the group, their bondedness, and their intimacy in sharing (or creating) these cultural details.

Nash (1973) has indicated that cliques of British youth can be distinguished by the nature and content of their interaction; and this content relates to their position within the school environment. Elwin (1947) notes that Indian boys develop secret languages to prevent outsiders from learning about their conversations. Boys at this age also create their own rules for leisure activities (Piaget, 1962). Cultural symbols can have the effect of providing the group with a unity that might have been absent otherwise. Indeed, friendship seems to motivate culture creation which in turn furthers friendship.

One must extend the analysis and inquire about how the specifics of the friendship culture become created. Shared fantasy can be quite extensive (Cottle, 1971; Giallombardo, 1974) but no rationale has been given for the particular form of these cultural elements in the friendship relationship.

Five determinants of the cultural elements seem particularly critical in this process, and each relates to the nature of the friendship relationship: the culture elements must be: (1) known; (2) usable; (3) functional; (4) appropriate to the group's status system; and (5) triggered by a specific event. First, for an item to be part of the friendship idioculture, it is necessary that at least one member be acquainted either with the cultural element or with the constituent features of which the cultural element is formed (creativity being the novel combination of previously known elements). The criterion of being *known* seems particularly important during the preadolescent period, as children are discovering much of interest about the world they live in, particularly in terms of the topic areas described above: socialization/adult roles, sex and aggression. When salient information is learned by a preadolescent, he quickly informs his intimates. Thus, in Sanford Heights, when one boy learned the anatomical term 'scrotum' from an older acquaintance, his friends were quickly educated; thus 'suck my scrotum' was made synonymous with the over-used 'suck my balls' in that friendship group, and other conversation gambits employing this new piece of specialized knowledge could be heard.

Information is readily spread in friendship groups as a function of classroom learning, learning from older (and wiser) associates, and media access. Sexual topics spread rapidly from one curricular generation to the next curricular generation. An example is provided by the word 'zoid', defined by its orginator as referring to a boy who is a 'loser' or has a poor reputation and is not a member of any group (Field notes, Sanford Heights, 5 July 1977). This word was created by a grade xii (18-year-old) boy in Sanford Heights and known to a group of his baseball friends. The word subsequently was learned and accepted by the originator's brother, and the brother (15-year-old), in grade ix, spread 'zoid' to his friends. One of this boy's friends had a brother playing Little League baseball (a 12-year-old in grade vi). This boy learned 'zoid' and used it in conversation with *his* friends. When we interviewed the 48 12-year-olds after the season, 11 others claimed that they had heard the term. Ten of these boys (91 per cent) were friends of this boy (according to his ratings). These 10 boys correspond to 53 per cent of the boys in the sample he considered to be his friends. Thus, the spread of 'zoid' among the Little Leaguers seems localized to segments of this boy's friendship network.

A second determinant of group culture is that the item be *usable* in group interaction, not tabooed or inappropriate. Since friendship is characterized by considerable intimacy, the range of allowable cultural content within this bond may be greater than that found in relationships which are less personal. Thus, the culture content of friendship-based idiocultures may be significantly more extensive than that found in other relationships.

This is particularly notable among preadolescent friendships, which are characterized by the selective loosening of certain cultural taboos and the selective tightening of others (as a function of knowledge and socialization). Preadolescents are likely to talk about topics laden with sexual and aggressive implications. These, however, will only be discussed in certain settings; preadolescents can be very proper, and even prudish in situations which they deem inappropriate for the topic, such as in the presence of adults. In Beanville, I was allowed to join several dirty-joke sessions; in these cases the participants watched for adults and changed the subject abruptly when an adult approached. This feature of friendship cultures can help explain the secret languages (Berkovits, 1970) developed by children (similar in function to adults speaking in foreign tongues or spelling words in front of children). These secret languages are found cross-culturally; for example, among Malay children, who employ 'backslang', based on transposed and inserted syllables, to keep their private talk private in front of adults or uninitiated peers (Evans, 1923).

A third element affecting the content of a group culture is the needs of the members of the relationship: that is, whether the cultural element will be *functional*. Here too, the culture found in friendships may differ substantially from that found in groups without strong affective ties, such as work groups or professional alliances. Preadolescent friendship culture in particular can be analysed from this perspective, because of the important psychological role of friendship during this period. The central aspect of friendship is not the spatial co-presence of two (or more) individuals, but the affective bonds that flow from companionship—affective bonds that derive from and are expressed in the content of interaction. Sullivan (1953) indicates the value of the chumship period in the creation of a joint mythology based upon shared fantasy:

> ... in this intimate interchange in preadolescence—some preadolescents even have mutual daydreams, spend hours and hours carrying on a sort of spontaneous mythology in which both participate—in this new necessity for thinking of the other fellow as right and for being thought of as right by the other fellow, much of this uncertainty as to the real worth of the personality, and many self-deceptive skills at deceiving others which exist in the juvenile era, may be rectified by the improving communication of the chums and, to a much lesser extent but nonetheless valuably, by confirmatory relations in the collaboration developed in the gang. (p. 251).

Stone and Church in describing the potency of children's culture argue that valuable lessons are learned within this cultural setting:

> The school-age child spends as much of his time as possible in the company of his peers, from whom he learns at firsthand about social structures, about in-groups and out-groups, about leadership and followership, about justice and injustice, about loyalties and heroes and ideals. (p. 364).

Sometimes the friendship culture may promote an escape from an undesirable present to a more desirable future (Cottle, 1971) or past (as when boys play knights or cowboys). Other times the needs served may be directly social, including support that boys receive from others when they enter a friendship pact. For example, six Hopewell grade vi boys formed the Hell's Angels, a friendship group based upon mutual support in fights with other boys and in dealings with girls. Their friendship culture was designed to support these ends, and they frequently recalled events which bolstered their collective social image. Because these individuals, as well as being unified were also high status (and physically adept), others accepted their dominance, and unlike many preadolescents with budding romantic interests these boys were teased rather little—because the consequences were obvious and painful. Their culture provided the basis for the continuation of the group and simultaneously provided support for its membership.

A fourth determinant of preadolescent friendship culture, and of group cultures generally, is the *appropriateness* of the culture. Does the content of the culture support the group's social (or sociometric) structure? Culture items will only be incorporated into the friendship structure of a group when that incorporation is supportive of the interpersonal network and power relations in the group.

This seems particularly relevant to preadolescence, a period in which there is a considerable range between boys who are popular and those who are outcasts or misfits, and often are treated with considerable cruelty (Knapp and Knapp, 1976). A low status boy may be subject to contradictory abuse, like the Sanford

Heights boy who was simultaneously accused of being a crybaby and of going out with a girl 2 years older than he.

The friendship culture is based upon the views of those in the group who rank highest in prestige (the chumship relation is a special case—an equal status bond). Among the Ngonde the friendship group (the basis of future age-villages) is highly structured and with the structure comes cultural authority. A tribesman states:

> When we herd cows as boys ... there is always one who is obeyed by his fellows whatever he says. No one chooses him, he gains his leadership and prestige by bodily strength. For always when we are all boys together among the cows, we vie with one another and dispute about going to turn back straying cattle or about fetching fire to cook the food we have brought with us. And so we start fighting until one of us beats all his fellows completely and so becomes the leader. And then it is he who sends others to turn back straying cattle, to fetch fire and to collect firewood. And he is greatly respected. He settles quarrels too ... This is always happening and then it is the part of the one who is leader to set those two on to fight. (Wilson, 1936, p. 270).

The leader sets the norms for the group, which are accepted because of his authority. These norms generally support his authority, such as a trial by strength in a group in which the leader is the strongest. Groups are most likely to accept a suggestion when made by the leader.

> Crane [the most popular boy in one of the Sherifs' camp groups] did not make all the suggestions for his group, but his approval was usually necessary for a suggestion to carry. The way in which his influence was exerted can be seen in a summary of the group's reaction to receiving ten dollars to spend as they pleased. Carlson (... centre of Bull Dog sociogram) first suggested improving the latrine. He was shouted down. Crane suggested wood for shelves. This suggestion received polite but unenthusiastic approval. Another boy suggested that orange boxes would do for this purpose. ... Bromley, one of the lowest-status members, then suggested a basket of fresh fruit. Crane endorsed this suggestion and then the others enthusiastically agreed. Lowe, of lower status, suggested blue hats. 'Yeah,' Crane said, 'and let's get some letters—B—to put on them'. This proposal was adopted. (Sherif and Sherif, 1953, p. 253).

This pattern has been repeated frequently in my observations of preadolescents. The high-status boy's opinion is at this stage generally sufficient to alter group opinion and to establish cultural content for the group. This is dramatically indicated in the case of preadolescent slang. Those words which become used are those which have been 'invented' or endorsed by the most popular boys.

> Several players tell me that most of the slang words that they use (that adults do not use) are made up by Bill; and that Chris Winfield makes up some. Jason Fowell tells me that the reason kids accept the words that Chris makes up is that: 'He's popular; a lot of kids listen to him'. From my observation Chris's popularity is evident, and I am aware of several words which can be traced to both him and Bill. (Field notes, Sanford Heights 7 May 1977).

Significantly, we find that Bill is the most popular boy in the league (on the basis of the midseason sociometric ratings) and Chris is the fifth best liked boy in the league (of 90 boys). Clearly the popularity of these two boys contributes to their role in the Sanford Heights preadolescent culture.

The final criterion relating to the culture of friendship is situational. For a cultural item to be incorporated in a friendship it must be *triggered* in the interaction. There needs to be some triggering event that provides a stimulus for the cultural response—a response which becomes traditional by being known, usable, functional, and appropriate for the group's status hierarchy.

These triggering events can take many forms, depending on the physical and social environment. Thus, a new haircut frequently spawns nicknames ('peach fuzz,' 'Buzz Conroy') or a physical error may produce a recurring teasing sequence (one boy being considered 'mental' after losing his temper). The increasing age segregation found in contemporary American life (Conger, 1972) affects the culture of the preadolescent group by making it more sub-cultural (Speier, 1973) and less similar to adult culture and values. Every group will, as a result of its proximate environment, create its own culture—a private culture—which differentiates it from other groups.

Network of friendship cultures

Having argued that friends share a common culture, albeit a variant culture of the larger society, it is necessary to explore how it is a variant of cultures shared by others. The private culture of friends while idiosyncratic to some degree, with its own lore based on its own history (significant triggering events), is also characteristic of a more general body of traditions. Several researchers (Elkin and Handel, 1972; Glassner, 1976; Goodman, 1970; Speier, 1973) have spoken of a children's culture: a set of traditions that are associated with childhood. This culture is known in its broad outline to preadolescents across the society being studied.

An explanation for this phenomenon is readily apparent in that children have a large number of 'friends' at any time and many more across a period of years. The private friendship culture that any one boy participates in with a friend will be duplicated with his other friends during this period; while each friendship is unique, it also conforms to a general pattern of friendship. The individual friendship interlocks with other friendships through boys who are members of several friendships and who have the influence and/or leader-ship to transfer information between groups or to get the groups to interact with each other (Sullivan, 1953, pp. 249–250). The fact that individuals have several friendships simultaneously implies that the idiocultures of these groups will be similar. There are only so many pranks, insults, teases and jokes that are in circulation at any one time. This explains the uniformity of a culture of child-hood within an area which is characterized by close interaction (a dense network of relationships according to Barnes, 1969).

However, children's culture is also similar across substantial areas, such as nation states (Knapp and Knapp, 1976; Opie and Opie, 1959). How can the similarity of preadolescent cultures be explained among children who do not regularly interact with each other? The mass media are obviously of great significance for the diffusion of certain types of cultural items to preadolescents. However, the media are controlled and sponsored by adults, and for this reason only a fraction of children's culture can be spread by this means. Without disputing its importance in some areas, the focus here is on interpersonal diffusion. Granovetter (1973) has pointed to an important, though relatively neglected, type of social relationship, that of the 'weak tie' or 'linkage-tie': that is, a personal tie between individuals who do not regularly interact. In considering the natural history of friendship these weak ties seem of more than anecdotal interest. Boys' friendships can span many miles, particularly when we consider those friendships which are not of the intense 'best friend' or 'chum' type, but rather are acquaintances to whom a boy feels positively (and thus is liable to consider as 'friends'). The practice of having pen pals is an example of a friendship tie over great distances (the greater the distance, the more exotic the relationship) in which interaction is totally absent, and in which the purpose of the tie is the exchange of information not shared by the other party. Once that information is transmitted across a geographical area, it can then be spread through the local communication channels, which are highly correlated with friendship. Pen pals are not the only distant friendship ties that a preadolescent may have: 'distant' cousins are one well known example in our mobile environment. Children learn about candies being test-marketed in other areas of the country by their cross-continental ties, and in some cases the contacts even provide the physical product (Fine, 1978); these network strands also provide a boon for beer-can collectors, whose collection may span areas beyond their ken.

Perhaps the best example of culture transmission from area to area is that of the mobile child who by his presence and past knowledge brings a rich harvest of cultural knowledge from his native area to his new locale. The points of contact in both communities will be the child's friends. The circumstance that Western societies are mobile (and thus children are mobile in these societies) has implications for the homogeneity of children's culture and this has implications for the activities and talk that children produce when they are with friends.

Social networks have traditionally been important for those examining the sociometric structure of children's relationships; however, these social networks are equally important for those attempting to understand the content of these relationships, and the comprehension and differences in behaviour both within a community (among friendship clusters) and across communities (in linkage friendship ties). Thus, children develop a subculture, and because many of the subcultural topics are not discussed with adults (for tactical reasons), it is a culture known only by children.

THE NATURAL DEVELOPMENT OF FRIENDSHIP

Researchers often abstract the components of friendship from the developmental dynamics of the process. Thus, researchers find that chronological age is associated with friendship (Furfey, 1927), or that geographical propinquity is (Gallagher, 1958), or that similar social class is (Neugarten, 1946), or that cognitive similarity is (Duck, 1973). However, these findings only point in valuable directions. They do not in themselves explain much about the *dynamics* of the friendship relation, because they do not attempt to explain behaviours: (1) on the interactional level (particularly in terms of the structure of interaction); and (2) in terms of the meaning of the friendship relation. It is on these two elements that the present discussion of the development of friendship ties now focuses.

The development of a friendship is based upon three factors. If any one of them is missing or minimal, the friendship will not develop or, if previously developed, may be redefined as an acquaintanceship, former friendship, or even, possibly, a relation of enmity. First, the potential friends must have the opportunity to spend time with each other, in order to get to know each other. This is primary to the establishment of a relationship and it can be described in terms of *structural constraints*. Second, once contact occurs some *individual propensity* for friendship must be present to allow a relationship to develop. It is here that personality, intelligence, race, religion, and ethnicity are directly relevant; these factors are of course indirectly relevant as structural constraints if they decrease the likelihood of contact. The third consideration relates to the *interaction results*: are the activities engaged in rewarding, satisfying, functional and need-fulfilling? Friendships that produce satisfying experiences are likely to continue. Those that do not, disappear. First, the individuals must meet, then they must perceive each other as potential friends, and finally the friendship must be built on satisfying experiences. This process is of course comparable to the formation and continuation of intimate relations generally (cf. Levinger and Snoek, 1972).

For a friendship to exist, all three of these factors, which are interrelated and affect each other, must *continue* to be present. The absence or rapid change in even one of these three is likely to produce dramatic shift in the quality of the bond.

Structural constraints

As noted, the first requirement of a potential friendship is that there be contact. Thus, many friendship pairs that are otherwise possible die unborn because the potential friends do not have the opportunity to meet. Three features seem particularly salient in defining the constraints within which the preadolescent friendship must develop: geographical proximity, activity sharing, and adult (parental) prerogatives.

Geography

The preadolescent boy is tied to his neighbourhood; indeed one geographer has argued that one can define a neighbourhood by the activity patterns of the 11-year-old boy (Bowden, 1972). Furfey (1927) has found, not unreasonably, that 89 per cent of 62 pairs of mutual chums lived in the same neighbourhood. Physical proximity is an excellent predictor of friendship. Two reasons can be suggested for this phenomenon: first, boys who live close together have similar backgrounds, experiences, and a similar known culture; second, and probably more important in practical terms, neighbours have more opportunities for interaction. They see each other more often, have more mutual friends, and have more opportunities for acquaintanceship than they do with boys who live outside of the neighbourhood. Because children tend to remain in their own neighbourhood, and tend to 'hang out' in particular locales, the potential for the development of friendship within the neighbourhood is continually present.

Activities

In addition to neighbourhood interaction, children in Western societies have a wide range of activities in which to participate. This leads them to have contact with children who live outside their neighbourhood. Schools which draw students from a city, or even a metropolitan area (as in the case of private day schools), or globally (as in the case of exclusive boarding schools) indicate the importance of contact in channelling friendship.

Extra-curricular activities also provide a setting in which friendships can occur, including sports teams, group lessons, church activities, and summer camps. Some of these may occur over limited time periods but for the time that the contact exists the tie may be quite intense. The institution of pen pals provides a case of intense 'communication' (though not precisely *interaction*) producing a friendship tie.

Parental constraints

Parental strictures may affect preadolescent friendship patterns, as parents may consider some potential companions as being inappropriate friends, and will encourage or coerce their offspring to choose other associates. This pheno-menon is not only familiar to modern class-conscious states, but to other status conscious societies as well (e.g. Cohen, 1966, describing the Jamaican commu-nity of Rocky Roads; Weltfish, 1965, among the Pawnee Indians). These parental restrictions may occur after the beginning of the relationship, and would in this case be a factor more relevant to the continuation of a relation-ship than to its beginning. However, parents may designate certain groups as off-limits a priori, and this restriction may be accepted by their offspring.

Individual propensities

If all that was necessary were some kind of contact to produce friendship, then children would find themselves with hundreds of friends. This, however, does not occur. The preadolescent is discriminating in terms of his friends. Friendships do not originate in the opening moments of acquaintance: that period is for sizing each other up and determining the likelihood of success of continued interaction. At the beginning of a relationship, factors like race, religion, class, or abilities prove particularly salient. A central explanation for the homogeneity of friendship is the desire for a set of common interests and experiences (e.g. Buechler and Buechler, 1971); a similar latent culture facilitates the development of a manifest friendship culture. By preadolescence, differences in culture stemming from demography and personality can influence the choice of friends, as sociometric studies have indicated. These differences can affect the natural history of a relationship at any point, but are probably most effective as filtering variables in the early stages of the relationship. As these variables have been discussed by others (e.g. Campbell, 1964; Hartup, 1978), we shall just note their importance as a determinant of successful relationships.

Interaction results

The third component of relationship success is the outcome of the interaction engaged in by its members. This natural history of the relationship is perhaps the single most important feature of friendship—although it is correlated with the situational constraints (how much time and support the friends have in their social surround) and with their propensities for friendship (success of interaction is directly based upon past experience, abilities, and personality). This emphasis on interaction reminds us that friendship is never content-free and that interaction is an essential component of friendship. Every boy has certain prior orientations and expertise in regard to the content areas of preadolescence sketched above—socialization, sex, and aggression, upon which much of preadolescent interaction is based. When the interaction is congruent with these orientations, friendship results; if the interactants differ sufficiently, a stable intimate bond will not develop.

One can analyse the success of the interaction from two perspectives— one internal to the interaction (the responses and satisfactions of the participants), and the other external to the interaction (the reactions of the significant others to the relationship and the interaction).

In terms of the internal contours of friendship, participants become closer to each other and more intimate over time—in that they come to trust one another and become less self-conscious. Children have a finely developed sense of 'presentation of self' in their interaction with others. While this impression management does not dissipate entirely in the presence of close friends, it need not be manipulated so consciously. Thus, friends are more able 'to be themselves'.

The personal satisfaction of the interaction is an important motivator of further interaction, and research has indicated that peer acceptance is correlated with the extent to which a child provides positive social rewards to others (Hartup, Glazer and Charlesworth, 1967), a finding which may be generalized to natural interaction. Children who share interests and thus can easily engage in activities which they find enjoyable are likely to wish to continue interaction, if structural considerations do not block them. One of the difficulties with friendships across age cohorts is this difference in interests, leading to different activity reward structures. However, although cross-age friendships occur at less than chance levels they do occur, and may play an important role in social development (Lougee, 1976; Powdermaker, 1933).

Friendships occur in a social world—a world comprised of many relationships—friendships, acquaintanceships, and enmities. Preadolescents have an international reputation of being candid about their feelings toward disliked others; thus if a boy begins to develop a friendship with another boy (or with a group) which his friends feel is inappropriate, he will be forced to defend that relationship. Depending on the strength of the relationship and the social standing of the accepted boy, the friendship can cause the disliked boy to become accepted, the liked boy to become a pariah (a cruel but not unheard of fate), or the inchoate relationship to falter. Thus, it is not only interaction within the relationship that produces rewards relevant to the continuation of the friendship, but interaction with others. The more time that a preadolescent chooses (or is able) to spend with one friend, the less time that can be spent with other friends in a fixed time schedule, unless that first friend is accepted into the peer group. Thus, the integration of friends into previously established groups becomes an important goal in friendship maintenance. If this incorporation is not possible, it is necessary to choose between the comparison levels of alternatives (Thibaut and Kelley, 1959).

The three elements sketched above: structural constraints, individual propensities, and interactional rewards are seen as determining the nature and strength of friendship development. All three are interdependent, but can be differentiated analytically in terms of whether their reference is to the situation, the individuals, or the interaction.

As described above, the friendship becomes more stable by the creation of a localized idioculture to which members refer as the basis for further interaction. The idioculture regularizes interaction, and institutionalizes satisfactions from friendship in feelings of cohesion and unity (cf. Fine, 1979). The existence of a friendship culture tends to stabilize the relationship by increasing each interactant's personal investment. However, this culture does not by itself define the relationship and does not directly affect its stability, which comes only through the on-going, negotiated interaction.

THE SOCIAL CONSTRUCTION OF FRIENDSHIP

Boys spend much time with other children. An examination of one day in the life of 7-year-old Raymond Birch (Barker and Wright, 1951) in a small town in Kansas reveals by my reanalysis that Raymond had contact with 32 children during the course of his day (it is impossible to ascertain which can be defined as friends), and spent a total of 3 hours and 22 minutes with them. A total of 24 12-year-old Little League baseball players in Bolton Park were interviewed in the course of my own research and asked to provide a time budget account of how they spent the previous Saturday (after the baseball season—during the months of September and October). These respondents spent an average of 4.2 hours with friends of their same age, as compared to 3.5 hours with their parents and 1.7 hours alone. Time with friends included such activities as bicycle riding, sports (soccer, football, basketball, bowling), playing games, 'hanging around', and watching television. This is the stuff of which friendships are made, yet it does not directly determine the meaning of friendship.

The defining of friendship may be very important to the preadolescent. In my research when I asked a boy who his best friends are he often made a big production of the answer, thinking very carefully, and then explaining why his best friends should be ranked in that particular order.

The membership initiation ceremonies in gangs (cf. Crane, 1942; Puffer, 1912) also emphasize the importance of the relationship and its definition. Secrecy may be used to define the extent of group membership—the protection of information makes the group seem of special importance to its members. Sherif and Sherif (1964) comment that for an adolescent group the relative secrecy of group members provides a good indicator of the group's solidarity, and this presumably can be generalized to preadolescents. It must be recalled that this secrecy is about something, the group idioculture, a culture which seems more central and extensive in secretive groups than in open ones.

Initiations and secrecy are private and internal to the group. However, there are occasions on which preadolescents are willing to declare their personal allegiance publicly. The ritual of pricking one's finger in swearing 'blood brotherhood' is a common tradition (Opie and Opie, 1959). One Sanford Heights duo decided to call themselves Starsky and Hutch, after the American television policemen, to indicate their solidarity (quickly converted by their peers to 'parsley and crutch'—indicating the danger of extended role plays). More fanciful bonding can occur, and become general to a culture, as for example China:

> The oath of friendship exchanged by the three warrior heros of *The Three Kingdoms*, Liu Pei, Kuan Yü and Chang Fei, still thrills Chinese youth. Sometimes friends gave each other a solemn oath of friendship in the temple of Kuan Yü ... 'If we are not born on the same day, we shall die on the same day. If we have wealth, we shall spend it together; if we have a horse, we shall ride together; if happiness comes, we shall enjoy

it together. The spirits should condemn us if we have two hearts and not a single one.'
(Lang, 1946, p. 324).

Or among Panamanian Indian tribes:

> The San Blas Indians have a peculiar custom of 'making a friend'. This is done in child-
> hood by both sexes. A boy will ask another boy: 'Will you be my friend?' If the one asked
> says that he will, then the first boy gives him a piece of cloth, enough to make a shirt;
> then he boils an egg and cuts it in two and they sit down and eat it together. Ever after
> that they are friends. The next day or week perhaps the second boy returns the compli-
> ment by giving to the other a shirt and boiling an egg . . . (Coope, 1917, p. 171).

Opie and Opie (1959) have pointed out that there also exists formulae for
breaking friendships formally and publicly.

Friendship as negotiated order

While there may be some cases in which the friendship relation becomes
formalized, generally it does not. Boys often gather together and are friends
in the analytic construction of the investigator, but may have an undefined
(and undefinable) relationship in their own eyes.

To the extent that there is instability in preadolescent friendship relations
(and the extent of this is an empirical issue) it may stem from the fact that
beyond one's closest friends one has friendly relations with many. These
relationships can easily be altered in the course of the interaction, and, since
they have many layers of content, they can easily be altered by an increased or
decreased emphasis on one or another level. This negotiation occurs continually,
since actions such as refusal to lend a 'friend' spare change may be cause for
a temporary break in a relationship.

Enmity poses a particularly interesting problem. While there are some
boys who are outcasts and disliked over a substantial period of time, many
boys lose favour over short periods of time as a function of certain situational
vagaries—such as suspected double dealing. It is these boys for whom particular
abuse is reserved. They seem to be the victims of pranks and insults, more than
the boy who is permanently outcast, ignored and scorned:

> I asked Larry how they decide whose house they should throw eggs at when he and his
> friends go egging. He claims that they only egg the houses of 'friends we hate'. (Field
> notes, Sanford Heights, 20 June 1977).

This category of 'friends we hate' is an important one for preadolescents, and
many boys fit into it in the leagues studied. These boys are the victims of ostenta-
tious silent treatment, pranks and verbal abuse; but they are not ignored.
The relationship is continually activated and often reverts to acceptance over

a short period of time. The previous friendship group of these victims is exerting a not very subtle form of coercion to force them to behave according to the norms of the group. The boy who is willing to accept the power of the group is welcomed back as a friend, and the ostracism is quickly forgotten. The content of interaction with the 'hated friend' is quite distinct from interaction with the outcast, although most conventional sociometric measures could not make this differentiation.

The preadolescent period is a time of intense negotiation for position. While popularity hierarchies exist before this age (Lee, 1973), they seem not to be consciously recognized by the peer cohort and are not used in interaction as symbolic of the group's social organization. Popularity, and along with it gossip (Fine, 1977), becomes an important topic. As a result popularity and status become problematic. Perhaps for this reason, as well as other psychiatric ones, the presence of a single chum on whom one can count or a group bound in blood brotherhood to support each other becomes a critical social marker.

CONCLUSION

The implications of friendship cannot be understood completely without a realization of the content of friendship ties as they exist in the social world that preadolescents inhabit. One must recognize the importance of friendships for the preadolescent male—friendships that may be with one other boy (a chumship), with a few (a clique or gang), and/or with many (a social network). While other age periods produce friendships, in none does the existence of friendships seem quite so important from a developmental standpoint.

Each friendship or friendship group develops its own culture, derived from past knowledge of members, norms of legitimate interaction, functional needs of the group, status and power considerations, and formulated by the particular events in which the group participates. This group culture is particular to the group and is used by members as a basis for categorizing and interpreting future events. As friendships are not confined to a small circle of friends, these cultural elements become spread throughout a larger population, and some of these cultural elements may come to characterize the preadolescent subculture.

The development of friendship depends upon the concatenation of three influences: (1) structural constraints have to be conducive to continued interaction; (2) personal inclinations must allow the friendship to develop despite different biographical contours; and (3) production of satisfying interaction must exist—based upon the content of the interaction of the friendship group itself and also upon the reaction of friends and acquaintances to the bond. If any of these three forces are not present, the relationship cannot exist successfully, and it will dissipate or change status.

Finally, friendships are continually subject to negotiation by members, such that they need not remain stable. Even in cases in which the relationship label of 'friendship' may continue to apply, the content of the friendship bond may have changed substantially, as is necessarily true in a relationship that spans a period of cognitive and emotional change. Friendship is an important relationship in preadolescence, because of its emotional effects and also because it provides a milieu in which cultural elements can be formed, learned, explored, played with, and discarded. This is particularly important for those topics and behaviours, such as sex and aggression, which may be unsuitable for adult – child interaction.

REFERENCES

Barker, R. G., and Wright, H. F. (1951). *One Boy's Day: A Specimen Record of Behavior*. New York: Harper.

Barnes, J. A. (1969). Networks and political process. In J. C. Mitchell (Ed.), *Social Networks in Urban Situations*. Manchester: The University Press.

Barnett, W. K. (1970). An ethnographic description of Sanlei Ts'un, Taiwan, with emphasis on women's roles, overcoming research problems caused by the presence of great tradition. Doctoral dissertation. Michigan State University. Ann Arbor: University Microfilms. (No. 71–2026).

Berkovits, R. (1970). Secret languages of children. *New York Folklore Quarterly*, **26**, 127–152.

Bowden, L. W. (1972). How to define neighborhood. *Professional Geographer*, **24**, 227–228.

Brittain, C. V. (1963). Adolescent choices and parent–peer cross-preferences. *American Sociological Review*, **28**, 385–391.

Brown, C. (1965). *Manchild in the Promised Land*. New York: Macmillan.

Buechler, H. C., and Buechler, J. M. (1971). *The Bolivian Aymara*. New York: Holt, Rinehart and Winston.

Campbell, J. D. (1964). Peer relations in childhood. In M. L. Hoffman and L. W. Hoffman (Eds.), *Review of Child Development Research*. Vol. I. New York: Russell Sage Foundation.

Cikler, J. (1967). The rise, the development and the extinction of a soccer team of boys. *International Review of Sport Sociology*, **2**, 33–46.

Cohen, R. (1967). *The Kanuri of Bornu*. New York: Holt, Rinehart and Winston.

Cohen, Y. A. (1966). A study of interpersonal relations in a Jamaican community. Doctoral dissertation, Yale University. Ann Arbor: University Microfilms. (No. 66–1209).

Conger, J. J. (1972). A world they never knew: the family and social change. In J. Kagan and R. Coles (Eds.), *Twelve to Sixteen: Early Adolescence*. New York: Norton.

Coope, A. (1917). *Sky Pilot to the San Blas Indians*. New York: American Tract Society.

Cottle, T. J. (1971). Prospect Street moon. In T. J. Cottle (Ed.), *Time's Children*. Boston: Little, Brown.

Crane, A. R. (1942). Pre-adolescent gangs: a topological interpretation. *Journal of Genetic Psychology*, **81**, 113–123.

Dressler, N. (1973). Telephone pranks. *New York Folklore Quarterly*, **29**, 121–130.

Duck, S. W. (1973). *Personal Relationships and Personal Constructs: A Study of Friendship Formation*. London: Wiley.

Elkin, F., and Handel, G. (1972). *The Child and Society*, second edition. New York: Random House.

Elwin, V. (1947). *The Muria and Their Ghotul*. Oxford: Oxford University Press.

Erikson, E. H. (1963). *Childhood and Society*, second edition. New York: Norton.

Evans, I. H. N. (1923). *Studies in Religion, Folklore and Custom in the British North Borneo and the Malay Peninsula*. Cambridge: Cambridge University Press.

Fine, G. A. (1977). Social components of children's gossip. *Journal of Communication*, **27**, 181–185.

Fine, G. A. (1978). Folklore diffusion through interactive social networks: conduits in a preadolescent community. Unpublished manuscript.

Fine, G. A. (1979). Small groups and the creation of culture: determinants of the development of idioculture. *American Sociological Review*, **44**, (in press).

Fine, G. A., and Glassner, B. (1979). The promise and problems of participant observation with children. *Urban Life*, **8**, 153–174.

Fortes, M. (1949). *The Web of Kinships Among the Tallensi*. Oxford: Oxford University Press.

Furfey, P. H. (1926). Some factors influencing the selection of boys' chums. *Journal of Applied Psychology*, **11**, 47–51.

Furfey, P. H. (1927). *The Gang Age*. New York: Macmillan.

Gagnon, J. H. (1972). The creation of the sexual in early adolescence. In J. Kagan and R. Coles (Eds.), *Twelve to Sixteen: Early Adolescence*. New York: Norton.

Gallagher, J. J. (1958). Social status of children related to intelligence, propinquity, and social perception. *Elementary School Journal*, **58**, 225–231.

Gamble, D. P. (1957). *The Wolof of Senegambia*. London: International African Institute.

Gesell, A., Ilg, F. L., and Ames, L. B. (1956). *Youth: The Years from Ten to Sixteen*. New York: Harper.

Giallombardo, R. (1974). *The Social World of Imprisoned Girls*. New York: Wiley.

Gladwin, T., and Sarason, S. B. (1953). *Truk: Man in Paradise*. New York: Wenner-Gren Foundation for Anthropological Research.

Glassner, B. (1976). Kid society. *Urban Education*, **11**, 5–22.

Goodman, M. E. (1970). *The Culture of Childhood*. New York: Teachers College Press.

Gorer, G. (1938). *Himalayan Village: An Account of the Lepchas of Sikkim*. London: Joseph.

Granovetter, M. (1973). The strength of weak ties. *American Journal of Sociology*, **78**, 1360–1380.

Gruenberg, S. M., and Krech, H. S. (1959). *Your Child's Friends*. Public Affairs Pamphlet, No. 285. New York: Public Affairs Committee.

Han, C. C. (1949). Social organization of Upper Han hamlet in Korea. Doctoral dissertation, University of Michigan. Ann Arbor: University Microfilms (No. 1245).

Hartup, W. W. (1978). Children and their friends. In H. McGurk (Ed.), *Issues in Childhood Social Development*. London: Methuen.

Hartup, W. W., Glazer, J. A., and Charlesworth, R. (1967). Peer reinforcement and sociometric status. *Child Development*, **38**, 1017–1024.

Helanko, R. (1969). The yard community and its play activities. *International Review of Sport Sociology*, **4**, 177–187.

Hilger, M. I. (1951). *Chippewa Child Life and its Cultural Background*. Washington: Government Printing Office.

Hilger, M. I. (1952). *Arapaho Child Life and its Cultural Background*. Washington: Smithsonian Institution Bureau of American Ethnology Bulletin 148.

Hilger, M. I. (1957). *Araucanian Child Life and its Cultural Background*. Washington: Government Printing Office.

Hunt, M. E. V. (1962). The dynamics of the domestic group in two Tzeltal villages: a contrastive comparison. Doctoral dissertation, University of Chicago, Chicago: University of Chicago Library Department of Photoduplication (Thesis No. 9048).

Kinsey, A. C., Pomeroy, W. B., and Martin, C. E. (1948). *Sexual Behavior in the Human Male*. Philadelphia: Saunders.

Knapp, M., and Knapp, H. (1976). *One Potato, Two Potato . . . : The Secret Education of American Children*. New York: Norton.

Kohen-Raz, R. (1971). *The Child from 9 to 13*. Chicago: Aldine-Atherton.

Konopka, G. (1976). *Young Girls*. Englewood Cliffs, New Jersey: Prentice-Hall.

Kurth, S. (1970). Friendship and friendly relations. In G. J. McCall, M. M. McCall, N. K. Denzin, G. D. Suttles, and S. B. Kurth (Eds.), *Social Relationships*. Chicago: Aldine.

Lang, O. (1946). *Chinese Family and Society*. New Haven: Yale University Press.

Lee, L. C. (1973). Social encounters of infants: the beginnings of popularity. Paper presented at the biennial meetings of the International Society For The Study of Behavioral Development, Ann Arbor, Michigan.

Lever, J. (1976). Sex differences in the games children play. *Social Problems*, **23**, 478–487.

Levinger, G., and Snoek, J. D. (1972). *Attraction in Relationship: A New Look at Interpersonal Attraction*. Morristown, New Jersey: General Learning Press.

Lougee, M. (1976). Age relationships in children's groups. Unpublished manuscript.

Lowie, R. H. (1935). *The Crow Indians*. New York: Farrar and Rinehart.

Maiskii, I. (1921). *Sovremennaia Mongoliia (Contemporary Mongolia)*. Irkutsk: Gosudarstvennoe Izdatel'stvo, Irkutskoe, Otdelenie.

Malinowski, B. (1929). *The Sexual Life of Savages in Northwestern Melanesia*. New York: Horace Liveright.

McBride, G. (1975). Interactions and the control of behavior. In A. Kendon, R. Harris and M. Key (Eds.), *Organization of Behavior in Face-to-face Interaction*. The Hague: Mouton.

Mead, M. (1930). *Growing Up in New Guinea*. New York: Morrow.

Nash, R. (1973). Clique formation among primary and secondary school children. *British Journal of Sociology*, **24**, 303–313.

Neugarten, B. L. (1946). Social class and friendship among school children. *American Journal of Sociology*, **51**, 305–313.

Newell, W. W. (1963). *Games and Songs of American Children*. New York: Dover (originally published 1883).

Opie, I., and Opie, P. (1959). *The Lore and Language of Schoolchildren*. Oxford: Oxford University Press.

Opie, I., and Opie, P. (1969). *Children's Games in Street and Playground*. Oxford: Oxford University Press.

Oxreider, J. (1976). The slumber party: transition into adolescence. Paper presented to the annual meeting of the American Folklore Society, Philadelphia, Pennsylvania, November.

Pepitone, J. (1975). *Joe, You Coulda Made Us Proud*. New York: Dell.

Petras, J. W. (1973). *Sexuality in Society*. Boston: Allyn and Bacon.

Piaget, J. (1962). *The Moral Judgment of the Child*. New York: Collier (originally published 1932).

Powdermaker, H. (1933). *Life in Lesu: The Study of a Melanesian Society in New Ireland*. New York: Norton.

Puffer, J. A. (1912). *The Boy and His Gang*. Boston: Houghton Mifflin.

Quain, B. H. (1937). The Iroquois. In M. Mead (Ed.), *Cooperation and Competition Among Primitive Peoples*. New York: McGraw-Hill.

Ransohoff, R. (1975). Some observations on humor and laughter in young adolescent girls. *Journal of Youth and Adolescence*, **4**, 155–170.

Redl, F. (1966). *When We Deal with Children*. New York: Free Press.

Rosen, B. C. (1955). Conflicting group membership: a study of parent–peer group cross-pressures. *American Sociological Review*, **20**, 155–161.

Schapera, I. (1930). *The Khoisan People of South Africa: Bushmen and Hottentots*. London: Routledge.

Shaw, C. R., McKay, H. D., and McDonald, J. F. (1938). *Brothers in Crime*. Chicago: University of Chicago Press.

Sherif, M., Harvey, O. J., White, B. J., Hood, W. R., and Sherif, C. W. (1961). *Intergroup Conflict and Cooperation: The Robbers Cave Experiment*. Norman, Oklahoma: University Book Exchange.

Sherif, M., and Sherif, C. W. (1953). *Groups in Harmony and Tension*. New York: Harper.

Sherif, M., and Sherif, C. W. (1964). *Reference Groups*. Chicago: Regnery.

Skrefsrud, L. O. (1942). *Traditions and Institutions of the Santals*, translated by P. O. Budding. Oslo: Oslo Ethnografiske Museum.

Smith, M. G. (1965). The Hausa of Northern Nigeria. In J. L. Gibbs, Jr. (Ed.), *Peoples of Africa*. New York: Holt, Rinehart and Winston.

Speier, M. (1973). *How to Observe Face-to-face Communication*. Pacific Palisades, California: Goodyear.

Spiro, M. E. (1949). Ifaluk: a South Sea culture. Unpublished manuscript.

Stevenson, M. (1920). *The Rites of the Twice-born*. Oxford: Oxford University Press.

Steward, J. H., Manners, R. A., Wolf, E. R., Seda, E. P., Mintz, S. W., and Scheele, R. L. (1956). *The People of Puerto Rico: A Study in Social Anthropology*. Urbana: University of Illinois Press.

Stone, L. J., and Church J. (1968). *Childhood and Adolescence*, second edition. New York: Random House.

Sullivan, H. S. (1953). *The Interpersonal Theory of Psychiatry*. New York: Norton.

Suttles, G. D. (1970). Friendship as a social institution. In G. J. McCall, M. McCall, N. K. Denzin, G. D. Suttles and S. B. Kurth (Eds.), *Social Relationships*. Chicago: Aldine.

Sutton-Smith, B., and Rosenberg B. G. (1961). Sixty years of historical change in the game preferences of American children. *Journal of American Folklore*, **74**, 17–46.

Thiabaut, J. W., and Kelley, H. H. (1959). *The Social Psychology of Groups*. New York: Wiley.

Thornburg, H. D. (1974). General introduction. In H. D. Thornburg (Ed.), *Preadolescent Development*. Tucson: University of Arizona Press.

Thrasher, F. M. (1963). *The Gang*. Chicago: University of Chicago (originally published 1927).

Wagley, C. (1949). The social and religious life of a Guatemalan village. *American Anthropologist*, **51**, 1–150.

Waldrop, M. F., and Halverson, Jr, C. F. (1975). Intensive and extensive peer behavior: longitudinal and cross-sectional analysis. *Child Development*, **46**, 19–26.

Wallis, W. D., and Wallis, R. S. (1955). *The Micmac Indians of Eastern Canada*. Minneapolis: University of Minnesota Press.

Weltfish, G. (1965). *The Lost Universe*. New York: Basic Books.

Wheeler-Voegelin, E. (1938). *Tübatulabal Ethnography*. Berkeley: University of California Press.

Whiting, B. B., and Whiting, J. W. M. (1975). *Children of Six Cultures*. Cambridge, Massachusetts: Harvard University Press.

Wilson, G. (1936). An introduction to Nyakyusa society. *Bantu Studies*, **10**, 253–291.

Wilson, M. (1951). *Good Company: A Study of Nyakyusa Age-villages*. London: Oxford University Press.

Wolman, B. (1951). Spontaneous groups of children and adolescents in Israel. *Journal of Social Psychology*, **34**, 171–182.

CHAPTER 12

Patterns of Cliquing Among Youth

MAUREEN T. HALLINAN

Numerous studies of popularity among schoolchildren (aged 6 to 12 years old) can be found in the literature on children's friendships. These studies investigate the relationship between social status or popularity and cognitive or social psychological characteristics such as achievement, athletic status, intelligence, and social class of children. A review of some of these studies is found in Glidewell, Kantor, Smith and Stringer (1966). Although research on the characteristics of popular and unpopular children may be useful, it sheds little light on the processes governing the interactions and social behaviour of a majority of the children in a school population. Popularity is a scarce resource and is available to only a small minority of pupils. In contrast, membership in a clique is obtainable by many pupils and may be even more desirable to an individual than being popular. Despite a pervasive interest in children's cliques, however, few systematic studies on cliques can be found in the literature. Neither can many studies be found on the determinants and consequences of the tendency of children to interact in cliques.

Research on children's friendship cliques is important for several reasons.

First, as children grow older, they become more socially oriented and turn to peers for normative and comparative reference groups and role models. Since peer groups exert pressure on the individual/member to conform to the group's norms and standards, an individual who belongs to a peer group or clique is likely to adopt the attitudes and values of its members. Thus, cliques can play a major role in the shaping of a child's value system and in influencing his academic and social behaviour.

Secondly, a study of friendship cliques may reveal a kind of isolation that is less easily perceived than that evidenced by the child who receives no friendship choices from his classmates. A child who has one or more friends may feel rejected because he is denied membership in a friendship clique to which he aspires to belong. This kind of isolation may be as detrimental to a child's self-image as actually having no friends. On occasions, a popular child may also be excluded from a clique for a variety of reasons and suffer a loss of self-esteem or self-confidence. Identifying classroom cliques and their membership should make this form of exclusion more explicit and may suggest ways of integrating students into friendship groups.

Finally, a study of change in clique membership over time can reveal the structure of an existing social system in a classroom and determine its stability. Classroom characteristics such as environment, ethnic composition and ability composition may be associated with the tendency for clique membership to change over time. Stability, in turn, may be related to cooperation, competition and morale. An understanding of the dynamics of a classroom's social structure is necessary before interventions for pedagogical and social purposes can be effective.

The aims of the present chapter are threefold: (1) to review research findings on children's friendship cliques; (2) to review methods of detecting and analysing clique structures; (3) to report results of a recent longitudinal study on the evolution of children's friendship cliques.

SELECTED STUDIES OF CHILDREN'S AND ADOLESCENTS' FRIENDSHIP CLIQUES

Two approaches to the study of friendship cliques can be found in the literature. The first is observation. This typically leads to case histories of friendship cliques within a single school or are used to describe the interaction patterns of a single friendship group or gang. The second type of study is based on data from sociometric questionnaires and aims to identify the structure of friendship patterns within one or more groups.

One of the earliest sociological case studies of the friendships of adolescents was conducted by Hollingshead (1949). The purpose of the study was to determine whether the social behaviour of adolescents was related to the position occupied by their families in the status structure of the community. The sample included 735 high school pupils aged 13–18 years old, most of whom attended the same high school in the community. Hollingshead observed the youths (i.e. boys and girls) over one academic year. They found that the majority of pupils interacted in small, somewhat exclusive cliques whose members were of the same social class and from the same age-grade in school. Individuals were assigned status within the clique and the cliques themselves formed a status hierarchy. Cliques were seen to have a major impact on the pupils' self-conceptions and sense of belonging. Moreover, the cliques effectively served as a means to isolate lower-class pupils in the social system of the high school.

Gordon (1957) studied the social structure of a suburban high school containing 576 students. Prestige-seeking behaviour by students was observed in the formal organization of the school, in extra-curricular activities and in the network of interpersonal relationships. Informal friendship networks were found to be most significant in determining behaviour with the peer group exercising autocratic control over individuals and their reputations. There was general consensus as to where classmates ranked in the social system and pupils associated only with peers of similar social status. Rank was determined by prestige gained from grades, organized activities, clique membership, dating, dress, morals and socioeconomic position of the family. Cliques were well-defined and were extremely important for defining individual status. Informal but well understood rules of behaviour guided action within the cliques. Most friendship cliques contained pupils of the same grade and sex.

Coleman's (1961) study of adolescent subcultures aimed to identify components of adolescent social climates, relate them to characteristics of schools and communities that may have caused them, and determine their influence on adolescent behaviours. The data included questionnaires on the attitudes and values of pupils at two points in time, as well as interviews with a subset of those pupils. The sample was drawn from 10 high schools located in geographic areas varying in size and socioeconomic status. The results of the study provided evidence of a strong subculture among adolescents. While some differences were found between schools, boys in general valued athletics and scholastic achievement while girls valued beauty and academic achievement. The highest ranked cliques in the schools contained pupils who excelled in these characteristics. The adolescent subculture was shown to affect the pupils' self-images, self-evaluations and achievements.

In a case study of friendship cliques in a senior high school of 1,100 pupils, Cusick (1973) investigated the way pupils perceived their high school experience, as well as the mediating role of friendship groups, on organizational characteristics of a school and pupils' attitudes and behaviours. He gave particular attention to 'Bill's group', of which he himself became a member observing how school authorities avoided confrontation by tolerating the way these youths ignored school rules. Cusick concluded that in general the pupils spent most of their school time interacting in cliques, that they engaged in activities having little to do with academic goals, and that cliques influenced the behaviours of teachers and other school personnel as well as pupils.

A particular kind of clique is a 'gang'; this is a friendship group governed by very elaborate codes of behaviour, often including delinquency or deviance. In his classic study of gangs, Thrasher (1927) examined 1,313 adolescent gangs in Chicago over a 7-year period. Although the study was not designed to test hypotheses, the data reveal some of the patterns of group formation and maintenance observed in other clique studies. One of Thrasher's main arguments was that the crowded urban conditions increased the likelihood of conflict among adolescents which in turn fostered gang formation. In general, adolescent gangs evolved from children's spontaneous play groups. Often a gang formed around close friends. Segregation or expulsion from a formal organization such as a school acted as a catalyst in gang formation. Adolescents with similar characteristics, including receiving the same label from peers or adults, were likely to become members of the same friendship group. The gangs studied tended to be unstable; several members left the gang and new ones joined over a period of time. Nevertheless, individuals' attitudes and behaviours were strongly influenced by group norms during their tenure in the gang. The study showed that among the benefits of adolescent membership in a gang was a feeling of solidarity, high morale, group awareness and attachment to local territory.

As part of a study of the social structure of an Italian slum, Whyte (1967) observed a small group of older adolescents who were members of a street gang. He addressed such questions as how a street gang is organized, how an individual attains leadership status in a gang, and how one gang exerts power and influence over another. Whyte found that the gang gave meaning, motivation and organization to members' lives. It also provided protection from other gangs. Members of the gang were assigned status based on an ability to fight and win respect for their behaviour from other members. Clear norms of dress and behaviour were enforced. The gang governed the leisure time of its members and played an important role in influencing future career decisions.

Although not an empirical study, Waller's (1932) treatise on the sociology of teaching contains a number of observations and generalizations about the peer subculture within a school environment. Waller argued that a peer subculture developed as a result of the isolationism of the schooling process. Organizational characteristics of a school such as age grading tended to constrain pupils to form friendships within classes or extracurricular activities. The intense involvement of youth in school activities led to the formation of cliques. Waller's analysis suggests that the experiences of pupils in formal and informal groups led to the establishment of norms and values that influence their attitudes toward authority and schooling. He notes that efforts on the part of teachers and other school officials to use friendship cliques for the purpose of control or to achieve academic goals generally have been unsuccessful.

A few field experiments examined the effects of clique membership on attitudes and behaviour. In one of these, Sherif, Harvey, White, Hood and Sherif (1961) studied 22 middle-class boys of about 12 years of age. The subjects were all in grade V and were of average and above average intelligence; they had no history of home or school problems. The boys were given tasks to accomplish which involved working toward goals that required task interdependency. Two friendship groups emerged among the boys centring around task activities. These two groups were then put in a competitive situation that encouraged frustration and friction and their behaviour was observed. Several generalizations about clique formation and evolution were made at the end of the study. Cliques were seen to form among individuals who must work interdependently to accomplish their goals. Status hierarchies and group norms developed as the group interacted over time. When cliques were placed in a competitive setting, within-group solidarity and cooperation increased while between-group relations became more negative. Hostility between groups was decreased by presenting the boys with a superordinate goal that required cooperation across groups for attainment.

In two separate field studies, Newcomb (1952, 1961) demonstrated the power of a friendship group or clique over an individual's attitudes and behaviour. The Bennington College study (Newcomb, 1952) was a field experiment in which the effect of membership groups and reference groups on attitude change was observed. The results showed that while attitudes were strongly influenced by membership in a friendship group or clique, they were also affected by one's reference group even when the student was not a member of that group. The greatest amount of change toward more liberal attitudes occurred among the women whose membership and reference groups were the same. Later Newcomb (1961) examined the determinants of friendship formation and maintenance among 34 college men. The study investigated the extent to which attitudes and sentiment relations were balanced. The findings revealed that persons similar in relevant characteristics were more likely to form a friendship group and that friends tended to agree on important attitudes. Positive interpersonal relations were seen to stabilize over time and with stability the relationship between agreement and attraction increased.

In a study of housing projects, Festinger, Schachter and Back (1950) found that the degree of conformity to group norms and uniformity of behaviour varied with the cohesiveness of the clique or friendship groups. Highly cohesive groups had a greater influence on the attitudes and behaviours of their members than less coherent groups.

While not all the studies reviewed shared the same perspective or examined the same kind of clique, they provide some insight into the process of clique formation and maintenance. A number of the findings are fairly consistent across studies and may be summarized as follows: (1) Members of friendship cliques are generally of the same sex, grade and social class. The effect of race or ethnicity on clique membership was not examined in the case studies reported primarily because the samples contained little, if any, racial or ethnic diversity; (2) Two informal ranking systems occur within a school or class. First, cliques are ordered on the basis of status stemming from the background characteristics and social behaviour of their members. Some between-school variance exists in source of status or prestige. Second, members of cliques are assigned hierarchical status determined by their adherence to the group norms and standards of the cliques; (3) Cliques exert a strong influence over the attitudes and behaviours of their members. Their influence is pervasive, governing academic achievement, educational aspirations, extra-curricular activities, leisure time activities, dating, attitudes toward authority and career decisions; (4) Membership of a clique has a positive effect on pupils' self-images and increases self-confidence and interpersonal skills; exclusion from a clique has a negative effect on persons' self-evaluations and may have negative consequences for their social and academic behaviour; (5) Efforts on the part of adults to penetrate the friendship cliques of older youth or to utilize them for academic purposes generally have had little success.

While observational studies (described above) provide valuable information about the determinants and consequences of cliquing in selected environments, they suffer from the limitations of all case studies, namely the difficulty of generalizing to a larger population. In addition, the studies lack quantitative measures of status, clique size and stability that would permit comparisons across groups.

The alternative approach to the study of friendship cliques involves using sociometric data to detect cliques. This approach avoids some of the weaknesses of observational techniques although at the same time it misses some of the richness of observational data. Numerous sociometric studies may be found in the literature but few of them actually identify friendship cliques. The great majority of these studies focus on popularity or on the distribution of friendship choices rather than on clique structures. The absence of research on sociometric cliques is most likely due to the lack, until recently, of analytic techniques for identifying structural characteristics of groups in data from large sociograms.

The few studies that do attempt to detect cliques in small groups generally use cross-sectional methods which preclude investigating change in the clique structure over time. An occasional longitudinal study may be found that examines clique structures at two points in time. These studies do not provide enough information to determine whether friendship structures are in a state of equilibrium.

In the present section some of the sociometric findings relevant to clique analysis are mentioned, followed by a brief review of some studies that actually examined clique structures based on sociometric data.

Several studies have investigated the relationship between ascribed and achieved characteristics of youth and their friendship choices. A consistent finding is that only a small number of cross-sex friendships are made among elementary and secondary school pupils (Damico, 1974; Durojaiye, 1969; Gronlund, 1959). Similarly, in ethnically mixed schools, the large majority of choices are to members of pupils' own ethnic groups (cf. Carter, this volume; Damico, 1974; Langworthy, 1959; Wyatt, 1977). These results suggest that cliques, which involve more exclusive friendship choices, are likely to manifest a sex and ethnic cleavage.

A number of sociometric studies show that social class is associated with friendships; that is, a pupil tends to choose the majority of his friends from the social class of which he is a member (Dahlke, 1953; Langworthy, 1959; Neugarten, 1946), a tendency to choose peers with higher status has also been reported (Langworthy, 1959). Since powerful or prestigious pupils are unlikely to select friends with lower status, the social class bias implies that cliques would tend to be differentiated by social class status. (However, Dahlke, 1953, reported that social class was important at the high school level but not at the elementary level contradicting a number of studies in this area.) The findings on social class correlates of friendship are consistent with those reported in the observational studies cited above.

Another fairly consistent finding of the sociometric literature is that socio-metric status remains fairly stable over an academic year (Bonney, 1942; Lippitt and Gold, 1959). In other words, a pupil receives approximately the same number of friendship choices at the beginning and the end of a school year. In particular, sociometric stars and social isolates do not change their position in the social structure of the class. While this finding might suggest that clique structures also remain stable over time, an unstable clique structure is consistent with a stable distribution of choices. Therefore, caution must be exercised in generalizing these findings to cliques.

Finally, sociometric studies show friendship choices to be associated with personal characteristics such as physical attractiveness (Dion and Berscheid, 1974), academic achievement (Damico, 1974) and athletic competence (Lever, 1974). These characteristics are also likely to be bases for clique formation as evidenced by the case studies described above.

While sociometric findings provide some information, at least by inference, about cliques and characteristics of their members, the studies which examine clique formation directly are more valid for this purpose. While research on sociometric cliques is meagre, the few studies that do exist can be divided into two categories: those that are concerned with devising methods to detect clique structures and those that describe characteristics of the membership cliques. Only the latter are of concern here; methods of detecting cliques are discussed in the following section.

In an early study of cliques among preadolescents and early adolescents, Hallworth (1953) reported that each of the sociometric cliques in a British grammar school could be characterized by a distinct set of values or a sub-culture. More recently, Roistacher (1973) found that members of the largest cliques in four urban and suburban junior high schools (11- to 15-year-olds) were distinguished by greater participation in sports and conformed more closely to clique norms than other pupils. In a study of 1,700 senior high school pupils (13- to 18-year-olds), Sweet (1971) showed that a typology of cliques could be made based on norms and personality traits including self-assertiveness, maturity and sociability.

Some studies have attempted to establish a relationship between cliques and academic achievement. Sweet (1971) found no relationship between type of clique and academic success. Damico (1974) found that cliques in a grade IX class (13- to 15-year-olds) were not formed on the basis of similar ability, although interestingly membership in a clique predicted school grades better than a measure of academic aptitude. She also reported that females who were new to the grade IX class had more difficulty making friends than males who, if rejected by an existing clique, formed a new one. In a study of 148 grade VIII students (12- to 14-year-olds) in a public junior high school, Benvenuto (1971) found slightly greater gains in achievement among pupils whose instructional groups coincided with their cliques than pupils in teacher-formed instructional groups.

Only a few studies have examined the stability of clique structures over time. Shapiro (1967) found that among 232 children of 8–15 years old in a summer camp, the formation of friendship cliques was associated with similarity while dissolution was related to dissimilarity. The younger children and females tended to dissolve cliques faster than older males. Damico (1974) reported that in a laboratory, school cliques did not dissolve between freshman and sopho- more years (13- to 16-year-olds) but that individual pupils joined and left the cliques frequently.

A recent, more comprehensive study of cliques based on sociometric data is reported by Cohen (1977). In a re-analysis of data from Coleman (1961), Cohen defined a clique as four or more persons each of whom was involved in a mutual choice relation with at least two other persons in the subgroup. He found 11 boys' cliques and 38 girls' cliques containing about 40 per cent of the school population. A clique was defined as stable if 50 per cent of its membership remained over the year. Analysis of the data from the following spring revealed that 37 of the 49 cliques detected in the autumn still existed in the spring—28 as cliques (four or more members) and nine as triads, plus an unspecified number of new cliques. Thus the main purpose of Cohen's study was to determine the differential effects of pressures toward conformity, homophilic selection and selective elimination of deviants or dissimilar group members on similarities among clique members. The results showed that initial homophilic selection was largely responsible for homogeneity in both the surviving autumn and new spring cliques. Initial homophilic selection explained the broad range of uniformity found in each clique. It was also largely responsible for membership changes whereas group leaving by deviates had no effect on membership change. Cohen's study is important not only for providing information on determinants of clique formation but also for identifying the factors that explain similarities that exist among members of the same clique in attitudes, values and behaviours.

The scarcity of studies utilizing sociometric data for clique analysis suggests the need for further research in this area. Not until clique structures are compared in large data sets across various settings and under differing conditions will the quantitative analysis of cliques yield as much valuable information about cliquing as case studies. Numerous data sets are available for this purpose as are methodological techniques for analysing sociograms. In the following section some of these methods are outlined.

THE DETECTION OF CLIQUES

Several traditional and newer methods of detecting friendship cliques from sociometric data are available; for a comparative review of some of these methods see Lankford (1974). These methods vary in usefulness according to the purpose of the investigator, the appropriateness of the underlying assumptions and restrictions imposed on the data by the analytical techniques. The most important of these methods of clique detection and their advantages and limitations are now discussed briefly.

Directed graphs and sociomatrices

The simplest and most common method of representing clique structures is by a graph that links members of a group by direct arrows. An arrow, which represents a relationship, initiates with the chooser and terminates with the person chosen. The arrows may be undirected, indicating symmetrical relationships but more often are directed to reveal asymmetrical or unreciprocated choices. Graph representation is purely a descriptive technique and visual analysis must be relied on to identify members of a clique. The limitations of a graphic depiction of cliques are obvious; in itself it provides little assistance in identifying dense clusters of relationships in any but small groups and offers no method for comparing clique structures across groups or within a single group over time.

A direct parallel to digraphs is found in the matrix representation of group structure. A matrix is a rectangular array of elements. If a group has n members, its structure can be depicted by a square matrix of order n in which the a_{ij} element is unity if person i chooses (or is related to) person j and zero otherwise. The a_{ii} element is usually defined to be zero. An advantage of the matrix representation of group relationships over digraphs is that matrices may be manipulated algebraically to provide greater ease in detecting cliques and identifying their members. The rows and columns of a sociomatrix can be permuted to place clique members in proximity. By arranging the rows and columns in such a way as to minimize the distance of the '1's' from the diagonal, dense clusters of choices representing cliques are obtained (Forsyth and Katz, 1946).

Festinger (1949) derived a method of identifying cliques by using matrix multiplication. The method identifies group members who are linked directly by a mutual choice or indirectly by being involved in a mutual choice with the same third person. Luce and Perry (1949) employed the method to obtain n cliques, that is, maximal complete subsets of a group whose members are connected by chains of length n or less, while Harary and Ross (1957) derived techniques to identify non-cliqual, unicliqual and cocliqual persons in a group. Hubbell (1965) improved on Luce and Perry's method by taking into account the strength of the relationship. Based on Leontief's (1941) input–output model for economic analysis, the method permits a relationship to assume positive or negative valence and to take on real values. Strongly connected and disjointed cliques are then defined on the basis of the density of interlocking relationships. Leik and Nagasawa (1970) give an example of the use of Hubbell's input–output technique.

The main limitation on most matrix multiplication methods for clique analysis is that they require mutual choices. This restriction considerably lessens its usefulness for most kinds of clique analysis of sociometric data which include asymmetric relationships.

Ordinarily, in clique studies based on graph analysis or sociomatrices, Luce and Perry's (1949) definition of clique is employed. That is, a clique is defined as a maximal complete subset all of whose members are connected by mutual choice relations. This definition is quite rigid. Efforts to weaken it have been made by Luce and Perry (1949) with their notion of an n clique and by Coleman (1961) and Alba (1972). (Luce and Perry's notion of an n clique was an attempt to weaken their own definition of clique.) The latter define a clique as a subset most of whose members are linked by mutual choices. Alba (1972) has written an algorithm to detect cliques according to this definition where the number of missing links permitted can be determined by the investigator. The empirical analysis reported in the last section of this chapter employs Alba's algorithm.

Factor analysis

A commonly used technique for the detection of cliques is factor analysis (Bock and Husain, 1950; MacRae, 1960). This method is based on the idea that persons who belong to the same clique are likely to give and receive choices among themselves and to ignore other group members. Factors are constructed to account for the variance in choices across group members. Members 'load' on the different factors in proportion to the amount they vary with the factors. Members of the same clique are those who have high loadings on the same factors. Overlapping cliques and social isolates are permitted.

Both direct factor analysis and factor analysis of the matrix of correlations among the choices given and received have the advantage of quick and easy computation and a degree of flexibility in determining the number of factors to be considered. Several disadvantages of the method are outlined by Hubbell (1965). Group members who are similar in patterns of choices given may not be similar in pattern of choices received; this necessitates a distinction between *choosing cliques* and *chosen cliques*. Subjective judgement is needed to set the number of factors and to determine rotational methods to be used. Sociometric data may not satisfy the assumption of interval data required by the factor analytic model. Finally, one questions whether similarity of choices given or received will always identify individuals who share the designated relationship to each other. A set of group members may all choose a small number of popular persons but may not be linked to each other.

Multidimensional scaling

Multidimensional scaling differs from the factor analytic approach to clique detection by employing a matrix of distances rather than a choice matrix or a correlation matrix. A metric is defined to establish the distance between any two individuals. A straightforward metric may be obtained for ranked socio-metric data by assuming that as the value or rank increases, the degree of closeness or friendliness of the two individuals decreases. Then the minimum dimensionality of the space is determined. Members of a group are located in the dimensional space and those who are within a given radius are defined as belonging to the same clique. Some scaling procedures allow overlapping cliques (e.g. Peay, 1974) while others do not (e.g. Johnson, 1967). Several examples of clique detection by multidimensional techniques may be found (e.g. Elliott and Hallinan, 1975; Lankford, 1974; Shepard, Romney and Nerlove, 1972; Torgerson, 1958).

Multidimensional scaling techniques may also be employed to obtain an ordering of cliques. A different group structure can be mapped for each metric or criterion value selected. If the group structure for each consecutive criterion value is obtained, the results provide a hierarchical arrangement of cliques, with cliques containing the closest or strongest relationships appearing as subsets of the larger and weaker cliques. This procedure is referred to as hier-archical clique analysis or hierarchical clustering (cf. Doreian, 1969; Jardine and Sibson, 1971; Peay, 1974).

An advantage of using multidimensional scaling as a clique detection tech-nique is its ability to utilize ordinal data which is the form in which sociometric data are frequently collected. Among the disadvantages are the difficulties in interpreting the data when dimensions greater than 3 are used and in selecting a meaningful metric for some kinds of data. Moreover, several steps are required to produce the cliques and this makes the technique inefficient.

Balance and transitivity models

Motivated by the early work of Heider (1958) on balanced cognitions and interpersonal sentiments, a set of models has been formulated that depict the structure of a group based on the amount of balance or transitivity it contains. These models are basically deterministic; however, some work has been done on developing random baseline models. Empirical data are compared to these baseline models to determine whether the data deviate from randomness in the direction of the deterministic model (Holland and Leinhardt, 1970). The simplest of the deterministic models of group structure are Cartwright and Harary's balance model (1956) and Davis's cluster model (1970). The balance model states necessary and sufficient conditions for a group to contain two disjoint subsets or cliques all of whose members are connected by symmetric relationships. The clusters model allows for the partition of a group into a number of disjoint subsets.

An elaboration of these two formulations is found in the transitivity model (Hallinan, 1974; Holland and Leinhardt, 1971), which also includes the ranked clusters model (Davis and Leinhardt, 1972) as a special case. In its deterministic form, the transitivity model depicts a structure that can be described as hierarchies of ranked clusters of cliques. The points of a graph are arrayed in such a way as to form disjoint clusters of cliques that are rank ordered.

While these models represent an interesting effort to portray group structure, they have limited usefulness as clique detection devices. At best they permit measurement of the tendency of a group to deviate from a random structure and approximate a deterministic model. If hierarchy is not of interest, the clusters model is the appropriate tool for this purpose. However, even if a strong tendency toward cliquing is observed, the model itself does not yield important characteristics of cliques such as number, size and membership. Moreover, these models, like the others mentioned in this section, yield only static representations of the data and provide no information about the stability of the group structure. On the other hand, the models are based on social psychological paradigms that serve to explain interpersonal attraction. It is possible that with modification and extension, this set of models could have greater utility for clique analysis.

Algebraic models

Another approach to the detection of cliques is found in algebraic models. The best known of these models was formulated by Boyle (1969). This model is a generalization of Friedell's (1967) semilattice algebra for the analysis of organizational structure. The major requirement of Boyle's model is that distance be preserved under transformation. Cliques are defined in terms of the distance of members from each other. The number and membership of the cliques obtained depends on the definition of distance employed. Boyle extends the clique model to include hierarchical relationships where hierarchy can be defined in terms of power or prestige. The model is deterministic and no algorithms have been written for the analysis of empirical data. Furthermore, the model is based on mutual choice relationships which limits its utility for empirical analysis.

Boyle's algebraic model represents a new direction in the analysis of clique structure. Algebraic models have the advantage of being based on powerful theorems about sets and relationships. However, considerable work remains to be done before algebraic modelling is easily employed as a clique detection device.

Blockmodelling

The most recent technique devised for the analysis of group structure and the detection of cliques is blockmodelling (Boorman and White, 1976; White, Boorman and Breiger, 1976). The aim of blockmodelling is to abstract the structure of a group based on several different social ties or relationships. Members of a group are partitioned into subsets in such a way that members of a subset are approximately equivalent in their relationships to each other and the subsets themselves occupy a similar place in the group structure across the various group ties. Blockmodelling differs from the other types of structural analysis described in this section in that it focuses on persons who are not related by any social ties (zero blocks). By so doing, blockmodelling can identify dense clusters of relationships only indirectly. The subsets defined by the partition that are not zero blocks contain individuals the majority of whom are connected by social ties. In general, the larger the number of zero blocks obtained by the partitioning, the denser the remaining subsets. A number of algorithms exist for finding zero blocks or approximations to zero blocks (Breiger, 1976; Breiger, Boorman and Phipps, 1975).

Although blockmodelling was not devised as a clique detection technique but rather as a device to detect subgroups linked by several ties, it can be adopted for clique analysis. The zero blocks obtained by the partition can be limited to those based on a single tie such as friendship. Utilizing block models in this way creates a tendency to define cliques empirically. This could lessen the utility of the method for comparing clique structures across groups.

One of the advantages of blockmodelling is that it permits considerable data reduction. However, questions can be raised concerning the meaning of the structure obtained from several diverse ties. A strong theoretical framework is essential before using this method for structural analysis other than the detection of cliques based on friendship or any other single relationship.

Of the clique detection methods described above, none emerges as clearly superior to all of the others for the analysis of sociometric data. Factor analytic techniques are among the most frequently used methods for clique analysis and can be used for large as well as small groups. Multidimensional scaling is growing in popularity as programmes for analysis become more accessible. Research on balance and transitivity models is shifting to an attempt to devise methods of examining change in group structure over time with emphasis on the dyad (Hallinan, 1976; Wasserman, 1977) and the triad (Holland and Leinhardt, 1977; Sørensen and Hallinan, 1976). Algebraic models are employed less frequently than the other methods of clique detection probably because a degree of competence in modern algebra is required to understand and manipulate the models. The importance of blockmodelling as a clique detection device remains to be seen. Some work is being done in this area but not enough to judge whether blockmodelling compares favourably with other clique detection techniques. One of the most accessible algorithms presently available for clique detection is based on Alba's clustering methods. The programme permits the researcher some flexibility in employing various definitions of cliques. The utility of this method is demonstrated in the following section.

LONGITUDINAL STUDY OF CHILDREN'S FRIENDSHIP CLIQUES

The remaining section of this chapter reviews the results of an empirical study (Hallinan, 1977) of the development of friendship cliques among pre-adolescents. The aim of the research was to identify and describe patterns in the evolution of children's cliques over a school year and to relate the observed patterns to personal characteristics of students and structural characteristics of classrooms.

Among the factors believed to affect the formation and evolution of children's cliques are propinquity and similarity. The effect of propinquity is straightforward. Persons who are near each other have more opportunities to interact and are more likely to become friends (Homans, 1950). The proximity of schoolchildren is constrained by structural layout and grouping practices. The effect of these variables is to place some children together more frequently than others which increases the chances that they will become friends and eventually form a clique.

Similarity among children is believed for several reasons to increase the likelihood that they form a clique. Similarity of attitudes, interests and values, for example, provides a person with a basis for approving another (Newcomb, 1956), helps one to validate his social identity (Schachter, 1959) and reduces areas of conflict (Sherif *et al.*, 1961). Consequently, children who are similar in characteristics they perceive to be relevant are likely to associate with each other and to form friendship cliques. Among the characteristics that are likely to be salient to schoolchildren are sex, race, age, athleticism and school achievement.

To investigate the effects of individual and classroom variables on clique formation and change over time, sociometric data were collected in 11 classes in seven public and private schools in the Midwest. The classes included four grade IVs (8- to 10-year-olds), three grade Vs (9- to 11-year-olds), and four grade VIs (10- to 12-year-olds). Data were gathered at least six times in each of the classes over the school year. The time intervals between collection points were varied from 5 to 7 weeks; in some of the classes equal time periods were used, while in others, the data were collected at uneven intervals. This method was important for certain methodological analyses not reported here (cf. Hallinan, 1976).

The subjects were given a list of the members of their class and asked to indicate whether each child on the list was a best friend, a friend or someone they knew but did not consider a friend. The respondents could list as many or as few names in each category as they wished. This sociometric technique is referred to as a 'free-choice questionnaire' with individual cut-off points, and it has the advantage of minimizing measurement error stemming from imposing a fixed number of choices on the subjects (cf. Hallinan, 1974; Holland and Leinhardt, 1973). The analysis reported here was on the best friend choices since cliques ordinarily are considered to contain close friends.

The mean size of the classes in the study was 31.8 pupils with a standard deviation of 12 and a range of 18–60. The classes were classified by age-grade and by organization. Four of the classes were designated as *open* based on Walberg and Thomas's (1972) scheme, three as *semi-open* and four as *traditional*. The open classrooms were characterized by considerable pupil interaction with almost unrestricted freedom to move about the room and talk to classmates. In the semi-open classes the pupils had some opportunity to interact but certain constraints were placed on them while those in the traditional classes had only infrequent opportunities to interact with peers.

Alba's (1972) algorithm for detecting cliques from sociometric data was used for the analysis. The cliques were detected in the following manner. First, the maximal complete subgroups with four or more members were obtained. Each member of the subgroup chose and was chosen as best friend by all the other members of the subgroup. Subgroups with fewer than four members were excluded since these are ordinarily not thought of as cliques. Secondly, subgroups that had two-thirds of their membership in common were combined. The purpose of this step was to weaken the traditional definition of clique. It resulted in forming subgroups that were not complete; that is, subgroups in which most but not all of the members were mutual best friends. These aggregated subgroups, as well as the denser groups created by the first step, were defined as cliques.

A descriptive analysis of the data revealed that the mean number of choices given and received in the 11 classes averaged over time was 5.4. The standard deviation of the number of choices given was 3.1 and of the number received was 2.7. Thus the range of best friend choices given and received was about 2–8.

Considerable variation was found in the number of cliques in each class over time. For example, a traditional grade VI with 26 members had four cliques while an open grade V with 29 pupils contained no cliques. Table 12.1 shows the average number of cliques over a school year by class size, grade/age and classroom organization. Large classes had a greater number of cliques on the average than smaller classes as might be anticipated. The average number of cliques per class varied directly with grade suggesting that a tendency toward cliquing increases as children mature, at least for the ages examined here. No clear relationship between classroom organization and number of cliques was observed in the data.

Table 12.1 also presents the average size of cliques over a school year. In general, larger cliques appeared in larger classrooms, as might be expected. Grade VI cliques were considerably larger than those in grades IV or V pointing to tighter friendship networks at the grade VI level. Cliques in the open classes were smaller than those in the semi-traditional and traditional classes possibly because the greater interaction permitted in these open classes produced less exclusive friendships.

Examining the effects of sex on the evolution of children's cliques revealed a complete sex cleavage in the cliques in all of the classes over the entire school year. On no occasion was a member of the opposite sex included in a friendship clique. Even in the open classrooms, where pupils were encouraged to interact and work together on shared projects, no cross-sex cliques were found. It is

Table 12.1. Average number and size of cliques over an academic year by size of class, grade/age and classroom organization

Size of class	Average number of cliques over school year		Mean size and standard deviation of cliques	
	$\bar{X}$	SD	$\bar{X}$	SD
Large (27–60) ($n = 7$)	3.7	1.4	5.6	1.6
Small (19–26) ($n = 4$)	2.0	1.8	5.0	2.1
Grade/age				
6/10–12 years ($n = 4$)	4.2	.5	6.3	.5
5/9–11 years ($n = 3$)	3.0	2.7	4.0	4.0
4/8–10 years ($n = 4$)	2.0	1.2	4.5	1.0
Classroom organization				
Traditional ($n = 3$)	3.3	2.1	6.0	2.0
Semi-traditional ($n = 4$)	4.0	.8	5.6	1.6
Open ($n = 4$)	2.0	1.8	4.0	2.8

interesting to note that sex cleavage occurred as early as grade IV and persisted through the grade VI where cross-sex friendships are likely to begin taking on a different meaning. While some cross-sex friendships were observed in the data at all grade levels, children apparently were reluctant to admit members of the opposite sex to their cliques probably because strong norms existed against it. Cliques are more public and visible than most dyadic friendships and sanctions for violating clique norms are likely to be severe. No sex differences in the number and size of cliques were observed when the sex ratio of the class was controlled.

The final analysis was an examination of the stability of cliques over a school year. A stable clique was defined as one that retains at least three of its members for the entire year. The joining and leaving of other pupils does not destroy the identity of the clique as a subgroup and hence its stability. While only six of the 34 cliques represented were stable over time, several other cliques were stable for most of the school year. Some cliques emerged and disappeared sporadically over the year. This phenomenon may be an artifact of the definition of clique employed in the analysis; a weaker definition is likely to result in more stable cliques. Other cliques formed at some point during the school year and, once established, remained stable for the rest of the year. Still other cliques were absorbed by already existing cliques. In general the cliques show considerable continuity as recognizable subgroups over the school year.

Examining the effect of grade on clique evolution showed that the grade VI classes contained the most stable cliques. Five of the six cliques that were stable throughout the entire year were in the grade VI classes while the sixth was in a grade V class. Two of the cliques in the remaining grade VI class were stable for all but one time period, the first and last time interval respectively. These findings suggest that 10–12 years (grade VI) might be the age range at which children begin to form the kinds of stable, tight knit and exclusive cliques found among adolescents. Class size and classroom organization apparently had no effect on clique stability, but these relationships do need to be examined on a larger sample.

More change occurred in the total membership of the cliques over time than in the existence of the cliques. Most clique members left their clique at some point during the year but many rejoined at a later time. Since pupils who appear in a clique for most of the year are likely to remain friendly with other clique members during the occasional times they do not appear as members, a weaker definition of clique may have included those students as clique members throughout the year. Moreover, based on the strength of the previous bonds linking clique members, pupils excluded from cliques for minor reasons are likely to be reinstated quickly. If an occasional absence of a pupil from a clique is interpreted as an artifact of the definition of clique, then the data showed that clique membership remained fairly constant over time. Pupils who joined a clique were likely to remain in it throughout the school year.

In summary, the study showed several patterns in the formation and evolution of children's friendship cliques. The incidence of cliquing among the children in the study was considerably less than anticipated; about half of the classes contained no cliques at all. The cliques that did form were somewhat stable over the school year although a number of pupils in each class left and rejoined the cliques at various times during the year. Sex cleavage in the cliques was total. These findings present additional empirical evidence of some of the patterns of cliquing observed in the case studies discussed earlier. It also provides fresh evidence as to some of the determinants of cliquing—such as age and classroom organization—which had been distinguished in a number of previous sociometric studies of children's friendships. Finally, the study presents data on the stability of all of the patterns observed at several points in time, a result not available in previous cross-sectional studies or in two-wave panel analyses of sociometric data.

CONCLUSIONS

The studies examined in this review demonstrate the presence of clearly identifiable friendship groups or cliques among youth both within and outside the school setting. Most studies have been concerned with adolescent cliques or gangs and show that cliquing is a pervasive structural characteristic of groups in this age range. Relatively fewer friendship cliques were found among elementary schoolchildren, but those that did form resembled the cliques of adolescents in terms of membership characteristics, size and stability. Organizational characteristics of the school were seen to impose some constraints on friendship patterns as evidenced by the high proportion of cliques that were homogeneous with respect to age and grade.

Many of the cliques described in the studies could be characterized by a distinct set of values or even a subculture. This is an important finding since much of the literature on youth assumes the existence of a single adolescent subculture while the studies reviewed indicate that many youth subcultures exist. Membership in a clique often required commitment to a set of beliefs and adherence to a code of behaviour that distinguished members of one clique from members of another as well as from non-members. The values of some cliques were less pronounced, especially among children who seemed to form cliques primarily on the basis of interpersonal attraction and shared interests.

Research consistently illustrates the importance of ascribed and achieved characteristics of students for admission to a clique. Most cliques are homogeneous with respect to sex and ethnicity. In some cliques members have the same ability or achievement levels while in others similarities stem from proficiency in extra-curricular activities such as sports. It is not clear from the studies reporting these findings whether the reward structure of the school or school climate were controlled for. In other words, when academic achievement or proficiency in sports or other activities are the basis for membership in cliques, students may be reflecting the values held by school authorities and other adults.

Based on the studies reported here and others not included in this review, at least four processes governing clique formation can be identified. Some cliques seem to evolve around a close friendship between two individuals. The dyad remains at the centre of the clique and friends of either member are included in interactions and activities. Other cliques form around a single individual who has certain skills or talents or who possesses certain resources that are valued by group members. In this case the central figure often becomes the leader and has considerable power over establishing rules and expectations. A third way cliques develop is within a formal structure such as an honours group or an extra-curricular activity. Here, students in the programme or activity are homogeneous with respect to a relevant characteristic; this increases the likelihood that close friendships will develop. Finally, students who share common interests are likely to form an informal group to engage in their preferred activity and over time become identified as a friendship group.

A number of questions about the process of clique formation and development remain unanswered. The relationship between organizational characteristics of schools and friendship patterns is not fully understood. Neither is it clear what factors determine the salience of certain personality or achieved characteristics in choosing clique members. Little is known about how a newcomer to a group is selected for membership in a clique or why the efforts of some new students to gain admission to an existing clique are ignored. Research is needed on the role of an informal leader in a clique and the extent to which that person is responsible for the stability of the clique. Comparative studies could help to identify causal agents in the cliquing process and to determine whether sex differences exist in the tendency to form and continue interacting in cliques. Finally, factors affecting stability of cliques over time require identification. To address these issues, systematic longitudinal research is needed. While several important case studies have already been conducted, they have not dealt with most of these questions. Besides additional field work, rigorous quantitative studies are necessary to identify cliques, to determine their structural characteristics, and to relate these to exogenous variables.

While recent advances in the methodology of clique detection makes research on cliques less difficult than in the past, new methods are needed to facilitate the analysis of longitudinal data. A few attempts to study change in dyadic and triadic structures over time have been made using discrete time and continuous time stochastic models. While stochastic models are useful for investigating change in small configurations, their utility for larger structures remains unclear. In the absence of more sophisticated analytical techniques, change in clique structures can be examined in careful panel studies. This approach should also have value for identifying factors affecting the clique process. The importance of friendship cliques in youth for shaping the attitudes and behaviours (of members and nonmembers alike) justifies the expenditure of considerable research effort in this area.

ACKNOWLEDGEMENTS

The author is grateful for support by NIMH Grant # R01–MH29208–02. She also wishes to express appreciation to Sally Brazil, Donna Mar, John Motulosky, Ed Russell and Bess Thrope for assistance in organizing the review.

REFERENCES

Alba, R. D. (1972). COMPLT—a program for analyzing sociometric data and clustering similarity matrices. *Behavioral Science*, **17**, 566–567.
Benvenuto, A. (1971). The use of sociometric grouping techniques for forming instructional groups. *Dissertation Abstracts*, **31**, 4029A.
Bock, R. D., and Husain, S. Z. (1950). An adoption of Holzinger's B-coefficient for the analysis of sociometric data. *Sociometry*, **13**, 146–153.
Bonney, M. E. (1942). A study of social status on the second grade level. *Journal of Genetic Psychology*, **60**, 271–305.
Boorman, S. A., and White, H. C. (1976). Social structure from multiple networks. II. Role Structures. *American Journal of Sociology*, **81**, 1384–1446.
Boyle, R. P. (1969). Algebraic systems for normal and hierarchical sociograms. *Sociometry*, **32**, 99–119.
Breiger, R. L. (1976). Career attributes and network structures: a blockmodel study of a biomedical research specialty. *American Sociological Review*, **41**, 117–135.
Breiger, R. L., Boorman, S. A., and Phipps, A. (1975). An algorithm for clustering relational data, with applications to social network analysis and comparison with multidimensional scaling. *Journal of Mathematical Psychology*, **12**, 328–383.
Cartwright, D., and Harary, F. (1956). Structural balance: a generalization of Heider's theory. *Psychological Review*, **63**, 277–293.
Cohen, J. (1977). Sources of peer homogeneity. *Sociology of Education*, **50**, 227–241.
Coleman, J. S. (1961). *The Adolescent Society*. New York: The Free Press.
Cusick, P. (1973). *Inside High School*. New York: Holt, Rinehart and Winston.
Dahlke, H. O. (1953). Determinants of sociometric relations among children in the elementary school. *Sociometry*, **16**, 327–338.
Damico, S. B. (1974). The relation of clique membership to achievement, self-concept, social acceptance and school attitude. *Dissertation Abstracts*, **35**, 2:717A.
Davis, J. A. (1970). Clustering and hierarchy in interpersonal relations: testing two graph theoretical models on 742 sociomatrices. *American Sociological Review*, **35**, 843–851.
Davis, J. A., and Leinhardt, S. (1972). The structure of positive interpersonal relations in small groups. In J. Berger, M. Zelditch and B. Anderson (Eds.), *Sociological Theories in Progress*. Vol. 2. Boston: Houghton Mifflin.
Dion, K., and Berscheid, E. (1974). Physical attractiveness and peer perception among children. *Sociometry*, **37**, 1–12.
Doreian, P. (1969). A note on the detection of cliques in valued graphs. *Sociometry*, **32**, 237–242.

Durojaiye, M. O. A. (1969). Patterns of friendship and leadership choices in a mixed ethnic junior school—a sociometric analysis. *British Journal of Educational Psychology*, **39**, 88–89.

Elliott, G., and Hallinan, M. T. (1975). An analysis of group structure by sociometric and multidimensional scaling techniques. Unpublished manuscript, University of Wisconsin, Madison.

Festinger, L. (1949). The analysis of sociograms using matrix algebra. *Human Relations*, **2**, 153–158.

Festinger, L. S., Schachter, S., and Back, K. (1950). *Social Pressures in Informal Groups: A Study of a Housing Project*. New York: Harper.

Forsyth, E., and Katz, L. (1946). A matrix approach to the analysis of sociometric data: preliminary report. *Sociometry*, **9**, 340–347.

Friedell, M. F. (1967). Organizations as semilattices. *American Sociological Review*, **32**, 46–54.

Glidewell, J., Kantor, M., Smith, L., and Stringer, L. (1966). Socialization and social structure in the classroom. In L. W. Hoffman and M. L. Hoffman (Eds.), *Review of Child Development Research*. Vol. 2. New York: Russell Sage Foundation.

Gordon, C. W. (1957). *Social System of the High School*. Glencoe, Illinois: The Free Press.

Gronlund, N. E. (1959). *Sociometry in the Classroom*. New York: Harper.

Hallinan, M. T. (1974). *The Structure of Positive Sentiment*. New York: Elsevier.

Hallinan, M. T. (1976). Friendship formation: a continuous time Markov model. Working Paper 76–5, Madison, Wisconsin: Center for Demography and Ecology, University of Wisconsin, Madison.

Hallinan, M. T. (1977). The evolution of children's friendship cliques. Paper presented at American Sociological Convention, Chicago.

Hallworth, H. J. (1953). Sociometric relationships among grammar school boys and girls between the ages of 11 and 16 years. *Sociometry*, **16**, 39–70.

Harary, F., and Ross, I. (1957). A procedure for clique detection using the group matrix. *Sociometry*, **20**, 205–215.

Heider, F. (1958). The *Psychology of Interpersonal Relations*. New York: Wiley.

Holland, P., and Leinhardt, S. (1970). A method for detecting structure in sociometric data. *American Journal of Sociology*, **75**, 492–513.

Holland, P., and Leinhardt, S. (1971). Transitivity in structural models of small groups. *Comparative Group Studies*, **2**, 107–124.

Holland, P., and Leinhardt, S. (1973). The structural implications of measurement error in sociometry. *Journal of Mathematical Sociology*, **3**, 85–112.

Holland, P., and Leinhardt, S. (1977). A dynamic method for social networks. *Journal of Mathematical Sociology*, **5**, 5–20.

Hollingshead, A. B. (1949). *Elmtown's Youth*. New York: Wiley.

Homans, G. C. (1950). *The Human Group*. New York: Harcourt.

Hubbell, C. H. (1965). An input–output approach to clique identification. *Sociometry*, **28**, 377–399.

Jardine, N., and Sibson, R. (1971). *Mathematical Taxonomy*. New York: Wiley.

Johnson, S. C. (1967). Hierarchical clustering schemes. *Psychometrika*, **32**, 241–254.

Langworthy, R. (1959). Community status and influence in a high school. *American Sociological Review*, **24**, 537–539.

Lankford, P. M. (1974). Comparative analysis of clique identification methods. *Sociometry*, **37**, 287–305.

Leik, R. K., and Nagasawa, R. (1970). A sociometric basis for measuring social status and social structure. *Sociometry*, **33**, 55–78.

Leontief, W. W. (1941). *The Structure of the American Economy—1919–1929*. Cambridge, Massachusetts: Harvard University Press.

Lever, J. (1974). Games children play: sex differences and the development of role skills. Unpublished doctoral dissertation, Yale University.

Lippitt, R., and Gold, M. (1959). Classroom social structure as a mental health problem. *Journal of Social Issues*, **15**, 40–58.

Luce, R. D., and Perry, A. D. (1949). A method of matrix analysis of group structure. *Psychometrika*, **14**, 95–116.

MacRae, D., Jr. (1960). Direct factor analysis of sociometric data. *Sociometry*, **23**, 360–371.

Neugarten, B. (1946). Social class and friendship among schoolchildren. *American Journal of Sociology*, **51**, 305–313.

Newcomb, T. M. (1952). Attitude development as a function of reference groups: the Bennington study. In G. E. Swanson, T. M. Newcomb and E. L. Hartley (Eds.), *Readings in Social Psychology*. New York: Holt, Rinehart and Winston.

Newcomb, T. M. (1956). The prediction of interpersonal attraction. *American Psychologist*, **11**, 575–581.

Newcomb, T. M. (1961). *The Acquaintance Process*. New York: Holt, Rinehart and Winston.

Peay, E. R. (1974). Hierarchical clique structures. *Sociometry*, **37**, 54–65.

Roistacher, R. C. (1973). Peer nominations, clique structures and exploratory behavior in boys at four junior high schools. *Dissertation Abstracts International*, **33B**, Number 9.

Schachter, S. (1959). *The Psychology of Affiliation*. Stanford, California: Stanford University Press.

Shapiro, B. Z. (1967). Dissolution of friendship ties in groups of children. *Dissertation Abstracts*, **27A**, Number 10.

Shepard, R. N., Romney, A. M., and Nerlove, S. B. (1972). *Multidimensional Scaling*. New York: Seminar Press.

Sherif, M., Harvey, O. J., White, B. J., Hood, W. E., and Sherif, C. W. (1961). *Intergroup Conflict and Cooperation: The Robber's Cave Experiment*. Norman, Oklahoma: University of Oklahoma Book Exchange.

Sørensen, A. B., and Hallinan, M. T. (1976). A small stochastic model for change in group structure. *Social Science Research*, **5**, 43–61.

Sweet, P. R. (1971). The influences of clique characteristics on academic achievement of Puerto Rican secondary school students. *Dissertation Abstracts International*, **32A**, Number 3.

Thrasher, F. M. (1927). *The Gang: A Study of 1,313 Gangs in Chicago*. Chicago: University of Chicago Press.

Torgerson, W. S. (1958). *Theory and Methods of Scaling*. New York: Wiley.

Walberg, H. J., and Thomas, S. C. (1972). Open education: an operational definition and validation in Great Britain and the United States. *American Educational Research Journal*, **9**, 197–208.

Waller, W. (1932). *The Sociology of Teaching*. New York: Wiley.

Wasserman, S. S. (1977). Mathematical models for graphs. School of Urban and Public Affairs. Pittsburgh, Pennsylvannia: Carnegie-Mellon University.

White, H., Boorman, S. A., and Breiger, R. L. (1976). Social structure from multiple networks. I. Blockmodels of roles and positions. *American Journal of Sociology*, **81**, 730–780.

Whyte, W. (1967). *Street Corner Society*. Chicago: University of Chicago Press.

Wyatt, D. L. (1977). The student clique system of a desegregated high school and its influence on the instructional process *Dissertation Abstracts*, **4457A**, Number 7.

CHAPTER 13

Social Interactions of Adolescent Females in Natural Groups

RICHARD
C. SAVIN-WILLIAMS

> Divergence is most marked and sudden in the pubescent period—in the early teens. At this age, by almost world-wide consent, boys and girls separate for a time, and lead their lives during this most critical period more or less apart . . . (Hall, 1904, p. 617).

Social scientists from a diversity of methodological and theoretical persuasions point to the peer group as a crucial determinant in 'healthy' development during the teenage years (Ausubel, 1954; Conger, 1973; Devereux, 1955; Douvan and Adelson, 1966; Dunphy, 1969; Elkind, 1971; Hartup, 1970; Horrocks, 1976; LeFrancois, 1976; Sherif and Sherif, 1964). Horrocks notes, 'An adolescent's relationship to his peers and his participation in their activities is usually one of the most important things in his life' (p. 512). Hartup (1976) concurs in assessing the significance of the relationships: he maintains that experience with peers is a universal component of adolescent development and that 'normal' social development cannot be achieved in the absence of such interaction.

Relations with peers apparently becomes increasingly important around the beginning of puberty (Dunphy, 1969; Hartup, 1970). At this time, the peer

343

group serves as the major socializing or character-forming agent for adolescent development (LeFrancois, 1976). Various writers have emphasized the following functions of the peer group: (1) it facilitates the transition from the nuclear family to a peer orientation (in psychoanalytic terms, transference of libido from primary to secondary objects); (2) it provides a number of diverse models for testing and reflecting upon the developing sense of identity, ideology, and value orientation; (3) it enhances a clear image of self by providing important feedback; (4) it provides for a variety of experiences with people and places, encouraging the development of competent social and interpersonal skills; (5) it socializes the expression of aggression and sexual attitudes and behaviours, paving the way for more mature relations; (6) it aids the interpretation of verbal and nonverbal cues concerning one's position and power; (7) it fills an emotional and social void; and (8) it provides an essential proving ground or normative regulator for attitudes and aspirations.

The peer group has a life of its own. The adolescent appears to be a different person when s/he is so associated rather than not; at least, different parts of the personality are displayed (Horrocks, 1976). Association can exist on a number of levels: (1) pairs—usually with 'best friends'; (2) primary group (cliques)—characterized by face-to-face interactions; a small number of members, usually similar in age, sex, and social class; unspecialized purpose; relative permanence; and a commonly shared set of likes and dislikes which ties the group together; (3) extended primary group (gang or crowd)—composed of a number of cliques or primary groups, usually modelled in an organized fashion with a special purpose; and (4) secondary groups—large, formalized organizations, for example, Girl Guides, YMCA, High School.

The second level (primary group) is the principal concern of this chapter. As Hollingshead (1949) has noted, 'On all levels, the clique is the social group within which persons work out most of their intimate, personal relationships during periods of leisure and recreation' (p. 80). An adolescent informed him, 'You can't understand those kids unless you get into their group' (p. 204). Even though the clique frequently has negative characteristics (e.g. snobbish, exclusive, condescending, intolerant of deviancy), its impact on the development of adolescents as the primary locus of self-esteem, confidence, security, and identity cannot be doubted (Ausubel, 1954).

The literature on adolescence is replete with accounts of male groups in novels (e.g. Golding, 1954), in gang studies (e.g. Thrasher, 1927), and in naturalistic research (Lippitt, Polansky and Rosen, 1952; Savin-Williams, 1976, 1977a; Sherif, Harvey, White, Hood and Sherif, 1961; Sherif and Sherif, 1953; Sherif and Sherif, 1964).

We now turn our attention to groups of female adolescents for which natural observation studies are almost non-existent. Despite its inadequacies, the scattered research does provide insight into the size, stability, structure, and function of adolescent female cliques.

First in this chapter, the nature of female groups in non-human primates and in other cultures is to be explored, providing the necessary background for the remaining sections of this review and for a recent observational study by the author of four female groups.

NON-HUMAN PRIMATES

Assuming the ethological perspective that social behaviour and its resultant impact on the social organization of a group are similar to, or at least continuous among, genetically related species, one may examine the non-human primate literature on group formation among adolescents for possible insights into human female adolescent behaviour and social structure. Although this literature is as sparse as its counterpart in humans, several trends are worth noting.

Adolescent female squirrel monkeys (Baldwin, 1971), talapoin monkeys (Rowell, 1973), vervet monkeys (McGuire, 1974), and green monkeys (Dunbar, 1974) all decrease their peer group interactions at the onset of puberty. When playing with fellow adolescents, the females become passive, especially when males are in the group. The social sphere is not, however, necessarily narrowed as interactions with adult females and infants increase. For example, langurs widen their radius of activities, developing a strong attachment both to adult females (with 4–5 hours per day spent in mutual grooming) and to infants (Jay, 1963; Poirier, 1970; Sugiyama, 1965).

These same patterns continue as one moves from the New to Old World monkeys and to the apes. Young orangutans of both sexes form 'brief social groups' while adolescent females, now pregnant, move from their mothers' sphere into their own territory, each with a male (Galdikas-Brindamour, 1975).

After puberty the level of peer play and associations drops dramatically in adolescent chimpanzee females, from 70 to 30 instances per hour of observations. At this stage, more time is spent with adult females, engaged in mutual grooming, or with infants whom they often 'kidnap'. While Goodall (1968) noted some instances of boisterous vocalizations, play, and grooming among female adolescent peers, she made no reference to peer group formation or structure.

An extensive review of the non-human literature on primate adolescence (Savin-Williams, in preparation) reveals no examples of females forming stable peer groups for any length of time. This is in direct contrast to the frequently reported 'bachelor' groups among many primate species. In these male adolescent groupings, usually formed at the periphery of the natal group, a systematic group dominance–submission structure can be clearly delineated. Except when in oestrus, female adolescents rarely engage in dominance interactions, usually ranking near the bottom and/or next to their mother in the total group dominance–submission hierarchy. The level of dominance interaction, giving more dyadic threats than receiving, and receiving more dyadic avoidances than giving, among the three adolescents in a troop of 25 Barbary macaques was low and inconsistent (Deag, 1977). While the *A* female dominated the *C* adolescent, the *A–B* and *B–C* dyadic relationships were slightly reversed.

A female may be 'kidnapped' by a male before or at puberty; in hamadryas baboons she is adopted or claimed by the time she is 2 years of age, before her first oestrus (Kummer, 1968). Macaca (Nishida, 1966), baboon (Rowell, 1969), orangutan (Cohen, 1975; MacKinnon, 1974), and chimpanzee (Goodall, 1968) adolescent females have been spotted living alone for short periods of time or shifting groups (usually during the first cycling period), but this is an individual and not a group effort.

In summary, while a non-human primate female at pubertal onset may decrease, maintain, or increase her radius of social contact in relation to former standards, her relations with peers of either sex dramatically *decreases* during adolescence. Adult females now become her 'reference' group and infants become her focus of attention. Perhaps due to social contact and hormonal changes (Baldwin and Baldwin, 1977), the adolescent female becomes more passive and withdrawn from aversive contingencies. She seldom asserts herself or is the recipient of antagonism, an adaptive strategy for protecting genetic potential. Unlike her male counterpart, the female adolescent seldom becomes a solitaire, forms a unisex group, relocates, or becomes peripheralized. Staying with the natal group is the norm; if this is abridged then it is usually just after the onset of pubescence and before the first parturition. This time lag between first swelling and conception is prolonged in many of the 'higher' non-human primates; in rhesus monkeys, baboons, and chimpanzees this period of cyclic irregularity and sterility has been documented (Graham, 1970). It is thought that this period, properly called *adolescence*, is a time to learn complex skills and cultural traditions. With males, these tasks are learned while in a peer group situation; with females, they are learned while in the company of adult females.

CROSS-CULTURAL STUDIES

Knowledge concerning the formation and structure of female adolescent groups in cultures other than American is extremely scant. Yet, such information is vital for a comprehensive understanding of the processes necessary to initiate and maintain a primary group among pubertal girls. A cursory outline of available anthropological data is provided below.

Chinese adolescent girls transcend from childhood to adulthood roles and status primarily through the family, and not the peer group. Hsu, Watrous and Lord (1961) noted that girls lack ' . . . the urge to cohere with their peer group because they had a far more tenacious relationship with their elders on the vertical plane' (p. 50).

While both Kibbutz (Spiro, 1965) and non-Kibbutz (Wolman, 1951) Israeli adolescent girls form same-sex cliques, they were far fewer in number than comparable groupings among adolescent males. Wolman's data were collected through questionnaires sent to over 2,500 8- to 20-year-olds. Thirty-eight per cent of the 8- to 12-year-olds but only 15 per cent of the 12- to 14-year-old 'gangs' were all-female. It appeared to Wolman that at the older age few of the gangs were all-female.

German 14-year-old girls were more apt to be observed by peers, teachers, and parents in pairs than in the larger, energetic play groups characteristic of 14-year-old boys and of girls at a younger age (Weise, 1976). This pattern was also characteristic of pubertal girls in East Africa (Edel, 1937), Samoa (Mead, 1928) and New Guinea (Mead, 1930). Samoan pre-teen and teenage boys had large and long-lasting associations; pre-teen girls formed loose-and-easy groups, but with puberty a girl was absorbed into the household. Mead (1930) noted that groupings of twos and threes were occasionally observed after pubertal onset in girls, the size was 'never more'. Magnus adolescents had much the same pattern. Girl play groups usually ended at 14 years of age and boys' play groups at 20 years of age. Mundugumor girls were observed in pairs, threes, or alone; boys were observed in larger groups (Mead, 1935). While Bathonga boys of South Africa roamed with large, all-male groups herding sheep and stayed with the same group in a 'dormitory', the adolescent girls remained with their mother or an adoptive woman (Goldman, 1937). Iroquois (Quain, 1937) and Dakota (Mirsky, 1937) Indian boys from the age of 8 years old until adulthood played in large and fortuitously composed games of war and hunting; the girls were under the guidance of their mother.

Similar activity patterns have also been noted in more westernized countries. After pubertal onset Israeli girls no longer 'ran wild'. They sat on the grass, talking or playing the harmonica, or went to a dance or a movie. An 'ambitious' girl usually stood out, as the leader—'Queen' (Wolman, 1951). While some German girls engaged in games with peers, most remained calm, walking or talking with each other. Contrary to 14-year-old boys, they displayed a degree of tenderness in interpersonal relationships (Weise, 1976).

Mead (1935) referred to leadership and dominance patterns in group structure in play groups of males, but not among girls. 'In the children's group, the relative dominance and submission among the boys is very noticeable. This is less marked among the girls, as the normal constellations are continually being disturbed by the exigencies of the avoidance tabus which are enjoined upon betrothed' (p. 221).

Based upon such cross-cultural sketches, one can conclude that pubescent girls forsake their childhood play groups either to join the household or to develop a personal friendship with another girl. Groups that do exist are small in size and infrequent in assemblage; activities become far less 'assertive' and 'energetic' than previously, and less so than among adolescent boys. Group structure is not easily recognized by the girls or by observers.

FREQUENCY AND SIZE OF FEMALE GROUPS

Drawing upon the preceding cross-species and cross-cultural data, one might hypothesize that female adolescent groups in the United States are to be found less frequently, and when so are smaller in size, than male counterparts. Theorists of adolescent development have not failed to take note of this sex difference. Ausubel (1954) maintained that adolescent girls form small cliques rather than gather in crowds like boys because they have less access to formal and public definitions of independent status in the adolescent peer culture, and because they are more interested than are boys in people and the subtleties of small, close interpersonal relationships. Adolescent girls are purported to be more status conscious, disdainful of out-group members, and jealous of risking such status to potential rivals. Thus, they do not form groups but have intense relationships with other girls in pairs or threesomes. Douvan and Adelson (1966) have argued much the same. The developmental tasks during adolescence for boys are dominated by needs for achievement and independence, best worked through in a group; for girls, developing interpersonal skills and love, which are best achieved in dyadic relationships.

Angrist (1969) has accounted for the size difference by noting that females from birth are oriented toward a contingency sex-role development. Rather than simply fitting into an organized group, girls negotiate interpersonal relationships in face-to-face interactions. Savin-Williams (1977b) found little difference among adolescent girls in traits attributed to ideal leaders and ideal friends: honest, trustworthy, fun, outgoing, relates to my problems, respectful of you, considerate, cooperative, sensible—all these traits emphasize the expressive, close-knit relationships desirable in both friendships and the peer group.

While theory concerning the frequency and size of adolescent female groups has not been lacking in exponents, the empirical evidence is considerably more sparse. Nevertheless, it tends to confirm the speculations of low frequency and small size. Same-sex, small cliques among adolescent girls apparently predominate during early adolescence, phasing out as heterosexual interests expand. Crane (1942) found through retrospective interview data that all-female groups were generally abandoned after 13 years of age. Observational studies indicate a slightly later break-up time of the exclusive same-sex female group. Hollingshead (1949) found that at 14 years old associations among girls were almost exclusively same-sex; by the end of the sixteenth year mixed-sex groupings were more prevalent. At this time, which he referred to as the 'latent phase of pals', the old group of girls may get together 'for old times' sake' and wonder why their relationship is no longer the same. Disappointments in love may bring a girl back to the clique, but only temporarily until a new 'dreamboy' comes along.

Dunphy (1969) noted that same-sex female cliques in 'early' adolescence give way to heterosexual cliques during middle and late adolescence. Boys are generally later in reaching these same developmental stages because, Ausubel (1954) hypothesized, of their later physical, emotional, and social maturation.

In Thrasher's (1927) study of 1,313 Chicago gangs, only six gangs were all-female. Girls gathered more often in a clique or set than in a gang, implying an entirely different type of collective behaviour. Thrasher found inadequate the explanation that girls lack the 'gang instinct' since several 'tomboy' girls were observed in otherwise all-male gangs; rather, he attributed the sex difference to the fact that an adolescent girl's social patterns of behaviour are more closely guarded and supervised by adults.

Zachry's (1940) contact with adolescents led her to conclude that girls seemed more interested than boys in establishing intimate relationships with same-sex peers; boys spent most of their time with a gang. Both patterns tended to break up after middle adolescence unless the individual was emotionally and socially immature.

Two non-observational studies in the early 1940s confirmed the earlier impressionistic accounts. Among 14-year-old females friendship selections were compact and separated into small cliques; boys displayed considerably more overlap in their choices, resulting in larger groupings (Jones, 1943). In the other study (Crane, 1942), questionnaires were given to a number of Australian college students asking for their recollection of childhood gangs. More males than females remembered belonging to such groups and the size of the male gangs was greater in range and average than the female gangs. In both sexes gang membership declined after 13 years of age.

Hollingshead's (1949) work is the one community study from the Chicago-based school of sociology that most explicitly and extensively documents the existence and size of female groups in natural settings. He recorded in his observation notebook that same-age girls were often seen walking together in groups of twos or threes, seldom more. Even when large groups were artifically created (e.g. through Cheer Club), 'They break up into little groups and, if you're not in one of the groups, you're left out of things' (p. 203). Existing groups were slow to accept new members. However, based on sociometric choices, Hollingshead reported that for both sexes the modal size of school and recreational cliques was four to five. The female range was 2–12 years; the corresponding male range, 2–9 years. No mention was made of the frequency with which the sexes entered into cliques. On the other hand, in River City, 'gangs' were found only among the adolescent boys. (Havighurst, Bowman, Liddle, Matthews and Pierce, 1962).

Jennings' (1950) study of 400 12- to 16-year-old girls in the New York State Training School for Girls reported the existence of small, compact groups of girls. Her sociometric data were not, however, concerned with group structure or maintenance but with interpersonal behaviour and characteristics of leaders and isolates based on choice selection of the girls and ratings by housemothers.

Based on sketchy observational data, Gesell, Ilg and Ames (1956) concluded that from the age of 10 to 16 years girls prefer several best friends rather than a large group for leisure-time activities and for emotional and social support. They reported that, even if she is a part of a large group from the age of 12 to 15 years, a girl will frequently leave the large group to be with one or two best friends, a replication of Hollingshead's findings. The same-age boys, while perhaps having a few best 'buddies', still prefer associations with large groups of boys. At Summerhill, adolescent girls were more likely than boys to entertain themselves in small groups (Neill, 1960). The preadolescent and early adolescent years for the girls was a time for cattiness, jealousy, and antagonisms—making large groups unfeasible. Four girl cliques were observed at Rome High School (Henry, 1963). Fourteen-year-old Lila reported, 'And as they grow toward adolescence, girls do not need groups; as a matter of fact, for many of the things they do, more than two would be an obstacle. Boys flock; girls seldom get together in groups above four whereas for boys a group of four is almost useless' (p. 150).

Coleman's questionnaire study (1961) of 10 high schools reported that the number of cliques among girls was greater than among boys; that is, girls were more likely to have more shared selections among themselves. The male groupings were more diverse (less 'connectivity') and thus larger. In a structural interview survey study of girl scout and boy scout adolescents, Douvan and Adelson (1966) found that the groups among girls were small in number, usually consisting of only a few close friends. The ties they did have with larger groupings were not strong, frequently going through breaking and re-joining cycles: 'Girls, on the other hand, even when they are part of a large group of friends, tend to form into centers of intimate two- and threesomes' (p. 194). Boys formed gangs, even when their number of friends was small.

Over a 14 month period in a large high school, a female observer was able to identify seven groups of girls on the basis of 'frequent and recurrent patterns of interaction within and outside of the school' (Sherif, Kelly, Rodgers, Sarup and Tittler, 1973, p. 316). These groups of 17-year-olds, averaging six or seven members, were observed, it would appear, because of their 'large' size and diversity of concerns (e.g. athletics, business, rural). There was no indication of how typical these female groups were in size or frequency. The data do clearly reveal, however, that medium-size groups of adolescent girls exist.

Recent urban studies of ethnic Americans corroborate the sex differences reported above. Suttles (1968) observed 16- to 19-year-old black and Mexican girls involved in gangs, but the mean size was considerably smaller than their male counterparts. Italian girls were occasionally seen in small groups, but these were not formalized gangs. Cronin (1976) reported the same pattern for several middle-class urban groups of 10- to 13-year-old Afro-American girls.

After reviewing the literature on sex differences and social behaviour, Maccoby and Jacklin (1975) concluded, 'Boys are highly oriented toward a peer group and congregate in larger groups, girls associate in pairs or small groups of agemates ... ' (p. 349). In addition, many investigators mentioned above found the incidence of female groups to be cited less frequently than in male counterparts when the definition of a group was a gang rather than a clique, regardless of social class, ecological variables, or other sociological data. This is most obvious in naturalistic observation studies, and can be reported by outsiders, informed others, and the adolescent participants. Sociometric data, while generally confirming the observational data, at times obscure these sex differences. The basic finding of girls in small cliques and boys in large gangs is fundamental input for a proper understanding of the next two issues to be discussed in this literature review: the internal structure and the function or purpose of these female groups.

INTERNAL STRUCTURE

The cross-species and cultural data provide few clues as to the internal organization of adolescent female groups, in part because either such groupings were seldom observed or they were so small as to render difficult any analysis of group structure. Research with regard to adolescent female group structure in American society is almost as difficult to interpret.

Hartup (1970) described the essentials of a group: ' ... it is not truly a group until leaders and followers have emerged or until labor has been divided in some way' (p. 370). The result is usually a hierarchical structure of status differentiations among group members. This group structure may become stabilized or polarized within minutes of initial social contact and is usually not rigid, but flexible by setting and over time. Hartup makes few age or sex distinctions in this basic orientation.

In summarizing the peer group literature Horrocks (1976) concluded, 'Girls' groups are not usually as well organized as boys' ... and they tend to operate without an identified leader' (pp. 521–522). Ausubel (1954) noted the basic equality of girl clique members, in part due to member sameness in personal attributes, values, social development, and physical maturity. However, he also maintained that girls are more accurate than boys in predicting how group members rank on acceptance–rejection sociometric exercises and that leadership within the female cliques carries over from one situation to another.

Researchers who have utilized various questionnaire methodologies— retrospective (Crane, 1942), sociometric (Coleman, 1961) and time-sampling (Larson, Mayers and Csikszentmihalyi, 1977)—report awareness among females, of who are the leaders in cliques, gangs and crowds. Female leadership is more formalized than male. In one study (Crane, 1942) adolescent females were more likely to appoint a leader while male leadership was more a matter of common concensus.

Observational studies are not unanimous in regard to the distinctiveness of leadership in the adolescent female group. Hollingshead (1949) found that group leadership was fluid, voluntary and informal. One girl, Gladys, said of her fellow clique member, 'Sometimes she dominates me and sometimes I dominate her'. Personalized accounts in Jennings (1950) and Gordon (1957), however, reveal an awareness, on the part of clique girls, of who are leaders, isolates and followers, but no such awareness of the entire order:

> Jacqueline can lead and not make the girls feel they are being overpowered but rather that they are doing things of their own accord . . . (Jennings, 1950, p. 193).

> There's nothing definite about her. She never takes sides on issues that come up . . . she'll let people put things over on her . . . It's almost as if she has no self-respect the way she lets people get her to do things for them. (Jennings, 1950, p. 168).

With regard to Sherif et al.'s (1973) observational study of 17 high school girls, although high and low status individuals were identifiable in each natural group, there was some difficulty in getting into their activities to clarify the role structures as had been done with boys. Female groups were quite cohesive and were generally highly male oriented, except for the 'long hairs' and 'athletes'.

The most explicit statements regarding group structure come from Dunphy's naturalistic study (1969) of Australian adolescent female crowds and cliques. When asked who were the leaders in the clique, girls disclaimed the existence of any such person: 'Oh, we're all equal!' But if asked in terms of specifics— for example, who arranges parties, who do you call to find out what is going on—then there was clear concensus on leadership. Diaries also confirmed status differentiations among the girls. Dunphy seldom, however, distinguished more than leaders and followers, even though he referred to the 'power structure' of the cliques, which should indicate a series of ordered positions beyond the first. The concern primarily was on the role the leader played in the clique and the larger crowd, an issue beyond the scope of this chapter.

While relatively little can be stated with any authority concerning the total group structure of female cliques or gangs, it is apparent that girls distinguish the broad categories of leaders and followers. This is still a relatively unexplored area.

ACTIVITIES AND FUNCTION OF FEMALE GROUPS

Observational reports of adolescent female groups have been most explicit in delineating the range of activities in which girls participate when with same-sex peers. In small groups of friends, girls joke, confide of loves or hoped-for-affairs, compare clothing, relax, tease each other, and just talk (in person or over the phone). Besides such activities, frequently summarized in America by the term 'hanging out together', such groups become involved in sports, attend dances and movies together, watch television or listen to records in each other's home, and go out smoking, drinking, or partying. Hollingshead (1949) found that from 64 per cent to 99 per cent of a girl's leisure time was with the clique. At school, girls gather in the halls, 'talking animatedly to one another about what they have done, or what they plan to do' (p. 167), and during classes they sit in adjacent seats. These activities were remarkably the same in the 1940s as in the 1970s and from upper-class to lower-middle class girls. Horrocks (1976) and Hartup (1970) summarized these activities as times when girls can escape the family and home to relax, pass the time, and have a good time. Few of the studies, however, give quantitative data, that is, how much time the groups are in which activities, or which are most meaningful to a girl's development.

At one level the basic purpose or function of groups among female adolescents is to offer an alternate environment for being oneself. Within this small grouping one finds mutual friendships, emotional support systems, intimacy, security, and belongingness (Hollingshead, 1949; Horrocks, 1976; Maccoby and Jacklin, 1975); novelty as well as sameness (Hollingshead, 1949); popularity (Douvan and Adelson, 1966); and development of social and interpersonal skills (Douvan and Adelson, 1966). In the peer group or small clique an adolescent girl sees a 'flesh-and-blood' mirror of herself—in terms of social relations, values, attitudes and personality (Jennings, 1950). Sherif et al.s (1973) suggest that the groups one joins reflects one's sense of identity.

In some respects, of course, peer group activities and functions are the same for male and female adolescents. However, the smaller size of the female groups, previously documented, encourages a more close-knit, intimate grouping. This exclusive, intimate characteristic is congruent with a basic developmental difference between the sexes as girls:

> rely more heavily on a close tie to a best friend, or to two or three good friends. They use the group as a source of narcissistic supplies ... or as a mechanism for finding girls with whom to build a more intimate relationship. But they do not generally value the authority or solidarity of the group qua group the ways boys often do (Douvan and Adelson, 1966, p. 201).

This sex difference is further explored in Douvan and Gold (1966):

> The group as such supports boys in their move toward independence: they depend on this source of strength and reciprocate with fraternal loyalty. Girls, less provoked by inner striving for freedom, have less need for group support and tend rather to conceive a group as a setting in which to find close dyadic relationships ... The two sex groups use social relationships differently to support and express these central concerns'. (pp. 494–495).

A NEW STUDY OF FEMALE GROUPS

In the summer of 1976 a project was undertaken by the author to help clarify the ontogenesis and function of female adolescent groups. The setting was a 5-week summer camp for girls between the ages of 10 and 17 years old. The methodology employed was primarily naturalistic observations with additional sociometric, questionnaire, and interview data available. After a brief sketch of the methodology (for more details see Savin-Williams, 1976, 1977b), the interpersonal dominance–submission relations of four cabin groups are detailed.

Methods

Setting

The camp was located in the north central section of the United States. Camp facilities encouraged a variety of recreational, instructional, and interpersonal activities, including handiwork and crafts, swimming, sailing, religious discussions, canoeing, and dramatic skits. The 300 girls were divided into age homogenous units, cabin groups of four to six girls and a college-age leader.

Subjects

Four groups of five girls between the ages of 12 and 14 years old were extensively observed over the 5-week camping session by their cabin counsellor. In most cases these girls shared a common upper-middle class, white and protestant orientation. They were mentally, physically, and emotionally healthy adolescents from intact families, living in Midwestern suburbs or small cities. Most had previously been to this particular camp, but many did not know their new cabin-mates (who were assigned randomly by the camp administration).

Procedures

Each female cabin counsellor, as participant observer, recorded by an event-sampling technique during 4 of every 5 days all episodes of dyadic verbal and physical expressions of dominance and submission occurring within the cabin group. Sampling of dominance interactions was systematically dispersed through the daily schedule: bedtimes, cabin clean-up, mealtimes, rest hour, and cabin activities, averaging 3 hours per observation day.

The focus was on dyadic interactions and the outcome of such encounters. Dominance and submission were categorized according to eight indices of behaviour, derived from observational studies of primatologists, social psychologists, and human ethologists and pretested in a pilot study (Savin-Williams, 1977a). The indices were: verbal directives, ridicule, physical assertiveness, recognition of other's status, physical threat, counter dominance (ignoring orders or shunning), and verbal rebuttals and arguments. Each index was subdivided and categorized as overt or indirect.

To allow for a more detailed analysis, the observational data were divided into three time periods, corresponding to temporal thirds of the total camp duration, usually 10 days each. Cabin members were rank ordered for each time period, summing indices and settings. The reversal rate, or transgressions against established status relationships, was the percentage of the total number of dominance behaviours occurring in a group in which the subordinates dominate higher ranking group members.

Two sociometrics were given to the girls during the first week of camp: (1) 'List the campers in the cabin, including yourself, in order of dominance' (also completed by junior counsellors after they assumed leadership over the cabin on the leader's day off); and (2) 'List in order your friends in the group'. The girls were also instructed to write the qualities that an ideal leader and an ideal friend should have, to reach a group consensus on these characteristics, and to rate each other on the traits.

In an attempt to discover the physical, behavioural, and social attributes which characterize the various dominance positions within a group, several tests, measurements, and observations were conducted during the camping session: body size, pubertal development, sleeping position in the cabin, family situation, demographic data (age, socioeconomic status, race, religion, years at camp, sibling order), intelligence, and athletic ability.

Results

Assessment of dominance structure

Members in all four cabin-groups ranked significantly ($p < .05$) the same on all eight indices of dominance; thus, the eight were aggregated to form the behavioural definitions of *dominance* and *submission*. A group hierarchy was inferred by summing the results of these dyadic interactions. The number one position was assigned to the girl who dominated the most cabin-mates in pair-wise interactions; the number two position to the next highest number, and so forth. In the case of ties, a girl was placed higher if she dominated the fellow tie-maker more than the reverse.

In all groups the girls behaved as if they recognized status differentiations among themselves. Thirty-five of the 40 dyadic pairings were significantly unidirectional ($p < .06$); three of the remaining five approached significance. In 11 of the 12 time periods transgressions against hierarchical relationships were significantly ($p < .05$) lower than the established status rankings.

Even though the dominance structure became more stable over time (reversal rates decreased), there were fluctuations in relative status over time. The most frequent shift occurred between the two top ranking girls during the middle third of camp. Last ranked girls remained least dominant during the entirety of the camping session. One of three situations was evident when a dyadic relationship was unstable: (1) a realignment of intra-cabin coalitions or friendships; (2) a girl withdrawing from cabin activities due to personal problems; or (3) the increasing involvement in the group social life by a first-year camper.

Frequency of dominance encounters

In the 402 hours in which the female groups were observed, slightly over 2,500 instances of dominance behaviours were recorded. The per hour average ranged from 4.85 to 8.46 dominance encounters in the four cabins; the overall average was 6.34. In three of the four groups the frequency rate increased as the camping session progressed.

Daily fluctuations from this average frequency rate were common. The 12 days in which the daily average was considerably above the group mean were times of extracurriculum events; for example, the formal banquet, the first beach night supper, and the first overnight sleepout.

Three categories of dominance behaviour formed the bulk of the observed number among the girls. These same three (ridicule, directives and recognition) were also the best indicators of relative status (see Table 13.1).

Dominance encounters were evenly divided between overt and indirect behaviour. The 48 per cent indirect ratio average became larger as the camping session progressed, significantly ($p < .01$) larger in two groups. During the last third of camp the usage of indirect behaviours was more frequent (54 per cent of the total) than overt strategies.

Table 13.1.   Frequency and reversal rate of dominance behaviours

Indices	% of the total behaviour observed for each index	Reversal rate for each index
Ridicule	28%	23%
Recognition	23%	28%
Directives	22%	18%
Counter dominance	13%	30%
Verbal control	7%	34%
Physical assertion	5%	35%
Threats	1%	26%
Displacement	1%	48%

Table 13.2.   Settings for dominance behaviours

Settings	Per hour frequency rate for each setting	Average reversal rate for each setting
Discussions	17.6	35%
Activities	11.1	24%
Bedtimes	7.5	31%
Clean-up	6.5	20%
Mealtimes	2.9	21%

Dominance behaviour in various settings

Regardless of the specific behavioural setting (rest hour, mealtime, etc.) in which the girls were observed, group members ranked significantly ($p < .01$) the same. The group structure was most stable during clean up and mealtimes, and least stable during cabin discussions and meetings. The first two were settings with a relatively low incidence of dominance interactions while dominance behaviours were most likely to occur during discussions. Thus, the best setting predictors of group status were those in which the frequency rate of dominance behaviour was lowest (see Table 13.2).

Sociometric assessment of dominance

On two of the four cabin dominance sociometric exercises, girls significantly ($p < .05$) agreed among themselves on relative rank. But only one of these was significantly related to the behaviourally derived dominance hierarchy. Non-group members (substitute counsellors) also had difficulty in rank ordering the girls. Of 10 such rankings only two reached significance ($p < .05$); the others ranged from -0.10 to $+0.80$ correlations, with most hovering around a low, positive mark.

Characteristics of the rank order

The rank order of girls on athletic ability and group leadership were the same as on dominance ($p < .05$). Those girls who were most popular among peers, who most frequently had someone sitting beside them, and who had reached a more mature level of pubertal development as compared with cabin-mates were also likely to be most dominant in the cabin (see Table 13.3).

Best friends tended: (1) to be close in dominance rank (43 per cent expected by chance; observed level—71 per cent); and (2) to sleep closest together (24 per cent expected by chance; observed level—47 per cent). The girls did

Table 13.3. The combined correlations of various physical, social and behavioural characteristics with the dominance hierarchy

Traits	r_s	Statistical significance
Leadership	0.82	0.05
Athletic ability	0.56	0.05
Sit beside	0.65	0.10
Popularity	0.63	0.10
Pubertal maturation	0.55	0.10
Chronological age	0.33	ns
Intelligence	0.30	ns
Physical size	0.28	ns
Socioeconomic status	− 0.10	ns
Overtness	− 0.30	ns
Bed position	− 0.51	ns

not necessarily interact most in dominance encounters with first- or last-ranked best friend, nor with a neighbouring ranked girl.

Styles of dominance and submission

There were similarities that spanned cabin groups among members in style of behaviour toward others and in physical and social traits. Not all 'types' were represented in each cabin; neither did all cabins have only one of each type. Some girls did not fit into any of the classifications below.

Maternal leaders

Frequently indirect, maternal leaders were most apt to give unsolicited advice on proper dress, manners and grooming. They were perceived by peers as a source of security and support and were described as confident, loyal, kindhearted and manipulative.

They were pubertally mature, physically large, and chronologically old in comparison to cabin-mates. Liked by both peers and adults, maternal leaders demonstrated intelligent behaviour and ideal leadership traits. Within their family, which was usually one of the cabin's lowest in socioeconomic status, they were the youngest children.

Antagonists

Antagonists were the most actively involved in cabin dominance encounters, frequently countering or refuting others. Cabin-mates frequently recognized the antagonists' superior status. Described by counsellors as the 'mood setters', antagonists were apt to utilize overt dominance strategies. They were portrayed by peers and adults alike as aggressive girls who imposed themselves on others, enticing others to join them in breaking camp regulations; as charismatic and spirited individuals; and as problem campers, that is, possessing negative leadership characteristics and continually contesting the authority of the counsellor.

In every female group the best athlete was an antagonist, who was in turn one of the most physically mature. The antagonist was always a returning camper, coming from a wealthy, but not necessarily stable family. All had older brothers and were amongst the youngest in their family. After an initial attraction, an antagonist usually lost her peer popularity as camp progressed. Not unexpectedly, she was frequently the cabin member least liked by the counsellor.

Amorphous miss average

Amorphous Miss Averages' distinguishing pattern was being modal in most indices and settings in their usage of and success at dominance behaviours. Usually they were the least involved in dominance interactions and, as camp progressed, they declined in their success dominations of others. Cabin-mates described them as non-descript, placid, shy, quiet, neat, 'just there', and 'the most forgettable character'.

Despite being amongst the youngest members of the cabin, the Miss Averages were usually the tallest and heaviest. On most other characteristics, however, they were average. Three of the four were first-year campers, all had large families, and all were liked by their cabin counsellors. Cabin-mates perceived them as having a potential for leadership that was not manifested behaviourally.

Compliant clingers

These girls frequently recognized the superior dominance status of cabin-mates by doing favours and giving compliments. When dominant—a rare event—they usually argued. Compliant clingers apparently set themselves up for being picked on, an almost universal reaction to them. This position of vulnerability was most obvious in their tendency constantly to minitor surrounds. Cabin-mates described this type of girl as friendly, talkative, and extraverted; however, they avoided her, considering her an embarrassment. If shown attention, the compliant held on physically like a 'leech'.

Compliant clingers were the worse athletes, the most pubertally immature, the shortest and the lighest. In most cases they were the oldest child in a wealthy family. Four of the six were first-year campers. They possessed few leadership traits, were not popular with peers and slept closest to the cabin counsellor.

Conclusion

None of the female cabin groups formed into a cohesive whole, the girls tended to split into pairs or threesomes. All four cabin leaders wrote of this development in their observational notebooks. For example:

> They did not seem to need each other . . . I saw much split allegiances with few girls seeing any reason to make the cabin work. Most did not give a damn about their tribe or their cabin group . . . Cabin families were a joke! We did not spend enough time together as a cabin group to develop any sense of family. The kids just were not interested in the cabin group as a group . . . They were willing, when I confronted them on numerous occasions, to bring the cabin group together as a group—but no one ever did anything!

During 'freetime' the girls were seldom together as a group; rather, they preferred to associate with sisters or cousins, home-town friends, extra-cabin friends, or one of their close cabin buddies. Apparently, at camp a premium was placed on promoting interpersonal relationships, skills and sensitivity—better accomplished in pairs than in groups.

Although the girls did not form into cohesive groups during the first five weeks of camp, each group did establish patterns of dyadic relations that remained stable by time and setting and can be summarized by reference to a dominance hierarchy. While it is not possible to determine the exact point in group life that relative status was apparent to the girls, opening day dyadic interactions set a 5-week pattern. As camp progressed the group structure became increasingly stable; that is, the reversal rates decreased. Although there were fluctuations in that some girls exchanged positions, few were dramatic alterations. What was setting-dependent was not relative rank but behavioural patterns utilized to assert or express dominance or to assume submission.

The most dominant girls were not only perceived by peers as possessing ideal leadership traits but they also acted as if they were the leaders. A leader might not necessarily suggest the most ideas but the ones vocalized by her were readily perceived by cabin-mates as 'the given'. Lower status girls frequently did not express their opinion or vote until higher ranking girls made their desires and judgements known. Physical, behavioural, and social characteristics of the various status positions have already been summarized, and are more explicitly spelled out elsewhere (Savin-Williams, 1977b).

While boys by and large assert their status by utilizing such power related acts as physical contact, verbal argument, physical displacement, and verbal-physical threats (Savin-Williams, in press), the adolescent girls in this study expressed their status by recognizing others, shunning, ignoring requests, and giving unsolicited advice. One could accurately predict the group hierarchy on the basis of athletic ability, pubertal maturation, and peer popularity.

It would appear that the net effect of a hierarchical group arrangement was to control conflict through a reduction of overt behaviour and to engender a clearly recognized division of labour. It did not necessarily enhance group cohesion or compatability as it did in male groups. The essential instrumental role was taken by the top-ranking girls, who were the leaders, organizers, decision-makers, and attention receivers. Lower ranking girls frequently did the day-to-day activities and duties necessary for some semblance of proper group functioning. Failure to perform these group obligations and roles implied the loss of the prestige that had been bestowed upon them by the group. In addition, most dominant girls also served an expressive function for other girls, who frequently approached them if there were problems in the cabin or if they were being personally picked on by other girls.

SUMMARY

Hollingshead (1949) noted that, 'This persistent relationship between a few boys or a few girls which carries over from one activity to another throughout the day, and day after day, is the most obvious thing about the behavior patterns of the high school pupils' (p. 205). Yet 'The area that has received least attention in research on adolescent friendship is the daily interaction, the content and concern of the relationship. . . . Unfortunately, no comparable description of the high school age group has appeared since Hollingshead observed the youth in Elmtown (1949)' (Douvan and Gold, 1966, p. 494).

Shortcomings are especially critical in two areas: naturalistic observation studies and data on females (Douvan and Gold, 1966; Hartup, 1970). Hartup (1970) is particularly revealing on these points. He notes that most research on groups concern adolescent males and not females. 'Our knowledge of peer influences and group behavior among girls is appallingly weak' (p. 437). Theorizing is heterogeneous with no parsimonious set of principles by which to integrate the research. What is needed is a more extensive gathering and a closer examination of existing anthropological data and a wider range and integration of research methods. In addition, from an ethological perspective, a serious consideration of non-human primate results orients the researcher of human female groups to potentially useful hypotheses and issues to explore.

This review and the study that has been summarized in this chapter are attempts to alleviate these shortcomings. Several major conclusions concerning adolescent female groups can be set forth, true not only for 'American girls' but also for cross-cultural and non-human primate pubescent females: (1) In comparison to their male counterparts, female adolescents are considerably less likely to form stable and consistent groups. (2) Groups that do form are likely to be cliquish (exclusive, intimate, intense) and small, usually pairs or three-somes. (3) If a group structure can be ascertained, then it is likely to be less structured than male adolescent groupings. The leader or 'most dominant' girl is clearly recognized, if not verbally then certainly behaviourally and informally. (4) The female group aids girls in developing highly prized socio-emotional and interpersonal skills and sensitivities; it offers a means of escaping the home to be with friends, to relax, and to spend time.

REFERENCES

Angrist, S. S. (1969). The study of sex roles. *Journal of Social Issues*, **25**, 215–232.

Ausubel, D. P. (1954). *Theory and Problems of Adolescent Development*. New York: Grune and Stratton.

Baldwin, J. D. (1971). The social organization of a semi-free-ranging troop of squirrel monkeys (*Saimiri sciurens*). *Folia Primatologica*, **14**, 23–50.

Baldwin, J. D., and Baldwin, J. I. (1977). The role of learning phenomena in the ontogeny of exploration and play. In S. Chevalier-Skolnikoff and F. E. Poirier (Eds.), *Primate Biosocial Development: Biological, Social, and Ecological Determinants*. New York: Garland.

Cohen, J. E. (1975). The size and demographic composition of social groups of wild orangutans. *Animal Behaviour*, **23**, 543–550.

Coleman, J. S. (1961). *The Adolescent Society*. New York: Free Press.

Conger, J. J. (1973). *Adolescence and Youth*. New York: Harper and Row.

Crane, A. R. (1942). Pre-adolescent gangs: a topological interpretation. *Journal of Genetic Psychology*, **81**, 113–123.

Cronin, C. L. (1976). Playground behavior as a function of rank in the dominance hierarchy. Paper presented at the Animal Behavior Society meeting, Colorado, June.

Deag, J. M. (1977). Aggression and submission in monkey societies. *Animal Behaviour*, **25**, 465–474.

Devereux, E. C. (1955). The world of the adolescent. In *Patterns for Modern Living: Psychological Patterns*. Chicago, Illinois: Delphian Society.

Douvan, E., and Adelson, J. (1966). *The Adolescent Experience*. New York: Wiley.

Douvan, E., and Gold, M. (1966). Model patterns in American adolescence. In L. W. Hoffman and M. L. Hoffman (Eds.), *Review of Child Development Research*. Vol. 2. New York: Russell Sage Foundation.

Dunbar, R. I. M. (1974). Observations on the ecology and social organization of the green monkey, *Cercopithecus subaeus*, in Senegal. *Primates*, **15**, 341–350.

Dunphy, D. C. (1969). *Cliques, Crowds and Gangs*. Melbourne, Australia: Cheshire.

Edel, M. M. (1937). The Bachiga of East Africa. In M. Mead (Ed.), *Cooperation and Competition among Primitive Peoples*. New York: McGraw-Hill.

Elkind, D. (1971). *A Sympathetic Understanding of the Child: Six to Sixteen*. Boston, Massachusetts: Allyn and Bacon.

Galdikas-Brindamour, B. (1975). Orangutans, Indonesia's people of the forest. *National Geographic*, **148**, 444–473.

Gesell, A., Ilg, F. L., and Ames, L. B. (1956). *Youth: The Years from Ten to Sixteen*. New York: Harper and Row.

Golding, W. (1954). *Lord of the Flies*. New York: Capricorn Books.

Goldman, I. (1937). The Bathonga of South Africa. In M. Mead (Ed.), *Cooperation and Competition among Primitive Peoples*. New York: McGraw-Hill.

Goodall, J. (1968). The behaviour of free-living chimpanzees in the Gombe Stream area. *Animal Behavior Monograph*, **1**, 161–311.

Gordon, W. (1957). *The Social System of the High School*. Glencoe, Illinois: Free Press.

Graham, C. E. (1970). Reproductive physiology of the chimpanzee. In G. H. Bourne (Ed.), *The Chimpanzee*. Vol. 3. Basel, Switzerland: Karger.

Hall, G. S. (1904). *Adolescence*. Vol. 2. New York: Appleton.

Hartup, W. W. (1970). Peer interaction and social organization. In P. H. Mussen (Ed.), *Carmichael's Manual of Child Psychology*. Vol. 2. New York: Wiley.

Hartup, W. W. (1976). Adolescent peer relations: a look at the future. In J. P. Hill and F. J. Monks (Eds.), *Adolescence and Youth in the Year 2000*. Guildford: IPC Science and Technology.

Havighurst, R. J., Bowman, P. H., Liddle, G. P., Matthews, C. V., and Pierce, J. V. (1962). *Growing Up in River City*. New York: Wiley.

Henry, J. (1963). *Culture Against Man*. New York: Random House.

Hollingshead, A. B. (1949). *Elmtown's Youth*. New York: Wiley.

Horrocks, J. E. (1976). *The Psychology of Adolescence* (fourth edition). Boston, Massachusetts: Houghton Mifflin.

Hsu, F. L. K., Watrous, B. G., and Lord, E. M. (1961). Culture pattern and adolescent behaviour. *International Journal of Social Psychiatry*, 7, 33–53.

Jay, P. C. (1963). The common langur of North India. In I. DeVore (Ed.), *Primate Behavior*. New York: Holt, Rinehart and Winston.

Jennings, H. H. (1950). *Leadership and Isolation* (Second Edition). New York: Longmans, Green.

Jones, H. E. (1943). *Development in Adolescence*. New York: Appleton-Century.

Kummer, H. (1968). *Social Organization of Hamadryas Baboons*. Chicago, Illinois: University of Chicago Press.

Larson, R., Mayers, P., and Csikszentmihalyi, M. (1977). Experimental sampling of adolescents' socialization: the concepts of family, friends, and being alone. Paper presented at the Conference on Research Perspectives in the Ecology of Human Development. Ithaca, New York: August.

LeFrancois, G. R. (1976). *Adolescents*. Belmont, California: Wadsworth Publishing.

Lippitt, R., Polansky, N., and Rosen, S. (1952). The dynamics of power: a field study of social influence in groups of children. *Human Relations*, 5, 37–64.

Maccoby, E. E., and Jacklin, C. N. (1975). *The Psychology of Sex Differences*. Stanford, California: Stanford University Press.

MacKinnon, J. (1974). The behaviour and ecology of wild orangutans (*Pongo pygmaeus*). *Animal Behavior*, 22, 3–74.

McGuire, M. T. (1974). The St Kitts vervet. In H. Kuhn (Ed.), *Contributions to Primatology*. Vol. 2. Basel, Switzerland: Karger.

Mead, M. (1928). *Coming of Age in Samoa*. New York: Morrow.

Mead, M. (1930). *Growing Up in New Guinea*. New York: Morrow.

Mead, M. (1935). *Sex and Temperament in Three Primitive Societies*. New York: Morrow.

Mirsky, J. (1937). The Dakota. In M. Mead (Ed.), *Cooperation and Competition among Primitive Peoples*. New York: McGraw-Hill.

Neill, A. S. (1960). *Summerhill: A Radical Approach to Child Rearing*. New York: Hart Publishing.

Nishida, T. (1966). A sociological study of solitary male monkeys. *Primates*, 7, 141–204.

Quain, B. H. (1937). The Iroquois. In M. Mead (Ed.), *Cooperation and Competition among Primitive Peoples*. New York: McGraw-Hill.

Poirier, F. E. (1970). The Nilgiri langur (*Presbytis johnii*) of South India. In L. A. Rosenblum (Ed.), *Primate Behavior*. Vol. 1. New York: Academic Press.

Rowell, T. E. (1969). Long-term changes in a population of Ugandan baboons. *Folia Primatologica*, 11, 241–254.

Rowell, T. E. (1973). Social organization of wild talapoin monkeys. *American Journal of Physical Anthropology*, 38, 593–598.

Savin-Williams, R. C. (1976). An ethological study of dominance formation and maintenance in a group of human adolescents. *Child Development*, **47**, 972–979.

Savin-Williams, R. C. (1977a). Dominance in a human adolescent group. *Animal Behaviour*, **25**, 400–406.

Savin-Williams, R. C. (1977b). Dominance–submission behaviors and hierarchies in young adolescents at a summer camp: predictors, styles, and sex differences. Unpublished doctoral dissertation, University of Chicago.

Savin-Williams, R. C. (in press). Dominance and submission during early adolescence: behaviors and hierarchies. In D. R. Omark, D. G. Freedman, and F. F. Strayer (Eds.), *Dominance Relations: Ethological Perspectives on Human Conflict*. New York: Garland Publishing.

Savin-Williams, R. C. (in preparation). Adolescence as a stage of life in non-human primates. Unpublished manuscript, Cornell University.

Sherif, C. W., Kelly, M., Rodgers, Jr., H. L., Sarup, G., and Tittler, B. I. (1973). Personal involvement, social judgment, and action. *Journal of Personality and Social Psychology*, **27**, 311–328.

Sherif, M., Harvey, O. J., White, B. J., Hood, W. R., and Sherif, C. W. (1961). *Intergroup Conflict and Cooperation: The Robbers Cave Experiment*. Norman, Oklahoma: Institute of Group Relations.

Sherif, M., and Sherif, C. W. (1953). *Groups in Harmony and Tension*. New York: Harper.

Sherif, M., and Sherif, C. W. (1964). *Reference Groups*. Chicago, Illinois: Regnery.

Spiro, M. E. (1965). *Children of the Kibbutz*. New York: Schocken.

Sugiyama, Y. (1965). Behavioral development and social structure in two troops of Lanuman langurs (*Presbytis entellus*). *Primates*, **6**, 213–247.

Suttles, G. D. (1968). *The Social Order of the Slum*. Chicago, Illinois: University of Chicago Press.

Thrasher, F. M. (1927). *The Gang*. Chicago, Illinois: University of Chicago Press.

Weise, G. (1976). Fourteen-year-olds' life-style examined. *The German Tribune*, No. 720, p. 12.

Wolman, B. (1951). Spontaneous groups of children and adolescents in Israel. *Journal of Social Psychology*, **34**, 171–182.

Zachry, C. B. (1940). *Emotion and Conduct in Adolescence*. New York: Appleton-Century.

CHAPTER 14

Friendship as a Factor in Male and Female Delinquency

ANNE C. CAMPBELL

Juvenile delinquency is perhaps one of the greatest social enigmas of our time. It has remained relatively impervious to forays by sociologists, psychologists, clinicians, educationalists and social workers. The academic machinery of social science has done nothing to depress the increasing number of juvenile crimes committed yearly. Its elusive quality has made it a natural target for the attention of warring factions of psychologists.

Both the psychoanalytic school and, subsequently, Bowlby have sought to place the main burden of responsibility on the family: Freud (1933) argued that a poor father–son relationship impaired the formation of conscience, while Bowlby (1969) and others believed that a failure to establish a long-standing attachment to a primary caretaker led to psychopathy. Learning theorists, such as Bandura and Walters (1959) and Trasler (1962) took a behaviourist line, arguing that the parents failed to become secondary reinforcers for their child's behaviour and that punishment schedules were too random to depress anti-social behaviour. Developmentalists maintained that moral development was impaired because of the child's early inability to take the

365

role of the parent and escape its own egocentricity. Variables concerned with overpunitive discipline, too little discipline, mother-smothering, mother neglect, breast-feeding, parental rejection, too much concern and too little concern have all been studied often with inconclusive, contradictory or non-replicable results.

A second faction of psychologists has placed the cause of delinquency firmly within the child's own internal personality predisposition. Extreme views in this area take a genetic line. Sheldon, Hartt and McDermott's (1949) typology of bodily structure was reminiscent of the atavistic theories of Lombroso and Ferrero (1958) and Burt (1925) who argued for the importance of 'dull or defective intelligence . . . or an over-development of some single primitive instinct' (Burt, 1925, p. 25). Subsequently Eysenck (1964) pointed to the inter-action of genetically determined personality traits with specific-learning experiences in the family. The enthusiasm for personality assessment and testing after the World War II resulted in the postulation of hundreds of variables which might discriminate 'delinquents' from 'normals'. Many of these were embedded in no theoretical or explanatory framework at all and ranged from inkblot tests through field dependency to IQ. Recent scepticism in the area of personality testing has persuaded some psychologists to adopt a social learning standpoint where delinquent behaviour is still viewed as an enduring characteristic of the individual but one which may be modified by implementing more 'appropriate' reinforcement contingencies. Within the limited confines of institutions, these programmes have met with some success.

A third group has chosen peer relations as the most critical factors in delin-quent behaviour. Sociologists as far back as Thrasher (1927) documented the very social nature of most delinquency and described the structure and opera-tion of juvenile groups. A psychologist, Sutherland, was one of the first to offer an explanation of this in terms of the individual learning both behaviours and attitudes conducive to delinquency within the peer group (cf. Sutherland and Cressey, 1970). The massive evidence on the importance of friendship in delinquency has persuaded many researchers that 'companionship is unquestionably the most telling force in male delinquency and crime' (Reckless, 1955). However, within this third faction, disagreement exists as to the nature of the influence which friends (or the lack of them) has on the individual's delinquent activities. This chapter addresses itself to this debate.

METHODOLOGICAL PROBLEMS IN THE STUDY OF FRIENDSHIP GROUPS

A 'friend', according to the *Oxford English Dictionary*, is 'one joined to another in intimacy and mutual benevolence independently of sexual or family love'. The amorphous quality of friendship effectively deterred research in the area for many years. The new scientific status of psychology could hardly deal with such a phenomenological and personal subject matter. To make it respectable it had to be translated into an operational definition; a prescribed and overt set of behaviours which could be quantified, measured and indexed. However arbitrary, however tenuously related to the experience and emotions of the individual, at least it objectified an internal experience and could be subjected to controlled laboratory experiments which were suitable material for journals and replication studies. In a monolithic effort to avoid actually asking people about their experiences, psychologists never stinted in their efforts to devise measures which the naive subject could not suspect to be related to friendship. In a single book (Cartwright and Zander, 1953) the following measures were reported: the number of times group members used the term 'I' instead of 'we', the number of statements showing discontent, group-mindedness or friendship, the extent of agreement of group norms, the ability of a group to overcome resistance to change, the degree of disruption caused when one member left the group. And industrial work on group cohesion took measures of absenteeism, turnover and payment of union dues. Klein and Crawford (1967) used average distance from members' homes to evening meeting sites as a measure of difficulties overcome to join in group activities in the delinquent gang. They sadly concluded that in 'some groups it is related to attendance figures, in others it is not' (p. 70).

It became clear that these kinds of measures were not only related to a number of other important variables apart from friendship but also that they were extremely hard to quantify in a natural field situation. There was no alternative but to ask subjects for information about their friends. The drive for quantitative rather than qualitative data was still strong and Moreno's (1934) technique of sociometry held an obvious appeal. The psychologist remained in charge, at a distance from his 'subjects'. He alone specified the criteria for choices, the number of others to be selected, the pool from which these choices should be drawn and ultimately drew up the finished group sociogram which was rarely shown to his original informants for their opinion. However, sociometrists sometimes failed to restrict themselves to simple structural description. Jennings (1950), for example, studied the friendship choices of girls in an American reformatory and from the resulting sociogram went on to give causal explanations of friendship choice in terms of the characteristics of leaders, isolates and so on. These are derived from her own personal and 'outside' view of the community with no attempt to check this against the girls' own perceptions. Her attributions of internal states and motivations (for example, 'Each leader ... is intellectually and emotionally "uncomfortable" when others are "unhappy" or "leftout"' p. 203) are no more than informed speculation. One of the major problems with the sociometric technique, particularly with respect to work on delinquency, is that the choice pool is often restricted and the individual is invited to select friends from within the confines of the school. It is a well-established fact that delinquents often underperform academically and show little interest in school either scholastically or socially. Since friendship is a reciprocal phenomenon, it is to be expected that an individual who nominates few friends is likely to receive few nominations himself and will therefore appear as a relatively isolated individual. From this set of information, researchers have often concluded that delinquents have severe social skill problems even to the point of pathological conditions. Croft and Grygier (1956), Sugarman (1968) and Kraft (1966) all reported that boys who were considered badly behaved by teachers were unpopular with their classmates. West and Farrington (1973) in a longitudinal British study tentatively concluded that 'boys who were popular with their classmates did not so often become delinquents as their less popular schoolfellows' (p. 106). Hargreaves' (1967) work in a Northern secondary modern school showed that even within a single school distinct subcultures existed and that delinquent boys were unpopular among the higher streams but popular with lower stream boys. There is a serious lack of studies which look at the delinquent in contexts other than school. Since many working-class adolescents live on housing estates or closed neighbourhoods, many of their friends may be at different schools, or unemployed, or they may be relatives. Campbell (1976) found that the highly delinquent girl preferred a greater number of male friends who were older than the girl herself and often already at work. Friendships were consolidated on the football terraces and in pubs and discotheques—not within the school walls.

A few steps have been taken into more qualitative research designed to explore the nature of the friendships of delinquent boys. These have been almost exclusively based on semantic rating methods. For example, Bhagat and Fraser (1970) asked Glasgow boys to rate their peers on 16 scales concerning judgements of evaluation, potency, activity and aggression. No significant differences appeared except on the evaluation items where offenders rated their friends less positively. However it should be noted that the specific scales on which the differences appeared were not mentioned and it can be misleading simply to sum over scales whose degree of intercorrelation has not been tested. There has also been a tendency to assume that when delinquents rate their friends as 'dishonest' it implies negative affect rather than an accurate appraisal of the others' characteristics. However, the major problem with this kind of technique is that the scales are chosen in advance of the study and may have little meaning to the subjects themselves. In fact, scales are usually chosen by reference to the work of Osgood, Suci and Tannenbaum (1957) who report that three major dimensions are sufficient to cover the psychological semantic space of most people. This has been shown to be untrue of many 'deviant' populations. It has also been pointed out that the factors which emerge from factor analytic studies may reflect more accurately the correlation between certain descriptive words (rather than interpersonal judgements) and this may account for the three primary clusters described by Osgood *et al.*

The repertory grid technique of Kelly (1963) avoids these objections because it allows the subject to nominate his or her own constructs. Their relevance is assured since they were generated for the very purpose of making discriminations between others. By its nature however the grid technique cannot yield general statements as it is an instrument geared to the individual. Results from work with delinquent girls (Campbell, 1976) suggest that they do not use the sorts of verbal labels suggested by the semantic differential. 'Mates of mine', 'people who get in trouble with me' and 'people who boss me about' were much more frequently employed to discriminate among others. Friendship may well be mediated by behavioural events between people rather than by abstract qualities.

Pike (1967) has coined the term 'etic' to describe analysis which is based on observation and inference by outsiders. In contrast stands 'emic' research in which social action is analysed 'in reference to the manner in which native participants in that behaviour react to their own behaviour and to the behaviour of their colleagues' (p. 55). Previously researchers developed coding categories in advance of a detailed understanding of the phenomenon in question and imposed them indiscriminately, viewing the subjects' own conceptual mode as 'noise' in the system to be eliminated as efficiently as possible. Newer style research, derived from social anthropology, has attempted to avoid a 'black box' view of people and to locate important aspects of the phenomenon in the words and actions of the people themselves. Patrick (1973) and Parker (1974) have done this by participant observation. The danger here is not only that the researcher may have a significant effect on the group he wants to study but also that the accuracy of his report may be difficult to corroborate. Daniel and McGuire (1972) have presented transcripts from recordings made of subjects' own words avoiding any attempt to interpret or question. Perhaps the best work has resulted from an active interchange between investigator and informant where they negotiate a description and interpretation of the informants' life styles. Behaviour is thus viewed from both 'inside' and 'outside' (see Harré, 1976; Marsh, Rosser and Harré, 1978).

So far this methodology has been talked about more than used. It has often been criticized as lacking in reliability and replicability. Yet it has a great deal to offer in both authenticity and meaningfulness.

FRIENDSHIP AND DELINQUENCY

The nature of the peer group's influence on individual member's delinquency is still in debate among sociologists and psychologists. Even the most fundamental question has not yet been fully resolved: are delinquents highly social individuals with strong positive bonds to their friends or are they 'loners' who, by nature of their disturbed background, are incapable of forming lasting affectional bonds with others? Anyone who has worked in an institution for young offenders will almost certainly reply that they have seen both. More complexly, they will add that some delinquents display all the trappings of good peer relations while showing a degree of ruthless egocentrism which belies it. Attempts have been made to develop typologies within the apparently heterogeneous field of delinquency based on this very distinction. At one extreme is the *psychopath*, characterized by a failure to show empathy for others and to maintain affectional bonds with anyone, and at the other is the *gang member* whose loyalty to his friends overrides any other consideration, even going to prison.

The sociable delinquent

Firstly, let us consider the theoretical background among those who see the delinquent as a highly social individual. Almost all writers in sociology and psychology who take this view have concentrated exclusively on boys. Girls are almost unanimously represented as social isolates, rejected not only by society but by their peer group also. The reasons for this are discussed in the following section on solitary delinquency. Meanwhile the literature on boys is discussed and the possibility of applying such formulations to girls is also considered. Both Cohen (1955) and Cloward and Ohlin (1960) see delinquency as a collective solution for boys who are in a state of stress. Both accounts draw attention to the fact that Western society (particularly the United States) encourages all members to strive for material rewards and financial success: 'All men are created equal' and the Protestant Ethic of hard work and delayed gratification are invoked to motivate every man and boy to climb the ladder of success. Status is correlated with achievement and wealth. Cohen goes on to argue that working-class boys are poorly equipped to succeed in this kind of competition. They have not learned to delay rewards nor to attach any positive value to forward planning, and control of emotions. In realistic terms, their chances of employment and long-term careers are low and their poor school performance (West and Farrington, 1973) reflects this despair as well as a failure on the part of the parents to place high value on academic success. However, it is virtually impossible for them to escape middle-class aspirations and values that are upheld by the school, the media and the very ideology of their country. As a result of this they find themselves in a state of frustration and anxiety which is dealt with by a process of collective 'reaction-formation'. The values and norms to which they cannot aspire are replaced by their very antithesis; anti-social, aggressive and destructive behaviour. In this way, the delinquent can achieve masculine status in the eyes of his peers, if not in the community at large. Aggression is legitimized, thus providing an expression for the internal frustration he experiences. Stealing becomes not just a way of getting something; it is a means that is the antithesis of sober and diligent 'labour in a calling'. For reaction formation to be successful it must be a collective enterprise since its purpose is to ensure the boy's status in the eyes of his friends. Peer bonds are seen as extremely strong: 'Relations with gang members tend to be intensely solidary and imperious . . . the gang is a separate, distinct and often irresistible focus of attraction, loyalty and solidarity' (Cohen, p. 31).

Cloward and Ohlin (1960) similarly see delinquency as a solution to status frustration. However, rather than producing reaction-formation, the response is a withdrawal of legitimacy from middle-class attitudes and lifestyle. Working-class youths still want the material rewards for which they are encouraged to strive but the impossibility of legitimately achieving these ends drives them to use illegitimate means such as theft, mugging and fraud. Cloward and Ohlin suggest that there are three distinct types of subcultural solution. The first is the conflict subculture and this is the most similar to the gang described by Cohen. Secondly, there is the criminal subculture in which younger boys are channelled into a life of crime via the close bonds in the community between the professional criminal and the street-corner boys. The third type of subculture is the retreatist or drug-oriented group in which the individual blames himself rather than society for his failure and cannot even succeed socially in the subcultural world around him. In these first two categories heavy reliance is placed on the group as a necessary part of the delinquent solution: 'The group members begin to exhibit a greater cohesiveness and sense of mutual dependence. They learn to define more closely those who are friendly or hostile to their activities. . . . The development of a delinquent solution thus depends not on the exploratory gestures that boys direct toward one another but also on their interaction with others in the community' (Cloward and Ohlin, pp. 142–143).

Miller (1958) offers an account of gang delinquency neither in terms of the individual's nor the group's reaction to middle-class values but in terms of the focal concerns of the working-class generally. His description resulted from a 3-year project in Boston talking to 21 'corner groups'. Working-class males are particularly concerned to assert their masculinity by demonstrating involvement in trouble (law-violating behaviour), toughness, smartness and excitement. Life is viewed as being controlled by both fate and luck but the 'smart operator' must also demonstrate autonomy in the form of disdain for authority figures. Among adolescent groups it is particularly important that the individual 'belongs' to a group and achieves status within it. This he does by demonstrating his prowess in the masculine requirements of his culture:

> The 'hanging' peer group is a unit of particular importance for the adolescent male. In many cases it is the most stable and solidary primary group he has ever belonged to; for boys reared in female-based households the corner group provides the first real opportunity to learn essential aspects of the male role in the context of peers facing similar problems of sex-role identification. (Miller, 1958, p. 14).

According to Miller these boys are drawn together in an attempt to try out adult masculine behaviours and to escape from predominantly female family units. He stresses that this is perfectly normal behaviour, not to be confused with pathology or social deviance. In fact, Miller applauds their social skills: 'The activity patterns of the group require a high level of intra-group solidarity; individual members must possess a good capacity for subordinating individual desires to general group interests as well as the capacity for intimate and persisting interaction' (Miller, 1958, p. 14).

Sutherland and Cressey (1970) also stress that delinquent behaviours and attitudes are learned in the adolescent group. They reject any notion of individual pathology and suggest that not only criminal behaviours but also the required attitudes, motives, drives and rationalizations are acquired within 'intimate personal groups'. Criminal behaviour is dependent on the individual learning an excess of definitions favourable to the violation of the law over definitions unfavourable to law breaking. Subsequently Akers (1973) has offered a more specific account of the processes of acquisition of these codes in terms of social learning theory. He views statements of justification as discriminative stimuli or cues for reinforcement. Sykes and Matza (1957) have suggested many of the ways in which delinquents justify and excuse their law-breaking activities. The existence of such rationalizations is integral not only to Sutherland's theory but also to Matza's (1964). Matza proposes that the distinction between delinquents and non-delinquents made by some subcultural theorists is too great. He points to the fact that most delinquents recognize what they do to be wrong and develop rationalizations to appease their guilt. He also points out that the 'delinquent group' is not engaged in full-time, law-breaking activities nor is it required of members that they do so.

An interesting question is—to whom do these boys justify their activities? Certainly, when questioned, they offer accounts to police, social workers, schools and sociologists, but do they feel the need to justify to one another or even to themselves? Both of these explanations take the importance of the gang or peer group to be axiomatic, suggesting that they provide the individual member with a coherent and sympathetic account of his own anti-social behaviour.

The evidence

A preliminary question must be concerned with the extent to which delinquency is in fact a group rather than solitary activity. It is now accepted that official crime statistics give an incomplete if not distorted view of delinquent activity. Police may be influenced in their decision as to whether simply to caution rather than 'book' an offence by such factors as the boy's past record, family background, race, distinctiveness of clothes and hairstyles and more importantly for the present argument, by the seriousness of his offence and whether or not he is in a delinquent group (Piliavin and Briar, 1964). Hindelang (1976) has also shown that 'offenders who engage in illegal behaviour in groups are more likely to have been picked up by the police than are offenders who tend to engage in illegal behaviour in isolation' (p. 123). Police account for this by pointing out that it is more difficult to caution groups of boys rather than individuals. The official statistics are further complicated by the relationship between seriousness of offence and whether or not it was committed in a group.

To gain a better idea of the true rate of group crime in the community some self-report studies of delinquency will be reviewed. This technique involves presenting groups of adolescents with a list of criminal offences couched in their everyday language and asking them to indicate whether or not they have ever done those things. Additional information may be sought as to whom they were with at the time.

Lerman (1967) worked with a sample of 555 American urban boys and girls aged 10–19 years old. He investigated developmental patterns of social inter-action among adolescents from urban 'slum' areas. Up to the age of 14 years old, the dominant social unit was the pair or triad, a regular larger group being second, with a few respondents considering themselves to be loners. From 14 to 16 years old membership of a regular group was the dominant behaviour. From 16 to 19 years old, the most common pattern was once again the pair or triad. Lerman also noted that the proportion of spare-time spent with the group was highest at 15 years of age, then decreased with age. When asked whether most of their self-reported illegal acts had been performed alone or with one or two others or in a regular group, the percentage reporting regular groups was small and did not increase with age. However, specific types of offences were not identified and the author relied on one global estimate on the respond-ents' part. The rate of group activity is likely to be intimately related to the type of delinquent act considered (Hindelang, 1976).

Erickson (1971) studied three groups of boys: 50 boys from a correctional institution, 50 boys who were on probation and 50 officially non-delinquent boys from a public high school. Group violation rates (defined as the proportion of all self-reported acts involving more than one person) differed considerably from offence to offence. The maximum was 0.91 for destruction of property and the minimum 0.17 for defying parents. The average group admission rate was 0.65. Probation officers and judges ranked the offences for seriousness and it was found that group violation rates bore a positive relationship to the serious-ness of the offence ($\varrho = .58, p < .001$).

Gold (1970) reports that only 25 per cent of offences admitted by his United States sample of 522 boys and girls were committed alone. Of these, a further 25 per cent were soon after described to a member of the peer group. He also reports a positive relationship between frequency of commission of an offence and the type of offence committed with others. Of all the offences committed with others, 41 per cent were with one other person, 23 per cent with two others, 15 per cent with three others, 9 per cent with four others and 12 per cent with five or more others.

Hindelang (1971) studied a sample of male, middle-class, high-school students in California with a mean age of 15 years 6 months. For each offence, he asked whether it was always committed alone, sometimes alone and sometimes with a friend or always with a friend. The figures for this last group ranged between 0.09 for theft of less than $10 to 0.36 for drinking alcohol under age. Offences committed 'sometimes alone and sometimes with a friend' accounted for the largest proportion of responses but without a more detailed analysis of the composition of this category, we can conclude little about the rates of group delinquency.

Hindelang's later study considered males and females in rural and urban schools in the United States (Hindelang, 1976). In this study there were four categories of response: always alone, usually alone, usually with a friend, always with a friend. There was a general tendency for the more serious acts in each category (theft, property destruction and fighting) to be associated with group rather than solitary commission. The only clear exception to this was the group of drug offences, where more serious acts (selling drugs, using heroin) were performed alone. Controlling for frequency and seriousness of offence, solitary offenders were less likely to be picked up by the police than were group offenders.

A British study by West and Farrington (1973) asked about the delinquent activities of respondents' friends. Friends' delinquent acts were positively related to a boy's own delinquency score, and to his present and future police convictions.

Shapland (1975), in a group of 11- to 14-year-old school boys in Oxford, found group crime (committed by more than one person) to be much more prevalent than solitary crime. Percentage of group involvement ranged from zero (taking money from home) to 91 per cent (letting off fireworks in the street). Interestingly many 'under-age' acts were first committed with an adult rather than with peers. Mean group involvement in crime was 60 per cent as compared to 65 per cent in the Erickson study.

This trend towards group crime is mirrored in official crime statistics. In the United States 70–80 per cent of all known offences are committed in groups (Erickson, 1971). Downes (1966) reports that in the Stepney and Poplar districts of London, group crimes account for 82 per cent of all offences committed by 13- to 16-year-olds. Bottoms (1970) reports that only 14 per cent of property damage offences and 33 per cent of violent crimes are committed alone under the age of 14 years old. By 20 years of age, however, the figures rise to 45 per cent and 67 per cent respectively. Having established that much juvenile crime is committed with others, it still remains to be shown whether or not delinquent boys belong to specific subcultures or gangs.

The existence of the delinquent gang has been widely held both in criminological and popular circles. Thrasher (1927) as far back as the 1920s described Chicago gangs, stressing as defining criteria their continuity over time, leadership, role allocation, initiation rites and common activities. Research in the United States has largely failed to confirm Thrasher's original description based on his sample of over one thousand Chicago gangs.

Instead, Yablonsky's (1962) study of a New York gang found an absence of defined members, of roles and norms, of leaders and specific activities; rather he reports 'a moblike collectivity that forms around violence in a spontaneous fashion'. Yablonsky refers to this as a 'near group', with only about 25 members, of which a handful constitute the core membership. Short and Strodtbeck (1965) similarly report small membership of their 16 Chicago gangs.

Cross-cultural factors are likely to be of some importance in gang research, so it is important to consider research into gangs within the United Kingdom. Spinley (1953) found London gangs to range from cliques of 3 to larger groups of 20. The boys carried weapons but rarely used them.

Scott (1956) developed a group typology based on his ten years experience with delinquents in London. He found adolescent street groups who were 'quite innocuous' and, secondly, gangs proper (i.e. with a leader, a definite membership, persistence in time, initiation rites and criminal objectives). Of 151 boys who had committed group offences, only 17 belonged to such a gang. Thirdly, there were loosely structured and diffuse groups; this category accounted for 86 per cent of his sample. Downes' (1966) study of delinquents in two London East End boroughs failed to find evidence of the classical gang. The average group size was four or five, with a few individuals on the periphery. 'While these street-corner groups persisted over time, and invariably possessed a dominant personality, all the other features commonly attributed to the delinquent gang were absent: i.e. leadership, role allocation, hierarchical structure, consensus on membership, uniform, and name' (p. 199).

Wilmott (1966) worked in the Bethnal Green area of London and reported similar findings to those of Downes. Most boys belonged to informal groups or mobs, in which all members were roughly equal in status and had neither leaders nor hierarchical structure. Although they cultivated an image of toughness, fighting between mobs was rare. Their main motive for violence and vandalism was, according to Wilmott, a desire to strike at society for its constant rejection of them as failures.

Between 1963 and 1966 Cohen studied the 'Mods and Rockers' disturbances on the south coast (cf. Cohen, 1972). He found little evidence of the gang warfare reported in the media: 'The groups were merely loose collectivities or crowds, within which there was occasionally some more structured grouping based on territorial loyalty, e.g. "The Walthamstow Boys", "The Lot from Eltham". Constant repetition of the gang image made these collectivities see themselves as gangs and behave in a gang fashion' (p. 282). He pointed to both the media and over-reaction by the authorities and the general public, in amplifying what were originally trivial incidences of uncooperativeness and high spirits.

White (1971) reported on the incidence of gangs in Birmingham, England. He concentrated on a description of the 'Quinton mob' who exhibited many attributes of the classical gang: leadership, roles, norms, violence, territoriality and endurance over time (at least 2 years in this case). He stressed the individual personality of different gangs around the city: 'The mobs' worlds are small and peculiar to the areas they spring from. The petrol-bombers of Bartley Green share nothing worth sharing with the Paki-rollers of Ladywood' (p. 763). Similarly, some groups were more structured and enduring than others: for example, the Smethwick Mob, who 'show no obvious loyalty to their leader, and seem confused about who are core members and who are fringe members' (p. 763). Interestingly, White noticed the existence of at least one female gang 'The Smethwick Boot Girls': 'These are not as terrifying as they sound. Although they ape skinheads' dress occasionally and match their language often, they depend on boys' gangs and do not move round alone' (p. 763).

Daniel and McGuire (1972) reported transcriptions of conversations with members of a London East End gang. During summer evenings, boys from various estates would congregate together on the lawn in front of a block of flats. No clear structure was ever present, boys joining and leaving as they wished. They had no leader and were hostile to the very idea of one: 'If he said "go and get that geezer" people wouldn't do as 'e said. I fucking wouldn't do it and there ain't no one who would do it, I don't think' (p. 33). The distinctive skinhead uniform was informally begun by the 'nutter' of the group:' 'e got 'is gear and we sort of thought "well he looks good" and just sort of copied. We all 'ad jeans and boots, we copied the 'aircut and then we started' (p. 33). The gang was exclusively male and their delinquent activities were violent and not for any financial profit. Although clashes did occur between groups (particularly at soccer matches) most violence was directed at groups of other youngsters such as hippies or Pakistanis. No evidence of the highly ritualized inter-gang fighting of American cities existed at all (Miller, 1975).

Finally, Patrick (1973) was a participant observer in a Glasgow gang for 4 months. He likened the gang structure to the 'near group', described by Yablonsky (1962), having half-a-dozen core members and a number of satellite members. Many of the gang names could be traced back to the 1920s. The groups were territorial, had definite leaders and although no specific initiation rites were defined, any member who did not exhibit sufficient violence was subject to sanctions. Inter-group fights accounted for a large part of the gang's activities and these were fought with knives, bottles, axes and occasionally guns. Several murders had thus occurred. There were normative prescriptions about behaviours which were frequently verbalized but not always adhered to; for example, no 'grassing', no cowardice (irrespective of the number of assailants), no house-breaking in your own neighbourhood and no hiding in wait for opponents 'up their close'.

An intense debate over the existence of structured gangs continues (cf. Hood and Sparks, 1970). Certainly young people commit many delinquent acts in groups rather than alone. Within large groups, friendship dyads and triads exist; this is a recurrent theme in the literature. Friendships and alliances change over time and the dynamic properties within groups have been very much ignored by many criminologists. The types of crimes also change depending on fads (Mods and Rockers), circumstances ('Paki bashing'), and opportunity (soccer violence). It seems that the most fruitful course of action would be to study friendships, rather than pursuing the search for the elusive gang. As Hood and Sparks note: 'All the evidence points to delinquency being mainly the product of the interaction between members of groups. It seems that what is often important is the significance of the delinquent act for the relationship between members . . . rather than as an end in itself' (Hood and Sparks, 1970, p. 138).

Little work has addressed itself to the *quality* of the friendship experienced by boys in these delinquent groups. Sociometric analyses exist of friendship networks within schools showing the delinquent boy as largely rejected by his brighter, more conforming classmates. However, Klein and Crawford (1967) looked at adolescent boys' friendship patterns in the community at large. This they did by asking detached youth workers to report the names of boys they saw each day round the city and to note the site, duration, mode of initiation, and the groupings of persons involved in any interaction situation. Results clearly indicated that the most delinquent boys interacted with each other more frequently, spent less time alone, and were more tightly knit into distinctive cliques than less delinquent groups. While this statistically confirms the close structure of the delinquent group, it fails to give any real feeling for what the boys' relationships are like. This can only be found in participant observation studies of youth groups.

For our purposes, we shall consider Parker's (1974) account of a Liverpool group 'The Boys', and Daniel and McGuire's (1972) reporting of the words of a group of London skinheads. In both cases, the boys came from around the same neighbourhood in working-class areas. The bulk of their leisure time was spent on the streets looking for excitement or just 'doing nothing'—an activity which Corrigan (1975) has shown to be a good deal more complex than might appear at first sight. The dynamic quality of intra-group relationships is something often ignored by sociologists. Cliques and dyads formed and broke up constantly, without radically affecting the overall identity of the group. Although there were no clear initiation rites, the local community was quite aware of who was in the group:

> The adolescents of both sexes in the area would be able to make a roll-call of the network, as would the bar staff and regular 'boozers' in the local pubs. Any member of the network could go into 'The Turk', ask 'Have you seen any of The Boys' and receive a sensible answer such as 'Colly and Jimbo were in a bit ago'. (Parker, 1974, p. 166).

Structure was evident in the locations where the boys met. In London it was at a housing estate with a green area for football. None of the boys lived there and because of this they felt able to cause trouble without fear of retribution from neighbours and the like. In Liverpool, each day was mapped out into a regular routine of venues so that any stray member could locate the rest of the boys. Daily visits were made to the Youth Club to play table tennis and to the pub for a few drinks and a game of darts. The rest of the time was spent standing on the corner, wandering about town, playing football or visiting the 'chippy'. Weekly events were superimposed on the daily routine—dole day, Friday lunchtime at the pub and football on Saturday. In both accounts, there was a clear longitudinal perspective to group membership. Younger boys joined the junior league group and grew up together to take over from the reigning gang. Their activities were viewed with paternalistic enjoyment by the older boys. Usually, they engaged in 'naughty' activities such as smashing things, raiding slot machines and petty theft. From this they graduated to selling stolen goods informally, and then on to planned theft done more for profit than for fun. For violence too, younger boys began with taunts and threats at their older colleagues who took it indulgently. In time, violent incidents occurred with other neighbouring street groups and became more serious in terms of actual physical harm.

Perhaps one indicator of the degree of closeness felt by the boys would be the degree of loyalty they demonstrated to one another. In both accounts there is clear evidence of the group closing ranks against officialdom, most particularly the police. The football terraces were another location where group solidarity was of particular importance. The London group cooperated in organizing buses to take them to 'away' matches where the trip and its attendant visits to pubs generated a strong sense of friendship and invincibility. The fact that the London supporters were clearly outnumbered at away matches made it particularly important that they should stick together: 'We used to go down the Shelf, and when we come out, we used to go out in a clink like and all run together and run down the street and if there was any supporters there we used to just trample over their heads or something' (p. 82). The telling and retelling of such exploits served to generate a strong sense of in-group feeling.

Occasionally things went wrong: perhaps one of the group was arrested. The boys would go in a body to the police station and attempt to bail him out but ultimately he would be expected to see it through on his own. On no account would one of the members ever 'grass' on the others. Even the 'nutters' of the group who started fights against outrageously poor odds would be supported through the violent encounters by his friends. It was the same with car radio theft among the Liverpool boys. It took three of them to complete the job and it was demarcated in such a way that they all took a comparable risk. One would do the look-out while the second boy forced the window or door and the third removed the radio by unscrewing the brackets and snapping the connecting wires. The first member, who had so far been in a safe situation, would then conceal the radio in his clothing and go off on his own to dump it. If he were to be picked up by the police, he would be expected to take the whole burden of responsibility on himself.

Girls alone were in the privileged position of being able to prise individual boys away from the group. Often a boy's departure into marriage was hastened by his girlfriend's pregnancy. Girls fell into three major categories. 'Someone's tart' was a regular girlfriend of one of the group members. She was expected to remain faithful although the boys themselves felt no compunction about casual sexual adventures if the chance presented itself. In time, the girl's sexual loyalty would finally be reciprocated prior to getting engaged. The second category was the 'dirty ticket'. These were local girls available for sexual experimentation who offered no threat to the cohesion of the group and in fact often reinforced it by being passed from one boy to another. The third category was known as the 'not having any's' comprising girls who intended to maintain their clean reputations until after marriage. Although the boys spent an increasing amount of time with their regular girlfriends as they grew older, they were still available for coach trips to football matches and a few nights a week 'down the pub'. However, they did become more cautious about their law-breaking activities and the excuse of 'the wife' was accepted as legitimate by the group members.

A good deal of generosity was apparent among the members, particularly in the Liverpool group where many were unemployed for long periods. They would buy stolen goods from the younger lads selling them at a profit to buy beer for the boys. Profits from car radio thefts were also spent on communal drinking. The boys had a distinct moral code about who could and could not be stolen from. One potential group member was excluded because he stole from neighbours and friends. This seems to go beyond the London boys' expedient concern with not making trouble 'outside your front door'. It reflects the existence of a certain moral concern based on community loyalty.

The sheer amount of time the boys spent together must be some indication of the strength of their friendship. Most grew up together from toddlers, and, in a community where the majority of adults of both sexes worked fulltime, spent the hours between school and bedtime roaming the streets and play areas generating fun. Their links with family, relatives, shopkeepers and publicans endured over years and showed no indication of any pathological social inadequacy. The friendships resulted from long association through similar circumstances and were based more on joint activities, anticipated and re-counted, than on intimate conversations. While middle-class children may forge their friendships through self-disclosure in one another's houses, these boys' loyalty develops from actions directed out towards society. Through these behaviours status is conferred, masculinity assured and an implicit loyalty forged between members.

Girls and delinquent friends

There is a complete absence of any theoretical formulations to explain group delinquency among girls. As can be seen later in this chapter, most writers on the subject have proceeded from the assumption that delinquent girls are isolates and misfits. There seems no reason why theories of male group delinquency could not usefully be applied to females. The only attempt to do this was by Morris (1964) who somewhat hastily made the assumption that while boys value prestige and wealth, girls are exclusively concerned with gaining boy-friends and husbands. Thus, by Cloward and Ohlin's (1960) formulation, boys might be expected to steal and girls to engage in acts of sexual promiscuity. However self-report and official figures show no significant differences between boys and girls with respect to petty theft and it is very likely that the apparent promiscuity of institutionalized girls is a reflection of judicial and moral bias. The very bases of the argument, regardless of the adequacy of the empirical testing, seem misguided from the start.

Only two self-report delinquency studies have looked at group violation rates among girls. Hindelang (1976) took five groups: institutionalized delin-quents, urban and rural males and urban and rural females. Urban females appeared as the most social non-institutionalized law-breakers averaging over all offences. They were, however, less likely than urban males to be picked up for these group offences (65 per cent of boys but only 23 per cent of girls had been questioned by the police). Offences were divided into four groups: always alone, usually alone, usually with others, always with others. For urban females, acts more likely to fall into this last category were: getting drunk (74 per cent), property destruction (72 per cent), smoking pot (54 per cent), drunken driving (53 per cent) and using force to obtain money (56 per cent). Campbell's (1976) study on British girls found a similarly high rate of group involvement. However, girls were asked to report only on the first occasion on which the act was performed. Items showing 100 per cent group admission rates were: smashing things on the street, breaking into shops and stores, housebreaking and bicycle theft. Under-age and theft acts had the highest rates of group commission, but the overall mean for the 43 offences was high (75 per cent).

There has been no systematic field work on gangs or groups of teenage girls. As McRobbie and Garber (1975) point out this may be because much all-girl leisure time is spent in one another's houses playing records, reading magazines and talking, together with the fact that entrée to a heterosexual group is often via their attachment to male members. White (1971) however, notes the existence of an all-female gang in Birmingham, England, and hastily assures us that they 'are not as terrifying as they sound' (p. 763). Adler (1975) similarly makes passing reference to girl gangs in London: 'Armed with switchblades, razors, clubs and fists, these girl gangs roam London streets attacking elderly women (a practice that is called "granny bashing") usually at night' (p. 48). As long ago as 1958, Cohen and Short deplored the absence of information on female groups while expressing certainty of their existence. In 1964, a journalist Kitty Hanson brought out a heavily dramatized account of a girl gang in a Spanish area of New York and the plot appears to owe much to *West Side Story* with gang 'rumbles', romance and a final tragic killing. The author claims that it is based on reports of street social workers familiar with the area but one suspects that much of this second-hand information was somewhat embroidered. She reports a fluid grouping of girls with five or six core members. The 'Dagger Debs' had a definite leader and councillor of war and internal rank was established by physical prowess. Female inter-gang fighting occurred and the female gangs were each affiliated with a male gang to whom they lent sexual and combative favours. The girls fought on each other's behalf and seemed to share with boys a disdain for self-revealing conversations with each other. The description given could equally well apply to any of the male gangs described in criminological literature except perhaps for the use of scratching and biting during fights.

With respect to the quality of these girls' friendships, little is known. Morris (1964) shows that delinquent girls believe their friends would disapprove of their delinquent behaviour more than do delinquent boys. However the specific delinquent acts they were asked to consider were different for the two sexes (for girls promiscuity and for boys theft and aggression). There were no differences in the number of delinquent friends nominated by delinquent boys or girls. Campbell (1976) showed that delinquent girls had more friends than non-delinquents and the composition of friendship groups was different. Delinquent girls predominately associated with a greater proportion of males and older adolescents who had left school, many of whom were in trouble with the police. They confided personal problems however to a smaller proportion of their group than did non-delinquent girls and were less static in their turnover of acquaintances. All this is at best only suggestive. An enormous amount of empirical work needs to be carried out in this area.

The solitary delinquent

In the opposing camp are those who believe the delinquent boy to be socially inept and incapable of forming adequate relations with the group. Yablonsky (1962) states: '... the defective socialization process to which he is subjected in the disorganized slum fosters a lack of social "feelings". At hardly any point is he trained to have human feelings of compassion or responsibility for another' (p. 196). Similarly Roach and Gurrslin (1965) state: '... it seems implausible

to assume that social actors who have cognitive restrictions, a deficient self-system and a limited role repertory, possess the requisite attributes for the elaboration of intricate cultural and social patterns' (p. 507).

Bandura and Walters (1959) argue that delinquent boys are negatively sanctioned for dependent behaviour towards their father. Through a process of generalization the boys' anxiety is transferred to their agemates. Aggressive delinquents more often than non-delinquent boys resist receiving help from their friends, feel rejected by them, experience less warmth of feeling toward them and confide in them less.

Hirschi (1969) argues that: 'the idea that delinquents have comparatively warm, intimate social relations with each other (or with anyone) is a romantic myth' (p. 159). His data however largely deal with non-delinquent boys and he has no direct evidence of gang membership since his questionnaire did not mention it. The forced choice format and the arbitrariness of his comparisons may well have selectively supported his *a priori* assumptions. Much of the solitary delinquent orientation derived directly from the post-World War II stress on the family and the interpersonal dynamics within it as being responsible for personality and character development. Bowlby (1953) and others who were influenced by his approach particularly focused on early mother–child relationships as the key to subsequent personality differences in children and adolescents. A failure of bonding in the early years was believed to affect all future relationships, at worst resulting in psychopathy. Much of the empirical work was performed on institutionalized children. Some studies looked at maternally deprived children in homes and searched for differences in later adjustment between these subjects and 'normal' children. However as Rutter (1972) has pointed out such studies are inconclusive since later differences may be attributable to a number of other factors concomitant with institutional life other than maternal deprivation. Other studies looked at delinquent adolescents in institutions and tried to establish retrospectively that they had experienced inadequate mother–child relationships. Results of such studies must be treated with caution since one of the selection criteria for institutionalization is the very fact that family relationships have broken down. Another confounding factor is that residential homes not only accept 'delinquent' children but also those who have been diagnosed as suffering from behavioural or emotional difficulties. In this way clinical disorder is confused with law-breaking behaviour and the results of such studies may be misleading. More studies of youth in the community are needed to clarify the results derived from institutionalized children.

This kind of theory presupposes that social deviance can be explained in terms of personal maladjustment. It also assumes that personality, once formed in childhood, remains relatively immutable. It is hard to ignore the practical and political implications of such a position. To explain deviant behaviour by recourse to clinical abnormality releases society from having to take seriously the statements and complaints that such groups may be trying to make. It divides the subculture into a set of 'disturbed' individuals whose particular problems result from various intra-family breakdowns. Liberal politics provide social workers and psychologists to diagnose, treat and rehabilitate thus leaving society securely intact. More right-wing views capitalize on the rigidity of personality suggested by such a theory in order to justify long periods of imprisonment or placement in mental institutions.

Many sociologists have suggested that the gang may function as a surrogate family (cf. Miller, 1958). In the United States, within the urban ghettos, family disorganization is fast becoming the rule rather than the exception (Collins, 1977). Single parent families, poverty, lack of employment opportunity, truancy and drugs are common (Mitchell, 1977). Within the gang, a boy may experience a greater sense of belonging, loyalty and continuity than he could within his home. Studies of early family experiences rarely go on to investigate the quality of relationships which the boy later develops with his peers. Too often such friendships are dismissed as pseudo-relationships lacking genuine concern or warmth (cf. Hirschi 1969). Better research techniques for investigating friendships are needed to help clinicians and researchers form judgements and attributions grounded more in facts than in *a priori* assumptions and theories.

Writers in the field of female delinquency have been virtually unanimous in their view of such girls as socially isolated and rejected. Major works by Cowie, Cowie and Slater (1968) and by Richardson (1969) do not even mention the peer group or friends as a factor of importance in female crime. The absence of research into these girls' friendships is noteworthy and suggests many implicit assumptions about female delinquents. Virtually all work in the area has used institutionalized girls as its data base. Both in Great Britain and the United States the majority of girls are placed in homes for 'status' offences— acts which would not constitute an offence if performed by an adult (Campbell, 1977). Although these go under different names (persons in need of supervision, children in moral danger or beyond parental control) in both countries they describe a common syndrome—sexually 'promiscuous' girls who can no longer be controlled within the family. Chesney-Lind (1973) has argued that even when a girl commits a criminal offence, she is more likely than a boy to have it converted into a 'status' offence for the purposes of the court. Writers who were unaware of this possible bias were equally unaware of the double standard of sexuality for boys and girls which punished females for behaviour which in a boy would be considered healthy and normal. The result of this confusion was that 'misused' sexuality was thought to represent the full extent of female juvenile crime (Cowie *et al.*, 1968; Konopka, 1966). This stress on sexuality opened the way very naturally to a psychoanalytic view of female delinquency. Such girls were thought to have made inadequate relationships with their fathers (Blos, 1957; Riege, 1972) and because of this, to have become engaged in a search for a surrogate. They use sex as a means of gaining the male approval and attention that they never received in the home. Such a view clearly directs attention to their early family life and to males who have 'taken advantage' of them sexually.

Historically, women have relied economically on men through the institution of marriage by which sex is traded for social and material benefits (cf. Klein, 1973). Perhaps because of this, women have been strongly condemnatory of females who freely engage in sex thus devaluing it as a bargaining tool for marriage. This is reflected in writers' assumptions that promiscuous girls were unlikely to have good relationships with other females and that their relationships with males must be based upon sexual exploitation. In this way, delinquent girls were seen as socially isolated as well as emotionally disturbed. Concern with adolescent girls' misuse of sexuality arose not only from prurient interest but also from the fact that subsequent pregnancies were likely to begin a whole new 'cycle of deprivation', ensuring another generation of promiscuous females. Concern arose too from the fact that sexual freedom was the first step on the road to a general moral decline often ending in full-blown criminality. The rationale for this seemed to be that such girls would fall under the influence of older men and be drawn into anti-social life styles. This is symptomatic of the general view of females as gullible and tractable. They are portrayed as the victims of unscrupulous men rather than as exercising any personal control over their lives.

Major work in the area of female crime can be divided into two types. Studies by Cowie *et al.* and Richardson focus on a population of institutionalized girls and present numerical data on a number of variables. The lack of a control group renders most of these figures uninterpretable. In neither case is any information provided on peer relations before the girl entered the institution. The second type of study presents vivid case histories of individual girls (Konopka, 1966; Thomas, 1967). The authors present no criteria for the choice of subjects and one suspects that they are chosen as much to fit in with the writers' preconceptions as for their sensationalism. In short, aside from researchers' assumptions concerning delinquent girls' social isolation, there are no studies of such girls' friendships in the community.

McRobbie and Garber (1975) comment on the 'invisibility' of the female delinquent in criminological literature and suggest that until recently teenage girls' friendships were confined to congregations in one another's bedrooms to listen to records and pay tribute to the latest pop hero. However, the greater freedom which has now extended to girls has given them access to street cultures, to discos and to bars and a much closer association with boys. A report by Collins (1977) of the New York City Police Department points out that at least half the city's gangs have female membership, although they are outnumbered by males in a ratio of 13 to 1. Such girls however remain marginal to the major activities of the group. They do not hold positions of authority within the group and do not fight amongst themselves to achieve dominance in the pecking order. Although some may be attached to a male member this is not a requirement for membership. The boys offer female members protection from assault by neighbouring gangs and in return the girls carry weapons for them, since they are immune to being searched by male police officers. Collins states:

> Females gravitate to the youth gangs for many of the same reasons as the male gang members ... Their home fails to provide the values and supervision that are needed to successfully guide them through the perilous years of adolescence. The girls recognise this void and seek out the gang for status, guidance, identity, protection, excitement and the attention they feel they need. (p. 5).

In a nationwide United States survey, Miller (1975) concurs with the New York findings. He suggests that females are involved in gang activities in one of three ways: as 'auxiliaries' of male gangs, as participants in sexually 'mixed' gangs and most rarely as all-female autonomous units. He estimates that only 10 per cent of all gang membership is female. So far, little research has gone beyond this initial observation. We still have no information on the quality of these girls' relationships with each other and with male members or on the function and importance of group membership to the girl. Collins' observations certainly suggest that the needs and aspirations of the girls are virtually identical to the boys but how these status and identification needs are met within the roles that are available to them is unclear. It is vital also to gain some understanding of the focal concerns of female working-class culture in the way that Miller has done for males.

There is a similar paucity of such work in the United Kingdom. Campbell (1976) analysed 16-year-old girls' own reports on their friendships with respect to basic variables such as age, sex, length of friendship and where friends were first encountered. Correlations between such variables and self-reported delinquency indicated that delinquent girls actually reported having more friends than girls in the non-delinquent range. Their friendship groups contained a greater proportion of males, of people who had left school early and people who often 'got in trouble'. Smith (1978) offers further observations on these mixed-sex delinquent groups. Ninety per cent of her sample of delinquent girls belonged to 'a group whose central requirement seems to be that of committing delinquent acts' (p. 85). The girls' involvement in such groups seemed to be as active as the males and they not only took part in, but instigated delinquent activities. Once again, further qualitative work is badly needed.

CONCLUSION

During the last 20 years, criminologists investigating male delinquency have turned from a pathological stance towards a functional and descriptive perspective. The dynamics of male groups have been investigated and the value of such gangs to boys growing up in disorganized social areas has been realized.

This has resulted in an appreciation of some of the positive aspects of such groups and an increasing willingness to take seriously the statements of discontent and alienation that they voice.

No such change has taken place with respect to girls. The female delinquent is a 'double deviant', rejecting not only the law but her sex role also. As such she has continued to be the focus of psychoanalytically-based clinical judgement, and her social isolation has been assumed rather than demonstrated. Changes in the female crime rate must soon direct more serious research into delinquent girls' relationships with each other and with boys. This can only be successfully done by embedding such analyses in the values and life-styles of working-class females generally. The increasing freedom now accorded to girls opens up access to the venues of 'delinquent' groups—bars, streets, football terraces and discotheques—and her presence there makes her 'visible' not only to the police but to social scientists. Future work may well domonstrate that she has moved on from her previous satisfaction with sexual attention from males and now demands recognition, status and a sense of belonging from her peers, both male and female.

REFERENCES

Adler, F. (1975). The rise of the female crook. *Psychology Today*, 9, 42–114.

Akers, R. L. (1973). *Deviant Behavior: A Social Learning Approach*. Belmont: Wadsworth.

Bandura, A., and Walters, R. (1959). *Adolescent Aggression*. New York: Ronald Press.

Bhagat, M., and Fraser, W. I. (1970). Young offenders' images of self and surroundings: a semantic enquiry. *British Journal of Psychiatry*, 117, 381–387.

Blos, P. (1957). Preoedipal factors in the etiology of female delinquency. *Psychoanalytic Studies of the Child*, 12, 229–249.

Bowlby, J. (1953). *Child Care and the Growth of Love*. Harmondsworth, Middlesex: Penguin.

Bowlby, J. (1969).*Attachment and Loss:* Vol. I. London: Hogarth.

Bottoms, K. (1970). *Report to Fourth National Congress on Research and Teaching in Criminology*. Cambridge: Institute of Criminology.

Burt, C. (1925). *The Young Delinquent*. London: University of London Press. Reprinted in J. B. May (Ed.), *Juvenile Delinquency, the Family and the Social Group*. London: Longman. (1972).

Campbell, A. C. (1976). The role of the peer group in female delinquency. Unpublished Doctoral Dissertation, University of Oxford.

Campbell, A. (1977). What makes a girl turn to crime? *New Society*, 39, 172–173.

Cartwright, D., and Zander, A. (1953). *Group Dynamics: Research and Theory*. New York: Row, Peterson.

Chesney-Lind, M. (1973). Judicial enforcement of the female sex-role: the family court and the female delinquent. *Issues in Criminology*, 8, 51–69.

Cloward, R. A., and Ohlin, L. E. (1960). *Delinquency and Opportunity*. Glencoe: Free Press.

Cohen, A. K. (1955). *Delinquent Boys: The Culture of the Gang*. Glencoe: Free Press.

Cohen, A. K., and Short, J. F. (1958). Research in delinquent subcultures. *Journal of Social Issues*, 14, 20–37.

Cohen, S. (1972). Mods, rockers and the rest. In J. B. Mays (Ed.), *Juvenile Delinquency, the Family and the Social Group*. London: Longman.

Collins, H. C. (1977). *Street Gangs of New York: A Prototype of Organised Youth Crime*. New York: New York City Police Department.

Corrigan, P. (1975). Doing Nothing. In T. Jefferson (Ed.), *Resistance through Rituals*. Birmingham: Centre for Contemporary Cultural Studies.

Cowie, J., Cowie, B., and Slater, E. (1968). *Delinquency in Girls*. London: Heinemann.

Croft, I. J., and Grygier, J. G. (1956). Social relationships of truants and juvenile delinquents. *Human Relations*, **9**, 439–466.

Daniel, S., and McGuire, P. (Eds.), (1972). *The Paint House*. Harmondsworth, Middlesex: Penguin.

Downes, D. M. (1966). *The Delinquent Solution: A Study in Subcultural Theory*. London: Routledge and Kegan Paul.

Erickson, M. L. (1971). The group context of delinquent behavior. *Social Problems*, **19**, 114–129.

Eysenck, H. J. (1964). *Crime and Personality*. London: Routledge and Kegan Paul.

Freud, S. (1933). *New Introductory Lectures on Psychoanalysis*. New York: Horton.

Gold, M. (1970). *Delinquent Behavior in an American City*. Belmont, California: Wadsworth.

Hanson, K. (1964). *Rebels in the Streets: The Story of New York's Girl Gangs*. Englewood Cliffs, New Jersey: Prentice-Hall.

Hargreaves, D. H. (1967). *Social Relations in a Secondary School*. London: Routledge and Kegan Paul.

Harré, R. (Ed.), (1976). *Personality*. Oxford: Blackwell.

Hindelang, M. J. (1971). The social versus solitary nature of delinquent involvement. *British Journal of Criminology*, **11**, 167–175.

Hindelang, M. J. (1976). With a little help from their friends: group participation in reported delinquent behaviour. *British Journal of Criminology*, **16**, 109–125.

Hirschi, T. (1969). *Causes of Delinquency*. Berkeley, California: University of California Press.

Hood, R., and Sparks, R. (1970). *Key Issues in Criminology*. London: Weidenfeld and Nicholson.

Jennings, H. H. (1950). *Leadership and Isolation*, second edition. New York: Longmans Green.

Kelly, G. A. (1963). *A Theory of Personality—the Psychology of Personal Constructs*. New York: Norton.

Klein, D. (1973). The etiology of female crime: a review of the literature. *Issues in Criminology*, **8**, 3–30.

Klein, M. W., and Crawford, L. Y. (1967). Groups, gangs and obsessiveness. *Journal of Research in Crime and Delinquency*, **4**, 63–75.

Konopka, G. (1966). *The Adolescent Girl in Conflict*. Englewood Cliffs, New Jersey: Prentice-Hall.

Kraft, A. (1966). Personality correlates of rebellion—behavior in school. *Adolescence*, **1**, 251–260.

Lerman, P. (1967). Groups, networks and subcultural delinquency. *American Journal of Sociology*, **73**, 631–672.

Lewis, H. (1954). *Deprived Children*. Oxford: The University Press.

Lombroso, C., and Ferrero, W. (1958). *The Female Offender*. New York: Philosophical Library. (Originally published 1895).

McRobbie, A., and Garber, J. (1975). Girls and subcultures: an exploration. T. Jefferson (Ed.), *Resistance through Rituals*. Birmingham: Centre for Contemporary Cultural Studies.

Matza, D. (1964). *Delinquency and Drift*. New York: Wiley.

Marsh, P., Rosser, E., and Harré, R. (1978). *The Rules of Disorder*. London: Routledge and Kegan Paul.

Miller, W. B. (1958). Lower class culture as a generating milieu of gang delinquency. *Journal of Social Issues*, **14**, 5–19.

Miller, W. B. (1975). *Violence by Youth Gangs and Youth Groups as a Crime problem in major American cities*. Washington: United States Government Printing office.

Mitchell, R. B. (1977). Changes in Bedford-Stuyvesant. *The Crisis*, **1977**, 12–16.

Moreno, J. L. (1934). *Who Shall Survive? A New Approach to the Problems of Human Interrelations*. Washington, DC: Nervous and Mental Disease Publishing Company.

Morris, R. (1964). Female delinquents and relational problems. *Social Forces*, **43**, 82–89.

Osgood, C. E., Suci, G. J., and Tannenbaum, P. H. (1957). *The Measurement of Meaning*. Illinois: The University Press.

Parker, H. J. (1974). *View from the Boys*. Plymouth: Latimer Trend.

Patrick, J. (1973). *A Glasgow Gang Observed*. Bristol: Eyre Methuen.

Pike, K. L. (1967). *Language in Relation to a Unified Theory of the Structure of Human Behaviour*. The Hague: Mouton.

Piliavin, I., and Briar, S. (1964). Police encounters with juveniles. *American Journal of Sociology*, **70**, 206–214.

Reckless, W. C. (1955). *The Crime Problem*, second edition. New York: Appleton Century Crofts.

Richardson, H. J. (1969). *Adolescent Girls in Approved Schools*. London: Routledge and Kegan Paul.

Riege, M. (1972). Parental affection and juvenile delinquency in girls. *British Journal of Criminology*, **12**, 55–73.

Roach, J. L., and Gurrslin, O. R. (1965). The lower class, status frustration and social disorganisation. *Social Forces*, **53**, 507.

Rutter, M. (1972). *Maternal Deprivation Reassessed*. Harmondsworth, Middlesex: Penguin.

Scott, P. (1956). Gangs and delinquent groups in London. *British Journal of Delinquency*, **7**, 4–24.

Shapland, J. M. (1975). *Behaviour and Personality in Delinquent Children*. Unpublished Doctoral Dissertation, University of Oxford.

Sheldon, W. H., Hartt, E. M., and McDermott, G. (1949). *Varieties of Delinquent Youths*. New York: Harper.

Short, J. F., and Strodtbeck, F. L. (1965). *Group Processes and Gang Delinquency*. Chicago: University of Chicago Press.

Smith, L. S. (1978). Sexist assumptions and female delinquency: An empirical investigation. In C. Smart and B. Smart (Eds.), *Women, Sexuality and Social Control*. London: Routledge and Kegan Paul.

Spinley, B. M. (1953). *The Deprived and the Privileged*. London: Routledge and Kegan Paul.

Sugarman, B. (1968). Social norms in teenage boys' peer groups: a study of their implications for achievement and conduct in four London schools. *Human Relations*, **21**, 41–58.

Sutherland, E. H., and Cressey, D. R. (1970). *Criminology*, eighth edition. New York. Lippincott.

Sykes, G. M. and Matza, D. (1957). Techniques of neutralisation: a theory of delinquency. *American Sociological Review*, **22**, 667–689.

Thomas, W. I. (1967). *The Unadjusted Girl*. New York: Harper Torchbook.

Thrasher, F. M. (1927). *The Gang: A Study of 1,313 Gangs in Chicago*. Chicago University Press.

Trasler, G. (1962). *The Explanation of Criminology.* London: Routledge and Kegan Paul.

West, D., and Farrington, D. P. (1973). *Who Becomes Delinquent?* London: Heinemann.

White, D. (1971). Birmingham's mobs. *New Society,* **473**, 760–763.

Wilmott, P. (1966). *Adolescent Boys of East London.* London: Routledge and Kegan Paul.

Yablonsky, L. (1962). *The Violent Gang.* New York: Macmillan.

Index